21 世纪英语专业系列教材

语言学高级教程

第二版

胡壮麟　姜望琪　主编

图书在版编目(CIP)数据

语言学高级教程 / 胡壮麟，姜望琪主编. —2版. —北京：北京大学出版社，2015.7
（21世纪英语专业系列教材）
ISBN 978-7-301-25825-5

Ⅰ.①语… Ⅱ.①胡… ②姜… Ⅲ.①英语—语言学—高等学校—教材 Ⅳ.①H31

中国版本图书馆CIP数据核字(2015)第097284号

书　　　名	语言学高级教程（第二版）
著作责任者	胡壮麟　姜望琪　主编
责 任 编 辑	刘文静
标 准 书 号	ISBN 978-7-301-25825-5
出 版 发 行	北京大学出版社
地　　　址	北京市海淀区成府路205号　100871
网　　　址	http://www.pup.cn　新浪微博：@北京大学出版社
电 子 信 箱	liuwenjing008@163.com
电　　　话	邮购部 62752015　发行部 62750672　编辑部 62754382
印 　刷 　者	三河市博文印刷有限公司
经 　销 　者	新华书店
	730毫米×980毫米　16开本　33.25印张　700千字
	2002年9月第1版
	2015年7月第2版　2019年12月第2次印刷
定　　　价	88.00元

未经许可，不得以任何方式复制或抄袭本书之部分或全部内容。
版权所有，侵权必究
举报电话：010-62752024　电子信箱：fd@pup.pku.edu.cn
图书如有印装质量问题，请与出版部联系，电话：010-62756270

第二版前言

在《语言学高级教程》(Linguistics: An Advanced Course Book)第二版付梓之际,我们谨在此汇报此次修订的过程和改动细节。

《语言学高级教程》第一版出版于2002年。随着岁月的流逝,有些内容逐渐陈旧,不再适应读者的需要。为此,我们从2011年秋天开始筹划该教程的修订。我们联系了各位作者,征求了修订意见,确定了修订方案。为了不增加读者的负担,这次修订的总原则是不增加篇幅,增添新内容,而且要相应地删减部分旧内容。

在各位作者的努力下,2013年5月完成修订,大多数章节都有一些改动。除了改正一些错误以外,变动比较大的是,原来的第二章(Phonetics)和第三章(Phonology)被合并成了一章,缩减了语音学的一些内容,更名为 Phonological Analysis;第七章 Linguistic Comparison(原第八章)增加了对比语言学一节;第九章(原第十章 Psycholinguistics)改成了 Cognitive Linguistics,以反映当代语言学新近的发展;第十章 Pragmatics(原第十一章)删减了一些内容,增加了一个新小节;第十二章 Computational Linguistics(原第十三章)删除了两个小节,充实了一个小节;原第十五章整章删除。

作者也略有变动,具体如下:

第一章	李战子	南京国际关系学院
第二章	史宝辉	北京林业学院外语学院
第三章	张维友	华中师范大学外语学院
第四章	何 卫	北京大学外语学院
第五章	钱 军	北京大学外语学院
第六章	姜望琪	北京大学外语学院
第七章	张德禄	同济大学外语学院
第八章	杨永林	清华大学外语系
第九章	卢 植	宁波大学外语学院
第十章	姜望琪	北京大学外语学院
第十一章	刘世生	清华大学外文系
第十二章	胡壮麟	北京大学外语学院
	李德俊	南京国际关系学院
第十三章	王初明	广东外语外贸大学
第十四章	封宗信	清华大学外文系

有人说,一部词典问世之日就是其内容老化之时。学术著作何尝不是如此?在信息爆炸的今天,在科学研究迅猛发展的语言学领域,著书永远赶不上研究的

步伐。因此,我们衷心希望语言学界各位朋友,使用本教程的各位老师、同学,一如既往关心、爱护我们。发现教程存在的问题、不足,能毫不留情地予以指正,以便下次修订能做得更好。

编者

2015 年 1 月

第一版前言

Linguistics: An Advanced Course Book《语言学高级教程》(以下简称《高级教程》)是为我国英语专业研究生,特别是国外语言学与应用语言学专业的研究生编写的语言学教材。这类教材在我国基本上处于空白,例如我国一些大学的研究生课程在较长时期内采用了从国外引进的教材,或是使用我们十余年前为本科生编写的《语言学教程》(以下简称《教程》)。《教程》虽经修订,在内容上对研究生终究显得单薄一些,不很合适。随着我国外国语言学与应用语言学硕士点、博士点和英语语言文学博士点的逐步增多,老师们期待着在我国出版适合于研究生层次的教材。其次,这也多少反映了汉语语言学与应用语言学的师生的需要,他们也需要了解国外语言学的现状、基本观点和学术动向。再者,我们认为培养研究生,与培养本科生比较,在要求上应该有所不同。如果给本科生教材以传授基本知识和着重操练为主,那么,供研究生用的教材应提供有关语言学各有关学科前沿性的最新进展的信息,让学生比较不同语言学理论和流派的利弊得失,启发学生独立思考和研究,从素质上提高有关专业研究生的水平。最后,对《语言学教程》的修订,也为我们对两本教材统筹安排和合理分流提供了良机,有的专题(如语音学、句法学、心理语言学、第二语言习得、外语教学等)可以比《教程》讲得细一些;有的专题根据培养的要求从《教程》移至《高级教程》(如历史语言学和比较语言学);有的做了一定的补充(如计算语言学、语言学理论和流派)等。

语言学教材的选题可窄可宽。本教材着眼于后者,内部语言学和外部语言学并重,理论语言学和应用语言学兼顾,尽管做得很不够。我们是这样考虑的,让我国的研究生有机会接触当代语言学及其应用学科的新进展,站在新世纪的高度去学习和思考本领域的主要问题。使用本教材的老师可以根据培养要求和教学时间,学习者完全可以根据个人的兴趣择要而学。本教材的使用者会发现,有些理论,有些观点,在不同章节中都有出现,一方面它们是在不同视角下出现的,另一方面我们相信这种章节之间的互参,反映了现代语言学多学科互相沟通的趋向,也可以起到触类旁通、加深影响的积极效果。

对象改变了,内容增多了,难度提高了,这必然要求对《高级教程》的编写方针有些调整。例如,问题和练习部分取消了,英汉词汇解释和索引去掉解释部分,推荐书目和参考文献合二为一,直接附在各章之后。此举是为新增章节和内容提供篇幅;降低印刷成本和书价。同时,也是基于这样的认识:研究生在入学或应考前应该已经熟悉《教程》和一些基本词汇,并动手做过一些练习,讨论过一些问题。

语言学的覆盖面很广,靠一个人的智力和精力难以胜任或保证质量,而这十多年来,在我国高校已形成了一批对某一学科颇有造诣的中青年学者,我们在《教程》的修订本中已反映了这个趋势。在《高级教程》中,我们保持这个做法,又邀请了国内更多专家学者参与编写。今后还要这样做。这里介绍一下《高级教程》的众作者,以各章序次排列。

第一章	李战子	南京国际关系学院
第二章	史宝辉	北京林业大学外语学院
第三章	史宝辉	北京林业大学外语学院
第四章	张维友	华中师范大学外语学院
第五章	何　卫	北京大学外语学院
第六章	钱　军	北京大学外语学院
第七章	姜望琪	北京大学外语学院
第八章	张德禄	青岛海洋大学外语学院
第九章	杨永林	清华大学外语系
第十章	索玉柱	北京大学外语学院
第十一章	姜望琪	北京大学外语学院
第十二章	刘世生	清华大学外语系
第十三章	胡壮麟	北京大学外语学院
第十四章	王初明	广东外语外贸大学国家语言学与应用语言学研究基地
第十五章	文秋芳	南京大学外语学院
第十六章	封宗信	清华大学外语系

应该承认,我们的知识和经验毕竟有限,撰稿者又是在较短时间内完成编写任务,他们还被告知,要勇于当枪靶子,尽量发表自己的哪怕是不很成熟的观点,以及适当地结合一定的汉语资料。这样,不论从内容和编排上都会有不足。当局者迷,旁观者清,我们希望语言学界的前辈们,各高校中使用本教材的老师和同学们,以及研究部门的有关专家将意见及时反馈我们,这既是参与了本教材的建设,也是对我们,特别是编者的鞭策。我们谨在此代表全体作者预致谢忱。

编者
2002 年 3 月

CONTENTS

Chapter 1 Linguistics—A Pilot Science (1)
  1.1 Why Study Linguistics? (1)
  1.2 What Is Language? —Defining the Object of Study (2)
  1.3 Origin of Language (3)
  1.4 Design Features of Language (4)
  1.5 Animal Communication Systems, Gesture and Other Language Forms (9)
  1.6 Perspectives of Language Studies (12)
  1.7 Functions of Language (15)
  1.8 Important Distinctions in Linguistics (20)
  1.9 Data of Linguistics (28)
  1.10 Status and Prospect of Linguistics (29)

Chapter 2 Phonological Analysis (34)
  2.1 Transcribing Speech Sounds (34)
  2.2 Consonants and Vowels (38)
  2.3 Phonemic vs. Phonetic Transcriptions (46)
  2.4 Distinctive Features and Rule Representation (49)
  2.5 Suprasegmentals and Feature Geometry (53)
  2.6 Optimality Theory (57)
  2.7 Conclusion (62)

Chapter 3 Morphology (68)
  3.1 Morphemes, Morphs and Allomorphs (68)
  3.2 Classification of Morphemes (70)
  3.3 Morphemization (73)
  3.4 Allomorphy (74)
  3.5 Word, Word-form and Lexeme (76)
  3.6 Morphology and Word-formation (78)
  3.7 Approaches and Problems (86)

Chapter 4 Generative Syntax (91)
  4.1 Generative Grammar: Some Basic Assumptions (91)
  4.2 Phrase Structure Rules (94)

4.3　Projection from Lexicon ……………………………… (101)
　　4.4　The Minimalist Approach …………………………… (130)

Chapter 5　Functional Syntax ……………………………… (148)
　　5.1　Vilém Mathesius ……………………………………… (148)
　　5.2　František Daneš ……………………………………… (162)
　　5.3　Michael Halliday ……………………………………… (172)
　　5.4　Summary ……………………………………………… (183)

Chapter 6　Semantics ………………………………………… (190)
　　6.1　Introduction …………………………………………… (190)
　　6.2　Meanings of "Meaning" ……………………………… (191)
　　6.3　The Referential Theory ……………………………… (192)
　　6.4　Sense Relations ……………………………………… (194)
　　6.5　Componential Analysis ……………………………… (199)
　　6.6　Sentence Meaning …………………………………… (202)

Chapter 7　Linguistic Comparison ………………………… (217)
　　7.1　Introduction …………………………………………… (217)
　　7.2　Comparative and Historical Linguistics …………… (217)
　　7.3　Typological Comparison …………………………… (232)
　　7.4　Contrastive Linguistics ……………………………… (245)

Chapter 8　Language, Culture, and Society ……………… (258)
　　8.1　Introduction …………………………………………… (258)
　　8.2　Language and Culture ……………………………… (259)
　　8.3　Language and Society ……………………………… (269)
　　8.4　Sociolinguistics and Language Teaching ………… (277)
　　8.5　Summary ……………………………………………… (290)

Chapter 9　Cognitive Linguistics …………………………… (296)
　　9.1　Introduction …………………………………………… (296)
　　9.2　Cognitive Abilities and Cognitive Processes ……… (298)
　　9.3　Cognitive Semantics ………………………………… (317)
　　9.4　Cognitive Grammar ………………………………… (324)

Chapter 10　Pragmatics ……………………………………… (341)
　　10.1　Introduction ………………………………………… (341)
　　10.2　Speech Act Theory ………………………………… (341)
　　10.3　The Classical Theory of Implicature ……………… (349)

10.4	Post-Gricean Theories	(353)
10.5	Recent Developments in Pragmatics	(361)

Chapter 11 Issues of Stylistics (370)
11.1	Introduction	(370)
11.2	Style and Stylistics	(372)
11.3	Style as Rhetoric: The Initial Stage of Stylistics	(373)
11.4	One Style or Several Styles?	(375)
11.5	Aspects of Style: The Writer-style as Writer's Individual/Personal Singularities	(377)
11.6	Aspects of Style: The Text-style as Linguistic Sameness (Structural Equivalence)	(380)
11.7	Aspects of Style: The Text-style as Linguistic Difference (Deviation or Foregrounding)	(383)
11.8	Aspects of Style: The Reader-style as Reader's Response	(387)
11.9	Aspects of Style: The Context: Style as Function	(389)
11.10	Aspects of Style: The Meaning: Style as Meaning Potential	(393)
11.11	Concluding Remarks: Linguistics, Literary Criticism, and Stylistics	(397)

Chapter 12 Computational Linguistics (403)
12.1	What Is Computational Linguistics?	(403)
12.2	Machine Translation	(404)
12.3	Corpus Linguistics	(413)
12.4	Information Retrieval	(420)
12.5	Looking into the Future	(424)

Chapter 13 Second Language Acquisition (430)
13.1	Introduction	(430)
13.2	The Role of Internal Mechanisms	(431)
13.3	The Role of Native Language	(440)
13.4	Input, Interaction and Output	(445)
13.5	Non-language Influences	(447)
13.6	Summary	(450)

Chapter 14 Modern Theories and Schools of Linguistics (454)
14.1	The Beginning of Modern Linguistics	(454)

14.2　The Prague School and the Copenhagen School …… (461)
14.3　The London School ……………………………… (469)
14.4　Halliday and Systemic-Functional Grammar …… (477)
14.5　American Structuralism ………………………… (487)
14.6　Chomsky and Transformational-Generative Grammar … (494)
14.7　Revisionist/Rebellious Theories ………………… (510)
14.8　Concluding Remarks …………………………… (518)

Chapter 1

Linguistics—A Pilot Science

We danced round in a ring and suppose, but the secret sits in the middle and knows.

——Robert Frost

1.1 Why Study Linguistics?

Very generally speaking, LINGUISTICS is the study of language. For some, language does not seem to be a worthy subject for academic study. It is treated as a tool for access to some other fields rather than as a subject in and of itself. This instrument fallacy hinders the public understanding of linguistics as the systematic study of language, though linguistics has been a field of academic enquiry in universities for many years now.

As a branch of science, linguistics has developed its own full fledged series of methodologies, which qualify it as "a pilot science." According to Saussure, the forefather of modern linguistics, linguistics is a radically interdisciplinary and self-reflexive enterprise and should not remain the business of a few specialists. (Saussure, 1959) It is indeed necessary to reconsider how much we really understand the nature of language and its role in our life. And one will be surprised to realize that some of our most damaging racial, ethnic, and socio-economic prejudices are based on our linguistic ignorance and wrong ideas about language.

With the advance of computer technology, linguistics has an increasingly important role to play in today's information age; and its educational implications can never be underestimated. We can all note that language plays a central role in our individual and social lives. However, if we are not fully aware of the nature and mechanism of our language, we will be ignorant of what constitutes our essential humanity. The understanding of language should not be confined to linguists, as it is a vital human resource that all of us share.

For instance, why does Chomsky's linguistic theory have such a great influence on humanities and social sciences? How is it that he makes the unknown to the public linguistic theory become the foundation of cognitive science, psychology, computer technology and artificial intelligence? We will have to acquire a systematic knowledge of the basic theories, research methodology, object and scope of the study, and main findings of linguistics in order to answer such questions. Two things need to be mentioned here to pave the way for our ensuing introduction. First, readers may refer to *Linguistics: A Course Book* (Hu et al., 1988/2001) for details of some relevant topics which are dealt with quite briefly in this new edition. Secondly, the problems discussed in this chapter involve varied approaches and viewpoints and it is our hope that readers will judge for themselves and delve further into the field. The journey of further exploration is bound to be rewarding, as a deeper understanding of language in general is fundamental for many sciences.

1.2 What Is Language? —Defining the Object of Study

When we discuss what is language, we face a problem of focus. Language involves at least three activities. It is a neural activity in the human brain and a muscular activity of the human body. More important, it also involves social activities which engage individuals interacting with one another and with the written language. Following Halliday and Matthiessen (2004: 20), we use "language" to mean natural, human, adult and verbal language. Natural as opposed to mathematics and computer languages, human as opposed to animal languages, adult as opposed to infant protolanguages, verbal as opposed to music, dance and languages of architecture and fashion, etc. All the other systems have some features in common with language proper, but none of them has all the features.

Different outlooks on language can lead to different research methods. For example the NATURALISTIC view of language held by the famous German philologist August Schleicher looks at language as an organism in the natural world. Consequently language has its growth and decay. He proposes to use Darwin's theory of the origin of species to study language and classify linguistics as belonging to natural sciences. Perceived in a more MENTALISTIC fashion, language is the capacity of one individual to alter, through structured sound, gesture or visual emission, the mental organization of another individual. (Mc Neill, 2000) The literary descriptions of the functions of language are beyond enumerating, e.g. in Chinese, we have "言为心声," etc.

To give the barest of definition, language is a means of VERBAL COMMUNICATION. It is rule governed in that speakers of the same language follow the grammar and communicative conventions. It is instrumental in that communicating by speaking or writing is a purposeful act. It is social and conventional in that language is a SOCIAL SEMIOTIC and communication can only take place effectively if all the users share a broad understanding of human interaction including such associated factors as non-verbal cues, motivation, and socio cultural roles. Language learning and use are determined by the intervention of biological, cognitive, psychosocial, and environmental factors. In short, language distinguishes us from animals because it is far more sophisticated than any animal communication system.

Here let us refer to a definition of language proposed by the famous Chinese linguist Chao Yuanren (赵元任, 1980/1999: 3): "人跟人互通信息,用发音器官发出来的,成系统的行为的方式。" He emphasizes the systematic aspect of language and by treating language as a BEHAVIOURAL pattern, he shows signs of being influenced by Bloomfieldian behaviorism. Perceived in today's views, Chao was correct in everything except that the focus now shifts from language as a behavioral pattern to language as an INTERACTIONAL pattern. We will dwell more on this in Section 1.6.4.

1.3 Origin of Language

Tracing the ORIGIN OF LANGUAGE is always an intriguing task as some scientists say that language is the very thing that makes us human. But when did we first start talking and how did language evolve over the millenniums into the diverse form of communication it is today? In religious canons we can find stories or parables about the origin of language. And various theories are proposed to account for or speculate about its origin, such as the *bow-wow theory*, the *pooh-pooh theory*, and the *yo-he-ho theory*, etc. Readers may refer to *Linguistics: A Course Book* (Hu et al. 1988/2001) for details of these theories.

William C. Stokoe (in McNeill, 2000) proposes a new interpretation of language origin: language may have begun with gestural expression. Instrumental manual actions may have been transformed into symbolic gestures, and vision would have been the key of language evolution: humans could have begun to represent the world they saw (namely, things and actions) by their own means. Vision would have been the key for syntax to slowly come up because of its great capability of parallel processing.

A more dynamic view of the origin of language holds that to trace the origin of language we must first ask ourselves "do we conceive of language as having sprung into existence full blown or as the result of the accretion of elements gradually coming to constitute something recognizable as language?" (McNeill, 2000)

Following this view, tracing the stages in the development of human language is not such an important inquiry. Instead of aiming for a precise dated origin of language, "we should recognize that language capacity was composed of mosaic of structural, anatomical, neural, behavioral and environmental features and be concerned to propose a plausible sequence of events in the evolutionary history of language." (McNeill, 2000) This of course goes beyond the limited space of our introductory chapter here. Readers may refer to Algeo and Pyle's *The Origins and Development of the English Language* (5th edition)(2009)for a very good introduction.

1.4 Design Features of Language

It is generally agreed that language is an intrinsic aspect of human inheritance. It thus differs in kind from other acquired but less essential skills such as chess playing, cycling and calculus. It is also advantageous over animal "languages." As a philosopher once observed, "No matter how eloquently a dog may bark, he cannot tell you that his parents were poor but honest." So what makes human language so complicated and flexible, so unrestrained by the immediate context and so capable of creating new meanings, in a word, so distinctive from languages used by other species? The features that define our human languages can be called DESIGN FEATURES. The following are the frequently discussed ones. We will have a more extended discussion on arbitrariness and mention others in passing, as there have always been some interesting arguments about how to understand arbitrariness

1.4.1 Arbitrariness

The widely accepted meaning of this feature, which was discussed by Saussure first, refers to the fact that the forms of linguistic signs bear no natural relationship to their meaning. Saussure's initial definition of the principle of ARBITRARINESS and its relationship to the sign is as follows:

> The link unifying signifier and signified is arbitrary or, even more, since we understand by the sign the total result of the association of a signifier with a signified, we can say more simply: the linguistic sign is arbitrary. (Saussure, 1959: 100)

For instance, we cannot explain why a book is called a /buk/ and a pen a /pen/. Recently some arguments have been going on in the serge of re-reading Saussure. Some scholars argue strongly in favor of non-arbitrariness of language while others insist on the total arbitrariness of language. Instead of going to extremes, more would agree that there seems to be different levels of arbitrariness.

1.4.1.1 Arbitrary Relationship between the Sound of a Morpheme and Its Meaning

ONOMATOPOEIA refers to words which are uttered like the sounds they describe, e. g. in Chinese "叮咚""轰隆""叽里咕噜" seem to have a natural basis. But in English, totally different words are used to describe the same sound. For example, dogs bark "bowwow" in English but "汪汪" in Chinese. As Sapir (1921/2004:4) put it succinctly, "They do not directly grow out of nature, they are suggested by it and play with it. Hence the onomatopoetic theory of the origin of speech, the theory that would explain all speech as a gradual evolution from sounds of an imitative character, really brings us no nearer to the instinctive level than is language as we know it today."

So there are some misunderstandings about the onomatopoeic effect. As a matter of fact, arbitrary and onomatopoeic effect may work at the same time. Widdowson cites a line from Keats' "Ode to a Nightingale" to illustrate this point:

(1) The murmurous haunt of flies on summer eves.

When reading it aloud, we may feel the connection between the sounds and the meaning. But the effect does not really result from the whispering sounds themselves, for we will have to know the meanings of the words "murmurous" "summer" "eves" before setting up such a connection. To test this, just think of using the similar sounding word "murderous" to substitute "murmurous," and no connection whatsoever will be established between the sounds and the little noises of the flying mosquitoes. "It is only when you know the meaning that you infer that the form is appropriate." (Widdowson, 1996:6) This also applies to many cases of the so called onomatopoeic words.

Some linguists in re-reading Saussure also hold that onomatopoeia is not really an exception to the general principle of arbitrariness. (Thibault,1997: 280ff.) Words such as "tick tock" "clang" "buzz" and so on are fully conventional in English. Linguistically, it is misleading to assume that these are motivated by a mimetic relationship with real world sounds, although there is a relationship of some kind, that needs to be explained by using many other words. For instance, it is not self evident why "轰隆" in Chinese means the sound of thunder or cannonballs. But after all, these examples of onomatopoeia, and many others, fully conform to the type categories of both Chinese phonology and lexicogrammar. Saussure has this to say about onomatopoeia:

> As for authentic onomatopoeia, not only are they not very numerous, but their choice is already to some extent arbitrary, since they are only the approximate and already half conventional imitation of certain noises. Furthermore, once introduced into the language system, they are more or less entrained in the phonetic, morphological, etc. evolution which other words are subject to... (Saussure, 1959: 102)

One of the challenges to the view of arbitrariness comes from the French linguist Pierre Guiraud. He studied the bunch of words with associative relations, such as "whirl" "twirl" "furl," and found that these words share the meaning "whirling" and that they have the same pronunciation with the corresponding parts of other words. But rather than a serious challenge to Saussure's views, his efforts appear more like an attempt to explore the degree of inner association and organization in lexis. (Gordon, 1996: 89)

1.4.1.2 Arbitrary at the Syntactic Level?

According to some functional linguists (Halliday, 1985/1994), language is not arbitrary at the syntactic level.

By SYNTAX we refer to the ways that sentences are constructed according to the grammar of arrangement. As we know, the order of elements in a sentence follows certain rules, and there is a certain degree of correspondence between the sequence of clauses and the real happenings. In other words, syntax is less arbitrary than words, especially in so far as word order is concerned. Compare:

(2) a. He came in and sat down.
   b. He sat down and came in.
   c. He sat down after he came in.

When we say (2)a, we mean the actions occurred in this order; if we say (2)b readers will take it as meaning the opposite sequence of real happenings—perhaps he got into his wheelchair and propelled himself into the room. In (2)c with the help of the word "after" we can reverse the order of the clauses. Therefore functionalists hold that the most strictly arbitrary level of language exists in the distinctive units of sounds by which we distinguish pairs of words like "pin" and "bin," or "fish" and "dish."

However, the opposite view underscores the AUTONOMY of syntax. "Human cognition embodies a system whose primitive terms are non-semantic and non-discourse derived syntactic elements and whose principles of combination make no reference to system external factors." (Newmeyer, 1998: 18) In other words, to these people, syntax is purely arbitrary.

1.4.1.3 Division of Reality Is Arbitrary

What is the relationship between the arbitrariness of the linguistic signs and the way language is used to classify reality? Let us look at Whorf's account:

> In English we divide most of our words into two classes, which have different grammatical and logical properties. Class I we call nouns, e. g. "house, man"; class 2 verbs, e. g. "hit, run." Many words of one class can act secondarily as of the other class, e. g. "a hit, a run," or "to man

(the boat),"but, on the primary level, the division between the classes is absolute. Our language thus gives us a bipolar division of nature. But nature herself is not thus polarized... (Widdowson, 1996: 81)

This is indeed an even more important and frequently misunderstood aspect of the arbitrary nature of language. Saussure emphasizes that a language is not a "NOMENCLATURE" that provides its own names for categories that exist outside language. We tend to assume that we have the words "books" and "chairs" in order to name books and chairs, which exist outside any language. But this is not the case. If words stood for pre-existing concepts, they would have exact equivalents in meaning from one language to the next, which is not at all the case.

We can summarize Saussure's theories as follows: he proposed that we divide up the world into arbitrary concepts, and we assign arbitrary labels (sound letter combinations) to those concepts. He argued that SIGNS depend for their value on the other signs in the language system. It is very hard for native speakers to perceive the division between the label and the concept; they perceive it as "natural" and arbitrariness is therefore invisible to them.

1.4.1.4 Arbitrariness and Convention

What then is the link between a linguistic sign and its meaning? It is a matter of convention. Here we have to look at the other side of the coin of arbitrariness, namely, CONVENTIONALITY. Arbitrariness of language makes it potentially creative. That is, it allows language to change. If the signs were not arbitrary, the new meaning of "mouse" (as a peripheral equipment of the computer) would not have come into being. This does not mean arbitrariness of language can facilitate the learning of a new language. On the contrary, the other side of arbitrariness—conventionality makes learning a language laborious. For learners of a foreign language, it is the conventionality of a language that is more worth noticing than its arbitrariness.

1.4.1.5 Arbitrariness and Iconicity

A theme pervading abundant work in the functionalist tradition is that language structure to a considerable degree has an "ICONIC" motivation. Roughly, this embodies the idea that the form, length, complexity, or interrelationship of elements in a linguistic representation reflects the form, length, complexity, or interrelationship of elements in the concept, experience, or communicative strategy that that representation encodes. (Newmeyer, 1998: 114) The major works dealing with ICONICITY in language are devoted primarily to defending three distinct claims, namely, grammatical structure is an iconic reflection of conceptual structure; iconic principles govern speakers' choices of structurally available options in discourse; and structural options that reflect discourse iconic principles become GRAMMATICALIZED. (Newmeyer,1998:115)

Just as arbitrariness, iconicity can also be observed widely in language, though we should not understand it at its face value. Arbitrariness defines the human language, while iconicity is our attempt to understand the resources of our language and the profound relationship between language and COGNITION. As the saying goes, the opposite of truth might not be fallacy—our language seems to incorporate both arbitrary and iconic elements. With more research findings in future, new insights will be revealed about this significant feature of language.

1.4.2 Duality

DUALITY is a property of communication systems in which meaningless units are combined to form arbitrary signs that, in turn, are combined to form new larger signs, each level having its own principles of organization. (O'Grady, et al. ,2001:713)

Roughly speaking, the elements of the spoken language are sounds which do not convey meaning in themselves. The only function of sounds is to combine with one another to form units that have meaning, such as words. We call sounds here secondary units as opposed to such primary units as words, since the secondary units are meaningless and the primary units have distinct and identifiable meaning. The property of duality then only exists in such a system, namely, with both elements (secondary units) and units. Many animals communicate with special calls, which have corresponding meanings. That is, their primary units have meanings but cannot be further divided into elements or secondary units. So we say most animal communication systems do not have this design feature of human language—the property of duality. Consequently, the communicative power of animal language is highly limited.

Now we can perceive the advantage of duality, which lies in the great productive power our language is endowed with. A large number of different units can be formed out of a small number of elements—for instance, tens of thousands of words out of a small set of sounds, around 48 in the case of the English language. And out of the huge number of words, there can be astronomical number of possible sentences and phrases, which in turn can combine to form unlimited number of texts.

1.4.3 Creativity

The CREATIVITY of language partly originates from its duality which we just discussed in the above section, namely, because of duality the speaker is able to combine the basic linguistic units to form an infinite set of sentences, most of which are never before produced or heard.

Language is creative in another sense, that is, its potential to create endless sentences. This is one of the major claims of Chomskian linguistics. The recursive nature of language provides a theoretical basis for this possibility. For example, we can write a sentence like the following and go on endlessly:

(3) He bought a book which was written by a teacher who taught in a school which was known for its graduates who...

According to computer estimation, to speak aloud all the possible sentences consisting of any 20 chosen words will take about 2000 times the age of the earth. From this we can claim that it is extremely impossible for one to hear again a 20 word sentence that he used to encounter. In other words, language is characterized by its creativity, as grammar enables us to produce infinite number of sentences.

1.4.4 Displacement

DISPLACEMENT means that human languages enable their users to symbolize objects, events and concepts which are not present (in time and space) at the moment of communication. Thus, I can refer to Confucius, or the North Pole, even though the first lived over 2,500 years ago and the second is far away from China.

Most animals respond communicatively as soon as they are stimulated by some occurrence of communal interest. For instance, a warning cry of a bird instantly announces danger. Such animals are under "immediate stimulus control."Human language is, unlike animal communication systems, stimulus free. What we talk about need not be immediately triggered by any external stimulus in the world or any internal state.

Displacement benefits human beings by giving them the power to handle GENERALIZATIONS and ABSTRACTIONS. Indeed words are often used not in such immediately physical context when they denote concrete objects. They are often used with a deference for referential application. Once we can talk about physically distant things, we acquire the ability to understand concepts which denote "no things" such as truth and beauty. In a word, the intellectual benefit of displacement to us is that it makes it possible for us to talk and think in abstract terms. (Fowler,1974:8)

1.5 Animal Communication Systems, Gesture and Other Language Forms

It is still not so easy to distinguish language from other FORMS OF COMMUNICATION. Animal communication systems and gesture are among the most widely studied forms of communication.

A brief look at animal communication systems can throw light on the nature of human language, and how language serves as a crucial divide between humans and other species. There are basically two types of animal communication systems: the first type is the remarkable system found in many species of bees; the second type is well represented by the calls of various monkeys and birds. Human language has something in common with each of these systems, but it differs in significant respects from both.

The first type is called point by point (unbounded analog) system: In such a system, each point along some real world continuum (e. g. distances or orientations in space) is associated with a point along a continuum of signals (e. g. time spent in the straight line portion of the dance, or orientation of the dancing bee in relation to the top of the hive).

The second major type is bounded discrete system, which is well represented by the calls of various species of monkeys. Such a system has only a limited number of signals, each triggered by a certain condition in the world (like the approach of a strange creature) or by an internal state of the animal (like fear) and thus communicating what that condition or state holds. Obviously this system can communicate only a limited number of messages:

```
signals (calls)          S1  S2  S3... Sn
                         ↑   ↑   ↑      ↑
eliciting conditions     C1  C2  C3... Cn
```

More recent research found that chimps also invent their own personal noises by using particular grunts to mean certain things, though such personal noises are not as obvious as gestures to human observers. "PROTOWORDS" of this kind are believed to be the first step toward language. The next would be for the symbolic noise to be picked up and used by all the members of a troop. Learned behaviors can spread through a troop, but they tend to spread most easily from mother to child. Countless generations of chimpanzees have probably made similar first steps toward speech without leading to anything substantial, for young chimps do not repeat the close relationship they have with their mothers when they grow up and mix with other adult chimps, who rarely take the necessary interest to learn from each other. (Macrone, 1991: 158)

If chimpanzees were seen as some ancestor of ours, it is more valuable to study its communication. Many researchers feel that chimps are developing toward threshold of speech. It is suggested that early man about two million years ago must have been at least as socially advanced as the modern chimp, and has since evolved to the language speaking societies like the ones we have today.

A program called "Can Chimps Talk?" explores the various experiments and issues involved in ape language. Mentioning a few of the findings may suffice here. Sherman and Austin are two chimps who are able to communicate specific information to each other through the use of symbols. Another Chimp learns about 150 different signs, and uses them spontaneously and without undue repetition. And it internalizes a minimal value system, using signs for GOOD and BAD in appropriate contexts. A chimp named Kanzi uses sentences, that is, he follows structured rules in his multi-word utterances (showing the property of duality). He even makes up his own rules, such as first using a "word picture" (LEXIGRAM) to specify an action and then using a gesture to specify an agent. Another chimp named Koko can even rhyme and joke. On one occasion she used a metaphor of an elephant to refer to herself when she pretended a long tube was her "trunk." We catch a glimpse of creativity here. If our readers are now intrigued by chimpanzee language, there are many chimpanzee internet resources they may turn to.

Communication can take many forms, such as sign, speech, body language and facial expression. Do body language and facial expressions of chimps share or lack the distinctive properties of human language? If we refer to the design features of language discussed in Section 1.3, body language and facial expressions of animals are found to be less arbitrary, less creative, limited in repertoire, emotionally oriented and lacking in duality.

In recent discussions on the Internet, KINESTHETIC-based human languages are being proposed. Some people argue that language may be more kinesthetically than visually oriented. For instance, some language families in indigenous North America may be a different *kind* of human language, where semantic PRIMES are *felt* rather than *pictured* from sound. (Linguist List: Vol—12—918. Apr. 1, 2001.)

Consequently, we have the question about the relationship between language and gesture—whether there is unity or duality. Adam Kendon (in McNeill, 2000) broaches a classical question in gesture studies: should we consider gesture and language as different and independent phenomena? Basing his own answer on a good number of examples that show different roles (such as pragmatic, contextualizing, propositional, and so on) that co-verbal gesture may play in communication, the author claims a unity for language and gesture, and believes that the two serve different but complementary roles in conversation.

Obviously, the generation of gestures is closely related and coupled with speech generation: the generation of gestures is implied by the creation of a preverbal sketch model.

Truth in established fields of science can be provisional and can be proven wrong in the light of later knowledge. Not to say "truth" about such a relatively less trodden area. Our knowledge and understanding of the nature of language and other related types of communication forms so far is limited and calls for ceaseless exploratory endeavor.

1.6 Perspectives of Language Studies

The fact that linguistic theories differ results from different perspectives. It is generally acknowledged that language involves neural activity in the human brain, muscular activity of the body and social activity of the kind which engages individuals interacting with one an other. Different definitions of language interrelate these three activities in different ways, and imply different views of exactly which neutral, muscular and social activities are involved. (Roy Harris,1998: 14)

1.6.1 Language as Innate Human Knowledge

Chomsky (1968) has argued that the structure of even the simplest of languages is incredibly elaborate—far too complex either to be taught by parents or to be discovered via simple trial and error processes by immature children. He therefore proposes that human beings are gifted with the LANGUAGE ACQUISITION DEVICE (LAD), an inborn model of the structure of human languages that allows any child who has acquired a sufficient vocabulary to combine words into new sentences. The task of the linguist is to find out how as a child grows up he activates his innate language ability and produces well formed sentences. There are two components which contribute to language acquisition. The innate knowledge of the learner (called UNIVERSAL GRAMMAR or UG) and the environment. The notion of UG has broad implications. It suggests that all languages operate within the same framework and the understanding of this framework would contribute greatly to the understanding of what language is.

Other linguists have different views. Dan Slobin (1985), for example, does not assume that children have any innate knowledge of language, but thinks that they have an inborn LANGUAGE MAKING CAPACITY (LMC)—a set of cognitive and perceptual abilities that are highly specialized for language learning. Presumably these innate mechanisms (LADs or LMCs) enable young children to process linguistic input and to infer the phonological regularities, semantic relations and rules of syntax of any language they are exposed to.

However, these views are not without challenges. Proponents of the interactional position acknowledge that children are biologically prepared to acquire language, but they stress that the environment plays a crucial role in language learning. Children need to have ample opportunities to converse with responsive companions who tailor their own speech to the children's levels of understanding.

1.6.2 Language as a Fixed Code

Language is a CODE, namely, it is the sets of phonological, morphological, syntactic and semantic rules that, together with the lexicon, can be used to construct any or all sentences of a language; when these sentences are combined into larger units, we get texts, but neither the sentences nor the texts are part of the code. They are rather the output of the code—what the grammar generates or produces. (Schiffman, 1996: 56)

Treating language as a fixed code assumes that a language, in virtue of its internal structure, establishes correlation between a set of fixed verbal forms and a set of fixed meanings. The combination of the two supposedly provides people with a fixed code for public use. Accordingly, understanding what another person says involves matching up the linguistic forms that person produces with the meanings the communal code provides. (Nigel Love in Roy Harris, 1998: 49ff.)

However, to look at language as a code can be a fallacy. We can raise at least the following two objections. 1) When a child learns a language, he eventually acquires the code. But he acquires it by observing and hearing utterances in situational and cultural contexts, not just observing the bare code. The utterances of discourse are loaded with values and beliefs and myths. "The language as a code" is just like the meat on the bone (the bone being "LANGUAGE AS INTERACTION"), as it is hard to learn the code separately. 2) If language is a fixed code, the code must be fixed before the language can be used. But the fixing of the code, namely, establishing the agreement among language users as to the relations between form and meaning must be done in language too.

1.6.3 Language as a System

The first implication of treating language as a SYSTEM is to treat it as a system of differences. Saussure declares that what makes each element of a language what it is, and what gives it its identity, is the contrasts between it and other elements within the system of the language. The most precise characteristic of a linguistic sign is to be what the others are not. As we discuss in the section on arbitrariness, language is not a "nomenclature" that provides labels for pre-existing categories; it generates its own categories. In this sense we say each language is a system of concepts as well as forms: a system of conventional signs that organize the world.

The second implication of language as a system is the major theoretical thrust of systemic functional linguistics. Let us first consider the traffic light system: red light stands for "stop," green for "go" and yellow for "pause."

There is a one to one form meaning correspondence with two levels only: the level of three colors of lights, the level of the meaning the colors stand for. With language, things are extremely complicated. In a "one to one" system such as traffic lights and some animal calls meanings and symbols are tied together absolutely; in a system which has duality, signs are freed from the load of carrying particular meanings.

Shall we compare language to a traffic light system? There are several limitations when we try to think about language as a system like traffic lights. First, there would only be one signal (group of letters or sounds) for every meaning. Second, there would be a limited number of meanings and signals available. But it should be obvious from the discussion so far that language is a far more complicated entity than traffic lights in that we can use it to create new meanings.

As Bolinger and Sears (1981: 3—4) put it, "Stratification—this organization of levels on levels—is the physical manifestation of the 'infinite use of finite means,' the trait that most distinguishes human communication and that provides its tremendous resourcefulness."

Systemic linguistics holds the same view that language has strata. In language, meanings are realized as wordings, which are in turn realized by sounds or letters. Technically: discourse semantics gets realized through the lexico-grammar, which in turn gets realized through phonology or graphology.

When we compare this model of language with our traffic lights, we see that language is a different kind of semiotic system because it has three levels, not just two. That is, language has two meaning-making levels, an upper level of content known as discourse semantics, and an intermediate level of content known as lexico-grammar. (Eggins, 1994: 21)

By far the most sophisticated and elaborate of all the semiotic systems is the system of language. Systemic linguists propose the following main theoretical claims about language: Language use is functional; Its function is to make meanings; These meanings are influenced by the social and cultural context in which they are exchanged; The process of using language is a semiotic process, a process of making meanings by choosing, namely, language involves sets of meaningful choices or oppositions. (Eggins, 1994: 3)

1.6.4 Language as Interaction

The notion that both oral and written use of language may be regarded as shaped by an INTERACTIVE process has gained strength through the theories of the Russian linguist and literary theorist Bakhtin. When dealing with the core of language meaning, he proposes that meaning is not a product of a self-contained and impersonal code, but is creative and fuzzy edged. The following are his insightful views:

Meaning does not reside in the word or in the soul of the speaker or in the soul of the listener. Meaning is *the effect of interaction between speaker and listener produced via the material of a particular sound complex*. It is like an electric spark that occurs only when two different terminals are hooked together. Those who... in attempting to find the meaning of a word, approach its lower, stable, self identical limit, want, in effect, to turn on a light bulb after having switched off the current. Only the current of verbal intercourse endows a word with the light of meaning. (Bakhtin, 1984 [1929]: 103)

One consequence of Bakhtin's theory is that the monolithic notion of the addresser's integrity is suspended. Just one piece of evidence. A textbook on pragmatics by Jenny Thomas (1995) is entitled *Meaning in Interaction*, written in the vein of Bakhtinian thought about the interactive aspect of meaning generation and comprehension. The title reflects the conception that the process of making meaning is a joint accomplishment between speaker and hearer.

Roy Harris also points out that "language as social interaction involves not just vocal behavior but many kinds of behavior, and to engage in face to face linguistic communication is, in the simplest type of case, to co-monitor with one other person a behavioral continuum along which a succession of integrated events can be expected to occur. To have grasped and be able to exploit these integrational connections is what makes us communicationally proficient members of a community." (Roy Harris, 1997: 13)

1.7 Functions of Language

Many categorizations of FUNCTIONS of language have been made, not in terms of the concrete specific functions that language is put to in our daily life, such as to chat, to think, to buy and sell, to read and write, to greet people, etc., but in terms of the more generalized functions language can perform in human communication. Functional linguists summarize these practical functions and attempt some broad classifications of the basic functions of language as will be listed below.

1.7.1 Theories of the Functions of Language

1.7.1.1 Jakobson's Classification

For Jakobson and the Prague school structuralists, language is above all, as any semiotic system, for communication. While for many people, the purpose of communication is referential, for Jakobson, REFERENCE is not the only, nor even the primary goal of communication. In his famous article, "Linguistics and Poetics," Jakobson defined the six primary factors of any speech event, namely: SPEAKER, ADDRESSEE, CONTEXT, MESSAGE,

CODE, and CONTACT. Based on these six key elements of communication, Jakobson established a well known framework of language functions, namely: REFERENTIAL (to convey message and information), POETIC (to indulge in using language for the sake of displaying its beauty or rhythm), EMOTIVE (to express attitudes, feelings and emotions), CONATIVE (to persuade and influence others through commands and entreaties), PHATIC (to establish communion with others) and METALINGUAL function (to clear up intentions, words and meanings). They correspond to such communication elements as context, message, addresser, addressee, contact and code. (See the following figure) Jakobson's views of the functions of language are still of great importance.

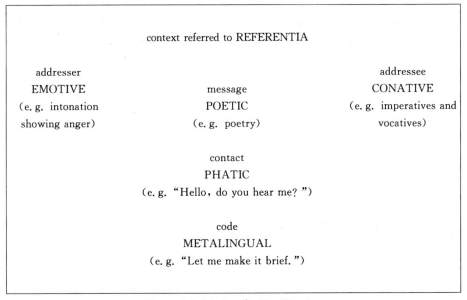

Figure 1.1 Jakobson's Classification

1.7.1.2 Halliday's Theory of Metafunctions

In his earlier works, Halliday proposed seven categories of language function, that is, instrumental, regulatory, representational, interactional, personal, heuristic and imaginative. For example, a baby may utter a particular noise to mean "Milk! I'm hungry—bring me the milk." This is the instrumental function of language which comes at a very early stage of life. Then the child may go on to learn the regulatory and other more advanced functions of language.

In the framework of functional grammar which he builds up and develops over the years, Halliday proposes a theory of METAFUNCTIONS of language, that is, language has IDEATIONAL, INTERPERSONAL and TEXTUAL functions. Ideational function construes a model of experience and constructs logical relations, interpersonal function enacts social relationships and textual function creates relevance to context. (Halliday, 1985/1994)

Still other classifications employ different categories and use different terms, but all share a great deal in common about the basic functions of language. Our list below is a summary for the convenience of presentation. The categories can still be somewhat overlapping.

1.7.2 Referential Function

The transmission of information is the first thing we think of when we consider the functions of language. INFORMATIONAL, or REFERENTIAL, or IDEATIONAL, function is associated with what objects and ideas are called and how events are described.

For most people the informational function is predominantly the major role of language. Language is the instrument of thought and people often feel need to speak their thoughts aloud when they are working on a math problem, for instance. The use of language to record facts is a prerequisite of social development. It is also called ideational function in the framework of functional grammar. Halliday notes that the ideational metafunction "is concerned with the content of language, its function as a means of expression of our experience, both of the external world and of the inner world of our own consciousness—together with what is perhaps a separate sub-component expressing certain basic logical relations." (Halliday & Mattiessen, 2004)

For example, for the same event—someone broke the vase in his colleague's house while the latter went to the other room to answer the phone, the following things can be said, "I broke the vase" "The vase was broken by me" "The vase broke," etc. And each represents a choice in the TRANSITIVITY system realizing the IDEATIONAL METAFUNCTION.

1.7.3 Interpersonal Function

In current linguistics we can observe a tendency to place greater stress on the INTERPERSONAL, variational and negotiable aspects of language in contrast to conventional concerns with the more ideational, content based and stable relations between forms and meaning.

In the framework of functional grammar, this function is concerned with interaction between the addresser and addressee in a discourse situation and the addresser's attitude toward what he speaks or writes about. For example, the ways in which people address others and refer to themselves (e.g. "Dear Sir" "Dear Professor" "Johnny" "yours" "your obedient servant") indicate the various types and degrees of interpersonal relations. In short, it is interactional and attitudinal.

Attached to the interpersonal function of language, is its function of the expression of identity. For example, the chanting of a crowd at a football match, the shouting of names or slogans at public meetings, the stage managed audience reactions to TV shows all signal who we are and where we belong. Language marks our identity, physically in terms of age, sex, and voiceprints; psychologically in terms of personality and intelligence; geographically in terms of accents and dialects; ethnically and socially in terms of social stratification, class, status, role, solidarity and distance. (David Crystal, 1992: 17) The interpersonal function is such a broad category that it is often discussed under various other terms as performative, emotive, expressive and phatic function of language. They emphasize different aspects of the interpersonal function.

1.7.4 Performative Function

This concept originates from the philosophical study of language represented by Austin and Searle, whose theory now forms the backbone of pragmatics. The PERFORMATIVE function of language is primarily to accomplish some act, as in marriage ceremonies, the sentencing of criminals, the blessing of children, the naming of a ship at a launching ceremony, and the cursing of enemies. The kind of language employed in performative verbal acts is usually quite formal and even ritualized. For example, when the sentence "I resign" is interpreted as an act of resignation.

The performative function can extend to the control of reality as on some magical or religious occasions. For example, in Chinese when someone breaks a bowl or a plate the host or the people present are likely to say "岁岁（碎碎）平安" as a means of controlling the forces which the believers feel might affect their lives.

1.7.5 Emotive Function

According to some investigations, though the conveying of some information occurs in most uses of language, it probably represents not more than 20 percent of what takes place in verbal communication. (Nida, 1998: 17) The emotive function of language is one of the most powerful uses of language because it is so crucial in changing the emotional status of an audience for or against someone or something. According to David Crystal (1992: 17), the EMOTIVE function is a means of getting rid of our nervous energy when we are under stress. For example, swear words, obscenities, involuntary verbal reactions to beautiful art or scenery; conventional words/phrases, like "God" "My" "Damn it" "What a sight" "Wow" "Ugh" "Ow,"etc.

It is also discussed under the term EXPRESSIVE function. The expressive function can often be entirely personal and totally without any implication of communication to others. For example, a man may say "Ouch!" after striking a fingernail with a hammer, or he may mutter "damn" when realizing that he has forgotten an appointment. Exclamations such as "Man!" "Oh boy!" and "Hurrah!" are usually uttered without any purpose of communicating to others, but as essentially a verbal response to a person's own feelings. Such expressive utterances can also be a communal response of a group of people who reinforce one another's expressive use of language to show their solidarity. (Nida, 1998: 21)

1.7.6　Phatic Communion

This term PHATIC COMMUNION originates from Malinowski's study of the functions of language used on Trobriand Islands. It refers to the social interaction of language, e.g.

(4) Mrs. P sneezes violently.
　　Mrs. Q: Bless you.
　　Mrs. P: Thank you.

We all use such small seemingly meaningless expressions to maintain a comfortable relationship between people without containing any factual content. Ritual exchanges about health or weather such as "Good morning!" "God bless you!" "Nice day!" often state the obvious. Yet they indicate that a channel of communication is open if it should be needed. And different cultures have different topics of phatic communion. According to David Crystal, the weather is not a universal conversation filler as the English might like to think. Rundi women (in Burundi, Central Africa), upon taking leave, routinely and politely say "I must go home now, or my husband will beat me." Some typical expressions of phatic communion in Chinese are: "好久不见了!" "祝你一路顺风!" and "过年好!" etc. Broadly speaking, this function is performed by expressions that help define and maintain interpersonal relations, such as slang, jokes, jargons, ritualistic exchanges, switches to social and regional dialects. We have to learn a large repertoire of such usage if we are to interact comfortably with different people.

1.7.7　Recreational Function

The RECREATIONAL function of a language is often overlooked because it seems restrictive in purpose and supposedly limited in usefulness. However, no one will deny the use of language for the sheer joy of using it, such as a baby's babbling or a chanter's chanting. In the Latin and Islamic worlds as well as in some areas of China, there is widespread use of verbal dueling, in which one singer begins a song of a few lines and challenges his opponent to continue the content or provide a rejoinder in a similar rhythm and rhyme scheme. Such verbal duels may last for a few hours and are performed for the sheer joy of using language.

When we observe a children's play, we can find nonsensical lyrics performing a recreational function in the game: the repetitive rhythms help to control the game, and the children plainly take great delight in them. Adults also have their way to appreciate language for its own sake. For instance, poetry writing gives them the pleasure of using language for its sheer beauty. We are getting very close here to Jakobson's poetic function.

1.7.8 Metalingual Function

Our language can be used to talk about itself. For example, I can use the word "book" to refer to a book or talk about the concept "book," and I can also use the expression "the word 'book'" to talk about the sign "book" itself. To organize any written text into a coherent whole, writers employ certain expressions to keep their readers informed about where they are and where they are going. For instance, instead of saying "The lion beat the unicorn all round the town." they say "All around the town the lion beat the unicorn." The change in linear order changes our perspective about the concerns of the clause. This is the METALINGUAL function of language, or in Halliday's term, the TEXTUAL FUNCTION.

This makes the language infinitely self-reflexive: We human beings can talk about talking and think about thinking, and in this sense we say only humans can ask what it means to communicate, to think, to be human.

We realize that while we are discussing the functions of language at length here, we might run the risk of orienting toward a functional view of language. Formalists would not take the trouble to enumerate the functions of language, not to say to explore how the function can help shape form. However, our understanding about the functions language performs can shed light on our understanding of the nature of language and the relationship between form and function. We are coming to the distinction between these two broad orientations—formalism and functionalism in Section 1.8.7.

1.8 Important Distinctions in Linguistics

It is helpful to sketch out a broad map of the terrain before one considers its more specific features on a smaller scale. The following pairs of concepts are among the most frequently mentioned in all branches of linguistics, and virtually form the backbone of linguistics. We hope our readers will take a critical view of these contrasts and make their own contributions.

1.8.1 Descriptive vs. Prescriptive

The distinction lies in prescribing how things ought to be and describing how things actually are. For example, concerning "It is I" and "It is me," the prescriptive view is that we should say the former instead of the latter because according to the rules in Latin "be" should be followed by the nominative case, not the accusative. Concerning (A) "Who did you speak to?" and (B) "Whom did you speak to?" one should say B instead of A. And concerning (A) "I haven't done anything" and (B) "I haven't done nothing," B is wrong because two negatives make a positive.

The DESCRIPTIVE views concerning the three cases are as follows. First, the Latin rule is not universal. In English, "me" is informal and "I" is felt to be very formal. Second, "whom" is used in formal speech and in writing, and "who" is more acceptable in informal speech. Third, language does not have to follow logical reasoning. Here two negatives only make a more emphatic negative. This sentence is not acceptable in Standard English not because it is illogical but because language changes and rejects this usage now. To sum up the two views, we can use the formulae—"Do/don't say X" and "People do/don't say X": the former represents the prescriptivist and the latter the descriptivist.

The essence of PRESCRIPTIVISM is the notion that one variety of languages has an inherently higher value than others, and that this ought to be imposed on the whole of the speech community. The areas in which prescriptivism pervades are pronunciation, grammar and vocabulary. In the field of rhetoric and writing styles, prescriptivism is also at work, though more subtly and implicitly. (Kaplan, 1966).

Though prescriptivism is still with us, an alternative point of view— DESCRIPTIVISM—wins more and more understanding. It proposes that the task of the grammarian is to describe, not prescribe, to record the facts of linguistic diversity, and not to attempt the impossible tasks of being language police and trying to stop language from changing, or imposing on members of a language community the so called norms of correctness. (David Crystal, 1992)

The reason why present day linguists are so insistent about the distinction between the two is simply that traditional grammar was very strongly normative in character, e.g. "You should never use a double negative" "You should not split the infinitive," etc.

In the 18th century, all the main European languages were studied prescriptively. The grammarians then tried to lay down rules for the correct use of language and settle the disputes over usage once and for all. Some usages were prescribed to be learned by heart, followed accurately or avoided altogether. It was a matter of black or white, right or wrong.

These attitudes are still with us, though people realize nowadays the facts of usage count more than the authority stipulated "STANDARDS." We can appeal neither to logic nor to Latin grammar when it comes to deciding whether something is or is not correct in English. Prescriptivism is an individual attitude. The related social attitude which goes to the extreme of prescriptivism is purism, which is something we should guard against. It is "a belief that there exists somewhere, perhaps in the past, or in a particular textual tradition, a state of 'PURITY' that the language can aspire to, or return to," and "a belief that purity is a good thing, capable of renewing or strengthening the moral fiber of the language, its linguistic culture, or its speakers." (Schiffman, 1996: 62)

Though the nature of linguistics as a science determines its preoccupation with description instead of prescription, it does not mean that there is no place at all for the establishment and prescription of norms of usage. "There are obvious administrative and education advantages, in the modern world, in standardizing the principal dialect that is employed within a particular country or region." (Lyons, 1981: 53) As Calsue Hagège (1999) rightly points out, linguists' participation in the appropriate amount of language planning and reform opens a wide field outside language teaching and information technology and makes their work truly influential and decisive. Language is not the private property of linguists, but they have the right and obligation to intervene when necessary and their intervention can to a certain extent affect the fate of the language and of the language users. For one thing, if there were no prescriptivism, language would change so fast that people might not understand each other. Prescriptivism serves to control the speed and extent of language change.

1.8.2 Synchronic vs. Diachronic

These are two fundamental and indispensable dimensions of linguistic study Saussure formalized and made explicit: "SYNCHRONIC," in which languages are treated as self-contained systems of communication at any particular time, and "DIACHRONIC," in which the changes which languages are subject to in the course of time are treated historically. (Robins, 1967: 200) It was Saussure's achievement to distinguish these two dimensions or axes of linguistics, synchronic or descriptive, and diachronic or historical, as each involving its own methods and principles and each essential in any adequate course of linguistic study or linguistic instruction.

Diachronic linguistics is the study of a language through the course of its history. Historical linguistics was a pervasive interest of the 19th century "Darwinists"; in the course of their historical researches into the development of the Indo-European tongues, the philologists instituted a firm tradition which had led to the production of much diachronic information about most of the culturally prominent, lettered languages of Europe.

A synchronic description takes a fixed instant (usually, but not necessarily, the present) as its point of observation. Most grammars are of this kind. If one takes something called *A Grammar of Modern Greek* from a library shelf, it will usually claim to be a synchronic grammar; likewise *The*

Structure of Shakespeare's English claims to be a synchronic description of a single past state of the language.

But linguists realize that synchrony is a fiction, for language changes as the minutes pass and grammar writing is a lengthy enterprise. However, the fiction of synchronic description is essential to linguistics. (Fowler, 1974: 34) In short, synchronic and diachronic linguistics are independent and yet interdependent. (Hu, 2000: 6)

1.8.3 Langue & Parole

In a celebrated series of lectures in the early 20th century, Saussure proposed that linguistics should concern itself with the shared social code, the abstract system, which he called LANGUE, leaving aside the particular actualities of individual utterances, which he called PAROLE. Langue was, on his account, a collective body of knowledge, a kind of common reference manual, copies of which were acquired by all members of a community of speakers.

Saussure distinguished the linguistic competence of the speaker and the actual phenomena or data of linguistics (utterances) as langue and parole. While parole constitutes the immediately accessible data, the linguist's proper object is the langue of each community, the lexicon, grammar, and phonology implanted in each individual by his up-bringing in society and on the basis of which he speaks and understands his language.

In the surge of re-reading Saussure, some linguists point out that the dominant reading of Saussure about the dichotomous relationship between langue and parole may not be correct. Neither is it necessarily appropriate to assume that Saussure's distinction between internal linguistics of langue and external linguistics of parole amounts to a description of the concrete reality of language. As Thibault (1997: 6) puts it, "this is a serious misreading of Saussure, which has given rise to a confusion between methodology, on the one hand, and ontology, on the other. A careful reading of Saussure does not necessarily lead to the rigid set of dichotomies which have predominated in subsequent thinking about these issues." The following is Saussure's account on the distinction between language and parole:

> If we could embrace the sum of word images stored in the minds of all individuals, we could identify the social bond that constitutes language (*langue*). It is a storehouse filled by the members of a given community through their active use of speaking (*parole*), a grammatical system that has a potential existence in each brain, or, more specifically, in the brains of a group of individuals. For language (*langue*) is not complete in any speaker; it exists perfectly only within a collectivity. In separating

language (*langue*) from speaking (*parole*) we are at the same time separating 1) what is social from what is individual; and 2) what is essential from what is accessory and more or less accidental. (Saussure, 1959: 13—14)

1.8.4 Competence and Performance

This fundamental distinction was first made by Chomsky in his *Aspects of the Theory of Syntax*. A language user's underlying knowledge about the system of rules is called his linguistic COMPETENCE. And PERFORMANCE refers to the actual use of language in concrete situations. (Chomsky, 1965: 3)

As a language user we all have intuitive grasp of the rules of language, and though we may not be able to state the rules explicitly, our performance demonstrates our adherence to them. If you have ever listened to an excited argument and tried to transcribe it, you will find that speakers do not always abide by linguistic rules. Instead there can be numerous false starts, deviations, and ungrammatical expressions even in the speech of a native speaker.

Even pre-school children know virtually all the rules of language except for some subtleties. They learn the rules by actually using the language. A child demonstrates by the way he uses words that he knows what a noun is long before he can define the term. We can also observe the discrepancy between competence and performance in normal language users. According to Chomsky, the task of a linguist is to determine from the data of performance the underlying system of rules that has been mastered by the language user.

Chomsky points out that this distinction is related to the langue parole distinction of Saussure; but he does not accept the view of seeing langue as a mere systematic inventory of items. For him, competence is closer to the conception of the famous German linguist Humbolt, that is, it should refer to the underlying competence as a system of generative processes.

Not all linguists agree with Chomsky in thinking that "linguistic theory is concerned primarily with an ideal speaker/listener, in a completely homogeneous speech community, who knows its language perfectly." (Chomsky, 1965: 3) Dell Hymes approaches language from a socio-cultural viewpoint with the aim of studying the varieties of ways of speaking on the part of the individual and the community. It is found that speakers vary their performance not at random but in a regular way. Thus it is possible to extend the notion of competence, restricted by Chomsky to knowledge of grammar, to incorporate the pragmatic ability for language use. This extended idea of competence can be called COMMUNICATIVE COMPETENCE. And the concept, though still not so clarified, has become very popular in EFL (English as Foreign Language) teaching in China in the past two decades.

There are many reasons for the discrepancy between competence and performance in normal language users. Some of them are ethnic background, socio-economic status, and regions of the country; and such short term factors as physical state changes within the individual, intoxication, fatigue, distraction, and illness.

Though competence and performance have been considered inter dependent, some recent writings express a belief in the autonomy of competence to performance. "Knowledge of language ('competence') can and should be characterized independently of language use ('performance') and the social, cognitive, and communicative factors contributing to use." (Newmeyer, 1998: 19)

Our view is that for students of English, competence needs to be nurtured in the process of enhancing performance, but competence calls for more efforts at the beginning stage while success in performance may motivate the acquisition of competence.

1.8.5 Actual and Potential Linguistic Choice

This distinction is interwoven with that between competence and performance, but oriented toward the systemic view of language, namely, language is a semiotic system with sets of oppositions and choices. The notion of language as a semiotic system enables us to interpret language behavior as choice. By CHOICE we mean the process of using language in a process of making meanings by choosing. Hence the pair of concepts—actual choice and potential choice. When making a choice from a linguistic system, what someone writes or says gets its meaning by being seen (interpreted) against the background of what could have been meant (said or written) in that context but was not. Through this distinction what people did do or did say on any particular occasion (their actual linguistic choices) is related to what they could have done or could have said (their potential linguistic choices). (Eggins, 1994: 22)

1.8.6 Etic vs. Emic

"Etic" and "emic" approaches (on the analogy of phon-*etic* and phon-*emic*) investigate, respectively, generalized phenomena of culturally patterned behavior, and phenomena peculiar to one language or culture system. The two terms were first used by the American linguist K. L. Pike in his 1954 book *Language in Relation to a Unified Theory of the Structure of Human Behavior*. Pike believes that the distinction and relationship between phonetics and phonemics in terms of "ETIC" and "EMIC" is also applicable to other linguistic levels and even the levels of human behavior. As we know, the abstract system of phonemic sounds was distinguished from the concrete phonetics of sounds in articulatory and auditory events. Similarly in ethnography, anthropology, psychology, sociology, archeology, and educational studies, the contrast between "etic" and "emic" is studied. Hu (2000: 99) summarizes the following dichotomies between what the two terms "etics" and "emics" stand for, namely, parole vs. non-parole, particular vs. general, based on observation vs. based on interview data, actual behavior vs. ideal behavior, description vs. theory, public vs. private, ethnographical vs. anthropological, cross-culturally non-comparable vs. cross-culturally comparable, hard-ware vs. soft-ware, and outsider's view vs. insider's view.

Anthropological linguistics adopts the distinction to mean that it is not sufficient for the investigator, no matter how much experience he has had with the verbal behavior of a particular speech community, merely to devise as detailed a list of speech acts and events as he can. Such a list runs the risk of being etic rather than emic, i.e. of making far too many, as well as behaviorally inconsequential, differentiations, just as was often the case with phonetic vs. phonemic analysis in linguistics proper. An emic set of speech acts and events must be one that is validated as meaningful via final resource to the native members of a speech community rather than via appeal to the investigator's ingenuity or intuition only.

In culture studies, emic perspective refers to determining what actions mean with a culture or cultural group, while etic perspective bears on concrete human actions and their motives and consequences. How to re-apply these terms to culture studies has been an issue of vivid disputes. For one thing, in the investigations, the "emic" might be associated with the insider's viewpoint (usually the native participant's) and the "etic" with the outsider's (usually an observer's). (Beaugrande, 1997: 526)

Significant as this pair of concepts is, views differ concerning their order of occurrence in research in the related fields. Pike proposes emic-etic-emic while Harris insists that etic analysis has its own independent significance. Hymes holds that the sequence should be $etic_1$-emic-$etic_2$, which seems to be more reasonable. (Hu, 2000: 94) Above all, etic and emic are mutually transferable, and further research is called for concerning the order of their occurrence in research and the causal relationship between them.

1.8.7 Formalism vs. Functionalism

General linguistic theory in the course of the 20th century has seen the emergence of two contrasting approaches. The mainstream approach has been, and remains, a segregational approach. Founded by Saussure, continued in the USA by Bloomfield and today by his generative successors, segregational analysis treats language and languages as objects of study existing in their own right, independently of other activities of communication and amenable to description in terms that are quite separate from those used in any other discipline. The alternative approach, the integrational approach sees language as manifested in a complex of human abilities and activities that are all integrated in social interaction, often intricately so and in such a manner that it makes little sense to segregate the linguistic from the non linguistic components. (Harris & Wolf, 1998: 6)

These two contrasting approaches are labeled as FORMALISM and FUNCTIONALISM. Formalists think that communication does not need gender marking, agreement rules, irregular verbs in order to be effective; while functionalists think that such grammatical phenomena may at first glance seem dysfunctional, but they may play an important role in discourse, for instance, the role in tracking referents. In other words, "in most external functionalist approaches, it is assumed that the links between form on the one hand and meaning and use on the other are 'natural' ones, in that the properties of the latter have helped to shape the former." (Newmeyer, 1998: 14)

Formalism holds that a central task for linguists characterizing the formal relationships among grammatical elements, independently of any characterization of the semantic and pragmatic properties of those elements. That is, it focuses centrally on linguistic form. In contrast, functionalism rejects that task on the grounds that the function of conveying meaning (in its broadest sense) has so affected grammatical form that it is senseless to compartmentalize it. (Newmeyer, 1998: 7) Advocates of extreme functionalism even believe that all of grammar can be derived from semantic and discourse factors—the only "arbitrariness" in language exists in the lexicon. (Newmeyer, 1998: 18)

While formalism makes very good sense about the rule-governedness of language and accomplishes a great deal in finding the universal aspects of languages, functionalism seems to be going on its own way by insisting on the mission of studying language in use. On the one hand, they emphasize the importance of context to the extent that they perceive language and context as inseparable. On the other hand, our ability to deduce context from text is a manifestation that language and context are interrelated. We are equally capable of predicting language from context, which provides further evidence of the language and context relationship.

Final evidence which emphasizes the close link between context and language is that it is often simply not possible to tell how people are using language if we do not take into account the context of use. Describing the impact of context on text has involved systemists in exploring in what ways context influences language and what aspects of language use appear to be effected by particular dimensions of context. Hence the REGISTER and GENRE theories. (Martin & Rose, 2008)

The following two quotes by the two representative figures of formalism and functionalism reveal the different emphasis or perspectives of language studies.

> ... modern generative grammar has sought to address concerns that animated the tradition; in particular, the Cartesian idea that "the true distinction" between humans and other creatures or machines is the ability to act in the manner they took to be most clearly illustrated in the ordinary use of language: without any finite limits, influenced but not determined by internal state, appropriate to situations but not caused by them, coherent and evoking thoughts that the hearer might have expressed, and so on. The goal of the work I have been discussing is to unearth some of the factors that enter into such normal practice, only some of these, however. (Chomsky, 2000: 17)

> So if we say that linguistic structure "reflects" social structure, we are really assigning to language a rule that is too passive. Rather we should say that linguistic structure is the realization of social structure, actively symbolizing it in a process of mutual creativity. Because it stands as a metaphor for society, language has the property of not only transmitting the social order but also maintaining and potentially modifying it. Variation in language is the symbolic expression of variation in society: it is created by society, and helps to create society in return. (Halliday, 1975 in Webster ed., 2007, Vol. 10: 255)

To summarize, formalists are correct in their commitment to characterize form independently of meaning and function, while functionalists have good reasons to believe that meaning and function can help shape form. Both these two orientations in linguistics have their strong points and inadequacies and a complementary approach should be possible if they are not taken as religious sects but alternative paths to approaching the truth.

1.9 Data of Linguistics

There are, broadly speaking, three sources of LINGUISTIC DATA we can draw upon to infer facts about language. To begin with, we can use introspection, appealing to our own intuitive competence as the data source. Some may doubt the validity or the representative nature of such intuitive sampling, and one alternative is to resort to elicitation. In that case, one uses other members of the community as informants, drawing on their intuitions. For instance, one might ask informants whether a particular combination of linguistic elements are grammatically possible in their language, or what would be an appropriate expression given a particular context.

If we recall the distinction between competence and performance, we may predict that elicitation can reveal what people know about what they do but not what they actually do. If the data of performance rather than competence is wanted, one needs to turn to the third way—observation.

The rapid progress of computer technology over recent years has made observation possible on a vast scale. Programs have been devised within corpus linguistics to collect and analyze large corpora of actually occurring language, both written and spoken, and this analysis reveals facts about the frequency and co-occurrence of lexical and grammatical items which are not intuitively accessible by introspection or elicitation.

As a science, linguistics now has a set of established theories, methods and sub-branches. As for its data, now the argument over intuition or corpus also fades as people realize the advantages of both and as corpus linguistics develops rapidly with the advent of computer technology. Lyons predicted three decades ago by pointing out that linguistics is empirical, rather than speculative or intuitive: it operates with publicly variable data obtained by means of observation or experiment. (Lyons, 1981: 38) It still rings true today. However, it is important to understand that there is no absolute validity of a particular kind of data. No one kind is more "real" than another. As Widdowson puts it, "It depends on what you claim data are evidence of, and what you are trying to explain." (Widdowson, 1996: 74—75)

1.10 Status and Prospect of Linguistics

Linguistics, conceived as an independent branch of academic study, embracing the entire range of observations and questions which relate to language, is a relatively recent development in the history of human culture. There have been arguments about whether linguistics is a science, especially when it was just coming into being. But now the arguments die away and linguistics has firmly established its place as a major branch of social science. As a recognized academic subject, it is an area with immense research potential, and a scholarly "industry" which produces a large amount of books, dissertations and papers every year; its preoccupations are expressed in such specialized journals as *Language*, *Applied Linguistics*, and at regular conferences. Web sites of linguistics also flourish, for example, http://www.linguist.org; and useful blogs on linguistics, for example, Linglish.net: Where English meets Linguistics (http://www.linglish.net/).

The justification for all these booming ventures should be obvious from our previous discussion. Language is so valuable to the individual, so critical to the efficient functioning of human societies, and in itself so impressively intricate and profound in structure, that it is bound to attract a great amount of intellectual attention. And since this attention must produce studies which have practical importance (e. g. in speech therapy, education, techniques of translation and many more "applied" concerns), linguistics is bound to be an academically and economically favored pursuit. It is also a subject of theoretical importance, for one thing, as we will discuss in later chapters, structuralism originating from Saussure's views has influenced many other related social sciences such as literary studies and social studies. In China the study of language has a long history but modern linguistics still has a long way to go to enjoy a "boom."

What will linguistics in the 21st century be like? J. H. Greenberg, once Chairman of the American Linguistics Association published an article in 1973 "Linguistics as a pilot science," which was echoed by linguists in China in the early 1980s. (Wu, 1994) If linguistics has not arisen to such a prominent position in social sciences in the 20th century China, it will in the 21st century. Some young scholars following Chomsky's grammar hold that linguists will be working in the language lab wearing white in the near future as they strive to solve the mystery of human brain and language; others argue that linguistics will further integrate with social sciences and play its role in social studies. Still others believe it will remain to be a core course in college English education, with its systematic methodologies exerting powerful influence on the neighboring disciplines.

This takes us back to an earlier similar argument. In the 1930s, Malinowski noted there was "the dilemma of contemporary linguistics," namely, whether we could treat language as an independent subject of study? And whether there is a legitimate science of words alone, of phonetics, grammar and lexicography? Malinowski's answer was "No." From what happened later in the field of language studies, we can predict at this stage that linguistics, while remaining an independent academic pursuit, will have to become more interdisciplinary in that social factors will have to be dealt with.

All in all, we should not stay satisfied with an over hasty rote memory of the technical terms in linguistic studies. Striving to understand the nature of language and its functions always seems to be more important than learning a bunch of technical terms without perceiving their relationship to the ultimate concern of linguistics. And the different voices we introduce here and in the following chapters will only serve to show the complexity of our object of study—the human language. And it may be helpful to remember that truth can be contradictory but complementary at the same time.

References

Algeo, J. & Pyles, T. 2009. *The Origins and Development of the English Language*.
    Beijing: Worlding Publishing Corporation.
Atkinson, Martin, David Kilby & Iggy Roca. 1982. *Foundations of General Linguistics*.

London: George Allen & Unwin.

Bakhtin, M. M. 1981. *The Dialogic Imagination*. Caryl Emerson & Michael Holquist (eds. and trans.). Texas: University of Texas Press.

Bakhtin, M. M. 1984. *Problems of Dostoevsky's Poetics*. Caryl Emerson (ed. and trans.). Minneapolis: University of Minnesota Press.

Beaugrande, Robert de. 1997. *New Foundations for a Science of Text and Discourse*. New Jersey: ABLEX Publishing Corporation.

Beedham. Christopher (ed.). 1999. *Langue and Parole in Synchronic and Diachronic Perspective*. Amsterdam: Pergamon.

Bolinger, Dwight & Sears, Donald A. 1981. *Aspects of Language*. San Diego: Harcourt Brace Javanovich.

Cogswell, David. 1996. *Chomsky for Beginners*. US: Writers and Readers Publishing Inc.

Clark, Virginia P. et al. (eds.) 1985. *Language-Introductory Readings*. New York: St. Martin's Press.

Chomsky, Noam. 1965. *Aspects of the Theory of Syntax*. Cambridge: MIT Press.

Chomsky, Noam. 1968. *Language and Mind*. San Diego: Harcourt Brace Javanovich.

Chomsky, Noam. 1975. *Reflections on Language*. New York: Pantheon Books.

Chomsky, Noam. 2000. *New Horizons in the Study of Language and Mind*. Cambridge: Cambridge University Press.

Crystal, David. 1992. *The Cambridge Encyclopedia of Language*. Cambridge: Cambridge University Press.

Eggins, Susanne. 1994. *An Introduction to Systemic Linguistics*. London: Pinter.

Fishman, Joshua A. 1977. *Sociolinguistics*. Massachusetts: Newbury House Publishers

Fowler, Roger. 1974. *Understanding Language*. London: Routledge & Kegan Paul.

Fromkin, V. et al. 2004. *An Introduction to Language*. (7th ed.). Beijing: Peking University Press.

Gee, James Paul. 1993. *An Introduction to Human Language-Fundamental Concepts in Linguistics*. New Jersey: Prentice Hall.

Gries, Stefan Th. 2010. *Statistics for Linguistics with R. Mouton*. Berlin: Walter de Gruyter & Co.

Gordon, Terrence. 1996. *Saussure for Beginners*. U.S.: Writers and Readers Publishing Inc.

Hagège, Calsu. 1999. *L'Homme De Paroles*. Zhang Zujian (trans.). Beijing: Sanlian Bookstore.

Halliday, M. A. K. "Language structure and language function," in John Lyons, 1970. *New Horizons in Linguistics*. New York: Penguin.

Halliday, M. A. K. "Language in a social perspective," *Educational Review* 1971(7).

Halliday, M. A. K. 1985/1994. *An Introduction to Functional Grammar*. London: Edward Arnold.

Halliday, M. A. K. 1978 "An interpretation of the functional relationship between language and social structure," in *Language and Society*. J. Webster (ed.). 2007. in *The Collected Works of M. A. K. Halliday*. Vol 10. Beijing: Peking University Press and U.S.: Continuum.

Halliday, M. A. K. & Mattiessen, C. 2004. *An Introduction to Functional Grammar*. (3rd ed.). London: Hodder Arnold.

Harris, Roy & George Wolf. 1998. *Integrational Linguistics: A First Reader*. Oxford: Pergamon.

Hartley, Anthony F. 1982. *Linguistics for Language Learners*. Kent: Multiplex Techniques Ltd.

Kaplan, R. 1966. "Cultural thought patterns in intercultural education," *Language Learning* 16: 1—20.

Kramsch, Clare. 2000. *Language and Culture*. Shanghai: Shanghai Foreign Language Education Press.

Lyons, John. 1981. *Language and Linguistics*. Cambridge: Cambridge University Press.

Martin, J. R. & Rose, D. 2008. *Genre Relations: Mapping Culture*. London: Equinox Publishing Ltd.

McCrone, John. 1991. *The Ape That Spoke: Language and the Evolution of the Human Mind*. New York: Avon Books.

McNeill, D. 1979. *The Conceptual Basis of Language*. Hillsdale, N. J. : Enbaum Associates.

McNeill, D. and E. Levy. 1982. "Conceptual representation in language activity and gesture," In *Speech, Place and Action*. R. J. Jarvella & W. Klein (ed.). New York: John Wiley. pp. 271—295.

McNeill, David (ed.) 2000. *Language and Gesture*. Cambridge: Cambridge UP.

Napoli, Donna Jo. 1996. *Linguistics*. New York: Oxford University.

Nida, Eugene A. 1998. *Understanding English*. Beijing: Foreign Language Teaching and Research Press.

Newmeyer, Frederick J. 1998. *Language Form and Language Function*. Cambridge & London: MIT.

O'Grady, et al. 2001. *Contemporary Linguistics*. Boston, New York: Bedford/St. Martin's.

Owens, Jr. Robert E. 1996. *Language Development*. Boston: Allyn and Bacon.

Pike, Kenneth L. 1967. *Language in Relation to a Unified Theory of the Structure of Human Behavior*. (2nd ed.). The Hague: Mouton.

Paul, Peter. 1993. *Linguistics for Language Learning*. South Melborne: Macmillan.

Qian, Jun. 1998. *Structural Functional Linguistics-The Prague School*. Jilin: Jilin Education Press.

Robin, R. H. 1967. *A Short History of Linguistics*. London: Longman.

Saussure, Ferdinand De. 1959. *Course in General Linguistics*. Charles Bally & Alvert Sechehaye (eds.). Wade Baskin (trans.). New York: Philosophical Library.

Sapir, E. 1921/2004. *Language: An Introduction to the Study of Speech*. Mineola, New York: Dover Publications, Inc.

Schiffman, Harold F. 1996. *Linguistic Culture and Language Policy*. London & New York: Routledge.

Slobin, Dan Isaac. 1971. *Psycholinguistics*. Illinois: Scott, Foresman and Company.

Slobin, Dan Issac (ed.). 1985. *The Crosslinguistic Study of Language Acquisition*. Vol. 2 Theoretical Issues. Hillsdale, N. J. : Erbaum.

Thibault, Paul J. 1997. *Re-reading Saussure—The Dynamics of Signs in Social Life*. London & New York: Routledge.

Thomas, Linda & Shan Wareing (eds.). 1998. *Language, Society and Power*. Routledge: London & New York.

Thomas, Jenny. 1995. *Meaning in Interaction: An Introduction to Pragmatics*. London &

New York: Longman.

Wardhaugh, Ronald. 1993. *Investigating Language-Central Problems in Linguistics*. Oxford UP & Cambridge USA: Blackwell.

Widdowson, H. G. 1996. *Linguistics*. Oxford: Oxford University Press.

胡壮麟,2000,《功能主义纵横谈》,北京:外语教学与研究出版社。

赵元任,1980/1999,《语言问题》,北京:商务印书馆。

伍铁平,1994,《语言学是一门领先的科学》,北京:北京语言学院出版社。

王　寅,1999,《论语言符号相似性》,北京:新华出版社。

Chapter 2

Phonological Analysis

The human being can make all kinds of sounds, but only some of these sounds have become units in the language system. Speech sounds had existed long before writing systems were invented, and even today there are still languages that have no writing systems. Therefore, the study of speech sounds is a fundamental aspect in the study of language.

The analysis of speech sounds can be approached on various levels. (Clark et al., 2007:1) At one level, it is a matter of anatomy and physiology, referring to speech organs and their functions, the production of speech sounds, acoustic waves carrying speech sounds, and the analysis and processing of the sounds by the listener. This is the level of phonetics, which can be further divided into anatomy and physiology of speech, articulatory phonetics, acoustic phonetics, and auditory or perceptual phonetics. On the second level, speech is seen as a "purposeful human activity," intended to convey meaning. (ibid:2) For this purpose, each specific language is equipped with its own repertoire of speech sounds and speech patterns, and the human language as a whole also displays certain sound patterns that are universally followed. The study of speech at this level is known as phonology, involving the study of rules and constraints, and theoretical considerations. Hardcastle et al. (2010) constitutes a full treatment of what phoneticians are currently engaged in and, for relevant theories and recent studies of phonology, see Goldsmith et al. (2011) and de Lacy (2007). In this chapter, we will discuss some of the major issues and theories in phonological analysis, beginning with the necessary phonetic foundation.

2.1 Transcribing Speech Sounds

2.1.1 The Need for Transcription

In some languages we can know their pronunciation by looking at the way they are written (e.g. Russian, Korean, Japanese, etc.), but in others the relation between pronunciation and writing is more complex. In English, for instance, the spelling does not always represent its pronunciation—the word *tick* contains four letters but there are three sound segments, with *ck* corresponding to only one sound. The correspondence between spelling and pronunciation is so irregular in English that George Bernard Shaw (1856—1950) said the word *fish* could as well be spelt as *ghoti* and still pronounced as *fish*, because *gh* is pronounced as [f] in *cough*, *o* as [ɪ] in *women*, and *ti* as [ʃ] in *nation*.

The reason for this divergence is complicated. In Old English, the relation between sound and symbol was much more regular. (Hogg, 1992: 85; for history of English writing and spelling, see Cook, 2004 and Upward & Davidson, 2011; for descriptions of Old English, see Wyatt, 1897; Quirk & Wren, 1957; Hogg, 1992, 2011; Smith, 2009; Lass & Anderson, 2010; Mitchell & Robinson, 2011) Some of the sounds, especially the vowels, have undergone changes in the development of English. (Baugh & Cable, 2002; Freeborn, 2006; Hogg & Denison, 2006; van Gelderen, 2006; Smith, 2007; Katamba & Kerswill, 2009; Algeo, 2010; Millward & Hayes, 2012) For example, in 1400 the words *put*, *bush*, *pull*, *cup*, *luck* and *mud* all had the vowel [ʊ], a high front vowel, for the Londoners. By about 1550, however, the vowel in *cup*, *luck* and *mud* had lowered to [ɤ], a mid-high back vowel, whereas [ʊ] was retained in *put*, *bush* and *pull*. Later, the lowered vowel in *cup*, *luck* and *mud* moved through a number of stages to the front to become [a], a low front vowel, in contemporary speech. This is a process of vowel split. (Figure 2.1, Radford et al., 2009: 65)

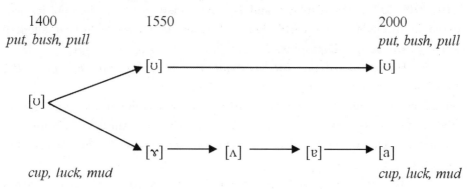

Figure 2.1 A Vowel Split in London

In some cases such change involves vowel merger, where two or three vowels have gradually merged into a single vowel in contemporary speech. For example, in East Anglian English, spoken in the east of England, certain diphthongs and triphthongs have combined to become monophthongs. (Figure 2.2, ibid.)

sure:	[ʃʊə]	→	[ʃɜː]
player:	[pleɪə]	→	[plæː]
fire:	[faɪə]	→	[fɑː]
tower:	[taʊə]	→	[tɑː]

Figure 2.2 Vowel Mergers in East Anglian English

Additionally, many English words have been borrowed from other languages throughout history and the irregularity of its spelling is made worse because of such borrowings (see Greenbaum, 1996: 400 – 412, for a quick summary of borrowings), and the divergence between spelling and pronunciation becomes greater when we consider the many accents of English used by people from different regions. (For varieties of English dialects, see Wells, 1982; Bauer, 2002; Finegan & Rickford, 2004; Labov et al., 2006; Britain, 2007; Amberg & Vause, 2009; Collins & Mees, 2013)

In order to capture the great diversity of speech sounds in all languages, it is necessary to devise sets of symbols that can be used for transcribing them. Several such systems are in use and the notation system of the International Phonetic Alphabet (IPA) is the most widely used.

2.1.2 The International Phonetic Alphabet

The IPA as a form of phonetic transcription was introduced in 1888 by the International Phonetic Association (also shortened as IPA), which was inaugurated in 1886 by a group of language teachers in France as the Phonetic Teachers' Association and changed to its present title in 1897. It has been revised several times (notably in 1951; 1979; 1996 and 2005; see Malmkjær, 2010: 270 – 273 for a display) and is now widely used in dictionaries and textbooks throughout the world. Some of its special letters have been adopted as part of the new orthographies for previously unwritten languages.

The *Handbook of the International Phonetic Association* (The *IPA Handbook*), published by Cambridge University Press in 1999, is a comprehensive guide to the use of the IPA. Produced collaboratively by leading phoneticians who have been on the Executive of the Association, it incorporates materials provided by numerous members of the Association worldwide.

The IPA chart consists of three tables of consonants, a vowel quadrilateral, a table of diacritics, and symbols for suprasegmentals. The sound segments are broadly grouped into consonants and vowels, which will be dealt with in the next section. The diacritics are additional symbols or marks used together with the consonant and vowel symbols to indicate nuances of change in their pronunciation. The suprasegmentals are used to represent stress and syllables, whereas the last group of symbols is used to show tonal differences and intonation patterns.

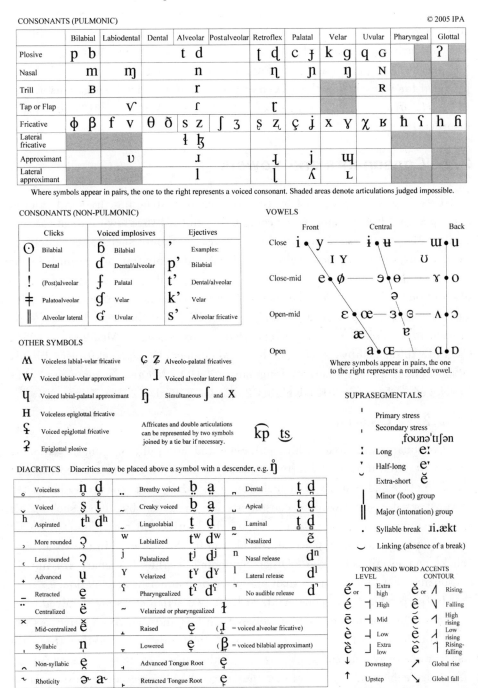

Figure 2.3 The International Phonetic Alphabet (revised to 2005)

At the 1989 Kiel Convention of the International Phonetic Association, two extension tasks were recommended: one was to develop a set of numbers for referring to IPA symbols in computer coding, and the other was to draw up recommendations for the transcription of disordered speech. The result was the IPA number chart and the ExtIPA Symbols for Disordered Speech. In the former, each symbol in the IPA chart is represented by a number, e. g. 101 for [p] and 301 for [ɪ], and in the latter, a large set of additional symbols are provided for transcribing the speech of people suffering from speech disorders. (*IPA Handbook*, 1999: Appendixes 2 and 3; see Vinson, 2012, for speech disorders)

2.2 Consonants and Vowels

Consonants are produced by constricting or obstructing the vocal tract at some place to divert, impede, or completely shut off the flow of air in the oral cavity. By contrast, a vowel is produced without such constriction or obstruction so no turbulence or total stopping of the airstream can be perceived. In this section we will discuss the major ideas and concepts for such description and more detailed description of consonants and vowels from various perspectives can be found in the IPA handbook and other good introductory books. (E. g. Laver, 1994; Ladefoged & Maddieson, 1996; Catford, 2001; Ashby, 2005; Ashby & Maidment, 2005; Bickford & Floyd, 2006; Lodge, 2009a; Reetz & Jongman, 2009; Ladefoged & Johnson, 2011; Ladefoged & Disner, 2012; Knight, 2012; Gick et al. , 2013; Zsiga, 2013)

2.2.1 Consonants

Consonants are divided into pulmonic and non-pulmonic ones. Pulmonic consonants are produced by letting out air from the lungs and are described in terms of place and manner of articulation, i. e. where and how air is obstructed or constricted. Non-pulmonic consonants are produced by either sucking air into the mouth (implosives), or closing the glottis and manipulating the air between the glottis and a place of articulation further forward in the vocal tract (clicks and ejectives). The "Other Symbols" in the IPA chart are mostly consonants that involve more than one place or manner of articulation.

In the production of consonants at least two articulators are involved. For example, the production of [b] involves both lips and that of [d] involves the blade (or the tip) of the tongue and the alveolar ridge. In addition there are also various ways of manipulating the articulators so that different sound effects are achieved. By examining the chart of pulmonic consonants we find there are three major ways of categorizing the consonants:

A. Manner of Articulation: ways in which articulation can be accomplished: the articulators may close off the oral tract for an instant or a relatively long period; they may narrow the space considerably; or they may simply modify the shape of the tract by approaching each other. Here are some of the major manners of articulation.

Plosive (or Stop): A three-phase articulation is involved in the production of a plosive or stop: (a) the *closing phase*, in which the articulators come together; (b) the *hold* or *compression phase*, during which air is compressed behind the closure; (c) the *release phase*, during which the articulators forming the obstruction come rapidly apart and the air is suddenly released. Technically this third phase is called plosion, hence the name "plosive," but because of the closure involved in the production of plosives, the alternative name "stop" is frequently used to refer to this category of sounds.

If the air is stopped in the oral cavity but the soft palate is down so that the airstream can go out through the nasal cavity, the sound produced is a nasal plosive/stop. Otherwise it is an oral plosive/stop. Although both types of sounds are plosives (or stops), phoneticians have retained the term "plosive/stop" for an oral plosive/stop and used the term "nasal" for a nasal plosive/stop. In English, [p,b,t,d,k,g] are plosives and [m,n,ŋ] are nasals.

All the sounds except the nasal plosives are oral sounds but oral sounds (particularly vowels) may be nasalized when they appear before or after a nasal.

Fricative: This refers to close approximation of two articulators so that the airstream is partially obstructed and turbulent airflow is produced. The audible friction defines this class of sounds and thus explains the label "fricative." [f, v,θ,ð,s,z,ʃ,ʒ,h] are fricatives in English.

A related concept is Affricates, which consist of a plosive followed immediately afterwards by a fricative at the same place of articulation. In English, the "ch[tʃ]" of *church* and the "j[dʒ]" of *jet* are both affricates. The legitimate position of [ts, dz, tr, dr] has been ejected from English because the first two are used only for suffixes and foreign words, while the latter two are often realized as two sounds in many people's speech. In Chinese, however, both [tsʰ] and [ts] are legitimate affricates as in words like "错 ('wrong')" and "做('do')" respectively.

Approximant: This is an articulation in which one articulator is close to another, but without the vocal tract being narrowed to such an extent that a turbulent airstream is produced. The gap between the articulators is therefore larger than for a fricative and no turbulence (friction) is generated. In English, this class of sounds include [w,ɹ,j] ([ɹ] often represented as [r] for ease of printing). As [j] and [w] can also be analyzed as vowels, it is an important point to note that this category overlaps with that of vowel.

Lateral: The obstruction of the airstream for such sounds is at a point along the center of the oral tract, with incomplete closure between one or both sides of the tongue and the roof of the mouth. As the lateral passage forms a stricture of open approximation and little noise of friction is produced, the result is that of approximants or fricatives. [l] is the only one lateral in English and Chinese. Unless marked "lateral," a sound is a central (or median).

Trill, tap, and flap: A trill (sometimes called roll) is produced when an articulator is set vibrating by the airstream. A major trill sound is [r], as in *red* and *rye* in some forms of Scottish English. The Spanish "rr" in *perro* (dog) [pero] is a trill [r]. (NB this is a different sound from the [r] of *red* in standard English, which is actually [ɹ] in IPA.)

If only one vibration is produced, i.e. the tongue makes a single tap against the alveolar ridge, the sound is called a tap or a flap. An example of the tap is the American substitution for /t/ in words like *city* [sɪɾɪ] and *letter* [leɾɚ], and /d, n/ in *ladder* and *tanner*. The flap [ɽ] is pronounced with the tip of the tongue curled up and back in a retroflex gesture and then striking the roof of the mouth in the post-alveolar region as it returns to its position behind the lower front teeth. In some forms of American English, the flap occurs in words like *dirty* [dɜːɽɪ] and *sorting* [sɔːɽɪŋ], after r-colored vowels in a stressed syllable. (Ladefoged & Johnson, 2011: 175—176)

B. Place of Articulation: where in the vocal tract there is approximation, narrowing, or the obstruction of airstream. Consonants may be produced at practically any place between the lips and the vocal folds. Eleven places of articulation are distinguished in the IPA consonant chart.

Bilabial: Bilabial sounds are made with the two lips. In English, bilabial sounds include [p, b, m], as in *pet*, *bet* and *met*. [w], as in *wet*, involves an approximation of the two lips (as in the lip-rounding of vowels) but is produced slightly differently: the tongue body is raised towards the velum at the same time and in the IPA it is treated as a labial-velar approximant, in "Other Symbols."

Labiodental: These are made with the lower lip and the upper front teeth. [f, v], as in *fire* and *via*, are produced by raising the lower lip until it nearly touches the upper front teeth.

Dental: Dental sounds are produced by the tongue tip or blade (depending on accent or language) and the upper front teeth. Only fricatives ([θ, ð]) are found to be strictly dental. Some speakers have the tip of the tongue protruding between the upper and lower front teeth whereas others have it closed behind the upper front teeth. Both are normal in English, and both may be called dental. (ibid: 12) The term interdental is sometimes used to describe the first kind to make a distinction.

Alveolar: Alveolars are made with the tongue tip or blade and the alveolar ridge. Sounds produced at this place include [t, d, n, s, z, ɹ, l] for English.

Postalveolar/Palato-alveolar: These are sounds made with the tongue tip and the back of the alveolar ridge. Such sounds include [ʃ, ʒ], as in *ship* and *genre*.

Retroflex: Retroflex sounds are made with the tongue tip or blade curled back (retroflexed) so that the underside of the tongue tip or blade forms a stricture with the back of the alveolar ridge or the hard palate. In Mandarin Chinese, the retroflex [ʂ] is found in "书('and')" [ʂʊ] and "事儿('matter')" [ʂɚ].

Palatal: Palatals are made with the front of the tongue and the hard palate. The only English sound made here is [j], as in *yes* and *yet*, but many speakers do use a palatal fricative [ç] for the "h" in *he* or *Hugh*.

Velar: Velars are made with the back of the tongue and the soft palate. In making such sounds, the back of the tongue is raised to touch the velum. Examples in English are velar plosives [k, g], as in *cat* and *get*, and velar nasal [ŋ], as in *sing*. The initial consonant in the Chinese word "和('and')" is the velar fricative [x], as is the pronunciation of *ch* in the Scots word *loch* [lɒx].

Uvular: Uvulars are made with the back of the tongue and the uvula, the short projection of soft tissue and muscle at the posterior end of the velum. In French, the letter "r" is pronounced as uvular fricative [ʁ], as in *votre* "your" [vɒtʁ].

Pharyngeal: Pharyngeal sounds are made with the root of the tongue and the walls of the pharynx. Arabic contains pharyngeal fricatives, [ħ, ʕ].

Glottal: Glottals are made with the two pieces of vocal folds pushed towards each other. The [h] in *hat* and *hold* is often described as a glottal fricative, although some people hold it may be more realistic to interpret it as a type of vowel because almost no friction is produced. The glottal plosive [ʔ] is formed by bringing together the vocal folds, building up pressure behind them as for a plosive and then releasing the airstream suddenly. Because of such a gesture, it is more of the lack of sound than a sound so it is more often called a "glottal stop." This is often perceived in words like *fat* [fæʔt] and *pack* [pæʔt], and many speakers of English have it for the "t" in words like *button* [bʌʔn], *beaten* [bɪʔn], and *fatten* [fæʔn]. (ibid: 62)

C. Voicing: the closing and opening of the vocal folds. For most phonetic purposes, the vocal folds can be 1) apart, 2) close together, or 3) totally closed.

1) When the vocal folds are apart, the air can pass through easily and the sound produced is said to be voiceless. Consonants [p, s, t] are produced in this way.

2) When they are close together, the airstream causes them to vibrate against each other and the resultant sound is said to be voiced. [b, z, d] are

voiced consonants.

3) When they are totally closed, no air can pass between them. The result of this gesture is the glottal stop [?].

In the IPA consonant chart, this is used to distinguish the plosives and fricatives that have the same place and manner of articulation. The voiced and voiceless distinction also applies to affricates, and the three classes of sounds are together called obstruents.

2.2.2 Vowels

As there is no obstruction of airstream in producing vowels, the description of vowels has to be done in a different manner, referring to the following criteria:

1) The part of the tongue that is raised-front, center, or back.

2) The extent to which the tongue rises in the direction of the palate. Normally, three or four degrees are recognized: high, mid (often divided into mid-high and mid-low), and low. In the IPA vowel chart, this is referred to as, respectively, close, close-mid, open-mid, and open, in reference to the degree in which the mouth is opened when producing sounds with different tongue heights.

3) The kind of opening made at the lips-various degrees of lip rounding or spreading.

The vowel chart is based on the idea of a system of cardinal vowels (CV), which was first suggested by A. J. Ellis in 1844 and taken up by A. M. Bell in his *Visible Speech* (1867). The system we are now considering here was put forward by Daniel Jones in a number of writings from 1917 onwards, e. g. in *An Outline of English Phonetics* (1922). For Jones, the cardinal vowels are a set of vowel qualities arbitrarily defined, fixed and unchanging, intended to provide a frame of reference for the description of the actual vowels of existing languages. When the cardinal vowels are explained, examples are usually given from various languages to help the student, but it should not be thought that the cardinal vowels are actually based on whatever examples or languages are given.

The cardinal vowel diagram (or quadrilateral), therefore, is a set of standard reference points based on a combination of articulatory and auditory judgments. The front, center, and back of the tongue are distinguished, as are four levels of tongue height:

1) The highest position the tongue can achieve without producing audible friction;

2) The lowest position the tongue can achieve; and

3) Two intermediate levels, dividing the intervening space into auditorily equivalent areas.

Chapter 2 Phonological Analysis

The system then defines eight "primary" cardinal vowels, conventionally numbered from one to eight: CV1 [ɪ], CV2 [e], CV3 [ɛ], CV4 [a], CV5 [ɑ], CV6 [ɒ], CV7 [o], CV8 [ʊ]. The first five of these are unrounded vowels while CV6, CV7 and CV8 are rounded ones.

A set of secondary cardinal vowels is obtained by reversing the lip-rounding for a given position: CV9 [y], CV10 [ø], CV11 [œ], CV12 [Œ], CV13 [ɒ], CV14 [ʌ], CV15 [ɤ], CV16 [ɯ]. Two further secondary cardinal vowels are then added: vowels which have tongue-positions half-way between [ɪ] and [ʊ] are represented as CV17 [ɨ] (unrounded) and CV18 [ʉ] (rounded).

The IPA also makes available some other symbols for frequently occurring vowels. The mid central vowel [ə], often referred to as schwa, is neither high nor low and neither front nor back. Other vowels include [ɪ, y, ʊ, ɘ, ɵ, ɜ, ɞ, ɐ, æ,] (see IPA vowel chart for the positions of these vowels). Note that where symbols appear in pairs, the one to the right represents a rounded vowel and the one to the left represents an unrounded vowel.

It should be pointed out that it is difficult to be precise about the exact articulatory positions of the tongue and palate because very slight movements are involved. Absolute values are not possible due to differences in the mouth dimensions of individual speakers. (See Beck, 2010, for a discussion of the organic variation of speech apparatus)

Languages frequently make use of a distinction between vowels where the quality remains constant throughout the articulation and those where there is an audible change of quality. The former is known as pure or monophthong vowels and the latter involves moving from one vowel to another. If a single movement of the tongue is involved, the resultant sound is a diphthong. A double movement produces triphthongs. Diphthongs in English can be heard in such words as *way* [weɪ], *tide* [taɪd], *how* [haʊ], *toy* [tɔɪ], and *toe* [təʊ]. Triphthongs are found in words like *wire* [waɪə] and *tower* [taʊə].

2.2.3 The Sounds of English

We have noticed that in many cases the pronunciation of English depends on speaker's accent and personal habit. There are different accents even within the UK, let alone outside it. Although no standard has been established on the way English should be pronounced, one form of English pronunciation is the most common model accent in the teaching of English as a foreign language. It is referred to as the Received Pronunciation (RP), and many people also call it King's/Queen's English, BBC English or Oxford English. RP originates historically in the southeast of England and is spoken by the upper-middle and upper classes throughout England. It is widely used in the private sector of the education system and spoken by most newsreaders of the BBC network. In

America the "standard" accent is known as "General American (GA)," used widely in news networks and education. Table 2.1 is a chart of English consonants as used by RP speakers.

Table 2.1 A Chart of English Consonants

Manner of Articulation	Place of Articulation							
	Bilabial	Labiodental	Dental	Alveolar	Postal veolar	Palatal	Velar	Glottal
Plosive/Stop	p b			t d			k g	
Nasal	m			n			ŋ	
Fricative		f v	θ ð	s z	ʃ ʒ			h
Approximant	(w)			ɹ		j	w	
Lateral				l				
Affricate					tʃ dʒ			

The consonants of English can be described in the following way:

(1) [p]voiceless bilabial plosive/stop

   [b]voiced bilabial plosive/stop

   [s]voiceless alveolar fricative

   [z]voiced alveolar fricative

When no distinction is made in voicing, only two values will be necessary. Therefore, [m] is a "bilabial nasal," [j] a "palatal approximant," and [h] a "glottal fricative." [l] may simply be called a "lateral" as there is only one lateral sound in English.

The differences in pronunciation among dialects are especially distinct in vowels. Even within RP the qualities of certain sounds have been changing too. And some of the symbols used in the IPA itself have also changed. All of these have resulted in the use of slightly different sets of pronunciation symbols in textbooks and dictionaries. In general, the RP English vowel system can be summarized in Figure 2.4.

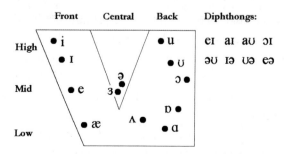

Figure 2.4 English Vowels (RP)

Table 2.2 shows a listing of RP and GA vowels with details of their differences from the IPA vowels indicated by diacritics.

Table 2.2 Classification of RP and GA Pure Vowels

	Front		Central		Back			
	Unrounded				Rounded		Unrounded	
	Tense	Lax	Tense	Lax	Tense	Lax	Tense	Lax
High	i̝	ɪ			u̝	ʊ		
Mid	e̝,ɛ̝		ɜ,ɝ	ə,ɚ	o̝,ɔ̝			ʌ̝
Low		æ		ɐ		ɒ̞	ɑ̞	

(Source: Roca & Johnson, 1999a: 190)
Note: Where symbols appear in pairs, the one to the right represents the GA counterpart.

Some explanations about Table 2.2 are necessary:

1. The idea of tenseness is introduced to indicate the difference between [i] and [ɪ], [ɜ] and [ə], etc. In the traditional classification of English vowels, they were said to be different in length, thus noting them as [iː] and [i], [əː] and [ə], and so on. Later, however, it was argued that the distinction was not just a matter of length: consider the difference in length of [i] in *beat* and *bead* and [ɪ] in *bit* and *bid*. As vowels tend to be shorter before voiceless consonants, the length of [ɪ] in *bid* is about the same as that of [i] in *beat*. *Bit* has the shortest vowel and *bead* has the longest. The difference in quality is however prominent: [i] and [ɪ] are simply different sounds, the former being pronounced with more tension. Therefore, in more recent notation different symbols are used to indicate the difference in quality between these pairs of sounds and the length symbol [ː] is often ignored. In some cases, differences in both quality and length are indicated so that [iː] and [ɪ], [ɜː] and [ə] are frequently found in the literature. In fact the length symbol was rejected in Ladefoged (1993) but was re-employed in Ladefoged (2001). In Ladefoged (2006) and Ladefoged and Johnson (2011), however, it was removed again. For a discussion of the various symbols used for English vowels, see Chapter 4 of Ladefoged (2006) or Ladefoged and Johnson (2011).

2. There are certain differences between the qualities of vowels in RP and GA. Notably, the central vowels [ɜ, ə] are *r*-colored or rhotic for GA, transcribed as [ɝ] and [ɚ], respectively. It means that they involve curling the tip of the tongue up in a gesture of retroflection, a phenomenon known as *r*-coloring or rhoticity. Another major difference is that in GA [ɑ] is used where it is [ɒ] in RP and [æ] replaces [ɑː] in RP. Furthermore, [ɔ] is pronounced at a slightly higher position and is more rounded in RP than in GA. Other minor differences exist but they do not lead to noticeable effects to the ordinary perception.

3. Diacritics are used to show the shades of difference between actual

vowel qualities in English and the hypothetical vowel qualities in the cardinal vowel system. For example, [i] in English is a little lower than CV1 and the vowel in *bed* is a little lower than CV2 for RP and a little higher than CV3 for GA. This explains why both [e] and [ɛ] are found in use for the phonetic transcription of English.

4. The low central vowel [ɐ] is often used by present-day RP speakers for the vowel in words like *but*, *mum* or *up*, instead of the more traditional [ʌ]. There are also other changes in the RP, including a lowered position for [æ] to the quality of CV4 [a], the use of [ʌɪ] for [aɪ], and [ɛː] for [eə].

Now we can describe the English vowels in the following manner:
(2) [iː] high/close front tense unrounded vowel
[ʊ] high/close back lax rounded vowel
[ə] mid central (lax unrounded) vowel
[ɒ] low/open back lax rounded vowel

Books abound for detailed descriptions of English sounds, including Aarts & McMahon (2006: Chapters 16−19), Culpeper et al. (2009: Chapters 2−4), Ladefoged & Johnson (2011: Chapters 3−4), Kreidler (1999; 2004), Gimson & Cruttenden (2008), Roach (2009), Ogden (2009), McCully (2009), Yavaş (2011), Tench (2011), Small (2012) and Carr (2013).

2.3 Phonemic vs. Phonetic Transcriptions

2.3.1 Phonemes

We have noticed that in English certain sounds are articulated in slightly different ways for different speakers. In fact many sounds are pronounced differently in different environments too, showing influences of their neighboring sounds. This is because speech is a continuous process, so the vocal organs do not move from one sound segment to the next in a series of separate steps. Consequently, sounds continually show the influence of their neighbors. While phonetic description aims at giving precise definitions of every possible speech sound, phonological analysis relies on the principle that certain sounds cause changes in the meaning of a word or phrase whereas others do not.

An early approach to the subject used a simple methodology to demonstrate this. It would take a word, replace one sound by another, and see whether a different meaning resulted. For instance, the word *tin* in English consists of three separate sounds, transcribed as [tɪn]. If we replace [t] by [d], we have a different word *din*. /t/ and /d/ are thus contrastive sounds in English because they enable us to distinguish *tin* and *din*, *tie* and *die*, and many other word pairs. Similarly, /i/ and /ɪ/ are contrastive units too as they distinguish between *beat* and *bit*, *bead* and *bid*, etc. This technique, called the "minimal pairs" test, can be used to find out which sound substitutions cause differences of meaning. The method has its limitations as it is not always possible to find pairs of words illustrating a particular distinction in a language, but it works well for English and leads to the identification of over 40 contrastive units. These "contrastive units" are called phonemes, which are transcribed using the normal set of phonetic symbols, but within slant lines instead of square brackets—/p/, /t/, /e/, etc. It shows that these units are seen as part of a language, instead of physical symbols.

Languages differ in the selection of contrastive sounds. In English, for example, the distinction between aspirated [p^h] and unaspirated [p] is not phonemic. They belong to the same phoneme /p/ but are realized as different phonetic sounds conditioned by different positions: the /p/ in *peak* is aspirated, phonetically transcribed as [p^h] while the /p/ in *speak* is unaspirated, phonetically [p]. In Chinese, however, the distinction between /p/ and /p^h/ is phonemic: "宾" (bīn, "guest") and "拼" (pīn, "to piece together") are transcribed in IPA as /pɪn/ and /p^hɪn/ respectively. Yavaş (2011: 37—45) gives a discussion of how English and a dozen or so other languages differ in the selection of phonemes.

The use of phonemic analysis is ancient but, according to Simpson (1979), the first explicit formulation of a phoneme theory was made only in the 1870s by Jan Baudouin de Courtenay and his student Mikolaj Kruszewski at Kazan. In early 20th century, the idea was developed by such renowned linguists as Daniel Jones in London, N. S. Trubetzkoy and the Prague School in Vienna, and numerous American linguists, including F. Boas, E. Sapir, L. Bloomfield, Y. R. Chao, and C. F. Hockett. The nature of the phoneme was hotly debated and several theories were put forward but, as Simpson (1979: 73) puts it, "For the practical task of describing sound-systems, the above question is of little importance, since identical phonemic analysis of a language might be made by holders of any of these views."

The "minimal pairs" test shows that the word *phoneme* simply refers to a "unit of explicit sound contrast": the existence of a minimal pair automatically grants phonemic status to the sounds responsible for the contrasts. (Roca & Johnson, 1999a: 53) As Spencer (1996: 3) notes, "[a] linguistic system is built on the idea of contrasts. By selecting one type of sound instead of another we can, for instance, distinguish one word from another." For full discussion of contrast in phonological theory, see Dresher (2009) and Lodge (2009b).

2.3.2 Allophones

The phonetic realizations of a phoneme can be illustrated by the difference of /s/ in *sea* and *Sue*. In the former the tongue is brought towards the front of the mouth in comparison with the latter, because /ɪ/ is a front vowel and /ʊ/ is a back vowel. The /s/ in *Sue* also shows lip-rounding as a result of the following vowel /ʊ/ being a rounded vowel. In both cases the difference is just physiologically inevitable.

Another example is nasalization. If a nasal consonant (such as /m/) precedes an oral vowel (such as /æ/ in *mass*), some of the nasality will carry forward so that the vowel /æ/ will bear a somewhat nasal quality. The reason is simple: in producing a nasal, the soft palate must be lowered to allow the airstream to flow through the nasal tract and, to produce the following vowel /æ/, the soft palate must move back to its normal position. As it takes time for the soft palate to move from its lowered position to the raised position, this process is still in progress when the articulation of /æ/ has begun. Similarly, when /æ/ is followed by /m/, as in *Sam*, the velum will begin to lower itself during the articulation of /æ/ so that it is ready for the following nasal.

To indicate that a vowel has been nasalized, we simply add a diacritic to the symbol /æ/, as [æ̃] (placed in square brackets as a phonetic realization). By the same token, we can use diacritics for transcribing other variations of the same sound, such as [pʰ] for *peak* and [p] for *speak*, using the diacritic "ʰ" for aspiration.

Fornon-technical purposes, it is not necessary to indicate such variations of a sound every time, e.g. dictionaries normally transcribe the words *peak* and *speak* as /piːk/ and /spiːk/ respectively. However, when the two words are actually pronounced, we know there is a rule in English that /p/ is unaspirated after /s/ but aspirated in other places:

(3) /p/ → [p] / [s] _____

    [pʰ] in other places

Unlike Chinese, [p, pʰ] are allophones of the phoneme /p/ in English. Allophones must be in complementary distribution and never occur in the same context: [p] occurs after [s] while [pʰ] occurs in other places.

To say that [p, pʰ] belong to the phoneme /p/ reduces the number of phonemes in English-the two sounds are attributed to only one phoneme. Of course, not all the phones in complementary distribution are considered to be allophones of the same phoneme: they must also be phonetically similar. Phonetic similarity means that the allophones of a phoneme must bear some phonetic resemblance—[p, pʰ] are both voiceless bilabial stops differing only in aspiration.

A phoneme may sometimes have free variants. For example, the final consonant of *cat* may be pronounced as [kʰætʰ], [kʰæʔ], or [kʰæt̚]. The difference may be caused by dialect or idiolect, though it is nearly always unrealised in cases like *the cat pushed* [ðə'kʰæt̚ 'pʰʊʃt]. (Ladefoged &

Johnson, 2011: 60) Regional differences for free variation can be exemplified by the word *either*, which is pronounced by most Americans as [iːðɚ] and by most British people as [aɪðə]. Individual differences may determine the use of [dɪˈrɛkʃn] or [daɪˈrɛkʃn] for the word *direction*. In dictionaries, free variants are often listed side by side, and special dictionaries in pronunciation give more free variants. (E.g. Wells, 2008; Jones et al., 2011)

When we use a simple set of symbols in our transcription, it is called a phonemic or broad transcription. And the use of more specific symbols to show more phonetic detail is referred to as a phonetic or narrow transcription. Compare the pairs of transcriptions in Table 2.3.

Table 2.3 Phonemic and Phonetic Transcriptions of English Words

Word	Phonemic	Phonetic	Phonetic detail
help	/hɛlp/	/hɛɫp/	Velarization
play	/pleɪ/	/pl̥eɪ/	Devoicing
tenth	/tɛnθ/	/tʰɛn̪θ/	Aspiration, dentalization
button	/bʌtn/	/bʌʔn̩/	Glottalization, syllabification

McMahon (2002) provides much descriptive detail of English phonemes and Giegerich (1992) gives a more advanced descriptive account of English phonology without requiring too much theoretical background on the part of the reader. Lass (2009) constitutes a study of English phonology and phonological theory from both synchronic and diachronic perspectives. For contrast, a good study of the phonology of Standard Chinese is Duanmu (2007).

2.4 Distinctive Features and Rule Representation

2.4.1 Features

So far speech sounds have been divided into classes according to a number of phonetic properties. For example, consonants are described according to their places and manners of articulation, and vowels are described according to their frontness or backness, roundedness and unroundedness, and so on. One property is "voicing," which plays an important part in distinguishing obstruents, and because voicing can distinguish one sound from another, it is a distinctive feature for English obstruents.

Features are binary in that sounds are grouped into two categories: one with this feature and the other without. The two values or specifications are denoted by "+" (plus) and "−" (minus) so voiced obstruents are marked [+voiced] and voiceless obstruents are marked [−voiced]. Sonorants are always

[+voiced] so the feature [±voiced] is redundant for such sounds. The feature [±nasal] is used for distinguishing nasals from non-nasals so the nasal sounds are marked [+nasal] and all other sounds are [−nasal]. In contemporary phonological analysis, some twenty such features are used to classify speech sounds from different perspectives.

The idea of distinctive features was first developed by Roman Jacobson (1896—1982) in the 1940s as a means of working out a set of phonological contrasts or oppositions to capture particular aspects of language sounds. Since then several versions have been suggested, notably by Chomsky & Halle (1968), Halle & Clements (1983) and Ladefoged (1982 and later editions). (See Clark et al., 2007: Appendix 2, for some early versions of features) More recent versions are discussed in Durand (1990), Carr (1993), Kenstowicz (1994), Spencer (1996), Roca & Johnson (1999a), Ewen & van der Hulst (2001), Jensen (2004), Odden (2005), Hayes (2009), Davenport & Hannahs (2010), and Gussenhoven & Jacobs (2011). Also, see Mielke (2008) for a specialized study of the emergence of distinctive features, and Kramer (2012) for a full discussion of underlying representations.

Below is a list of features that are widely used in recent studies.

A. Major Class Features

consonantal ([± **cons**]): Consonantals are produced with a major obstruction in the oral cavity. Consonants are [+cons] while vowels are [−cons].

syllabic ([± **syll**]): These are sounds that can form a syllable peak, including vowels, liquids and nasals.

sonorant ([± **son**]): Such sounds are produced with a vocal tract configuration in which spontaneous voicing is possible. Obstruents are [−son], and all other sounds are [+son].

approximant ([± **approx**]): These sounds are made with an oral tract constriction which is less than that required to produce friction. Vowels, glides and liquids are [+approx], other sounds are [−approx].

Table 2.4 shows the classification of sounds using major class features and their relation with the phonetic classifications.

Table 2.4 Major Class Features

Vowels	Glides	Liquids	Nasals	Obstruents
[−cons]	[+cons]			
	[+approx]		[−approx]	
	[+son]			[−son]
[+syll]	[−syll]		[+syll]	[−syll]

B. Vocalic Features

high: This feature distinguishes the high vowels from all other vowels. The consonants that have this feature include [j, k].

low: These include the low vowels and the glottal consonants like [ʔ,h].

back: This distinguishes the back vowels and all other vowels, and includes consonants [k,g,ŋ].

front: These include the front vowels.

round: This distinguishes the rounded sounds from unrounded ones.

tense: This feature is used to distinguish between long vowels and short vowels.

advanced tongue root ([±ATR]): These are vowels made by drawing the root of the tongue forward, thus enlarging the pharyngeal cavity, tending to raise the tongue body, and tending to give the sound a more tense articulation, e.g. [i,e,ɜ,o,u]. [−ATR] sounds lack this gesture, e.g. [ɪ,ɛ,ɔ,ʊ,a,ɑ].

C. Consonant Place Features

labial ([±lab]): Such sounds involve a constriction of the lips to give either a labial (labiodental) consonant or a rounded vowel.

coronal ([±cor]): Coronal sounds are produced with the front of the tongue raised from the neutral position, including the dentals, alveolars and palatals.

anterior ([±ant]): These are sounds produced in the front of the mouth, including the labials, dentals and alveolars.

D. Manner Features

continuant ([±cont]): The primary constriction is not narrowed so much that airflow through the oral cavity is blocked. Plosives and nasal stops are [−cont]; other sounds (including laterals) are [+cont].

delayed release ([±del rel]): This distinguishes affricates from other [−cont] segments.

strident ([±strid]): This means that sounds are produced with a construction with greater noisiness. Stridency is only defined for fricatives and affricates: Labiodentals, sibilants and uvular fricatives/affricates are [+strid]; all other fricatives/affricates are [−strid].

nasal ([±nas]): The velum is lowered which allows air to escape through the nose.

lateral ([±lat]): The mid section of the tongue is lowered at the side.

E. Laryngeal Features

voiced ([±voice]): The vocal folds vibrate.

spread glottis ([±spread], or [±s. g.]): The vocal folds are spread far apart. Aspirated (voiceless) consonants, breathy or murmured voiced consonants and voiceless vowels/glides are [+spread]; other sounds are [−spread]. Because of this, they are also known as aspirated.

Tables 2.5 and 2.6 show the distinctive feature specifications for vowels and consonants in English. For full specifications of sounds in all languages, see Chapter 4 of Hayes (2009).

Table 2.5 Feature Specifications for English Vowels
(Source: Davenport & Hannahs, 2010: 113)

	iː	I	uː	ʊ	ɔ	ɔː	ɒ	ɑː	ʌ	æ	eː	ɛ	ə	ɜː
high	+	+	+	+	−	−	−	−	−	−	−	−	−	−
low	−	−	−	−	−	+	+	+	+	−	−	−	−	−
back	−	−	+	+	+	+	+	+	−	−	−	−	−	−
front	+	+	−	−	−	−	−	−	−	+	+	+	−	−
round	−	−	+	+	+	+	+	−	−	−	−	−	−	−
tense	+	−	+	−	−	+	−	+	−	−	+	−	−	+

The idea of distinctive features is to organize certain sound segments into a natural class. That is to say certain segments almost always behave in similar ways. For example, Chinese syllables allow coronal and dorsal nasals in the coda position but not the labial nasal, and the English fricatives (not plosives) go through a devoicing process when preceding a voiceless consonant. Using the distinctive features, we can capture such classes through a matrix of features and exclude all other sounds from our matrix.

Table 2.6 Feature Specifications for English Consonants
(Source: Davenport & Hannahs, 2010: 112)

	p	b	t	d	ɾ	k	g	ʔ	tʃ	dʒ	f	v	θ	ð	s	z	ʃ	ʒ	x	h	m	n	ŋ	ɹ	l	w	j
syll	−	−	−	−	−	−	−	−	−	−	−	−	−	−	−	−	−	−	−	−	−/+	−/+	−/+	−/+	−/+	−	−
cons	+	+	+	+	+	+	+	+	+	+	+	+	+	+	+	+	+	+	+	+	+	+	+	+	+	−	−
son	−	−	−	−	−	−	−	−	−	−	−	−	−	−	−	−	−	−	−	−	+	+	+	+	+	+	+
cor	−	−	+	+	+	−	−	−	+	+	−	−	+	+	+	+	+	+	−	−	−	+	−	+	+	−	+
ant	+	+	+	+	+	−	−	−	−	−	+	+	+	+	+	+	−	−	−	−	+	+	−	+	+	−	−
cont	−	−	−	−	−	−	−	−	−	−	+	+	+	+	+	+	+	+	+	+	−	−	−	+	+	+	+
nas	−	−	−	−	−	−	−	−	−	−	−	−	−	−	−	−	−	−	−	−	+	+	+	−	−	−	−
strid	−	−	−	−	−	−	−	−	+	+	+	+	−	−	+	+	+	+	−	−	−	−	−	−	−	−	−
lat	−	−	−	−	−	−	−	−	−	−	−	−	−	−	−	−	−	−	−	−	−	−	−	−	+	−	−
del rel	−	−	−	−	−	−	−	−	+	+	−	−	−	−	−	−	−	−	−	−	−	−	−	−	−	−	−
voice	−	+	−	+	+	−	+	−	−	+	−	+	−	+	−	+	−	+	−	−	+	+	+	+	+	+	+
high	−	−	−	−	−	+	+	−	+	+	−	−	−	−	−	−	+	+	+	−	−	−	+	−	−	+	+
low	−	−	−	−	−	−	−	−	−	−	−	−	−	−	−	−	−	−	−	+	−	−	−	−	−	−	−
back	−	−	−	−	−	+	+	−	−	−	−	−	−	−	−	−	−	−	+	−	−	−	+	−	−	+	−
round	−	−	−	−	−	−	−	−	−	−	−	−	−	−	−	−	−	−	−	−	−	−	−	−	−	+	−
	Stops								Affricates		Fricatives										Nasals			Liquids		Glides	
	Obstruents																				Sonorants						

2.4.2 Rules

If we reexamine rule (3) in 2.3.2, we see that, obviously, this rule also applies to /t/ and /k/, as in *tool* vs. *stool* and *cool* vs. *school*. Using features, we can group /p, t, k/ into a class:

(4) /p, t, k/ = $\begin{bmatrix} -\text{voice} \\ -\text{cont} \end{bmatrix}$

Then rule (3) can be rewritten as

(5) $\begin{bmatrix} -\text{voice} \\ -\text{cont} \end{bmatrix}$ → [−spread] / [s] _____

   [+spread] in other places

Such rules can be used to capture other phonological phenomena, e. g. the present tense third person singular -*s* ending and the regular past tense form -*ed* ending in English.

(6) The present tense -*s* ending rule:

/z/ → [əz] / $\begin{bmatrix} +\text{strid} \\ +\text{cor} \end{bmatrix}$ _____   (Epenthesis Rule)

      [s] / $\begin{bmatrix} -\text{voice} \\ +\text{cons} \end{bmatrix}$ _____   (Devoicing Rule)

      [z] in other places

(7) The past tense -*ed* ending rule

/d/ → [ɪd] / $\begin{bmatrix} +\text{cor} \\ -\text{cont} \\ -\text{nas} \end{bmatrix}$ _____   (Epenthesis Rule)

      [t] / [−voice] _____   (Devoicing Rule)

      [d] in other places

The epenthesis rule (i. e. the insertion of a vowel between two consecutive similar segments) is an instance of a more general rule:

(8) *Obligatory Contour Principle* (OCP)

   No identical adjacent autosegments. (Goldsmith, 1976)

The rules above are known as linear or derivational rules, with the pattern X → Y / A ____ B. They are particularly useful for representing the rules that apply to a class of sound segments when they have the same kind of allophonic distribution. Linear rules are results of Generative Phonology, developed in Chomsky & Halle (1968) based on the phoneme theory, feature theory and transformational grammar. The theory has undergone much change in technicalities but it is not at all dated, with the essence being carried on till today. For recent accounts, see Odden (2005), Hayes (2009) and Davenport & Hannahs (2010).

2.5 Suprasegmentals and Feature Geometry

It was found that the linear rule representation was unsatisfactory when describing suprasegmentals. For example, the stress patterns of long words may have a primary stress, a secondary stress and a number of other syllables. Although these other syllables are said to be unstressed, they do not have the same degree of strength and weakness. In this section, we will look at some of the ideas and outcomes that were developed along the lines of what is know as non-linear phonology.

2.5.1 The Foot Structure and Stress Assignment

The foot structure can be illustrated by a line of a poem, such as

(9) We **would** sit **down** and **think** which **way**
    To **walk**, and **pass** our **long** love's **day**;
    (Andrew Marvell, "To his coy mistress," c. 1660; quoted in Gregoriou, 2009: 10)

In this example, each line consists of four recurring patterns of "unstressed-stressed" units: we **would**, sit **down**, and **think**, which **way**, etc. Each such unit is called a foot. In this case, it is an iambic foot (or iamb), consisting of two syllables, the first being unstressed and the second stressed.

Words that have two or more syllables are also said to make up "feet," e.g. be**gin** is an iamb, *wai*ter *is a trochee, and* **Me**xico is a dactyl.

The assignment of word stress in English is extremely complex, as shown in Chomsky & Halle (1968: Chapter 3), Roca & Johnson (1999: Chapters 11—16), Hammond (1999: Chapters 5—8), Gimson & Cruttenden (2008: Chapter 10), Roach (2009: Chapters 10—11), Yavaş (2011: Chapter 7), Carr (2013: Chapter 8). However, many other languages are fairly regular in this respect.

Take Maranungku, an Australian language, for example:

(10) a. tíralk 'saliva'
     b. mérepèt 'beard'
     c. yángarmàta 'the Pleiades'
     d. lángkaràtetì 'prawn'
     e. wélepènemànta 'kind of duck'

We can see disyllabictrochaic feet easily in (10)a, (10)c and (10)e, but in (10)b and (10)d the last syllable does not form a complete foot. This kind of incomplete foot is called degenerate foot. The way foot is formed in this language is clear:

(10') *Stress assignment algorithm in Maranungku*
      Construct left-headed binary feet from left to right, the stressed syllable being the first in each foot.

Another language, Weri, spoken in South America, gives us the following data:

(11) a. nintíp 'bee'
     b. kùlipú 'hair of arm'

c. ulùamít 'mist'
d. àkunètepál 'times'

Obviously, the stress assignment in Weri is the other way round:

(11') *Stress assignment algorithm in Weri*
   Construct right-headed binary feet from right to left, the stressed syllable being the last in each foot.

The case with another South American language, Warao, is a little more complicated:

(12) a. yàpurùkitànehàse 'verily to climb'
   b. nàhoròahàkutái 'the one who ate'
   c. yiwàranáe 'he finished it'
   d. enàhoròahàkutái 'the one who caused him to eat'

The assignment of stress in this language is the same as Weri except that we must ignore the last syllable in each word, which is always unstressed. Such syllables ignored systematically are called extrametrical or extraprosodic, and are "adjoined to the nearest suitable prosodic category, in this case the foot." (for a detailed discussion of these languages, see Spencer, 1996: 244—248)

To sum up, we can reach a more general rule that covers the assignment of stressed syllables in the discussion above:

(13) *End Stress Rule*
   Stress is assigned to the left or right of the syllable.
   End stress (L): Maranungku
   End stress (R): Weri, Warao

2.5.2 Metrical Grid

The Metrical Grid is a method of representing syllable and stress structure: a * or an x is used to stand for a syllable and more *'s or x's are used to mean more stress. For example,

(14)   *   *   Stress line
       *   *   *   *   Baseline
     (to) contact   (a) contact

Longer words have secondary stress:

(15) *   Stress line 2
     *   *   Stress line 1
     * * *   Baseline
     marmalade

And for compounds:

(16)   *   Stress line 3 (compound/phrase)
             *   *   Stress line 2 (word)
          * *   *   Stress line 1 (foot)
          * * * * *   Baseline

Crocodile Dundee

This accounts for the change of stress position in some compounds or phrases, known as stress retraction, which follows a rhythm rule, subject to stress clash and OCP.

(17)　　　*　　　Stress line 3
　　　*　←　*　　　Stress line 2
　　　*　*　*　　*　Stress line 1
　　　*　*　*　*　*　Baseline

Dundee marmalade

As a result, though we often say *research* with stress on the last syllable, in *research paper*, it is preferred to place stress on the first syllable for *research*. Other examples of stress retraction include: *antique chair*, *fifteen children*, *bamboo table*. Things become complicated with *antique dealer*, *sports contest*, *tax increase*, which may involve no stress movement (in the case of *antique dealer* because *ti* has the primary stress), or movement to the right (*sports contest*, *tax increase*). See Roca & Johnson (1999a: Chapter 11) for full discussions.

2.5.3　Feature Geometry

The idea of multi-levels is then extended to the segmental domain, and features are organized into tree structures, known as feature geometry. (Davenport & Hannahs, 2010: 155) Figure 2.5 is an example of feature geometry.

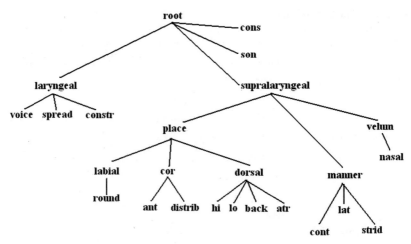

Figure 2.5　An Example of Feature Tree
(Source: Davenport & Hannahs, 2010: 155)

The non-linear representations of the rules of English verbs in (6) and (7) in 2.4.2 would go as in Figures 2.6. Obviously, these representations are more complex than the linear rules and cannot capture more than their linear counterparts, which perhaps explains why linear representation is still widely taught and used.

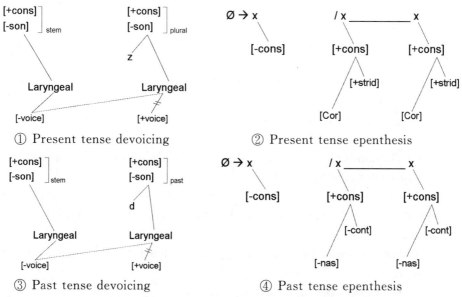

Figure 2.6 Non-linear Representation of Verb Ending Rules
(Based on: Roca & Johnson, 1999a: 622)

However, non-linear phonology involves a series of studies in a full range of topics in phonology and various attempts have been made to explain the topics in a wide array of languages. For further studies, Spencer (1996) and Roca & Johnson (1999a) are good places to start. Other relevant sources that are devoted extensively or fully to such theories include Durand (1990), Goldsmith (1990), Ewen & van der Hulst (2001), Gussmann (2002) and Gussenhoven & Jacob (2011).

For studies of suprasegmentals under various theoretical frameworks, see Gordon (2006) and Duanmu (2008) for syllable, Burzio (1994), Hayes (1995) and Kahnemuyipour (2009) for stress, Bolinger (1986, 1989), Cruttenden (1997), Yip (2002), Gussenhoven (2004), Wells (2006), Chen (2007) and Ladd (2008) for tone and intonation, and Fox (2000) for a general discussion of prosodic features and prosodic structure.

2.6 Optimality Theory

2.6.1 Constraints vs. Derivation

Optimality Theory (OT) was developed by Alan Prince and Paul Smolensky (Prince & Smolensky, 2004, based on earlier versions of 1993 and 2002) and has been the leading model of phonological research in the past two decades. (See de Lacy, 2007) OT presents a very different view of phonological studies and is also used in the study of morphology, syntax and language acquisition. This is a constraint-based approach instead of the derivational approach as has been outlined in the sections above, which takes the form "X becomes Y in the context of A and B" (X→Y/A___B). The following rules are typical of derivational rules that we have seen so far:

(18) a. **Devoicing**: A voiced obstruent becomes voiceless after a voiceless obstruent.
　　b. **ə-insertion**: Insert [ə] between two adjacent sibilants in the same word.

The constraint-based approach is based on the following assumptions:
1) Constraints are universal.
2) Languages differ in the importance they attach to the various constraints so the phonology of a language is given by the ranking of the set of universal constraints.
3) Constraints may be contradictory and violated-the higher ranked one has priority.

The constraints take the following format:
(19) a. *__SIBSIB__: Sequences of sibilants are prohibited within the word.
　　b. **MAX-IO**: Deletion of segments is prohibited.
　　c. **DEP-IO**: Insertion of segments is prohibited.
　　d. *α**VOICE** $-\alpha$**VOICE**: Sequences of obstruents within the syllable must agree for voicing.
　　e. **IDENT-IO**: A segment in the input is identical to the corresponding segment in the output.

The OT grammar consists of three components:
1) Lexicon: contains lexical representations (or underlying forms) of morphemes, which form the input to:
2) Generator: generates output candidates for some input, and submits these to:
3) Evaluator: the set of ranked constraints, which evaluates output candidates as to their harmonic values, and selects the optimal candidate.

Such a grammar is an input-output mechanism:
(20) **Gen** (**input**) => {cand$_1$, cand$_2$... cand$_n$}
　　Eval {cand$_1$, cand$_2$... cand$_n$} => **output**
　　(Kager, 1999: 19)
which is shown in Figure 2.7.

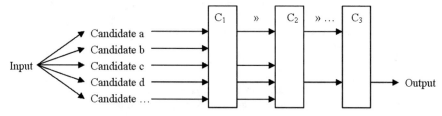

Figure 2.7 Mapping of Input to Output in OT
(Source: Kager, 1999: 8)

2.6.2 Constraints and Tableau

There are two types of constraints:

1. Markedness constraints: require that output forms meet some criterion of structural well-formedness. They take the form of prohibitions of marked phonological structures (19) a-c. Other examples of markedness constraints include:

(21) a. Vowels must not be nasal.
 b. Syllables must not have codas.
 c. Obstruents must not be voiced in coda position.
 d. Sonorants must be voiced.
 e. Syllables must have onsets.
 f. Obstruents must be voiced after nasals.

2. Faithfulness constraints: require that outputs preserve the properties of their basic (lexical) forms, requiring some kind of similarity between the output and its input (19)d-e. Other examples of faithfulness constraints are:

(22) a. The output must preserve all segments present in the input.
 b. The output must preserve the linear order of segments in the input.
 c. Output segments must have counterparts in the input.
 d. Output segments and input segments must share values for [voice].

Some basic notions of OT are:

1) Universality: constraints are universal.

2) Violability: constraints are violable, but violation must be minimal.

3) Optimality: an output is "optimal" when it incurs the least serious violations of a set of constraints, taking into account their hierarchical ranking.

4) Domination: the higher-ranked of a pair of conflicting constraints takes precedence over the lower-ranked one.

The ranking of constraints can be demonstrated by a tableau demonstrated in Figure 2.8:

Constraint 2	Input	Constraint 1
a. ☞ Candidate a		*
b. Candidate b	*!	

Figure 2.8 A Tableau of Simple Domination

Let us now see how the constraints interact with each other by way of two examples:

1. A markedness constraint:

(23) * VOICED-CODA

Obstruents must not be voiced in coda position.

2. A faithfulness constraint:

(24) IDENT-IO(voice)

The specification for the feature [voice] of an input segment must be preserved in its output correspondent.

We will use these two constraints to analyze the neutralization of voicing contrast in Dutch and the preservation of voicing contrast in English. Examples in(25) shows neutralization in Dutch:

(25) a. i /bɛd/ → [bɛt] 'bed'

a. ii /bɛd-ən/ → [bɛ. dən] 'beds'

b. i /bɛt/ → [bɛt] '(I) dab'

b. ii /bɛt-ən/ → [bɛ. tən] '(we) dab'

(Kager, 1999: 16)

This shows that in Dutch word-final consonant must not be voiced. In English, however, the voicing is maintained in this position, contrasting words such as *bed* and *bet*. Therefore, in English, the faithfulness constraint, Ident-IO(voice) is in dominant position:

(26) Preservation of voicing in English

Ident-IO(voice) 》 * Voiced-Coda

It is represented by the tableau in Figure 2.9:

Candidates	Ident-IO(voice)	* Voiced-Coda
a. [bɛt]	*!	
b. ☞ [bɛd]		*

Figure 2.9 Tableau for the Input /bɛd/ in English

In Dutch the domination is the opposite:

(27) Neutralization of voicing in Dutch

* Voiced-Coda 》 Ident-IO(voice)

This is represented by the tableau in Figure 2.10.

Candidates	*Voiced-Coda	Ident-IO(voice)
a. [bɛt]		*
b. [bɛd]	*!	

Figure 2.10 Tableau for the Input /bɛd/ in Dutch

2.6.3 Is OT better?

Let us re-examine the verb rules in Figure 2.6, using OT tableau, in Figure 2.11.

/kɪsz/	OCP	Dep-IO	*αvoice −αvoice
a. [kɪsz]	*!		*
b. [kɪsəz]		*	
c. [kɪzz]	*!		
b. [kɪss]	*!		

(1) Present tense epenthesis

/bækz/	OCP	Dep-IO	*αvoice −αvoice	Ident (F)
a. [bækəz]		*!		
b. [bækz]			*!	
c. [bæks]				*

(2) Present tense devoicing

/wɒntd/	OCP	Dep-IO	*αvoice −αvoice
a. [wɒntd]	*!		*
b. [wɒntɪd]		*	
c. [wɒndd]	*!		
b. [wɒntt]	*!		

(3) Past tense epenthesis

/wɔːkd/	OCP	Dep-IO	*αvoice −αvoice	Ident (F)
a. [wɔːkɪd]		*!		
b. [wɔːkd]			*!	
c. [wɔːkt]				*

(4) Past tense devoicing

Figure 2.11 Tableau for the Verb Inflection in English

It can be seen that in these four tableaus, one thing is in common: the ranking of the constraints captures all four rules, as in

(28) *Ranking of some constraints in English*

OCP 》DEP-IO 》 *αvoice-αvoice 》IDENT(F)

This is surely an advantage. Of course many tasks still remain before we can work out the full system of constraint ranking in English, not to say in all languages. Hammond (1999) is a full OT study of English phonology. Kager (1999) is still the best textbook to embark on a serious study of OT, but McCarthy (2008) also aims at the beginning student. Katamba (2006) contains much work on how OT can be related to the study of English morphology. For advanced studies, see Goldsmith (1999), McCarthy (2002; 2004) and Lombardi (2010). The Rutgers Optimality Archive (ROA) at http://roa.rutgers.edu/ has over a thousand papers and monographs that can be downloaded.

2.7 Conclusion

In this chapter we have reviewed some of the basic issues in phonological studies, including the necessary phonetic foundations. Since Chomsky & Halle (1968), modern phonology has undergone a series of exciting developments and it is impossible to outline them all in one chapter of this introductory nature. Therefore, we have referred to a number of textbooks and monographs as we go along. For exercises with problems in phonology, Halle & Clements (1983) and Roca & Johnson (1999b) provide excellent resources. We have covered basically all the three major theoretical approaches to phonology, i.e. the linear theory, non-linear theory, and OT. This chapter should have provided enough background for further work in phonology.

References

Aarts, Bas & April McMahon (eds.). 2006. *The Handbook of English Linguistics*. Malden, MA: Wiley-Blackwell.

Algeo, John. 2010. *The Origins and Development of the English Language*. (6th ed.). Boston, MA: Wadsworth.

Amberg, Julie S. & Deborah J. Vause. 2009. *American English: History, Structure and Usage*. Cambridge: Cambridge University Press.

Ashby, Michael & John Maidment. 2005. *Introducing Phonetic Science*. Cambridge: Cambridge University Press.

Ashby, Patricia. 2005. *Speech Sounds*. 2nd ed. Cambridge: Cambridge University Press.

Bauer, Laurie. 2002. *An Introduction to International Varieties of English*. Edinburgh: Edinburgh University Press.

Baugh, Albert C. & Thomas Cable. 2002. *A History of the English Language*. (5th ed.). London: Routledge.

Beck, Janet Mackenzie. 2010. *Organic Variation of the Vocal Apparatus*. Hardcastle, et al. (eds.). pp. 155−201.

Bell, Alex. Melville. 1867. *Visible Speech: The Science of Universal Alphabetics; or Self-

interpreting Physiological Letters, for the Writing of All Languages in One Alphabet. London: Simplin, Marshall & Co.

Bickford, Anita C. & Rick Floyd. 2006. *Articulatory Phonetics: Tools for Analyzing the World's Languages*. (4th ed.). Dallas, TX: SIL International.

Bolinger, Dwight L. 1986. *Intonation and Its Parts*. Stanford: Stanford University Press.

Bolinger, Dwight L. 1989. *Intonation and Its Uses*. Stanford: Stanford University Press.

Britain, David (ed.). 2007. *Languages in the British Isles*. Cambridge: Cambridge University Press.

Burzio, Luigi. 1994. *Principles of English Stress*. Cambridge: Cambridge University Press.

Carr, Philip. 1993. *Phonology*. Basingstoke: Macmillan.

Carr, Philip. 2013. *English Phonetics and Phonology: An Introduction*. (2nd ed.). Malden, MA: Wiley-Blackwell.

Catford, J. C. 2001. *A Practical Introduction to Phonetics*. (2nd ed.). Oxford: Oxford University Press.

Chen, Matthew Y. 2007. *Tone Sandhi: Patterns Across Chinese Dialects*. Cambridge: Cambridge University Press.

Chomsky, Noam & Morris Halle. 1968. *The Sound Pattern of English*. New York: Harper & Row.

Clark, John, Colin Yallop & Janet Fletcher. 2007. *An Introduction to Phonetics and Phonology*. (3rd ed.). Malden, MA: Blackwell Publishing.

Collins, Beverley S. & Inger M. Mees. 2013. *Practical Phonetics and Phonology: A Resource Book for Students*. (3rd ed.). London: Routledge.

Cook, Vivian. 2004. *The English Writing System*. London: Arnold.

Cruttenden, Alan. 1997. *Intonation*. (2nd ed.). Cambridge: Cambridge University Press.

Culpeper, Jonathan, Francis Katamba, Paul Kerswill, Ruth Wodak & Tony McEnery (eds.) 2009. *English Language: Description, Variation and Context*. Basingstoke: Palgrave Macmillan.

Davenport, Mike & S. J. Hannahs. 2010. *Introducing Phonetics and Phonology*. (3rd ed.). London: Hodder Education.

de Lacy, Paul (ed.). 2007. *The Cambridge Handbook of Phonology*. Cambridge: Cambridge University Press.

Dresher, B. Elan. 2009. *The Contrastive Hierarchy in Phonology*. Cambridge: Cambridge University Press.

Duanmu, San. 2007. *The Phonology of Standard Chinese*. (2nd ed.). Oxford: Oxford University Press.

Duanmu, San. 2008. *Syllable Structure: The Limits of Variation*. Oxford: Oxford University Press.

Durand, Jacques. 1990. *Generative and Non-linear Phonology*. Harlow: Longman.

Ewen, Colin J. & Harry van der Hulst. 2001. *The Phonological Structure of Words*. Cambridge: Cambridge University Press.

Finegan, Edward & John R. Rickford. 2004. *Language in the USA: Themes for the Twenty-first Century*. Cambridge: Cambridge University Press.

Fox, Anthony. 2000. *Prosodic Features and Prosodic Structure: The Phonology of Suprasegmentals*. Oxford: Oxford University Press.

Freeborn, Dennis. 2006. *From Old English to Standard English: A Course Book in*

Language Variations Across Time. (3rd ed.). London: Palgrave Macmillan.

Gick, Bryan, Ian Wilson & Donald Derrick. 2013. *Articulatory Phonetics*. Malden, MA: Wiley-Blackwell.

Giegerich, Heinz J. 1992. *English Phonology: An Introduction*. Cambridge: Cambridge University Press.

Gimson, A. C. and Alan Cruttenden. 2008. *Gimson's Pronunciation of English*. (7th ed.). London: Hodder Education.

Goldsmith, John A. 1976. *Autosegmental Phonology*. MIT: PhD Dissertation. Published by Garland Publishing, New York, 1979.

Goldsmith, John A. 1990. *Autosegmental and Metrical Phonology*. Oxford: Blackwell.

Goldsmith, John A. 1999. *Phonological Theory: The Essential Readings*. Malden, MA: Blackwell Publishing.

Goldsmith, John, Jason Riggle and Alan C. L. Yu (eds.) 2011. *The Handbook of Phonological Theory*. (2nd ed.). Malden, MA: Wiley-Blackwell.

Gordon, Matthew Kelly. 2006. *Syllable Weight: Phonetics, Phonology, Typology*. London: Routledge.

Gregoriou, Christiana. 2009. *English Literary Stylistics*. Basingstoke: Palgrave Macmillan.

Greenbaum, Sidney. 1996. *The Oxford English Grammar*. Oxford: Oxford University Press.

Gussenhoven, Carlos. 2004. *The Phonology of Tone and Intonation*. Cambridge: Cambridge University Press.

Gussenhoven, Carlos & Haike Jacobs. 2011. *Understanding Phonology*. (3rd ed.). London: Hodder Education.

Gussmann, Edmund. 2002. *Phonology: Analysis and Theory*. Cambridge: Cambridge University Press.

Halle, Morris & George N. Clements. 1983. *Problem Book in Phonology: A Workbook for Courses in Introductory Linguistics and Modern Phonology*. Cambridge, MA: MIT.

Hammond, Michael. 1999. *The Phonology of English: A Prosodic Optimality-theoretic Approach*. Oxford: Oxford University Press.

Hardcastle, William J., John Laver & Fiona E. Gibbon (eds.) 2010. *The Handbook of Phonetic Sciences*. (2nd ed.). Malden, MA: Wiley-Blackwell.

Hayes, Bruce. 1995. *Metrical Stress Theory: Principles and Case Studies*. Chicago: University of Chicago Press.

Hayes, Bruce. 2009. *Introductory Phonology*. Malden, MA: Wiley-Blackwell.

Hogg, Richard M. 1992. *The Cambridge History of the English Language*. Vol. 1: The Beginnings to 1066. Cambridge: Cambridge University Press.

Hogg, Richard M. 2011. *A Grammar of Old English*. Vol. 1: *Phonology*. Malden, MA: Wiley-Blackwell.

Hogg, Richard & David Denison (eds.). 2006. *A History of the English Language*. Cambridge: Cambridge University Press.

International Phonetic Association. 1999. *Handbook of the International Phonetic Association: A Guide to the Use of the International Phonetic Alphabet*. Cambridge: Cambridge University Press.

IPA Handbook. = International Phonetic Association, 1999.

Jensen, John T. 2004. *Principles of Generative Phonology: An Introduction*. Amsterdam:

John Benjamins.
Jones, Daniel. 1922. *An Outline of English Phonetics*. Leipzig/Berlin: B. G. Teubner.
Jones, Daniel, Peter Roach, Jane Setter & John Esling. 2011. *Cambridge English Pronouncing Dictionary*. (18th ed.). Cambridge: Cambridge University Press.
Kager, René. 1999. *Optimality Theory*. Cambridge: Cambridge University Press.
Kahnemuyipour, Arsalan. 2009. *The Syntax of Sentential Stress*. Oxford: Oxford University Press.
Katamba, Francis & Paul Kerswill. 2009. Phonological Change. In Culpeper, et al. (eds.): 259−285.
Katamba, Francis & John Stonham. 2006. *Morphology*. Basingstoke: Palgrave Macmillan.
Kenstowicz, Michael. 1994. *Phonology in Generative Grammar*. Oxford: Blackwell.
Knight, Rachael-Anne. 2012. *Phonetics: A Coursebook*. Cambridge: Cambridge University Press.
Kramer, Martin. 2012. *Underlying Representations*. Cambridge: Cambridge University Press.
Kreidler, Charles W. 1997. *Describing Spoken English*. London: Routledge.
Kreidler, Charles W. 2004. *The Pronunciation of English: A Coursebook*. (2nd ed.). Malden, MA: Blackwell Publishing.
Labov, William, Sharon Ash & Charles Boberg. 2006. *The Atlas of North American English: Phonetics, Phonology and Sound Change*. Berlin: Mouton de Gruyter.
Ladd, D. Robert. 2008. *Intonational Phonology*. (2nd ed.). Cambridge: Cambridge University Press.
Ladefoged, Peter. 1982. *A Course in Phonetics*. (2nd ed.). Fort Worth, TX: Harcourt, Brace, Jovanovich.
Ladefoged, Peter. 1993. *A Course in Phonetics*. (3rd ed.). Fort Worth, TX: Harcourt Brace.
Ladefoged, Peter. 2001. *A Course in Phonetics*. (4th ed.). Fort Worth, TX: Harcourt.
Ladefoged, Peter. 2006. *A Course in Phonetics*. (5th ed.). Boston, MA: Wadsworth.
Ladefoged, Peter & Sandra Ferrari Disner. 2012. *Vowels and Consonants*. (3rd ed.). Malden, MA: Wiley-Blackwell.
Ladefoged, Peter & Keith Johnson. 2011. *A Course in Phonetics*. (6th ed.). Boston, MA: Wadsworth.
Ladefoged, Peter & Ian Maddieson. 1996. *The Sounds of the World's Languages*. Malden, MA: Blackwell Publishing.
Lass, Roger. 2009. *English Phonology and Phonological Theory: Synchronic and Diachronic Studies*. Cambridge: Cambridge University Press.
Lass, Roger & John M. Anderson. 2010. *Old English Phonology*. Cambridge: Cambridge University Press.
Laver, John. 1994. *Principles of Phonetics*. Cambridge: Cambridge University Press.
Lodge, Ken. 2009a. *A Critical Introduction to Phonetics*. London: Continuum.
Lodge, Ken. 2009b. *Fundamental Concepts in Phonology: Sameness and Difference*. Edinburgh: Edinburgh University Press.
Lombardi, Linda (ed.). 2010. *Segmental Phonology in Optimality Theory: Constraints and Representations*. Cambridge: Cambridge University Press.
Malmkjær, Kirsten (ed.) 2010. *The Routledge Linguistics Encyclopedia*. (3rd ed.).

London: Routledge.

McCarthy, John J. 2002. *A Thematic Guide to Optimality Theory*. Cambridge: Cambridge University Press.

McCarthy, John J. (ed.). 2004. *Optimality Theory in Phonology: A Reader*. Malden, MA: Blackwell Publishing.

McCarthy, John J. 2008. *Doing Optimality Theory: Applying Theory to Data*. Malden, MA: Blackwell Publishing.

McCully, Chris. 2009. *The Sound Structure of English: An Introduction*. Cambridge: Cambridge University Press.

McMahon, April. 2002. *An Introduction to English Phonology*. Edinburgh: Edinburgh University Press.

Mielke, Jeff. 2008. *The Emergence of Distinctive Features*. Oxford: Oxford University Press.

Millward, C. M. & Mary Hayes. 2012. *A Biography of the English Language*. (3rd ed.). Boston, MA: Wadsworth.

Mitchell, Bruce & Fred C. Robinson. 2011. *A Guide to Old English*. (8th ed.). Malden, MA: Wiley-Blackwell.

Odden, David. 2005. *Introducing Phonology*. Cambridge: Cambridge University Press.

Ogden, Richard. 2009. *An Introduction to English Phonetics*. Edinburgh: Edinburgh University Press.

Prince, Alan & Paul Smolensky. 2004. *Optimality Theory: Constraint Interaction in Generative Grammar*. Malden, MA: Blackwell Publishing.

Quirk, Randolph & C. L. Wren. 1957. *An Old English Grammar*. London: Methuen.

Radford, Andrew, Martin Atkinson, David Britain, Harald Clahsen & Andrew Spencer. 2009. *Linguistics: An Introduction*. (2nd ed.). Cambridge: Cambridge University Press.

Reetz, Henning & Allard Jongman. 2009. *Phonetics: Transcription, Production, Acoustics, and Perception*. Malden, MA: Wiley-Blackwell.

Roach, Peter. 2009. *English Phonetics and Phonology: A Practical Course*. (4th ed.). Cambridge: Cambridge University Press.

Roca, Iggy & Wyn Johnson. 1999a. *A Course in Phonology*. Oxford: Blackwell.

Roca, Iggy & Wyn Johnson. 1999b. *A Workbook in Phonology*. Oxford: Blackwell.

Simpson, J. M. Y. 1979. *A First Course in Linguistics*. Edinburgh: Edinburgh University Press.

Small, Larry H. 2012. *Fundamentals of Phonetics: A Practical Guide for Students*. (3rd ed.). Upper Saddle River, NJ: Pearson Education.

Smith, Jeremy J. 2007. *Sound Change and the History of English*. Oxford: Oxford University Press.

Smith, Jeremy J. 2009. *Old English: A Linguistic Introduction*. Cambridge: Cambridge University Press.

Spencer, Andrew. 1996. *Phonology: Theory and Application*. Oxford: Blackwell.

Tench, Paul. 2011. *Transcribing the Sounds of English: A Phonetics Workbook for Words and Discourse*. Cambridge: Cambridge University Press.

Upward, Christopher & George Davidson. 2011. *The History of English Spelling*. Malden, MA: Wiley-Blackwell.

van Gelderen, Elly. 2006. *A History of the English Language*. Amsterdam: John Benjamins.

Vinson, Betsy Partin. 2012. *Language Disorders across the Lifespan*. Clifton Park, NY: Delmar-Cengage.

Wells, John. 1982. *Accents of English*. Vols. 1—3. Cambridge: Cambridge University Press.

Wells, John. 2006. *English Intonation: An Introduction*. Cambridge: Cambridge University Press.

Wells, John. 2008. *Longman Pronunciation Dictionary*. (3rd ed.). Harlow: Pearson-Longman.

Wyatt, A. J. 1897. *An Elementary Old English Grammar (Early West Saxon)*. Cambridge: Cambridge University Press.

Yavaş, Mehmet. 2011. *Applied English Phonology*. (2nd ed.). Malden, MA: Wiley-Blackwell.

Yip, Moira. 2002. *Tone*. Cambridge: Cambridge University Press.

Zsiga, Elizabeth C. 2013. *The Sounds of Language: An Introduction to Phonetics and Phonology*. Malden, MA: Wiley-Blackwell.

Chapter 3

Morphology

MORPHOLOGY is a branch of linguistics that deals with the internal structure of words. It is generally divided into two fields: inflectional morphology and derivational morphology, with the former studying inflections of words and the latter word formation. Morphology can refer to morphemics, a term used by American structuralists in the 1940s and 1950s, which emphasizes synchronic morphemic analysis, but more generally it designates morphological analysis which involves both synchronic and diachronic studies. In its modern sense, however, morphology is essentially synchronic, primarily concerned with the forms of words through the use of morpheme construct. (Matthews 1991:2—9, Bauer 1983:13, Crystal 1985:200)

3.1 Morphemes, Morphs and Allomorphs

Traditionally, words are treated as the minimal basic units of a language to make sentences, which are combinations of words according to syntactic rules. Structurally, however, a word is not the smallest unit because a majority of words can be separated into even smaller meaningful units. Take *decontextualization* for example. This word can be broken down into *de-*, *con-*, *text*, *-al*, *-ize*, *-ation*, each having a meaning of its own. And none of these segments. can be further divided; otherwise, they would not make any sense. Though *-ation* has a number of variants such as *-tion*, *-sion* and *-ion*, they belong to the same suffix as they have the same meaning and grammatical function. The different forms occur to adapt to different phonetic environments These minimal meaningful units are known as MORPHEMES (Morph is the Greek word for "form"; *-eme* as in "pheme" means "class of"). In view of word formation, the morpheme is seen as "the smallest functioning unit in the composition of words." (Crystal, 1985) Syntactically, a morpheme is the minimal form of grammatical analysis. For instance, each of the word-forms *studies*, *studying*, *studied*, consists of the morpheme *study* +; the forms *-es* in *studies*, *-ing* in *studying*, and *-ed* in *studied* are morphemes, which express grammatical concepts instead of deriving new words. (See Section 3.3)

Morphemes are abstract units, which are realized in speech by discrete forms known as MORPHS. "They are actual spoken forms, minimal carriers of meaning." (Bolinger and Sears, 1981:43) In other words the phonetic or orthographic strings or segments which realize morphemes are "morphs." (Bauer 1983: 15) The morph is to a morpheme what a phone is to a phoneme. Most morphemes are realized by one morph like *bird*, *tree*, *green*, *sad*, *want*, etc. These morphemes coincide with words as they can stand by themselves and function freely in a sentence. Words of this kind are called monomorphemic words. Some morphemes, however, are realized by more than one morph in relation to their phonological context in a word. For instance, the morpheme of plurality {s} has a set of morphs in different sound context, e. g. *cats* /s/, *bags* /z/, and *matches* /ɪz/. The alternates /s/, /z/ and /ɪz/ are three different morphs. The same is true of the link verb morpheme {be}. Its past tense is realized by two distinct orthographic forms *was* and *were*, each of which happens to be a word-form, realizing {preterite} and {singular}, and {preterite} and {plural} respectively and each has its own phonetic forms /wɒz/, /wəz/ and /wɜː/, /wə/. Therefore, both *was* and *were* and their respective phonetic forms are morphs. (See discussion in Bauer, 1983: 15)

An ALLOMORPH refers to a member of a set of morphs, which represent the same morpheme. Just as we class phones together as allophones of a single phoneme, so we class morphs together as allomorphs of a single morpheme. Take the plural morpheme {s} again. Phonetically, it is realized by /s/, /z/, /ɪz/, which are thus said to be allomorphs of {s}. In English, many morphemes can have more than one allomorph, particularly those freestanding morphemes operating as functional words. Once they occur in connected speech, they may be realized by different forms, depending on whether they are accented or weakened (See the data in the table below).

Table 3.1 Mopheme and Allomorph

Morpheme	Allomorph	
	Strong	Weak
{am}	/æm/	/əm/, /m/
{was}	/wɒz/	/wəz/, /z/
{have}	/hæv/	/həv/, /v/
{would}	/wʊd/	/wəd/, /əd/, /d/
{he}	/hiː/	/hɪ/, /ɪ/
{his}	/hɪz/	/ɪz/, /z/
{for}	/fɔː/	/fə/
{to}	/tuː/	/tʊ/, /tə/, /t/

Then what is the difference between morphs and allomorphs? The relationship can be illustrated by the diagram below.

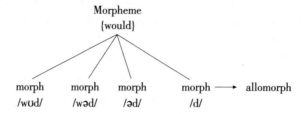

3.2 Classification of Morphemes

Morphemes vary in function. Accordingly, we can classify morphemes into several general categories: free versus bound, derivational versus inflectional, and lexical versus grammatical. However, their boundaries are not as clear-cut as they appear to be due to some overlapping. For the sake of discussion, we shall define each type in terms of its characteristics.

3.2.1 Free and Bound Morphemes

This is the most preferred classification in morphological studies, discussed in Hatch & Brown (1995), Crystal (1985), Fromkin & Rodman (1983), Bauer (1983), Bolinger & Sears (1981) and Matthews (1991). Morphemes which can stand alone are "free." These morphemes can be used as free grammatical units in sentences. They are identical with words, for example, *man*, *earth*, *wind*, *car* and *anger*.

Morphemes which cannot occur as words are "bound." They are so named because they are bound to other morphemes to form words or to perform a particular grammatical function. BOUND MORPHEMES are mainly found in derived words. Let us take *recollection*, *idealistic* and *ex-prisoner* for example. Each of the three words comprises three morphemes: *recollection* (re-collect-ion), *idealistic* (ideal-ist-ic), *ex-prisoner* (ex-prison-er). Of the nine morphemes, *collect*, *ideal* and *prison* can stand by themselves and thus are FREE MORPHEMES. All the rest *re-*, *-ion*, *-ist*, *ex-* and *-er* are bound as none of them are freestanding units.

Free morphemes are all ROOTS, which are capable of being used as words word-building elements to form new words, whereas bound morphemes consist of both roots and AFFIXES, most of which can be used to create new words like *re-*, *-ion*, *-ic*, and *ex-*. But there are a few affixes, which only indicate grammatical such concepts as "tense" "aspect" "number" and "case," for example, the *-ing* in *watching*, *-er* in *easier*, *-s* in *books*, and *-ed* in *worked*.

The English language possesses a multitude of words made up of merely bound morphemes, e. g. *antecedent*, which can be broken down into *ante-*, *-ced-* and *-ent*. Among them, *-ced-* is a root meaning "approach, go to," *ante-*, a prefix meaning "before" and *-ent*, a noun suffix meaning "a person, a thing," thus the whole word *antecedent* meaning "something that goes before." This example shows clearly that bound morphemes can be root (See Root, Stem & Base) and affix (See Affix).

3.2.2 Derivational and Inflectional Morphemes

Morphemes used to derive new words are known as DERIVATIONAL MORPHEMES because when these morphemes are conjoined, new words are derived. In English, DERIVATIVES and COMPOUNDS are all formed by such morphemes. For example, *a + mor + al, clear + ance, life + like* and *homo + gen + eous* are results of morphological processes.

INFLECTIONAL MORPHEMES, in contrast, indicate syntactic relationships between words and thus function as grammatical markers. In English, inflectional morphemes are all suffixes. For instance, the regular plural suffix *-s* (*-es*) is added to nouns such as *machines, fridges, desks, radios* and *potatoes*; the same forms call be added to verbs to indicate the simple present for the third person singular such as *likes, works* and *goes*; the form *-'s* is used to denote the possessive case of nouns such as *children's library*, the *man's role* and the *mother-in law's complaints*; the suffixes *-er*, *-est* are usually attached to simple adjectives or adverbs to show their comparative or superlative degrees like *happier, happiest; harder, hardest*. And the past tense marker *-ed* and progressive marker *-ing* are added to verbs. The characteristics of inflectional and derivational morphemes can be summarized as follows (See Hatch & Brown 1995: 266):

Table 3.2 The Characteristics of Inflectional and Derivational Morphemes

Inflectional morpheme	Derivational morpheme
1. does not change meaning or part of speech of the stem.	1. changes meaning or part of speech of the stem.
2. indicates syntactic or semantic relations between words in a sentence.	2. indicates semantic relations within the word.
3. occurs with all members of some large class of morphemes.	3. occurs with only some members of a class of morphemes.
4. occurs at margins of words.	4. occurs before any inflectional morpheme.

Inflectional morphemes are of paramount importance in AGGLUTINATING or INFLECTIONAL languages such as Latin, Russian and German as all the grammatical aspects of words are marked by these morphemes. However, inflectional morphemes are not found in ISOLATING languages like Chinese, in which the grammatical concepts are indicated by lexical means. Nouns and verbs are not subject to change in morphology to show inflections. Compare:

 (1) He often *writes letters*.
  他常写信。
  We often *write letters*.
  我们常写信。
  He *wrote a letter* yesterday.
  他昨天写了一封信。
  We *wrote two letters* yesterday.
  我们昨天写了两封信。

In the English versions, the forms of verbs and nouns are affected by person, number and tense whereas in Chinese the nouns and verbs remain the same except for the addition of some other words to indicate person, number and tense.

3.2.3 Lexical and Grammatical Morphemes

On a semantic and syntactic basis, morphemes can fall into lexical (also known as content by Traugott & Pratt, 1980: 91) and grammatical morphemes (Bolinger & Sears, 1981: 66—71; Hatch & Brown, 1995: 267). LEXICAL MORPHEMES are used, as we see above, to derive new words, so also known as derivational morphemes. These morphemes, whether free or bound, whether roots or affixes, all contribute to the formation of new lexical entities, hence the name. GRAMMATICAL MORPHEMES, on the other hand, are grammatical in nature. They function primarily as grammatical markers to show syntactic relations. They encompass both inflectional morphemes and such free morphemes as *in*, *and*, *do*, *have*, *they*, *while*, *where*, *but* and *that*, which are traditionally known as FUNCTIONAL WORDS.

The boundaries between lexical and grammatical morphemes, however, are not always clear. The English noun suffix like *-tion*, adjective suffix like *-eous*, and adverb suffix *-ly* are added to stems to convert them into different classes. Are they grammatical or lexical? This is an arguable case. In fact they do not add much lexical meaning to the stems but they function as markers of part of speech. Even a full noun like *man* can pose some difficulty as in "Why is he on trial?" "Because he killed a man." In this case, the word *man* is a little more than "somebody," filling an empty grammatical slot just like a pronoun. (Bolinger & Sears, 1981: 69)

3.3 Morphemization

MORPHEMIZATION is the process of creating a new morpheme, using a word or part of a word. This is a common linguistic phenomenon going on in natural languages, unfortunately largely neglected. For example, so far this term is hardly found in the mainstream literature on morphology and word-formation in relation to Indo-European languages. However, the process has never ceased to function. Take -gate for example. Originally, the form is part of the American place name Watergate in Washington, D.C. related to a political scandal leading to American President Nixon's resignation. Later, the form -gate was segmented from Watergate to signify "political scandal." Then the form was used to derive new words referring to any similar political scandal, like *Irangate*, *Koreangate*, etc. When -gate was introduced to Chinese, it was translated into 门 (literal meaning "gate"), as a result the Chinese character 门 (a new morpheme now in Chinese) took on the same meaning "scandal," leading to free generation of words with this form. The process of -gate developing as a word-forming element is morphemization, for -gate is no longer regarded as a word relating to the freestanding root morpheme *gate* but a new morpheme which cannot stand alone and needs to be affixed to the end of a stem or base to form words. More examples are -*scape* from *landscape* in *skyscape*, *moonscape*, etc. and -*bot* from *robot* in *bugbot*, *sexbot* and so on.

New morphemes are generally created in two ways: 1) using an existing word (mostly monomorphemic) like *speak* "idiosyncratic way of speaking or special terminology" as in *Clintonspeak* in the first sense and *computerspeak*, *cyberspeak* in the second, and *in* "mass demonstration esp. to protest, etc." as in *live-in*, *bike-in* and *love-in*; 2) using a segment of a word (generally monosyllabic) like -*gate* (from *Watergate*), -*scape* (from *landscape*) and -*bot* (from *robot*). Look at some Chinese examples 打的(take taxi), 的哥(male taxi driver); 网吧(Internet bar), 茶吧(tea house). 的 originally borrowed from Cantonese phonological translation of taxi 的士 became morphemized still denoting "taxi"; likewise 吧 sound copying of English *bar* now is used as a new morpheme to refer to any place of similar size for specialized use, hence 网吧 and 茶吧. Different from English, morphemization is common in Chinese in relation to borrowings through translation and in fact there is a large body of literature on morphemization. (See 周洪波, 1995; 苏新春, 2003; 郭鸿杰, 2002; 杨锡彭, 2004 等)

A newly morphomized form should have characteristics of morphemes. First, since it is a morpheme, it should be productive, i.e. the form can be used to create new words with stems or bases as exemplified above. Second, the form should have no part of speech (but Chinese is an exception) even though the original form was a word. Take -*speak* and -*in* again. The original word *speak* is a verb and *in* a preposition, but the morphomized forms both function as noun suffixes. The same is true of the new morphemes *info-* from *information* and *e-* from *electronic*, both functioning as formatives with no relation to the original part of speech. Third, semantically new morphemes may keep the meanings of their parent words like *info-* as in *infonet*, *infocenter*, *info-education*, and *e-* as in *e-book*, *e-commerce*, *e-readingroom*. More often than not, the new morphemes may acquire new meanings as *-gate* in *prisoner-gate* and *zipper-gate*, and *-in* as in *teach-in* and *wed-in*. In the former case, *-gate*, which is not politically oriented, means "infamous event," and in the latter, *-in* has no connotation of "protesting" but simply "a mass gathering." Nevertheless, their identity as affixes or combining forms is still arguable, yet there seems to be no disagreement that these forms have morphemic status-resultant of morphemization.

3.4 Allomorphy

ALLOMORPHY is concerned with the ways in which morphemes are related to phonological forms, in other words, with the principles governing the range of variation in shape shown by particular morphemes. (Anderson, 1992:13) It deals with the relation between morphs and morphemes. (Matthews 1991:107) It is closely parallel to the study of allophonic variation in phonology, also known as MORPHOPHONOLOGY or using American terminology, MORPHONEMICS—analysis and classification of the phonological factors which affect the appearance of morphemes. (Crystal 1985: 200)

3.4.1 Phonological Conditioning

As is already known, morpheme is an abstract notion. In the actual context it is realized by morphs called ALLOMORPHS. A morpheme may consist of a single allomorph like *bomb* /bɒm/ or more than one allomorph like *bombard* /bɒm'bɑːd/. The letter b occurs twice in both cases, yet the second b is silent in the former but is sounded in the latter. The plural morpheme {s} has three main allomorphic variants /s/, /z/ and /ɪz/, the occurrence of which is predictable as each is closely related to a particular sound context: /s/ occurs after the voiceless consonants /t, p, k/ as in *packs*, *cheats* and *shapes*; /z/ after the voiced consonants /d, h, g, l/ as in *beds*, *bottles* and *bags*, and /ɪz/ after /s, z, ʃ, ʒ, tʃ, dʒ/ as in *classes*, *dishes* and *garages*, etc. This is called PHONOLOGICAL CONDITIONING, which also accounts for the phonic variants of past tense morpheme {ed} and prefix morpheme {in} as follows:

(2)   {ed}   {ɪn}
       worked, helped   /t/   improper, immovable, imbalance   /ɪm/
       tried, warmed   /d/   irreconcilable, irresistible   /ɪr/
       wanted, landed   /ɪd/ illegal, illegible   /ɪl/
                               inaudible, incapable, inactive   /ɪn/

The rules for the plural morpheme {s} are also applicable to the past tense {ed}, which is realized by /t/ after a voiceless consonant, /d/ after a voiced consonant, and /ɪd/ after alveolar plosives /t/ and /d/. The prefix {ɪn} has four variants as illustrated above: /ɪm/ occurs before labial consonants /m/, /p/, /b/; /ɪr/ before /r/, /ɪl/ before /l/, and /ɪn/ before all other sounds.

3.4.2 Morphological Conditioning

There are cases where the allomorphs of the noun plural morpheme are unusual:

(3) a. ox-oxen
    b. child-children
    c. brother-brethren
    d. phenomenon-phenomena, insigne-insignia, jinnee-jinn, schema-schemata, datum-data, alumnus-alumnae
    e. foot-feet, goose-geese, man-men, mouse-mice
    f. sheep-sheep, deer-deer

Each of the six classes is unique in its plural formation. The first three classes share the same morpheme {en} attached to the end of the stem, but (3)b involves the addition of the letter r before it, and 3(c) involves both vowel change and addition. (3)e is characterized by vowel change and (3)f by the addition of a zero morph /ø/. Words of (3)d are all borrowed from Latin, Greek or Hebrew, therefore their plural formation is governed by their original rules. Since these are exceptional cases and have their own rules of allomorphy, they are said to be morphologically (grammatically, morphemically, lexically) conditioned. (See discussion in Bolinger & Sears, 1981:44−47; Traugott & Pratt, 1980: 92−94; Katamba, 1993: 23−31; Matthew, 1991: 114−119)

Let us consider the genitive singular of the definite article in German. The form of the genitive singular definite article for a masculine noun like *Mann* "man" or a neuter like *Kind* "child" is *des*; for a feminine noun like *Frau* "woman," the article is *der*. The form of the genitive singular definite article is not conditioned by the phonological shape of the noun, nor by specific lexemes, but by a grammatical feature of the noun it is used with, namely gender. This is typical GRAMMATICAL CONDITIONING. (Bauer 1983:15−16)

Morphological conditioning embraces the paradigm of irregular verbs, each of which undergoes a special internal vowel change to indicate the past tense or past participle as *get-got-got*, *sing-sang-sung* and *drive-drove-driven*, each of which involves internal changes /e→ɒ/, /ɪ→æ→ʌ/, /aɪ→ou→ɪ+n/ (for reasons of such change, see Bynon, 1977: Ch. 1). Like zero plural morph for *deer* and *sheep*, the past tense and past participle of some irregular verbs are also realized by zero morph such as *hit-hit-hit* and *cut-cut-cut*. However, some scholars rationalize the phenomenon by attaching the past marker /t/ to the stem * hit-t or * cut-t, resulting in the present forms *hit* and *cut*, the last letter t in each word entailing the past marker /t/. This also accounts for the forms of *keep-kept*, *deal-dealt*, *catch-caught*, *tell-told* and *sell-sold*. The first three examples involve vowel change plus the past marker /t/ and the last two vowel change plus the past marker /d/. (Matthews, 1991: 125—142)

Apart from vowel change and addition in the realization of the past tense, a totally different form may be borrowed to represent the past tense morph, for instance, *go-went*. Historically, the Old English form "go" is *gan* and *went* is related to the Old English *wendan* "turn." Now *wen-* is the form that *go* takes before the past tense marker /t/. This phenomenon is known as SUPPLETION, the realization of a single morpheme by sound sequences that have no phonological similarity. (Traugott & Pratt, 1980: 94) Other examples of this kind include the comparative form of *better* for *good*, and *worse* for *bad*, where the base form and the comparative are two different roots. (Katamba, 1993:30—31)

3.4.3 Stylistic Conditioning

It is known that the allomorphs of a morpheme are the result of complementary distribution in connected speech. In each context, a different morph might occur in compliance with the situation. This is called STYLISTIC CONDITIONING. (Bolinger & Sears, 1981: 47—48) For instance, the functional words *you*, *he*, *she*, *am*, *are*, *is*, *have*, *has* and *not* each have one form in formal and accented position, but take completely different forms when they are contracted in informal speech as in *she's*, *you're*, *haven't* and *isn't*. In such cases as *I wanna go* (I want to go), *Drinka pinta milka day* (Drink a pint of milk a day), *"emah frien"* (He is my friend), *fightin'* (fighting), *partik'lar* (particular), *agen'* (against), the phonological variants represented by the unconventional spelling all result from the styles of speaking.

3.5 Word, Word-form and Lexeme

The term WORD is so extensively used that its meaning becomes vague and its use is often confusing. Conventionally, a "word" is a unit of expression which is intuitively recognized by native speakers in both spoken and written language. Consider the sentence or utterance: *A cat eats rats*. In visual terms a word is a meaningful letter or a group of letters printed or written on paper. Accordingly, the italicized utterance consists of four words. Phonologically, a word is viewed as a sound or combination of sounds, which are made voluntarily with human vocal equipment to convey meaning and its boundaries are indicated by pauses. Along this line the same utterance would be represented as [ə kæt i ː ts ræts]. But problems arise here. Do we consider the forms *eat*, *eats*, *ate*, *eaten*, *eating* five different words or one word? If the same form appears more than once in a sentence or utterance, do we count them as one word or more than one? Orthographically, each of the forms *eat*, *eats*, *ate*, *eaten*, *eating* is a "word" in the sense of word-form. Semantically, however, the five forms share the same basic meaning, and grammatically the five forms are the inflectional variants in the paradigm of the verb EAT. "Word" used in this sense is known in linguistics as LEXEME, i. e. "a minimal free form" in Bloomfield's terminology. A lexeme is a word in an abstract sense. When it "occurs" in context, it is a word-form, which has a particular phonological or orthographical shape. Such are the two senses of the "word." (Lyons, 1981: 101; Matthews, 1991: 26, 30; Bauer, 1983:1−12, Gramley & Pätzold, 1992:11−12; Crystal, 1985: 333)

In addition, the "word" has another sense: grammatical word or morphosyntactic word. For instance, the form *ate* represents the lexeme EAT and the past tense of EAT, and *eats* represents the "third person" and "singular" of EAT. Therefore, *eats* and *ate* are two words in a grammatical sense. From this perspective, a word can be defined as a grammatical unit. (Bauer, 1983: 12; Crystal, 1985: 334)

According to Cruse (1986), a word has two fairly general and constant characteristics. The first is that a word is typically the smallest element of a sentence which has positional mobility, i. e. it can move around without destroying the grammaticality of the sentence.

(4) John saw Bill.
Bill saw John.
Bill, John saw.

This characteristic of the word does not apply to morphemes which constitute a word like *unfriendly*, which cannot be rearranged as * *friendlyun*, *lyfriendun*, *friendunly*, because the morphemes have fixed positions in the word.

The second characteristic is that a word defies insertion of new material between the constituent parts. The sentence "His coolness was unbelievable" allows the insertion of material between *his*, *coolness*, *was*, *unbelievable* like "His *great* coolness *in the face of danger* was *quite* unbelievable." However, nothing can be inserted within each of the forms *his*, *coolness*, *was* and *unbelievable.* (Cruse, 1986:35 — 36) This justifies the word-status of *his*, *coolness*, *was* and *unbelievable.*

Nevertheless, these two rules are not applicable to languages in involving "infix," nor to Chinese. In Chinese, the redistribution of characters lead to different words such as 算盘(abacus)—盘算(calculate), 和平(peace)—平和 (gentle, mild). Many words do allow insertion of other elements such as 鞠躬 (bow)—鞠三个躬(bow three times), 倒霉(have bad luck)—倒八辈子的霉(be extremely unlucky).

3.6 Morphology and Word-formation

3.6.1 Root, Stem and Base

Words can be analyzed into morphemes. In word-formation morphemes are conventionally known as root, stem, base and affix.

A ROOT is the basic form of a word which cannot be further analyzed without total loss of identity. (Crystal, 1985:267) It is that part of the word that remains when all affixes have been removed. (Bauer, 1983: 20) A root can be free or hound. Whether free or hound, it carries the main component of word meaning. All free morphemes are FREE ROOTS such as *man*, *earth*, *wind*, *car* and *anger*. In the word *internationalists*, removing *inter-*, *-al*, *-ist*, *-s* leaves the free root *nation*, which defies further analysis.

A BOUND ROOT is a form that cannot stand alone but has to combine with other morphemes to make words. Take *-diet-* for example. It is a Latin root, meaning "say or speak," but it is not a word in its own right. Yet with affixes, it can create quite a number of words. With prefixes *contra-* "against" and *pre-* "before," it produces verbs *contradict* "speak against" and *predict* "tell beforehand"; with the additional suffix *-ion*, it forms *contradiction* and *prediction*; and with the suffix *-or*, it yields *contradictor* and *predictor*. Apart from these, *dictum*, *dictate*, *dictation*, *dictator*, *diction*, *dictionary* are all derived from the same root *-diet-*. Likewise, *-gen-* in *homogeneous* and *am-* in *amiable* are bound roots.

Some linguists make a distinction between simple root like *black*, *bird* and complex or compound root like *blackbird* from the viewpoint of INFLECTIONAL MORPHOLOGY. (Crystal, 1985:287) Many others hold that these terms contradict the unanalyzability of root. Therefore, another term STEM was introduced. Though the term was reserved by some linguists for the part of the word that remains when inflectional morphemes have been removed. (Bauer, 1983: 20) It is used to refer to the form of the word to which both inflectional and derivational morphemes can be added. (Matthews, 1991:64, 176) A stem can be a root like *-dict-*, *black*, *desk* and *am-*, called simple stem, or a form bigger than a root like *predict*, *prediction* and *darkroom*, known as complex or compound stems.

Finally, mention should be made of a related term BASE, used as an alternative to root or stem. (Crystal, 1985: 31) It is a form to which affixes of any kind can be added. Some scholars like Bauer (1983: 20) prefer the term "base" when they reserve stem for the form of the word only in terms of inflectional morphology.

3.6.2 Affix

AFFIXES are forms that are attached to bases or stems to change or modify meaning or function. All affixes are bound morphemes because none of them can stand as words on their own. According to the function of affixes, we can divide them into INFLECTIONAL AFFIXES like *-s*, *-ed* and *-ing*, and DERIVATIONAL AFFIXES like *pre-*, *ex-*, *de-*, *less*, *-dom* and *-ic*. Derivational and inflectional affixes are identical with derivational and inflectional morphemes on a morphological basis. In view of their distribution in the formation of words, affixes can be further divided into PREFIX and SUFFIX. Prefixes in English are all derivational, i. e. they are used to form new words, whereas suffixes are both derivational and inflectional. Accordingly, the above-mentioned affixes can be further grouped into prefixes: *pre-*, *ex-* and *de-*, and suffixes: *-less*, *-dom*, *-ic*, *-s*, *-ed* and *-ing*.

Occasionally, terms like INFIX and CIRCUMFIX might be heard. Infix is an affix attached inside a base or stem. The use of infixes and circumfixes are common in some of the non-Indo-European languages. In Bontoc, a Philippine language, for example, *fikas* means "strong," but *f. um. ikas* means "he is becoming strong"; similarly, *fusul* means "enemy" while *f. um. usul* means "he is becoming an enemy." In both cases, a form *-um* is inserted just after the initial consonant, expressing the same sense. (See discussion in Bauer, 1983: 18) In Indonesia, *ke-...-an* seems to constitute one unit, for the two forms are seldom used separately but occur together. For example, *kebisaan* meaning "capability" is derived from *bisa* "be able" rather than by prefixation of *ke-* to * *bisaan* or by suffixation of *-an* to * *kebisa*. Thus *ke-...-an* can be considered a circumfix, i. e. involving both a prefix and suffix in one unit. (Anderson, 1992: 53) As Bauer (1983: 18) notes, "infixation is virtually unknown in English, and comparatively rare throughout the Indo-European." There are a few extreme eases like *-bloody-*, *-bloomin (g)-*, and *-fuckin (g)* which are occasionally inserted into the middle of certain words to achieve special effect, such as *im. fucking. possible*, *propa. fucking. ganda*, and *al. bloody. mighty*. (Bauer, 1983: 89—91) These are exceptional rather than common, and in fact such words never survive and enter standard dictionaries.

3.6.3 Hierarchical Structures of Words

3.6.3.1 Word-formation Rules

Words can be simple and complex. Simple words consist of only a single root or stem. Simple words can take inflectional affixes to indicate grammatical concepts such as "person" "number" "tense" and "aspect." (See Section 4.2.2) Complex words can be analyzed into morphemes. According to structuralists, every word is composed exhaustively of morphemes and morphemes are arranged into a hierarchical IC (Immediate Constituent) structure. (Anderson, 1992: 13) When morphemes are combined to form words, they observe word formation rules. First, the stems with which a given affix may combine generally belong to the same part of speech. For instance, the suffix *-able* is freely attached to verbs to form adjectives, but not to adjectives or nouns, thus we can add it to *accept, love, depend* and *imagine*, but not to *nice, happy, empty, sky, earth* and *book*. Second, the words formed by the addition of a given affix also belong to the same part of speech. For instance, *symbolize, moralize, memorize* and *pressurize* are all verbs, and *brainless, childless, endless* and *restless* are all adjectives. (Clark et al., 1994: 352—353)

A POLYMORPHEMIC WORD can be segmented linearly into morphemes, for example, *untouchable*: un + touch + able. It seems that the prefix and suffix are attached to the verb stem at the same time. However, this is not the case because, as is stated already, each affix can only combine with stems of particular part of speech, the addition of a given affix normally depends on the occurrence of another affix. The suffix *-able* should combine with a verbal stem, and the prefix *un-* normally attaches to adjective stems. Before the verbal stem takes *-able*, *un-* cannot be added. Therefore, *-able* attaches first to the stem *touch* to create *touchable*, and then *un-* is added to form *untouchable*. The whole process involves two steps. We can map the process in terms of immediate constituents (IC) like [un [[touch] able]]. The hierarchical structure of the word can also be indicated by a tree graph:

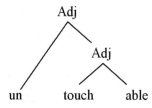

All the words can be analyzed in terms of immediate constituents. Take a more complex word: *oversimplification* [[over [[simple] ify]] (c)ation]

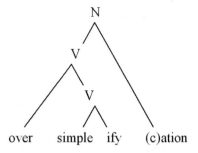

3.6.3.2 Suppletion

Every complex word is the combination of more than one morpheme, which are separable from the stem and from each other. When the morphemes are segmented, they should be identical with the original forms. But there are exceptions. Take *simplify* for example. To change it into a noun, we need to add the suffix *-ation* (which has variants like *-tion*, *-sion*, *-ion*). The result would be * *simplifiation*, but the accepted form is *simplification*. The same happens to all other words ending in *-ify* and *-ply* as *application* from *apply*, *multiplication* from *multiply*, *qualification* from *qualify* and *classification* from *classify*. This is applicable to adjectives formed from nouns ending in *-y* as *geographical* (geography + al) and *philosophical* (philosophy+ al). To accommodate such phenomena, linguists have come up with different ways of description, ranging from a quasi-phonological rule of "re-adjustment'" to lexical SUPPLETION within lexical entries of individual verbs, i. e. the addition of certain sound to meet the allomorphic need. (Anderson, 1992: 188—189)

3.6.3.3 Truncation

It is observed that there are cases in which affixation involves the deletion of certain element of the stem or base in the formation of new words. This is called TRUNCATION by Aronoff. (See discussion in Anderson, 1992:187—188) Consider the suffix *-able/-ible* again. According to the rule, we attach this suffix to any verb stem to create an adjective, for example, *read* + *able* → *readable*, and *obtain* + *able* → *obtainable*. But in *demonstrable*, *navigable* and *formulable*, when the suffix *-able* is removed, what remains are *demonstr-*, *navig-*, and *formul-* rather than the verbs *demonstrate*, *navigate*, and *formulate*. In the derived words, the sequence of *-ate* is deleted. Aronoff argues that in truncation what is deleted is always a FORMATIVE (a form used to form words like prefix and suffix) before other formatives. Therefore, *debate* cannot be changed into * *debable*, because *-ate* in *debate* is not a formative. However, this argument is not convincing. As a matter of fact, truncation occurs often in the formation of words, particularly when proper names are changed into common words or nationality words into adjectives such as *Faraday → farad*, *Denmark → Danish*, *Switzerland → Swiss*, and *Tentalus → tentative*. In these words what is deleted or replaced are non-formatives, and the changes are made to conform to the English way of pronunciation and spelling.

3.6.4 Productivity

If something has a creative capacity of producing things in large numbers, it is productive. In word formation, a process can be labeled PRODUCTIVE if it can be used synchronically in the production of new words. An affix is productive if it can be used freely by native speakers to form new words with other word-building elements like stem or affix. The productivity of word-formation processes are changing and so are word-building elements. Diachronically, some formatives which used to be productive have now become dead whereas other forms may have come to be productive with the development of language. For instance, the affixes *de-*, *non-*, *-teria* and *-wise* are now productive, as we can attach *de-* freely to verbs to create new verbs meaning the reversal of the action like *defrost*, *decentralize* and *defeather*. The prefix *non-* finds over 500 more recently occurring formations in the *Supplement to Oxford English Dictionary*. (Bauer, 1983: 279) On the other hand, *-th* which was active in Old English and found in the formation of *warmth*, *length*, *depth*, *width* and *breadth* derived from *warm*, *long*, *deep*, *wide* and *broad* is no longer used to form new words, and thus *coolth* is not acceptable.

According to the degree of productivity, the active word-formation processes can be arranged in the order of affixation, compounding, conversion, followed by the minor ones like shortening including clipping, acronymy, blending and back-formation. (Pyles & Algeo, 1991) But of course, linguists may not agree. Bolinger and Sears hold that the productivity of compounding is limitless whereas derivation is less productive. (1981: 61 — 63) This view is justified by Cannon's data (1987), which show that composite forms (words created by affixation and compounding) constitute 54.9 percent, followed by shifts with 19.6 percent and shortenings 18 percent. Conversion is not our concern in morphology because the process does not involve the addition or deletion of morphemes. New words are created in a semantic and grammatical sense but not in a morphological sense.

3.6.5 Word-formation Processes

3.6.5.1 Compounding

COMPOUNDS usually consist of two free morphemes like *dump show*, *hot seat*, *childhood* and *sweetheart*. They are formed on a variety of patterns, which yield three major classes of words: nouns, adjectives and verbs, e. g. *sunrise* (n+ v), *pickpocket* (v + n), *harddisk* (adj + n), *have-not* (v+ adv), *upstart* (edv+v), *warweary* (n+adj), *icy-cold* (adj+ adj). There are also a small number of words which combine with only bound forms as in *biochemistry*, *sociolinguistics*, *telethon* and *anglophone*, in which *bio-*, *socio-*, *tele-* and *anglo-*are combining forms, which function like *prefixes* but are actually stems.

According to semantic criteria, compounds fall into four classes. The first class is called ENDOCENTRIC COMPOUNDS comprising words like *armchair* (a kind of chair) and *houseparty* (a kind of party). In each, one constituent is the center and the other is the modifier. The second class is EXOCENTRIC COMPOUNDS (also known as bahuvrihi compounds in Sanskrit), consisting of words like *redskin* (not a type of skin) and *birdbrain* (not brain of the bird), in which there is no focal element and the whole refers to something else rather than what either of the constituents denotes. Words like *girlfriend* (a girl and also a friend) and *woman lawyer* (a woman and a lawyer) are termed APPOSITIONAL COMPOUNDS. The final class COPULATIVE COMPOUND (also known dvandava compound in Sanskrit) is exemplified by *French-German* and *aural-oral*, each of which shows a coordinating relationship and it is often difficult to decide which of the two is the focal element. (Bauer, 1983:30—31; Gramley & Pätzold, 1992: 28; Quirk *et al.*, 1985:1576—1578)

Compounds are semantically similar to idioms but characterized by their "one-wordness," which, in spoken form, is embodied by stress. The stress of a compound normally falls on the first element such as "*fat lady* not *fat*" *lady*, and "*mad man* not *mad*" man. The "one-wordness" can be manifested by inflectional morphology. A compound verb can take *-s* or *-ed* to show third person singular and past tense like *badmouths* or *badmouthed*. But the first adjective element can not undergo inflectional change, thus *redtape* is a compound whereas *reddertape* is not. (Bolinger & Sears, 1981: 62—63)

At present, there is a tendency of using combining forms (which are boundroots but function like affixes) to create new words. They are particularly common in scientific terms, such as *micro-*, *immuno-*, *photto-* and *neuro-*. Combining forms in end position are productive such as *-naut*: *cosmonaut*, *aquanaut*, *hovernaut*, *oceanaut*; *-crat*: *autocrat*, *nonocrat*, *Eurocrat* and *physiocrat*. However, their productivity cannot compare with suffixes. (Gramley & Pätzold,1992:29—30)

In Chinese, compounding is the most productive word-building process due to the unique characteristics of the language. The basic units are characters which function as morphemes but in most cases are different from morphemes in synthetic languages. The rules for compounding are identical with grammatical rules, by which characters are combined without any morphological change, for example, "love peace" is a verb phrase which can be made into an adjective as *peace-loving* in English whereas their Chinese equivalents 爱和平(verb phrase) becomes 爱和平的 (adjective), in which the original characters and word-order are the same, and only the adjective marker 的 is added to it. Other examples are 负责(take charge), 吃饭(eat), 朋友 (friend), 道路(road), 餐车(dining car), etc.

3.6.5.2 Affixation

AFFIXATION is also known as DERIVATION, a process of producing new words by adding affixes to stems or bases. As infixes are unknown in English, all the affixes can be classified into prefixes and suffixes and the processes involving them are called prefixation and suffixation. Prefixes and suffixes differ in two ways: 1) prefixes change the meaning of bases but normally not part of speech, 2) suffixes change part of speech and alter the meaning (usually grammatical meaning) as well. For instance, *obey*, *treat* and *distribute* are verbs and remain verbs after *dis-*, *real-* and *re-* are added to them: *disobey*, *maltreat* and *redistribute*. However, if suffixes are affixed to them, their part of speech will all change as *obedient*, *treatment* and *distributor*. Affixation in Chinese is not as productive as that in English. In the following examples, the second character in each of the words 妻子(wife), 读者(reader), 律师(lawyer), 职员(staff member), 球迷(fans), 园丁 (gardener), 匪徒(bandit) is a suffix. (吕叔湘,1979:48；任学良,1981: 6) But their productivity is very limited in the number of words created, far from the English agential suffix like *-er*, which can be attached to almost any verb to form a new word denoting either a person or an object.

Prefixes are not class-changing morphemes with the exceptions like *a-*, *be-*, *en-* (*em-*), which do change part of speech such *alive*, *awash*, *befriend*, *endanger* and *embitter*. In contemporary English, however, class-changing prefixes grow in number. The prefixes like *de-*, *un-*, *anti-*, *inter-*, *post-*, *pre-* and *out-* can all change the stem of one part of speech into that of another, for example, *unmask*(n→v), *postwar* (n→adj), *inter-city* (n→adj), *de-scale* (n→v), and *antipollution*(n→adj). But the change is simple either from nouns to adjectives or from nouns to verbs.

Complex forms are often the result of two processes (affixation and compounding) operating together. Take *information highways* for example. Information is the result of suffixation by adding the suffix *-ation* to the base *inform* and *highway* is the result of compounding by joining *high* with *way*; then *information* is combined with *highway* into *information highway*; finally the inflectional suffix *-s* is added, hence *information highways*. The steps can be illustrated as [[[inform] ation] [[high] [way]]]s].

3.6.5.3 Shortening

SHORTENING used in this context is a cover term referring to any process of word formation to create words by making the original shorter in various ways. Shortening is also rule-governed, and what is deleted often depends on the English convention of spelling or pronunciation. BLENDS are words formed by combining elements of two stems, either part of both words or part of one with the whole of the other or vice versa. For example, *comsat* is the result of blending the initial syllable of *communication* and *satellite*, each representing the original base form. The manner of blending varies such as *camcorder* (camera + recorder), colaholic (cocacola + alcoholic), telequiz (telephone + quiz), and lunarnaut (lunar + astronaut). All these examples are nouns. Words of other classes are rare though there are verbs and adjectives like *guesstimate* (guess + estimate) and fantabulous (fantastic + fabulous).

ACRONYMS and ABBREVIATIONS are the combinations of initial letters of a noun phrase but they are different mainly in formation and pronunciation. Acronyms are pronounced like an ordinary word, for example, *laser* (lightwave amplification by stimulated emission of radiation) and *dinky* (dual income, no kids + y). In order to make the word pronounceable, some words might be omitted like the formation of *laser* and sometimes two letters might be taken from one word like the formation of radar (radio detecting and ranging). Abbreviations (also known as INITIALISMS) are pronounced letter by letter as UN (the United Nations) and VIP (very important person).

CLIPPINGS are shortened forms of words by cutting a part off the original. There are two major types of clipping, front-and back-clipping, with the second being more frequent like *quake* (earthquake) and *memo* (memorandum). Medial clipping and front-back clipping are also possible but not so frequent like *vegan* (vegetarian), *veggies* (vegetables), and *van* (advantage), *flu* (influenza). The forms *mike* (microphone), *coke* (cocacola), *telly* (television), *comfy* (comfortable) are clippings with additional change for the sake of pronunciation and spelling.

Another kind of word creation by means of reduction is BACK-FORMATION. The existence of suffixation suggests that a complex noun presupposes a verb. That is, since a suffix can be attached to a verb to create a noun, conversely by removing the suffix a noun can be changed back into a verb. Logically, *enthuse* and *televise* are derived from *enthusiasm* and *television* by removing -*iasm* and -*ion* respectively. Accordingly, *automate* (from *automation*), *laze* (from *lazy*), *auth* (from *author*) and *bant* (from *banting*) have come into existence. The difference between back-clipping and back-formation lies in the fact that in the former case what is deleted can be any segment of a word whereas in the latter what is deleted is normally identifiable with a suffix.

3.7 Approaches and Problems

In the study of morphology, there are a variety of approaches or models that have been put forward and employed. The ones which have been widely discussed are the models of description formulated by Hockett in 1954 in his article "Two models of grammatical description" published in *Word*. (Matthews, 1991: 21) Apart from these, two other approaches formulated in the analysis of Chinese morphology are to be introduced.

3.7.1 Item and Arrangement

ITEM AND ARRANGEMENT (IA) —one of the models of description used in morphology for the analysis of words-took as its basic unit the morpheme which includes roots, inflections, derivational affixes and other formatives. In this morpheme-based approach, words are seen as linear sequences of morphs or "items." (Crystal, 1985: 166) In other words the morphs are arranged in a liner manner in terms of the surface structure, e. g. the word *internationalists* can be analyzed as *inter* + *nation* + *al* + *ist* + *s*, each being a separate morph. Naturally, the past tense form *worked* is arranged as *work* + *ed* and the comparative degree of the adjective *happy* is *happy* + *er*. This is effective in the description of languages like Chinese but not so attractive to a specialist in Latin. (Matthews, 1991: 22) But the actual practice finds this approach problematic. How can we analyze *men* and *sheep* or the past form *ate*? Since each is a single morpheme containing two morphs which are inseparable, the alternative suggested is *men* [man + plural], *sheep* [sheep + plural] or [sheep + 0] and *ate* [eat + past tense]. The other problem is related to the structure of composite forms, which, by analysis, can be separated linearly but fails to reveal the hierarchical nature of word structure.

3.7.2 Item and Process

The model of description which includes morphological processes is called ITEM AND PROCESS (IP), formulated as an alternative approach to morphology. Along this line, the relationships between words or items are seen as processes of derivation, e. g. the item *drove* is derived from *drive* just as *walked* from walk. Since its formulation, it has been used in different ways to refer to any kind of derivational processes. If a rule has an input (e. g. *drive*, *walk*) and an output (e. g. *drove*, *walked*), then it presents a process picture of language. This approach which is still morpheme-based has been widely adopted by generativists. For example, *mice* is presented as [mouse + plural] morphologically with vowel change and phonologically it can be represented as [... [aʊ]...]$_n$→[aɪ]. Similarly, *sang* [sing + past tense] with vowel change is phonologically realized by [... [ɪ] v→[æ]. In both cases, the derivation of one item from the other undergoes a process of vowel change. This process model is applicable to other words or items as well. It "allows all forms, both regular and exceptional, to be described naturally and consistently." (Matthews, 1991: Ch. 7; Crystal, 1985: 166)

3.7.3 Word and Paradigm

WORD AND PARADIGM (WP) is a word-based model, i. e. the word being its central unit. This traditional model of description is appropriate in dealing with inflectional languages, in which each lexeme has variant forms which constitute its paradigm to indicate "person" "number" "mood" "tense" "gender" "case" and so on. This paradigm can be learned by analogy. Consider the following paradigms of Latin verbs *armo* (love) and *puto* (think):

(5)   'I x'   'you x'   'he xes'   'we x'
  "love"   amo   amas   amat   amamus
  "think"   puto   ____   ____   _____
                (Note: x refers to the verb)

The significance of this model is limited in analytic languages such as English and is not applicable to Chinese at all. From the point of view of derivational morphology or word formation, this model is even less significant.

3.7.4 Character-based Approach

IA and IP models are morpheme-based, and WP is word-based. They were formulated as a result of the studies on agglutinating or polysynthetic languages of the Indo-European. They have been proved effective in describing and accounting for the linguistic phenomena in most of the Indo-European languages though each has its weaknesses. Since the morphological theories were introduced to China, many Chinese scholars and researchers have made endeavour to apply these theories to the Chinese language. But they have selected only the phenomena which are theoretically accountable and neglected those which are difficult to interpret such as classification of words. It was against this background that Xu Tongqiang(徐通锵, 1993: 244 – 274), later followed by Pan Wenguo (潘文国, 2002), proposed the CHARACTER-BASED APPROACH. According to Xu, the Chinese character is different from the Indo-European morpheme and it is a linguistic unit in a phonological, lexical, syntactic and semantic sense. Each character is a syllable embracing consonant, vowel and tone. The true value of a character can be mapped into the formula: 1 x 1 = 1. That is in each character, no matter how many consonants and vowels occur, the result is one syllable, which can be utilized in communication as each is a free-standing unit.

Conversely, languages like English are poly-morphemic in nature. A morpheme is the minimal meaningful unit, but not free in most cases. Although a considerable number of morphemes coincide with words, most of them are word-building elements. The relationship between different morphemes is complicated and therefore important as different distribution of morphemes gives shape to different words. As a result, means of word formation have a very important role to play. However, this is not the case in Chinese, in which characters are free minimal units in their own right. Each is a root and, just like roots in Indo-European languages, can combine with other roots to make new words. This accounts for the overwhelming majority of compounds in Chinese. Xu argues that Chinese does not need means of word formation as it used to do. Such affixes as 子, 儿, 头 and the like came into being in the course of language development, and as a result of fossilization of phrases as well as of shifting words to affixes. For instance, in 妻子(wife), 嫂子(sister-in-law), 女儿(daughter), 孩子(child), removing 子 and 儿 from the words does not affect the original meaning at all.

Another important factor is that in morpheme based languages, the morphological changes of the words indicate such grammatical aspects as "gender" "number" "case" "tense" "aspect" "mood" and "person," which, however, are marked by separate characters in Chinese. From the morphological perspective, words of English and other Indo-European languages are easily classified into nouns, verbs, adjectives, adverbs and so on because each class has distinctive morphological features and one class can be converted into a different class just by adding or deleting affixes. In Chinese, however, since words do not generally involve morphological transformation, word classes are extremely difficult to determine. Some have identified 17 classes while others have agreed on 9. (傅雨贤, 1988: 85) The tremendous difference in word-classification itself suggests the discrepancy between Chinese and English. Of course, character-based approach is still controversial among Chinese academics. Yet there is one thing for sure that morphological approach does have its limitations. Chinese is unique and should have its own linguistic theories.

3.7.5 X-bar Approach

X-bar theory was first proposed by Chomsky (1970) and further developed by Jackendoff (1977) to deal with syntax of phrases. The theory claims that among phrasal categories, all languages share certain structural similarities, including one known as the "X-bar," which does not appear in traditional phrase structure rules for English or other natural languages. The advantage of the X-bar theory recognizes the syntactic status of all the intermediate categories of a phrase, as in the NOUN PHRASE *the very fast car*, namely, *very fast*, *very fast car*, which are larger than the noun but smaller than the phrase. (Crystal, 1985: 336—337) This theory is now employed to account for word-formation by Selkirk (1982), Sadock (1991) and Packard (2000). (See discussion in Packard, 2000: 136—148) Packard proposes two rules based on the X-bar theory to deal with Chinese word-formation:

Rule 1 $X^{-0} \to X^{-0,-1,(w)}, X^{-0,-1,(w)}$

Rule 2 $X^{-0} \to X^{-0}, G$

Rule 1 deals with derivational morphology which is to be discussed in more detail and Rule 2 is concerned with inflectional morphology (not to be discussed further). According to the rule, X^{-0} stands for a gestalt word and a free root as well and X^{-1} for a bound root, and X^w for an affix. Accordingly, 马路 (road) can be analyzed as $N^{-0}N^{-0}$, 电脑 (computer) as $N^{-0}N^{-1}$, 念头 (idea) as $V^{-1}N^w$, and 开化 (civilize) as $V^{-0}V^w$. In the examples N stands for noun root, and V for verb root, because most Chinese morphemes can be identified as different class categories. If a form's class category is unclear, X is used. For example, 无线电 (radio) and 核武器 (nuclear weapon) can be analyzed respectively as follows:

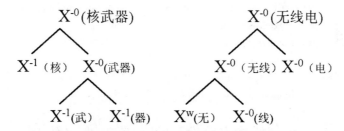

This model is applicable to morphological structures of English words. Take *anti-Clintonism* and *decapitate* for example.

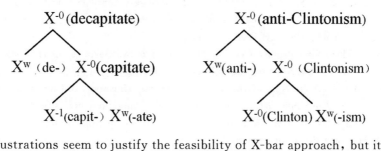

The illustrations seem to justify the feasibility of X-bar approach, but it proves problematic when it is applied to the analysis of irregular verbs like *go-went-gone*, *teach-taught-taught* and irregular nouns like *man-men*, *sheep-sheep* as well as irregular forms of comparatives and superlatives of adjectives and adverbs such as *bad-worse-worst* and *little-less-least*. Nor can it account for some derivatives with truncation like *demonstrable* and *navigable*.

References

Anderson, Stephen R. 1992. *A-Morphous Morphology*. Cambridge: Cambridge University

Press.

Bauer, Laurie. 1983. *English Word-formation*. Cambridge: Cambridge University Press.

Bynon, Thepdora. 1977. Historical Linguistics. Cambridge: Cambridge University Press.

Bolinger, Dwight & Donald A. Sears. 1981. *Aspects of Language*. (3rd ed.). New York: Harcourt Brae Jovanovich, Inc.

Cannon, G. 1987. *Historical Change and English Word-formation*. New York: Peter Lang. International Academic Publishers.

Chomsky, Noam 1970. Remarks on nominalization. In R. Jacobs & P. Rosenbaum (eds.). *Reading in English Transformational* Grammar. Waltham: Ginn. pp. 184—221

Clark, Virginia P., Paul A. Eschholz & Alfred F. Rosa. 1994. *Language, Introductory Readings*. New York: St. Martin's Press.

Cruse, D. A. 1986. *Lexical Semantics*. Cambridge: Cambridge University Press.

Crystal, David. 1985. *A Dictionary of Linguistics and Phonetics*. Oxford: Basil Blackwell Ltd.

Fromkin, Victoria & Robert Rodman. 1983. *Introduction to Language*. New York: Holt, Rinehart and Winston.

Gramley, S. & Kurt-Michael Pätzold. 1992. *A Survey of Modern English*. Reprinted 1995. New York: Routledge.

Hatch, Evelyn & Cheryl Brown. 1995. *Vocabulary, Semantics, and Language Education*. Cambridge: Cambridge University Press.

Jackendoff, Ray. 1977. *X-bar Syntax: A Study of Phrase Structure*. Cambridge, MA: MIT Press.

Katamba, Francis. 1993. *Morphology*. New York: St. Martin's Press.

Lyons, John. 1981. *Language and Linguistics*. Reprinted 1982. Cambridge: Cambridge University Press.

Matthews, P. H. 1991. *Morphology, an Introduction to thee Theory of Word-structure*. (2nd ed.). Cambridge: Cambridge University Press.

Packard, Jerome L. 2000. *The Morphology of Chinese: A Linguistic and Cognitive Approach*. 北京:外语教学与研究出版社/Cambridge:Cambridge University Press.

Pyles, T., & J. Algeo. 1991. *The Origins and Development of the English Language*. (4th ed.). New York: Harcourt Brace Jovanovich.

Quirk, R., Sidney Greenbaum, Geofrey Leech & Jan Svartvik. 1985. *A Comprehensive Grammar of the English language*. London: Longman.

Sadock, J. M. 1991. *The Autolexical Syntax*. Chicago: University of Chicago Press.

Selkirk, E. 1982. *The Syntax of Words*. Cambridge: Cambridge University Press.

Traugott, Elizabeth C. & Mary L. Pratt. 1980. *Linguistics for Students of Literature*. New York:Harcourt Brace Jovanovich, Inc.

傅雨贤,1988,《现代汉语语法学》,广州:广东高等教育出版社。

吕叔湘,1979,《汉语语法分析问题》,北京:商务印书馆。

潘文国,2002,《字本位与汉语研究》,上海:华东师范大学出版社。

任学良,1981,《汉语造词法》,北京:中国社会科学出版社。

徐通锵,1993,《徐通锵自选集》,河南教育出版社。

苏新春,2003,当代汉语外来单音语素的形成与提取,《中国语文》(6):1—11。

孙继善,1995,无义音节语素化的形成及特点,《语文学刊》(5):32—34。

杨锡彭,2004,《汉语语素论》,南京:南京大学出版社。

周洪波,1995,外来词译音部分的语素化,《语言文字应用》(4):63—65。

Chapter 4

Generative Syntax

Syntax, as generally defined, is the study of how sentences are properly formed out of words of a language. For those who are interested in abstract formal systems like formal logics, syntax is the study of the structural properties of well-formed formulas of that system. It includes a complete specification of the primitive symbols that are accepted as the basic vocabulary and the formation rules by which these symbols are combined to form a well-formed formula.

For linguists, grammar—the overall description of human language—consists of three components: 1) phonology, to specify pronunciation of sentences; 2) syntax, to specify the proper construction of sentences and 3) semantics, to specify the meaning of the sentences. Among the three components of grammar, syntax is the generative part, hence, generative grammar, in the sense that it is responsible for generating sentences that are regarded as grammatically well-formed in the language. A generative grammar G_L of some language L is a system of rules and principles that are at the bottom of all grammatical sentences of the language—in other words, it generates the sentences of language L.

4.1 Generative Grammar: Some Basic Assumptions

4.1.1 Generative Grammar and Chomsky

GENERATIVE GRAMMAR, or Transformational Generative Grammar as it is also called, refers to the work in syntax by Noam Chomsky and his followers from mid-1950s. Early work in generative grammar (up to mid-1970s) was inspired by the formal sciences in the 20th century and focused on providing a formal framework for axiomatic description of natural language. In the course of its development, the focus gradually shifted from language itself to the native speaker's knowledge of language. Thus, the main goal of generative grammar is to provide a cognitive explanation for the nature of human linguistic system. The generative linguist wishes to set up a model of the *grammatical competence* of the fluent native speaker of the language. Such competence is reflected in native speakers' intuition of grammaticality and interpretation, representing what native speakers tacitly know about the grammar of their language.

4.1.2 E-language and I-language

In line with this cognitive orientation, Chomsky (1986, 1995) makes a distinction between *E-language* and *I-language*. A language L can be regarded as a set of sentences a native speaker could use. Chomsky calls such a set E-language, where E suggests the external, observed language specified in extension. What he is interested in is the cognitive system internalized within human brain/mind, i.e. I-language, the "internal" "individual" "intensional" linguistic system by which E-language is derived. As Chomsky (1995) points out:

> The concept of language is internal, in that it deals with an inner state of [a native speaker's] mind/brain, independent of other elements in the world. It is individual in that it deals with [a native speaker] and with language communities only derivatively, as groups of people with similar I-languages. It is intensional in the technical sense that the I-language is a function specified in intension, not extension: its extension is the set of SDs (what we might call the *structure* of the I-languages).

Thus, the ultimate goal of generative grammar is to characterize the nature of the internalized linguistic system. The target for generative linguistics is not the observed language (E-language), but intuitions about language (I-language) and the goal of generative linguistics is not description of languages but explanation of language.

4.1.3 Criteria of Adequacy

Descriptive Adequacy. A grammar G_L is a model of the grammatical competence of a native speaker of a particular language L. G_L is said to be *descriptively adequate* if

i. it can distinguish the grammatical sentences of the language from ungrammatical sequences of words; and

ii. it does not only provide rules to describe linguistic data but also provides an account of a native speaker's intuitive knowledge of his language.

We can think of G_L as representing an abstract machine that works according to grammatical rules of G_L. The input of such a machine is some expression S constructed over the vocabulary of language L and its output is either:

i. yes, if S is in L, or no, if it is not, or

ii. an analysis of S, if it is in L.

Chapter 4 Generative Syntax

Such a machine can recognize all expressions of L and those expressions only. On the other hand, it allows us to reconstruct the process by which a grammatical expression is derived. Thus, it not only describes the expressions or linguistic data as observed but also represents our inner knowledge about the grammar of the language. Any G_L is said to meet the condition of *descriptive adequacy* if it can be used in an abstract machine whose analyses of expressions of L corresponded to native speakers' intuitions about the structure of those expressions.

Explanatory Adequacy. A theory of language reaches *explanatory adequacy* if it does not only account for the phenomena of a particular language but also explains how knowledge of these facts arises in the mind of a native speaker. Explanatory adequacy is a higher criterion placed on a linguistic theory, which enables us to choose between two possible grammars if they are both descriptively adequate.

An explanatorily adequate linguistic theory should meet the condition of *universality*. According to a basic generative assumption about human language, all human beings are genetically endowed with the language faculty. I-language, for instance, is one component of the language faculty that is involved particularly with the generation of structural descriptions, or the expressions of the language. The language faculty has the initial state S_0, which is represented in a fixed system of universal principles. The initial state S_0 is genetically determined and common to all human languages. A particular language like English or Chinese is an instantiation of the initial state S_0, or a state the language faculty attains in the mental development of a child. Thus to attain explanatory adequacy, a theory of language should go beyond the specification of a particular language (state attained) and provide an account for the initial state S_0 of the language faculty and show how it maps experience to the state attained. In generative tradition, the theory of state attained (a particular language) is called grammar. The theory of the initial state S_0 is called Universal Grammar, or UG for short.

Universal Grammar provides a basis for the explanation of learnability of a particular language. In a standard model of language acquisition, the initial state S_0 is taken as a function from primary linguistic data (PLD) to a language. UG contains a set of absolute universals or invariant principles of S_0, and some permissible variation called parameters. It follows that language learning is only involved with the parametric variation, or with parameter setting as it is often called in literature of generative linguistics. This generative view of language acquisition can be represented as follows:

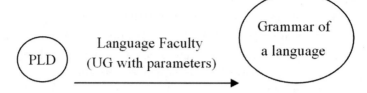

UG of the language faculty is thus regarded as a function whose input is experience (PLD) and whose output is Grammar of the language. One's language is uniquely determined by the input of PLD. Thus, an *adequate* theory of language should be *universal, explanatory, restrictive, minimally complex* and be able to provide *learnable* grammars.

4.1.4 The Development of Generative Grammar: Three Theoretical Models

The fundamental question we have to answer in syntax is this: How is a sentence constructed out of words in a language? In the history of generative grammar, three main theoretical models have been devised to address this question: 1) phrase structure rules approach, 2) lexical projection approach and 3) the minimalist approach. Phrase structure grammar dominated the field from its beginning until roughly the early 1980s. However, some conceptual difficulties inherent in the theory became explicit over time and eventually led to its rejection. Lexical projection approach maintains that syntactic structure is determined by the intrinsic formal properties of words, and is hence projected from the lexicon. The most recent work, as summarized in *The Minimalist Program* by Chomsky, is characterized by a commitment to "explanation through minimalization"—an endeavor aiming at maximizing the explanatory power of grammar by minimizing the theoretic apparatus.

4.2 Phrase Structure Rules

From the 1960s through the early 1980s, syntactic structure was thought to be generated by phrase structure rules.

4.2.1 Rule-generated Language: A Simple Example

To understand how grammar rules work to generate sentences, let's first look at some languages of simple nature. Given vocabulary $\Sigma=\{a, b\}$, we can construct $\Sigma*$, a set of all strings or "sentences" over Σ, i.e. $\{a, b\}* = \{\Lambda, a, b, aa, ab, ba, bb, aaa, aab, aba, abb, baa...\}$. A language can be defined as a set of "sentences" formed over Σ, that is, a subset of $\Sigma*$. Here are some examples of languages over $\{a, b\}$:

(1) L1=$\{\Lambda, a, aa, aab\}$

Chapter 4   Generative Syntax

L2 = {bxb | x ∈ {a, b} * }

L4 = {x | x ∈ {Λ, a, aa, aaa, aba, abba, b, bb, bab, baab...}}

L1, a very simple language indeed, contains only four "sentences," including a NULL string symbolized as Λ. L2 is an infinite set whose members are whatever strings from {a, b} * with b added to each end, e.g. {bb, bab, bbb, babb, bbab, baaab...}. L4 represents a more interesting language, i.e. a set of all palindromes (strings that are the same read both ways). We shall call it PAL. It is obviously impossible to specify PAL by enumerating palindromes one by one, since PAL contains infinitely many elements. However, we can describe PAL more efficiently by resorting to certain grammar rules, by which strings in PAL can be generated automatically. Such a grammar would look like this:

(2) a. S → a | b | Λ
   b. S → aSa | bSb

The rules in (2) say actually two things:

1) S could take the value a, b, or, Λ and
2) S could take the value aSa, or bSb, where the new S is yet to be computed.

In terminology we are adopting, S is a variable, representing any arbitrary element of PAL, a and b are terminal symbols, and → a rewriting rule, meaning "could take value." We start with the variable S, replace it with other strings and stop until we finally get a string consisting of only terminals.

4.2.2   Context Free Phrase Structure Rules

The nature of Σ * varies, depending on what elements we include in Σ. Suppose, for example, that Σ is a finite set of all English words, Σ * may be regarded as the collection of all "sentences" formed over Σ. The English language, which is a set of grammatically well-formed sentences, is obviously a subset of Σ *.

The rule system that can distinguish grammatical sentences of English from ungrammatical ones would be similar to that which we see in (2). From mathematic point of view, such rules are part of Context Free Grammar and can be defined as a 4-tuple G = (S, T, Σ, P), where

T and Σ have no members in common;
S ∈ T is the start symbols; and
P is a finite set of productions of G or grammar rules.

The idea here is that Σ is a set of terminal symbols, or you may think of it as a lexicon containing all allowed words in a language. T stands for a set of variables or non terminal symbols, i.e. the grammatical categories like N (oun), V(erb), A(djective), NP, VP, AP, etc. These are used to describe parts of sentences but are not actually in the language. The start variable S stands for an arbitrary sentence in our language. P is a set of productions or grammar rules, of the form $l \rightarrow r$, where l stands for the symbols appearing on the left-hand side of the arrow, and r for those appearing on the right-hand side. The symbol → stands for a production relation of G, meaning "could take the value" or "can be rewritten as." The statement $l \rightarrow r$ is called a production of G. A production is CONTEXT- FREE if $l \in T$ (that is, l is a single non-terminal from T) and $r \in (V \cup \Sigma)*$ (i.e. r is finite sequences of terminal or non-terminal symbols). A grammar G is context-free if all it's production rules are context-free.

To put our discussion on a concrete footing, let $\Sigma = \{$the, this, man, story, will, not, believe, know...$\}$ (there could be many more), T = {S, N, V, Art, Adv, NP, VP, Aux,} and suppose that P is the set containing a list of productions as follows:

(3) a. S→NP Aux VP
    b. NP→Det N
    c. VP→Adv V NP
    d. Det→ the, this
    e. N→ man, story
    f. Aux→will, shall,
    g. Adv → not, quickly
    h. V→believe, know

Now suppose we have a sentence "The man will not believe the story." To prove that this sentence is syntactically correct, we can have the following sequence of substitutions:

(4) S
    NP Aux VP
    Det N Aux VP
    Det N Aux Adv V NP
    Det N AuxAdv V Det N
    The N AuxAdv V Det N
    The man AuxAdv V Det N
    The man will Adv V Det N
    The man will not V Det N
    The man will not believe DetN
    The man will not believe the N
    The man will not believe the story

Such a sequence is called a derivation of a sentence. The first line of the derivation is the start symbol S. Each succeeding line rewrites one non-terminal symbol in the preceding line, until a sentence is generated when the derivation terminates with a line containing only terminal symbols.

The derivation can be modeled as graph structures called trees:

(5)

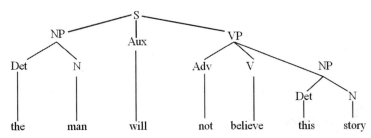

A deviation tree, also called a phrase marker, or structure description (SD for short), represents the constituent structures of a sentence as a set of nodes, each carrying a label and is related to the other either in a mother-daughter relation or as sisters. In technical terms, we say a mother node immediately dominates a daughter-node, and dominates all other nodes under a daughter node. The nodes immediately dominated by the same (mother) node are sister to each other.

Sometimes, we may want to represent a deviation using labeled bracketing, as in (6) below:

(6) [$_S$[$_{NP}$ The [$_N$ man]] [$_{Aux}$ will] [$_{VP}$[$_{Adv}$ not] [$_V$ believe] [$_{NP}$[$_{Det}$ this] [$_N$ story]]]]

(6) is equivalent to (5), less easy to read but saving space.

To say a sentence structure is grammatically well-formed simply means that it is a string constructed out of legal words from vocabulary Σ (e.g. it is an element in $\Sigma *$, i.e. $x \in \Sigma *$) and it can be derived from S by finite steps of substitutions according to the rules specified. The set of all sentences that can generated by a grammar G constitute a language L_G, defined as follows:

$$L_G = \{x \in \Sigma * | S \Rightarrow_G x\}$$

(where $S \Rightarrow_G x$ means x can be derived from S using G in finite steps of substitution)

One good thing about the context free grammar is that the rule system can be extended to include more rules so that more sentence structures can be described. We can revise, for instance, a rule in G, to allow NP to be rewritten as N, Det Adj N, or Det Adj N S, and VP to be rewritten as V, V NP NP, or V PP. Thus the revised version of rule 3 and rule 4 in (3) would include some alternate rules, as is shown in (7) below:

(7) a. NP → N| Det Adj N| Det N S
    b. VP→ V | V NP | V NP NP |V NP PP

What we have in (7)a or (7)b are not one single rule but several alternate rules. With the extension in (7), we can easily prove that the sentences in (8) are all grammatical sentences in L_G. In fact, linguists have proved that the rule system of the free phrase structure grammar, if worked out carefully enough, can generate the basic structures in English.

(8) a. John loves Mary.
   b. The wise man will not believe.
   c. I really enjoy the book you gave me the other day.
   d. John *gives Mary a book*.
   e. He is waiting for someone.

4.2.3 Transformation

While the phrase structure grammar G is adequate for a small set of the language, it fails to recognize many grammatical sentences. For example, (9) is a grammatical sentence, but is not included in L_G generated by G:

(9) Which book do you like best?

It is possible to extend the rule system to cover the entire language, but this can only be done at the cost of simplicity of grammar and, for that matter, the explanatory adequacy of the syntactic theory. To address this drawback, Chomsky suggested that the phrase structure rules would not generate a sentence directly, but only a sequence of symbols known as a kernel string. This string, together with the tree representing its derivation, is called deep structure of a sentence. To obtain a grammatical sentence, a deep structure must be submitted to further grammatical operations, known as transformations, and be transformed into a surface structure. Thus, a grammar for a natural language like English must go beyond phrase structure rules to include transformational component that converts one structural representation into another. The architecture of grammar during this period looks like this:

(10)

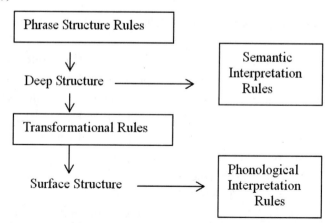

Under this assumption, no sentence can be derived directly by using Phrase Structure Rules. To derive a typical active declarative (kernel) sentence like *The man sold his car*, an obligatory tense readjusting transformation has to be applied to its deep structure, as given in (11)a, yielding (11)b, where the tense suffix is placed after the verb *sell* (*sold*):

(11)

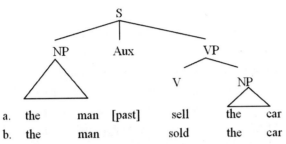

```
                S
      ┌─────────┼─────────┐
     NP        Aux        VP
      △                ┌───┴───┐
                       V       NP
                                △
   a. the     man [past]  sell   the   car
   b. the     man         sold   the   car
```

(By convention, we draw a triangle under a node to indicate that the detail of the derivation is omitted.)

The formation of more complicated grammatical constructions like passives, interrogatives, etc. involves more (optional) transformations. The passive form of (11)b, *The car was sold by the man*, for example, is constructed by applying a transformational rule known as Passivization to the same corresponding deep structure in (11)a. We have the process illustrated here in (12):

(12)   the man [past] sell the car.
    NP—   Aux   —V—   NP
    1   2   3   4
    4   2be+en   3   by1
    the car was sold   by the man

Again, we can think of a transformation as a function, or an abstract machine, which uses a (deep) structure as input and produces another (surface) structure as output. By applying different transformational rules, we can obtain different surface structures from the same deep structure as in (11)a:

(13) the man [past] sell the car =>
    1) the man didn't sell the car   (Negative Rule)
    2) did the man sell the car   (Interrogative Rule)
    3) which car did the man sell
    4) who sold the car

In the 1970's and 1980's, more and more transformational rules were found, adding greatly to the descriptive adequacy of the phrase structure grammar.

4.2.4 Subcategorization

Phrase Structure Grammar, with all the extensions made so far, is still capable of generating ungrammatical sentences:

(14) a. * The Paris is the capital of France.
   b. * I will put you an answer.
   c. * They waited me at gate.
   d. * They are trying to hit at me.

The problem here is caused by a notational deficiency of the rule system. The phrase structural rules we have so far discussed are category-based. It means that the rule system does not provide any device to deal with the subcategorial differences between words belonging to the same grammatical category.

To cope with this situation, we need to incorporate into the lexical entry of each word the proper information about its categorial and subcategorial properties. Chomsky (1965) suggests that this type of information be encoded in a unitary way by using a binary feature system, as was originally used in phonology. As a result, the subcategorial difference, say, between *Paris* and *book*, can be encoded in terms of a matrix of grammatical features, as in (15):

(15) Paris   [+N, PROPER]
    news   [+N, −PROPER, −COUNT, −PLURAL]
    book   [+N−PROPER, +COUNT, +_ PLURAL]

The subcategorial differences between verbs can be dealt in a similar way. Traditionally, verbs are divided into three subcategories: intransitive verbs that take no object, transitive verbs that take one object and ditransitive verbs that take two. In predicate logic, objects, taken together with subjects, are referred to as the arguments of the predicate verb. An intransitive verb is called one-place predicate in the sense that it involves only one argument; a transitive verb is described as a two-place predicate because it takes two arguments; and ditransitive verb is a three-place predicate in that it takes three arguments. So in logic notation sentences in (16) a, b, c is assigned the presentations in (16)a',b',c':

(16) a. We eat.
    b. John kissed Mary.
    c. John gave Mary a kiss.
    a' P(x)   (where P stands for Predicate of any kind, and x,
    b' P(x, y)   y, z for the arguments the Predicate could take.)
    c' P(x, y, z)

In generative tradition, however, the information about the argument structure is incorporated, among other things, into each verb's lexical entry and represented as subcategorization frames as encoded in (17):

(17) a. put   [+V, __ NP PP]
    b. tell   [+V, __ , ___ NP NP, ___ NP PP]
    c. devour   [+V, ___ NP]
    d. waited   [+V,___]
    e. eat   [+V, ___, ___ NP]

The blank line represents the position of the verb, and remaining syntactic categories(NP, PP) represent the numbers of objects a verb could take. This model, however, does not include Subject in the subcategorization frame. *In Head Driven Phrase Structure Grammar* (Pollard,C and I. Sag. ,1992), the subject is included as a member of the subcategorial list:

(18) die   [NP]
     hit   [NP_0 NP_1]
     go   [NP PP]
     think [NP,S']
     give   [NP_0 NP_1 PP]
     tell   [NP_0 NP_1 S']

With subcategorization frames, the problem posed by sentences like those in (14) can be solved in an efficient way by checking the verb's subcategorization frame against the categorical rules at the point of lexical insertion.

4.3 Projection from Lexicon

Phrase Structure Grammar underwent several major revisions since it was first developed in the mid-1950s. (See Chomsky, 1957; 1965; 1981) However, some conceptual inconsistency inherent in the theory became explicit over time. During the 1970s on through the 1980s, much effort has been made to solve the problems inherent in the system, which eventually lead to the elimination of the phrase structure rules and give rise to LEXICAL PROJECTION APPROACH, according to which sentence structures are projected from the lexicon according to the syntactic features carried by each lexical item.

4.3.1 Some Conceptual Difficulties with Phrase Structural Rules

The system of phrase structure rules, along with subcategorization frames, recorded a number of achievements. However, it was eventually discarded for some conceptual difficulties inherent in the architecture of a grammar based on the rules system.

First, the rule system of phrase structure syntax is too restricted, in the sense that the types of categories it allows are too limited in number. The system recognizes only two types of categories:

(19) i. Lexical categories: N,V,P, A, Adv, AUX, DET,etc. and
     ii. Phrasal categories: NP,VP,PP,AP,ADVP,S, etc.

In this system, structure units that are larger than the word and smaller than the phrase cannot be properly described. To illustrate, let's consider the structure of a Noun Phrase like that in (20) below:

(20) the lovely little girl

Within the system of phrase structure syntax, (20) could probably be assigned the structure (21):

(21)

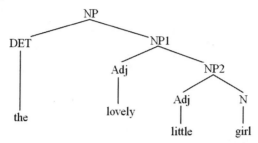

The syntactic status of the intermediate NP1 and NP2 is dubious. Obviously, they cannot be identified with ordinary NPs because they do not have the typical distribution of an NP. The intermediate phrases like *little girl* and *lovely little girl* cannot occupy the NP positions in any subcategorization frames, as we can see in (22):

(22) I like *the lovely little girl*.
　　* I like *lovely little girl*.
　　* I like *little girl*.
　　* I like *girl*.

However, it seems equally implausible to identify an intermediate structure unit with the lexical category N. Although the nominal complex *lovely little girl* behaves more like a single noun than a noun phrase, it is still a different unit than the lexical item *girl*. Then how is an intermediate constituent differs from N at the lower level and form NP of the higher level? In later development of generative grammar, X-bar Theory has the capacity of dealing with the structure unit at the intermediate level, but the syntactic identity of the intermediate structure constituent remains a baffling enigma.

While the system of phrase structure rules is criticized for being too restricted, it can also be condemned as being excessively unconstrained. It is unconstrained in that there is no device in the context-free grammar to prevent such "crazy" derivations as those in (23):

(23) a. NP → V Adj
　　　b. VP → Adj

John Lyons (1968) is the first person to make the observation. He argues that a good grammar should provide a theoretic apparatus to rule out the possibility of such crazy rules. What is needed here is a convention that will ensure a phrase of a particular type contains a lexical item of that same type: a Noun Phrase contains a Noun as its lexical head; a Verb Phrase contains a Verb as its lexical head, etc. Following the convention used by Lyons and

adopted by Chomsky, we need to restrict Phrase Structure Rules universally to the schematic form:
(24) XP→...X...
Informally, every X-Phrase must have an X as its head word.

The worst problem, however, is that a heavy redundancy is observed to exit between categorial rules and the lexicon. (Chomsky, 1982) The rules, it turned out, are a sheer repetition of the subcategorization information given in the lexicon as the subcategorization frames:

(25) VP→V　　　　　　　　die [+V, __]
　　 VP→V NP　　　　　　 hit[+V __ NP]
　　 VP→V PP　　　　　　 go [+V __PP]
　　 VP→V S　　　　　　　think [+V, __S']
　　 VP→V NP NP　　　　　give [+V NP NP]
　　 VP→V NP NP | V NP S　tell [+V __NP NP, __ NP S]

Such redundancy reveals a serious conceptual inadequacy of the grammar Chomsky (1965) outlined in *Aspects*. The phrase structure rules turn out only a superfluous device, the basic information about syntactic structure already ineliminably represented in the lexicon. To remove the redundancy from the system, the phrase structure rules have to be eliminated from the architecture of the grammar.

4.3.2　Projection Principle

The idea that syntactic structure is determined by the idiosyncratic properties of the lexical item is summed up in the Projection Principle (Chomsky Lectures, 1981d: 29):

(26) Projection Principle
　　　Representations at each syntactic level (i. e. LF, D-and S-Structure) are projected from the lexicon, in that they observe the subcategorization properties of lexical items

One consequence of the Projection Principle is that lexical items, or words from the lexicon, come to play an important role in the architecture of grammar. Lexical items, under Principle of Projection, are taken as atomic elements (primes). Each prime is a feature complex, carrying important information about its sound, meaning, and structure, from which other objects (representations at phonetic, semantic and syntactic levels) are constructed. In the course of a derivation, the lexical information is first represented at an abstract syntactic level called D-Structure. Words from the lexicon are arranged there in a way that conforms to their intrinsic formal properties, yielding the D-Structure representation. Transformations then apply, converting the D-Structure representation to the S-Structure representation, leaving behind traces when one constituents (words or phrases) are moved out of its original place. There the deviation splits into two directions, yielding Phonetic Form (PF) representation and Logic Form (LF) representation, each an interface of syntax with the system of language use.

Generative grammar divides words from the lexicon into two main categories: 1) the lexical categories and 2) functional categories. The former categories consist of the content words like verb, adjective, noun and proposition; and the latter, of function words like particles, auxiliaries, determiners, pronouns, etc. The information about the syntactic properties of a word is represented, among other things, as a matrix of grammatical features—among them, the lexical categorial features N(oun), V(erb), A (djective), P(reposition) and functional categorical features I(FLT), D(eterminers), etc. For the moment, we will focus on the lexical categories.

Since syntactic structure originates in the lexicon, the structural unit like, say, VP is no more a primitive presupposed by the rule system, but rather a structure projected from the intrinsic grammatical properties of verbs. This can be represented as in (27) below:

(27)

a. VP
    |
    V
    |
   eat

b. VP
   / \
  V   NP NP
  |
 give

c. VP
   / \
  V   NP
  |
 beat

What we have in (27) is not rule-generated structures that are built up in a top-down fashion by applying rewrite rules of the phrase structure grammar. Instead, they are endocentric structures headed by verbs, each projected from head verbs in a way that satisfies the subcategorization requirements of the verbs. In (27) above, the lexical category V is derived from the grammatical feature [+V] of the lexical item, and is hence called the lexical or minimal projection. The phrase category VP is the phrasal or maximal projection of the lexical item.

4.3.3 Extended Projection Principle

The subcategorization frame specifies how many Objects a verb is likely to take but does not list the Subject as an element in the frame. That is, the projection principle does not guarantee the presence of the Subject. From logic point of view, the subject is an argument of a predicate verb. In languages like English, the Subject position must be filled even the verb does not have an obvious subject. In (28) below, for example, the subject position is filled by such dummy words like *it* or *there*:

(28) It was raining.

It is likely that he will come.

There are four people in my family.

To cope with this situation, as structural constraint is placed on projection principle, which says to the effect that

(29) All clauses have a subject. (Chomsky Lectures, 1981d: 27)

This structural requirement, combined with the Projection Principle, is called Extended Projection Principle(Chomsky, 1982: 10)

(30) Extended Projection Principle

Lexical requirements and structural requirements must be uniformly satisfied at all syntactic levels

As the Projection Principle requires, the projection of a lexical head must specify the information characteristic of the head and at the same time satisfy the structural requirement that a Clause should have a Subject. It is then important to notice that some critical information is still missing in the VP structures in (27)a-c, i.e. they fail to reflect the complete argument structure of the head verbs because the information about the Subject has not been incorporated in the VP structures.

The simplest way to encode the information about the argument structure is to incorporate an NP subject into the tree as a daughter of a VP node, yielding structures as in (31)a-c:

(31)

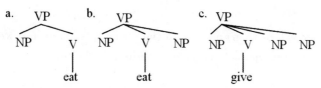

The NP subject then presents itself as the left-most daughter of VP and a sister of V and NP objects. However, this possibility has already been ruled out in generative grammar. Chomsky in *Aspects* (1965) defined the subject as the NP directly dominated by S and the object as the NP directly dominated by VP:

(32)

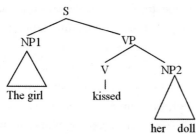

The idea here is that subjects and objects are hierarchically defined. They are constituents at two different projection levels and cannot be represented as

sisters dominated by the same mother. In generative tradition, the hierarchical relation between subjects and objects is referred to as a c-command (constituent command) relation, where c-command is defined as:

(33) α c-commands β iff
α does not dominate β and
every γ that dominates α also dominates β
(Chomsky, 1986b:8)

Thus in a sentence like (32), VP c-commands NP1, NP1 c-commands VP and all its daughters—V and NP2, which c-command each other but not NP1.

In short, a subject c-commands an object but an object does not c-command a subject. To incorporate this information into VP, we need to introduce an intermediate projection level between minimal projection V and maximal projection VP, so that V and its NP objects (if any) can be grouped together as sisters c-commanding one another. The additional projection level is conventionally labeled as V' (read as V-bar), as is in (34):

(34)

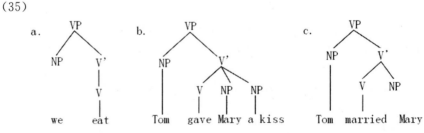

Assign proper values to arguments in the structures above and we may get what we want: the grammatical sentences, as in (35) below:

(35)

We eventually come up with an assumption that views Sentence as a maximal projection of a verb. One might find it uncomfortable to identify Sentence with VP, which is taken traditionally as a constituent part of a sentence. However, such an assumption is an unavoidable theoretical consequence of Projection Principle. After all, the lexical entry of a verb contains everything we need to construct a grammatical sentence.

Now to sum up, we say that the lexical item projects syntactic structure. The head of the projected structure—in our examples, V—is referred to as the lexical or minimal projection. The sister of the head, if any, is called complement; V' is the intermediate projection, and VP is the phrasal or maximal projection. The sister of the intermediate projection V' is called specifier. The specifier of VP, shorten as Spec (VP), is the Subject of a sentence; the complement, if any, is what we traditionally called object. The specifier and complement, taken together, are referred to as the arguments that a head verb takes, and, following Chomsky (Lectures, 1981:47), we may refer to the positions that arguments occupy in a sentence structure as the "A-positions."

4.3.4 Adjunction

As one might have already noticed, there seems no particular reason at all to device an intermediate level V' for intransitive verbs like "eat" in (35)a. Then what are the theoretic grounds and empirical evidence for us to assume there exists such a level? Before answer this question, let's first look at two sentences in (36):

(36) a. We eat everyday.
  b. We eat an apple everyday.

We may be tempted to represent the structures of (36)a, b as follows in (37)a,b:

(37)

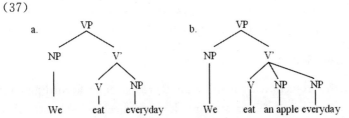

A further scrutiny, however, reveals that structural descriptions for (36) a, b as represented in (37) are wrong ones. We know, by looking up in the lexicon, that *eat* can be used in two ways: 1) as an intransitive (one-argument) verb that takes no complement, and 2) as a transitive (two-argument) verb that takes one complement. However, (37) wrongly represents "everyday" as a complement to "eat," which amounts to saying that "eat" is a transitive verb in (37)a and a ditransitive verb in (37)b.

To avoid this undesirable result, it is suggested that a further bar level be incorporated, as in (38) below:

(38)

The extra V' added in (38) is a level under which we can place such an expression as "everyday"—what is known as an NP adverbial, or more generally as modifier / adjunct. The process to enter adjuncts into syntactic structure is called adjunction. The relation between adjuncts, complements, and the specifier can be illustrated as follows in (39):

(39)

Relation to Head	Sister to	Daughter to
Complement	Head (V)	Intermediate Projection (V')
Adjunct	Intermediate Projection (V')	Intermediate Projection (V')
Specifier	Intermediate Projection (V')	Maximal Projection (VP)

As we can see from the table, the structural units are all hierarchically defined: complements as sister to V; Adjuncts as sister and daughter to V'; and Specifier as sister to V' but daughter to VP. It is then theoretically sound, and empirically correct, to assume that all verbs, including the intransitive ones, undergo at least one intermediate projection. Or else we have to place an adjunct under V' as a sister of V (as in (38)a). In that case, we have to eat not only apples but also "everyday," which is, I'm afraid, not very tasteful.

4.3.5 X-bar Schema

In accord with Projection Principle, all words project according to their intrinsic lexical properties. Thus a three-level projection schema of more general nature is suggested for all lexical categories {N, A, P, V}:

(40)

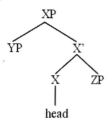

In (40), X, Y, and Z are variables ranging over {N,A,P,V}. Known as X-bar schema, the tree can also be represented as the category-neutral rewrite rules, as illustrated in (41):

(41) XP → YP X'
　　　X' → X' ZP

YP, a daughter of XP and sister of X', is the Specifier of XP (often shortened as Spec ⟨XP⟩); ZP, a daughter of X' and sister of X, is the complement.

The empirical evidence often cited to support the hypothesis is the cross-categorial parallels between VP (sentence, that is) and NP, as

exemplified in (42):
>(42) a. The Romans destroyed the city
>b. the Romans' destruction of the city

With the X-bar schema, (42)a, b can be represented as (43)a, b:
>(43)

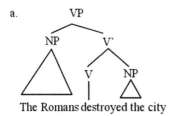

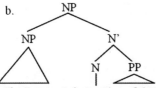

Although the node-labels along the projection line X, X', and XP vary according to the categorical features of the lexical item, the over-all pattern of the projection configuration in (43)a, b is the same.

The difference between NP and VP is that a verb projects an obligatory Specifier, while for a NP, Specifier is only optional, as in (44) below:
>(44)

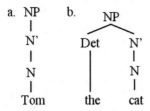

As with verbs, the three-level projection is supposed for NP. Even Proper Nouns like Tom, which takes neither complement nor specifier, project three levels. The motivation for this is that the intermediate level N', as with V', is a level reserved to anchor a complement, which N may take as sister. The maximal level NP is a level to anchor Specifier, which is a sister of N'. Between N' and NP another bar level can be insert for adjuncts.

We may look at the examples in (45): (cited from Radford, 1981 with modification)
>(45) a. a student of physics
>b. a student with long hair

The phrases in (45) a, b seem to have the same structure, but a closer examination proves that we would be wrong in thinking so. In fact we can

combine (45)a, b, yielding (46)a but not (46)b:
    (46) a. a student of physics with long hair
        b. * a student with long hair of great courage
The difference between (45)a and (45)b may be further illustrated by the examples cited in (47):
    (47) a. I prefer a student with short hair to one with long hair.
        b. * I prefer a student of chemistry to one of physics.
The implicit intuition here is that *the student of physics* forms closer constituent than *the student with long hair*. This can be spelled out in an articulated way by inserting another bar-level of projection, where the proposition phrase "with long hair" may be added as adjunct, as is in (48):
    (48)

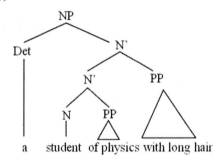

Obviously, sentences in (45)a, b are of quite different structure, with PP as complement for one, and as adjunct for the other.

More generally, adjunction can be applied to X-bar schema, so we can extend (48) to (49):
    (49)

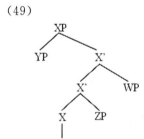

The X-bar schema conveys two types of information about the internal structure of constituents across all lexical categories: 1) that a lexical item projects a three-level structure, running from the head to maximal projection; 2) each node making up the projection spine is of different level (X being the head, X' the intermediate projection, and XP the maximal projection). Although we have not yet tackled the projection of P(respositon) and A(djective), we can assume that they will project structures in the similar way as V and N. (We will leave the details as exercises for students.)

4.3.6 Extending X-bar Schema to Functional Categories

Up to now, we have simply assumed, quite unwarrantedly though, that only Lexical categories {V, N, A, P} project according to the X-bar schema. However, generative grammar during this period recognizes also functional categories {I, C, D} and therefore, we need to generalize X-bar Schema to all syntactic categories, in line with the general requirement of the Projection Principle.

I(NFL): Among the set {I, C, D}, I— shortened from INFL—is category whose members include auxiliaries and modal words (like *will*, *would*, *may*, *might*, *can*, *could*, *must*, etc., which are INFLected for tense/agreement). This group also includes INFL particle *to*.

Let's assume for the moment that the functional category I projects in the same way as lexical categories. Substitute I for X along the projection spine in (40), we get (50):

(50)

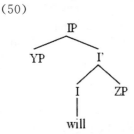

Let's further propose that IP takes a VP complement and an NP specifier, and then we can identify a sentence with IP, as in (51):

(51)

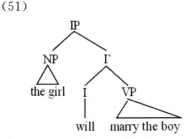

(51) produces a grammatically correct sentence but at the same time causes some undesirable result. For one thing, the subject "the girl" is an argument of a two-place predicate "marry" and should take the position of Spec(VP). However, in (51), it is represented as in Spec (IP).

As a way out, a fairly reasonable suggestion is made to explain the new position of the argument NP. The theoretic assumption, known as the VP-internal subject hypothesis, postulates that subjects originate within VP in Spec(VP), and are subsequently moved into Spec(IP) by a movement operation called subject raising (also known as subject to subject raising or raising for short). Thus, the correct representation of (51) should be (52):

(52)

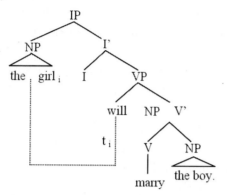

By subject movement, the subject originating in Spec (VP) is moved into Spec (VP), and leaves in the original position a trace (symbolized as t) bearing the same index.

Tense/AGR: The functional category I projects a three-level structure: I, I', IP. However, it was observed that the category IP "has the strange property of 'being double-headed'" (Chomsky & Lasnik, 1993:530), in that auxiliaries inflect (overtly or covertly) for Tense and Agreement features:.

(53)

```
              IP
            /    \
          NP      I'
          |     /    \
          We   I      VP
               |     /   \
          Tense/AGR  NP   V'
               |     |    |
        [Present]/[Plural] t   won
               |
             have
```

It is then suggested (Pollock, 1989; Chomsky,1993) that the category I be further split into two different heads: Tense and Agreement (shortened as T and AGR respectively). Under the assumption that all heads project, T and AGR project phrases of their own, each with the typical X-bar structure: T, T' TP and AGR, AGR', AGRP. In a language like English, where AGRP dominates TP (Chomsky, 1991c), an finite clause like (53) would be represented as the AGRP in (54):

(54)

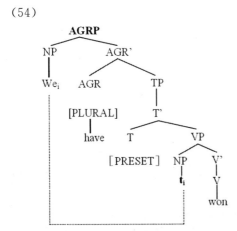

As for TP, it is identified with a not-finite clause headed by infinitival *to*, which bears a Tense feature [-tense], but no Agreemont feature. A TP thus derived is often used as the complement of such verbs as *want*, *expect*, etc. , as illustrated in (55):

(55)

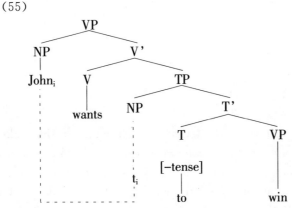

In fact, IP has been split into many more specific phrases. To name just a few, AGRsP (Subject Agreement Phrase), AGRoP (Object Agreement PHRASE), NegP (Negation Phrase, Pollock, 1989 and Chomsky, 1991c), Modal Phrases, Aspect Phrases (Ouhalla, 1991). However, the term IP continued to be used as a general heading for these different phrases and we will keep to this convention in our later discussion.

Complementizers: The functional category C, shorten from COMP or complementizer, refers to a category of clause introducing words such as *that* /*if*/for, as used in sentences (56)a, b, c:

(56) a. I'm glad that he will come.
b. I wonder if she knew.
c. It's time for you to go.

Obviously, Complementizers takes IP (that is, Clause) complements, and project to CP, as is illustrated in (57) below:

(57)

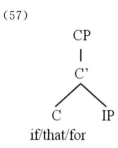

The maximal projections of C (that is, CP) in turn can be used as the complements of verbs, nouns, adjective, and so on. An example is provided in (58) below

(58)

```
        NP
        |
        N'
       / \
      N   CP
      |   |
     time C
         / \
        C   TP
        |  / \
       for NP  T'
           |  / \
          you T  VP
              |  |
              to go
```

The complementizer for differs from if/that in that while if/that takes an AGRP complement, for as a complementizer can only take a tenseless infinitival TP as complement. For convenience, we sometimes refer to AGRP as finite IP (IP[+fin]), as projected from a finite I (I[+fin]) and the tenseless TP as infinite IP (IP[−fin]), as projected from an infinitival I (I[−fin]).

Determiners and DP Hypothesis: The functional category D, shortened for Det or Determiner, consists of articles (a/an/the), demonstrative adjective/pronouns (this/that, these/those), quantifiers (some, all, both, etc.) and personal pronouns (she, he, we, you, they, her, his our, your their, etc.).

We have up to now presumed that determiners do not project (see example in ⟨34⟩b). But this is conceptually inconsistent with the X-bar Schema, which requires that Spec(NP) be filled not by a head but by a maximal projection YP. To avoid this conceptual inconsistency, it is supposed that determiners also project DP with the normal X-bar structure. (Abney, 1987; Fukui, 1986) Some determiners take no complement and project in a way as illustrated in (59):

(59)

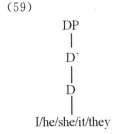
I/he/she/it/they

Other determiners (like a⟨n⟩/the/my) require complements, and they project in a way as illustrated in (60) below:

(60)

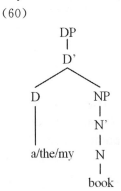

Demonstratives (like *this/that*, *these/those*) and certain pronouns (like *we/you*) may or may not take complements, and they have the following projections:

(61)

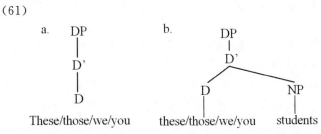

A direct consequence of D projection is that nominal groups, what we used to call NP, is no more viewed as a structure headed by N, but rather a DP headed by D, hence the DP hypothesis of noun phrase.

The Null Determiner: It suggested that all bare nominals are headed by a silent null determiner, ϕ. The conceptual grounds for such a stipulation are, again, the DP hypothesis of noun phrase structure. Consider the sentences in (62) and (63):

(62) a. The/we/ students] worked very hard.
  b. [The water] in the bottle is not drinkable.
(63) a. Students] should work hard.
  b. [Students] worked] very hard.
  c. [Water] is indispensable to life.

d. I had [water and bread] for breakfast

Whereas the nominal groups in (62) can be described as DP structures headed by determiners, the bare nominals in (63) present a serious problem. It is important to notice that the nominals in the two groups have very different interpretations. In (62), the sentences have specific reference, but those in (63) are interpreted in a quite different way. The bare nominals in (63)a, c have generic reference, that is, they are interpreted as "students/or water in general." In sentences (63)b, d, however, *students* and *water* are said to have existential interpretation, meaning they refer to "some students" or "some water." To suggest that bare nominals are headed by generic/existential null determiners enables us to represent all nominal groups in a unified way as DP and in a way "saves" the DP hypothesis.

4.3.7 Theta-theory

Up to now, we have presumed that all syntactic structures are projected from the lexical head according to X-bar schema. A sentence, for example, is the maximal projection of a head verb. This presumption, however, is quite unwarranted. In (64) below, the verb *sell* projects in a way that strictly conforms to its subcategorization requirements, but yields two different results:

(64) a. The book sold well.
      [Patient]
  * b. The book sold the author.
      [Agent]

(64)b is ungrammatical even though *sold* can also be used as a two-place predicate that takes two arguments. The problem here lies in the fact that in (64)b *the author*, the person selling the book (hence, the agent of the action) and *the book* being sold (hence, the patient of the action) are placed in the wrong places of the sentence. In linguistics, the grammatical functions such as agent, patient, etc. are grouped under the general heading of thematic role. The theta-theory, or θ-theory, is devised to deal with the complicated relation between an argument and the thematic role (or semantic function) the argument plays in relation to its predicate.

The examples in (64) seem to suggest that, to form a grammatical sentence, a verb does not only select the right syntactic category to fill an argument position, it also needs to assign the right semantic function, or thematic role, to each NP argument it takes. In generative grammar, the first procedure is often referred to as category-selection (hence, c-selection), and the latter, the semantic selection (hence, s-selection). It follows that, to make a right choice, both c-selection and s-selection properties should be included in the lexical entry of a verb. For example, the lexical entry of *sell* would be expanded to provide more detailed information:

(65) sell [NP] <Patient>
     [NP₀, NP₁] <Agent, Patient>

On most occasions, the c-selection properties are inferable from s-selection properties, in that each NP is a referring phrase that points beyond itself to its θ-role. It is then suggested that c-selection be reduced to s-selection and the subcategorization frame be removed from the lexicon. (Pesetsky, 1982; Chomsky, 1986a:88—90)

Linguists today use different terms to label thematic roles. We will adopt the terms traditionally used to describe a range of different roles. The list is given below in (66), together with a brief definition and illustrative example (with the specified role in bold print):

(66)

Theta-role	Definition	Example
Agent	doer or instigator of some action	**The girl** kisses her doll.
Patient/theme	entity undergoing the effect of some action	**The stone** rolled down the hill.
Experiencer	entity experiencing some psychological state	**I** love this game.
Recipient	entity receiving or possessing some entity	John gave **Mary** a book.
Goal	entity towards which something moves	Let's go **home**.

Obviously, the semantic role an argument plays is determined by the intrinsic semantic property of the verb. In terms we are adopting here, we say a verb assigns a thematic role or θ-role to each of its arguments. Or we may say a verb theta-marks /θ-marks its arguments by assigning each a θ-role and an argument is theta-marked by the verb that assigns it a θ-role.

In *Barries*, Chomsky (1986b) places a structural restriction on the theta marking, supposing that theta-role assignment takes place only between the sister nodes in a tree. For example, the head verb *kiss* assigns the θ-role of Patient to its complement *her doll* and then the V-bar *kiss her doll* assigns the θ-role of Agent to the subject *the girl* (see ⟨67⟩ for example).

(67)

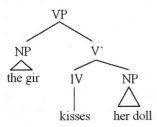

Thus, the head *kiss* θ-marks its complement directly and its subject indirectly. For this reason, the complement is often referred to as the internal argument, meaning it receives a θ-role directly from V. The subject, on the other hand, is called the external argument for being indirectly θ-marked by V through the intermediate level of V'.

It is important to notice that each argument can only take one thematic-role as its unique value. That is to say, in a sentence, an argument plays one and only one θ-role and a θ-role is assigned to one and only one argument. This principle of θ-role assignment is generally known as the θ-criterion. (Chomsky, 1981a:36) θ-criterion requires that NP arguments, each a referring phrase in itself, be interpreted by taking one and only one value from the set of semantic roles. To illustrate, let's look at the sentences in (68) below:

(68) * a. The girl loves.
  * b. The girl kissed her doll *her friend*.

In (68)a the lexical entry for *loves* lists two θ-roles, e.g. Agent and Patient, but the θ-role of Patient has nowhere to go, since one NP argument is missing in the structure. In (68)b, the predicate *kissed* has the capacity to assign two θ-roles to its arguments, the Agent role to *the girl* and the Patient role to *her doll* and there is no other value left for the superfluous element *her friend*. Thus, both sentences are ungrammatical because they violate the θ-criterion.

Again, as always, language exhibits an obstinate unwillingness to yield. The θ-criterion seems refutable when confronted with the evidence from the sentence in (69):

(69) He expected to enjoy the play.

In (69) above, there are two theta markers, *expected*, *enjoy the play*, but only one argument (*he*) is ready for role assignment. One solution to the problem is to loosen up our standard a bit by allowing one argument to take more than one θ-roles. For example, the subject *he* could take the role of Agent and Experiencer once at the same time from the theta markers. However, the suggestion is implausible, because constantly changing our theory to accommodate the obstinate data would cause inconsistency somewhere else in the grammatical system.

As an alternative solution to the problem, it is suggested that there exists a silent pronominal determiner PRO (big PRO) in sentence (69). PRO is an empty category that has no overt phonetic form and is hence silent. However, the existence of such a hidden pronominal determiner is evident from (70)b, where the same position of the invisible element is filled by an overt pronominal determiner *you*.

(70) a. He expected [PRO] to enjoy the play.
  b. He expected you to enjoyed the play.

In traditional grammar, the pronoun *he* is called the logic subject of infinitive verb. In generative grammar, however, the subject position of the infinitive IP *to enjoy the play* is filled by a silent PRO. The understood subject *he* is referred to as an antecedent that controls PRO (hence, the controller of PRO). Verbs, such as like, try, want, which take an infinite complement with a PRO subject, are called control verbs. Evidently, in (70) a as well, at least two subjects are involved with θ-role assignment. The PRO subject is assigned the role of EXPERIENCER by the infinitive IP *enjoy the play*; its antecedent *he*, on the other hand, is (indirectly) assigned the θ-role of AGENT by the verb *expected*.

Underlying the θ-criterion is the fundamental concept of the mathematical function. In mathematics, a function f from A to B, denoted as f: A→B, is relation from A to B such that for each argument $a \in A$, f(a) contains one unique $b \in B$. Functions are also called transformations or mappings, for they are often geometrically viewed as rules that assign each element $a \in A$ a unique value $b \in B$. This matching yields a set of pairs <a, b>, with *a* taken from A (the domain of the function) and *b* from B (the co-domain). With the θ-criterion, a verb is thus viewed as a function that relates set of phrase structures to a set of theta-roles, so that for each argument defined as NP at the syntactic level there is one unique value (a theta-role) determined at the semantic level. Pursuing this line of argument, Chomsky (1972a, p. 17) believes that "each language can be regarded as a particular relationship between sounds and meaning." This means that a linguistic expression can be described as an ordered pair <π, λ>, with π interpreted at the phonetic level as a sequence of sounds and λ at semantic level as meaning. The pairing between sounds and semantic value rules out the possibility of any uninterpretable, superfluous element in syntactic structures. In the later development of generative grammar, such a pairing is said to be able to meet the condition of Full Interpretation. The θ-criterion, as a special case of such a pairing, can be reduced to Principle of Full Interpretation (FI) and be deleted from Grammar.

4.3.8 Movement and Trace

So far we have assumed that, in the course of syntactic derivation, words from the lexicon are first arranged in the way that strictly conforms to the X-bar schema and the fundamental notion of θ-theory, forming the so called D-structure representations. Trans-formations apply to convert the D-structure representations into the S-structure level representations, leaving behind the traces when syntactic constituents are moved out of their original position. The empty category trace is a S-structure phenomenon that is particularly related to movement operations.

As we have seen in the projection of IP (see), the subject, *the girl*, originates within VP to receive θ-role assignment from the V'. Then, by subject raising, it moves to a new subject position in Spec (IP), leaving behind a trace bearing the same index in its original position and yielding a typical S-structure representation, as in (71):

(71)

```
                    IP
                   /  \
                 NP    I'
                 |    /  \
           the girl_i I    VP
                     |   /   \
                   will NP    V'
                        |    /  \
                        t_i V    NP
                            |    |
                          marry the boy
```

The empty traces are also found to exist in a sentence like (72):

(72)   [_IP The fish does [_VP t seems [_IP t to [_VP t be happy]]]].

Well, *The fish does seem to be happy*. It has a pretty good reason to be—our fish first had its home in a small pond (labeled as VP) and then it began to swim, as it were, first to a bigger pond (labeled as IP), then to a lake, and finally to the open sea, leaving behind a trace of itself in every place it once stayed. The word *seem*, that which gives our little fish the inner drive to migrate, is called a RAISING VERB.

However, it is important to note that the fish cannot swim backward from bigger places to smaller ones. To explain this, let's switch back to our less romantic but more practical way of speaking. We may say that the constituent together with any traces associated with it forms a chain. The elements of the chain are called links. The higher link is also referred to as the antecedent of the lower links t_i. In our example, (the fish$_i$, t_i, t_i) forms a chain, and the link *the fish* is the antecedent of its traces. In a chain formed by movement, the antecedent must c-command its traces, which amounts to saying that movement always raises an element but never moves it sideways or downwards to a low position in a tree. That explains the migration pattern of our little fish.

Now it is important to tell an empty trace from another empty category PRO, the difference between the two by no means straightforward. Compare the following to sentences:

(73) a. John$_i$ expected PRO$_i$[to enjoy the play].
     b. John$_i$ was expected t_i[to enjoy the play]. (Chomsky,1995)

The empty categories in the two sentences may look quite similar at the first sight, but deep down they are completely different structural elements. In (73)a, *expect* is a subject control verb that takes an infinitival complement with a PRO subject. In (73)b, however, the sentence is headed by *seemed*, a subject raising verb that takes an infinitive complement with a trace subject.

The difference between the two kinds of verbs boils down to this: control verbs like *expect* θ-mark and hence control their subjects, but raising verbs like *seem* don not θ-mark and hence do not control their subjects. Thus, in (73)a, there are two control verbs and according to θ-criterion, at least two subjects are involved with θ-rule assignment. The PRO subject is assigned the role of EXPERIENCER by the verb *enjoy*; its antecedent *he*, on the other hand, is assigned the θ-rule of AGENT by the verb *expected*. With the sentence in (73)b, however, there is only one control verb, *enjoy*, so only one subject is involved with the role assignment. This subject, *He*, originates within the VP as Experience of *enjoy the play*. And since the raising verb *seemed* cannot control its subject—*He* still plays the same role when raised out its original position.

More empirical evidence for such distinction comes in (74) and (75), where sentences in (74) are headed by raising verbs and those in (75) by control verbs:

(74) a. I happened to find the book in our library.
   b. There happened to be such a book in our library.
   c. We need to solve the problem by Friday.
   d. There needs to be a solution by Friday.

(75) a. *I hope to see the film*.
   b. * *There hoped to a film*.
   c. *I tried to help her*.
   d. * *There tried to help her*.

The difference between the two kinds verbs boils down to this: control verbs like *expect* θ-mark and hence control their subjects, but raising verbs like *seem* do not θ-mark and hence do not control their subjects. Thus, control verbs are more fussy about their subjects: they refuse take *there* as their subjects. This is because *there* cannot be assigned any θ-role and θ-criterion will be violated if it is used as the subject of a control verb. As a result we can always safely use the expletive *there* as the most reliable diagnostic tool in deciding whether a verb is a raising verb or a subject control verb. However, it is important to remember that difference between the two kinds empty categories is of theoretic nature: a trace is a S-structure phenomenon involved with movement operations and PRO a D-structure phenomenon involved with θ-role assignment.

In the theoretic model developed in 1980s, the movement transformation is no more a grammatical operation governed by a particular transformation rule, but rather "an invariant principle of computation," known as alpha movement

(Move α). (Chomsky and Lasnik, 1993:522) Move (α) in effect states that any category (symbolized as α) can be moved anywhere in a sentence. Thus, besides NP-movement we have so far discussed, other types of movement recognized during this period are Wh-movement and Verb-movement

Wh-subject questions, for example, involve Wh-movement within IP, as in (76):

(76)

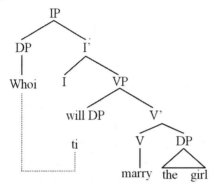

In (76), the wh-phrase *who* originates in Spec (VP) and is consequently moved into Spec (IP), leaving behind a trace bearing the same index.

In short, traces are language phenomena particularly related to the movement transformations and hence are typical of the S-Structure representation. Move (α), as a general rule, allows us to move any category to any place in a sentence. But it is important to remember that the specific movement operation is always carried out under certain constrains. So traces are not left just anywhere in a tree—their positions are generally determined by the kind of movement they undergo. We will come back to the problem of movement later.

4.3.9 Case Theory

While the Theta-theory deals with the relation between the NP argument and its interpretation at the semantic level, CASE THEORY deals with the relationship between elements within a tree. It explains how NPs receive Case from Case as signers such as Verb and Preposition and provides a principled explanation of NPs movement.

The traditional syntactic idea of case tries to capture the relationship between NPs and case-assigning elements in a sentence as being indicated by their morphology. In some languages, case is morphologically realized. For example, German, Russian, Latin have fully-developed case systems and recognize a wide range of case forms for different verbs or prepositions: dative, accusative, instrumental, etc. In other languages, however, case has little or no overt realization. English personal pronouns have three different case forms: nominative case (*I, we, he, they*, etc.), objective case (*me, us, him, them*) and genitive case (*my, our, his, their*), but NPs in English are morphologically insensitive to case differences. In a language like Chinese, case differences usually do not have apparent morphological realization so words may have exactly the same form, whether in Nominative or Accusative case.

However, case is regarded as a structural relationship that universally holds between NPs and other elements in a sentence, so it is assumed that abstract Case is assigned to all (phonetically realized) NPs, whether the case forms are morphologically realized or not. In nominative/accusative languages, the subject is assigned nominative Case by AGR in a finite clause; the object of a transitive verb or preposition is assigned Accusative Case. To illustrate, let's look at (77):

(77)

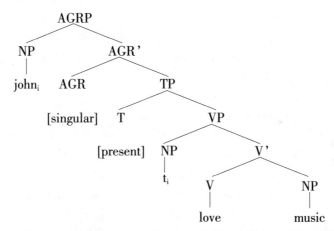

From (77) above, both arguments, *John* and *music*, are Case-marked although they bear no morphological manifestations. Nominative and Accusative Cases are structurally determined (hence structural Case) in that they are assigned to NPs according to their positions. *John* appears in the Spec (AGRP) and receives nominative Case from AGR; and *music* receives accusative Case from the verb as complement of V. We refer to the position where NPs receive their Cases as Case Marked positions.

The principle that requires Case to be assigned to all NPs is known as the CASE FILLER. (Chomsky, 1986: 74) It conveys the simple idea that any sentence will be regarded as ungrammatical and then filtered out unless it has the NPs case-marked. Compare the sentence in (78):

(78) a. I'm sorry if I have confused you.
   b. * I'm sorry I have confused you.
   c. I'm sorry to have confused you.

In (78) a, the adjective *sorry* takes a CP complement, where the subject *I* appears in a Case-marked position, Spec (AGRP), and receive Nominative Case from AGR. In (78)b, the adjective *sorry* takes an infinitival complement. The infinitival clause is headed by a tense element *to*, and it requires a null-case PRO subject instead of a covert NP subject. The appearance of an overt *pronoun I* in Spec (TP) (a non-case-marked position) violates the Case Filter and is ruled out as ungrammatical. So, in a structure like (77), NP originating within VP has to be moved out to Spec (AGRP), the only position where the NP in question can receive Nominative CASE.

4.3.10 Types of Syntactic Relations

In generative grammar, syntactic elements and the structural relation between them are often configured graphically as labeled nodes and paths in a tree diagram. The most common relation holding between syntactic elements is that of DOMINANCE and SISTERHOOD—each node appears in a tree either as the MOTHER, a DAUGHTER, or a SISTER of some other nodes.

C-command: A more restricted configuration relationship on the tree is called c-command, defined in (34) and repeated here as (79)

(79) α c-commands β if and only if
   i. α does not dominate β and
   ii. every γ that dominates α also dominates β

As the term suggest, c-command refers to the relation between the constituents dominated by the same structural unit γ. When γ is a maximal projection, the c-command relation is also referred to as M-COMMAND, m standing for the maximal or phrasal projection. The c-command domain of (e. g. the set of all possible element c-commanded by) an element α would be defined as the minimal phrasal projection in which α appears. (Chomsky, 1995: 93) Take (80) for example:

(80)

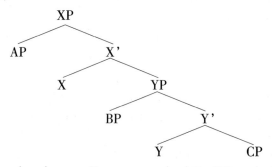

In (80), the element X c-commands AP, YP and all the other notes under them, as all these elements are contained in XP, the nominal phrase projection dominating X. BP, on the other hand, c-commands Y' and everything under Y' but not X and AP because the two nodes are not contained in YP.

Government: GOVERNMENT is a more "local" version of c-command. It explains how lexical heads (i. e. N, V, A, P, AGR) are formally related to other syntactic elements, and how this formal relation influences the syntactic behaviors of these other elements. There exist several equivalent definitions of government in the generative literature. Here we adopt one according to which a head governs its Specifier and Complement, as specified in (81) below:

(81) α governs β iff
   i. α is a governor (i.e. the heads N, V, A, P, C, AGR)
   ii. α and β mutually c-command each other.

As compared with the c-command relation, government is subjected to two formal constraints: 1) α, the governor, is limited to a small set of head features (i.e. N, V, A, P, etc.); and 2) the commanding domain of the governor has a lower as well as a upper bound, as illustrated in (82)

(82)

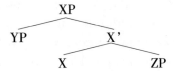

In (82) X is the governor ranging over {N, V, A, P...}, and YP and ZP are the only two elements that are governed by X. Here YP, the specifier, and ZP, the complement, set up the upper and lower bounds to the c-command domain of X—anything beyond YP and ZP is beyond the reach of the governor and hence fails to be governed by X.

In (83) below, the governors are given in bold print, each with an arrow pointing to its governee.

(83)

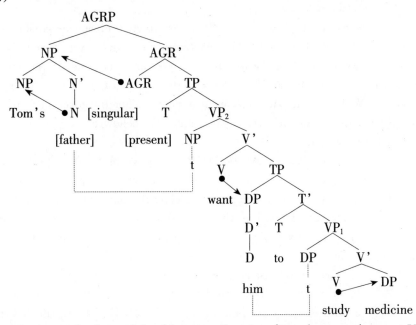

Four governors can be located in this tree. Starting from bottom they are V (*study*) in VP_1, V (*want*) in VP_2, AGR and N (*father*) under AGRP. The V head, *study*, governs its DP complement *medicine* and determines its syntactic behavior by assigning it Accusative Case. By definition, the same head V also governs the DP in Spec (VP$_1$). However, V does not Case-mark its Specifier and this forces the DP to move to a position where it can be Case-marked. In our example, the DP moves to Specifier of TP, where it is assigned nominatives case by the governor AGR. Finally, in the NP *Tom's father*, the N head (*father*) governs its specifier, the genitive NP *Tom's*.

In (83), the TP complement of the verb *want* is an EXCEPTIONAL CASE MARKING (ECM) construction, so called because the subject of the TP, *him*, is exceptionally assigned Accusative Case instead of the normal Nominative Case. The accusative subject *him* in the ECM construction causes certain difficulty, for the DP specifier *him* lies within the maximal projection TP, and is beyond the reach of the governor (the V head *want*) according to the present definition of government. To solve this problem, it is argued that the TP, which does not need Case, is invisible for government, and as a result Accusative Case is passed on through the mediating TP to its specifier. This process is referred to as the MEDIATED CASE ASSIGNMENT.

To explain the Mediated Case Assignment, it seems that we need to make an extension to the notion of government so that case assignment in ECM constructions can be accounted for uniformly in terms of government relation. This can be done by adding one more rule to the definition of government, as in (84) bellow:

(84) α governs β only if there is no γ governed by α and governing β
(Chomsky, 1995:90)

The government relation in an ECM construction obviously satisfies the extra condition specified above. The TP complement, governed by a V or C head (i.e. Complementizer *for* as in *We decided for you to go*), does not govern its own specifier. It follows that any head that governs a TP must also govern the specifier of that TP. With such an extension, we may now redefine the government relation in a simpler and more straightforward way, as in (85) bellowed:

(85) Government
A head (N, V, A, P, AGR, C) governs its NP specifier, its NP complement, and the NP specifier of its TP complement.

Government, as a fundamental syntactic relation, plays an important role in what has come to known as the GB framework of Generative Grammar. In Case Theory, for example, it is suggested that Case is assigned under government according to the rules given in (86) as follows:

(86) a. Nominative Case is assigned by AGR to the NP specifier that it governs
b. Genitive Case is assigned by N to the NP specifier that it governs; and
c. Accusative Case is assigned by V, P, C [for] to the NP that they govern

The formal requirement that Case be assigned under government is generally known as the CASE ASSIGNMENT PRINCIPLE. This principle places a strict formal restriction on Case assignment, and provides a formal explanation for NP movement: Case requirements drive an NP to move from its original position to a new case-marked position to receive Case from the Governor. In Minimalist approach, however, it is suggested that Case feature is checked in a Head-Specifier agreement, in a way that satisfies the general requirement of Full Interpretation. As a result, the notion of Government turns out to be eliminable from the structure of grammar.

Binding and Binding Theory. BINDING is a special case of c-command relation, where the commanding and commanded elements are c-referential expressions that bear the same index. A case in point is the chain formed by movement. In such a chain the moved constituent c-commands a CO-INDEED TRACE, as in (87)

(87) John$_i$ got arrested t$_i$.

To use our newly introduced term, we may say that, in (87), *John*, the antecedent, binds its trace t$_i$, or the trace t$_i$ is bound to its antecedent John$_i$. A more formal definition of binding is given in (88) as follows:

(88) α binds β if and only if
  i. α c-commands β and
  ii. α and β are coindexed.

By definition, binding relation satisfies two conditions: 1) the binding element α c-commands the bound element β and 2) they both are bound to the same semantic value or interpretation (indicated by the coindexation).

Binding, as first used in logic, specifies how variables are interpreted in relation to certain logic operators known as quantifiers. Take (89) for example:

(89) Clever students admire themselves.

In the standard notation of predicate logic, nominal expressions (e.g. pronouns, full NPs, etc.) can be treated as QUANTIFIED EXPRESSIONS and sentence (89) would be represented as (90):

(90) $\forall$ x [Student (x) $\land$ Clever(x)→Admire (x,x)]

The symbol $\forall$ is the universal quantifier (the other being the existential quantifier $\exists$), with the meaning *every/all*. The quantified expression in (91) would read as

(91) For every x it holds that if x is a student and x is clever, then x admires x.

The square brackets [ ] in (90) or that-clause in (91) constitutes the binding scope of the universal quantifier $\forall$. Any variable x falling in this scope is bound to the quantifier, and is hence called a QUANTIFIED or BOUND VARIABLE. Bound variables always have the same interpretation, for they are bound to the same semantic value. Thus whatever value that is assigned to Student (x) and Clever (x) is also assigned to Admire (x, x), which mounts to saying "*Clever students*" and "*themselves*" are co-referrential (e.g. referring to the same individuals).

On the contrary, variables not bound to a quantifier are FREE in the sense that they can take any value. For example, in (92) below,

(92) $\forall x [Student(x) \wedge Clever(x) \rightarrow Admire(x,x)]$

The occurrence of x in Admire (x, x) is free (e.g. not included in the scope of $\forall$). In that case, (92) may mean "For every x it holds that if x is a clever student, then teachers admire themselves." The value of the variables in *Admire* (x, x) is independent of the value of the x's that are inside the binding scope.

In natural language, nominal expressions occupying argument positions behave like variables and we need to explain the coreference properties of these expressions in terms of structural relations holding among them. Binding Theory is developed for the special purpose to deal with the relations among NPs "that have to do with such semantic properties as dependence of reference, including the connection between a pronoun and its antecedent." (Chomsky, 1988:22) With the binding relation defined in (88), the structural aspects of coreference properties of nominal expressions are revealed by the three Binding Principles, as given in (93) below:

(93) Binding Principles
    A. An anaphor is bound in a local domain.
    B. A pronoun is free in a local domain.
    C. An r-expression is free. (Chomsky, 1986a: 166)

Binding principles specify how different types of nominal expressions are actually interpreted in a sentence. Anaphors are expressions that are traditionally termed as RECIPROCALS and REFLEXIVES, such as *himself*, *themselves*, *each other*, etc. R-EXPRESSIONS are referring to phrases like proper names and full NPs (or rather DPs), which may refer directly to extra-linguistic, real-world entities. The terms "LOCAL DOMAIN" can be roughly defined as the minimal clause in which an anaphor or pronoun appears.

Principle A in (93), also known as Condition A of Binding Theory, places a structural constraint on the coreference relation between an anaphor and its antecedent—the expression an anaphor is bound to must appear in a c-commanding position and it must appear close enough, e.g. in the local domain of an embedded clause. Take (94) for example:

(94) Mary thinks [*Jane's sister* is proud of *herself*.]

In (94), *Mary* cannot be taken as the antecedent of *herself*. It satisfies the c-command condition but is not in the local domain. The genitive *Jane's* cannot serve as the antecedent either, because it fails to c-command *herself* although it appears in the local domain. The only possible element to which the anaphor *her* is bound is *Jane's sister*, which c-commands her and is at the same time in the same domain.

Principle B, or Condition B of Binding Theory, states that there are no structural restrictions on the coreferennce relation between a pronoun and its antecedent. To say a pronoun is free in its local domain simply means that it is not syntactically bound to any commanding element in its own clause and is hence free in interpretation. Consider sentence (95).

(95) Mary thinks Jane's sister is proud of *her*.

Since the personal pronoun *her* is not bound to *Jane's sister*, the commanding element in the local domain, it is free to have other interpretations. It can refer, for example, to *Jane* in its local domain, *Mary* in the main clause, or any other person mentioned somewhere else.

Finally, Principle C of Binding Theory says that full NPs are always free to have their own interpretations. Full NPs are referring phrase and to refer freely, they cannot be syntactically bound to any particular semantic value. Unless the identity is directly asserted, referring phrases are always free to refer to different entities. Compare (96) and (97):

(96) a. $Cramer_i$ is $Cramer_i$.
  b. $John_j$ is the $winner_j$.
(97) a. $Cramer_i$ vs. $Cramer_j$.
  b. $John_i$ hates the $winner_j$.

Although Cramer is always Cramer by law of identity (as is asserted in, (96a)), Cramer vs. Cramer cannot be a lawsuit Cramer brought up against himself. The repetition of the same name does not guarantee the coindexation of the name repeated. Thus, in (97)a, the coindexation of the name Cramer in two different positions cannot be asserted. Names are free referring expressions and in (97)a the name Cramer refers to two different individuals, who happen to have the same name as husband and wife. Similarly, in (96)b, the coindexation between $John_j$ and the $winner_j$ is a matter of contingency— John happened to be the winner and this fact has nothing to do with the syntactic relation holding between the expressions. Thus, to say a referring expression is free simply means that the coreference properties of a full NP cannot be syntactically defined. We have, after all, no syntactic principle by which the semantic value of full, referring NPs can be determined.

To summarize: starting in the 1970s and on through the 1980s, generative grammar underwent great changes. We have so far discussed the theoretic and empirical motivations for such changes. In addition, we have also introduced the main theoretic assumptions during this period: that syntactic structure is projected from lexicon in line with the general requirement of projection principle; that all lexical and functional categories project three bar-levels in accord with X-bar schema and that an argument is interpreted (i. e. chooses its value) in a range of semantic roles. These assumptions, brought together with a couple of more, accumulate into the GB model of generative grammar, named after Chomsky's Lectures on Government and Binding (1981).

According to the GB model, a language L is a generative procedure that derives an infinite set of structural descriptions (SD) or linguistic expressions at four levels, i. e. the levels of D-Structure, S-Structure, Phonetic Form (PF), Logic Form (LF), as illustrated in (98):

(98)　　　D-Structure　←　Lexicon
　　　　　　　↓
　PF　←　S-Structure
　　　　　　　↓
　　　　　　　LF

(Based on Chomsky 1995)

The most prominent feature of the GB model is that Lexicon is separated from the syntax or the computational rule of the language. In GB framework, the lexicon is a repository containing all important information about particular lexical items: the representation of phonetic forms of each word, the specification of its syntactic properties and semantic characteristics. Since the phrase structure rules are only a dubious device to recapitulate the grammatical information already presented in lexical entries, it follows that representations at the syntactic levels (D-Structure, S-Structure, LF in a narrow sense of syntax) must all originate from the lexicon.

D-structure is the level through which the lexicon is associated with the computational systems of the language. In the course of a syntactic derivation, words from the lexicon are arranged at the D-structure level, in a way that conforms to fundamental notions of X-theory and Theta-theory. Transformations apply to alter the D-structure representation, leaving behind traces in case of movement transformations, and eventually produce the S-structure. There the derivation continues into two directions, producing the PF representation and LF representation, respectively. The PF representation carries formal instructions on how a speech sound is articulated and perceived, and is said to be an interface relating language to the Articulatory-Perceptual (AP) system of human performance. The LF representation carries semantic information about how a sentence is to be interpreted, and is said to be an interface relating language to the Conceptual-Intentional (CI) system. This new model provides a new way to look at human language, and drastically changes our view as to how phrases structures are generated.

4.4 The Minimalist Approach

In generative tradition, a good grammar should meet the basic requirements of explanatory and descriptive adequacy. However, the extremely rich and complex phenomena of human language create an essential tension between the two goals. On one hand, to attain the goal of explanatory adequacy (i. e. to explain how it is possible for a child to acquire his mother tongue so quickly and on the basis of such limited evidence), linguistic theories should provide a grammar that is as simple as possible. On the other hand, to attain the goal of descriptive adequacy (i. e. to cover as many linguistic phenomena as possible), a grammar should be complex enough. Up to the 1980s, much work in syntax is involved with the postulation of ever more complex structures and principles. To resolve the problem Chomsky has taken the minimalist approach since 1990s. The aim is to seek a unified explanatory theory to minimize the burden of excessive theoretic apparatus and maximizes the explanatory power and learnability of grammar.

Such a grammar, as outlined by Chomsky in *The Minimalist Program*, consists of a Lexicon and a computational system. The lexicon is the indispensable component of the grammar, representing important information about the sound, meaning and syntactical properties of lexical items (words) listed in the lexicon. The information is encoded as feature sets attached to the lexical entry of words. The syntactic-feature set, among others, contains the categorical features (i. e. N, V, A, P, etc.) and φ-features (i. e. person, gender, number, etc.). These features identify the syntactic status of each lexical item and provide instructions to computational operations.

4.4.1 Merge / Move

The computational system of human language consists of two simple concatenating (structure building) operations: Merge and Move. Each of these operations is binary by nature, taking two and only two objects, concatenating them and forming a third. The operations can be performed iteratively until the constituent structure we desire is finally built. As an example, we have the process illustrated in (99):

(99)

```
                              CP
Step 10          D         C'
                 |        / \
Step 9          who_i    C       IP
                         |      / \
Step 8                  do_j   D      I'
                               |     / \
Step 7                        you   I     VP
                                    |    / \
Step 6                            [do]  V      IP
                                        |     / \
Step 5                                 t_j think DP    I'
                                                |     / \
Step 4                                        [who]  I     VP
                                                     |    / \
Step 3                                             t_i will V      DP
                                                            |     / \
Step 2                                                    marry  D     NP
                                                                 |    / \
Step 1                                                         the   A    N
                                                                  run-away bride
```

As we can see, the tree in (99) is built bottom-up in 10 steps by applying Merge and Move iteratively. In Step 1, an adjective *run-away* is merged with a noun *bride*, yielding a third constituent *run-away bride*, labeled as NP. In Step 2 a determiner *the* is merged with NP *run-away bride*, yielding still another constituent *the run-away bride*, labeled as DP. The same operation is repeated in Step 3 through Step 8, each concatenating a lexical item with an already constructed phrase, until an IP *you think who will marry the run-away bride* is formed. (Notice that a wh-subject question will be yielded if the process stops at Step 5.)

Step 9 and Step 10 involve Move. Such an operation takes an element from within the constructed tree and concatenates it with that tree, leaving behind a trace in original position out of which the element moves. Minimalist Program distinguishes two main types of Move operation: 1) head movement whereby a word moves from one head position to another, and 2) operator movement whereby an operator moves into Spec (CP).

A special case of head movement is illustrated by Step 9 in (99), where the auxiliary *do* moves from I to C. The operation involved would be referred to as auxiliary inversion in tradition grammar, but here we simply call it I (-to-C) movement. Yes-no questions are believed to be generated by I movement and we will leave the derivation for the students as an exercise. Step 10 in the derivation of (99) involves operator movement, a Move operation that is applied to wh-determiners (known also as interrogative operators) and negative words (negative operators such as none, hardly, no). In our example in (99), this operation picks up the interrogative operator *who* from within the tree, concatenates it to the tree as the Spec (CP), and finally yields a CP. Except for wh-subject questions, the formation of wh-questions in general is connected with operator movement.

It is worth noticing that movement transformations do not move a constituent simply to any place in the tree but are subjected some strict constrains. As we have seen before 4.3.7, all movement transformations must satisfy the c-command condition on binding—the general principle requiring that all constituents moved c-command their traces.

In addition to that, shorter movements are preferred over longer ones out of economy considerations. This restriction is generally known as the principle of shortest movement or, equivalently, the minimal link condition. A case in point is the locality constrain on head movement, which requires a head only move into a head position in the next highest phrase within the structure. For example, in (99) we cannot move *will* across the lower IP to position C, yielding (100)a instead of (100)b:

(100) a. * Who *will*$_i$ you think t_i marry the run-away bride?
      b. Who *do*$_i$ you t_i think will marry the run-away bride?

In a multiple wh-questions where two or more wh-operators are involved, the one nearest to C moves to satisfy the shortest movement condition. An example is given here in (101):

(101) a. Who$_i$ do you think t_i will marry who?
b. * Who$_i$ do you think who will marry t_i?

In case where wh-determiners take a complement, moving a wh-operator by itself without its complement would be regarded as an illegal operation, as illustrated in (102) below:

(102) * Which$_i$ do you like t_i book best?

The reason for this is that in chain (Which$_i$, t_i) formed by the movement, the links are not consistent with each other. The higher link, *which*, is obvious a maximal projection labeled as DP, however, its trace is only minimal projection labeled as D. The two links simply refer to different grammatical objects. This is said to have violated the chain uniformity condition, which requires that the links of a chain be of the same structural status.

Now to meet the chain uniformity condition, the whole DP headed by *which* has to move together into Spec (CP), yielding a structure as shown in (103):

(103)

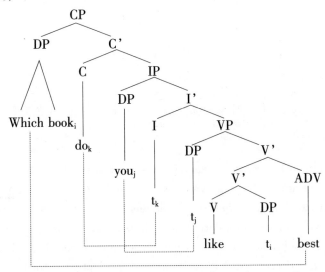

When the wh-determiner *which* moves, it lures its complement *book* to move with it, leaving a DP trace t_i in the original site. In allusion to the story of the pied piper who lured rats by playing his pipe, a wh-determiner is said to pied-pipe its complement when it moves into Spec (CP).

In the minimalist framework, constraints on grammatical operations are formulated out economy considerations. The principle of Full Interpretation, for example, can be reduced to the more general principle of economy, because derivation that violate FI yields superfluous representations that must be ruled out for economy reasons. The *minimal link* and *chain uniformity conditions on Move* are also economy principles, which in effect state that if we have to move anything at all, "move the smallest constituents possible the smallest distance." (Radford, 1997: 140)

4.4.2 Minimizing to Bare Essentials

The minimalist approach to phrase structures differs from the traditional theoretic models in a tremendous way. While the category particular rewrite rules of the Phrase Structure Grammar build up structures in top-down direction, Merge/Move constructs structures pair-wise in a bottom-up in fashion. The shift from the top-down rewrite rules to bottom-up system of Merge/Move marks a fundamental change in the view as to how sentences are formed. First, the category labels such as S, NP, DP, AP, VP, N, D, A, V, etc. are no more given as theoretical primitives of rule systems. They turn out to be some derived notions that can be reduced to syntactic features listed in a lexical entry in the lexicon. Thus, structure like the *run-away bride*, which would be represented as (104) under DP hypothesis, can be given a tree representation as in (105):

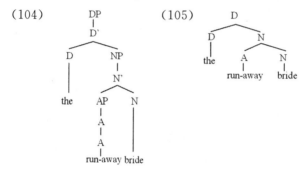

The presentation in (105) conveys exactly the same information about syntactic status of the expression. Merging A*run-away* with N *bride*, the noun head, we get a noun phrase *run-away bride*, also labeled as N. Merging the resulting N with D, the head *the*, we get a determiner phrase, carry the category label of the head D. Here label distinctions between projection levels (X for heads, X' for immediate projection, and XP for maximal projection) turn out to be redundant. Such distinctions are inferable from the dominating relation between nodes.

In a more radical treatment, it suggested that (105) be represented as (106), for the information about category status of each word is already listed in the lexicon, encoded as syntactic features set:

(106)

The system used in (106) is based on "bare essentials"—basic syntactic, phonological and semantic information encoded as features. Thus, the category-based rule system of the Phrase Structure Grammar is eliminated in favor of the featured-based "bare phrase structure" theory. In the minimalist theory the traditional category labels are still used, and we will keep to this convention, too. Nevertheless, it is important to keep in mind that these labels are no more used as the primitive terms of the system and that they have no theoretical status whatsoever in the computational system of human language.

Theoretical fundamentals of X-bar theory—the notion of projection level—are also held to critical scrutiny. In X-bar theory, bar levels are absolute concepts defined in terms of the top-down rewrite rules of X-bar schema. (We have it in 41, but reproduce it here as ⟨107⟩):

(107) XP→ YP X'
      X'→ X ZP

In a descriptive system that uses (107), the three levels of projection X-X'-XP is guaranteed by X-bar schema. NP, for example, is always represented as N-N'-NP, even there may exist no specifier or complement. In the bottom-up phrase building system of Merge/Move, the projection level of a syntactic structure is a derived notion, definable only in relation with other constituents surrounding it. Thus the minimal projection, X, is defined as a syntactic object that is not projected from some other constituent. The maximal projection, XP, is a structural constituent that does not project any further. A constituent that is neither maximal nor minimal is called an intermediate projection, X'. In (106), for example, *bride*, the head that is not projected from anything else, is the minimal projection, N. *Run-away bride*, a projected object that projects no further, is the maximal projection NP. Interestingly, the adjective *run-away* is, by virtue of definition, both minimal and maximal. There might be no intermediate level N' unless the head *bride* takes a complement, like in, say, *run-away bride in white*. As a result of the elimination of X-bar theory, the structural building device of grammar is minimized and limit to some formally simple operations like Merge and Move.

4.4.3 Checking and Checking Theory

The minimalist endeavor to minimize the burden of too many theoretic apparatus seems quite successful, except for one problem: we have nothing at disposal to prevent the computational system to generate undesirable structures. To illustrate, we cannot prevent Merge to take an adjective *happy* to concatenate with a verb *go*, yielding a third object *happy go*. Traditionally, a generated structure is globally defined by the top-down rewrite rules, and the grammaticality is guaranteed by the rule system. Ungrammatical combination such as *happy go* can be avoided, at least in theory, if we strictly follow the rules. However, such possibility is no more available after we abandon the rule system for a formally simple device such as Merge. It is true that operation Move is subjected to formal constrains, among others, c-command condition, minimal link condition and chain uniformity condition. These constrains eventually become a part of the definition of movement operations. However, no formal constrains whatsoever are placed on Merge.

CHECKING THEORY is proposed particularly to address the problem. We have to check the grammatical features carried by each word in a sentence to see whether the sentence in question is grammatical or not. To understand how the checking process works, lets return to our *happy go* example, which is not very happy to go together. As operation Merge can combine any two legitimate grammatical objects to form a third, combining *happy* with *go* to form *happy go* turns out to be a legitimate operation. There are two possible interpretations for the grammatical status of the new object. If *happy* is taken as the head, the projected target *happy go* is an AP. Otherwise, it is projected by *go* and is a VP. We have the two possible structures in (108):

(108)

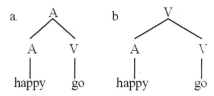

Unfortunately, neither is correct. This is because an adjective like *happy* may take a CP or PP complement but never takes a bare verb as complement. Thus *happy to go*, *happy you go*, *happy about it* all count as grammatical AP but *happy go* does not. In a similar way, the verb *go* does not take an A as its specifier, thus *happy go* cannot be a legitimate VP either.

In making the above analysis, we have in fact followed through on the procedure of a checking operation. Now let's try to formulate the whole process of checking in a more precise way. We have presumed that all words carry three feature-sets, containing information about the pronunciation, meaning, and syntactic properties of the words respectively. Let's further suppose that the syntactic feature-set contains three subsets: 1) head-features, 2) complement-features and 3) specifier-features. Head features specify the grammatical properties of the head itself. The complement features specify the range of possible complements the head is allowed to take. The specifier features determine the range of specifiers the head is allowed to take. The types of features involved are tense or participle features in case of V or I and Case/agreement features (person, number, gender) in case of N or D. The relevant features are encoded as feature matrix placed under each word in a sentence. We give a simple example in (109) to show how this can be done:

(109)

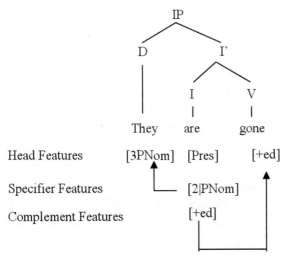

In (109), the I(NFL)*are* has its grammatical properties expressed as follows: 1) it carries the head feature [Pres], indicating it is in present tense form; 2) its Specifier features [2Pnom] tells us that it requires for a second person (encoded as [2]) or plural ([P]) subject in nominative case ([Nom]); and 3) the complement feature [+ed] means that it must take a complement headed by a verb carrying past participle inflection +*ed*.

In the course of a derivation, we have the Specifier Features of a head checked with the Head Features of its specifier, and the Complement Features of a head with the head features of its complement. If all the features being checked are compatible with each other, the sentence derived is grammatical; otherwise, it is ungrammatical. Obviously, the structure in (109) can pass the feature checking and is a grammatical sentence.

Checking Theory is motivated by the ambitious plan to minimize the theoretic apparatus of linguistics, so it can be best understood in connection with the basic minimalist assumptions about human language. As we know, in the eye of a native speaker, a linguistic expression—a word, a phrase, or a sentence—is always a sound/meaning combination. Then how does a linguistic expression come to be pronounced and understood the way it is? A standard minimalist assumption is that when the syntax derivation generates a linguistic expression, it produces two and only two levels of representation: 1) Phonetic Form representation and 2) Logic Form representation. (There is no D-Structure or S-Structure anymore). The former is a formal specification of sound, telling us how an expression is pronounced, and the latter, of the linguistic aspects of meaning, telling us how an expression is interpreted. It is further assumed that PF representation carries information that is only phonetically interpretable and the LF representation carries information that is only semantically interpretable, hence, satisfying the principle of full interpretation (FI). Apparently, a large part of grammatical information (encoded as features) turns out to be irrelevant to the pronunciation and understanding and is therefore not interpretable at the phonetic or semantic level. If such uninterpretable features are subjected to further processing at PF or LF level, they violate the FI and cause the derivation to crash, yielding an ungrammatical sentence as a result. However, if no uninterpretable grammatical features are brought up to PF or LF level, the derivation is said to converge (at PF or LF) and hence is grammatical.

Thus, the operation of feature checking is in order. Nonetheless, it does not simply check grammatical features to see if they match or not in a fashion sketched out in (109). It checks and eventually erases all matched features, unless these features are interpretable at PF or LF level. According to Checking Theory, head features such as person/number/gender are interpretable, but the case feature is not. (For example, with pronouns *she*, *he*, *they*, *I*, *we*, feature difference in person/ number/gender effects different interpretations.) On the other hand, with *they* and *them* (as in *I waited for them but they didn't show up*) case properties features make no difference in interpretation. In case of Vs head features like tense inflections ([Pres], [Past]) are interpretable; whereas, verb inflections other than tense (such as [+ing],[+ed]) are not. Specifier features and complement features of a head are uninterpretable, in that they are actually the features of some other words and reveal nothing about the intrinsic nature of the head itself. Now, subject (109) to the checking procedure outlined above, and we get (110) below:

(110)

```
                        IP
                       /  \
                      D    I'
                      |   /  \
                      |  I    V
                      |  |    |
                    They are gone

Head Features    [3P̶n̶om]  [Pres]   [+̶e̶d̶]
Specifier Features         [2P̶N̶o̶m̶]
Complement Features         [+̶e̶d̶]
```

Here, all features not interpretable at the interface level, PF or LF, are checked and eventually erased before the derivation reaches the point Spell-out. The remaining feature information disappears when [3P] is phonetically interpreted as *they* (instead of as *you*, *we* or *she*), and [Press2P] as *are*

Chapter 4 Generative Syntax

(instead of as *were*, *am*, or *is*). They are all gone—grammatical features, the D-structure, S-structure, category or phrasal labels. What we eventually get is a "clean" linguistic expression that converges at both PF and LF levels, or more simply, a sentence—something a native speaker intuitively takes as a sound/meaning combination.

With Checking Theory, the notion of Case Marking is reduced to that of CASE-CHECKING. NPs (or DPs) certainly do not move to case-marked positions to "receive" Case from the case-assigning elements. In the minimalist approach, words enter into the computation system with their Case-marked position. Nor is there any possibility for ECM, which assumes that Accusative Case may be assigned by a Verb to the Specifier of its TP complement under government relation. In fact, there would be no place in a clause to have the Accusive case checked off, although it is always possible for the subject NP (or DP) to move into the Spec (AGRP) to have its Nominative feature checked with the specifier feature of AGR. In minimalist framework, this problem is solved by introducing an extra Object Agreement Phrase (henceforth AGRoP) into the basic clause structure. It is assumed that the functional category I can be split into two distinct X-bar structure (T) projection. In addition, its AGRoP is introduced into the clause structure as the sister to T, its AGRo head taking a VP complement. So a clause would assume the following typical structure.

(111)

```
          CP
         /  \
       Spec   C
             / \
            C   ABRsP
               /    \
             Spec    AGRs'
                    /     \
                  AGRs     TP
                          /  \
                         T    AGRop
                             /    \
                           Spec    AGRo'
                                  /    \
                                AGRo    VP
```

The AGRs is obligatory, because every clause must have a subject according to the Extended Projection Principle (EPP). AGRo, however, is only optional. If VP is headed by an intransitive V, there is no AGRo and no AGRoP would be projected. Only when the VP is headed by a transitive Verb with a DP complement, AGRoP will be projected, with V raised to AGRo and the DP to

Spec (AGRoP). The right word order (Verb-object instead of Object-verb) will be produced by raising of the main verb V to a light verb v, to which we will return in the vp-shell analysis in the next section. In case of the so-called ECM, where V takes a TP complement, the Verb raises to AGRo and the Specifier of TP to Spec (AGRoP) to have their Accusative Features checked in Spec-head agreement.

Checking Theory produces many other favorable theoretical results. For one thing, the EPP requirement that all clauses have subjects can be restated in terms of feature checking. Chomsky (1995: 232) recognized strong features—the ones carried by a nonsubstantive category like I, C, etc., which would cause a crash at PF unless checked and thereby deleted before the derivation reaches Spell-out. The functional category I carries a strong D-feature, which must be checked by a DP move to the specifier of I. "Thus, the Extended Projection Principle (EPP) plausibly reduces to a strong D-feature of I." (Chomsky, 1995: 232)

The Spec-head agreement also provides a unified way to account for the Head and Operator Movement. In the Minimalist Program, Chomsky (1995: 289) suggests that clause types are determined by the formal features of the functional category C. Consider (112) below:

(112) IP The *man* I will *t* marry the run-away bride

A declarative sentence can be taken as a CP headed by a convert C. In (112), the DP *the man* raises to the Spec (IP) to have the strong D-feature of I checked off, and it is not required to move any further because the complementizer C is covert and does not to be checked.

In an interrogative clause, however, the complementizer C bears the feature Q. Such a feature is interpretable at LF and need not be checked. In English, however, Q happens to be a "strong" feature—it cannot be passed on to PF without causing the derivation to crash (at PF). As a result, an element has to be moved into its checking domain to have the Q feature checked and eliminated. This can be done by adjoining I to Q in an I-to-C movement, as in the derivation of yes-or-no questions:

(113)

```
                    CP
                   /  \
                  C    IP
                 / \
               will  Q    the man t marry the run-away bride
```

Here, the strong feature Q is believed to be affixal in nature and its attracts an auxiliary to move from I to C to adjoin it.

Or alternatively, the wh-phrase carrying the Q feature [wh-] may move to

the Spec (CP) to check with C, yielding a wh-question as in (114):
(114)

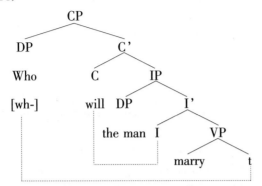

In this example, Q is taken as the specifier feature carried by C. The wh-phrase enters the Spec (CP) position to have its head feature [wh-] checked with the specifier feature of C, resulting in the deletion of the strong Q, with the head feature [wh-] left for further processing at LF.

From the above analysis, we can see that movements are made to satisfy the sole need to check off and thereby erase the uninterpretable features associated with inflected elements (e. g. I, AGR, T, etc.) and the complementizer C. It follows that a syntactic constituent will never move unless for the "selfish" purpose to check off its own features. Thus, elements that do not need checking do not move because they do not have to. This constitutes another economy constrains on operation Move, known as the PRINCIPLE OF GREED. In addition, syntactic derivation is conducted step-wise and in each step economy of derivation allows only a minimum of transformation activity. Thus, contrary to the industrious motto "Don't leave today's work for tomorrow," checking requires that movements always be postponed as long as possible in the derivation, if movements have to happen at all. This can be formulated as another economy principle, known as PROCRASTINATE. (Chomsky, 1993:33)

4.4.4 VP Shells

Within the minimalist framework, the computational system of human language consists only of two simple operations, Merge/Move, which build up structures in a pair-wise fashion. The binary operation of Merge, however, does not seem to hold for ternary structures where verbs take two complements or one complement plus an adjunct (see ⟨115⟩ for example):

(115) a. The sea rolls its waves onto the sands.

Since Merge can only form a large unit out of two, in (115) merging N *waves* with a PP *on the sands* would yield an NP *waves on the sands*. That is obviously implausible, because *onto the sands* is a PP adverbial and, with X-bar schema, it can only be adjoined to V' to form an extended V' structure.

However, to reintroduce the X-bar schema into the computational system is even more implausible, for the inconsistency it is likely to cause.

Fortunately, the verb *roll* happens to belong to a group known as ERGATIVE VERBS, which can also be used intransitively as a one-place predicate, as in (116)

(116) Its waves roll onto the sands.

Here, *roll* merges with its complement *onto the sands* to form a V' *roll onto the sands*, which in turn merges with a DP *its waves*, yielding a VP. Although the DP *its waves* occupies the subject position in one sentence and the object position in the other, it plays exactly the same thematic role in both cases, e. g. as the entity that undergoes the rolling motion. A closer observation may further reveal that *roll* in its transitive use is comparable with a causative construction, which is usually formed by merging causative element such as *make* with a VP complement. Thus (116) can be paraphrased as "The sea makes *its waves roll onto the sand*," and represented as (117) below:

(117)

```
                    IP
                   /  \
                 DP    I'
                 △    /  \
              The sea I   VP₂
                         /   \
                        DP    V'
                              / \
                             V   VP₁
                             |   / \
                          makes DP  V'
                                △  / \
                           its waves V  PP
                                     |  △
                                   roll onto the sands
```

In (117), the verb *makes* in VP₂ assigns the agentive role to *the sea*, which is then raised to Spec (IP) to have its Case checked. The verb roll originates in VP₁, where it assigns the Theme role to *its waves*.

Although no overt causative element is directly observable in (115), it is assumed that the position occupied by the causative *make* in (116) is filled by an abstract causative light verb ɸ. A further assumption is that the light verb ɸ is a strong feature, affixal by nature (as the tense feature *-ed* in TP or the **Q** feature of C in a question), and will draw the verb ɸ *roll* to join it in the causative position. Thus, sentence (115) will be represented as (118).

According to (118), the verb *roll* originates in VP, where it assigns the Theme role to DP *its waves*. Then it moves out of VP to join the light verb ɸ and assigns the causative role to *the sea*, which is inserted in the tree by Merge and then moves into Spec (IP) to have its case checked. By convention, the lower case letters are used to denote the light verb and its projection: v, v', and vp. Here, the lower case vp is called the vp shell, in contrast to the capitalized VP core.

(118)

```
                    IP
                   /  \
                  DP   I'
                  |   /  \
              The sea I   vp
                         /  \
                        DP   v'
                        |   /  \
                        t  v    VP
                          / \  /  \
                        roll φ DP   V'
                              |    /  \
                          its waves V   PP
                                    |   / \
                                    t  onto the sands
```

The light verb analysis can also be applied to the ditransitive verbs and help to solve the problem of the binary merge operation with double-object constructions. Consider the following sentences:

(119) They sent her some flowers.

In (119), *her* and *some flowers* are two independent structural elements and they cannot be merged to form a single structural unit. With vp-shell configuration, sentence (119) can be derived by the binary merge operation, without making the two independent complements a single unit. (120) shows how this can be done:

(120)

```
              vp
             /  \
            DP   v'
            |   /  \
          They  v    VP
               / \  /  \
              V   φ DP   V'
              |     |   /  \
            sent   her  V    DP
                        |   / \
                        t  some flowers
```

Here, we assume that *sent* originates within VP, where it takes *some flowers* as its complement and *her* as its specifier. It then moves to join the agentive light verb φ, and assigns the Agent role to the DP specifier *they*. Consequently, double-object structures are assumed to be a complex v-VP configuration, which v is a light verb to which the main verb V moves to adjoin. In such a structure, the external argument (e.g. the subject) originates within the outer vp as the Specifier of v and the internal arguments (e.g. the objects) within inner VP, occupying the positions of Specifier and Complement of V.

Based on the assumption that the external subject is θ-marked by v rather than V, Chomsky (1995) suggests that the light verb analysis can be extended to transitive verb constructions generally. Consider, for example, the sentence in (121) below:

(121) a. She sings us a song.
   b. She sings a song.
   c. She sings the song badly.

The verb *sings* has different uses (121)a and (121)b, but the two sentences can be derived in a unified way as in (122) below:

(122)

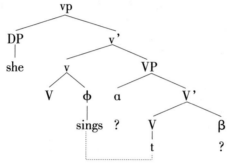

Here again, the external argument (e.g. the subject *she*) remains high up in Spec (vp). The light verb φ is said to have a performative interpretation, meaning roughly *She performs the action of singing*. The Agent role of the subject is understood as being assigned to the v-VP configuration by v. With the double-object construction in sentence (121)a, internal argument positions are both filled, α by *us* and β by *a song*. In (121)b, however, the verb *sings* merges with only one complement, yielding a VP directly since no specifier α is involved in the derivation. The resulting VP *sings a song* merges with the light verb φ, which projects from v' and then vp.

However, it is important to note that β, the sister of V, is no more a position reserved exclusively for a DP argument, but rather a position that can also be occupied by a PP or Adverb. In fact, adverbs are regarded as the innermost complement of V. (Larson, 1988; 1990) So in (121)c, the verb *sings* first merges with its adverb complement *badly*, yielding a V' *sing badly*. This V' merges with the DP specifier *the song* and θ-marks it as Theme, forming the VP *the song sing badly*. The inner VP core is in turn merged with a light verb φ, to which the verb *sing* adjoins. This operation results in a v', which merges with the DP *she* and projects into a vp *She sings the song badly*.

With the vp-shell construction, the traditional VP-internal subject

Chapter 4 Generative Syntax 145

hypothesis seems quite unwarranted and needs to be reexamined. In fact, to say that the external argument originates in vp shell rather than in the VP core simply means that the subjects can only be inserted directly by operation Merge in Spec-vp, where it is θ-marked as Agent by the performative light verb. It would be wrong to suppose that the external argument first originates within VP and then moves to Spec-vp—such a raising always entails a violation of the θ-criterion and hence "causes the derivation to crash, by failure to satisfy FI." (Chomsky, 1955:315)

The only exception is perhaps unaccusative verbs, whose subjects originate within the VP core as the internal argument. Examples of such verbs are given in (123) as follows:

(123) a. There *goes* the bell for us to get strapped in.
   b. There *remains* nothing more for us to do.
   c. There *stands* a danger of flooding if this heavy rain continues.
   d. There once *lived* a poor widow who had a beautiful daughter.
   e. Suddenly there *entered* a strange figure dressed all in black.
   f. There *followed* an uncomfortable silence.

An unaccusative verb typically expresses existence, movement, occurrence, or change of state, which is not actively initiated by the subject of the sentence. UNACCUSATIVES are believed to have the simple VP structures for they do no assign the agent role to the external argument. (Chomsky, 1995)

Nevertheless, Radford (1997) argues that the unaccusative verbs may also involve a vp headed by v. Consider the following:

(124)

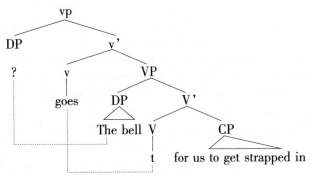

(124) suggests that the unaccusative *goes* originates as a V head but is raised to the v position of vp. After that, the sentence may derive in two possible ways. Either the subject *the bell* is raised to Spec-vp, yielding *The bell goes for us to get strapped in*. Or the subject may remain *in situ*, with the Spec-vp filled by the dummy *there*, yielding an expletive structure *There goes the bell for us to get strapped in*. This is because the Spec-vp in (124) is a

none-θ position and filling it with an argument (like, *say*, *he*) would cause the sentence to crash.

References

Akmajian, A. & Heny, F. W. 1975. *An Introduction to the Principles of Transformational Syntax*. Cambridge: MIT Press.

Borsley, Robert. 1999. *Syntactic Theory: A Unified Approach*. London and New York: Arnold.

Chomsky, Noam. 1957. *Syntactic Structures*. Mouton: The Hague.

——1965. *Aspects of the Theory of Syntax*. Cambridge: MIT Press.

——1970. "Remarks o Nominalization," In *Readings in English Transformational Grammar*. Roderick Jacobs & Peter Rosebaum (eds.). Waltham, MA: Blaisdell.

——1972. *Language and Mind*. (enlarged ed.). New York: Harcourt Brace Jovanovich.

——1981. *Lectures on Government and Binding*. Dordrecht: Foris.

——1986a. *Knowledge of Language: Its Nature, Origin and Use*. New York: Praeger.

——1986b. *Barries*. Cambridge, Mass: MIT Press.

——1988. *Language and the Problems of Knowledge: The Managua Lectures*. Cambridge, Mass: MIT Press.

——1991a. "Linguistics and adjacent fields: a personal view," In *The Chomskyan Turn*. A. Kasher (ed.). Oxford: Blackwell. pp. 5—23.

——1991. "Some notes on economy of derivation and representation," In *Principles and Parameters in Comparative Grammar*. R. Freidin (ed.). Cambridge, Mass: MIT Press. pp. 417—545.

——1993. "A minimalist program for linguistic theory," In *The View from Building* 20. K. Hale & S. J. Keyser (eds.). Cambridge, Mass: MIT Press. pp. 1—52.

——1995. *The Minimalist Program*. Cambridge, Mass: MIT Press.

Chomsky & Lasnik. 1993. "Principles and parameters theory," In *Syntax: An International Handbook of Contemporary Research*. J. Jacobs, A von Stechow, W. Sternefeld & T. Vennemann (eds.). Berlin: de Gauyter. pp. 506—569.

Cook, Vivian James & Mark Newson. 1996. *Chomsky's Universal Grammar: An Introdution*. Oxford and Cambridge, MA: Blackwell.

Cowper, Elizabeth. 1992. *A Concise Introduction to Syntactic Theory: The Government-Binding Approach*. Chicago: University of Chicago Press.

Culicover, Peter. 1997. *Principles and Parameters: An Introduction to Syntactic Theory*. Oxford: Oxford University Press.

Kolman, B. et al. 1996. *Discrete Mathematical Structures*. (3rd ed.). London: Prentice Hall.

Jackendoff, R. 1977. *X' Syntax: A Study of Phrase Structure*. Cambridge, MA: MIT Press.

Lyons, John. 1968. *Introduction to Theoretical Linguistics*. Cambridge: Cambridge University Press.

Lyons, John. 1991. *Chomsky*. London: Fontana Press.

Martin, John C. 1991. *Introduction to Language and the Theory of Computation*. New York: McGraw-Hill, Inc.

Ouhalla, J. 1991. *Functional Categories and Parametric Viriation*. London: Routledge.

Pinker, Steven. 1994. *The Language Instinct: How the Mind Creates Language*. New York: Morrow.

Pollard, C. & I. Sag. 1994. *Head-Driven Phrase Structure Grammar*. Chicago: University of Chicago Press.

Pollock, J. Y. 1989. "Verb movement, universal grammar, and the structure of IP," *Linguistic Inquiry* 20: 365—424.

Quirk, Randoph, et al. 1985. *A Grammar of Contemporary English*. London: Longman.

Radford, A. 1988. *Transformational Syntax: A First Course*. Cambridge: Cambridge University Press.

Radford, A. 1997. *Syntax: A Minimalist Introduction*. Cambridge: Cambridge University Press.

Radford, A. et al. 1999. *Linguistics: An Introduction*. Cambridge: Cambridge University Press.

Santorini, Beatrice. 2000. *Introduction to Transformational Grammar*. Des. 12, 2000. http://www.ling.upenn.edu/~beatrice/150/

Chapter 5

Functional Syntax[①]

This chapter makes an introduction to functional syntax with a focus upon some relevant studies by Vilém Mathesius, František Daneš, and Micheal Halliday. It discusses some basic aspects of their theories with a view to giving a state of the art presentation and indicating what may be further explored.

5.1 Vilém Mathesius

Vilém Mathesius (1882—1945), a Czech linguist, was one of the founding members and life-long chairman of the Prague Linguistic Circle. (Trnka, 1946; Vachek, 1966; 1972; 1980; 1982; 1983; 1994; 1995; 2002; Toman, 1995; Daneš, 2003a; 2003b); His ideas of functional syntax can be found in his posthumous publication *A Functional Analysis of Present Day English on a General Linguistic Basis* (1975) as well as in his papers written between 1920s and 1940s. (Mathesius, 1927; 1928; 1929a; 1929b; 1936; 1939; 1941; 1942) Our discussion concentrates upon his ideas of subject, predication, object, subject-predicate relations, object-predicate relations, and functional sentence perspective (FSP).

5.1.1 Subject

Mathesius's ideas of subject are noteworthy in two ways. One is the function of the subject, the other is the subject selection principle.

In present-day English, the subject can perform the function of both the agent and patient of the action expressed by the predicate. Historically, the grammatical subject might have originated from a formally fixed manner of expressing the theme of the utterance, and the theme of the utterance expressed the agent of the action that was predicated by the verb. Out of the communicative need to have the non-agent element as the theme and also the need to resolve the conflict between the requirement of grammatical word order (agentive subject precedes the predicate) and the requirement of functional

---

① This chapter is based on Chapter 2 of Qian, 2001a, with numerous revisions made.

sentence perspective (e. g. to postpose the agentive subject) English has developed passive constructions. And this is also one of the reasons for a relatively higher frequency of passive constructions in English. Contrastive studies reveal that the subject in Czech has largely preserved the function of the agent while the subject in English "has to a considerable extent acquired thematic function, i. e. the function of expressing the agent of the action has been appreciably weakened in favour of the function to express the theme of the utterance." (1975:101)①Compare the following sentences:
    (1) a. The blacksmith forged the horseshoe.
         b. The horseshoe was forged by the blacksmith.
    (2) a. I feel cold.
         b. Czech:*Je mi zima.* (Is to-me cold.)
         c. German:*Mir ist kalt.* (To me [dative] is cold.)
    (3) a. I am sorry.
         b. Czech:*Je mi lito.* (Is to-me sorry.)
         c. German: *Es tut mir leid.* (It makes me [dative] sorry. I am sorry.)

In English the subject of the predicative verb can express the person affected by the mental or physical state. In Czech, sentences describing physical or mental states are subjectless, which help to prove that the Czech subject has largely preserved the function of the agent.

Mathesius (1975:100, 102) holds that English tends to choose something concrete as the subject of the sentence, especially words denoting persons. Wherever there is a possibility of choice between a person and an inanimate subject, English prefers the former. This hierarchy may be regarded as a subject selection principle, and it needs further research. (Qian, 2004a)

5.1.2 Predication

Mathesius divides predication into four types: 1) actional, 2) qualifying, 3) existential and 4) possessive.

5.1.2.1 Actional Predication

Mathesius tackles the issue from the formal and semantic points of view respectively. From the formal point of view, the question is in what manner actional predication is expressed. In English, there are two ways, i. e. the finite verb form and the verbo-nominal predication. Verbo-nominal predication is "a predication that combines a verb and a noun to express what Czech denotes by the verb alone."

---

① See Firbas, 1996 for a detailed discussion of Mathesius's use of the term theme.

The forms of verbo-nominal predication can be divided into two categories. One is that "the action and its agent or patient are not expressed separately by the grammatical predicate and the grammatical subject but are merged in a synthetic expression operating as the grammatical subject, while the finite verb designates merely the existence of what the synthetic expression describes." For example:

(4) The white fog was there before there was any buying and selling in the London market.

(5) a. There was a steady coming and going of his aunts and uncles.
 b. His aunts and uncles came and went in a steady manner.

By Mathesius' analysis "any buying and selling in the London market" in (4) is the grammatical subject, and "a steady coming and going of his aunts and uncles" in (5)a is the grammatical subject, which results from the merging of the agent ("his aunts and uncles") and the action ("came and went"). If the meaning of (5)a is to be expressed by means of the grammatical subject and the grammatical predicate separately, presumably the sentence would be something like (5)b.

When *there*-constructions are used, there may exist such reasons as 1) the subject is unknown or need not be expressed, 2) requirement of the FSP (cf. Quirk et al., 1972:958—959), 3) tendency to conceive action as a mere fact. (See Kuno & Takami, 2004, for another functional approach to the *there*-construction.)

The other category is subdivided into four types: 1) possessive, 2) causative, 3) adverbial, and 4) adjectival. The four types are respectively illustrated in (6)—(11):

(6) I have a wash every day. (possessive)
(7) I have no hesitation in stating that you are wrong. (possessive)
(8) He has received a good education. (possessive)
(9) Well, you shall do the shopping and I shall do the cooking. (causative)
(10) They are now in full control of the state. (adverbial)
(11) They are frankly critical of the new move. (adjectival)

With possessive type, "the action is expressed by a noun which is joined to the grammatical subject by the copula *to have* or another verb of a similar meaning," (1975:105) as in (6)—(8). The reason for Mathesius to regard the verb *to have* as a copula is that it functions more as a link verb than express a possessive meaning. The fact that (6)—(7) can be rewritten as (12)—(13) implies that the semantic focus in (6)—(7) is on the verbal noun:

(12) I wash every day.
(13) I do not hesitate in stating that you are wrong.

The reason for the use of *have* + a noun of activity (e.g. *to have a smoke*, *to have a shave*) is that this construction helps "to permit the activity to be regarded as a unitary event which can be numbered," (Nida, 1993:39) just as Nida (1993:39) believes that the verbs *make* and *do* are "semantically empty" in such phrases as *to make a talk* and *to do a dance*. Furthermore, this construction offers one more alternative to qualify the activity. (cf. Jespersen's 〈1924:137—138, 1927:234—235〉 discussion of the cognate object construction. Also see Wierzbicka, 1987, for her discussion of why *to have a drink* is acceptable while *to have an eat* is unacceptable.) However, the term "possessive" is misleading, for nothing can be regarded as possessed in (6)—(8). (6) expresses a unitary activity and (8) is pseudo-active in that it is active in form but passive in meaning. "Education" is a process rather than a tangible object that can be affected by an action, and (8) may be rewritten as "He is well educated," which clearly shows the patient role of the grammatical subject "he."

With causative type, the action is "expressed by a noun which is joined to the subject by the verbs of the meaning *to do*, *to perform*," as in (9). However, verbs are basically doings and beings. *To do* is generic in meaning. Why is "do the shopping" causative? If it is causative in the sense that the subject causes himself to do the shopping, then "I walk every day" may as well be regarded as causative, for "to walk" is a kind of doing and the subject causes himself to walk.

With adverbial type, "the action is again expressed by a noun, which, however, in this case has adverbial form, i.e. it is construed as a prepositional phrase, the verb merely denoting that the subject is in some relation to the action." However, (10) is not an action but rather a state. And a prepositional phrase is not necessarily an adverbial form. Although a prepositional phrase may often function as an adverbial, it may also function as a predicative, attributive, and even occasionally as a subject and as a prepositional complement. (Quirk et al., 1972: 304—305) Observe the following sentences:

(14) Between six and seven will suit me. (Quirk et al., 1972:305)
(15) He crawled out from under the table.

With adjectival type, the action is expressed by an adjective as in (11). In Mathesius's view (1975:106), "English can express action by an adjective," since the English adjective can denote both a permanent quality and a temporary feature, valid only with respect to the situation which the predicate expresses. It is arguable whether (11) is an action or not.

Mathesius attempts a formal classification here; however, "possessive" and "causative" are semantic terms and "adverbial" and "adjectival" are grammatical terms.

The verbo-nominal predication is a case of nominal tendency of Modern English. This becomes clearer particularly through Czech-English contrastive studies. (Vachek, 1961)

In addition to the formal classification of actional predication as shown above, Mathesius also attempts a semantic classification by dividing actional predication into active and passive, active being further subdivided into causality as (16)—(18) and perceptivity as (19), and passive being further subdivided into five groups. The five groups of passive actional predication are: 1. be + -ed, 2. qualifying, 3. adverbial, 4. possessive (subject being directly or indirectly affected), and 5. perceptive, and these five groups are illustrated in (20)—(24). Observe the following sentences:

(16) Modern means of travel have shrunk our world.　(active: causality)
(17) He made her cry.　(active: causality)
(18) I will have it sent to you.　(active: causality)
(19) He saw that.　(active: perceptivity)
(20) The book is bound by the binder.　(passive: be+-ed)
(21) They were subject to a cruel persecution.　(passive: qualifying)
(22) The ships are under construction.　(passive: adverbial)
(23) He had a country rearing.　(passive: possessive)
(24) He saw his fortune engulfed by the flood.　(passive: perceptive)

5.1.2.2 Qualifying Predication

The most frequent type of qualifying predication is the copulative type (be + noun, be + adjective, be + adverb of time, place, manner, etc., be + of, etc.) as in (25)—(28):

(25) He is a dreamer.　(be + noun)
(26) Are you quite serious?　(be + adjective)
(27) The girl was blue-eyed.　(be + adjective)
(28) Dinner was over.　(be + adverb of time)

5.1.2.3 Existential Predication

The existential predication refers to the *there* construction, "which states the existence of something." Noteworthy is that Mathesius attempts to account for this construction from the perspective of FSP. In his view, this construction helps to reconcile the conflicting requirements of FSP and the English grammaticalized word order, i.e. the English word order requires that the subject should precede the predicate in declarative sentences, but sometimes FSP requires that both the subject and the predicate carry new information. Since the English subject has largely acquired a thematic function, the SV word order may not work well to realize a FSP. Observe (29):

(29) There (Theme) // is a strong wind blowing outdoors (Rheme).

5.1.2.4 Possessive Predication

Possessive predication involves the possessor and the thing possessed (cf. Halliday's terms "possessor" "possessed"). Mathesius points out that either the possessor or the thing possessed may be taken as a starting point as in (30). And this suggests that two sentences may differ in focus although they are ideationally synonymous. Observe the following sentences:

(30) a. My father has a house.
 b. This house belongs to my father.

5.1.3 Object

Under this heading, Mathesius discusses 1) object of the accusative type, 2) object of the dative type, 3) object of the genitive type, and 4) other types of object.

5.1.3.1 Object of the Accusative Type

Object of the accusative type consists of three subtypes, i. e. 1) the category of affected object, 2) the category of created object, and 3) the category of temporary object.

In terms of the relations between the verb and the direct object, affected object means that the action expressed by the verb affects this object whose existence precedes the starting of the action, e. g. *to whitewash a room*, *to correct the homework*.

Created object means that "the action of the verb results in the creation of an object which continues to exist after the action of the verb has ceased," e. g. *to build a house*, *to paint a portrait*, *to write a letter*.

Temporary object means that "the object expresses merely the content of the action with which it both comes into existence and ceases to exist," e. g. *to play a game*, *to weep tears*. When viewed closely, the semantic relation between *to play* and *a game* is different from that between *to weep* and *tears*. *a game* specifies the content of the action of playing since one can also play a piano, but *tears* rather indicates the extent of the action of weeping.

Within the category of affected object, Mathesius makes further subdivisions. One is the category of perception verbs. With these verbs it is the subject that is affected, e. g. *to see something*, *to hear something*. The semantic relation is that of affectee—perception—causer. Another is the category of the goal, i. e. the object is the goal towards which the action proceeds, or reaches, or departs from, for instance, *to enter a house*, *to approach a house*, *to approach somebody*; *to leave the house*. The semantic relation is that of agent—action—place. And *to whitewash a room* and *to leave a room* are not exactly the same with reference to the semantic relation although Mathesius puts them into one class. Yet another is the category of instrumental object which includes objects that denote instruments (cf. Jespersen 1927:236—237), e. g. *to throw stones at somebody*, *to point one's finger at somebody*. *Stones* may be regarded as the content of the action of throwing and both *stones* and *somebody* may be regarded as affectee. In the corresponding Czech expressions, the objects are in the instrumental case.

The category of created object contains a subsidiary category, i. e. the category of quantitative complement. Observe Mathesius's illustrations:

(31) He paid five shillings for it.

(32) He answered a few words.

(33) He answered nothing.

Compared with *to build a house* and *to write a letter*, *five shillings* is not the result of paying in the sense that its existence precedes the action of paying. Rather, five shillings is one of different ways to pay for something. And *nothing* in (33) could hardly be regarded as a created object.

The category of temporary object may consist of two subclasses. One includes "instances where the temporary object expresses a content closely related to or identical with what is denoted by the verb." For instance, *to weep tears*, *to play a game*, *to laugh a short ugly laugh*, *to run a race*. In these expressions there is a close semantic relation between the verb and the object. The meaning of the object is already implied in the verb, therefore, these objects are often left out. When these objects are present, there may be a need to count the action (e. g. *to have a smile*) or to qualify the action (e. g. *to cough two dry coughs*). Another subclass includes objects that are not "predetermined by the semantics of the verb," e. g. *to look daggers*, *to nod approval*, *to smile a welcome*. In these expressions, what is normally expressed by verbal action (i. e. *to say*) is expressed by visual action.

5.1.3.2 Object of the Dative Type

From the view of syntactic structure, the object of the dative type in English is expressed in two ways. One is by the fixed construction with the preposition *to* (e. g. *to belong to*, *to happen to*, *to seem to*, *to yield to*, *to adhere to*, *to object to*), the other is by the so-called positional dative (e. g. *to find somebody a seat*, *to sing somebody a song*, *to give somebody something*, *to tell somebody something*) or its variable, the so-called variable prepositional dative (e. g. *to give something to somebody*, *to teach something to somebody*, *to tell something to somebody*). From the examples we can see that positional dative and variable prepositional dative are what some linguists label internal dative and external dative. (Wierzbicka, 1988)

From the view of semantic types, Mathesius discusses *dativus commodi* (dative of advantage), *dativus incommodi* (dative of disadvantage), *dativus ethicus* (ethical dative), *dativus sympatheticus* (dative of sympathetic interest) and *dativus judicantis* (dative of reference).

Dative of advantage and dative of disadvantage refer to the dative "denoting a person to whose advantage or disadvantage something is done." For example:

(34) a. I bought my son a coat. (positional dative)
b. I bought a coat for my son. (variable prepositional dative)
(35) a. I have bought a coat for myself.
b. I have bought myself a coat.
c. I have bought me a coat.

English uses the positional dative, variable prepositional dative or the prepositional *for* to express dative of advantage. In Mathesius's view (1975: 126-127), "*dativus commodi* referring to the subject is never expressed by the positional dative," i. e. when the subject and dative of advantage are identical, positional dative is not used as in (35)c, and this observation is similar to that made by Jespersen (1927:284), who, in discussing "*I buy me clothes*," points out that "this use of a pronoun of the same person as the subject (a reflexive pronoun without *self*) as an indirect object is not now so usual as in former times, and even the corresponding use of the pronouns with *self* is not very frequent, though by no means rare: the pronoun is generally felt as superfluous." However, some native speakers regard (35)c as perfect.

Dative of disadvantage is reflected in English constructions like *to take something from somebody, to steal something from somebody*. In addition to the adverbial adjunct with the prepositional *from*, the person afflicted can be expressed by the possessive as in (36):

(36) They stole all his money.

Ethical dative "expresses the speaker's interest in what he says about a person or thing or by which he intends to arouse the interest of the listeners." Mathesius believes that ethical dative does not exist in present-day English. In discussing *dativus ethicus* in his monumental English grammar, Jespersen (1927:285) thinks that it is better to regard *dativus ethicus* as "the affective (emotional) indirect object." Jespersen holds that *dativus ethicus* "is used to enliven the style by introducing a personal element, where it is not really necessary for the thought" and his examples are from Shakespeare, Sheridan, and Thackeray (e. g. He could knock *you* off forty Latin verses in an hour. W. M. Thackeary, Vanity Fair.).

Dative of sympathetic interest "denotes a person a part of whose body (or attire, etc.) is affected by the action expressed by the verb." It is expressed with the genitive case or possessive adjective in English. Observe the following sentences:

(37) He cut off the giant's head.

(38) He broke his leg.
(39) The oculist looked in my eyes.
(40) She looked me tenderly in the eyes.
(41) She looked at me severely. (W. Somerset Maugham, *The Moon and the Six Pence*)
(42) She looked at me with good-humoured contempt. (W. S. Maugham, *The Moon and the Six Pence*)

A noteworthy phenomenon is that a body part in the part-whole relation conceived as affected by the action may be expressed in two ways. In Mathesius's view (1975:127), the positional dative in (40) is marked with emotional colouring and the corresponding possessive construction in (39) is an objective unemotional one. Theoretically speaking, the difference between *to look in somebody's eyes* and *to look somebody in the eyes* might be one as Mathesius suggests. However, if (39) is unemotional in colouring, it is largely because of the fact that an oculist is not supposed to look at someone with emotion. If (40) is emotional in colouring, it is largely because of the presence of the word *tenderly*. In other words, the two words *oculist* and *tenderly* contribute considerably to the meaning suggested by Mathesius, and the structural meaning of these two constructions needs further verifying. In connection with this, compare (39)—(40) with (41)—(42) taken from Maugham's novel. In addition, what kinds of action can be viewed as affecting one's body part is worthy of interlingual contrastive studies.

Dative of reference "expresses the person to whom the evaluation applies." For example:
(43) Silence was a hell to me.
(44) It is difficult for me to tell him the truth.

5.1.3.3 Object of the Genitive Type

The object of the genitive type is expressed by the construction with the preposition *of*. The meaning of this construction, physical or figurative, is more or less appropriate to the partitive genitive as (45). With some verbs in this construction, the genitive meaning is lacking (e.g. *to think of*, *to speak of*, *to complain of*). Observe the following sentences:
(45) They partook of our meal.
(46) He has never tasted of success.
(47) He has drunk deeply of flattery.

5.1.3.4 Other Types of Objects

Other types of objects include 1) prepositional (e.g. *to believe in him*, *to comply with the rule*), 2) infinitival (e.g. *to learn to write*), 3) gerundal (e.g. *to like singing*). They are here formally classified, however, they may have different semantic relations. For example, *to learn to write* expresses mental action—content, and *to like singing* represents mental disposition—content.

Mathesius also discusses the double object of the verb in English. It may be classified as 1) dative + accusative, e. g. *to give somebody something*; 2) dative + genitive, e. g. *to tell somebody of something*; 3) accusative + genitive, e. g. *to accuse somebody of something*. In both groups 1) and 2), *somebody* may be regarded as the benefactee and *something* as the content of the action. In discussing the following sentences, Mathesius regards them as of the type accusative + accusative and (49) as double accusative proper,[①] however, they seem to differ in semantic relations. (48) appears to have a semantic relation of agent—action—affectee—content and (49) contains an idiom which may be regarded as describing the manner of the action of binding:

(48) He asked the boys a few questions.

(49) They bound him hand and foot.

5.1.4 Subject-predicate Relations

In Mathesius's view (1975:74—75), subject-predicate relations may be classified as 1) performance of an action, 2) suffering of an action, 3) experiencing of an action. Observe the following sentences:

(50) I looked at the picture.

(51) I was scolded.

(52) I saw him on the street when I went shopping.

In (50), the subject does the action of looking of his own will. There is an active relation between the subject and the predicate and the subject stands as an agent in relation to the predicate. In (51), "the subject is affected by an action issuing from some other agent." In (52), "the action may not be an activity performed by the agent of his own will, but he may merely be experiencing what is not within his power." In Mathesius's view, the semantic relation between the subject and the predicate constitutes a scale of performing—experiencing—suffering. Observe the verbs *continue*, *read*, and *fail* in the following sentences:

(53) He continued his walk. (agent, performing)

(54) Even when he was ill, he continued to be visited by his old friends. (experiencing)

(55) He reads English very well. (agent, performing)

(56) This book reads very well. (goal)

(57) He failed to come at the fixed hour. (agent, performing)

---

① Mathesius's analysis of (48) as accusative + accusative may result from the fact that in Old English *ascian* took two accusatives. (cf. Jespersen, 1924:175)

(58) He tried to persuade her but he failed in doing so. (experiencing)

In (53), the verb denotes an intentional activity whose realization depends upon the will of the subject. *Continue* also indicates the aspect of the action, ① and (53) may be rewritten as "he walked continuously." In (54), "the verb *continue* does not express an action dependent on the will of the subject, but merely denotes being in a neutral relation to a continuing activity." The subject *he* is neither the agent nor the patient in relation to the verb *to continue*. It is a patient in relation to the verb *to visit*.

In (55), the verb *reads* denotes an intentional activity and the subject is the performer of this action while in (56) the subject is the goal or the content of the action.

In (57), if the verb *failed* is understood to mean "He was expected to come but he did not do so," the subject then is the agent as "the result may be dependent on the will of the subject." In (58), the meaning of *failed* "is not an active relation between the subject and the action but something that resembles experiencing, which depends on conditions beyond the agent's power."

The point is that no matter what the semantic relation between the subject and the predicate may turn out to be, English verbs can pass from one category into another without any formal change. And this is in contradistinction to Czech, for "In Czech it is usually clear at first sight to which of the above categories a verb belongs."

5.1.5 Object-predicate Relations

In relation to this issue, Mathesius discusses 1) subjective verbs (= intransitive verbs), 2) objective verbs (=transitive verbs), and 3) reflexive verbs.

A subjective verb expresses an action which is complete in itself (e.g. *to sleep*), and an objective verb expresses "an action that is not complete in itself, but requires a complement." (e.g. *to beat*) Observe the following sentences:

(59) Everyone can apply this rule to a special case.
(60) This rule applies to many special cases.
(61) He visited Boston last year.
(62) They are visiting in Boston.
(63) We attended the meeting.
(64) In addition to the representatives of the army, many civil officials attended.

The point is that many English verbs can be used both transitively and intransitively without any formal change. And this is different from Czech, for instance, the Czech verb *navstevovat nekoho* (to visit somebody) is only

---

① Mathesius (1975:68—73) discusses verbal aspect and treats it as an aspectual modification of verbs, the other two aspectual modifications of verbs being tense and mood.

transitive while the English verb *to visit* is used both transitively and intransitively. Another point is that the transitive and intransitive meanings of one and the same English verb sometimes are expressed with different verbs in Czech as in (65)—(67). (Mathesius 1975:77):

(65) to run vt. to cause something to run, keep going: *ridit*
to run vi. to move faster than at a walking speed: *bezet*
(66) to grow vt. to cultivate (e. g. to grow wheat): *pestovat*
to grow vi. increase in size, weight, length, etc. : *rust*
(67) to shrink vt. to make something smaller: *zmensit*
to shrink vi. to become smaller: *scvrkat se*

5.1.6 Functional Sentence Perspective (FSP)

Mathesius (1975:79) holds that "the central issue of functional syntax is the problem of the sentence." The issue concerns the definition of the sentence, arrangement of sentence elements, and analysis of grammatical syntactic functions. Approaching the sentence from the functional point of view and examining it as a tool of communication, Mathesius believes that a majority of sentences (he confines his research to declarative sentences) contain two basic elements. One is the element about which something is stated, the other is what is stated about that element. Mathesius calls the former **"the basis of the utterance"** (*vychodiste vypovedi*) and the latter **"the nucleus of the utterance"** (*jadro vypovedi*). In his Czech writings, Mathesius used three terms in discussing theme, *vychodiste* (point of departure), *tema* (theme), and *zaklad* (basis, foundation). Later, he dropped the term *vychodiste* and used the terms *tema* and *zaklad* synonymously. (Firbas, 1987; 1992; 1996) The terms have come to be replaced by "theme" and "rheme," which were introduced in 1957 by Jan Firbas.

In Mathesius's view, the patterning of the sentence into the theme and the rheme is the **functional sentence perspective (FSP)** "because this patterning is determined by the functional approach of the speaker." Mathesius's (1939) original Czech term is *aktualni cleneni vetne* (actual sentence division), which has come to be replaced by the term "functional sentence perspective," introduced by Jan Firbas. (Daneš et al., 1974:219—220; Daneš, 1987b: 24; Firbas, 1992:336; Qian, 2001b; 2002; 2004b; 2007; 2008)[1]

---

[1] It should be noted that Mathesius uses the term perspective in different senses. In addition to functional sentence perspective, he (1975:125—126) also talks about "the object perspective," e. g. in the constructions *to hang pictures on the wall* and *to hang the wall with pictures* "the object perspective is changed without any accompanying formal change in the verb." In the expressions *to run a business* (directly affected object), *to run a race* (temporary object), *to run a risk* (object of goal) "the same verb allows three different object perspectives."

The two elements of theme and rheme may be arranged in different ways. If the addresser takes the addressee into account, the addresser probably starts from what is known and proceeds to what is new. This theme-rheme order conforms to our usual cognitive procedure, and it is usually used in unemotional narration. Mathesius calls this order **"objective order."** If the addresser starts with the new element and adds the known element afterwards, this rheme-theme order is **"subjective order"** and it is usually used in emotional narration.

Theme and rheme belong to functional analysis of the sentence and subject and predicate belong to formal analysis of the sentence. Mathesius believes that they are not the same and should be strictly distinguished from each other. Grammatical subject and predicate may have evolved from a fixed manner of expressing the theme and the rheme, however, such correspondence could not have been of a long duration. If there lacks a correspondence between FSP and formal sentence structure, it is to be studied how different languages resolve the conflict between the formal patterning of the sentence (which is relatively fixed) and the functional patterning of the sentence (which is to adapt the formal patterning to the needs of a momentary situation). Compare the following sentences:

(68) a. *Tatinek* (T) // *napsal tenhle dopis* (R).
 b. Father (T) // wrote this letter (R).
(69) a. *Tenhle dopis napsel* (T) // *tatinek* (R).
 b. * This letter wrote (T) // father (R).
 c. This letter was written by father.
 d. It was father who wrote this letter.

In Czech, flexible word order is the most important device available for the clear expression of FSP. In English, word order has a grammatical function and the theme and the rheme of the utterance are often expressed by the grammatical subject and predicate respectively. Because of that, (69)a can not be rendered into English word for word since that would violate the English grammatical rule. To overcome this conflict between grammatical structure and FSP, English uses passive construction and syntactic periphrasis as in (69)c—d.

From the above discussion, some of Mathesius's characteristic features of his linguistic studies may be summarized as follows:

1. The principle of functional approach. "Functional linguistics takes the standpoint of the speaker." (Mathesius, 1929/1983:131) Functional

Chapter 5   Functional Syntax

linguistics, "relying on its experience with present-day language,[①] starts from the needs of expression and inquires what means serve to satisfy these communication needs in the language being studied. It thus proceeds from function to form." (Mathesius, 1929/1983:123) With this in mind one may understand why the question of the nature of encoding is the main topic of Mathesius' analysis of Present Day English and why the encoding process is divided into two parts: (a) functional onomatology, (b) functional syntax.

2. The principle of synchronic approach. Mathesius (1911/1983: 42) believes that "the procedure leading from the static to the dynamic issues [i. e. from synchronistic to diachronistic issues, J. V.] is the safest in linguistics."[②] In his (1927/1983:48−49) view the synchronic approach plays an important role in the following areas: 1) the study of problems connected with the expresssive and communicative function of language, 2) a full analysis of the basic grammatical functions (e. g. the function of the subject and of predication), 3) the study of meaning and of emotional elements in language, 4) "the study of the interdependence of two or more coexistent linguistic facts" (e. g. the interdependence of rhythm and word order), 5) the role of linguistic tendencies, 6) linguistic characterology.

It is to note that the Praguians' focus upon the functional and synchronic aspects of language in their linguistic research in no way implies an underestimation of the formal and diachronic aspects of language. Functional approach (from function to form, or from the needs of expression to the means of language, cf. Mathesius, 1929/1983:123) and formal approach (from form to function, cf. Mathesius, 1929/1983: 123) are just two approaches in linguistics, they differ in perspectives and complement each other. (Havránek 1928/1983:65)

3. The principle of contrastive approach. The contrastive approach permeates Mathesius' monograph (1975). In fact, his characterization of

---

[①]   Trnka (1948/1982:59), a Czech linguist and a founding member of the Prague Linguistic Circle, notes that Mathesius prefers "to observe language experience and speak only of language trends or tendencies." In his view, "The very concept of function would be unclear if one did not consider the factor of language internalizaiton." (Trnka, 1948/1982:58) "The observation of linguistic development leads to the recognition that language cannot be judged only from the standpoint of logical, intellectual values and relations. For a linguistic system to be a language it must be internalized. Only to the extent to which it is internalized, takes on the necessary expressiveness, becomes part of our self does it become a dynamic system capable of continuing development in time and space. We can experience linguistic internalization when we learn a foreign language." (Trnka, 1943/1982:41) "Suffice it to say that our concept of language internalization has a broader meaning because it includes the internalizing not only of affective but also of intellectual elements of language." (Trnka, 1948/1982:58)

[②]   The terms "static" and "dynamic" in Mathesius, 1911, is interpreted by his student Josef Vachek as "synchronistic" and "diachronistic," e. g. Vachek, 1983:3, 30, 43.

English is inseparable from his analytical comparison. (e.g. his discussion of the function of the subject in English, his characterization of different hierarchies of word order principles in English and Czech.) Take his discussion of the accusative object for example. Through comparison Mathesius (1975: 124—126) finds out three differences between English and Czech or German. Firstly, English uses the accusative object "in many instances where Czech and German have the dative." Secondly, English uses the accusative object where Czech and German use an adverbial adjunct. Thirdly, "English allows a change in the object perspective with the verb retaining the accusative construction" (e.g. *to hang pictures on the wall*, *to hang the wall with pictures*) while "Czech and German usually employ a derived or an altogether different verb." It is through analytical comparison that Mathesius was able to make shrewd observations and insightful remarks. Vachek (1980) states a fact when he regards Mathesius as forerunner of contrastive linguistic studies.

4. The principle of textual approach. Mathesius was "one of the forerunners of modern textological research." (Vachek, 1994) In his functional analysis of Prenent Day English Mathesius takes a textual approach in that he studies utterances rather than sentences.[①] For example, in exploring the function of the subject in English he (1975: 101) bases his discussion on an analytical comparison of a Czech utterance. In studying the two constructions of the verb *steal* (*to steal something from somebody*, *to steal somebody's something*) as related to *dativus incommodi*, he (1975: 127) points out that the tendency is to use the possessive construction "if the thing taken is the rheme of the utterance." (cf. *He had the sum of £20 in his pocket, but a thief stole it from him. He travelled alone, but was met by a thief who stole all his money*.)

As Hu (1994: 137; 2000: 12) and Jiang (2011: 18) observe, the Prague School not only initiated the functional approach but also laid the foundation for discourse analysis (or text linguistics) in modern linguistics.

5.2 František Daneš

František Daneš (1919—), a Czech linguist, is an important

[①] The Prague School makes a distinction between sentence and utterance. cf. "... we believe that it is useful to distinguish first of all the following two concepts of sentence: 1) the sentence as a minimal situationally anchored speech event, and 2) the sentence as a usual, standardized grammatical form of such an event. To prevent terminological confusion, we use the term *utterance* in the first sense, in accordance with a tradition that is deep-rooted in Czech linguistics; cf. e.g. Mathesius (1942: 59) definition: 'The sentence as the expression of a topical attitude to a fact is an utterance,' whereas the technical term *sentence* is left only for a typical syntactic form of utterance, characteristic of a given language." (Dokulil & Daneš, 1958/1994: 25) representative of the present-day Prague School. In 1964, Daneš published a paper entitled "A three-level approach to syntax." He believes that "much confusion in the discussions of syntactic problems could be avoided if elements and rules of three different levels were distinguished." The three levels are 1) level of the grammatical structure of sentence, 2) level of the semantic structure of sentence, and 3) level of the organization of utterance. Since 1964, Daneš (1970a—b; 1974) has written a series of papers devoted to the third level. He has also written some papers on the relation between the syntactic structure and the semantic structure of sentence (e.g. 1968; 1978; 1987a). Of the latter ones, Sentence Patterns and Predicate Classes (1987a) is quite representative. The following discussion focuses upon these two papers.

5.2.1 A Three-level Approach to Syntax

In 1962, Noam Chomsky published a paper entitled "The logical basis of linguistic theory." Daneš believes that there exists a confusion of concepts in Chomsky's discussion of "grammatical relation," for example:

(70) John is easy to please.
(71) John is eager to please.
(72) Did John expect to be pleased by the gift?
(73) The gift pleased John.

Chomsky states that in (70) "*John* is the direct object of *please* (the words are grammatically related as in *This pleases John*)," in (71) *John* "is the logical subject of *please* (as in *John pleases someone*)" and in (72) the expressions *John*, *please* and *gift* are grammatically related as they are in (73). As Daneš (1964:225) points out, "it is even the terminology ('direct object' 'grammatically related' 'logical subject') that reveals the confusion of notions."

By our usual practice, direct object is a syntactic concept, logical subject is a semantic concept, and grammatical relations refer to formal grammatical features including direct object. Therefore, from the syntactic perspective, *John* in (70)—(71) are both grammatical subjects. From a semantic point of view, *John* in (70)—(71) might be called logical object and logical subject; however, these terms are actually not used in our analysis of the semantic structure of the sentence and such terms as agent and patient are used instead. Jespersen (1924:150) also objects to assigning a "logical" and "psychological" meaning to the term "subject" and maintains that the term "subject" should refer to the grammatical subject.

Chomsky's problem lies in that he seemed to have confused the grammatical structure with the semantic structure of the sentence and he seemed not to have distinguished the terms applicable on different levels and not to have distinguished the grammatical relation from the logical relation. In

Chomsky's view, for instance, the grammatical relation among *John*, *please* and *gift* is the same in (72)—(73); but *John* functions as a grammatical subject and object in (72)—(73) respectively and stands in different grammatical relations to the other sentence elements. What Chomsky was driving at, one may suppose, is that the two sentences with an identical syntactic structure may not necessarily have an identical semantic relation as in (70)—(71) and the two sentences with different syntactic structures may not necessarily have different semantic relations as in (72)—(73). This certainly deserves adequate attention.

To avoid the confusion in the discussion of syntactic problems, different levels of syntax are to be distinguished, elements and rules of different levels are to be distinguished, and different terms are to be used in the description of elements of different levels. Hence Daneš puts forward his idea of three different levels of syntax: 1) level of the grammatical structure of sentence, 2) level of the semantic structure of sentence, and 3) level of the organization of utterance.

5.2.1.1 The Grammatical Level

Daneš (1964:227) thinks that the grammatical level "can be characterized by the fact that it is autonomous, and not onesidedly dependent on the semantic content; consequently, it is a rather self-contained and determining component. Thus, the grammatical categories such as subject etc. are not based on the semantic content, but on the syntactic form only." What is noteworthy is that this view is similar to that of Chomsky's (1957). But how could it be proved that the grammatical level is autonomous? Daneš (1964:227) holds that "the autonomy of the grammatical form reveals itself in the fact of diversity of languages (while the semantic categories, being extra-linguistic, seem to be universal, or nearly so)."

5.2.1.2 The Semantic Level

Daneš (1964:226) thinks that the elements of the semantic structure are the generalizations of concrete lexical meanings and these generalizations are abstract categories (e.g. living being, individual, quality, action) or relations between these categories (e.g. action as feature of an individual). The sentence structure is based on the semantic relations, and these semantic relations are derived from nature and society and may be classified into certain kinds such as 1) actor—action, 2) the bearer of a quality/state—state, and 3) action—an object resulting from the action or touched by it. At the end of his paper, Daneš mentions his concept of the semantic pattern ("on the level of syntactic semantics") and he mentions in passing five semantic patterns without examples: 1) process, 2) agent—action—the object of action, 3) the bearer of state—state, 4) individual—predication of a feature to it, and 5) individual—placing it into a class.

Daneš seems not to have attempted a detailed classification of semantic patterns and he neither illustrates the semantic patterns nor defines the semantic elements (therefore one is not sure whether or not his actor and agent are identical). Now each of the five semantic patterns mentioned above are illustrated with one sentence as follows:

(74) *Prsi.* (rains. cf. It is raining)

(75) He broke the window.

(76) He sat in a chair.

(77) He is kind.

(78) He is a poet.

Judging from his remarks, Daneš's Process refers to that kind of Czech sentences which refer to natural phenomena. "In Czech such sentences have a special form, viz. the verb without subject, no subject being conceivable." (Mathesius, 1975:83) They are subjectless and do not permit an insertion of a pronominal element as the subject. In contrast, another kind of Czech sentences permits both absence and presence of the pronominal element (as the subject). In English, French and German, sentences that refer to natural phenomena have a formal grammatical subject. (cf. *It rains. Il pleut. Es regnet.*)

5.2.1.3 The Organizational Level

The issue to be studied at this level is "how the semantic and grammatical structures function in the very act of communication, i.e. at the moment they are called upon to convey some extra-linguistic reality reflected by thought and are to appear in an adequate kind of perspective." (Firbas, 1962; Daneš, 1987b:23—26) With Daneš, the term sentence may refer to the notion of a sentence pattern which can be filled in with particular words and sentence patterns are realized through concrete utterances in the act of communication. "The utterance refers to a concrete piece of reality, to a particular situation and is an organic constituent of a discourse (text)." (Daneš, 1970:133) This distinction between sentence and utterance can be found in other Prague School linguists as well.

One reason to regard the organization of utterance as a level lies in that special means of organizing utterances have been wrongly classed with grammar (syntax) or stylistics. Through the distinction of this level, Daneš attempts "a theory of utterance" and a study of "all non-grammatical means and processes of organizing utterance and even context should be treated (together with grammatical ones)." (Daneš, 1964:228) One important means of organizing utterance is functional sentence perspective (FSP), which has been a focus of the Praguian syntactic studies ever since Mathesius. (Firbas, 1957; 1962;

1987a; 1987b; 1991; 1992; 1996a; 1996b; 1997; 1998; Daneš, 1964; 1970a; 1970b; 1974a; 1974b; Sgall, 1967; 1979; 1987a; 1987b; 2003)①

Daneš's three-level theory (syntactic, semantic, discourse) finds an echo in other linguists (Firbas, 1987:55), for instance, Dik's (1980:49—50) belief that "functional grammar gives a prominent role to three distinct 'layers' of functional notions," i. e. semantic functions (Agent, Goal, etc.), syntactic functions (Subject, Object, etc.), and pragmatic functions (Theme and Tail, Topic and Focus); Halliday's (1974; 1985) three metafunctions; and Panfilow's three levels. (Helbig, 1973:105)

5.2.2 Sentence Patterns and Predicate Classes

Daneš (1987a:3) admits that "My attempt at the syntactico-semantic analysis, description, and interpretation of the sentence structure derives, in principle, from Mathesius' concept of functional onomatology and functional syntax." He points out three assumptions which he regards as especially relevant to Mathesius: 1) the distinction between the sentence as a unit of the grammatical system and the sentence as a minimal utterance from the textual point of view, 2) "the construction of sentences is based on predication, whereby particular naming units are put into mutual relations by means of a predicate; thus the central task of functional syntax is seen to be the study of predicates," and 3) the structure of sentence types "may be best performed in terms of sentence patterns."

5.2.2.1 GSP, SSP, and CSP

With these assumptions Daneš attempts a study of sentence patterns and predicate classes. His central idea is that "the structure of the sentence may be described by means of the correlation of a formal grammatical (syntactic) sentence pattern (GSP) and a semantic (propositional or ideational) sentence pattern (SSP). Such a correlation of patterns will be called complex sentence pattern (CSP)." (Daneš, 1987a:4) For example:

(79) The farmer killed a duckling.

      CSP N/Agent $<=$ VF/Action $=>$ N/Patient

In this formula, the elements on the left side of / are of GSP, those on the right side of / are of SSP, $<=$ $=>$ denotes the dominance (valency) relation, and VF stands for *verbum finitum* (finite verb). The so-called CSP refers to the correlation between GSP and SSP, i. e. what kind of SSP a GSP represents and how a SSP is realized through a GSP. In fact, GSP and SSP are concomitant. Daneš combines the

---

① Many of Firbas' papers published in *Brno Studies in English* (BSE, 1959-present) are now available in their full electronic versions at http://www.phil.muni.cz/wkaa/home/publikace/bse-plone-verze/.

syntactic and semantic formulas and gives their correspondences; however, a GSP is normally described in terms of SVO instead of NVN.

In Daneš's view, the finite verb (in the predicate function) represents the organizing centre of sentence structure. On the grammatical level, its valency properties determine the number of the functional positions (i. e. subject, object, etc.). On the semantic level, the finite verb determines the number and roles of the involved participants. Therefore, "any attempt at ascertaining the system of sentence patterns of a given language has to be based on a systematic inquiry into the syntactically relevant properties of verbs, functioning as predicators (predicate expressions)." (Daneš, 1987a:5) Take the English verb *to kill* for example. Its semantic valency determines that the process involves two participants, an agent and a patient. Its GSP is N <=VF => N, its SSP is Agent <=Action=> Patient, and its CSP is N/Agent <= VF/Action = > N/Patient. "Generally speaking, with any predicator, its valency potential (corresponding to a certain GSP), its field of intention (corresponding to a certain SSP), and a correspondence rule correlating the two structures, are associated and should be ascertained." (Daneš, 1987a:6)

Nevertheless, there lacks a one-to-one relation between GSP and SSP. (Daneš, 1964:227) One and the same GSP may represent different SSPs. For instance, N < = VF = > N (i. e. SVO) can describe the following three different kinds of SSP:

(80) <kill: farmer, duckling>
   The farmer killed a duckling.
   SSP: Actor-Material Process-Goal
(81) <contain: milk, water>
   The milk contains water.
   SSP: Possessor-Relational Proc. -Possessed
(82) <hate: father, lie>
   Father hates lie.
   SSP: Sensor-Mental Proc. -Phenomenon

As Daneš does not offer a detailed analysis, (80)−(82) is analyzed according to Halliday (1985).

GSP has a polysemous character. On the one hand, one and the same GSP can represent different SSPs; on the other hand, one and the same syntactic element may be performed by different semantic elements. If one GSP could express only one SSP, then the system of sentence patterns would be rather complicated and that would violate the principle of economy in communication.

5.2.2.2 The Issue of Synonymy

Observe the following sentences:
(83) a. The farmer killed the duckling.

b. The duckling was killed (by the farmer).

The two GSPs of (83) are filled with an identical set of lexical items and identical role distribution. *Farmer* and *duckling* are agent and patient in both respectively. If the lexical items are identical while the role distributions are different, e.g. *the duckling killed the farmer*, then the semantic function of *duckling* changes. In Daneš's view (1987a:6), "there may exist couples or triads of GSPs that yield, when filled with an identical set of lexical items and identical role distribution, an identical SSP; such GSPs may be regarded as synonymous." However, the syntactic and semantic structures in (83) are not identical in terms of linear arrangement. As Daneš says, this synonymy does not mean a full equivalence and the two GSPs in (83) reveal a different semantic hierarchization of their participants. If two GSPs are completely identical, the semantic difference may be reflected through phonological means instead of word order, for instance, intonation and accent.

Intralingual contrast in (83) indicates that two synonymous sentences may reveal a difference in perspective. One wonders whether there exists a similar difference when an experience is expressed in different languages. Observe the following sentences:

(84) a. Peter stole a book from his brother.
　　b. *Peter stahl ein Buch seinem Bruder.*

Daneš (1987a:7) thinks that these sentences "differ, at least, in the way of presenting the legal possessor of the stolen thing." In his view, "*Peter*" is presented in (84)a "as 'source of acquisition,' since the verb *steal* is evidently classed with verbs of acquisition (*buy, borrow...*)"; and in (84)b "as the person to whose detriment the action (classed as deprivation) has been performed (cf. the dative case)."

It seems that the English wording here fails to express what Daneš intends to say. In correspondence to his view, Daneš is expected to have contrasted *his brother* with *seinem Bruder*, but he talks about *Peter* instead and mistakes *Peter* (it should be *seinem Bruder*) for the person to whose detriment the action has been performed.

Daneš does not discuss the issue why an identical concept (*to steal something from somebody*) or an identical experience is differently encoded in English and German and whether this difference is related with different world views. Neither does he explain why the so-called verbs of acquisition have different syntactic structures (e.g. *to steal something from somebody, to buy somebody something, to buy something for somebody, to borrow something from somebody*) and what the correlations there are between the relevant GSPs and SSPs. (84)b may be accounted for with reference to the fact that some Indo-European languages use nouns, dative pronouns in particular, to express misfortune, i.e. the so-called "dative of misfortune." (Wierzbicka, 1988:

278—279) Observe the following sentences:
- (85) a. *Ihm ist die Frau gestorben.* (Wierzbicka, 1988:278)
    (to-him is the wife dead.)
  b. His wife died on him.
- (86) a. *Ils lui ont tué sa femme.* (Wierzbicka, 1988:279)
    (they to-him have killed his wife.)
  b. *Sie haben ihm seine Frau getötet.*
    (They have to-him his wife killed.)
  c. They have killed his wife.
- (87) a. *Jan ztratil klice.* (Daneš, 1987a)
    (John lost his keys.)
  b. *Janovy klice se ztratily.*
    (John's keys got lost.)
  c. *Janovi se ztralily klice.*
    (to-John got lost keys.)

5.2.2.3 Description with Semantic Formula

Daneš attempts to describe predicates with semantic formula. Take (84) for example. *stealing* is an action in which a person (agent) brings it about that a thing passes from its initial legal possessor to the causer of this change. It might be formulated as follows:

$$x \ A \ ((z \ LC \ y) \ T \ (z \ LC \ x))$$

x denotes an agent, y the initial possessor, z the held thing, and A an action. The content of this action consists of an initial situation (z LC y) and a final situation (z LC x), and these two situations are related by the relator of transition T. And these two situations represent two-place relations of local-occurence LC. The formula may be read as follows: "x brings about that z passes from the initial situation, in which it is held by y, to the final situation, in which it is held by x." (Daneš, 1987a:11) x is agent in respect to A and new possessor in respect to LC. z is the held thing in respect to LC and also patient. y is possessor in respect to LC. Semantic formula reveals that agent and patient appear to be the primary role of x and z respectively.

Semantic formula can represent a set of predicates similar in meaning. For example, *clean*, *pump* and *empty* all mean *removal of co-occurrence* (i.e. to clean is to remove dirt from a dirty thing, to pump is to remove water out of the well, and to empty is to remove the contents of the vessel). Of the two co-occurring items, y is a "container" and z its "contents." The final situation is a negation of the initial situation as in (88). A counterpart to this set of predicates is the set of predicates of "co-occurrence accomplishment", e.g. *load*, *fill*. With these predicates, the situation changes from the initial one of non-cooccurrence to the final one of co-occurrence as in (89):

x A ((y LC z) T (y LC z))

(88) a. She cleaned the cloth (of the stain).

b. She cleaned the stain (from the cloth).

x A ((y LC z) T (y LC z))

(89) a. We loaded the boxcars with wheat.

b. We loaded the wheat into the boxcars.

(88) and (89) indicate that an experience may be represented from two perspectives. There may exist different syntactic choices correlated with different perspectives. Therefore, different syntactic structures in describing an experience as in (88)—(89) indicate that they are not absolutely synonymous. In Daneš's view, similar cases exist in other languages such as German, Czech and Russian, however, he does not illustrate this point. ①

5.2.2.4 Predicate Classes

Daneš classifies predicates according to their syntactically relevant semantic structures. He describes and represents the types of predicate structures by means of a Semantic Formula (a modified relational logic notation). He divides predicates into two major classes: static and dynamic.

Static predicates are subdivided into three groups: 1) two-place predicates, 2) one-place predicates, and 3) unarticulated predicates.

Two-place predicates consist of 1) location in space (x L y: *be placed, be situated, stand*), 2) local co-occurrence (x LC y), 3) possession (P: *have, belong*), 4) mental possession (MP: *know*), 5) qualification (x QL y: *He is rich. She appeared tired*), 6) quantification (x QN y: *His reasons were many*) and some other relations.

One-place predicates consist of 1) existence, nonexistence (x E: *There are no gods*), 2) position (x POS: *She was kneeling*), and some other relations.

Unarticulated predicates refer to the Czech subjectless sentences that describe natural phenomena.

Dynamic predicates are divided into two classes: processes and mutations. Processes are subdivided into two groups: action processes and non-action

---

① One thing that Daneš does not deal with is the semantic difference between (88)a and (88)b or that between (89)a and (89)b. It is noticed by numerous linguists (e.g. Jespersen, 1924; Fillmore, 1968, 1977) that some English verbs allow two perspectives or a choice of perspectives to present one and the same event, e.g. *to present something to somebody, to present somebody with something*. In some cases the difference seems to be related to the partitive-holisitc view of the event, e.g. (a) He sprayed paint on the wall. (b) He sprayed the wall with paint. Cf. Jespersen's (1927:214) examples: the garden swarms with bees = bees swarm in that place. This stream abounds in fish = fish abounds in this stream. Jespersen (1927:215) believes that "similar shiftings are frequent in other languages" such as German, Danish, and Swedish.

processes. Action processes are subdivided into close actions and open actions and non-action processes are subdivided into close processes and open processes. Observer:

 close actions: x PR p
 (90) He is jumping.
 (91) He often sings.
 open actions: x A p(y), x A p(y,z)
 (92) He greeted her.
 (93) He attacked the enemy.
 close processes: x B p
 (94) The sun is shining.
 (95) He coughed.
 open processes: x B p(y), x B p(y,z)
 (96) The air carries sound.
 (97) It smells after onion.

Close actions involve the participant processor (PR) only as in (90) — (91). Open actions involve two participants at least as in (92) — (93) and the SF reads as "x performs a process p implying right-hand participants y, z." However, this reading offered by Daneš (1987:14) does not appear to match his semantic formulas and his illustrations, for it implies two right-hand participants (y, z) whereas his semantic formulas imply that the right-hand participants involved in an open action may be one or more than one.

Close processes imply the participant "bearer (of process)" (B) only as in (94) — (95). And open processes imply two participants at least as in (96) — (97). As (90) — (97) indicate, the difference between action processes and non-action processes lies in that x (i.e. grammatical subject) in action processes is usually an agent while x in non-action processes is usually the bearer of the process.

Another kind of dynamic predicates is mutations. "They imply a process of change that can be interpreted as a transition (T) from an initial or opening situation (o) to a final or closing one (c)." (Danes, 1987a:15). Daneš divides mutations into two kinds: agentive mutations and non-agentive mutations. Agentive mutations are "mutations in which the change process T will be conceived of as an (intentional, purposeful) action of a personal element, as a change brought about by an 'agent'" while non-agentive mutations "conceive of the transitional process as a simple, spontaneous change of entity, disregarding possible agents or causes." (Daneš, 1987a:16 — 17). Daneš's discussion of mutations may be summarized as follows:

 Agentive mutations:
  (i) Existence: x A ((y E) T (y E)), e.g. *create, build, construct*
  (ii) Non-existence: x A ((y E) T (y E)), e.g. *annihilate, dissolve*

(iii) Location: (y L z), e. g. *take out*, *remove*, *insert*, *place*
(iv) Position: (y POS z), e. g. *seat*
(v) Qualification: (y QL z), e. g. *close*, *open*, *press*, *repair*
(vi) Possession: (y P z), e. g. *acquire*, *borrow*, *buy*, *gain*, *give*, *sell*
(vii) Local-cooccurrence: (x LC y), e. g. *clean*, *load*, *pump*
Non-agentive mutations:
(viii) Existence: (x E), e. g. *arise*, *be born*, *cease*, *die out*
(ix) Location: (x L y), e. g. *appear*, *disappear*
(x) Position: (x POS z), e. g. *fall*
(xi) Qualification: (x QL y), e. g. *soften*, *become tame*, *grow black*
(xii) Possession: (x P y), e. g. *get*
(xiii) Local-cooccurrence: (x LC y), e. g. *lose (one's keys)*

This table indicates that the semantic categories involved in agentive and non-agentive mutations are more or less the same, however, there are some problems. First, Daneš regards existence and nonexistence as two types in classifying agentive mutations while he puts existence and nonexistence into one type in classifying non-agentive mutations (cf. ⟨i⟩, ⟨viii⟩). And he offers no reason for this inconsistency. Second, Daneš's notion of possession consists of subgroups like "taking" and "giving" in (vi) and it excludes "giving" in (xii). Third, the boundary between Location and Position appears unclear (cf. ⟨iii⟩, ⟨iv⟩, ⟨ix⟩, ⟨x⟩). As Daneš neither gives his criteria of these classifications nor defines these semantic categories, it would be difficult to apply his theory to practice.

With his focus upon classification of predicates, Daneš appears to have paid less attention to the semantic roles of participants and less attention to verb-noun relations. (cf. the study of verb-noun relations by Fillmore, 1968; 1977) In his view (1987a:19—20), the semantic roles of participants may be arrived at on different levels of abstraction and generalization, and the multi-level character of semantic sentence structures may result in combined or double roles. Therefore, Daneš regards the labeling of roles as "an issue of a mnemonic significance only" and prefers to ground his investigation on the analysis and classification of predicate structures.

5.3 Michael Halliday

Michael Halliday (1925—) is a British linguist. He is probably the most important representative of the Systemic-Functional School. He is closely associated with the London School and the Prague School. (Halliday, 1985: xxii; Daneš, 1987a—b) His contribution to syntactic semantics is "of a fundamental and pioneering character." (Daneš, 1987a:3) The following introduction focuses on his idea of transitivity.

Halliday holds that language has three metafunctions, ideational, interpersonal and textual. Language in its ideational function represents patterns of experience of the world, or in Halliday's (1985:101) terms, it enables human beings "to build a mental picture of reality, to make sense of their experience of what goes on around them and inside them." Halliday calls this reflective, experiential aspect of meaning TRANSITIVITY.

Transitivity is a grammatical system. It "specifies the different types of process that are recognized in the language, and the structures by which they are expressed." The basic semantic framework for the representation of processes consists of three components 1) the process itself, 2) participants in the process, and 3) circumstances associated with the process.

5.3.1 Processes

Halliday recognizes six process types: 1) material processes, 2) mental processes, 3) relational processes, 4) behavioural processes, 5) verbal processes, and 6) existential processes. He (1985:128) regards the first three types as principal ones and the last three types as subsidiary ones. Of the three subsidiary types, behavioural processes are intermediate between material and mental processes; verbal and existential processes are close to mental and relational processes respectively. Halliday's (1985:131) view on the relations among these process types may be represented like this: material-behavioural-mental-verbal-relational-existential.

5.3.1.1 Material Processes

Material processes are processes of doing, for instance,

(98) The lion sprang. (Actor-Process)

(99) The lion caught the tourist. (Actor-Process-Goal)

The material process involves an actor and often a goal as well. "The Actor is the 'logical subject' of older terminology, and means the one that does the deed," and the term "Goal" implies "directed at." (Halliday, 1985: 102—103) Actor and Goal correspond to Agent and Patient respectively.

5.3.1.2 Mental Processes

Mental processes are processes of sensing, for example:

(100) Mary liked the gift. (Senser-Process-Phenomenon)

(101) The gift pleased Mary. (Phenomenon-Process-Senser)

A mental process consists of two potential participants, Senser and Phenomenon. "The senser is the conscious being that is feeling, thinking, or seeing. The Phenomenon is that which is 'sensed' —felt, thought or seen." (Halliday, 1985: 111) The category of mental process consists of three principal subtypes 1) perception (seeing, hearing, etc.), 2) affection (liking, fearing, etc.)and 3) cognition (thinking, knowing, understanding, etc.).

5.3.1.3 Relational Processes

Relational processes are processes of being. "The central meaning of clauses of this type is that something is." Halliday (1985:112—113) classifies relational process into different types: 1) intensive "x is a," 2) circumstantial "x is at a," and 3) possessive "x has a." Each of these types come in two modes: (ⅰ) attributive "a is an attribute of x," (ⅱ) identifying "a is the identity of x." Observe the following sentences:

attributive mode (Carrier-Process-Attribute)

(102) Sarah is wise. (intensive)

(103) The fair is on a Tuesday. (circumstantial)

(104) Peter has a piano. (possessive)

identifying mode (Identified-Process-Identifier)

(105) Tom is the leader. (intensive)

(106) Tomorrow is the tenth. (circumstantial)

(107) The piano is Peter's. (possessive)

An essential difference between the attributive and the identifying modes is that the identifying clause is reversible whereas the attributive clause is not. Observe the following sentences:

(108) a. Tom is the leader.

　　　b. The leader is Tom.

(109) a. Sarah is wise.

　　　b. *Wise is Sarah.

Halliday's (1985:114) account runs thus: in the attributive clause there is only one participant (the Attribute is not a participant); whereas in the identifying clause there are two participants. A general principle of English grammar is that any participant can become the subject, hence the identifying clause may have either the Identified or the Identifier as the subject. In his view, the reversible form of the identifying clause (in which the Identifier becomes the subject as ⟨b⟩) is in fact a passive clause. This seems to imply that as the verb *to be* has no special passive form, one has to resort to other means to express a passive meaning when called for.

5.3.1.4 Behavioural Processes

Behavioural processes are of physiological and psychological behaviour, such as breathing, dreaming, smiling, coughing. The process usually has one participant, the Behaver. Observe the following sentences:

(110) He neither laughs nor smiles. (Behaver-Process)

(111) He sighed deeply. (Behaver-Process-circumstance)

(112) He weeps for you. (Behaver-Process-circumstance)

5.3.1.5 Verbal Processes

Verbal processes are processes of saying. A verbal process may consist of three participants, the Sayer, the Receiver, and the Verbiage. The Sayer is the addresser, and it may be a human being or something related with symbolic exchange of meaning. The Receiver is the addressee "to whom the verbalization is addressed." The Verbiage is the verbalization itself or the content of message. Observe the following sentences:

(113) He said that. (Sayer-Process-Verbiage)

(114) The notice tells you to keep quiet. (Sayer-Process-Receiver-Verbiage)

(115) She asked me some questions. (Sayer-Process-Receiver-Verbiage)

5.3.1.6 Existential Processes.

Existential processes represent that something exists or happens (cf. Mathesius' existential predication). It is usually realized by *there*-construction. The Existent in the process may be an event, an object or a human being. Observe the following sentences:

(116) There was a storm.   (Process-Existent)

(117) On the wall there hangs a picture.   (circumstance-Process-Existent)

(118) There's a man at the door.   (Process-Existent-circumstance)

5.3.2 Participants

Halliday deals with participants in his discussion of process types, for example, Actor and Goal in a material process, Behaver in a behavioural process, Senser and Phenomenon in a mental process, Sayer, Receiver and Verbiage in a verbal process, Token, Value, Carrier, Attribute, Identified and Identifier in a relational process, and Existent in an existential process.

Halliday's Actor corresponds to logical subject, Goal to logical direct object, Beneficiary to logical indirect object, and Range to logical cognate object. (Halliday, 1985: 132) He gives a more detailed discussion of Beneficiary and Range.

5.3.2.1 Beneficiary

Halliday (1985: 132) defines his Beneficiary as "the one to whom or for whom the process is said to take place." Beneficiary appears in material and verbal processes, and sometimes in relational processes. In a material process, the Beneficiary is specified as Recipient (one that goods are given to) or Client (one that services are done for); in a verbal process, the Beneficiary is specified as Receiver; and in a relational process, it is referred to just as Beneficiary without being specified likewise. Therefore, Beneficiary is an umbrella term.

In a material process, Recipient and Client each may appear with or without a preposition, depending on its position in the clause (cf. Mathesius' positional dative and variable prepositional dative, Wierzbicka's internal dative and external dative). If it is an external dative, Recipient is associated with the preposition *to* and Client the preposition *for*. For example:

(119) a. He gave her a book. (Actor-Process-Beneficiary: Recipient-Goal)

b. He gave a book to her. (Actor-Process-Goal-Beneficiary: Recipient)

(120) a. He bought a present for her. (Actor-Process-Goal-Beneficiary: Client)

b. He bought her a present. (Actor-Process-Beneficiary: Client-Goal)

However, this does not imply that any clause that contains a prepositional phrase *to* or *for* necessarily contains a Beneficiary. One way to probe, as Halliday (1985:132) suggests, is to see if it can occur naturally without the preposition. Compare:

(121) a. She sent her best wishes to John.

b. She sent John her best wishes.

(122) a. She sent her luggage to her husband.

b. She sent her husband her luggage.

(123) a. She sent her luggage to London.

b. *She sent London her luggage.

(124) a. He painted John a picture.

b. He painted a picture for John.

(125) a. He built Mary this house.

b. He built this house for Mary.

(126) a. He did all this for Mary.

b. *He did Mary all this.

In (121), *John* is Beneficiary; in (123), *London* is not Beneficiary. *London* is neither positively nor negatively affected if someone sends his luggage there. By contrast, someone would be affected if to him one's luggage is sent. Therefore, it seems that with the verb *to send* the location appears less likely to be perspectivized. In other words, the constructional meaning of the internal dative construction excludes the possibility of having a locative element in the indirect object position. (cf. Wierzbicka, 1988; Goldberg, 1995) In (126), *Mary* is not a Client but a type of Cause, i.e. Behalf. An issue that remains is how to account for the fact that the Beneficiary with different verbs are syntactically realized through different prepositions (*to* and *for*) and whether this is semantics-based.

As shown above, the Beneficiary may be a human being. And it may also be a plant or an abstract entity. The "benefit" (i.e. goods given to or services done for the Beneficiary) is not necessarily beneficial. Observe the following sentences:

(127) He gave the tree some water.

(128) They never gave the plan a fair trial. (Zandvoort, 1957:200)

(129) Loyalty is owed some recognition.

(130) He gave her a dose of poison.

In a verbal process, "the Beneficiary is the one who is being addressed." Observe the following sentences:

(131) He said to Mary.

(132) He told Mary a story.

The preposition associated with the Beneficiary in a verbal process is *to*, as Halliday believes. Nevertheless, the case is somewhat complicated as there are other prepositions in addition to the preposition *to*. Observe the following sentences:

(133) He notified Mary of the decision.

(134) He informed us of his plan.

In a relational process, a Beneficiary may sometimes be found in the following constructions:

(135) She made him a good wife.

(136) It cost him a pretty penny.

5.3.2.2 Range

Halliday defines his term Range as "the element that specifies the range or scope of the process."

In a material process, the Range may be an entity and indicates the domain over which the process takes place. Observe the following sentences:

(137) He climbed the mountain.

(138) He played the piano.

(139) A mouse crossed the court.

In traditional terminology, *mountain* and *piano* are "affectum objects" (Fillmore, 1968:4), and they are independent of the processes of climbing and playing. As a mountain is a natural product, and a piano, by contrast, is a man-made product for a specific purpose, there is a difference between them. Even so, a piano is also independent of the process of playing, and in both cases they are Range/entities.

If one plays the piano, the piano is affected in that it produces tunes as a result of being played and so is the player in that he is spiritually satisfied. If one climbs a mountain, what is affected is rather the climber. And this difference may be largely due to the difference between the piano as a man-made product and a mountain as a natural product. By contrast, although a mountain is an entity, it is also highly suggestive of location, as it localizes the action process. So is a court. Theoretically, any entity is a location since it is three-dimensional in space. *Mountain*, *court* and the like actually draw a boundary within which the acts of climbing and crossing take place.

One question concerning the Range function of *the mountain* in (137) is that how this function is determined, by its collocates or something else? Compare:

(140) They moved the mountain.

From a semantic point of view or in terms of change of state (Fillmore, 1977), *the mountain* in (137) is less affected than that in (140) which is drastically affected. Theoretically, when two entities come into contact or are brought into contact, both of them are affected, and the difference lies in the degree of being affected. Conventionally, some entities, though affected as well, are not thus considered, and *the mountain* in (137) is a case in point. *The mountain* in both (137) and (140) are perspectivized, in (137) for being the element specifying what the act of climbing extends to (i.e. if one climbs, one must climb something, though this semantic element may not be realized in syntactic structure), in (140) for undergoing the change of state. Therefore, both of them enter the nuclear grammatical relations.

In Halliday's (1985: 134 − 136) view, there is not a "doing" relationship in (137), which suggests that *the mountain* in (137) is not the target of the acting, and it is where the acting takes place. Hence it is location. By contrast, *the mountain* in (140) is the target of the acting, i.e. the acting of moving is to affect the mountain in some way. Because of this semantic difference, syntactic constructions in (141−142) are not likely while those in (143−144) are likely:

(141) ? What he did to the mountain was climb it.
(142) ? What a mouse did to the court was cross it.
(143) What they did to the mountain was move it.
(144) What they did to the court was clean it.

A constructional constraint also implies this semantic difference. When the semantic relation is that of doing something to a target, the construction *to have something done* can be used. When the semantic relation is that of action and Range/entity, this construction can not be used. Observe the following sentences:

(145) a. He climbed the mountain.
      b. ? He has the mountain climbed.
(146) a. They moved the mountain.
      b. They have the mountain moved.

This constructional constraint suggests that the semantic relations have close relations with syntactic constructions. Although *the mountain* in (137, 140) are both entities and the actions are transitive, there may exist certain syntactic constructions to reveal the potential semantic difference. Hence an important issue is how different semantic relations are realized in syntactic constructions and how syntactic constructions encode and reveal

Chapter 5 Functional Syntax

semantic relations.

Structurally speaking, Process+Range and Process+Goal have the same syntactic construction, i.e. Predicate+Object. If one claims that the semantic structure determines the syntactic structure, then why do different semantic structures here have the same syntactic structure? Firstly, theoretically, there is an asymmetric character of language. (Karcevskij, 1929) This character implies that between the semantic structure and the syntactic structure there often lacks a one-to-one correspondence. One syntactic structure may embody more than one semantic structure. (Daneš, 1978) Secondly, sometimes the difference in semantic structures may not be evident within a single sentence. Nevertheless, the difference emerges at the intersentential level. (Fillmore, 1968:4) For instance, "the Range cannot be probed by *do to* or *do with*, whereas the Goal can." (Halliday, 1985:136) In other words, there may still be syntactic constraints somewhere to correspond to the difference in the semantic structural relations; for example, the Range element cannot take a resultative attribute whereas the Goal element can. Observe the following sentences:

(147) ? They crossed the field flat. (Process+Range/entity)

(148) They trampled the field flat. (Process+Goal)

The Range may also express the process itself. A difference between Range/entity and Range/process is that Range/entity exists independently of the process whereas Range/process depends upon the process (cf. Mathesius' temporary object); for example:

(149) They played tennis.

(150) They sang a song.

(151) They played games.

Tennis is not an entity but the act of playing it. Similarly, song is the act of singing, and game is the act of playing. Song and game appear to be "effectum objects" in traditional terminology. The function of this structure is to "enable us to specify further the number or kind of processes that take place." (Halliday, 1985:135; cf. Nida, 1993:39)

Semantically, a Range element is not a participant in the process, but grammatically, it is treated as if it was. (Halliday, 1985:136) In other words, a Range element is not a target of the acting as a Goal is. Since it is not a target, a Range element is sometimes similar to a circumstantial element (Extent) in a way. The complexity and the fuzzy boundary involved with the Range element points to the fact that language is a system where everything adheres. ("*langue est un system ou tout se tient*") As a result, a Range element, and in fact any semantic element, stands in close relation to its neighbouring elements (e.g. Goal, Extent) and in varied relation to other elements within the same system. Hence the notion of potentiality (Mathesius,

1911) may work where cases of indeterminacy exist.

In a mental process, the verb bears no relation to an Actor and Goal structure, and somehow resembles a pattern based on the concept of Range. (Halliday, 1985:136) For example:

(152) He likes it.

In (152), *it* (Halliday's Phenomenon) specifies the domain of one's liking and may be regarded as a kind of Range element.

In a verbal process, the Range element expresses the class, quality or quantity of what is said as follows:

(153) She speaks German.

(154) He asked a difficult question.

(155) He made a long speech.

5.3.3 Circumstances

Circumstantial elements consist of Extent and Location in time and space, Manner (Means, Quality and Comparison), Cause (Reason, Purpose and Behalf), Accompaniment, Matter, and Role.

5.3.3.1 Extent and Location

Extent is related with the notion of distance and duration (a stretch, a period) whereas Location is related with the notion of place and time (a spot, a point). Both of them can express spatial and temporal meanings; for example:

(156) He walked (for) two miles. (Extent: spatial)

(157) He stayed (for) two hours. (Extent: temporal)

(158) He worked in the kitchen. (Location: spatial)

(159) He gets up at six o'clock. (Location: temporal)

5.3.3.2 Manner

The circumstantial element of Manner consists of three subcategories: Means, Quality, Comparison.

Means refers to the means or instrument whereby a process takes place. For example:

(160) He came by train.

(161) a. The pig was beaten with the stick.

　　　b. She beat the pig with the stick.

(162) a. The pig was beaten by the stick.

　　　b. The stick beat the pig.

　　　c. *She beat the pig by the stick.

Halliday (1985:139) holds that "the instrument is not a distinct category in English grammar; it is simply a kind of means." In his view, *with the stick* in (161) is a circumstantial expression of Manner, (161)b being the corresponding active form of (161)a. In (162)b, which Halliday regards as the corresponding active form of (162)a, *the stick* has the function of Actor. By classifying the instrument as of circumstantial elements, Halliday seems to imply that the instrument is not a participant of a process whereas the agent is a participant in a process. By analysing *the stick* in (162)b as having the function of Actor, Halliday appears to regard the instrument as a participant since he (1985:32-37,102) defines Actor as "the one that does the deed." This may illustrate Halliday's view that "the line between agent and instrument is not always very sharp" since the category of means includes, "in principle, the concepts of both agency and instrumentality." In relation to our concern with the semantic-syntactic relations, this means that one can view an object as instrument like *the stick* in (161) or view it as an actor like *the stick* in (162). And the different views or conceptions of *the stick* are syntactically realized through different prepositions, *with* and *by*.

Perhaps there would be more sense in probing the semantic-syntactic relations than arguing whether the instrument should be treated as a participant or not. Observe the following sentences:

(163) a. She was pleased by the gift.

b. She was pleased with the gift.

(164) a. He pleased her with his gift.

b. He pleased her by his gift.

Halliday (1985:139) believes that there is no real difference in function between (163)a and (163)b. In terms of representational function, (163)a and (163)b reflect the same experience and the same relationship. Nevertheless, the difference is there, through it appears to be a lexical one. However, if this difference could be overlooked, then an overlook of the difference between *The pig was beaten with the stick* and *The pig was beaten by the stick* might be justified as well, since the difference here is of a similar kind (i.e. preposition) as that between (163)a and (163)b. True, the representational function may remain the same in spite of the surface structural difference. If it is so, it is once again a case of asymmetry, namely, one function may be realized through more than one structure. Relation is not linear, for one can make different choices without changing the nature of the relationship. Take a possessive relation for instance. One can choose the possessor or the possessed as point of departure, hence makes different semantic and syntactic arrangements. Syntactic structure, a kind of postsemantic processing, is linear.

The instrument involved in a process may be inherent in the acting, and needs not be there in the surface structure. Similarly, the actor may also be implicit. The point is that not everything involved in a scene needs to be syntactically realized, and that would be not only unnecessary but also impossible. (Mathesius, 1975:15) Some elements are so closely associated with a particular scene that they have become conventionalized, so to speak; and to syntactically realize them would mean to foreground or mark them. For example, to play football implies the involvement of foot, to play volleyball that of hand, and to knock at the door that of one's fingers. Observe the following sentences:

(165) He knocked at the door (with his fingers).

Quality expressions represent various meanings such as degree. They "characterize the process in respect of any variable that makes sense." Observe the following sentences:

(166) It puzzled him too much

(167) It was raining heavily.

(168) He said in a calm tone.

Comparison represents the meaning of similarity or difference. It is typically expressed by a prepositional phrase with *like* or *unlike*:

(169) He worked like a slave.

(170) He signed his name differently.

5.3.3.3 Cause

The circumstantial element of Cause comprises three subcategories: Reason, Purpose and Behalf.

Circumstantials of Reason represent the reason for which a process takes place. Circumstantials of Purpose represent the purpose for which a process takes place. Circumstantials of Behalf represent the entity, "on whose behalf or for whose sake the action is undertaken." Observe the following sentences:

(171) They left because of the drought. (Cause: Reason)

(172) He died of starvation. (Cause: Reason)

(173) Let's go for a walk. (Cause: Purpose)

(174) He put in a word on John's behalf. (Cause: Behalf)

The category of the Behalf includes in principle the concept of the Beneficiary. (Halliday, 1985: 140) A difference between them is that the Beneficiary is treated in the grammar as a participant and it may be brought into the nuclear grammatical relations as the subject in the passive or internal dative in the active. By contrast, the Behalf can not be perspectivized in the same way. Compare:

(175) a. She gave up her job for her children. (Cause: Behalf)
   b. *She gave her children up her job.

(176) a. She built a new house for her children. (Beneficiary)
   b. She built her children a new house.

5.3.3.4 Accompaniment

This semantic element represents the meanings *and* (positive *accompaniment*), *not* (negative accompaniment) as circumstancials. It is expressed by prepositions or prepositional phrases, e. g. *with*, *without*, *instead of*. Observe the following sentences:

(177) He came with/without her.
(178) He set out with/without his umbrella.
(179) He came as well as she.
(180) He came instead of her.

5.3.3.5 Matter

This element corresponds to the interrogative "what about?" and is expressed by prepositions or prepositional phrases, e. g. *about*, *concerning*, *with reference to*:

(181) I worry about her health.
(182) They're talking about the weather.

5.3.3.6 Role

This element corresponds to the interrogative "what as?" and is expressed by prepositions and prepositional phrases, e. g. *as*, *by way of*:

(183) I come here as a friend.
(184) They leave the place untidy by way of protest.

5.4 Summary

The above introduction shows the rich resources of functional syntax, though we have not yet discussed Jan Firbas (1992), Petr Sgall (Sgall, 2006; Sgall et al., 1969; 1973; 1986), and Susumu Kuno (1987; 1993; 2004). If one searches for an invariance from out of these variations or a unity in diversity, that would be "FUNCTIONAL SYNTAX is a subarea of functional linguistics in which syntactic structures are analyzed with emphasis on their communicative function." (Kuno, 1980:117)

References

Chomsky, Noam. 1957. *Syntactic Structures*. The Hague: Mouton.
Chomsky, Noam. 1964. "The logical basis of linguistic theory," In Lunt, Horace G. (ed.). *Proceedings of the IXth International Congress of Linguists.* (Cambridge, Massachusetts, 1962) 1964: 914—1008.
Daneš, František. 1964. "A three-level approach to syntax," *Travaux Linguistiques de Prague* 1: 225—240.
Daneš, František. 1966. "The relation of centre and periphery as a language universal," *Travaux Linguistiques de Prague* 2: 9—22.
Daneš, František. 1968. "Some thoughts on the semantic structure of the sentence," *Lingua* 21: 55—69. Reprinted in Luelsdorff, Philip, Jarmila Panevová & Petr Sgall (eds.).

1994. *Praguiana*: 1945—1990. Amsterdam: John Benjamins. pp. 71—85.(《布拉格学派：1945—1990》,英文影印本列为西方语言学原版影印系列丛书 5,北京:北京大学出版社,2004。)
Daneš, František. 1970a. "One instance of Prague school methodology: functional analysis of utterance and text," In Garvin, Paul (ed.). *Method and Theory in Linguistics*. The Hague: Mouton. pp. 132—140.
Daneš, František. 1970b. "Zur linguistischen analyse der textstruktur," *Folia Linguistica* 4: 72—79.
Daneš, František. 1970c. "Semantic considerations in syntax," In *Actes du Xe Congress international des linguistes* II: 407—413.
Daneš, František. 1971. "On linguistic strata(levels)," *Travaux Linguistiques de Prague* 4: 127—144.
Daneš, František. 1974a. "Functional sentence perspective and the organization of the text," In Daneš, František (ed.). *Papers on Functional Sentence Perspective*. Prague: Academia. pp. 106—128.
Daneš, František (ed.) 1974b. *Papers on Functional Sentence Perspective*. Prague: Academia.
Daneš, František. 1978. "Satzglider und satzmuster," In Helbig, Gerhard. (Hrsg.) *Beitrage zu Problemen der Satzglieder*. Leipzig: VEB Verlag Enzyklopadie. pp. 7—28.
Daneš, František. 1987a. "Sentence patterns and predicate classes," In Steele, Ross &. Terry Threadgold (eds.). *Language Topics*. Amsterdam: John Benjamins. pp. 3—21.
Daneš, František. 1987b. "On Prague school functionalism in linguistics," In Dirven, René &. Vilém Fried (eds.). *Functionalism in Linguistics*. Amsterdam: John Benjamins. pp. 3—38.
Daneš, František. 1991. "A functional model of the system of sentence Sstructures," In Ventola, Eija (ed.), *Functional and Systemic Linguistics: Approaches and Uses*. Berlin: Mouton de Gruyter. 1991, pp. 63—79.
Daneš, František. 1994. "The sentence-pattern modal of syntax," In Luelsdorff, Philip (ed.). *The Prague School of Structural and Functional Linguistics: A Short Introduction*. Amsterdam: John Benjamins. pp. 197—221.
Daneš, František. 2003a. "The double basis of the Prague functional approach: Mathesius and Jakobson," In Hladky, Josef (ed.). *Language and Function: to the Memory of Jan Firbas*. Amsterdam: John Benjamins. pp. 57—69.
Daneš, František. 2003b. "Vilém mathesius' konzeption der funktionalen Linguistik," In Nekula, Marek (ed.). *Prager Strukturalismus: Methodologische Grundlagen = Prague Structuralism: Methodological Fundamentals*. Heidelberg: Winter. pp. 31—47.
Dik, Simon C. 1980. "Seventeen sentences: basic principles and application of functional grammar," In Moravcsik, Edith A. &. Jessica R. Wirth (eds.). *Current Approaches to Syntax* (Syntax and Semantics, vol. 13). New York: Academic Press. pp. 45—75.
Dokulil, Miloš &. Františe Daneš. 1958. "On the so-called semantic and grammatical structure of the sentence," In Luelsdorff, Philip, Jarmila Panevová &. Petr Sgall (eds.). *Praguiana*: 1945—1990. Amsterdam: John Benjamins. pp. 21—37.
Fillmore, Charles J. 1968. "The case for case," In Bach, Emmon &. Robert T. Harms (eds.). *Universals in Linguistic Theory*. New York: Holt, Rinehart and Winston. pp. 1—88.

Fillmore, Charles J. 1977. "The case for case reopened," In Cole, Peter & Jerrold M. Sadock (eds.). *Grammatical Relations* (Syntax and Semantics Vol. 8). New York: Academic Press. pp. 59—81.

Firbas, Jan. 1957. "Some thoughts on the function of word order in old English and modern English," *Sbornik praci brnenske univerzity* A5: 72—100.

Firbas, Jan. 1962. "Notes on the function of the sentence in the act of communication," *SPFFBU* 10: 133—148.

Firbas, Jan. 1987a. "Thoughts on functional sentence perspective, intonation and emotiveness," Part Two. *Brno Studies in English* 17: 9—49.

Firbas, Jan. 1987b. "On some basic issues of the theory of functional sentence perspective II," (On Wallace L. Chafe's views on new and old information and communicative dynamism) *Brno Studies in English* 17: 51—59.

Firbas, Jan. 1987c. "On the delimitation of the theme in functional sentence perspective," In Dirven, René & Vilém Fried (eds.). *Functionalism in Linguistics*. Amsterdam: John Benjamins. pp. 137—156.

Firbas, Jan. 1991. "On some basic issues of the theory of functional sentence perspective III: on discreteness in functional sentence perspective," *Brno Studies in English* 19: 77—92.

Firbas, Jan. 1992. *Functional Sentence Perspective in Written and Spoken Communication*. Cambridge: Cambridge University Press. (《书面与口语交际中的功能句子观》,英文影印本收入西方语言学与应用语言学视野丛书,北京:世界图书出版公司北京公司,2007。)

Firbas, Jan. 1996a. "Exploring Vilém Mathesius' use of the term *theme* (I-III)," *Linguistica Pragensia* 1996 (1): 5—23.

Firbas, Jan. 1996b. "Exploring Vilém Mathesius' use of the term *theme* (IV-VIII)," *Linguistica Pragensia* 1996 (2): 63—86.

Firbas, Jan. 1997. "On some basic issues of the theory of functional sentence perspective IV: some thoughts on Marie Luise Thein's critique of the theory," *Brno Studies in English* 23: 51—86.

Firbas, Jan. 1998. "On some basic issues of the theory of functional sentence perspective V: some more thoughts on Marie Luise Thein's critique of the theory," *Brno Studies in English* 24: 11—32.

Goldberg, Adele E. 1995. *Constructions: A Construction Grammar Approach to Argument Structure*. Chicago: The University of Chicago Press.

Halliday, Michael A. K. 1974. "The place of functional sentence perspective in the system of linguistic description," In Daneš, František (ed.). *Papers on Functional Sentence Perspective*. Prague: Academia. pp. 43—53.

Halliday, Michael A. K. 1985. *An Introduction to Functional Grammar*. London: Edward Arnold.

Havránek, Bohuslav. 1928. "Trends in present-day linguistic research," (This article originally appeared as the introductory chapter of Havránek's Czeck work *Genera verbi v slovanskych jazycích* I [Genera Verbi in Slavic Languages]. Prague: Kr. Česká spol. Nauk. pp. 3—4.) Translated into English by Libuše Dušková. Included in Vachek, Josef (ed.). 1983. *Praguiana: Some Basic and Less Known Aspects of the Prague Linguistic School*. Prague: Academia. pp. 65—75.

Helbig, Gerhard. (Hrsg.) 1971. *Beitrage zue Valenztheorie*. Haag: Mouton.

Helbig, Gerhard. 1973. *Geschichte der neueren Sprachwissenschaft: Unter dem besonderen Aspekt der Grammatik-Theorie*. 2Aufl. München: Max Hueber.

Jespersen, Otto. 1924. *The Philosophy of Grammar*. London: Allen and Unwin.

Jespersen, Otto. 1927. *A Modern English Grammar on Historical Principles*. Part III Syntax. Second Volume. Heidelberg: Carl Winter/ London: Allen and Unwin.

Karcevskij Sergej. 1929. "Du dualisme asymétrique du signe linguistique," (The Asymmetric Duallism of the Linguistic Sign) *Travaux du Cercle Linguistique de Prague* 1: 88—92. Reprinted in Vachek, Josef (ed.). 1964. *A Prague School Reader in Linguistics*. Bloomington: Indiana University Press. pp. 81—87. English translation by Wendy Steiner in Steiner, Peter (ed.). 1982. *The Prague School: Selected Writings*, 1929—1946. Austin: University of Texas Press. pp. 49—54.

Kuno, Susumu. 1980. "Functional syntax," In Moravcsik, Edith A. & Jessica R. Wirth (eds.). *Syntax and Semantics, Volume* 13: *Current Approaches to Syntax*. New York: Academic Press. pp. 117—135.

Kuno, Susumu. 1987. *Functional Syntax: Anaphora, Discourse and Empathy*. Chicago: University of Chicago Press.

Kuno, Susumu & Ken-ichi Takami. 1993. *Grammar and Discourse Principles: Functional Syntax and GB Theory*. Chicago: University of Chicago Press.

Kuno, Susumu & Ken-ichi Takami. 2004. *Functional Constraints in Grammar: On the Unergativce-Unaccusative Distinction*. Amsterdam: John Benjamins.

Mathesius, Vilém. 1911. "O potenciálnosti jevů jazykovych," (On the Potentiality of the Phenomena of Language) *Věstnik Královské České Společnosti nauk, třida filio. -histor.* 1911, Sect. II, 1—24. Prague. English translation by Josef Vachek & in Vachek, Josef (ed.). 1964. *A Prague School Reader in Linguistics*. Bloomington: Indiana University Press. pp. 1—32 and also in Vachek, Josef (ed.). 1983. *Praguiana: Some Basic and Less Known Aspects of the Prague Linguistic School*. Prague: Academia. pp. 3—43.

Mathesius, Vilém. 1927. "New currents and tendencies in linguistic research," *MNHMA Sbornik věnovany na pamětčtyřicetiletého učitelského pů sobeni profesora Josefa Zubatého na Universitě Karlově* 1885—1925. Praha: Jednota českych filologů. pp. 188—203. Reprinted in Vachek, Josef (ed.). 1983. *Praguiana: Some Basic and Less Known Aspects of the Prague Linguistic School*. Prague: Academia. pp. 45—63.

Mathesius, Vilém. 1928. "On linguistic characterology of modern English," *Actes du Premier Congrès International de Linguists à la Haye du* 10—15 *avril* 1928. Leiden: A. W. Sijthoff. pp. 56—63. Reprinted in Vachek, Josef (ed.). 1964. *A Prague School Reader in Linguistics*. Bloomington: Indiana University Press. pp. 59—67.

Mathesius, Vilém. 1929a. "Functional linguistics," Translated into English by Libuše Duškov and included in Vachek, Josef (ed.). 1983. *Praguiana: Some Basic and Less Known Aspects of the Prague Linguistic School*. Prague: Academia. pp. 121—142.

Mathesius, Vilém. 1929b. "Zur satzperspektive im modernen Englisch," *Archiv für das Studium der neueren Sprachen und Literaturen* 155: 202—210.

Mathesius, Vilém. 1936. "On some problems of the systematic analysis of grammar," *Travaux du Cercle Linguistique de Prague* 6: 95—107. Reprinted in Vachek, Josef (ed.). 1964. *A Prague School Reader in Linguistics*. Bloomington: Indiana University Press. pp. 306—319.

Mathesius, Vilém. 1939. "O tak zvaném aktuálnimčleněni věty," (On information-bearing structure of the sentence) *Slovo a slovesnos* 5: 171—174. English translation by Tsuneko Olga Yokoyama and included in Kuno, Susumu (ed.). 1975. *Harvard Studies in Syntax and Semantics*, Volume 1. Cambridge, Mass. pp. 467—480. "关于句子的所谓实际切分",张惠芹、武爱华、于淑杰译,《话语语言学论文集》,王福祥,白春仁编。北京:外语教学与研究出版社。1989,第 10—17 页。

Mathesius, Vilém. 1941. "Základní funkce pořádku slov včeštině," (The basic function of word order in Czech) *Slovo a slovesnos* 7: 169—180. "捷克语词序的基本功能",丛林译,《话语语言学论文集》,王福祥,白春仁编。北京:外语教学与研究出版社。1989,第 18—37 页。

Mathesius, Vilém. 1942. "Ze srovnávacich studii slovoslednych," (From comparative word order studies)*časopis pro moderni filologii* (Journal for Modern Philology) 28: 181—190, 302—307.

Mathesius, Vilém. 1975. *A Functional Analysis of Present-Day English on a General Linguistic Basis*. Josef Vachek (ed.). Libuše Dušková (trans.). The Hague: Mouton/Prague: Academia.

Nida, Eugene A. 1993. *Language, Culture, and Translating*. Shanghai: Shanghai Foreign Language Education Press.

Quirk, Randolph, Sidney Greenbaum, Geoffrey Leech, & Jan Svartvik. 1972. *A Grammar of Contemporary English*. London: Longman.

Sgall, Petr. 1967. "Functional sentence perspective in a generative description," *Prague Bulletin of Mathematical Linguistic* 2: 203—225.

Sgall, Petr. 1979. "Towards a definition of focus and topic," *Prague Bulletin of Mathematical Linguistics* 31: 3—25; 32 (1980): 24—32.

Sgall, Petr. 1987a. "The position of Czech linguistics in theme-focus research," In Steele, Ross & Terry Threadgold (eds.). *Language Topics*. Amsterdam: John Benjamins. pp. 47—55.

Sgall, Petr. 1987b. "Prague functionalism and Topic vs. Focus," In Dirven, René & Vilém Fried (eds.). *Functionalism in Linguistics*. Amsterdam: John Benjamins. pp. 169—189.

Sgall, Petr. 2003. "From functional sentence perspective to Topic—Focus articulation," In Hladky, Josef (ed.). *Language and Function*. Amsterdam: John Benjamins. pp. 279—287.

Sgall, Petr. 2006. *Language in Its Multifarious Aspects*. Charles University in Prague: The Karolinum Press.

Sgall, Petr et al. 1969. *A Functional Approach to Syntax in Generative Description of Language*. New York: American Elsevier.

Sgall, Petr, EvaHajičová & Eva Benešová. 1973. *Topic, Focus, and Generative Semantics*. Kronberg: Scriptor.

Sgall, Petr, Eva Hajičová & Jarmila Panevová. 1986. *The Meaning of the Sentence in its Semantic and Pragmatic Aspects*. Dordrecht: D. Reidel.

Toman, Jindřich. 1995. *The Magic of a Common Language: Jakobson, Mathesius, Trubetzkoy, and the Prague Linguistic Circle*. Cambridge, Mass.: MIT Press.

Trnka, Bohumil. 1943. "Obecné otázky strukturálniho jazykozpytu," (*General Problems of Structural Linguistics*) *Slovo a slovesnos* 9: 57—68. English translation by Philip H. Smith, reprinted in Trnka, Bohumil. 1982. *Selected Papers in Structural Linguistics*.

Vilém Fried (ed.). Berlin: Mouton. pp. 32—48.

Trnka, Bohumil. 1946. "Vilém mathesius," (*Journal for Modern Philology*) *Časopis pro moderni filologii* 29: 3 — 13. Translated by Vladimir Honsa. Included in Sebeok, Thomas A. (ed.). 1966. *Portraits of Linguists: A Biographical Source Book for the History of Western Linguistics*, 1746—1963. *Volume Two: From Eduard Sievers to Benjamin Lee Whorf*. Bloomington: Indiana University Press. pp. 474—489.

Trnka, Bohumil. 1948. "Jazykozpyt a myšlenková struktura doby," (Linguistics and the Ideological Structure of the Period) *Slovo a Slovesnost* 10: 73—80. Translated by Josef Vachek, in Vachek, Josef. 1966. *The Linguistic School of Prague*. Bloomington, Indiana: Indiana University Press. pp. 152—166. Reprinted in Trnka, Bohumil. 1982. *Selected Papers in Structural Linguistics*. Vilém Fried (ed.). Berlin: Mouton. pp. 49—60. Reprinted in Vachek, Josef (ed.). 1983. *Praguiana: Some Basic and Less Known Aspects of the Prague Linguistic School*. Prague: Academia. pp. 211—229.

Vachek, Josef. 1961. "Some less familiar aspects of the analytical trend of English," *Brno Studies in English* 3: 9—78. Reprinted in Vachek, Josef. 1976. *Selected Writings in English and General Linguistics*. The Hague: Mouton. pp. 311—385.

Vachek, Josef (ed.). 1964. *A Prague School Reader in Linguistics*. Bloomington: Indiana University Press.

Vachek, Josef. 1966. *The Linguistic School of Prague*. Bloomington, Indiana: Indiana University Press.

Vachek, Josef. 1972. "The linguistic theory of the Prague school," In Fried, Vilém (ed.). 1972. *The Prague School of Linguistics and Language Teaching*. London: Oxford University Press. pp. 11—28.

Vachek, Josef. 1976. *Selected Writings in English and General Linguistics*. Prague: Academia/The Hague: Paris: Mouton.

Vachek, Josef. 1980. "Vilém Mathesius as forerunner of contrastive linguistic studies," *Papers and Studies in Contrastive Linguistics* (Poznan) 11: 5—16.

Vachek, Josef. 1982. "Vilém Mathesius' living heritage to world linguistics," *Philologica Pragensia* 25 (3): 121—127.

Vachek, Josef(ed.). 1983. *Praguiana: Some Basic and Less Known Aspects of the Prague Linguistic School*. Prague: Academia.

Vachek, Josef. 1994. "Vilém Mathesius as one of the forerunners of modern textological research," In Čmejrková, Světla and František Šticha (eds.). 1994. *The Syntax of Sentence and Text: A Festschrift for František Daneš*. Amsterdam/Philadelphia: John Benjamins. pp. 67—71.

Vachek, Josef. 1995. "Vilém Mathesius 1882—1945," *Linguistica Pragensia* 1995 (2): 57—59.

Vachek, Josef. 2002. "Prolegomena to the history of the Prague school of linguistics," *Prague Linguistic Circle Papers* (*Travaux du Cercle Linguistique de Prague*, nouvelle série) 4: 3—81.

Vachek, Josef (ed.). 2003. *Dictionary of the Prague School of Linguistics*. In collaboration with Josef Dubsky; translated from the French, German and Czech original sources by Aleš Klégr, Pavlina Saldová, Markéta Malá, Jan Cermák, Libuše Dušková; edited by Libuše Dušková. Amsterdam: John Benjamins.

Wierzbicka, Anna. 1988. *The Semantics of Grammar*. Amsterdam: John Benjamins.
Zandvoort, Reinard Willem. 1957. *A Handbook of English Grammar*. (7th ed.). London: Longmans.
胡壮麟,1994,《语篇的衔接与连贯》,上海:上海外语教育出版社。
胡壮麟,2000,《功能主义纵横谈》,北京:外语教学与研究出版社。
姜望琪,2011,《语篇语言学研究》,北京:北京大学出版社。
钱 军,2001a,*Towards a Relational-Perspective Approach to Syntactic Semantics*,北京:人民教育出版社。
钱 军,2001b,"Towards a history of linguistic ideas: a note on Jan Firbas and the Prague school," *Prague Bulletin of Mathematical Linguistics* 76: 5—12.
钱 军,2002,句子的实际切分,《语言学研究》第1辑,第8—20页。
钱 军,2004a,主语的问题,《语言学研究》第2辑,第32—50页。
钱 军,2004b,《布拉格学派1945—1990》导读,*Praguiana 1945—1990*,第1—42页。北京:北京大学出版社。
钱 军,2007,《书面语与口语交际中的功能句子观》导读,*Functional Sentence Perspective in Written and Spoken Communication*,第13—31页。北京:世界图书出版公司北京公司。
钱 军,2008,《普通语言学基础上的当代英语功能分析》导读,*A Functional Analysis of Present Day English on a General Linguistic Basis*,第13—63页。北京:世界图书出版公司北京公司。

Chapter 6

Semantics

6.1 Introduction

SEMANTICS is generally defined as the study of meaning, which has always been a central topic in human scholarship. There were discussions of meaning in the works of the Greek philosopher Plato as early as the fifth century before Christ. In China, Lao Zi had discussed similar questions even earlier. The fact that over the years numerous dictionaries have been produced with a view to explaining the meaning of words also bears witness to its long tradition. But a distinction is usually made between two different approaches to meaning. The approach in which more attention is paid to the meaning of linguistic units themselves, words and sentences in particular, may be called LINGUISTIC SEMANTICS. The approach more concerned with the relationship between linguistic expressions and the phenomena in the world to which they refer, and the conditions under which such expressions can be said to be true or false, and the factors which affect the interpretation of language used may be called PHILOSOPHICAL SEMANTICS or LOGICAL SEMANTICS.① And the present chapter will be mainly on the former, touching on the latter only at the end.

Despite the long history of the study, the term "semantics" is only a little over a hundred years old. The French linguist Michel Bréal coined the term "sémantique" in 1893. In 1894, a paper entitled "Reflected meanings: a point in semantics" was read to the American Philological Association. In both cases, however, the term referred to the development of meaning, or historical semantics. It was in his book *Essai de Sémantique* published in 1897 that Bréal first used the term in its present day sense as the science of meaning. Its English version came out in 1900.

As the study of meaning, semantics assumes an important position in the study of language. We make sounds, words, sentences, not for the sake of making them. We make them in order to mean something, to express some

---

① A further distinction may be made between philosophical semantics and logical semantics by defining the latter in a narrower sense as the study of meaning in terms of logical systems of analysis, or calculi.

meaning. But meaning is intangible. It is more difficult to study than sounds, and the forms of words and sentences. At the present, semantics is the least known area in linguistics, compared with phonetics, phonology, morphology and syntax.

6.2 Meanings of "Meaning"

One difficulty in the study of meaning is that the word "meaning" itself has many different meanings. In their book *The Meaning of Meaning* written in 1923, C. K. Ogden and I. A. Richards presented a "representative list of the main definitions which reputable students of meaning have favoured." (186) There are 16 major categories of them, with sub-categories all together, numbering 22. G. Leech in a more moderate tone recognizes 7 types of meaning in his *Semantics* (23), first published in 1974, as follows:

Table 6.1 7 Types of Meaning

1. Conceptual meaning	Logical, cognitive, or denotative content
Associative meaning	
2. Connotative meaning	What is communicated by virtue of what language refers to.
3. Social meaning	What is communicated of the social circumstances of language use.
4. Affective meaning	What is communicated of the feelings and attitudes of the speaker/writer.
5. Reflected meaning	What is communicated through association with another sense of the same expression.
6. Collocative meaning	What is communicated through association with words which tend to occur in the environment of an other word.
7. Thematic meaning	What is communicated by the way in which the message is organized in terms of order and emphasis.

Leech says that the first type of meaning—CONCEPTUAL MEANING—makes up the central part. It is denotative in that it is concerned with the relationship between a word and the thing it denotes, or refers to. In this sense, conceptual meaning overlaps to a large extent with the notion of reference. But the term "CONNOTATIVE" used in the name of the second type of meaning is used in a sense different from that in philosophical discussions. Philosophers use "connotation," opposite to "denotation," to mean the properties of the entity a word denotes. For example, the denotation of "human" is any person such as John and Mary, and its connotation is "biped," "featherless," "rational," etc. In Leech's system, however, as is the case in daily conversation, "connotative" refers to some additional, especially emotive, meaning. The difference between "politician" and "statesman," for example, is connotative in that the former is derogatory while the latter is favourable. This type of meaning and the following four types are collectively known as ASSOCIATIVE MEANING in the sense that an elementary associationist theory of mental connections is enough to explain their use. The last type, THEMATIC MEANING, is more peripheral since it is only determined by the order of the words in a sentence and the different prominence they each receive.

But even when "meaning" is understood in the first sense above, there are still different ways to explain the meaning of a word. In everyday conversation, there are at least the following four ways. Suppose you do not know the word "desk," and ask what it means. One may point to the object the word stands for, and answer "This is a desk." Alternatively he may describe the object as "a piece of furniture with a flat top and four legs, at which one reads and writes." Or he may paraphrase it, saying that "a desk is a kind of table, which has drawers." If he is a teacher of English, then he may more often than not give you its Chinese equivalent—书桌. The first method is usually used by adults to children, since their vocabulary is small and it is difficult to explain to them in words. The second and the third are the usual methods adopted in monolingual dictionaries, which sometimes may also resort to the first by illustrating with pictures. And the fourth is the kind of explanation provided by bilingual dictionaries and textbooks for teaching foreign languages.

6.3 The Referential Theory

The theory of meaning which relates the meaning of a word to the thing it refers to, or stands for, is known as the REFERENTIAL THEORY. This is a very popular theory. It is generally possible, as we have shown in the previous section, to explain the meaning of a word by pointing to the thing it refers to. In the case of proper nouns and definite noun phrases, this is especially true. When we say "The most influential linguist Noam Chomsky teaches at MIT," we do use "the most influential linguist" and "Noam Chomsky" to mean a particular person, and "MIT" a particular institution of higher learning. However, there are also problems with this theory. One is that when we explain the meaning of "desk" by pointing to the thing it refers to, we do not mean a desk must be of the particular size, shape, colour and material as the desk we are pointing to at the moment of speaking. We are using this particular desk as an example, an instance, of something more general. That is, there is something behind the concrete thing we can see with our eyes. And that something is abstract, which has no existence in the material world and can only be sensed in our minds. This abstract thing is usually called CONCEPT. ①

A theory which explicitly employs the notion "concept" is the SEMANTIC TRIANGLE proposed by Ogden and Richards in their book *The Meaning of Meaning*. They argue that the relation between a word and a thing it refers to is not direct. It is mediated by concept. In a diagram form, the relation is represented as follows: ②

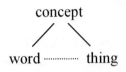

Figure 6.1 **Semantic Triangle**

Now if we relate this discussion with the four ways of explaining the meaning of a word mentioned in the last section, we may say that the first method of pointing to an object corresponds to the direct theory of the relation between words and things, while the second corresponds to the indirect theory. By saying "desk" is "a piece of furniture with a flat top and four legs, at which one reads and writes," we are in fact resorting to the concept of "desk," or summarizing the main features, the defining properties, of a desk. And the third and fourth methods are even more indirect, by involving the concept of another word, " table" or 书桌.

Leech also uses "SENSE" as a briefer term for his conceptual meaning. This usage is justifiable in that as a technical term "sense" may be used in the same way as "connotation" is used in philosophy. It may refer to the properties an entity has. In this sense, "sense" is equivalent to "concept." The definition of "desk" as "a piece of furniture with a flat top and four legs, at which one reads and writes" may also be called the sense of "desk." So the distinction between " sense" and " REFERENCE " is comparable to that between "connotation" and "denotation." The former refers to some abstract properties, while the latter refers to some concrete entities. In other words, Leech's conceptual meaning has two sides: sense and reference. There is yet another difference between sense and reference. To some extent, we can say every word has a sense, i. e. some conceptual content, otherwise we will not be able to use it or understand it. But not every word has a reference. Grammatical words like "but" "if" "and" do not refer to anything. And words like "God" "ghost" and "dragon" refer to imaginary things, which do not exist

---

① It is in this sense that Leech calls his first type of meaning conceptual meaning.

② The term Ogden and Richards used for "word" is "symbol," that for "concept" is "thought or reference," and that for "thing" is "referent."

in reality. What is more, it is not convenient to explain the meaning of a word in terms of the thing it refers to. The thing a word stands for may not always be at hand at the time of speaking. Even when it is nearby, it may take the listener some time to work out its main features. For example, when one sees a computer for the first time, one may mistake the monitor for its main component, thinking that a computer is just like a TV set. Therefore people suggest that we should study meaning in terms of sense rather than reference.

6.4 Sense Relations

Words are in different SENSE RELATIONS with each other. Some words have more similar senses than others. For example, the sense of "desk" is more closely related to that of "table" than to "chair." Conversely we can say the sense of "desk" is more different from that of "chair" than from "table." And the sense of "desk" is included in the sense of "furniture," or the sense of "furniture" includes that of "desk." As a result the sense of a word may be seen as the network of its sense relations with others. In other words, sense may be defined as the semantic relations between one word and another, or more generally between one linguistic unit and another. It is concerned with the intra linguistic relations. In contrast, as we alluded to earlier, reference is concerned with the relation between a word and the thing it refers to, or more generally between a linguistic unit and a non-linguistic entity it refers to. There are generally three kinds of sense relations recognized, namely, sameness relation, oppositeness relation and inclusiveness relation.

6.4.1 Synonymy

SYNONYMY is the technical name for the sameness relation. English is said to be rich in synonyms. Its vocabulary has two main sources: Anglo Saxon and Latin. There are many pairs of words of these two sources which mean the same, e. g. "buy" and "purchase," "world" and "universe," "brotherly" and "fraternal." But TOTAL SYNONYMY is rare. The so called synonyms are all context dependent. They all differ one way or another. For example, they may differ in style. In the context "Little Tom _____ a toy bear," "buy" is more appropriate than "purchase." They may also differ in connotations. That is why people jokingly say "I'm thrifty. You are economical. And he is stingy." Thirdly, there are dialectal differences. "Autumn" is British while "fall" is American. The British live in "flats" and take the "underground" or "tube" to work while the Americans live in "apartments" and take the "subway."

6.4.2 Antonymy

ANTONYMY is the name for oppositeness relation. There are three main sub-types: GRADABLE ANTONYMY, COMPLEMENTARY ANTONYMY, and CONVERSE ANTONYMY.

6.4.2.1 Gradable Antonymy

This is the commonest type of antonymy. When we say two words are antonyms, we usually mean pairs of words like "good : bad," "long: short," "big: small." As the examples show, they are mainly adjectives. And they have three characteristics.

First, as the name suggests, they are gradable. That is, the members of a pair differ in terms of degree. The denial of one is not necessarily the assertion of the other. Something which is not "good" is not necessarily "bad." It may simply be "so so" or "average." As such, they can be modified by "very." Something may be "very good" or "very bad." And they may have comparative and superlative degrees. Something may be "better" or "worse" than another. Some thing may be the "best" or "worst" among a number of things. Sometimes the intermediate degrees may be lexicalized. They may be expressed by separate words rather than by adding modifiers. For example, the term for the size which is neither big nor small is "medium." And between the two extremes of temperature "hot" and "cold," there are "warm" and "cool," which form a pair of antonyms themselves, and may have a further intermediate term "lukewarm."

Second, antonyms of this kind are graded against different norms. There is no absolute criterion by which we may say something is "good" or "bad," "long" or "short," "big" or "small." The criterion varies with the object described. "A big car" is in fact much smaller than "a small plane." A "microcomputer" is giant by the standard of "microorganism."

Third, one member of a pair, usually the term for the higher degree, serves as the cover term. We ask somebody "How old are you?" and the person asked may not be old in any sense. He may be as young as twenty or three. The word "old" is used here to cover both "old" and "young." The sentence means the same as "What is your age?"

Technically, the cover term is called UNMARKED, i.e. usual; and the covered MARKED, or unusual. That means, in general, it is the cover term that is used. If the covered is used, then it suggests that there is something odd, unusual here. The speaker may already know that somebody/something is "young" "small" "near" and he wants to know the extent in greater detail. This characteristic is also reflected in the corresponding nouns, such as "length" "height" "width" "breadth" and "depth," which are cognates of the cover terms.

6.4.2.2 Complementary Antonymy

Antonyms like "alive : dead" "male : female" "present : absent" "innocent : guilty" "odd : even" "pass : fail (a test)" "hit : miss (a target)" "boy : girl" are of this type. In contrast to the first type, the members of a pair in this type are complementary to each other. That is, they divide up the whole of a semantic field completely. Not only the assertion of one means the denial of the other, the denial of one also means the assertion of the other. Not only "He is alive" means "He is not dead" "He is not alive" also means "He is dead." There is no intermediate ground between the two. A man cannot be neither alive nor dead. The Chinese expression 半死不活 can only be used for somebody who is still alive. If he is really not alive, then he is dead completely, not just half dead. In other words, it is a question of two term choice: yes or no; not a multiple choice, a choice between more or less. So the adjectives in this type cannot be modified by "very." One cannot say somebody is * "very alive" or * "very dead." And they do not have comparative or superlative degrees either. The saying "He is more dead than alive" is not a true comparative. The words "dead" and "alive" are not used literally here. The sentence actually means "It is more correct to say that he is dead than to say he is alive." After all we do not say "John is more dead than Peter." An example supporting this view is that we can say "John is more mad than stupid" in the sense that "It is more correct to say John is mad than to say John is stupid." The word "mad" is not used in the comparative degree, since its comparative form is "madder."

To some extent, this difference between the gradable and the complementary can be compared to the traditional logical distinction between the contrary and the contradictory. In logic, a proposition is the contrary of another if both cannot be true, though they may both be false; e.g. "The coffee is hot" and "The coffee is cold." And a proposition is the contradictory of another if it is impossible for both to be true, or false; e.g. "This is a male cat" and "This is a female cat." In a diagram form this difference may be represented as follows:

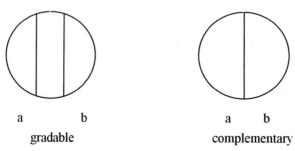

Figure 6.2 Gradable Antonymy and Complementary Antonymy

Secondly, the norm in this type is absolute. It does not vary with the thing a word is applied to. The same norm is used for all the things it is applicable to. For example, the criterion for separating the male from the female is the same with human beings and animals. There will be no such a situation that a creature is male by the standard of human being, but female by the standard of animal. And the death of a man is the same as that of an elephant, or even a tree, in the sense that there is no longer any life in the entity. If anything, the difference between the death of a man and that of a tree is a matter of kind, not of degree.

Thirdly, there is no cover term for the two members of a pair. If you do not know the sex of a baby, you ask "Is it a boy or a girl?" not * "How male is it?" The word "male" can only be used for boys, it cannot cover the meaning of "girl." As a matter of fact, no adjective in this type can be modified by "how." This is related to the fact that they are not modifiable by words like "very." Now the pair of antonyms "true : false" is exceptional to some extent. This pair is usually regarded as complementary. "True" equals "not false," and "not true" equals "false." But there is a cover term. We can say "How true is the story?" And there is a noun "truth," related to this cover term. We can also use "very" to modify "true." It even has comparative and superlative degrees. A description may be "truer" than another, or is the "truest" among a number of descriptions, though "false" cannot be used in this way.

6.4.2.3 Converse Antonymy

Pairs of words like "buy : sell" "lend : borrow" "give : receive" "parent : child" "husband : wife" "host : guest" "employer : employee" "teacher : student" "above : below" "before : after" belong to this type of antonymy. They show the reversal of a relationship between two entities. "X buys something from Y" means the same as "Y sells something to X." "X is the parent of Y" means the same as "Y is the child of X." It is the same relationship seen from two different angles. This type of antonymy is typically seen, as the examples show, in reciprocal social roles, kinship relations, temporal and spatial relations. It is in this sense that they are also known as RELATIONAL OPPOSITES. There are always two entities involved. One presupposes the other. This is the major difference between this type and the previous two.

With gradable, or complementary, antonyms, one can say "X is good," or "X is male," without presupposing Y. It is, as it were, a matter of X only, which has nothing to do with Y. But with converse antonyms, there are always two sides. If there is a buyer, there must also be a seller. A parent must have a child. Without a child, one cannot be a parent. If X is above Y, there must be both X and Y. Without Y, one cannot talk about the aboveness of X. And one cannot simply say "He is a husband." One must say whose husband he is. Similarly, one cannot simply say "He is a son" without mentioning his parents.

Now some people may argue that we can say "He is a child." However, this is a different sense of "child." The word "child" here means "somebody under the age of 18." In this sense, it is opposite to "adult." When a man is above 18, he is no longer a child. In contrast, used in the sense of "child" opposite to "parent", a man is always a child to his parents. Even when he is 80, he is still a child to his father and mother. Another word which may cause some trouble is "teacher." It can be used in the sense of a profession. So one can say "He is a teacher," as against any other occupation, such as, journalist, writer, actor, musician, or doctor. In the sense opposite to "student," however, a man is a teacher only to his students. To other people, he is not a teacher. And to his own teacher, he becomes a student.

The comparative degrees like "bigger : smaller" "longer : shorter" "better : worse" "older : younger" also belong here, since they involve a relation between two entities.

6.4.3 Hyponymy

The term HYPONYMY is of recent creation, which has not found its way to some small dictionaries yet. But the notion of INCLUSIVENESS is not new. For example, the meaning of "desk" is included in that of "furniture," and the meaning of "rose" is included in that of "flower." In other words, hyponymy is a matter of class membership.

The upper term in this sense relation, i.e. the class name, is called SUPERORDINATE, and the lower terms, the members, HYPONYMS. A superordinate usually has several hyponyms. Under "flower," for example, there are "peony" "jasmine" "chrysanthemum" "tulip" "violet" "carnation" and many others apart from "rose." These members of the same class are CO-HYPONYMS.

Sometimes a superordinate may be a superordinate to itself. For instance, the word "animal" may only include beasts like "tiger" "lion" "elephant" "cow" "horse" and is a co-hyponym of "human." But it is also the superordinate to both "human" and "animal" in contrast to "bird" "fish" and "insect," when it is used in the sense of "mammal." It can still further be the superordinate to "bird" "fish" "insect" and "mammal" in contrast to "plant."

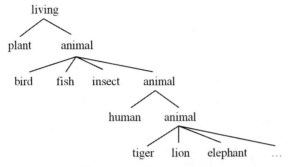

Figure 6.3 Superordinate

From the other point of view, the hyponym's point of view, "animal" is a hyponym of itself, and may be called auto-hyponym.

A superordinate may be missing sometimes. In English there is no superordinate for the colour terms "red" "green" "yellow" "blue" "white," etc. The term "colour" is a noun, which is not of the same part of speech as the member terms. And the term "coloured" does not usually include "white" and "black." When it is used to refer to human races, it means "non-white" only. The English words "beard" "moustache" and "whiskers" also lack a superordinate. Hyponyms may also be missing. In contrast to Chinese, there is only one word in English for the different kinds of uncles: 伯伯、叔叔、舅舅、姑父、姨父. The word "rice" is also used in the different senses of 稻、谷、米、饭.

6.5 Componential Analysis

In the discussion so far, we have been treating meaning as a property of the word, in line with the traditional approach. In what follows we shall introduce some modern approaches to the study of meaning. And this section is devoted to a discussion of meaning in terms of units smaller than the word meaning, while the next section will be concerned with the meaning of a unit larger than the word, namely, the sentence.

On the analogy of distinctive features in phonology, some linguists suggest that there are SEMANTIC FEATURES, or SEMANTIC COMPONENTS. That is, the meaning of a word is not an unanalysable whole. It may be seen as a complex of different semantic features. There are semantic units smaller than the meaning of a word. For example, the meaning of the word "boy" may be analysed into three components: HUMAN, YOUNG and MALE.① Similarly "girl" may be analysed into HUMAN, YOUNG and FEMALE; "man" into HUMAN, ADULT and MALE; and

---

① The semantic elements are usually enclosed in square brackets like [HUMAN]. In order to save some effort, in this chapter we do not use them.

"woman" into HUMAN, ADULT and FEMALE.

To be economical, we can combine together some semantic components. The components YOUNG and ADULT may be combined together as ADULT, with YOUNG represented as ∼ADULT; MALE and FEMALE may be combined together as MALE, with FEMALE represented as ∼MALE.

Words like "father" "mother" "son" and "daughter," which involve a relation between two entities, may be shown as follows:

father = PARENT (x, y) & MALE (x)①
mother = PARENT (x, y) & ∼MALE (x)
son = CHILD (x, y) & MALE (x)
daughter = CHILD (x, y) & ∼MALE (x)

Verbs can also be analysed in this way, for example,

take = CAUSE (x, (HAVE (x, y)))②
give = CAUSE (x, (∼HAVE (x, y)))
die = BECOME (x, (∼ALIVE (x)))
kill = CAUSE (x, (BECOME (y, (∼ALIVE (y)))))
murder = INTEND (x, (CAUSE (x, (BECOME (y, (∼ALIVE (y)))))))

It is claimed that by showing the semantic components of a word in this way, we may better account for sense relations. Two words, or two expressions, which have the same semantic components will be synonymous with each other. For example, "bachelor" and "unmarried man" are both said to have the components of HUMAN, ADULT, MALE and UNMARRIED, so they are synonymous with each other. Words which have a contrasting component, on the other hand, are antonyms, such as, "man" and "woman," "boy" and "girl," "give" and "take." Words which have all the semantic components of another are hyponyms of the latter, e.g. "boy" and "girl" are hyponyms of "child" since they have all the semantic components of the other, namely, HUMAN and ∼ADULT.

These semantic components will also explain sense relations between sentences. For example, (1), (2) and (3) are all self-contradictory, as there are words, or expressions, which have contradictory semantic components in them.

(1) *John killed Bill but Bill didn't die.
(2) *John killed Bill but he was not the cause of Bill's death.
(3) *John murdered Bill without intending to.

But a more important sense relation between sentences is entailment, exemplified by the (a) and (b) sentences in (4), (5), and (6).

(4) a. John killed Bill.

---

① This is a usual expression in logic. In plain English, it means "x is parent of y, and x is a male." For the details of logical semantics, see section 6.6.2.

② This expression means "x causes x to have y."

b. Bill died.

(5) a. I saw a boy.

   b. I saw a child.

(6) a. John is a bachelor.

   b. John is unmarried.

　The member sentences of each pair are in such a relationship that the truth of the second sentence necessarily follows from the truth of the first sentence, while the falsity of the first follows from the falsity of the second. In terms of semantic components, we can say it is because (a) sentences contain words which have all the semantic components of a word used in (b) sentences. ①

　Now there are also difficulties in the approach to analyse the meaning of a word in terms of semantic components. One difficulty is that many words are POLYSEMOUS. They have more than one meaning, consequently they will have different sets of semantic components in different sentences. A case in point is the word "man," which is usually said to have a component MALE. But it may also be used in a generic sense as in "Man is mortal," which applies to both sexes.

　Secondly, some semantic components are seen as binary taxonomies. MALE and FEMALE is one, and ADULT and YOUNG is another. But as we have learnt in the discussion of antonymy above, the opposition between MALE and FEMALE is different from that between ADULT and YOUNG. The former is absolute while the latter is relative. In English, though both "boy" and "girl" are marked as YOUNG or ~ ADULT, the distinction between "boy" and "man" is very different from that between "girl" and "woman." Very often, the former distinction is relatively clear cut while the latter is rather vague. There is a considerable overlap between "girl" and "woman." A female person may often be referred to by both.

　Thirdly, the examples we have seen are only concerned with the neatly organized parts of the vocabulary. There may be words whose semantic components are difficult to ascertain. Then there is the question of whether they are really universal, whether the vocabulary of every language may be analysed in this way. And even if the answers to these questions are all positive, there is still the question of how to explain the semantic components themselves. As it stands, semantic components like HUMAN, ADULT, MALE are not ordinary words of English, they belong to a META-LANGUAGE, a language used for talking about another language. The

---

　① There seems to be an exception as shown by the sentences in (1) below. (1)a entails (1)b, but "boys" has all the semantic components of "children," not the other way round. However, this exception is more apparent than real. The reason for this entailment comes from the use of "all" rather than the sense relation between "boys" and "children." If "some children" or "children" is used in (1)a, it will no longer entail (1)b, which is also born out by the sentences in (2).

attempt to explain the meaning of "man" in terms of these components is simply a translation from English to the meta-language. To someone who does not know the meta-language, his translation explains nothing.

6.6 Sentence Meaning

The meaning of a sentence is obviously related to the meanings of the words used in it. But it is also obvious that the former is not simply the sum total of the latter. Sentences using the same words may mean quite differently if they are arranged in different orders. For example,

(7) The man chased the dog.
(8) The dog chased the man.

Even when two sentences mean similarly as (9) and (10), there is still the difference in what Leech calls thematic meaning.

(9) I've already seen that film.
(10) That film I've already seen.

With sentences like (11), we need not only know the linear order of a sentence, but also the hierarchical structure.

(11) The son of Pharaoh's daughter is the daughter of Pharaoh's son.

This shows that to understand a sentence, we need also knowledge about its syntactic structure. In other words, this is an area where word meaning and sentence structure come together.

6.6.1 An Integrated Theory

The idea that the meaning of a sentence depends on the meanings of the constituent words and the way they are combined is usually known as the principle of COMPOSITIONALITY. The first theory which tries to put this principle into practice was advanced by J. Katz and his associates in the framework of transformational grammar some 50 years ago.

In 1963, Katz and Fodor wrote an article "The structure of a semantic theory," arguing forcibly that semantics should be an integral part of grammar, if, as Chomsky claims, grammar is to be a description of the ideal speaker hearer's knowledge of his language. And they set out to describe in some detail the internal structure of the semantic component. In the following year, Katz and Postal further elaborated their proposal in "An integrated theory of linguistic description."

Their basic idea is that a semantic theory consists of two parts: a DICTIONARY and a set of PROJECTION RULES. The dictionary provides the grammatical classification and semantic information of words. The grammatical classification is more detailed than the traditional parts of speech. For example, "hit" is not just a verb, but a transitive verb, written as Vtr;

"ball" is not just a noun, but a concrete noun, written as Nc. Terms like Vtr and Nc are called GRAMMATICAL MARKERS, or SYNTACTIC MARKERS. The semantic information is further divided into two sub-types: the information which has to do with the more systematic part, or is of a more general nature, is shown by semantic markers, such as (Male), (Female), (Human), (Animal). The information which is more idiosyncratic, word specific, is shown by DISTINGUISHERS. For example, the word "bachelor" has the following distinguishers:

a. [who has never married]
b. [young knight serving under the standard of another knight]
c. [who has the first or lowest academic degree]
d. [young fur seal when without a mate during the breeding time]

The projection rules[1] are responsible for combining the meanings of words together. We learn in the chapter on syntax that in Chomsky's theory a sentence like "The man hits the colorful ball" will have a syntactic description as in Figure 6.4.

The semantic description of this sentence, Katz and his associates suggest, is built on this basis. That is, they will first combine the meanings of "colorful" and "ball," then those of "the" and "colorful ball," and "hits" and "the colorful ball," and so on. This effectively provides a solution to the integration of syntax and semantics. Sentences made up of the same words but in different orders like (7) and (8) above will surely be given different semantic interpretations.

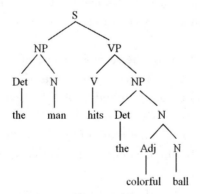

Figure 6.4

---

[1] Katz and Fodor (1972 [1963]: 475) argues "Since a fluent speaker is able to use and understand any sentence drawn from the *infinite* set of sentences of his language, and since, at any time, he has only encountered a *finite* set of sentences, it follows that the speaker's knowledge of his language takes the form of rules which project the finite set of sentences he has fortuitously encountered to the infinite set of sentences of the language."

In order to block the generation of sentences like "Colorless green ideas sleep furiously," they also introduce some SELECTION RESTRICTIONS as constraints on the combination process. For example, "colorful" has the selection restrictions, enclosed in angle brackets, in addition to grammatical markers, semantic markers and distinguishers, as follows:

colorful {Adj}
    a. (Color) [abounding in contrast or variety of bright colors]⟨(Physical Object) or (Social Activity)⟩
    b. (Evaluative) [having distinctive character, vividness, or picturesqueness] ⟨(Aesthetic Object) or (Social Activity)⟩

Given that "ball" has the following three readings:

ball {Nc}
    a. (Social Activity) (Large) (Assembly) [for the purpose of social dancing]
    b. (Physical Object) [having globular shape]
    c. (Physical Object) [solid missile for projection by engine of war]

a projection rule will be in effect to combine the features of "colorful" and "ball," resulting in the four readings of "colorful ball":

    a. (Social Activity) (Large) (Assembly) (Color) [abounding in contrast or variety of bright colors] [for the purpose of social dancing]
    b. (Physical Object) (Color) [abounding in contrast or variety of bright colors] [having globular shape]
    c. (Physical Object) (Color) [abounding in contrast or variety of bright colors] [solid missile for projection by engine of war]
    d. (Social Activity) (Large) (Assembly) (Evaluative) [having distinctive character, vividness, or picturesqueness] [for the purpose of social dancing]

The other two combinations of the second reading of "colorful" and the second or the third of "ball" are blocked by the selection restrictions. Then the distinguisher [some contextually definite] of "the" will be added to those of "colorful ball" by another projection rule. By the same token, the meanings of "hits" and "the colorful ball", and those of "the" and "man" will be established respectively. In the end, the meanings of the whole sentence will be composed as shown below:

    a. [some contextually definite] (Physical Object) (Human) (Adult) (Male) (Action) (Instancy) (Intensity) [collides with an impact] [some contextually definite] (Physical Object) (Color) [abounding in contrast or variety of bright colors] [having globular shape]
    b. [some contextually definite] (Physical Object) (Human) (Adult) (Male) (Action) (Instancy) (Intensity) [collides with an impact] [some contextually definite] (Physical Object) (Color) [abounding in

contrast or variety of bright colors] [solid missile for projection by engine of war]

c. [some contextually definite] (Physical Object) (Human) (Adult) (Male) (Action) (Instancy) (Intensity) [strikes with a blow or missile] [some contextually definite] (Physical Object) (Color) [abounding in contrast or variety of bright colors] [having globular shape]

d. [some contextually definite] (Physical Object) (Human) (Adult) (Male) (Action) (Instancy) (Intensity) [strikes with a blow or missile] [some contextually definite] (Physical Object) (Color) [abounding in contrast or variety of bright colors] [solid missile for projection by engine of war]

In other words, "the sentence is not semantically anomalous; it is four ways semantically ambiguous ... ; it is a paraphrase of any sentence which has one of the readings [listed above]; and it is a full paraphrase of any sentence that has the set of readings [listed above]." (Katz & Fodor 1971 [1963]: 508—509)

However, there are problems in this theory. First, the distinction between semantic marker and distinguisher is not very clear. Katz and Fodor themselves pointed out that the feature (Young) in the dictionary entry for "bachelor," which we quoted earlier, was included in a distinguisher, but it could be regarded as a semantic marker, since it represents something general. In Katz and Postal (1964: 14), even (Never Married), (Knight), (Seal) are treated as semantic markers. And eventually Katz dropped this distinction completely.

Second, there are cases in which the collocation of words cannot be accounted for by grammatical markers, semantic markers or selection restrictions. Katz and Fodor (1971 [1963]: 513) argue that features (Male) and (Female) are involved in the different acceptability of "The girl gave her own dress away" and " * The girl gave his own dress away." Presumably, they would also say the acceptability of "He said hello to the nurse and she greeted back" shows that "nurse" has a feature (Female). But "My cousin is a male nurse" is a perfectly normal sentence while "My cousin is a female nurse" is decidedly odd.

The most serious defect concerns the use of semantic markers like (Human) and (Male), which, more usually called semantic components as we mentioned in the last section, are elements of an artificial meta-language. To explain the meaning of "man" in terms of (Human), (Male) and (Adult), one must go on to explain the meaning of these semantic markers themselves, otherwise it means nothing.

6.6.2 Logical Semantics

The second promising theory to put the principle of compositionality into practice has been developed by logicians. In order to understand it better, in this sub-section, we introduce some basic concepts in logical semantics, especially the concepts in propositional logic and predicate logic.

PROPOSITIONAL LOGIC, also known as PROPOSITIONAL CALCULUS or SENTENTIAL CALCULUS, is the study of the truth conditions for propositions: how the truth of a composite proposition[①] is determined by the truth value of its constituent propositions and the connections between them. According to J. Lyons (1977: 141—142), "A proposition is what is expressed by a declarative sentence when that sentence is uttered to make a statement." In this sense, we may very loosely equate the proposition of a sentence with its meaning.

A very important property of the proposition is that it has a TRUTH VALUE. It is either true or false. And the truth value of a composite proposition is said to be the function of, or is determined by, the truth values of its COMPONENT PROPOSITIONS and the LOGICAL CONNECTIVES used in it. For example, if a proposition p is true, then its negation $\sim p$ is false. And if p is false, then $\sim p$ is true. The letter p stands for a simple proposition; the sign $\sim$, also written as $\neg$, is the logical connective negation; and $\sim p$, signalling the negation of a proposition, is a COMPOSITE PROPOSITION. There are four other logical connectives: CONJUNCTION &, DISJUNCTION $\vee$, IMPLICATION $\rightarrow$ and EQUIVALENCE $\equiv$. They differ from negation in that two propositions are involved, hence the name two place connective. In contrast, negation $\sim$ is known as one place connective. The truth tables for the two place connectives are as follows:

Table 6.2 Propositional Logic

p q	p&q	p∨q	p→q	p≡q
T T	T	T	T	T
T F	F	T	F	F
F T	F	T	T	F
F F	F	F	T	T

The LOGICAL CONNECTIVE CONJUNCTION &, also symbolized as $\wedge$, corresponds to the English "and." The truth table for it shows that when both p and q are true, the formula p & q will be true. This is both a necessary and a sufficient condition. That is, only when and as long as both conjuncts are true, the composite proposition will be true. The CONNECTIVE DISJUNCTION $\vee$ corresponds to the English "or." Its truth table shows that only when and as long as one of the constituents is true, the composite proposition will be true. The connective implication $\rightarrow$, also known as

---

① J. Lyons (1995) has introduced this term to cover both compound and complex propositions.

conditional, corresponds to the English "if ... then." Its truth table shows that as long as the consequent is true, or both the antecedent and the consequent are false, the composite proposition will be true. And the last logical connective equivalence ≡, also called BICONDITIONAL and symbolized as .., is a conjunction of two implications. That is, $p \equiv q$ equals (p → q) & (q → p). It corresponds to the English expression "if and only if ... then," which is sometimes written as "iff ... then." The condition for the composite proposition to be true is that if and only if both constituent propositions are of the same truth value, whether true or false.

Now one may notice immediately that the truth functions of the logical connectives are not exactly the same as their counterparts in English—"not" "and" "or" "if ... then" and "if and only if ... then" respectively. We mentioned in Section 6.4.2 that antonyms are of different types. With complementary antonyms, it is true that the denial of one is the assertion of the other. With gradables, however, that is not necessarily the case. When "John isn't old" is false, its negation "John is old" is not necessarily true. And the truth table for conjunction shows that if two propositions p and q are both true, then the composite proposition made up of them, p & q, will definitely be true. The order of the constituent propositions is not important. But "and" in English is used in a different way. "He arrived late and missed the train" may be true in a situation while "He missed the train and arrived late" may not, though both of their constituent propositions may be true. The difference between the implication connective → and "if ... then" is even greater. The logical connective takes no account of the nature of the relation between the antecedent and the consequent. The truth table shows that as long as two propositions are both true, the composite proposition made up of them, p → q, is true. That is, any true proposition would imply any other true proposition. Not only the composite proposition "If he is an English man, he speaks English" is valid in logical terms, but that "If snow is white, grass is green" is also valid. What is more, according to the truth table a composite proposition will be true, as long as its consequent is true. In other words, even a false antecedent proposition may imply a true consequent proposition, such as, "If snow is black, grass is green." In a natural language, however, there must be some causal or similar relationship between the two. The composite proposition "If snow is white, grass is green" sounds odd. And nobody would accept "If snow is black, grass is green" in daily conversation. If one wants to make a counterfactual proposition, then he would have to use the subjunctive mood, e.g. "If snow were black, grass would be red."

As is shown, propositional logic, concerned with the semantic relation between propositions, treats a simple proposition as an unanalyzed whole. This is inadequate for the analysis of valid inferences like the syllogism below:

(12) All men are rational.
Socrates is a man.
Therefore, Socrates is rational.

To explain why these inferences are valid, we need to turn to predicate logic, also called predicate calculus, which studies the internal structure of simple propositions. In this logical system, propositions like "Socrates is a man" will be analyzed into two parts: argument[①]and predicate. An ARGUMENT is a term which refers to some entity about which a statement is being made. And a PREDICATE is a term which ascribes some property, or relation, to the entity, or entities, referred to. In the proposition "Socrates is a man," therefore, "Socrates" is the argument and "man" is the predicate. In logical terms, this proposition is represented as M(s). The letter M stands for the predicate "man," and s the argument "Socrates." In other words, a simple proposition is seen as a function of its argument. The truth value of a proposition varies with the argument. When Socrates is indeed a man, M(s) is true. On the other hand, as Cupid is an angel, the proposition represented by the logical formula M(c) is false, where c means "Cupid." If we use the numeral 1 to stand for "true" and 0 for "false," then we can represent these two examples as the formulas: M(s) =1, M(c) = 0.

In "John loves Mary," which may be represented as L(j, m), we have two arguments "John" and "Mary." If we classify predicates in terms of the number of arguments they take, then "man" is a one place predicate, "love" a two place predicate. And "give" is a three place predicate in "John gave Mary a book," the logical structure of which being G(j, m, b). But propositions with two or more arguments may also be analyzed in the same way as those with one argument. "John loves Mary," for example, may also be represented as (Lm)(j),[②] in which there is a complex predicate (Lm), (consisting of a simple predicate "love" and an argument "Mary") and a single argument "John." And there are even suggestions that a predicate may take propositions[③] as arguments. A case in point is the componential analysis of words like "take" and "kill." Recall that the componential analysis of "kill" is CAUSE (x, (BECOME (y, ($\sim$ALIVE (y)))), which may be simplified now as C (x, (B (y, ($\sim$A (y))))). That is, the predicate "cause" takes a simple argument x and a propositional argument "y becomes non-alive." The latter itself may be analyzed as consisting of a predicate "become" and a propositional argument "y is non-alive," which is itself made up of a predicate "non-alive" and a simple argument y.

---

① It is also referred to as "name" or "individual."
② This particular form of representation is mine, not conventionally used by logicians.
③ As will be pointed out in note 1 on page 251, these are not really propositions, since the relevant arguments do not refer to particular entities as proper nouns to.

Now propositions like "All men are rational" are different. First there is a quantifier "all," known as the universal quantifier and symbolized by an upturned A — ∀ in logic. Second, the argument "men" does not refer to any particular entity, which is known as a variable①and symbolized by the last letters of the alphabet such as x, y. So "All men are rational" will be said to have a logical structure of ∀x (M (x) → R (x)). In plain English it means "For all x, it is the case that, if x is a man, then x is rational."

There is another quantifier—the existential quantifier, equivalent to "some" in English and symbolized by a reversed E — ∃. This is useful in the logical analysis of propositions like "Some men are clever," which, for example, is represented as ∃x (M (x) & C (x)). That is, "There are some x's that are both men and clever," or more exactly, "There exists at least one x, such that x is a man and x is clever."②

Notice that the logical structures of these two types of quantified propositions not only differ in the quantifier but also in the logical connective: one uses the implication connective → and the other the conjunction connective &. That is, the universal quantifier is conditional and does not presuppose the existence of an entity named by the argument. What it asserts is that if there is an entity as named then it will definitely have the property as specified. There is no exception to this rule. But the existential quantifier carries the implication that there must exist at least one such entity and it has the relevant property specified, otherwise that proposition is false. In fact the universal and existential quantifiers are related to each other in terms of negation. One is the logical negation of the other. "All men are rational" means the same as "There is no man who is not rational," which in logical terms may be represented as: ∀x (M (x) → R (x)) ≡ ~∃x (M (x) & ~R (x)). More generally, we can have the following equivalences.

(13) ∀x (P (x)) ≡ ~∃x (~P (x))
~∀x (P (x) ≡ ∃x (~P (x))
∃x (P (x)) ≡ ~∀x (~P (x))
~∃x (P (x)) ≡ ∀x (~P (x))

That is, "It is the case that all x's have the property P" is equivalent to "There is no x, such that x does not have the property P"; "It is not the case

---

① In contrast, arguments expressed by proper nouns like "Socrates" are known as constants.

② The quantifiers are indispensable in expressions with variables. In logical terms, expressions like "Men are rational" are not acceptable. The argument "men" does not refer to a particular entity as "Socrates" does, therefore the expression does not have a truth value and is not a proposition proper. And such expressions are called open sentences, or sentential functions, propositional functions. So there are no ambiguous expressions like "Children are a nuisance" in logic, as we touched on in note 1 on page 241. In this sense the logical formulas used in componential analysis like PARENT (x, y) & MALE (x) do not represent propositions, but propositional functions.

that all x's have the property P" is equivalent to "There is at least an x, such that x does not have the property P"; "There is at least an x, such that x has the property P" is equivalent to "It is not the case that all x's do not have the property P"; and "There is no x, such that x has the property P" is equivalent to "It is the case that all x's do not have the property P."

When analyzed in this way, the validity of inferences like (12) will be easily shown. That is, the logical structures of the three propositions involved are respectively:

(14) $\forall x \ (M(x) \rightarrow R(x))$
  $M(s)$
  $\therefore R(s)$

On the other hand, the following inferences are not valid. In (15), the antecedent and the consequent are reversed. An entity which is rational is not necessarily a man. In (16), the major premise is existential, which does not guarantee that any entity which is a man is clever.

(15) $\forall x \ (M(x) \rightarrow R(x))$
  $R(s)$
  $\therefore M(s)$

(16) $\exists x \ (M(x) \ \& \ C(x))$
  $M(s)$
  $\therefore C(s)$

The validity of inferences involving the universal and existential quantifiers may also be shown in terms of set theory. In the left figure below, the large circle represents the set of entities which are rational and the inner small circle represents the set of entities which are men. It is obvious that any entity which is a member of the set M is also a member of the set R, but not vice versa. That is, the set M is a subset of R. And this explains why (14) is valid, but (15) is not. The figure on the right represents the scope of the existential quantifier as E, which is the intersect of the two sets M and C. In other words, not all the members of the set M are members of the set C. And this is why (16) is invalid.

Figure 6.5 The Validity of Inferences Involving the
Universal and Existential Quantifiers

Now the analysis in terms of predicate logic is also divergent from that in natural languages. For one thing, common nouns like "man" in "Socrates is a man" are treated in the same way as adjectives like "rational" in "Socrates is rational" and verbs like "run" in "Socrates ran." All three are one place predicates, while in English they belong to three different word classes. For another, there are more quantifiers in natural languages than "all" and "some," such as, "many" "most" "dozens of" "several" "a few" in English. But there is no adequate provision for them in predicate logic.

6.6.3 Montague Semantics

MONTAGUE SEMANTICS, or MONTAGUE GRAMMAR, is the approach to the analysis of natural languages which originated with the American logician Richard Montague in the late 1960s.

Logicians before Montague usually study formal, artificial, or logical languages, such as is done in propositional logic and predicate logic. And their findings there, we noted in the previous sub-section, are not necessarily applicable to natural languages. But Montague holds that there is no important theoretical difference between natural languages and the artificial languages of logicians. The methods used for the analysis of logical languages may also be applied to natural languages. His basic idea is that we can treat logical languages and natural languages as the two extremes of a spectrum, and construct a number of intermediate languages between them, some of which are more like logical languages and others more like natural languages. In the end we will arrive at a language in the middle, which is like logical languages on the one hand and natural languages on the other. To achieve this aim, he set out to narrow the gap between grammar and logic by introducing revisions on both sides.

On the grammar side, Montague used as the basis of his theory a kind of CATEGORIAL GRAMMAR, initially proposed by the Polish logician Kazimierz Ajdukiewicz. In this grammar, there are two primitive categories: sentence (abbreviated as S) and name (abbreviated as N). Other categories are all derived from these two. For example, in transitive verbs are of the category S/N. That is, they are of the category which combines with an N to form an S.[1] And transitive verbs are of the category (S/N)/N, the category combining with an N to form an intransitive verb, in the more usual sense of a predicate. But Montague changed the names of the primitive categories in his theory to t (the category of truth value expressions, or declarative sentences) and e (the category of entity expressions, or individual expressions). And some of his derived categories are:[2]

---

[1] To understand the symbol S/N more easily, we may see the slant/as equivalent to the minus sign-. In other words, IV (intransitive verb) = S—N.

[2] Montague defined different categories in different papers. What follows are from his "The proper treatment of quantification in ordinary english," the last paper he had written.

IV, or the category of intransitive verb phrases, is to be t/e. ①
T, or the category of terms, is to be t/IV. ②
TV, or the category of transitive verb phrases, is to be IV/T. ③
IAV, or the category of IV modifying adverbs, is to be IV/IV.
CN, or the category of common noun phrases, is to be t//e. ④ (1974: 249—250)

The syntactic rules in Montague's theory take the following form:

If $\zeta \in P_{CN}$, then $F_0(\zeta), F_1(\zeta), F_2(\zeta) \in P_T$,
where $F_0(\zeta) =$ **every** ζ,
$F_1(\zeta) =$ **the** ζ,
$F_2(\zeta)$ is **a** ζ or **an** ζ according as the first word in ζ takes **a** or **an**. (ibid.: 251)

The Greek letter ζ could be anything, though in this context we may say it refers to a phrase. The sign $\in$, as used in set theory, means "is a member of." P_{CN} is the abbreviation of "the set of common noun phrases," with P standing for "phrase." The letter F refers to a syntactic function, or a syntactic mode of combination of the constituent phrases. And the subscripts of F, namely, 0, 1, 2, serve to distinguish one function from another. P_T, like P_{CN}, means "the set of term phrases." In plain English, the whole rule means "If anything is a member of the set of common noun phrases, then, it will follow 'every' by the operation of F_0, 'the' by F_1, and 'a' or 'an' by F_2; and the resultant phrases are all members of the set of terms."

On the logic side, Montague made some revision to INTENSIONAL LOGIC, a more advanced logical system than predicate logic, with more logical operators than the two quantifiers and the logical connectives. The term "INTENSION" and its antonym "EXTENSION" are usually used in the senses of "connotation" and "denotation," or "sense" and "reference." That is, the intension of a word is something abstract while its extension is more concrete. For example, the intension of "desk" is the defining properties of the thing it

---

① The symbol t/e means this is a category which may be used together with an entity expression to form a truth value expression. For example, "run" may be used with "John" to form a sentence "John runs."

② Similarly, t/IV means this is a category which may be used together with an IV expression to form a sentence, e.g. "John" in "John runs." The establishment of this category effectively leaves the category of entry expression *e* redundant. Except for defining the category IV, the category *e* has no other uses. But, as we shall see later, *e* as a semantic type is not redundant.

③ This means a transitive verb like "love" may be used together with a term "Mary" to form a predicate as in "John loves Mary," just as "run" does in "John runs."

④ One may remember "Socrates is a man" is logically represented as M (s). That is, "man" here, like "run" in "John runs," is a predicate. In other words, common nouns like "man" may also be used with a term to form a sentence. In order to separate this category form that of IV, Montague used a double slant here.

stands for, such as "a piece of furniture, with a flat top and four legs, at which one reads and writes." And its extension is the class of objects which have the relevant properties, i.e. all kinds of desks. Something new in Montague's intensional logic is that the notion "possible world" is also involved here. By a possible world is meant a possible state of affairs. We know that there are many factors contributing to the present state of affairs. Any difference in one of the factors may lead to a different state of affairs, or a different world. So it is advisable to discuss not only the actual world, but also the possible worlds.

The introduction of this notion greatly facilitates the discussion of meaning in terms of reference, or extension. We mentioned in Section 6.3 that one of the problems with the referential theory of meaning is that there are words, such as "God" "ghost" and "dragon," which refer to imaginary things and do not have actual existence. Now that we have the notion of possible worlds, we may say these things have existence in a possible world, in an imaginary world, in the world of Christianity or of Chinese culture. In other words, the reference, or the extension, of a word may be defined as what it stands for in a possible world, not necessarily in the actual world. Consequently, the intension of a word may also be changed somewhat. In set theory, a definition in terms of defining properties is equivalent to an exhaustive listing of the members. For example, in the sentence "The integers bigger than 5 and smaller than 10 are 6, 7, 8 and 9," the subject is a description of the defining properties of a set and the predicative a list of the members of the set. Usually, the first method is used for sets with infinitely large members. So human being is defined by descriptions like "a featherless biped" "a rational being" or "an articulate mammal." The second method, on the other hand, is used for finite sets such as the English alphabet. Now with the introduction of the notion possible world, the distinction between the two methods may be blurred. We may relate intension with extension in that the intension of a word may be defined as the extension in all possible worlds. That is, we may define human being as all the persons together, whether living in the present, past or future, whether living on the earth or elsewhere. ①In logical terms, the intension of a word is said to be the function, understood in the sense of a rule, formula or operation, which determines its extension in all possible worlds. Conversely, we may define the extension of a word as its intension in a possible world. Given a possible world, the intension of a word tells us whether there is an extension in it, and if there is, what it is. In this sense, intension is the function from possible worlds to extension. This interdefinability between

---

① In this sense, the intension of a word is also seen as an aspect of denotation. The distinction between intension and extension, therefore, is no longer comparable to that between connotation and denotation.

intension and extension makes it possible to represent the meaning of a word in terms of its intension only.

Corresponding to the syntactic categories on the grammar side, Montague also has two primitive units on the logic side-t (truth value) and e (entity). But they are called types, or more clearly, SEMANTIC TYPES, to be distinguished from the syntactic categories. So a proposition, which has a truth value as its reference or extension, is of type t; and an argument or a name, which refers to an entity, is of type e. The intension of a proposition, on the other hand, is a function form possible worlds to a truth value, which is represented as $\langle s, t \rangle$.① And the intension of an argument is a function from possible worlds to an entity, represented as $\langle s, e \rangle$. The derived types may be worked out recursively. For example, the extension of a one place predicate is of type $\langle e, t \rangle$, which means that with e as an input, a one-place predicate may produce an output of type t. And its intension is of type $\langle s, \langle e, t \rangle \rangle$. The extension of a two place predicate is of type $\langle e, \langle e, t \rangle \rangle$, whose intension is similarly of type $\langle s, \langle e, \langle e, t \rangle \rangle \rangle$.

Now predicates are of different kinds in that some presuppose the existence of the objects they take while others do not. Verbs like "kick" in (17) are of the former kind, known as extensional in the sense that their objects have extensions in the actual world; and verbs like "seek" in (18) are of the latter kind, known as non-extensional, or intensional, in the sense that their objects may not necessarily have extensions in the actual world.

(17) John kicked a dog.

(18) John sought a unicorn.

To solve this problem, Montague chose to raise all the types one level higher. That is, the extensions of one place predicates will no longer be of type $\langle e, t \rangle$, but $\langle \langle s, e \rangle, t \rangle$; and their intensions will be of type $\langle s, \langle \langle s, e \rangle, t \rangle \rangle$. The extensions of two place predicates will be changed to type $\langle \langle s, e \rangle, \langle \langle s, e \rangle, t \rangle \rangle$, and their intensions will be of type $\langle s, \langle \langle s, e \rangle, \langle \langle s, e \rangle, t \rangle \rangle \rangle$. This effectively means that all the logical form tells us is that the expression concerned has such and such intensions, whether there are also extensions we do not know. In situations where it is important to show that there are also extensions, there is a rule, called MEANING POSTULATE, to allow the extensional predicates to change back to their original types.

In Montague's theory, there is a third part to translate English expressions into logical expressions. The general principles are as follows:

---

① Montague did not explain what exactly the letter s here stands for. According to his usage, there are two possible explanations. One is that it stands for the Latin word saeculum, meaning "world." The other is that s is mnemonic for "sense."

$$f(e) = e,$$
$$f(t) = t,$$
$$f(A/B) = f(A//B) = \langle\langle s, f(B)\rangle, f(A)\rangle \text{ whenever } A, B \in Cat.$$
(ibid. :260)

The letter f stands for "function." The expressions enclosed in round brackets on the left side of the equation are syntactic categories, while those on the right are semantic types. And *Cat* is the abbreviation of "category." In other words, $f(e) = e$ means the syntactic category e has its corresponding semantic type e as its value, and $f(t) = t$ means the syntactic category t has the semantic type t as its value. One will remember that the double slant // is used to separate the intransitive verb from the common noun, though they are the same in the sense that both may be used together with a term, such as a proper noun "Socrates," to form a sentence like "Socrates ran" and "Socrates is a man." That is why $f(A/B) = f(A//B)$. And either of them equals $\langle\langle s, f(B)\rangle, f(A)\rangle$. If we substitute t for A, and e for B, we can see the reasoning very clearly. That is, the third equation above means $f(t/e) = f(t//e) = \langle\langle s, f(e)\rangle, f(t)\rangle$. To go one step further, i.e. to substitute e for $f(e)$, and t for $f(t)$, we arrive at $\langle\langle s, e\rangle, t\rangle$, an intensional type of a one-place predicate (or an argument) at the lower level. This shows that the syntactic categories of English correlate very neatly with the semantic types of intensional logic. There are also translation rules to correlate with the syntactic rules. It is for this reason that Montague's theory is referred to as either Montague semantics or Montague grammar.

Montague's theory is very complicated. Our presentation here has left out many technical details. But the basic idea, we hope, is clear. That is, to repeat, Montague tried to narrow the gap between logic and grammar, to apply logical analysis to natural languages. And he succeeded in this attempt to some extent.

PS. In recent years, the study of meaning has been advanced greatly by cognitive linguists. But to avoid possible overlaps, we will not add anything on cognitive semantics in this chapter. Readers interested in that aspect may read the chapter on cognitive linguistics for the details.

References

Akmajian, A., Demers, R. A. & Harnish, R. M. 1984. "Semantics: the study of meaning and reference," In *Linguistics: An Introduction to Languages and Communication.* (2nd ed.). Cambridge, Mass.: MIT Press. pp. 236—285

Allwood, J., Andersson, L-G., & Dahl, O. 1977. *Logic in Linguistics.* Cambridge: Cambridge University Press.

Atkinson, M., Kilby, D. & Roca, I. 1988. "Semantics," In *Foundations of General Linguistics.* (2nd ed.). London: Unwin Hyman. pp. 188—223.

Katz, J. J. & Fodor, J. A. 1963. "The structure of a semantic theory," In *Language* 39: 170—210. Reprinted in Rosenberg, J. F. & Travis, C. (eds.). 1971. *Readings in the Philosophy of Language.* New Jersey: Prentice Hall, Inc. pp. 472—514.

Katz, J. J. & Postal, P. M. 1964. *An Integrated Theory of Linguistic Descriptions*. Cambridge, Massachusetts: MIT Press.

Lyons, J. 1977. *Semantics*, 2 vols. Cambridge: Cambridge University Press.

Lyons, J. 1995. *Linguistic Semantics: An Introduction*. Cambridge: Cambridge University Press.

Leech, G. 1981. *Semantics: The Study of Meaning*. (2nd ed.). Harmondsworth: Penguin.

McCawley, J. D. 1981. *Everything that Linguists have always Wanted to Know about Logic*. Oxford: Basil Blackwell.

Montague, R. 1974. *Formal Philosophy: Selected Papers of Richard Montague*. By R. H. Thomason. (ed.). New Haven: Yale University Press.

Ogden, C. K. & Richards, I. A. 1923. *The Meaning of Meaning*. London: Routledge & Kegan Paul.

Palmer, F. R. 1981. *Semantics: A New Outline*. (2nd ed.). Cambridge: Cambridge University Press.

Partee, B. H. (ed.). 1976. *Montague Grammar*. New York: Academic Press.

Saeed, J. I. 1997. *Semantics*. Oxford: Blackwell.

方 立,1987,《蒙太古语义学导论》评介,《外语教学与研究》第3期。转载于方立(1993)《美国理论语言学研究》,第97—142页。北京:北京语言学院出版社。

方 立,2000,《逻辑语义学》,北京:北京语言文化大学出版社。

姜望琪,1991,True or False?《北京大学学报(英语语言文学专刊)》第2期。

徐烈炯,1995,《语义学》,第二版,北京:语言出版社。

邹崇理,1995,《逻辑、语言和蒙太格语法》,北京:社会科学文献出版社。

Chapter 7

Linguistic Comparison

7.1 Introduction

Linguistic comparison refers to a branch of linguistics, in which the primary concern is to make statements comparing the characteristics of different languages, different varieties of the same language or different historical states of a language. It forms an important part of general linguistics and of our understanding of the working and development of the world languages.

Generally speaking, linguistic comparison is concerned with the discovery of the identical or similar, or different aspects or characteristics of different languages, different varieties or different stages of the same language by bringing the linguistic data or evidence from them into comparison. In this case, it will be related to several branches of linguistics: the comparative and historical linguistics, linguistic typology between languages and within a language, language universals and contrastive linguistics. The identical or similar aspects of different languages show that these languages share features in common, and if they are proved to be shared by all the languages of the world, they are linguistic universals; if they are proved to be shared by a certain number of languages, then these languages are said to belong to the same type at least in these aspects, or they may be descendents of the same mother language, and if they are proved to be different in certain aspects, they are said to be contrastive.

Comparative and historical linguistics, linguistic typology and contrastive linguistics are based on rather different principles and with different ends in view. So it is necessary to understand the bases and methods of these three types of linguistics.

7.2 Comparative and Historical Linguistics

7.2.1 The Emergence of the Branch of Linguistics

Comparative and historical linguistics, also called "comparative philology" dominated the field during the nineteenth century in Europe. This is partly because of the stimulus derived from the discovery of Sanskrit, the ancient classic language of India, by Western scholars and the demonstration at the end of the eighteenth century of the indisputable historical connection of this language with Latin, Greek and German.

This inspires the Western scholars to develop a set of theoretical hypotheses on the relationships between languages and on the development of language, and to pursue the discovery of the affinal relationships between languages in Europe, including the relationship between Sanskrit and the European languages, and traced their common ancestry.

7.2.2 The Stages of Development

The development of comparative and historical linguistics can be briefly summarized into the following stages: 1) the observation of correspondence, 2) the explanation of correspondence, 3) the reconstruction of proto-language, 4) the representation of affinal relations between languages, 5) the identification of language families, and 6) the explanation of exceptions.

7.2.2.1 The Observation of Correspondence

The linguistic evidence, the facts on which comparative and historical studies are based, is in part very obvious. **Word forms** in languages are in the great majority of cases only conventionally linked with their referents or with their semantic functions; this has been expressed by speaking of the essentially arbitrary nature of linguistic forms. However, among different languages greater or smaller numbers of words, whose meanings are related or similar, exhibit **manifest similarities** of phonetic form. Some examples from European languages will illustrate this (see Table 7.1).

Table 7.1 Phonetic Similarity in Groups of European Languages

Meaning	English	German	French	Italian	Spanish
'hand'	hand /hænd/	Hand /hant/	main /mẽ/	mano /ˈmano/	mano /ˈmano/
'life'	life /laɪf/	Leben /ˈleːben/	vie /vɪ/	vita /ˈvɪtɑ/	vida /ˈvɪda/
'summer'	summer /ˈsʌmə/	Sommer /ˈzɒmer/	ete /ete/	estate /eˈstate/	estio /esˈtɪo/
'give'	give /gɪv/	geben /ˈgɜːben/	donner /dɒne/	donare /doˈnare/	donar /doˈnɑr/

It will be seen from these examples that **English and German** constitute one group, and **French, Italian, and Spanish** another group, in which these word forms of similar meanings show obvious similarities with one another, but not between languages of the different groups. We may now consider the examples in Table 7.2.

Chapter 7 Linguistic Comparison

Table 7.2 Phonetic Similarities in European Languages

Meaning	English	German	French	Italian	Spanish
'foot'	foot /fʊt/	Fuss /fuːs/	pied /pje/	piede/pɪˈɛde/	pie /ˈpɪe/
'two'	two/tuː/	zwei /tsvaɪ/	deux /dø/	due /ˈdʊe/	dos /dos/
'three'	three/θriː/	drei/draɪ/	trots/tma/	tre/tre/	tres/tres/
'me'	me/miː/	mich/mɪg/	moi/mwa/	me/me/	me/me/

In these word forms it is clear that, while the similarities within the two groups of languages mentioned above are closer, a general similarity in at least some part of each word unites all five languages into a larger group in terms of this evidence.

The immediately apparent basis for this sort of lexical comparison is similarity of word forms, but further examination reveals that similarity is only a special case of **systematic and regular correspondences** between component sound segments in semantically related words. Single pairs of similarly sounding words of the same sort of meaning are of no significance unsupported by others, and can be found between almost any two languages. The significance of Italian *piede* and English *foot* is not so much the similarity between /p/ and /f/, as the fact that the correspondence is matched by such further pairs as *padre* /ˈpadre/ and *father*, *pesce* /ˈpeʃʃe/ and *fish*, and that /d/ and /t/ correspond in *due* and *two*, *dieci* /dɪˈɛcɪ/ (ten) and *ten*, and other pairs; and the same thing applies to all the other examples quoted. Examples of such correspondences become cumulatively weightier as their number multiplies.

When the series of words exhibiting correspondences of this sort between languages is set out and examined, it is found that they are far too numerous to be plausibly explained away as coincidental (as single unsupported examples could be), and that they are each confined to certain groups of languages. Languages can be grouped together on the evidence of these correspondences.

7.2.2.2 Explanation of Correspondence

Since the particular correspondences and similarities by which languages may be grouped in this way are not universal as between all languages, nor reasonably regarded as coincidental, an explanation is required, and comparative and historical linguistics is an explanatory discipline. The only plausible explanation is that the different word forms related by one or more correspondences of phonetic composition are the result, after varying intervals of time, of the gradual divergence of the languages involved from an earlier linguistic situation in which their predecessors in time constituted something like a single language (itself, of course, like all languages, an abstraction and no doubt divided by isoglosses into regional dialects). This is what is meant by saying that, historically a language is derived from an earlier language. That is to say, that the derived languages from an earlier language were once dialects of that language, and they became separate languages in the historical process of development. By the same way, particular words in it are derived from particular earlier words.

The causes of this continuous process of change are as yet not fully understood, but two sets of factors may be distinguished, external influences and internal processes. External causes of linguistic change are the contacts between the speakers of different languages, of the sort that occur when a foreign language is imposed on a people by conquest or by political or cultural domination, or when cultural and other factors produce a high degree of bilingualism between adjacent speech areas. Under such conditions speakers who acquire a second language in adulthood will inevitably bring into their use of it, phonetic, grammatical, and some lexical habits of their own first language. In the course of time such habits, passed on from generation to generation, becomes standardized and acceptable. External factors of one sort or another have been held responsible for many of the differences in languages that take place when an original language is diffused over wide areas displacing languages spoken there before, as happened with the spread of Latin over much of the western half of the Roman Empire and of English, Spanish, and Portuguese over large areas of the world in more modern times.

Internal causes of linguistic changes lie in the nature of the transmission of speech habits from one generation to another. Apart from all external influence, gradual changes appear to be inevitable, and in the processes some general tendencies are found repeatedly at work in various times and areas. It must be remembered that a language as such is wholly acquired by exposure to utterances in the language of those closest to the infant and young child, normally its biological parents. The general ability to acquire and to use a language is innate, biologically inherited, and with it certain restrictions on the form that languages can take, but the actual sounds, grammatical forms, syntactic constructions and lexical meanings are culturally transmitted, mostly in the child's early years. Herein lies the scope for small and gradual, but cumulative, changes at all levels.

Among all the systematic and regular sound changes so far discovered, there are two most celebrated ones: **the First Germanic Consonant Shift**, and **the Great English Vowel Shift**.

The First Germanic Consonant Shift applied to prehistoric times in Proto-Germanic to a number of the consonants inherited from PIE, and familiarly known as **the Grimm's Law**. Jacob Grimms, in 1822, found this sound-shift:

(a) $p > f$ (b) $b > p$ (devoicing)   (c) $bh > b$ (deaspirating)

t > ρ(θ)   d > t   dh > d
k > x   g > k   gh > g

In the following Table, Latin, Greek and Lithuanian, which did not undergo the shift, are used to illustrate the consonants of IIE, while Gothic, Old English, and Old Norse represent the shifted consonants of Proto-Germanic.

Table 7.3 The First Germanic Consonant Sift

PIE	Gothic	Old English	Old Norse	Meaning
Latin: piscis	Fisks	fisc	fisk	'fish'
Latin: tu	Pu	pu	pu	'thou'
Sanskrit: bharami	Baíran	beran	bera	'bear'
Greek: thyra	—	duru	—	'door'
Latin: ego	Ik	ic	ek	'I'

The Great Vowel Shift in English is a term given to a series of far-reaching and interrelated changes in vowel articulations that took place in English principally during the fifteenth century, as part of the passage from Middle English to early modern English and thence to present-day English. It was the earlier long vowels that were most affected. Leaving aside many details, what happened was a related raising of all the long vowels except for /iː/ and /uː/, which could not be raised further. These were kept distinct by diphthongization, first to /əɪ/ and /əʊ/ and then to /ɑɪ/ and /ɑʊ/. These changes may be diagrammed like this:

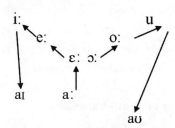

Figure 7.1 The Great Vowel Shift

Later /eː/ from Middle English /ɛː/ fell together with /iː/ from Middle English /eː/, /oː/ became /oʊ/ (/əʊ/), and /ɛː/ became /eɪ/.

7.2.2.3 The Representation of Correspondence

The correspondences are between sound segments, not letters, though in dead languages the written letters may be only evidence for the existence in the words concerned, of the sounds; and the attested correspondences of sound segments in the different languages in which they appear in the words may for convenience be summarily represented by a single symbol, usually prefixed by an asterisk, to distinguish it from the representation of an actual sound in a particular language, and referred to as a "starred letter." Thus *p represents the series: Sanskrit /p/ (pita /pɪtaː/, father), Latin /p/ (/ˈpater/), Ancient Greek /p/ (pɪtā /pɪta/, father), Ancient Greek /p/ (παλήρ /patéːr/), English /f/ (/ˈfaːλðə/), German /f/ (vater /ˈfaːter/), and so on in the other I-E languages; and in the same way *e represents the series: Sanskrit /a/ (asti /astɪ/ is), Ancient Greek /e/ (εστί/estí/), Latin /e/ (/est/), etc.

When the same procedure is applied to several segments in the series of words compared in this way and showing regular correspondences of this sort, the series of related words may be jointly represented by a sequence of starred letters to give what is called a "starred form," usually representing what appears to be common among the several languages concerned either to the root of the words, or, if any of them are variable words, to a similarly related series of bound affixial elements. Thus *septm represents the sound correspondences in several words meaning "seven": Sanskrit sapta /sáptá/, Latin /septem/, Ancient Greek ἑπτά/heptá/, German sieben /ˈziːben/, English /ˈsevən/ etc, and *nti represents those in the third person plural forms of present tense paradigms of verbs in such words as Sanskrit bharranti /bharantɪ/ (they) carry, Greek Φέρονσι /pʰérousɪ/ (Doric dialect Φέροντι /pʰéroutɪ/), Latin /ferʊnt/, and Gothic bairand /ˈbɛrand/.

It must be stressed that starred word forms can be set up from a series of actual attested words because the sound correspondences found between them are paralleled by the same correspondences in the same languages in other word series. Not every vowel and consonant in each member of a series of related words can necessarily be brought into a set of correspondences; but where a number of segments in each of the words can be so related the starred form is constructed to summarize these related segments.

7.2.2.4 The Reconstruction of Proto-Languages

The existence of systematic correspondences allowed us to make at least educated guesses about the sounds that must have been present in particular words in ancestral proto-languages. Then we can go much further than this in several directions: 1) to work out, not just the individual ancestral sounds, but all the ancestral sounds in individual words, 2) as an immediate consequence, to work out roughly what whole words must have sounded like in the ancestral languages, 3) as a further consequence, to work out what the entire phonological system of the ancestral language must have been like. This process is called the reconstruction of the proto-language. Broadly speaking, there are two methods to do this. One is called **the comparative reconstruction**, and the method used **the comparative method**; the other is called **the internal** reconstruction, and the method used **the internal method**.

7.2.2.4.1 The Comparative Reconstruction

The comparative method is the single most important tool in the historical linguist's toolkit, and we have in many cases enjoyed great success in reconstructing important aspects of unrecorded proto-languages. Rasmus Rask laid down fundamental principles of comparison in 1814. The comparison was made in three aspects:

(1) Inflectional endings.

(2) Systematic correspondence between sounds of the "most essential, concrete, indispensable words" of two languages.

(3) Similarities of vocabulary.

Informally, the comparative method works like this:

1. Decide by inspection that certain languages are probably genetically related and hence descended from a common ancestor.

2. Place side by side a number of words with similar meanings from the languages we have decided to compare.

3. Examine these for what appear to be systematic correspondences.

4. Draw up tables of the systematic correspondences.

5. For each correspondence found, posit a plausible-looking sound in the ancestral language, one which could reasonably have developed into the sounds that are found in the several daughter languages.

6. For each word surviving in the various daughters, look at the results of 5 and thus determine what the form of that word must have been in the ancestral language.

7. Finally, look at the results of 5 and 6 to find out what system of sounds the ancestral language apparently had and what the rules were for combining these sounds.

This, of course, is a vastly oversimplified picture of what happens in practice, but it gives you the general idea of what's going on. Table 7.4 lists, in phonemic transcription, a number of words from four western Romance languages: Portuguese, Spanish, Catalan, and French.

Table 7.4 Western Romance

No.	Portuguese	Spanish	Catalan	French	meaning
1	pajíš	país	pəís	pei	'country'
2	šūbu	plomo	plom	plɔ̃	'lead' (metal)
3	kopa	kopa	kop	kup	'cup'

We now begin setting up systematic correspondences.

Table 7.5 Correspondences Involving Voiceless Plosives

No.	Portuguese	Spanish	Catalan	French
1	p-	p-	p-	p-
2	š-	p-	p-	p-
3	-p-	-p-	-p	-p

For correspondences NO. 1 and NO. 3 we can clearly reconstruct *p. But NO. 2 is a slight problem. We would also like to reconstruct *p here, but Portuguese is a problem, since it doesn't show the expected /p/. Before trying to reconstruct something different, though, let's look for a conditioning factor. Note that, in item NO. 2, all the languages except Portuguese have an /l/ following the initial /p/, while Portuguese has no /l/ either. Hence the correspondence is more accurately stated as P /š-/; S /pl-/; C /pl-/; F /pl-/, and we can therefore reconstruct initial *pl in this word, with *pl developing into /š-/ in Portuguese.

So we have reconstructed *p. The other consonants can be reconstructed in the same way. Finally, we can reconstruct all the consonants of the Proto-Western Romance, such as *k, *b, *d, *g, *v, *m, *n, *s, *š, *f, *r, *rr, *l, *λ, apart from one or two puzzling forms which may be placed aside as problems.

Then we can also reconstruct the vowels in the same way. These we can represent as *i, *e, *ɛ, *a, *ɒ, *o, and *ʊ. When we have finished, we can then display the reconstructed PWR forms. With just a couple of outstanding puzzles, the forms will appear to represent the best available reconstructions. You can see that Spanish appears to be the most conservative of the four languages and French the least conservative.

However, we do not mean that the reconstruction is the definitive last word on Proto-Western Romance. Examination of a much wider set of data has shown that we have oversimplified in a few places, and specialists in fact reconstruct a couple of or more consonants in addition to the ones we have identified here, and they make different reconstructions in several cases.

7.2.2.4.2 Internal Reconstruction

The comparative method is the most important of the historical methods, but it can be used only when we have identified two or more languages sharing a common ancestor. It cannot be applied to a language with no known relatives, and it may be of minimal use with a language whose only identifiable relatives are very distantly related to it. In such circumstances, we must fall back on a second method, one which requires no data from related languages. This is the **internal method**, which can sometimes be applied to a single language so as to allow us to reconstruct important characteristics of earlier

Chapter 7 Linguistic Comparison

stages of that language; such reconstruction is **internal reconstruction.**

The term internal reconstruction is in fact applied to several slightly different procedures. In the simplest and most central of these, we proceed as follows:

1. Note that a certain pattern is visible in the language.
2. Note that some forms are exceptions to this pattern.
3. Hypothesize that the exceptional forms originally conformed to the pattern.
4. Posit an ancestral stage of the language with no exceptional forms.
5. Identify the changes that disrupted the original perfectly regular pattern and led to the introduction of exceptional cases.

Here is a simple example. A certain class of Latin verbs forms its first-singular present by suffixing-o to the stem, its infinitive by suffixing-ere, its first-singular perfect by suffixing-si, and its supine by suffixing-tum. (Note that Latin x represents [ks] and is equivalent to cs.)

Table 7.6 Latin Verb Forms

No.	first singular present	infinitive	first singular perfect	supine	Meaning
1	carpo	carpere	carpsi	carptum	'pluck'
2	dico	dicere	dixi	dictum	'say'
3	repo	pepere	repsi	reptum	'creep'
4	scalpo	scalpere	scalpsi	scalptum	'carve'

However, some anomalous forms can be found in some verbs in this class.

Table 7.7 Latin Verbs Showing Anomalous Form

No.	First singular present	infinitive	first singular perfect	supine	Meaning
1	figo	figere	fixi	fictum	'fix'
2	fingo	fingere	finxi	fincum	'form'
3	nubo	nubere	nupsi	nuptum	'marry'
4	pingo	pingere	pinxi	pictum	'paint'
5	tego	tegere	texi	tectum	'cover'

On the basis of the stem exhibited in the first two columns we would have expected * figsi, * figtum for 'fix,' * nubsi, * nubtum for 'marry,' and so on throughout the list. Let us therefore posit that these were the forms in some ancestral variety of Latin. What changes do we now have to recognize on the way to classical Latin? A voiced plosive *b* or *g* is devoiced when it is followed by a voiceless consonant like *s* or *t*. This is a perfectly natural phonological change, one of voicing assimilation in clusters. To prove our hypothesis, we need to look to see if there are any Latin words with clusters like *bs* and *gt*. As it happens, there are none, exactly as our account predicts. All such clusters, wherever they existed, must have undergone voicing assimilation.

By the same way, we can reconstruct the verb for 'cover' as the originally entirely regulartego, tegere, * tegsi, * tegtum, by the process of internal reconstruction, and we posit a single phonological change, a voicing assimilation applying to obstruent clusters. Of course, there are verbs which exhibit other anomalous forms, but these can all be explained by phonological conditioning, alternations in the forms of particular stems and affixes, the characteristics of the language and the historical development of the language, etc.

7.2.2.5 The Neogrammarians

The maintenance of strict standards of regular correspondences between the component sounds of the words adduced as evidence of genetic relations between two or more languages is a key point in the scientific standing of historical linguistics. The need for this "Strict regularity hypothesis" was emphasized by a group of German scholars in the latter half of the nineteenth century (altogether four members; August Leskien, Berthold Delbruck, Hermann Osthoff & Karl Brugmenn). The name is a translation of *Junggrammatiker*, a nickname given to those who first insisted on this principle and from them what is called the "neogrammarian" a hypothesis or theory has, in a modified form, become part of the accepted theory of comparative and historical linguistics.

As first formulated, the hypothesis was that "sound laws" were without exceptions; that is to say, within certain geographical limits and between certain dates a change of one sound in a language to another would affect in the same way all words containing the sound in the same phonetic environment of other sounds. It was soon seen that geographical and temporal limits in matters like this are hazy and indeterminate; one is dealing not with things, but with changes in rules and in habits, the ways people pronounce particular words. These changes cannot be expected to affect all words simultaneously, and on the borders between languages or dialects, some words may be subject to the change while others escape it or are affected by a different change. Broadly speaking four types of explanation may be called for:

(i) Words apparently belonging to a correspondence series are historically unrelated. Thus Latin /dɪeːs/ *day*, and the English word *day*, though similar in their initial consonants, and in their meanings, are not regarded as the result of divergence from a single word form, as the correspondences that regularly appear in such word pairs are Latin /d/ and English /t/ (/duo/ *two*; /ed-/ *eat*;

/decem/ *ten*, etc, part of the more general correspondences system known as Grimm's Law).

(ii) The rules, by which the correspondences were stated were not drawn up strictly enough and must be modified by a number of subsidiary and more exact statements to account for all word series properly falling within their scope. For example the correspondence of voiceless plosive and fricative does not apply when the sounds concerned follow a fricative in the word: Latin /tenʊɪs/, English thin /θɪn/, but Latin /sta-/, English stand /stænd/, Latin /est/, German ist /ʔɪst/. Another important modification to Grimm's Law is known as Verner's Law, from the name of the scholar who first worked it out; within the correspondences known under the general title of Grimm's Law some medial consonants show different correspondences according to the position of the accented (stressed) syllable of the word in the early period of LE unity. This is most readily illustrated from Sanskrit and Gothic. We may compare Sanskrit /ˈbhra:tar-/, *brother*, with Gothic /ˈbro:θar/, and Sanskrit /pɪˈtar-/, *father*, with Gothic, /fadar/, with the Sanskrit accented syllables marked as they were pronounced in the earlier stages of the language. We see the different correspondences of the Germanic languages such as English and German have obscured the earlier correspondences. The effect of differential stress placement on consonant articulation can be noticed in the English pair exercise, /ˈeksəsaɪz/, and exert /egˈzɜ:t/.

(iii) The apparently exceptional word is a loan word that entered the language at a period subsequent to the operation of the sound change responsible for the particular form the correspondence takes. Loans entering a language after a sound change has ceased to operate are not affected by it; conversely, loans entering before or during its operation will be affected in the same way as any other words containing the sound segments subject to the change.

(iv) The operation of the sound change in the particular word or words concerned has been prevented or reversed, or a different change has taken place, under the influence of analogy. In its widest sense analogy is at work in every utterance and understanding of a sentence not hitherto heard by either party, and in the similar use of forms of variable word paradigms that have not so far occurred with a particular root in the experience of a particular speaker.

The replacement of an irregular or suppletive form within a grammatical paradigm by a new form modeled on the forms of the majority of members of the class to which the word in questions belongs is the work of analogical creation. Individual examples of this are repeatedly found in the speech of children and foreign speakers with incomplete command of a language; 'seed' /si:d/ and 'hitted' /ˈhɪtɪd/, as mistaken past tense forms of *see* and *hit*, are analogical creations. Some such individual variations persist and are adopted by others in widening circles until they come to be accepted beside and ultimately to replace the older forms. The virtual supersession of *kine* by *cows* as the plural of cow is an example of successful analogical creation, and so are the more modern regular past tense forms *helped*, *climbed*, and *snowed*, for the earlier *holp*, *clomb*, and *snew*.

7.2.2.6 Representation of Genetic Relations between Languages

Not all the genetically related languages are equally closely related. For example, English is fairly close to Dutch but much more distant from Icelandic. Frisian is often singled out as the closest living relative of English, while Gothic is the Germanic language that is most different from all the others. Like any language family, then, the Germanic family has an internal structure, with some languages being particularly closely related and perhaps forming subgroups within the family. It is desirable to have some way of representing such internal structures. The most widely used device is **the tree diagram**, introduced by the German linguist August Schleicher in the middle of the nineteenth century.

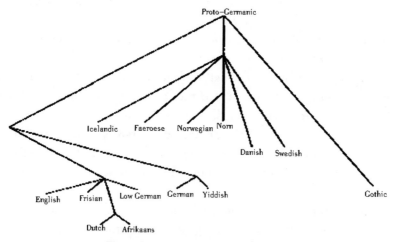

Figure 7.2 The Germanic Family Tree

Figure 7.2 shows the tree which is commonly drawn for the Germanic languages. This figure displays vividly some things we know to be true. For example, we can see at a glance that Dutch and Afrikaans are very closely related indeed, having diverged only about three centuries ago, when Dutch speakers settled in South Africa, and that Gothic is very different from all the other languages, having already diverged from them 2000 years ago, which is when the Goths begin to appear in Greek and Roman records.

Tree diagrams like these are very convenient, and they are widely used in historical linguistics. They have the great advantage of displaying the connections between languages vividly and at a glance. But they also have one great drawback: they are not very realistic. In particular, the branching structure of a tree suggests that a single rather homogeneous ancestral language at some point split suddenly and decisively into two or more separate daughter languages, which thereafter went their separate ways and had nothing further to do with one another. But we already know that this is not what really happens.

In 1856, the German linguist Johannes Schmidt therefore proposed a very different way of representing language families, the so-called wave model. A wave-model diagram looks something like a dialect map. The language names are spread about the page in some convenient arrangements, and each significant change which has occurred in some languages is represented by a closed curved line surrounding those languages. Figure 7.3 shows the example of the Germanic languages, classified in terms of a number of changes which Germanic specialists consider to be particularly significant.

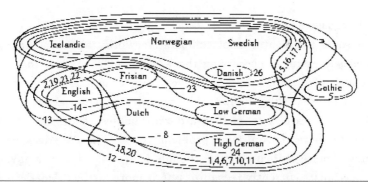

1 /æː/ backed to /aː/	15 extensive assimilation of consonant clusters
2 /aː/ from earlier /æː/ restored	16 suffixed definite article introduced
3 sharpening,	17 mediopassive introduced
4 /z/ > /r/	18 verbal infinitive becomes a noun
5 /fl-/ > /θl-/	19 vowel "breaking" introduced
6 masculine singular-s lost	20 consonant gemination in certain circumstances
7 masculine plural-s lost	21 palatalization and assimilation of /k, g/ before front vowels
8 reflexive pronoun lost	22 metathesis of /r/
9 reduplicating verbs lost	
10 inflected passive lost	23 final /-n/ lost in inflections
11 umlaut introduced	24 High German consonant shift
12 dental fricatives lost	25 pitch accent introduced
13 /n/ lost before /s/	26 pitch accent converted to glottalization
14 /n/ lost before any voiceless fricative	

Figure 7.3 A Wave Diagram of the Germanic Family

A wave diagram like this one therefore shows quite graphically the continuing contact between dialects and languages which have already begun to diverge, and thereby demonstrates the unreality of the sudden and decisive splits required by the tree model. Nonetheless, the wave diagram still reveals the reality of the major splits posited in the tree diagram: you can see here that Gothic still comes out as the most divergent Germanic language, while both the Scandinavian languages and the West Germanic languages still appear to form coherent groupings, and even English and Frisian appear to form a valid subgroup.

In spite of its obvious advantages, however, the wave model also possesses a few shortcomings. Most obviously, it does not allow us to represent earlier and later stages of languages at the same time, something which the tree diagram does very easily. Wave diagrams are also tedious and cumbersome to prepare and to draw, and they are much harder on the eye. In practice, therefore, historical linguists generally use wave diagrams only when we want to draw attention to particular facts which cannot otherwise be easily presented; the rest of the time we use the simpler and more vivid trees.

7.2.2.7 Language Families

After some two centuries of comparative work, historical linguists have been rather successful at classifying the world's 6000 or so living languages, plus a number of recorded dead languages, into genetic families, often with a good deal of internal subgrouping. The majority of languages in Europe have been assigned to scarcely more than a dozen families, and some of them very large, though there remain some problem areas. The Americas have so far proved much more difficult: even though it has far fewer languages than Europe, specialists currently recognize 140 or more distinct American families. No doubt further research will reduce this number to some extent, but it really does appear that the Americas are linguistically far more diverse than most of the rest of the world.

Here we will briefly review some of these families.

I. Indo-European family: This family is conventionally divided into ten branches. They are: Germanic; Italic (the Romance group); Celtic, divided into two branches: Brythonic, Goidelic; Balto-Slavic, divided into the Baltic and Slavic groups; Albanian; Greek; Thraco-Phrygianl Indo-Iranian, divided into three branches. The Iranian languages, The huge Indo-Aryan branch and the small Dardic branch Anatolian; Tocharian,

II. The Uralic family. This is divided into the Samoyed languages of Siberia and the Finno-Ugric branch.

III. Altaic. This is divided into three branches: the Turkic branch; the Mongolian branch, and the Tungusic branch.

IV. The Sino-Tibetan family. This includes the several Chinese languages (called "dialects," by the Chinese), plus Tibetan, Burmese, and many other less well-known languages.

V. The large Dravidian family, whose best-known member is Tamil.

VI. The Austro-Asiatic family, whose main branch is Mon-Khmer, The Munda languages of eastern Asia, and Nicobarese are two smaller branches.

VII. The Tai family (also called Daic), which includes Thai, Lao, and dozens of other languages.

VIII. The Miao Yao family is scattered across much of southern China.

IX. The Austropzesian family (once called "Malayo-Polynesian"), stretching from Madagascar to Easter Island.

X. Pama-Nyungan family, spoken in most of Australia.

XI. Africa and most of the Middle East are occupied by just four families, two of them are very large: the Afro-Asiatic family (formerly called "Hamito-Semitic") ; the ancient Egyptian; the Berber languages, and Chadic.

XII. The Nilo-Saharan' family, whose most famous member is Maasai in Kenya.

XIII. The vast Niger-Congo (or Niger-Kordofanian) family, which occupies most of the African continent below the Sahara.

XIV. Finally, there remain the isolates, single languages which do not appear to be related to anything else at all. Most famous of these is Basque, spoken at the western end of the Pyrenees in Western Europe.

XV. There are two of the major languages of Asia, Japanese and Korean. These two languages constitute one of the biggest problems of all. For generations each of them has been regarded as an isolate. Recently, however, a number of linguists have begun to argue that there is clear evidence that Korean and Japanese are in fact related to each other, and that both of them are moreover related to the nearby Altaic family, perhaps most closely to its Tungusic branch. So far, however, the proponents of the Altaic link have not succeeded in convincing the majority of specialists that their evidence is good enough to support the hypothesis, and the issue continues to be debated.

XVI. As shown above, the Americas are linguistically far more diverse than Europe, with at least 140 families being commonly recognized. Some of these families, however, are quite large such as the Eskimo-Aleut family the Na-Déné family, the Algonquian family, the Iroquoian family, the large Siouan family, and the sizeable Muskogean family. There are many other North American families: Tunican, Salishan, Waka, Shan, and Chimak. Much of Mexico and the southwestern USA are occupied by another large family, Uto-Aztecan. Much of northern South America and the Caribbean are (or were) occupied by the Carib family, which gives its name to the Caribbean Sea. In the Andes, we find the Quechuan family.

It is clear that there is still a great deal of work to do in the Americas. From time to time someone proposes to group two or three existing families into one larger family, and some of these proposals have won widespread acceptance.

7.3 Typological Comparison

Apart from historically orientated linguistic comparison, comparative and historical linguistics, or comparative philology, it is, however, possible to compare languages simply by reference to any significant general features of form or structural organization that they share at any level of analysis. Such comparisons group languages together in that they jointly exhibit features of some sort in common, other than those features which are exhibited in common by all languages and so form part of the nature of language itself. Comparison of languages on this basis is termed *typological comparison*.

The term typology has a number of different uses in linguistics. The broadest and most unassuming linguistic definition of "typology," refers to *a classification of structural types across languages*. In this definition, a language is taken to belong to a single type, and a typology of languages is a definition of the types and an enumeration or classification of the languages into those types. This definition of typology is called *typological classification*. The morphological typology of the nineteenth and early twentieth centuries is an example of this use of the term. This definition introduces the basic connotation that "typology," has to contemporary linguists: typology has to do with cross-linguistic comparison of some sort.

A more specific definition of "typology" is that it is *the study of linguistic patterns that are found cross-linguistically, in particular, patterns that can be discovered solely by cross-linguistic comparison*. The classic example of typology under this definition is the *implicational universal*. Under this definition, typology is a subdiscipline of linguistics with a particular domain of linguistic facts to examine cross-linguistic patterns. Typology in this sense began in earnest with Joseph H. Greenberg's discovery of implicational universals of morphology and word order.

There is a final, still more specific definition of "typology." In this view, typology represents *an "approach," to the study of language that contrasts with prior approaches*, such as American structuralism and generative grammar. In this third and last definition, typology is an approach to linguistic theory, or more precisely a methodology of linguistic analysis that gives rise to different kinds of linguistic theories than other "approaches." This view of typology is closely allied to functionalism, the hypothesis that linguistic structure should be explained primarily in terms of linguistic function (the Chomskyan approach is contrastively titled formalism). For this reason, typology in this sense is often called the *(functional-) typological approach*, which is primarily associated with Talmy Givón, Paul Hopper and Sandra

Thompson, though it has well-established historical antecedents.

7.3.1 Linguistic Typology and Linguistic Universals

Clearly, features at any level are of major interest in typology if they characterize the language as a whole either by being themselves of major relevance throughout a level or by forming part of a set of such features. This quest for typological features of wide significance has been termed "holistic typology."

Certainly basic word order is of considerable importance in itself, but it has become much more so since researches have shown a strong correlation, though a variable one with other features. Languages with a basic SOV order mostly use postpositions to mark the syntactic and semantic relations marked in SVO languages by prepositions. Considerations of this sort, set out by Greenberg in 1961, raise an important point. Typological classification is not an all or none question. For example, the distinction between tonal and non-tonal languages is not absolute and languages may share ergative and non-ergative syntactic structures.

This relative indeterminacy of typological classes has led to the formulation of **hierarchical tendencies** in regard to some features. As an example, some languages in Australia and elsewhere having both nominative, accusative, and ergative constructions, it can be shown that some nominals are more likely to occur as subjects in nominative constructions but that others are more likely to appear as ergatives in similar semantic relationships, and that the preferential ranking of nominal sets of words and phrases appears along the same hierarchy in quite unrelated languages.

There is a twofold relationship between linguistic typology and linguistic universals, depending on the conception of universals that is under consideration. In part this depends on the standpoint taken on the distinction between the "internalist," and the "externalist" approaches to the study of language as a human capability and activity. Many consider universals of language, linguistic universals, as a biologically inherited set of constraints characterizing the "language organ" of the brain rather as the human liver, kidneys, etc. Comparable constraints on the phonetics of human speech are more readily understood, through an inspection of the physiological capabilities and limitations of the human vocal tract.

Such a set of universals can, it is asserted, be inferred from the examination of a few or even of one language, as a working hypothesis to be tested, but to be accepted until falsified. These universals act as restraints on the ways and on the extent of language variations. But many linguists today aim at drawing the boundaries much more firmly and in greater precision. For example, phonetically, the physiology of the human vocal organs sets limits on the types of sounds that can be produced, and the physiology of the ear and the perceptual centres of the brain sets limits on the degree to which sounds used in continuous discourse may be acoustically similar and yet serve efficiently as phonologically distinctive units and features. Speech consists of serial events occurring in time, and the signaling devices in languages must, therefore, be such as can be manifested by means of a series of sounds and sound features, just as in writing they are manifested in linear successions of letters, syllable signs, or characters. Moreover, spoken communication must take account of the limits of short-term memory; otherwise the hearer will "lose his or her way," in trying to follow what is being said. Spoken sentences must be adequately structured and these structures adequately signaled by means available to the speaker and accessible to the hearer. The hearer cannot "go back," as the reader can, which is why, of course, sentences composed purely for silent reading may be both longer and more complicated than sentences intended to be spoken or read aloud.

On the other side, however, the sorts of clusters of features, or typological implications, being investigated by typologists following the proposals of Greenberg, also appeal to universals of language. These are inductive universals, not assumed as essential to the very existence of language, but arrived at from the analysis and comparison of many languages, in line with the "externalist," approach to linguistic science. For example, any language must be adequate for the communication needs of its speakers. The distinctive sound differences must be combinable in a sufficiently diverse number of separate word and morpheme forms to provide for an adequate word stock or lexicon; and these lexical resources of a language must be organized into a sufficiently flexible and productive grammatical system to produce sentences of the different types and patterns required for communication, readily understandable by other speakers of the same language. The double structuring of all languages in phonological and grammatical systems is the means whereby the physiologically limited possibilities of sound production and recognition can be made to serve the unlimited demands that languages have to meet in fulfilling the diverse and ever-changing needs of speech communities.

Within these limits of speech production and speech requirements, languages differ in the ways in which they fulfill their purposes; and these differences may be observed at every level of language and linguistic analysis. This sort of comparison gives rise to typological classification, languages being assigned to typological classes. Languages are typologically classified according to the similarities of form they exhibit with other languages at any level or levels. This type of linguistic comparison is best explained by illustrations from the main levels in which similarities of formal constitution are exhibited.

7.3.2 Typological Classification

Typological classification is the process of describing the various linguistic types found across languages for some grammatical parameter, such as grammatical number or the formation of relative clauses.

Typological classification is historically the first manifestation of typology in modern linguistics, starting with the morphological classification of languages in the nineteenth century. The notion of a linguistic type has changed somewhat since that time, particularly under the impact of structural linguistics

7.3.2.1 The Concept of Linguistic Type (strategy)

The usual procedure for initiating a cross-linguistic comparison of a particular grammatical phenomenon for the purposes of a typological analysis is to survey the range of structures used for the phenomenon in question. In morphosyntax, the phenomenon is generally a grammatical construction, which is usually defined on an external basis precisely because of the degree of structural variation actually found in languages. Thus, given a particular external definition of a category, one may then classify the linguistic structures found across languages to express or manifest that external definition. These structures are called **types or strategies**. This is typology in the first sense, a cross-linguistic structural classification.

Typology, in the sense of a cross-linguistic classification of types, is often considered to be a classification of languages into types, that is, a classification of language types. For example, Mam is an indexing genitive language type, and Bulgarian is an adpositional genitive language type, etc. The notion of a "language type" originates in the nineteenth century view of the morphological typology of languages. In the vast majority of cases, however, a classification of language types is difficult, if not impossible. Most languages have at their command several different structural types for a given construction, such as the genitive.

Then, we can say that a structural type is represented by a particular construction in a particular language. We will call this a classification of linguistic types. A language may have more than one construction representing more than one linguistic type. Technically, therefore, one cannot say that languages are of one type or another, or that languages use one strategy or another. This point is crucial in evaluating claims concerning entities like "OV languages," or "ergative languages." In most cases, such claims must be identified with the actual constructions in which OV word order or ergative morphology is used.

Although it is impossible to say in general that a language belongs to a particular structural type, such as the adpositional genitive type, it is very often possible to determine which of the many structural types a language uses is the basic type. A language's basic type may be useful in making typological generalizations; for example, there has been a good deal of success in making typological generalizations on basic word order types. Thus, there may be a legitimate sense in which we may be able to speak of a language belonging to a "language type," as opposed to a construction belonging to a structural type. This raises the question of determining which of several structural types a language uses for a given function is the **basic one.**

Linguistic types based on individual structural features form the foundation of most typological analysis. Each structural feature represents the independent variables on which cross-linguistic generalizations are based. Thus, the structural analysis of types is essential to typological analysis.

7.3.2.2 Morphological Typology

The first typological classification of languages (i.e. classification by structure rather than by genetic affiliation) is the so-called morphological typology, developed in the 19th century. The original formulation, by Friedrich von Schiegel, divided languages into two types: *affixal* and *inflectional*. Although it is not clear what criteria Schlegel used, the distinction may be characterized roughly as the simple combination of morphemes vs. the phonological alteration of morphemes in combination. Schlegel's brother, August, added a third type: languages with "*no structure*," (i.e. no affixation or inflection) with modern Chinese being the paradigm example. Wilhelm von Humboldt added a fourth type, "*incorporating*," to designate languages such as those of North America that treat the verb and the object as a whole word. The incorporating type did not figure in the "classical" formulation of the morphological classification, by August Schleicher, into the three types isolating, aggluatinative and inflectional, corresponding to Auguest von Schlegel's "no structure," affixal and inflectional respectively. Under the classical formulation, isolating languages did not use affixes at all; agglutinative languages used affixes that denoted single grammatical categories (such as number), and were concatenated with relatively little phonological alteration; and inflectional languages used affixes which often fused together several grammatical categories (such as number, gender and case) into a single morpheme, and which often underwent major phonological alterations when combined with roots.

The typological classification of languages at the time differs from the modern concept of typological classification in two important respects: first, the classification recognized only a single parameter on which languages varied, the morphological structure of words; second, it was a classification of languages as a whole, not as parts of a language. Both of these characteristics can be attributed to what is called the neo-Humboldtian view of language. In this view, each human language has its organic unity which manifests an "inner form." The morphological type of a language was a manifestation of its organic character.

The structuralist movement in linguistics altered the view of the morphological typology of languages. By postulating that languages had a synchronic structure, it made it possible to examine parts of language in isolation and make a typological classification of various features of language. Thus, one could typologize different parts of language, and one could typologize languages in different ways.

The idea that typological classification involves a particular construction, not the language as a whole, is a more recent one, though there is some presentiment of this in some Prague School work. (see Greenberg, 1974:46, n. 9) Although the traditional morphological typology is generally applied to a language as a whole, it could just as easily be applied to different parts of the linguistic system. For instance, the nominal system of a language may be agglutinative while the verbal system is inflectional.

The current concept of a linguistic type is a characteristic of what Greenberg (1974) called the generalizing approach to typological classification, the classification of languages, or more precisely elements of a language, by structural features of maximal generality. The individualizing approach, taken to its extreme, defines languages by their individual and perhaps unique combination of grammatical features. The truth has to be somewhere in between, since languages are different structurally, though not so different as to be incommensurable. However, the individualizing as well as the generalizing approach contains the seeds of modern typology, the study of cross-linguistic patterns of variation. If language as a structure does hang together in a certain way, then the identification of one structural feature—the feature defining the linguistic type—would imply the presence of certain other structural features. The generalizing approach to typological classification, with its emphasis on single morphosyntactic features rather than the language as a whole, also contribute to modern typology. It does so by separating the typological classification of logically independent grammatical properties of languages from the discovery and explanation of relationships between features across languages.

7.3.3 Implicational Universals

7.3.3.1 Restrictions on Possible Language Types

The first step beyond typology as the classification of types and towards the explanation of the cross-linguistic variation that classification describes is the discovery of *restrictions* on possible language types. Linguistic theory in any approach, "formalist," or "functional-typological," has as its central question, what is a possible language? This question can in turn be paraphrased as: of the logically possible types of languages, how do we account for what types actually exist?

One of the features that distinguishes the typological method of discovering constraints on possible language types is the strongly **empiricist method** applied to the problem. If a typologist wants to find restrictions on possible relative clause structures, for example, he or she gathers a large sample of languages and simply observes which of the possible relative-clause types are present and which are absent. That is, the restrictions on logically possible language types are motivated by the actually attested language types. If there is a gap in the attested language types, then it is provisionally assumed that the gap represents a constraint on what is a possible language, and explanations are sought for the gap.

Another important point about the empiricist method that should be mentioned here is that theoretical significance also accrues to the frequency of a language type, not just to whether it is attested or unattested. If one language type is extremely rare and another type extremely common, this distribution merits explanation even though both types are classed as "attested." For example, the first universal listed in Greenberg's original paper on implicational universals is "*In declarative sentences with nominal subject and object, the dominant order is almost always one in which the subject precedes the object.*" (Greenberg, 1966:77; my italics)

7.3.3.2 Unrestricted and Implicational Universals

An unrestricted universal is an assertion that all languages belong to a particular grammatical type on some parameter, and the other types on the same parameter are not attested (or are extremely rare). Unrestricted universals characterize the distribution of languages along a single parameter, for example, the order of subject and object, or whether or not a language has oral vowels. The parameter allows for the logical possibility of more than one type, but only one type is attested.

The number of unrestricted universals is relatively small. Most unrestricted universals are built into the frameworks of linguistic theories because they are true of all languages. Nevertheless, unrestricted universals require deeper explanation just as much as implicational universals or other more complex cross-linguistic patterns do. For example, why do all languages distinguish consonants and vowels, and nouns and verbs, apparently without exception? Why do virtually all languages appear to have words, phrases and clauses, have subject and object in that order, the protasis and apodosis of conditionals in that order, etc. ? Although the subject-object order question has been discussed extensively, and the noun-verb question has been addressed recently, many of these other questions could be investigated much further.

Implicational universals differ from unrestricted universals in that they do not assert that all languages belong to one type. Instead, they describe a restriction on logically possible language types that limits linguistic variation but does not eliminate it. We may illustrate this with a simple implicational universal, "If a language has noun before demonstrative, then it has noun before relative clause." (Hawkins, 1983: 84,-Universal XI ') This implicational universal cover the following four logically possible types:

Type 1. demonstrative and relative clause both follow the noun (NRel, NDem);

Type 2. relative clause follows the noun and demonstrative precedes the noun (NRel, DemN);

Type 3. relative clause precedes the noun and demonstrative follows the noun (RelN, NDem);

Type 4. demonstrative and relative clause both precede the noun (RelN, DemN).

The implicational universal restricts language variation to three types 1, 2, 4 by excluding the third type 3. Thus, implicational universals capture a pattern in language variation, and differ from unrestricted universals, which account for uniformity, not variation. As such, implicational universals cannot even be discovered without cross-linguistic comparison.

What makes implicational universals more interesting than unrestricted universals above all, however, is that they state a dependency between two logically independent parameters. The four logically possible language types described in the preceding paragraph actually represent two independent parameters, demonstrative-noun order and relative clause-noun order. Each parameter has two values: the modifier precedes or the modifier follows.

Another important feature of both unrestricted and implicational universals is that they are universal, not language-specific. In the case of implicational universals, the universal dependencies between grammatical properties may not even be apparent in individual languages taken one at a time, because they are patterns of variation. Even so, since implicational universals cover all human languages, the forces that account for their existence must be operating in the grammars of individual languages. Implicational universals represent an application of propositional logic to typology.

A standard implicational universal is a generalization over a tetrachoric table in which three types are attested and one type is not. It is important to remember that the pattern of attested and unattested language types in a tetrachoric table (or larger table) is the central fact, and that an implicational universal is only a convenient low-level description of that pattern. There are other possible patterns of attested language types in which only two types are attested, or even just one type is attested.

The concept of an implicational universal has had its greatest impact in the area of word order. Although broader theoretical concepts have been invoked to account for typological patterns of word order, implicational universals still remain a basic unit of typological analysis. Implicational universals of word order illustrate the basic elements of the typological method in their simplest form. The first step is the enumeration of logically possible language types by the structural parameters involved, illustrated by the tetrachoric table. The second step is the discovery of the empirical distribution of attested and unattested types, illustrated by the pattern of gaps in a tetrachoric (or larger) table. The third step is developing a generalization that 1) restricts variation in language types without eliminating it—i. e. allows for the various attested types while excluding the unattested types, and 2) reveals a relationship between otherwise logically independent grammatical parameters—in this case the implicational relationship. At this point, typologists from Greenberg onward have observed more far-reaching relationships between the word order parameters, such as harmony and dominance, than could be captured by simple implicational universals. The final step in the analysis is to seek a deeper (possibly external) explanation for the relationship, such as heaviness, mobility and the various proposals for explaining the existence of harmony.

7.3.4 Functional Typological Classification

The functional typological classification is concerned with the relationship between typology and external explanation, or more precisely, external motivation for language structure. This brings us to typology in the third sense, the functional typological approach to linguistic theory and explanation.

The relationship between typology and functionalism can be summarized quite simply at the broadest level. Functionalism seeks to explain language structure in terms of language function. It assumes that a large class of fundamental linguistic phenomena are the result of the adaptation of grammatical structure to the function of language. In grammatical basics, the function of language is universal across cultures: roughly, language is the general-purpose communication device. As a consequence, functionalism ought to try to account for those facts about language that are universal across all languages. Typology is a primary source for those universals, particularly those universals which are not unrestricted.

7.3.4.1 Markedness and Economic Motivation

Greenberg (1966: 65—69) argues that in the case of morphosyntax, *textual frequency* is the source of the markedness criteria. The most frequent grammatical value has zero or minimal expression (the structural criterion), because it is the most common form and the uncommon form (marked value) is given a distinctive mark. The hidden assumption for the connection between frequency and zero expression is *the principle that people will shorten the linguistic expressions that are used most commonly for economy, that is to simplify their linguistic utterances.*

This principle is sometimes called "Zipf's Law," after the linguist who popularized it:"High frequency is the cause of small magnitude." (Zipf, 1935: 29) John Haiman has called it economic motivation or economy (Haiman, 1985), and he argues that it pervades grammatical expression. Most markedness patterns can be analyzed as economically motivated, and economic motivation probably plays a role in other aspects of grammar and typology.

Haiman, following Meillet (Haiman, 1985: 157), offers another suggestion for markedness: the origin of cross-cutting categories in unmarked rather than marked values. Frequent combinations tend to be "run together," and eventually phonologically fused, that is, frequent expression is economized by being physically shortened. This may occur only for the most frequent, that is unmarked-values in a paradigm, hence the greater inflectional versatility of unmarked forms. This is essentially a diachronic account of markedness.

The final criteria for markedness are typological frequency and typological distribution (dominance). The typological frequency criterion is relatively simple to account for: if a grammatical/semantic category is very infrequent, it simply will not be expressed as a distinct grammatical category in as many languages. Typological distribution is more problematic. There does not seem to be a general explanation in terms of economy, or any other functional motivation for that matter. In the case of dominant word order, it does not appear that economic motivation can play any role, and the "preferred word order" (other things being equal) presumably has to do with factors such as the heaviness of the constituent and the pragmatics of word order. Both of these may be functionally motivated, but not by economy. However, explanations of preferred word order will not help to explain the "preference" for number inflection manifested in the universal "If nouns inflect for gender, then they inflect for number."

It appears that economic motivation can easily provide a functional explanation of morphosyntactic markedness for the structural, typological frequency and the inflectional behavioral criteria, using text (discourse) frequency as the causal source. It may also account for the distributional, behavioral criterion. However it does not account for the typological-distributional criterion. In itself, this does not question the validity of the latter two criteria as criteria of markedness. But it does suggest that markedness is more than just one manifestation of economic motivation.

There are more external explanations. First, not all markedness patterns are directly associated with frequency. Second, even if frequency is the immediate cause of markedness patterns, it is worth investigating in turn the cause of the frequency of certain grammatical values and combinations in speech. One may ask, for example, why the singular category is more frequent in discourse, that is why singular entities are more spoken about than plural collections of those entities. In other words, the functionally oriented typologist may seek justification of the prominence or salience of particular semantic categories to human beings: those constructions that involve less formal [structural] markedness linguistically correspond to those extralinguistic situations which—in fact or in our conceptualizations—are more expected. On the other hand, all that is necessary for invoking economic motivation to explain linguistic markedness is reliable frequency data. Only in the case of prototypes does there appear to be enough independent psychological evidence to make it worth venturing farther afield in the functional justification of typological patterns.

Hopper and Thompson then argue that the *foregrounding-backgrounding distinction* is the explanation for the grammatical transitive prototype. That is, "transitive" encodes the foregrounding of information, and "intransitive" encodes the backgrounding of information. The remaining correlations follow because foregrounded information tends to be telic, punctual, volitional, etc., and backgrounded information tends to be stative, durative, non-volitional, etc.

7.3.4.2 Iconicity

The other major type of external motivation for linguistic structure is iconicity. The intuition behind iconicity is quite simple: the structure of language reflects in some way the structure of experience, that is to say, the structure of the world, including (in most functionalists' view) the perspective imposed on the world by the speaker. The structure of language is therefore motivated or explained by the structure of experience to the extent that the two match. As we have already seen, there are other motivations which destroy the parallelism between linguistic structure and external structure in the name of economy: an unmarked concept often has no corresponding linguistic entity referring to it.

Iconicity of linguistic structure to external or experiential structure can be divided into two aspects: the correspondence of parts and the correspondence of relations between parts. Haiman calls these "isomorphism" and "motivation."

7.3.4.2.1 "Isomorphism" and Polysemy

Haiman interprets "isomorphism" as referring to the hypothesis of "one form, one meaning." This is the correspondence of parts of the linguistic structure (including the linguistic construction as a whole) to parts of experience, and represents an unrestricted universal of human language. Haiman observes that this requires the explanation of four types of exception or "mismatch" (Haman, 1985:21):

1) one form to zero meaning: empty morphemes;

2) zero form to one meaning: zero morphemes;

3) many forms to one meaning: synonymy;

4) one form to many meanings: homonymy (including polysemy).

7.3.4.2.2 Iconic Motivation

Hainan's narrow use of the term (iconic) "motivation" is defined by him as the parallelism between the relations among parts in linguistic structure and relations among parts in the structure of what is signified. (Haiman, 1985:11) The distinction between "isomorphism" and iconic motivation is not entirely clear, as we will see from the following illustrations of iconic motivation.

The primary difficulty in evaluating arguments in favor of iconicity is that the structure of what is signified, "experience" as we put it above, is not well established.

There are three very general aspects of grammatical structure that can be, and have been, studied from a typological perspective. Each of these has its corresponding hypothesis for iconic motivation.

1) *Simple vs. complex expressions.* One can study what concepts are expressed cross-linguistically by simple grammatical structures—single morphemes, single words, single clauses—as opposed to what concepts are expressed by complex structures—multiple morphemes, compound words, complex sentences. The iconicity hypothesis would propose that the concepts which are always, or frequently, expressed by simple grammatical structures are cognitively primitive and those expressed by complex structures are cognitively complex.

2) *Categorization.* One can study what concepts are placed into the same grammatical category. This resembles the typological notion of polysemy: in this instance, the assignment of concepts to the same grammatical category (e.g. "auxiliary") implies conceptual similarity or relatedness. Two general classifications will concern us here. The first is the classification of concepts into specific grammatical categories, such as noun, verb, adverb, etc. The iconicity hypothesis would propose that the concepts that fall into the same grammatical category are cognitively similar in some respects. The second question is the more general classification of concepts into two types of grammatical categories: either a closed-class, usually bound-morpheme

"function word" category or an open-class, usually free morpheme "content word" category. The iconicity hypothesis would propose not only that the concepts falling into each of these two categories are cognitively similar but that the distinction in grammatical structure and behavior corresponds to some cognitive distinction.

3) *Structural isomorphism*. One can study the range of structures (types or strategies) used for the expression of complex concepts across languages, looking for similarities and regularities in the types used. The iconicity hypothesis would propose that (to the extent that structures are universal) the structure of a grammatical construction will reflect the structure of the complex concept it expresses.

The study of any one grammatical structure frequently involves more than one of these aspects. The examples used here will therefore sometimes illustrate two or three of these aspects at once.

7.3.4.3 Competing Motivations

Different motivations may also compete with each other, for example, the economy motivation competes with the iconicity motivation in various ways. In this case, the resolution of the conflict gave rise to the phenomenon of polysemy. It is important to note that the competition between economy and iconicity has different possible resolutions, that is, it allows for cross-linguistic variation. Either polysemy occurs, signalling the predominance of economy; or separate forms for each concept occur, signalling the predominance of iconicity. The competing motivation model of economy and iconicity excludes one logically possible type: the uneconomic and un-iconic presence of more than one form for a given concept. This is synonymy, whose existence Haiman, Bolinger and other linguists have argued against. Thus, competing motivations provide an important class of explanations for both typological variation and constraints on that variation.

A competing motivation analysis also underlies markedness patterns, at least structural markedness. But markedness is not an unrestricted universal.

7.3.4.4 Concluding Remarks

In the above, we have examined external explanations for typological patterns, focusing chiefly on economy, iconicity and communicative function. The principle of economy provides explanation for those many aspects of markedness patterns (including hierarchies and prototypes) that can be traced to frequency. The principle of iconicity, including "isomorphism" and iconic motivation, along with the principle of communicative function can be used to account for the typology of form-function relations. The empirical study of cross-linguistic patterns of form-function relations is basically in its infancy.

This area is currently attracting considerable attention in typological research.

7.4 Contrastive Linguistics

7.4.1 Introduction

Contrastive Linguistics may be roughly defined as a subdiscipline of linguistics which is concerned with the comparison of two or more languages (or subsystems of languages) in order to determine both the differences and similarities that hold between them (Fisiak et al., 1978; cf. Jackson, 1976), more importantly, it focuses more on the differences than similarities. It is also called "**comparative descriptive linguistics**" by Ellis (1966), "**linguistic confrontation**" by Akhmanova & Melencuk (1977), but the term "contrastive linguistics" or "**contrastive analysis**" is the most frequently used and occurs in most languages which have been the subject of this type of investigation.

The tradition of contrastive linguistics is not long and goes back only to the fifties and early sixties of the last century (Rusiecki, 1976), and it is primarily associated with language teaching. But Contrastive Linguistics has much longer roots than the fifties or even the forties of the last century. Although it was not called so until 1941 (Whorf), it goes back at least to the last decade of the 19th century and the beginning of the 20th century. Interestingly enough, the first published studies were predominantly theoretical in orientation. (Grandgent, 1892; Vietor, 1894) The applied aspect was not totally neglected (e.g. Vietor, 1903) but was accorded a more peripheral importance. Theoretically oriented contrastive studies were continued from the late twenties throughout the interwar period by Prague School linguists, notably V. Mathesius (1928, 1936), and also later by his followers well into the sixties. (Vachek, 1961; Firbas, 1964)

The Second World War aroused great interest in the applied aspect in the United States. Contrastive studies were recognized as an important part of foreign language teaching methodology and, as a result, more applied relevance was assigned to CL. Just as Fries (1945) says, "The most efficient materials are those that are based upon a scientific description of the language to be learned, carefully compared with a parallel description of the native language of the learner." (Fries, 1945: 9)

Contrastive linguistics as a systematic branch of linguistic science is of fairly recent date. The publication in 1957 of Robert Lado's *Linguistics across Cultures* marks the real beginning of modern applied contrastive linguistics. Lado on the first page of his book quotes Charles C. Fries, the American structuralist who took the lead in applying the principles of linguistic science to the teaching of English. Lado supports this contention with the following words: "Textbooks should be graded as to grammatical structure, pronunciation, vocabulary, and cultural content. And grading can be done best after the kind of comparison we are presenting here." (Lado, 1957:3) Two years later work was started on the *Contrastive Structure Series*, edited by Charles A. Ferguson. The series has as its aim the description of similarities and differences between English and each of the five foreign languages most commonly taught in the U. S. A.: French, German, Italian, Russian and Spanish. In the meantime work in the field of contrastive linguistics has steadily increased.

Concerning the general characteristics of contrastive analysis (CA), we need to ask three questions: 1) Is CA concerned with language in general or with particular languages? 2) Is it concerned with immanent features or comparison? 3) Is it diachronic or synchronic? The answers to these questions, with respect to contrastive analysis are not clear-cut. First, CA is neither only concerned with general features shared by all languages nor with the particular language, but somewhere intermediate on a scale between the two extremes. Likewise, CA is as interested in the inherent genius of the language under its purview as it is in the comparability of languages. Yet it is not concerned with classification, but, as the term contrastive implies, more interested in differences between languages than in their likenesses. And finally, although it is not concerned either with language families, or with other factors of language history, nor is it sufficiently committed to the study of "static" linguistic phenomena to merit the label synchronic. CA seems, therefore, to be a hybrid linguistic enterprise. In terms of the three criteria discussed here we might say that CA is a linguistic enterprise aimed at producing contrastive (not comparative) two-valued typologies (as CA is always concerned with a pair of languages), and founded on the assumption that languages can be compared.

7.4.2 Major Branches of Contrastive Linguistics

Contrastive linguistics is thus not a unified field of study. The focus may be on general or on language specific features. The study may be theoretical, without any immediate application, or it may be applied, i.e. carried out for a specific purpose. The term "contrastive linguistics," or "contrastive analysis," is especially associated with applied contrastive studies advocated as a means of predicting and/or explaining difficulties of second language learners with a particular mother tongue in learning a particular target language. In the Preface to his well-known book, Lado (1957) expresses the rationale of the approach as follows: "The plan of the book rests on the assumption that we can predict and describe the patterns which will cause difficulty in learning and those that will not cause difficulty. It was thought that a comparison on different levels (phonology, morphology, syntax, lexis, culture) would identify points of difference/difficulty and provide results that would be important in language teaching."

The most efficient materials are those that are based upon a scientific description of the language to be learned, carefully compared with a parallel description of the native language of the learner. (Fries, 1945:9) The high hopes raised by applied contrastive linguistics were dashed. There are a number of problems with the approach, in particular the problem that learning cannot be understood by a purely linguistic study. So those who were concerned with language learning instead turned to the new disciplines, such as **error analysis, performance analysis** or **interlanguage** studies, and contrastive analysis was rejected by many as an applied discipline. In spite of the criticism of applied contrastive linguistics, contrastive studies were continued, and their scope was broadened.

7.4.2.1 Theoretical Orientation

The task of finding out the differences and similarities between languages can be approached in many different ways depending on what theory of language the investigator adheres to. The results of investigation will differ considerably because the task itself, especially the terms "difference" and "similarity," will be understood differently in different theories. For instance, the structural linguist will apply these terms to the structural phenomena such as sentence structure, modification structures, and the like. The analyst who thinks in terms of the transformational theory of language will compare rules which relate the common deep structure to different surface structures rather than compare directly the surface elements of two languages. The functionalists will compare how the different functions of language will be realized in the grammar, lexis and sound patterns of different languages.

Secondly, differences can also be found in the philosophical assumptions underlying each school. These differences will influence the final goal of the investigations. It may be expected that structuralists will emphasize the differences in grammar, lexis, phonology, etc. among languages, whereas transformationalists will look for the evidence that languages are finally of the same pattern in deep structures. Since American descriptivism has its roots in anthropology, it not only retained some of the methods of this discipline but also the general view about the diversity of human cultures reflected at least to some extent in languages.

The structurarist's philosophical outlook is mainly relativistic, accepting generally the weaker version of the Sapir-Whorf hypothesis, while the transformational school has close connections with some trends of modern philosophy and logic. Its method is mainly deduction rather than induction employed by structuralists, and its philosophical basis, stemming from the

Cartesian line of thought, is absolutist, that is, when analyzed at a high level of abstraction, languages share universal structures. The search for universal linguistic features is the primary objective of transformational grammar.

If transformational grammar were already adequately formulated, the task of CA would be to compare the ways in which common underlying structures are realized as different surface structures. But since such objectives cannot constitute reasonable immediate goals, given the present state of the transformational theory, intermediate goals have to be formulated. One of such goals is finding sub-universals by comparing pairs and larger groups of languages. Proper contrastive studies should be based on a universal grammar and particular grammars should be constructed by means of the same theoretical apparatus for all languages.

The functionalists will assume that languages share the same functions, but are expressed in different ways in different situations. It starts from perceived similarities of meaning across two or more languages, and seeks to determine the various ways in which these similar or shared meanings are expressed in different languages. It represents one general approach to CA, the functional approach, in the sense that it is based on meaning, and looks at the ways meanings are expressed. The perspective is from meaning to form. Research using this methodology also aims to specify the conditions (syntactic, semantic, pragmatic etc.) which govern the use of different variants, and ultimately to state which variant is preferred under which conditions. Broadly speaking, the approach is thus a paradigmatic one, with a Hallidayan-type focus on the options that speakers have in expressing meanings. It is in fact a kind of cross-linguistic variation analysis.

The existence of **sociolinguistics** presupposes recognition of language variation. Language variation, in turn, may be conceived of basically in terms of: 1) the ideal speaker-hearer's knowledge of communicative rules and his potential ability to apply these rules, and 2) the actual performance as can be investigated on a group of speakers strictly defined by social and geographical parameters.

These two views of language variation bring to light the fundamental question of sociolinguistics, namely, what is it that the sociolinguist studies, or should study? The choice of 1) or 2) does not necessarily answer the question posed, but it definitely imposes on the linguist methodological requirements and constraints pertaining to the collection of data.

Contrastive Sociolinguistics (henceforth CS) seems to be best understood in terms of an approach toward sociolinguistics. The underlying objective of CS is twofold: 1) to provide a systematic juxtaposition of equivalent and non-equivalent sociolinguistic patterns, and 2) to provide an analytical framework for the formation of theories of language use, i. e., performance theories.

The contrastive sociolinguist oriented toward performance analysis will question some of the methodological assumptions that the "orthodox" contrastive linguist will accept. The few contrastive sociolinguistic studies available as well as the bulk of nonsociolinguistic contrastive analyses carried out to date have purported to provide facts pertaining to two languages, which in fact have been some nonspecified varieties of either of the languages compared.

In view of the facts discussed above we want to concede that contrastive sociolinguistic analyses cannot be undertaken until the necessary levels of comparability have been established and clearly defined.

In order to establish the levels of comparability one has to take recourse to the distinction made by Halliday et al (1964) between language variety according to user, and language variety according to use.

The interaction between the two involves the necessity to make choices and establish comparability with respect to *both* the user and the use. The first decision will concern the national varieties the linguist wishes to study. Since language varies from social group to social group, upon analyzing a language the sociolinguist then ought to make his choice with regard to the social group he wishes to study. In a contrastive analysis the language variety of an equivalent social group of the other culture should be juxtaposed. In other words, choices must be made with respect to the sociolectal variety which may in practice be narrowed down to such small group varieties as those of professional groups.

The sociolectal varieties can be made according to various criteria that can divide the social groups, and these include the social status, age, gender and race, etc. Language variation according to user includes also the regional dimension, but it is of little use for contrastive purposes.

Contrastive Sociolinguistics will also have to take account of situations where members of sociolect 1 of L1 communicate with members of sociolect 2 of L1, what is usually called **cross-culture communications.** In such a case speakers of both 1 and 2 apply a number of adaptive rules which modify their speech with respect to the rules which are used when in-group members are addressed. CS will be interested in looking at those adaptive strategies as they function in a pair of languages.

Variation according to use is translatable into the individual speaker's or a relatively homogeneous group of speakers' linguistic repertoire out of which the appropriate linguistic forms are selected in varying extralinguistic circumstances. The set of registers that speakers have at their disposal involves a large variation of linguistic forms which are subsumable and differentiated categories. It is important therefore to state which of these categories of language use are being considered in a contrastive sociolinguistic study. These categories, according to Halliday (1973; 1978), include the field of study, such as linguistics, art and literature, the tenor, the relationship between the speaker and the listener, and the style proposed by Joos (1959) and the mode, the role language plays in the situation.

Contrastive psycholinguistics (Osgood, 1953) compare the equivalent features of the two languages in order to explain the differences between the different effects when the equivalent features of the two languages are different or similar, so Osgood (1953) says, "When two sets of materials to be learned are quite different or are easily discriminated by the learner, there is relatively little interaction, that is, learning one has little effect upon learning the other. If they are similar in such a way that the learning of one serves as partial learning of the other, there may be facilitation, or positive transfer. If, however, the similarities either of stimuli or responses are such that responses interfere with one another, then there will be greater interference as similarity increases." Initially, CA was associated with behaviorism, and this association with behaviorism gave CA academic respectability, providing a theoretical foundation for the approach. In this viewpoint, language acquisition is simply habit formation.

7.4.2.2 Practical Orientation

For practical purposes, contrastive analysis can be applied to two major areas of practical research: foreign and second language teaching and **translation**. First, for foreign and second language teaching, CA is developed to make foreign language teaching more effective on the assumptions that 1) Foreign language learning is based on the mother tongue as the speaker has already mastered the language system of the mother tongue; 2) if the mother tongue and the foreign or second language are similar in certain aspects, it will result in **positive transfer**, that is, the skills of mother tongue will naturally be transferred to the target language; 3) if the mother tongue and the foreign or second language are different, it will result in **negative transfer** or **interference**, that is, the differences will serve as interference factors for learning the target language. The differences and similarities are to be discovered via CA, and so the problems in language teaching and learning can be predicted through CA and should be considered in the curriculum. In this sense, contrastive linguistics is seen as an applied branch of linguistics, used for serving practical purposes in foreign and second language teaching.

The general procedure for CA consists of the following steps:
1) Description: first, the items for comparison is selected and then described to determine the characteristics of items in terms of their own essential features independent theoretical model.

2) Juxtaposition: secondly, after a careful description of the items, cross-linguistic equivalents are sought for comparison.
3) Comparison: the supposed equivalents are compared for the specification of degree and type of correspondence between compared items in the two languages.

The bulk of the SLA field was concerned with the prediction of errors. The most simplistic version was the belief that linguistic differences based simply on similarities and differences alone could be used to predict learning difficulties.

However, the contrastive analysis hypothesis version of CA, that is, the predictive version ran into some problems. Sometimes, it mispredicts the errors, specifically, the supposed ability of contrastive analysis hypothesis to predict errors was not supported by the facts, and sometimes, it underpredicted the errors, that is, it failed to predict some errors; and at other times, it overpredicted the errors, that is, it predicted some errors that failed to occur. Of course, it also got some right. The reason is that, just as Long and Sato (1984) pointed out, one cannot depend upon the analysis of a linguistic product to yield meaningful insight into a psycholinguistic process. The failure discussed thus far is the failure of contrastive analysis hypothesis, not the failure of CA.

Wardhaugh (1970) proposed a distinction between the strong and the weak version of the CA. The strong version predicts the same as contrastive analysis hypothesis does, while the weak version deals with learner errors and uses CA, when applicable, to explain them.

This set off the theory of error analysis, that is, the detection of the source of errors. Thus, the next approach was to limit the analysis to the examination of errors that students actually made. Under the influence of Chomsky's theory of language acquisition, researchers began studying the speech of children learning English as their L1. They attempted to use these to write a grammar of what the children were producing, So-called "**rule formation.**" For example, "* She doesn't wants to go" "* I eated it" "* geeses" "* wented." Such forms cannot be the product of imitation. They are called "**developmental' errors.**" SLA researchers found that in SL study, the learners committed similar "developmental" errors, errors that were not apparently due to L1 interference.

Errors found to be traceable to L1 interference were termed **interlingual errors.** CA was used to explain them. A large number of similar errors, however, were found to be committed by SL learners regardless of their L1. These were termed intralingual errors. (Richards, 1971) These were analyzed to see what sort of strategies were being used, such as overgeneralization, simplification, etc.

Secondly, for translation, CA can be an effective aid to determine the translation equivalents between the target language and the source language. The headache of any contrastive study has been finding the so-called *tertium comparationis* (TC), that is, the common ground on which two languages can be compared to be able to establish (dis)similarities. In James (1980), **translation equivalence** is seen as the best TC for contrastive analysis. James sees translational equivalence in light of Halliday's (e.g. 1994) three metafunctions of language, and writes: "For two sentences from different languages to be translationally equivalent they must convey the same ideational and interpersonal and textual meanings." (James, 1980: 178)

However, total translation equivalents between languages in all the three meanings are rare. They may be the same in ideational meaning, but different in interpersonal or textual or both interpersonal and textual meanings, or they may be different in the scope of meaning or in the number and type of referents. Contrastive analysis can be made to determine in what aspects or areas of meaning TC can be established, and differences in the scope and type of meanings can be ascertained.

For the sake of establishing translation equivalents between the source language and the target language, CA can be made at different levels. At the phonological and the graphological level, the existing sounds and sound patterns and the graphic symbols and their patterns in the two languages can be compared to determine the phonological and graphological translation equivalents, used in what Catford (1956:56) called "restricted translation"; by the same way, at the lexical and grammatical levels, contrastive analysis can be made to determine the lexical and grammatical translation equivalents again as a kind of "restricted translation."

7.4.3 Major Areas of Contrastive Analysis

Although Lado (1957) included a comparison of cultures, early contrastive studies focused on what has been described as **microlinguistic contrastive analysis** (James, 1980: 61ff.): phonology, grammar and vocabulary. With the broadening of linguistic studies in general in the 1970s and 1980s, contrastive studies became increasingly concerned with **macrolinguistic contrastive analysis** (James, 1980:98ff.): text linguistics, discourse analysis and pragmatics.

7.4.3.1 Microlinguistic Contrastive Analysis

Microlinguistic contrastive analysis focuses on the contrastive study of the sound and sound system, vocabulary, and grammar.

7.4.3.1.1 Phonetics and Phonology

Phonetic contrastive analysis focuses on the contrast of the production, reception and transmission of the sounds between languages. In the

International Phonetic Alphabet, there are about 70 consonants, and more than thirty vowels, but in each language, the number of consonants and vowels are much smaller and of different types. CA aims to find out the different distribution of sounds in different languages, their relations with each other, especially whether they can correspond to each other or not. For example, in English we can find about 48 consonants and vowels, but in Chinese we have only about 28, and they have different characteristics, and are pronounced differently, for example, in Chinese, many consonants are pronounced with a retroflex and many vowels are nasalized.

Phonological contrastive analysis focuses on the contrast of the distribution of phonemes in the sound system, their phonological patterns, and the distribution and patterns of suprasegmental features. In English, we have more phonemes than in Chinese, and they are distributed differently. In English, a syllable can be formed of at most three initial consonants, such as [spraɪt] (sprite), one vowel and vocalic consonant, and at most four final consonants, such as [sɪksθ] (sixths), while in Chinese, a syllable consists of one initial consonant, and optionally a final nasal consonant, such as [kaːŋ] (康). Suprasegmentally, in Chinese, for each syllable, there is a tone: level, rise, fall-rise, and fall, but in English, tones can only be found in tone groups, a series of the feet with one tonic syllable. These differences will be significant for language learning and teaching.

7.4.3.1.2 Lexis

Lexis refers to the items that can be put into the syntactic structures to form sentences and clauses. However, in different languages, they may behave differently. In English, words can behave differently when they are inflected differently with different grammatical affixes, such as *work*, *works*, *working and worked*, while in Chinese, their functions can only be determined by their positions in the syntactic structures, such as"他做事情""他做的事情""事情的由来."

Secondly, words in a language can form systems, such as the kinship terms, and different languages may have different lexical systems. For example, the kinship system in Chinese and that in English are vastly different from each other. There are more than 50 terms in Chinese in terms of generation, age, maternity versus paternity, male versus female, consanguinity versus affinity, while there are only about 10 in English.

Thirdly, words are distributed differently in different languages in structures. Words co-occurring in one language may not co-occur in another. For example, the most characteristic feature of Chinese is its power of classification by words, that is, in most of the words, there is an element which shows which type it belongs to, such as 榆树,柳树,槐树,柏树,松树 etc., but we can not find their counterparts in English: elm, willow, locust, cypress, pine, etc. Also, *bay* in *bay horse* can only co-occur in such a pair, while its lexical translation equivalent 栗色 is not restricted in such a way; in English we say "kill the motion," and in Chinese we say "否决提案."

7.4.3.1.3 Grammar.

Grammar is usually divided into morphology, the formation of words, and syntax, the formation of sentences. Firstly, morphological contrastive analysis can be made between languages of different types, such as isolating, inflectional, agglutinative and synthetic. Although both English and Chinese are of the same type: isolating, they are still on the continuum from the isolating to the inflectional. In English, we still have many words that are formed by inflection and derivation, such as *act vs acts*; *act, action, react, reaction, reactionary,* and *reactionaries*, while most of the Chinese words are formed by compounding, such as 来回、树木、红色, etc. The second part of these words are somewhat like affixes, but actually they are more like words added to the end of other words to form a new word, as each can stand independently as a separate word.

Grammatical contrastive analysis is more complicated than that at other levels. First, the contrast can be made from different perspectives, such as formal, functional, cognitive, etc.; secondly, it can be made on the basis of different theories, such as TG theory, systemic functional linguistics, case grammar, cognitive grammar, etc., thirdly, it can focus on different aspects of language, such as the system or categories of languages concerned, or the structure of those languages. Here, we are mainly concerned with the CA of the characteristics of the system and structure of different languages concerned.

First, as far as system is concerned, different languages may have different systems. For example, In English, there are the case differences among the nominative, the accusative, the oblique, and the possessive, etc., such as "He hit me in the head"; "He gave him his book," etc., the number differences between singular, plural and mass; the tense differences between the present, past and future, the aspect differences between progressive and perfective, etc. But all these systems are absent in Chinese. Secondly, as far as structure is concerned, different languages may exhibit different structures, or the same structure may express different meanings, or the same structure may be distributed differently in different languages. (Lado, 1957) For example, in terms of mood structure, in the interrogatives in English, auxiliaries or modal verbs and wh-elements have to be moved to the initial position, such as, "Are you going to town?" "Where are you going?" but in Chinese, it is realized as the repetition of the verb or the addition of a mood marker, such as, "你去不去城里?" "你到哪儿去呀?" When the utterances in the two languages share the same structure, they may mean very differently. For example, "Chicago saw a big fire" mean "there was a big fire in Chicago," but its correspondent in Chinese "芝加哥看到一场大火" can only mean

"Chicago as a human being witnessed a big fire." Furthermore, the same structure may be distributed differently in different languages. The Chinese version may be a common sentence structure, and so can occur regularly in daily conversation, but the English version may be metaphorical, so is mainly found in written language.

7.4.3.2 Macrolinguistic Contrastive Analysis

Macrolinguistic contrastive analysis focuses on the contrastive study of cultural, situational and pragmatic aspects of language.

7.4.3.2.1 Discourse Analysis

Discursive contrastive analysis focuses on the differences and similarities of the discourse structures, and their internal organizations in terms of cohesion and coherence. Cohesion is the means whereby sentences cohere with each other to form a complete text, and there are five categories of cohesive devices: reference, ellipsis, substitution, conjunction and lexical cohesion. (Halliday & Hasan, 1976) However, the number and the scope of these devices are significantly expanded in later research. (Halliday & Hasan, 1985/1989; Hu Zhuanglin, 1994; Zhang Delu, 2003) In this aspect, Chinese texts exhibit significant differences in various aspects, such as conjunction, reference, lexical cohesion, ellipsis and substitution etc. from its English counterpart. For example, Chinese favours parataxis over hypotaxis, the juxiposition of textual elements that are organized in hypotactic relations. At the same time, the relations between elements are often kept implicit in Chinese texts, while in their English counterparts, they are made explicit as temporal, spatial, causal, conditional, accompanying relations. Also, in Chinese, recurrence of items are manifested as repetition, or simply ellipsis, but that in English are often shown as reference, or substitution.

Discursive contrastive analysis can also be made on the textual patterns and genre structures, which exhibits not only the different cultural behaviours and ways of doing things, but also the thought patterns as a result of a long cultural history. It is said that the English thought patterns are direct, linear and analytic, while the Chinese ones are spiral and synthetic. These different thought patterns will inevitably influence and also are reflected in their discourse patterns and structures.

7.4.3.2.2 Pragmatics

Pragmatic contrastive analysis focuses on the similarities and differences between languages in terms of how the social and communicative factors affect the use of language. It means that different languages may exhibit different types of deixis, presuppositions, speech acts, pragmatic principles, etc. These are proper areas of CA. For example, first, in Chinese, politeness principles play a more important role than that in English. If the communicative intent is in collision with the politeness principle in terms of benefit or social hierarchy, then the quantity and quality maxims will give way to the politeness principle in Chinese, and the speaker has to say things in a round-about way, while in their English counterpart, they may have to observe the cooperative principle. There are numerous instances of this type.

References

Akhmanova, O. S. , Melencuk D. A. 1977. *The Principles of Linguistic Confrontation*. Moscow: Izdat.

Croft, W. 1990. *Typology and Universals*. Cambridge: Cambridge University Press.

Crystal, D. 1985. *A Dictionary of Linguistics and Phonetics*. Oxford: Basil Blackwell.

Diderichson, P. 1974. "The foundations of comparative linguistics: revolution or dontinuation?" in Dell Hymes (ed.). 1974. *Studies in the History of Linguistics*. Bloomington: Indiana University Press.

Firbas, J. 1964. "From comparative word-order studies," In: *Brno Studies in English*. Vol. 4. Brno: Masaryk University Press. pp. 111—128.

Fisiak, Jacek, Maria Lipinska-Grzegorek, & Tadeusz Zabrocki. 1978. *An Introductory English-Polish Contrastive Grammar*. Warsaw: PWN.

Fisiak, Jacek. 1980. "Some notes on contrastive linguistics," *AILA Bulletin* 1 (27): 1—17.

Fisiak, Jacek. 1980. *Theoretical Issues in Contrastive Linguistics*. Amsterdam: John Benjamins B. V.

Fries, Charles C. 1945. *Teaching and Learning English as a Foreign Language*. Ann Arbor: University of Michigan Press.

Fromkin, V. & Rodman, R. 1974/1993. *An Introduction to Language*. London: Harcourt Brace College Publishers.

Grandgent, C. H. (1892). *German and English sounds*. Boston: Ginn.

Greenberg, Joseph H. 1966. *Language Universals, with Special Reference to Feature Hierarchies*. The Hague: Mouton.

Greenberg, Joseph, H. 1974. *Language Typology: A Historical and Analytic Overview*. The Hague: Mouton.

Haiman, John. 1985. *Natural Syntax*. Cambridge: Cambridge University Press.

Halliday, M. A. K. 1976. *Explorations in the Functions of Language*. London: Edward Arnold.

Halliday, M. A. K. 1978. *Language as Social Semiotic: The Social Interpretation of Language and Meaning*. London: Edward Arnold.

Halliday, M. A. K. 1994. *An Introduction to Functional Grammar*. London: Edward Arnold.

Halliday, M. A. K. og Hasan, R. 1976. *Cohesion in English*. London: Longman (English Language Series 9).

Halliday, M. A. K. og Hasan, R. 1985. *Language, Text and Context*. Geelong, Vic.: Deakin University Press.

Halliday, M. A. K., Machintosh, A. & Stevens, P. 1964. *The Linguistic Sciences and Language Teaching*. London: Longman.

Hawkins, John A. 1983. *Word Order Universals*. New York: Academic Press.

Hu Zhuanglin, Liu Runqing, Li Yanfu (eds.). *Linguistics: A Course Book*. Beijing: Beijing University Press.
Jackson, Howard. 1976. "Contrastive linguistics—what is it?" *ITL* 32: 1–32.
James, Carl. 1980. *Contrastive Analysis*. Harlow: Longman.
Joos, Martin. 1959. "Process and relation verbs in English," Paper read at the 34th Annual Meeting, Linguistic Society of America.
Keenan, E. & B. Comrie. 1977. "Noun phrase accessibility and universal grammar," *Linguistic Inquiry* 8: 63–99.
Lado, R. 1957. *Linguistics across Cultures: Applied Linguistics for Language Teachers*. Ann Arbor: University of Michigan Press.
Long, M. & Sato, C. 1984. "Methodological issues in interlanguage studies: an interactionist perspective," in A. Davies, C. Criper and A. Howatt (eds.). *Interlanguage*. Edinburgh: Edinburgh University Press.
Mathesius, V. 1928. "On the linguistic characterology of modern English," *Actes du Premier Congrès International de Linguistes á la Haye*. Leiden: Sijthoff. pp. 59–67.
Mathesius, V. 1936. "On some problems of the systematic analysis of grammar," In *Travaux du cercle linguistique de Prague* 6: 95.
Nickel, Gerhard. 1957. *Papers in Contrastive Linguistics*. Cambridge: Cambridge University Press.
Osgood, C. Egerton, 1953. *Method and Theory in Experimental Psychology*. Oxford: Oxford University Press
Richards, J. "Error analysis and second language strategies," *Language Science* 1971(17): 12–22.
Robins, R. H. 1964/1989. *General Linguistics*. London: Longman.
Rusiecki, Jan. 1976. "The development of contrastive linguistics," *Interlanguage Studies Bulletin*, Utrecht 1(1):12–24.
Trask, R. L (ed.). 1996. *Historical Linguistics*. London: Edward Arnold (Publishers) Limited.
Trosborg, A. 1997. *Text Typology and Translation*. Amsterdam: John Benjamins Publishing Company.
Vachek, J. 1961. "Mathesius as a contrastive linguist," In *Papers and Studies in Contrastive Linguistics*. Poznań: Adam Mickiewicz University. Vol. 11. pp. 5–16.
Verschueren, J. 1999. *Understanding Pragmatics*. London: Edward Arnold (Publishing) Limited.
Viëtor, W. 1894. *Elemente der Phonetik des Deutschen, Englischen und Französischen*. Leipzig: Reisland.
Viëtor, W. 1903. *German Pronunciation: Practice and Theory*. Leipzig: Reisland.
Wardhaugh, Ronald. 1970. "The contrastive analysis hypothesis," *TESOL Quaterly* 4(2): 123–130.
Whorf, Benjamin Lee. 1941. "Languages and logic," *Technological Review*: 43.
Yule, G. 1985/1996. *The Study of Language*. Cambridge: Cambridge University Press.
胡壮麟，1994，《语篇的衔接与连贯》，上海：上海外语教育出版社。
张德禄，2003，《语篇连贯与衔接理论的发展及应用》，上海：上海外语教育出版社。

Chapter 8

Language, Culture, and Society

8.1 Introduction

It has long been recognized that language is an essential and important part of a given culture, and that the impact of culture upon a given language is something intrinsic and indispensable. This interpretation of the relationships between language, culture, and society leads one to such a belief that language can never function independently if there are no social contexts to fit it in. (Alptekin, 1993)

In the same vein, the association or integration of linguistic analysis, cultural research, language learning, and anthropological fieldwork has long been witnessed and well recognized in a more general enterprise as Hall's view of communication systems suggests. (Hall, 1959; Byram, 1986)

A study of these relationships, rather, inter-relationships, is generally called SOCIOLINGUISTICS. As we will show below, though the endeavor in the pursuit of the inter-relationships has never been dormant in the development of linguistic science, "this very embedding of language in society and culture has been the focus of intense and sustained research efforts since the 1960s." (Apte, 1994: 2000) In order to provide the student with an opportunity to know more about the situation, we introduce this chapter and focus our discussion on the relationships among LANGUAGE, CULTURE and SOCIETY. This attempt can be alternatively understood as an effort to provide a different perspective to the study of language science in general and applied linguistics in particular in terms of some new tendencies and developments observed in the field of sociolinguistics. The direct motivation for this arrangement of discussion lies in the fact that sociolinguistics has been proven over the past decades to be an additional momentum, first in a theoretical sense, to the study of language use in a socio-cultural setting, and then in a practical sense, to some fundamental changes in the field of applied linguistics, rather, language teaching. Bearing these points in mind, we organize our discussion in the following three parts: language and culture, language and society, sociolinguistics and language teaching. Put more explicitly, we want to know more about the nature of language by virtue of exploring these pairs of relationships.

8.2 Language and Culture

The first type of the relationships we want to look at is the relationships between language and culture. A general consensus sociolinguists and anthropologists may share is that the relationships between language and culture can never be over-emphasized, and that the importance of the relationships has recently received much more attention. On the other hand, a new scientific pursuit of the relationships in a broader sense, identified as cultural studies, has been observed and emphasized as well.

Important as the study of these relationships is, a difficulty one may have in the task we are now undertaking is that culture appears to be a concept full of divergent interpretations. This is especially the case when we notice that this terminology is often used in a rather loose sense, with pub culture, music culture, wine culture, and even drug culture being included sometimes. Some definitions that may appear to be more relevant to our discussion here may include the following four types, though it must be admitted that this list is far from complete and highly likely to be expanded to some extent.

Culture is a semiotic system.

Culture is a communication system.

Culture is a history of achievements and types of civilization produced.

Culture is an epitome of values, beliefs, knowledge, behavioral patterns, ways of thinking members of a speech community share.

Viewing the diversity in defining the term, in our discussion below, we are going to develop a more language-related framework to illustrate our understanding of the issue in question. Consequently, the focuses of our discussion will be:

How does language relate to culture?

What more should we know about the Sapir-Whorf hypothesis—a classical assumption concerning the relationships between language and culture?

What evidence can we give to show the close relationships between language and culture?

To what extent do we need culture in linguistic study in general and in language teaching in particular?

8.2.1 How Does Language Relate to Culture?

It has become axiomatic to state that there exist close relationships between language and culture. More evidence can be gathered to substantiate this claim if we have a brief survey of what has happened in the field of linguistics over the past century—a historical perspective thus being taken.

Ever since the beginning of the 18th century, the linguistic inquiry of language has been either comparative and historical or structural and formal in nature. Some change, however, was observed at the start of the 20th century: An ANTHROPOLOGICAL ORIENTATION in the study of language was developed both in England and in North America. What characterized this new tradition was its focus on studying language in a socio-cultural context. While Bronislaw Malinowski and John P. Firth can be regarded as the pioneers of this movement in England, Franz Boas, Edward Sapir, and Benjamin Lee Whorf are naturally seen as the representatives of a parallel but independent tradition from North America. With their innovation, commitment, and perseverance, a lot of important and creative work has been done and documented in the research of the relationships between language and culture. More importantly, a paradigm was thus set up, which has led to a diversity of research of the issue in the following years. Take the latter group for example. Their extraordinary work completed during the "Golden Age of Native American Indian Linguistics" (Werner, 1994: 3656) has laid a firm foundation for an anthropo-linguistic pursuit of the correlation between language, culture, and society. Let us start first with the British tradition in this respect.

As early as in the 1920s, a school of ANTHROPOLOGICAL STUDY OF LINGUISTICS came into being in England. This has much to do with the work of Malinowski, a well-known anthropologist at the London School of Economics. When he did his field work on the Trobriand Islands off eastern New Guinea, Malinowski observed that in this primitive culture the meaning of a word greatly depended upon its occurrence in a given context, or rather, upon a real language situation in life. Take the word "wood" for example. In this culture, the word might be used either to refer to the solid substance of a tree as its English equivalent suggests, or more specifically, to designate a "canoe," which served as a useful means of transportation to these islanders and therefore played an important role in the daily life of this SPEECH COMMUNITY. The second interpretation of this word was, however, turned out to be heavily situationally or culturally specified and might not be easily captured by an outsider from a different cultural background. Based on phenomena like this, Malinowski claimed that "In its primitive uses, language functions as a link in concerted human activity... It is a mode of action and not an instrument of reflection." (1923: 312)

Needless to say, the work by Malinowski paved the way for a cultural, rather, a contextual study of language use in Britain. Strongly influenced by this anthropological view of language and being fully aware of the importance of the context in the study of language use, Firth, a leading figure in a linguistic tradition later known as the London School, tried to set up a model for illustrating the close relationships between language use and its co-occurrent factors. In the end, he came up with his own theory of CONTEXT OF SITUATION, which can be summarized as follows. (Firth, 1950: 43—44[Palmer, 1981:53—54])

 A. The relevant features of the participants:Persons, personalities:
  (i) The verbal action of the participants.
  (ii) The non-verbal action of the participants.
 B. The relevant objects.
 C. The effects of the verbal action.

 In relation to the focus of our discussion given above, two points can be made to show the strong culturally specific implication of this theory. Like his American colleague Sapir, though far less directly, Firth here seemed to imply the creativity and diversity of linguistic idiosyncrasy in language use. (cf. Darnell, 1994: 3655) On the other hand, what Firth emphasized in this theory is quite similar to a more updating sociological axiom in language use, namely, "who speaks (or writes) what language (or what language variety) to whom and when and to what end." (Fishman, 1972: 46) Later on, the Firthian tradition in this respect was further developed by the founder of systemic functional linguistics, M. A. K. Halliday. The contributions Halliday has made to sociolinguistics could be better seen from his understanding of language from a socially semiotic or interactional perspective, his functional interpretation of grammar as a resource for MEANING POTENTIAL, and his linguistic model in the study of literature. (Downes, 1998)

 A parallel but independent pursuit of language and culture-related issues was spotted on the other side of the Atlantic Ocean as well. This is especially the case when we notice that linguists from the North American side began to make some substantial contributions to the study of the relationships between language and culture around the early 1920s. In fact, when we talk about a cultural study of language in America, we'll soon realize the fact that the American Indian culture formed an extremely fruitful source for early American anthropologists to look at this subject matter. From the 1920s to the 1940s, when engaged in a demanding but significant task—the reconstruction of American Native languages, those anthropologists such as Boas, Sapir, and Whorf came to know the significance of culture in the study of language use. For instance, from their field work, a lot of language data were collected, pooled and documented, providing much first hand evidence to show how the interpersonal relationship is related to linguistic forms chosen by these American Indians in their daily communication. If things like this were not to be appropriately described and correctly understood, it would be very difficult to interpret some variation in the structure of these languages. Due to their marvelous work in this reconstruction project, the anthropological approach they developed to the study of language and culture laid a firm foundation in the history of linguistic development. The potential impact of this tradition can still be felt when we talk about the ETHNOGRAPHY OF COMMUNICATION, an authoritative research framework of our time in a linguistic study of social and cultural factors. (Hymes, 1962)

Having talked so much about the heritage concerning the study of language and culture, now let us move on and introduce a very influential but controversial theory that has ever been made in the study of the relationships between language and culture. As one may expect, this attempt will inevitably lead us to an important figure in American ANTHROPOLOGICAL LINGUISTICS—Benjamin Lee Whorf and his famous hypothesis concerning language, thought, and culture.

From the early 1920s, as an amateur linguist, Whorf began to show an interest in language, anthropology, and archaeology. Later on, he went to Yale University and attended some linguistic courses offered by Sapir there. By taking these courses, he "found particular resonance between his own ideas and those of Sapir." (Stam, 1994: 4983) This experience and his study of Hopi, an American Indian language, helped Whorf form his unique understanding of linguistic relativity, which is now widely known as the SAPIR-WHORF HYPOTHESIS. What this hypothesis suggests is like this: Our language helps mould our way of thinking and, consequently, different languages may probably express speakers' unique ways of understanding the world. Following this claim, Sapir assumed that there is an indispensible connection between language and culture, and that evidence for this connection lies in vocabulary:

> Human beings do not live in the objective world alone... but are very much at the mercy of the particular language which has become the medium of expression for their society. The worlds in which different societies live are distinct worlds, not merely the same world with different labels attached. (cited in Mandelbaum, 1963: 162)

Following Sapir, Whorf developed a similar understanding of the relationships between language and culture, this time evidence from grammatical systems being provided. His comparative study between an American Indian language Hopi and some European languages finally led him to an explicit assertion that "... the grammar of Hopi bore a relation to Hopi culture, and the grammar of European tongues to our own 'Western' or 'European' culture." (1939: 73) Based on these arguments, two important points could be captured in his theory. On the one hand, language may determine our thinking patterns; on the other, similarity between languages is relative, the greater their structural differentiation is, the more diverse their conceptualization of the world will be.

Chapter 8 Language, Culture, and Society

For this reason, this hypothesis has alternatively been referred to as LINGUISTIC DETERMINISM and LINGUISTIC RELATIVITY—a view which "was first expounded by the German ethnologist, Wilhelm von Humboldt." (Crystal, 1985: 262)

Before we end this historical survey of the relationships between language and culture and move on to a more detailed illustration of the Sapir-Whorf hypothesis, we should not miss some brilliant points made by Eugene Nida, a well known linguist and translation theorist, on the same topic. What makes his discussion of language and culture more meaningful to the issues we are talking about here is the fact that for many years he has been involved in the Bible translation work across different languages. His rich experience in this respect led him to claim that, as translators, if we want to do a good job in CROSS-CULTURAL COMMUNICATION, there are five types of sub culture we should be fully aware of:

Ecology
Material culture
Social culture
Religious culture
Linguistic culture (Nida, 1964)

More recently, by following a situational and cultural understanding of language use, Nide (1998: 32−45) focuses his research attention more on a contextual or situational study of semantics and generalizes the following five features possessed by English words:

Words are polysemantic.
Words are sometimes idiomatically governed.
Words are stylistically governed.
Words are sometimes culturally specific.
One to one equivalents are possible but few.

Furthermore, by providing some interesting examples, Nide (1998: 32) illustrates nicely how we can disambiguate the meaning of a word by virtue of relevant information from the context:

The traditional view about the meaning of *run* is to say that *run* has a number of different meanings and that different contexts point to the right meaning in each case. For example, in the following series:

the man is running,
the motor is running,
the water is running,
the office is running efficiently,
the line ran off the page,
Tom is running for mayor.

There are obviously different kinds of *running* involved. But how do we know this? Precisely from the contexts. This does not mean that the verb *run* possesses all these different meanings and that the contexts simply point to the specific meaning in each context. In each case there is a combination of meaning coming from both the verb *run* and the context. (1998: 32)

8.2.2 What More Should We Know about the Sapir-Whorf Hypothesis?

As has been shown above, what this classical hypothesis primarily suggests is that our language will mould our view of the world. Before going deeper, we would like to point out one thing: Nowadays few people would possibly tend to accept the original form of this theory completely. Consequently, two versions of the SAPIR-WHORF HYPOTHESIS have been developed, a strong version and a weak version. The strong version of the theory refers to the claim the original hypothesis suggests, emphasizing the decisive role of language as the shaper of our thinking patterns. The weak version of this hypothesis is a modified type of its original theory, suggesting that there is a correlation between language, culture, and thought, but the cross-cultural differences thus produced in our ways of thinking are, however, relative, rather than categorical. Put alternatively, these differences are in fact a matter of degree but not a matter of kind.

When we go over the literature concerning the hypothesis more thoroughly, we'll soon discover that this theory has aroused more controversy than consensus. While some researchers claim that they have found reliable evidence to justify its validity, others argue that they have obtained enough counter evidence to jeopardize its feasibility. Facing a situation like this, we must be careful and do not rush to any hasty conclusion before we really obtain some reliable evidence in our research work to support or reject the hypothesis. What we put below are two cases that can be utilized to further show the complexity and controversy of the theory.

The first case is quoted from Hopi, an American Native language spoken in Arizona, while the other case is taken from Dugum Dani, a Papuan language spoken in the central highlands of Irian Jaya. As far as the former is concerned, it serves as a good example to show how languages may differ from each other, possibly providing some positive evidence to support the hypothesis. On the other hand, by looking at the basic color word system in Dani language from an evolutionary perspective, we will have an opportunity to get to know that linguistic relativity may equally meet some cross-cultural counter examples, thus forming a challenge to the theory hence formed.

In Hopi, there is something very special about its grammar. (cf. Fasold, 1999[1990]: 51—52) One of these features that separate it from other languages is that Hopi does not use the same means to express time, and hence is metaphorically dubbed a "timeless language." Sampson (1980: 86) describes it in this way:

> ... the language does not recognize time as a linear dimension, which can be measured and divided into units like spatial dimensions... Furthermore, Hopi verbs do not have tenses comparable to those of European languages. And since there is no concept of time, there can be no concept of speed, which is the ratio of distance to time: Hopi has no word for "fast," and their nearest equivalent for "He runs fast" would translate more literally as something like *He very runs*.

With an understanding of Hopi language like this, we may inevitably have a big question to think about: If we have from the Hopi culture a physicist, who is as innovative as Albert Einstein is, can we expect this physicist to tell us the same thing as Einstein did in discussing the relativity theory? Admittedly, we may say that if this happened, this Hopi physicist would definitely find his/her way to express the principles suggested by the theory. But a more crucial question involved here is how his linguistic representation could be compared in relation to those linguistic patterns of which we are either native speakers or fully aware. Considerations like this imply that when dealing with a cross-cultural question like this, we have to be cautious and do not always evaluate a language system against the criteria we are familiar with in our mother tongue.

As a matter of fact, one of the criticisms to the Sapir-Whorf hypothesis is that the theory is based on establishing European languages as a model against which all comparisons are made. The undertone behind this criticism is that when we examine linguistic issues from a universal perspective, what we are actually doing is to look at linguistic properties by a criterion of similarity and difference; hence, it is a process of recategorization, but not by a criterion of an already established model language. Furthermore, for the convenience of observation and comparison, it is justifiably argued that when we search for LINGUISTIC UNIVERSALITY, we'd better begin with the similarities possessed by most languages, instead of their assumed differences. (Greenberg et al., 1978) Having said so much about Hopi language, let us move on and introduce our second example derived from Dani language to reveal the other side of the Sapir-Whorf hypothesis.

In the late 1960s, two American scholars, Brent Berlin and Paul Kay conducted a large cross-linguistic investigation of basic color vocabulary, which involved 98 languages in the world. The most striking finding in this research is that color word systems in different languages are not like what has been assumed by the Sapir-Whorf hypothesis, being culturally determined and hence absolutely different from one another. Contrary to this assumption, Berlin and Kay showed that different languages might well undergo A UNIVERSAL EVOLUTIONARY PROCESS OF DEVELOPMENT which, in turn, made the basic color system in one language different from that in another only in terms of the stages of their evolution. This evolutionary process can be specified as follows.

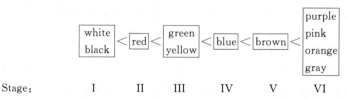

Stage: I   II   III   IV   V   VI

Figure 8.1   Evolutionary Stages of Basic Color Words
(Berlin & Kay, 1991[1969]: 4)

What Figure 8.1 above implies is this: If a language has two basic color terms, it is identified as staying in the first stage of evolution, possessing two basic color words "white" and "black"; if a language has three basic color words, it is assumed to be in the second stage of evolution, possessing three basic color words "white" "black" and "red." According to this evolutionary theory, English has all the eleven basic color words so it reaches the last stage of evolution concerning its color system. The good thing about this theory is that it neatly captures a kind of generalization in basic color words of language. Because it was found that for the whole of 98 languages examined, there were only about 30 combinations of basic color words, varying from two to eleven in number and governed by their stages of evolution. If there is not a linguistic universality in the basic color word system of language, as this theory predicts, a free combination of these eleven basic color words will produce over two thousand random combinations, which was not, however, supported by Berlin and Kay's survey.

    This evolutionary theory gains strong evidence in our second example from Dani, a language which has become well known for its highly restricted system of basic color words. For instance, there are only two basic color words in this language: *Modla* for light, bright, hence, white, and *mili* for dark, dull, hence, black. (Berlin & Kay, 1991: 46) In relation to this specific language, an interesting question can be raised: What will a native Dani speaker do if he/she wants to designate colors other than black and white? Or, alternatively, do "white" and "black" always mean white and black linguistically? A further investigation of the basic color word system in Dani revealed that the native speakers of this culture use this white versus black contrast to convey more messages about their color perception than we may assume. For instance, it turns out that they use *modla* as a general color term to include all warm colors such as red and yellow and use *mili* as another umbrella color word to cover all the cold colors such as blue and green. Therefore, the contrast between *modla* and *mili* in fact is a contrast between "whitewarmness" versus "blackcoldness," rather than a simple achromatic contrast between *white* and *black* in their pure sense.

Furthermore, these results uncover two facts: First, the color word system in Dani remains in its first stage of evolution; second, by using this whitewarmness vs. blackcoldness contrast plus other types of color words, say, color words derived from object names, animals, plants, and so on, the speakers from this culture can equally express any colors labeled by distinct color words in another culture. The explanatory force of linguistic relativity, as the strong version of the Sapir-Whorf hypothesis advocates, is hence greatly reduced if we also take into our consideration the issue of language use.

8.2.3 What Evidence Can We Give to Show the Close Relationships between Language and Culture?

As a matter of fact, a constellation of examples could be picked up from different levels of language analysis to illustrate the interplay of language and culture. Moreover, this selection may range from textual structure to phonological variation. A relevant case can be found in Kaplan's study (1966) in which he claims that the structural or rhetorical organization of a text tends to be culturally specific. Some interesting experimental studies have also been conducted to test the sensitivity of the speakers to conditional clauses in a cross-linguistic context, though no consensus results have been observed yet. (Bloom, 1981) A cross-cultural study of the meaning of some idioms or metaphorical uses in a cultural context can definitely provide an optimal opportunity to examine the issue in a lifelike way. This choice of observation may partially explain why Nida, when summarizing some intrinsic features of vocabulary in relation to semantic, translating and cultural studies, states that words are sometimes "idiomatically governed" and "culturally specific." (1998: 32—45) Additionally, this observation also implies that there comes an important new force (i.e., the study of metaphor) in the pursuit of the relationships between language and culture. (Lakoff & Johnson, 1980)

Following this line of discussion, we choose to turn to our personal exposure to the American culture for more direct evidence. (Yang, 1993) Informal as these cases are, we believe that they will serve the purpose of our discussion well.

1) When you "get your hands dirty," it does not necessarily mean in the American culture that you've done some manual work and need to wash your hands.

Interaction Milieu: Professor Tulai, an American linguist, and Professor Yang, a visiting scholar from China, were talking about the relationships between teaching and doing research in the office.

Prof. Tulai: To do research means to get your hands dirty.

Prof. Yang: So you think teaching is worthier than doing research? Does the phrase "to get your hands dirty" have some pejorative connotations?

Prof. Tulai: Oh, no! I didn't mean that. When I was saying that, I simply meant "you are practicing something," or "you are engaged in doing something."

2) When you "have enough dumbbells," it does not necessarily mean that you keep pairs of this instrument for regular physical practices.

Interaction Milieu: Mr. Goodell, Mr. Yang's American landlord, and Mr. Yang were cleaning up the apartment. Mr. Yang pointed to the dumbbells on the floors and asked Mr. Goodell if he would have any use of them for the time being.

Mr. Goodell: I guess I'd better put them in the garage. I've had enough dumbbells in my office.

Mr. Yang: Really? Can you do dumbbell practice in your office?

Mr. Goodell: Definitely not! I was joking. What I really meant is that there have been a lot of stupid guys in my office.

8.2.4 To What Extent Do We Need Culture in Linguistic Study in General and in Language Teaching in Particular?

Our Hopi, Dani, and case examples above partially provide a good answer to the subtitle question. In what follows, we are going to take up an example from English which is more structure related to indicate that a study of linguistic issues in a cultural setting can greatly promote our understanding of MOTIVATION and DIRECTIONALITY in language change. Moreover, by introducing a study like this, we will have an opportunity to show how to "do linguistics" in a cultural context.

Ever since the early 1970s, along with the disclosure of the notorious political scandal dubbed the Watergate event, a bunch of derived words has been rushing into the English language. Words like "Billygate" "Debategate" "Cattlegate" "Ricegate" are some of these compounding forms. In this situation, one may feel that a sociolinguistic study of the combining form-*gate* and its derivations is necessary for us to examine the semantic, structural, and functional development concerning these nonce words and know more about the correlation of these related factors in the study of word formation. (Yang, 1997) A careful study of this phenomenon reveals the following facts:

This suffix enjoys a rich productivity in American English.

Words derived from this source inevitably take on a culturally pejorative implication to refer to "the disclosures of misconduct in highplaces" (Barnhart & Barnhart, 1981: 2364), hence, a synonym to scandals of different types, political or economical.

A variety of derivational processes (i. e. , antonomasia, conversion and affixation) can be explained in the study of the productivity of this compounding form. Based on these findings, we may draw some tentative conclusions as follows:

"Watergate," as a word taking on a pejorative implicature to refer to any political scandal at the high rank, will stay in English for quite a long time.

Its structural status in the language becomes rather stable through the rich derivational processes it has undergone in word formation.

The semantic implicature it possesses will stay with the word for quite a long time.

This compounding form has become so generalized in its form and meaning that some -*gate* words have even gone out of the American society and been used to refer to political, business, and secular scandals in other cultures as well. This explains why we have found so many -*gate* related events and new expressions ("'门'字事件"及其表达) in China over the past decade. (Yang, 2008)

8.3 Language and Society

The second association we attempt to look at is the relationships between language and society. A convenient support for an effort like this can be found in a well written article by Cem Alptekin (1993: 141): "Language has no function independently of the social contexts in which it is used." Moreover, as Halliday (1977) elegantly illustrates, this understanding of language has a long tradition in the history of language science and reflects an ever lasting contrast between a Platonic view of language study and an Aristotelian view of language study. (cf. Hu, 1990) From an ecological point of view, either Saussure's contrast between langue and parole, or Chomsky's original distinction between competence and performance, and his later dichotomy between I(nternalized) language and E(xternalized) language can be regarded as some natural deviations of the original parallel concepts derived from the Greek tradition. For example, Aristotle notices the correlation and difference existing between the mental structure that underlies the abstract language system we inherit biologically and the formal variation that distinguishes languages we speak everyday. He expresses his linguistic understanding of this contrast by the following statement.

> Spoken sounds are symbols of impressions in the mind, and what is written are symbols of what is spoken. Speech, like writing, is not the same for all mankind, although the mental impressions directly expressed

by these signs are the same for all, as are the things of which these mental impressions are likenesses (De Interpretatione I [quoted by Harris & Taylor, 1997: 21]).

Unfortunately, the social and functional understanding of language has not received as much attention as it should have deserved for long. What we want to do here is first to recall this tradition in language study and then to illustrate its resurrection in a newly developed subfield called sociolinguistics. Below are the four issues we are going to deal with in this section.

How does language relate to society?
What do we mean by a situationally and socially variationist perspective?
What more should we know about sociolinguistics?
What implications can we get from sociolinguistics?

8.3.1 How Does Language Relate to Society?

The relationships between language and society have long been recognized and examined. Evidence for this claim, discrete as it might be, can be conveniently gathered from the works by those great philosophers and grammarians either in the Graeco-Roman tradition or in the Indian history. (Harris & Taylor, 1997[1989]; Apte, 1994) During the whole 20th century, a great deal of efforts has been taken to treat the inquiry of linguistics as a MONISTIC or AUTONOMOUS PURSUIT of an independent science. Strongly influenced by this dominant view of linguistic science, a separation of the structural study of language from its social context of usage was claimed, justified, and reinforced. The resurrection of a DUALISTIC VIEW of linguistic inquiry, however, came into being in the 1960s, along with the development of sociolinguistics as an opposition to the dominant theory of Chomskyan linguistics.

8.3.2 What Do We Mean by a Situationally and Socially Variationist Perspective?

As far as the situational variation in language use is concerned, Geertz (1960) provides a good example to illustrate the diversity and richness of some stylistic variants available for a Javanese speaker to choose when engaged in different types of communicative events. For instance, even a simple interrogative sentence like "Are you going to eat rice and cassava now?" will, as the following example shows, situationally admit several Javanese translations, starting from a rather lower level of style and moving to a comparatively higher level of style:

    Are   *apa/napa/menapa*
    you   *kowé/sampéjan/pandjenengan*

going	arep/adjeng/dadé
to eat	mangan/neda/daharé
rice	sega/sekul
and	lan/kalijan
cassava	laspé
now	saiki/saniki/samenika

The copiously potential selection of linguistic forms in this Javanese community shows this fact: Appropriate language use in any social interaction not only has something to do with structural rules, but also involves some socially institutionalized norms in usage. In this sense, the choice of one linguistic form over another is both stylistically and socially governed. This conceptualization of linguistic variation, in relation to what will be discussed below, is likely to provide an innovative and more comprehensive understanding of the issue in general.

When we talk about linguistic variation, we may notice that there has been a maxim in sociolinguistics which claims that "You are what you say." (Lakoff, 1991) Following this claim, we may expand the scope of our observation by introducing some social factors that are believed to influence our language behavior in a social context. The following list documents some major ones:

Class
Gender
Age
Ethnic identity
Education background
Occupation
Religious belief

A thorough discussion of each of these factors will need much more space than we can afford here. Consequently, we are going to focus on the first two factors, namely, class and gender, in our discussion below and show their impact upon one's language use.

In the middle of 1960s, William Labov, a famous sociolinguist, conducted a rather meticulous survey at several departments in the City of New York. The objective for having this sociolinguistic investigation was to examine the relationships between speakers' social status and their phonological VARIATION. The results of this investigation were later reported in his work *The Social Stratification of English in New York City* (1966), which has now become a new classical work in sociolinguistics. In this study, it turned out that class and style were two major factors influencing the speakers' choice of one phonological variant over another. Based on these findings, Labov explicitly delineated the patterns of stratification by class and style and, more importantly, successfully introduced class as an indispensable sociolinguistic variable in the study of language use. Ever since its publication in the middle of the 1960s, this research paradigm has become the mainstream in sociolinguistics, being alternatively referred to as "the quantitative paradigm, sociolinguistics proper, variationist studies, urban dialectology and secular linguistics." (Mesthrie, 1994: 4900; Bolton, 1992: 14; Milroy, 1994: 4859; Fasold, 1999[1990])

Over the past decades, in addition to the study of linguistic variation produced by class, the investigation of gender effects upon one's linguistic behavior has also been proven to be a rich resource for examining the correlation of language and society, though the awareness of this issue seems to be an older story which can be traced back to two millenniums ago at least. For instance, many precious examples reflecting gender differences in speech have been found in some Ancient Greek dramas. (Gregersen, 1979) Nonetheless, it is generally believed that a real sociolinguistic inquiry of this issue began with Robin Lakoff's (1973) retrospective study of gender differences in American English in the early 1970s, though a cross-linguistic study of the same issue could be found in the early works of Jespersen (1922). Inspired by this very seminal article, the following years have seen a lot of publications either to support or challenge the hypotheses Lakoff put forward concerning the linguistic behavior of females in the American society. What these hypotheses predict is that there exists a WOMEN REGISTER in the language that takes on the following features:

Women use more "fancy" color terms such as "mauve" and "beige."

Women use less powerful curse words.

Women use more intensifiers such as "terrible" and "awful."

Women use more tag questions.

Women use more statement questions like "Dinner will be ready at seven o'clock?" (with a rising intonation at the end)

Women's linguistic behavior is more indirect and, hence, more polite than men's.

More importantly, it is further argued that these differences in language use are brought about by nothing less than women's place in society. The underlying point for this argument is rather significant: If we are not satisfied with some practices in language use, say, LINGUISTIC SEXISM, and want to reform the language, then the first thing we need do is to try to change society rather than language. Because, as Lakoff correctly suggests, it is not language but women's lower place in society that makes them linguistically behave in a particular way. Hence, the relationships between language and society can be further illustrated by raising the following questions:

Is a certain linguistic form more likely to be used by females than by their male peers?

If so, why should it be so?

The natural connection of these issues also explains why the study of gender differences has become an ever-lasting focus in sociolinguistics since the 1970s when the women liberation movement gained a glorious victory.

8.3.3 What More Should We Know about Sociolinguistics?

Sociolinguistics, as an interdisciplinary study of language use, attempts to show the relationships between language and society. More specifically, in this discipline we have two important things to think about: Structural things and their uses in a sociocultural context. In the same vein, when we conduct a sociolinguistic survey of language use, we have two big issues to deal with. First, we want to show how these two factors, language and society, are related to each other, and second, we attempt to know why it should be so. Put another way, we want to look at structural things by paying attention to language use in a social context. Meanwhile, we also try to understand sociological things of society by examining linguistic phenomena of a speaking community.

These dual objectives make this new type of linguistic study as an interdisciplinary or multidisciplinary enterprise in nature. (Bolton & Kwok, 1992) The pluralism and diversity of the field make it difficult to delineate the scope of this practice. Overlapping with other types of scientific research is another striking property we can observe in a sociolinguistic study: If we prepare to examine the structure of the whole sociolinguistic edifice, we can either classify sociolinguistic studies by means of a hierarchical division, or alternatively, by means of an orientational categorization. For convenience of discussion, we choose the latter approach to continue our survey of the relationships between language and society. This selection could be further specified as two related but not identical perspectives of observation identified as a SOCIOLINGUISTIC STUDY OF SOCIETY and a SOCIOLINGUISTIC STUDY OF LANGUAGE, respectively. (Fasold, 1984)

Methodologically, if we want to know more about a given society or community by examining the linguistic behavior of its members, we are doing a sociolinguistic study of society. That is, we are doing sociolinguistics at a macro level of investigation. If we turn to Fasold (1984) again, we may say that at this level of discussion things that we are interested in include bilingualism or multilingualism, language attitudes, language choice, language maintenance and shift, language planning and standardization, vernacular language education, to name some important ones.

On the other hand, if we want to know more about linguistic variation in language use by turning to potential sociocultural factors for a detailed description and explanation, we are doing a sociolinguistic study of language. Consequently, we are more interested in examining micro linguistic phenomena such as structural variants, address forms, gender differences, discourse analysis, Pidgin and Creole languages, and other more language-related issues. The interested reader can find more discussions concerning some of these heated sociolinguistic issues. (Yang, 1988; 1990a; 1990b; 1991; 1996; 2000)

What we will present below are some important features and developmental issues of this new linguistic enterprise. We will first show how theoretical linguists look at sociolinguistics and then review how sociolinguists define this new enterprise. To help you form a complete picture of the situation, we will also discuss stages of its development.

Initially being as an opposition to generative linguistics, the development of sociolinguistics has been a rather uneven one. As late as in the 1970s, this pursuit was still regarded as a job of butterfly sample collection in linguistics, which could hardly make any significant contribution to the formation of linguistic theory. (Chomsky, 1977) After four decades of collective and persevering labor and effort, the professional position of sociolinguistics has become secured and this school of linguistic study is now viewed as a legitimate academic pursuit in linguistics. (Chomsky, 1995)

As you can fully understand, the choice of terms and definitions means a lot to any science during its development. The same thing is true to sociolinguistics. Ever since the 1960s, efforts have been made to define the term of sociolinguistics in the field. For instance, Susan Ervin Tripp (1971 [1969]) defines the subject as "the systematic study of the relation of linguistic forms and social meaning," while Hymes (1973: 315) asserts that "The term 'sociolinguistics' means many things to many people, and of course no one has a patent on its definition. Indeed not everyone whose work is called 'sociolinguistic' is ready to accept the label, and those who do use the term include and emphasize different things." In fact, a variety of definitions and descriptions have been given to the subject, each trying to look at the discipline from a slightly different perspective (Fishman, 1972; Berns, 1990; Chambers, 1995; Downes, 1998). More recently, Hymes comments that "the distinctive mark of sociolinguistics as a whole, I think, has been insistence on attending to linguistic features in any and all aspects of social life, and presumably will continue to be so." (2000: 313)

Clearly, it seems still premature at present for any one to provide a definition that is broad enough to include everything which can be justifiably dubbed a sociolinguistic study of language. In a dilemma situation like this, the best thing we can do, perhaps, is to provide a series of descriptors that will help capture some fundamental characteristics of this dynamic school of linguistics. And these features can be summarized as follows:

Sociolinguistics has a wide inclusion.

Sociolinguistics is characteristic of a multi-dependent subject.

Sociolinguistics emphasizes a situational study of linguistic items and their social functions.

Sociolinguistics focuses on examining the interplay between language, culture, and society.

Sociolinguistics, different from a pure structural perspective in linguistics, attempts to provide a description and explanation of language-related issues by exploring the social meaning or significance in language use.

Having illustrated some important features that characterize the discipline, we'd better look back and examine its developmental issues so that a more complete picture can be formed concerning this new subject. Roughly speaking, there exists a series of six developmental stages in sociolinguistics and each of these stages can be briefly summarized as follows.

The first stage started from the early 1920s and lasted to the late 1940s. Some major anthropological linguists of this period could be regarded as the representatives of the early pioneering stage of a socially and culturally oriented perspective in linguistic study.

It is generally believed that the Ninth International Congress of Linguistics at the University of California at Los Angles, which was held in 1964, indicates a sudden rising of a new discipline in linguistics—sociolinguistics. (Samarin, 2000) In fact, this conference played such an important role that it marked a new epoch in the history of linguistics by gathering a group of scholars who shared a belief that linguistic research should not only be confined to descriptive or structural linguistics, and that the study of language use in social contexts should also be taken into serious consideration. (Hymes, 2000)

When it came to the 1970s, a rapid development was witnessed in the domain of sociolinguistics. Strongly influenced by the women's liberation movement and the similar political awareness of some social problems and conflicts, researchers from different academic backgrounds, began to develop an interest in looking at linguistic behavior of different speech communities, expecting to provide a social, rather than a pure structural, explanation for their observations.

From the late 1970s to early 1980s, some weaknesses were, however, found in the current paradigm of sociolinguistics. Different criticisms were heard from both inside and outside critics. The major problem facing the field at this time was its inefficiency in theory and methodology development. With great efforts from theorists and practitioners, problems in these two respects were attenuated and improved in the late 1980s. This is an indication that sociolinguistics was moving to a stage of gradual maturity.

When we compare sociolinguistic research completed in the 1990s with those studies conducted in its earlier stages, we will notice that a variety of positive changes have taken place. With its emphasis of the correlation with other sciences in a broad sense and also with its further improvement in theory and methodology, this new discipline has gained much acknowledgement and academic reputation, and has gradually become a comparatively independent and professional study in the field of linguistics. (cf. Chomsky, 1995)

The new millennium has brought a constellation of innovative things to different fields of scholastic pursuit and technological research. As a multi disciplinary study of language-related issues, sociolinguistics has gained much momentum both from theoretical linguistics and from ethno-linguistics. Recent developments in linguistics predict that linguistic studies in the new century will become more fruitful if an evolutionary, cognitive, and interdisciplinary perspective is taken in its theoretic pursuit. (Hauser, Chomsky & Fitch, 2002) On the other hand, a new framework, the linguistic landscape, has been introduced to look at the informational and symbolic functions public and commercial signs may serve in a given linguistic community. (Landry & Bourhis, 1997; Backhaus, 2005 & 2007; Shohamy & Gorter, 2009)

8.3.4 What Implications Can We Get from Sociolinguistics?

The past decades have witnessed a rapid development in sociolinguistics and the findings in this field have greatly enriched our understanding of the relationships between language and society. Along with the gradual maturity and acceptance of this school of linguistics, there has been an ever-growing possibility for us to have a new daughter discipline called "applied sociolinguistics." (Trudgill, 1984) Some more successful practices of this attempt have been found in language class rooms, law courts, and clinical settings, respectively.

Following this line of discussion, we will first have a brief look at sociolinguistics in language classrooms and some detailed discussion of these relationships will be given in the fourth part of this chapter. Before we take up this issue, we'd better start our pursuit by raising a question like this: What is wrong with the traditional perspective in language teaching? By asking this question, we are in fact making a choice between training our students as GRAMMARIANS and training them as ACTIVE LANGUAGE USERS. This contrast reflects two different views of philosophy in language teaching. We witnessed, however, a dramatic change in language teaching in the middle of the 1970s when Hyme's theory of COMMUNICATIVE COMPETENCE was introduced into the field as an antagonism to the traditional philosophy in language teaching. Consequently, as the name of this theory indicates, language teachers began to pay more attention to the question of how to train their students as active and successful language users in a real language context.

Still with an applied perspective, now let us take a look at sociolinguistics in law courts. The inquiry of the relationships between language and law has opened another avenue for the application of sociolinguistic findings to some more practical issues in society. Some fruitful practices of this attempt have been observed in this respect. For instance, the important role of linguists in the analysis of language data gathered as evidence in law courts has been recognized by more and more people. Meanwhile, the joint work by sociolinguists and legislators in the preparation of some legal documents is proven to be helpful to increase the readability of this text and therefore appreciated. (cf. Fasold, 1999[1990]) On the other hand, investigations of language use in a law court background also have revealed some interesting results which, in turn, greatly enrich our understanding of the relationships between the concept of POWER and LANGUAGE IN USE. (O'Barr & Atkins, 1980)

Our last case comes from a sociolinguistic study of discourse in clinic settings. The analysis of dialogues between doctors and patients in a hospital context has also attracted the interest of some sociolinguists. Similar to our case in the law court, the study of this type is also employed to illustrate things such as how the concept of power is encoded and decoded through language use in a hierarchical society and what pragmatically related patterns and forces in reference and implication are involved in such a speech event. For this reason, rewarding efforts have been taken in a sociolinguistic analysis of discourse patterns in a clinic setting. Because it is believed that in a highly hierarchically ordered communicative situation like this, through the study of language use by doctor and patient, more implications can be obtained in terms of the impact of some sociological factors upon the linguistic behavior of the members of a speech community.

8.4 Sociolinguistics and Language Teaching

The relationships between sociolinguistics and language teaching are the last association we set up to explore in this chapter. This association is so important and colorful that we would like to say more about it, compared to other types of relationships we have examined so far.

Strongly influenced by the rapid development of sociolinguistics over the past decades, the enterprise of language teaching has gradually developed into a well established subfield in linguistic science, which is alternatively referred to as applied linguistics in a broad sense. What makes the inclusion of the relationships between sociolinguistics and language teaching more relevant to our discussion in question is that a survey of the relationships will further justify the necessity for adopting a tripartite model in linguistic research, with language, culture, and society being examined as a whole, rather than discrete subjects. Put another way, a glimpse of what has happened in the field of language teaching over the past four decades will provide us with a further opportunity to see how these three important factors are related to each other in linguistic research in general and in applied linguistic study in particular. In traditional linguistics, for instance, issues concerning meaning and communication have been ignored for a long time. The discussion given below will, nonetheless, indicate that with a due consideration of meaning production and communicative competence development in a language learning situation, plentiful useful implications can be gathered from a social and cultural study of some issues in the language classroom so that further contributions from the sociolinguistic side can be made to the study of linguistics in general.

To better understand possible contributions sociolinguistics can make to linguistics in general and to applied linguistics in particular, we must know something about the traditional way of language teaching. A general assumption behind this statement is that if everything works well with the original paradigm of language teaching, there would not be any necessity to introduce something new, as Kuhn's theory of paradigm shift rightly suggests. (Kuhn, 1962 & 1970) Consequently, five crucial issues have been spotted and will be dealt with in this section:

How are some leading sociolinguistic theories related to language teaching?

Why should we teach cultural things in our classroom?

What should we teach about culture in our classroom?

How can we use public signs to enhance learners' awareness of cultural differences in language learning?

What contributions has sociolinguistics made to the field of language teaching?

8.4.1 How Are Some Leading Sociolinguistic Theories Related to Language Teaching?

By raising a question like this, we need to recall what has happened in the field of language teaching over the past three decades or so. Chomsky (1965: 3) argues:

> Linguistic theory is concerned primarily with an ideal speaker listener, in a completely homogeneous speech community, who knows its language perfectly and is unaffected by such grammatically irrelevant conditions as memory limitations, distractions, shifts of attention and

interest, and errors (random or characteristic) in applying his knowledge of the language in actual performance.

Being unsatisfied with the dominance of the Chomkyan linguistics, Hymes (1972[1966]) puts forward a theory of COMMUNICATIVE COMPETENCE. This new theory suggests that good mastery of grammar can never independently make an appropriate language user in a real social context of language use, and that a serious linguistic study should not only confine itself to the inquiry of the formation of linguistic competence of the speaker, but also need to pay enough attention to the development of communicative competence of the speaker. What is entailed by this new theory can be recapitulated as the following four possibilities (1972[1966]):

Whether (and to what degree) something is formally possible.

Whether (and to what degree) something is feasible in virtue of the means of implementation available.

Whether (and to what degree) something is appropriate (adequate, happy, successful) in relation to a context in which it is used and evaluated.

Whether (and to what degree) something is in fact done, actually performed, and what its doing entails.

A good starting point for one to illustrate the validity of these possibilities or features goes to a tentative analysis of a classic example taken from the generative paradigm, namely, "Colorless green ideas sleep furiously." Following Hymes, a general statement can be made about this example sentence: It is grammatically possible, and idiomatically feasible, but semantically either inappropriate or absurd, and practically rarely, if not never, used in a real language interaction situation. In the same vein, the overemphasis of the structural training and reinforcement in the traditional language teaching paradigm could inevitably lead the learner to producing a variety of sentences that are formally acceptable but stylistically heavy, pragmatically inappropriate and practically rare. Consequently, a similar parallel flaw was identified in language teaching as it is the case with theoretic linguistics—the study of meaning and language use has been greatly, if not completely, ignored.

As soon as the theory of communicative competence was made known, it received a warm welcome among language teachers. The reason for this appeal could be multiple. But one thing that should never be over-emphasized is the fact that what implies by this theoretic framework is exactly what has long been sought but in vain in the domain of applied linguistics and language teaching. The sharp contrast thus formed between Chomskyan linguistics and Hymesian linguistics finally led to a paradigm shift in the language teaching enterprise, with the latter successfully initiating a movement from a pure structural tradition in language teaching to a new sociolinguistic perspective in language teaching. The difference between these two orientations can be better illustrated by examining the different goals of language training in each of these traditions, which can be further defined as two parallel concepts with one focusing on "mastery of language structure" and the other spotlighting "mastery of language use." (Newmark & Reibel, 1968: 232) For the former, language learning is regarded as a subject that shares a lot of similarities with other well established subjects such as history and mathematics. The goal of language training in this framework is to encourage learners to accumulate as much grammatical knowledge as they can, while the function of communication is by and large ignored.

Contrasting with the formal perspective of language teaching is a sociolinguistic theory of language training where the subject of language learning is regarded as a process of communicative competence development. The training goal in this new model is not to make learners become grammarians but active language users. This contrast, as Berns (1990: 342) summarizes, reflects two different philosophies in language teaching: In the former paradigm, "language learning is treated as a process of acquiring knowledge, like studying history or mathematics. The end result is that learners will know something about the language in the same way a linguist does, but will know little about the language used by others." In the latter paradigm, language learning is regarded as a process of picking up knowledge and skills for linguistic communication rather than purely formal principles and rules.

If we can say that a sociolinguistic understanding of the relationships between performance and competence, as Hyme's theory of communicative competence suggests, has greatly changed our view of language teaching and learning in general, then we may have enough reason to state that it is Halliday's theory of SOCIOLOGICAL SEMANTICS (1973) that helps us see more about the relationships between structure, meaning, and function in language acquisition in particular. Put another way, by turning to Halliday, we can redefine language as a system that represents MEANING POTENTIAL and regard language acquisition or language learning as a sociological process of how to select from a variety of linguistic options to produce a given meaning that is socially or contextually appropriate. Hence, the validity of a famous philosophical understanding of an important role of language, namely, we do things with language, is reinforced. (cf. Austin, 1962) To illustrate how his view of sociological semantics works, Halliday puts forward a tripartite model to show the interdependency of the three factors that are assumed to guarantee the operation of the semantic networks in an actual social interaction. Figure 8.2 below illustrates this relationship.

Chapter 8 Language, Culture, and Society

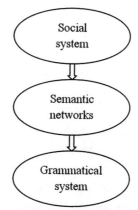

Figure 8.2 The Interdependent Relationships between Social, Semantic, and Grammatical Realization

Elsewhere, Halliday (1978) further explains the importance of a sociological view of semantics in language study:

> These networks are what we understand by "semantics." They constitute a stratum that is intermediate between the social system and the grammatical system. The former is wholly outside language, the latter is wholly within language; the semantic networks, which describe the range of alternative meanings available to the speaker in given social contexts and settings, form a bridge between the two. (quoted in Brumfit & Johnson, 1979: 44)

In relation to language teaching, what Halliday stresses here is in fact a sociolinguistic understanding of why we should include social and cultural things in our language teaching and how language could be more efficiently learned and taught by adopting a functional or sociolinguistic approach, if we want to train our students as successful communicators rather than pedantic grammarians. More importantly, as J. B. Pride (1968:1) correctly points out, "Meaningful use of language, among other things, is that which appropriately reflects its social and cultural milieu, and conveys social and cultural purpose." Following this line of argument, we may better appreciate the important role that the semantic networks could play in quality teaching. This is because "the time is once more with us when we as language teachers can bring meaning and purpose into our discourse without an apology or a blush." (Lott, 1975: 271)

Having said so much, we may have enough reason to assume that one culture's meat could be another culture's poison. The choice of an expression over another in some cases is culturally, semantically and functionally specific. In the same sense, we may state that language is a loaded weapon. (Bolinger, 1980) In relation to a language learning situation, the meaning we can read between the lines of this statement is: If learners from a given cultural background are not fully aware of the relevant constraints socially and functionally institutionalized in another society, they may easily get themselves hurt when involved in some socially interactive activities. Consequently, a purposeful selection of a linguistic form from the semantic networks available in the target language to convey an appropriate meaning in a certain social setting becomes all important and indispensable in language learning. Below is a bad experience undergone by a group of Chinese girls in New York. Here is a clue question for you to quickly understand the bad situation these girls had linguistically: According to your understanding of English, what is the appropriate usage a native speaker would use if he or she wants to attract the attention of others in a public situation like this?

  A group of Chinese girls who just arrived at the United States for their university education decided to visit the city of New York together. Since their school was not very far from the city, so they planned to take a Greyhound bus to go there at weekend. Saturday morning, they got up early and after two hours' drive they got to the downtown of the city. They stayed there for a couple of hours, shopping and sightseeing happily. Everything seemed OK until it was the time for them to go back—they suddenly realized that they lost their way back to the Greyhound bus station. What made the situation worse was that it was getting darker. In despair, they stopped at a corner on the street and decided to ask for help. At this moment they saw a young couple passing by so they said "Hello!" to this couple. To their surprise, the couple looked at them coldly and hustled on. Having no way out, they approached to a next group of passersby and tried a louder "Hello" this time. Again they got nothing but a cold shoulder from these metropolitan people.

With the help of the clue question, we believe that you got the answer for sure. In fact, what bothered this group of Chinese girls was not their English grammar but their awareness of some culturally specific usage. As you can fully understand, these Chinese students performed satisfactorily on their TOEFL and GRE tests and did not have much difficulty understanding their professors' lectures in university. But, as this sad story indicates, they did have some difficulty in choosing an appropriate linguistic form from their English repertoire to meet with their semantic end in this particular social context. More specifically, as you may assume, it is a convention for native speakers of English to say "Excuse me" rather than "Hello" to attract others' attention in such a public setting as the one these women students were in.

  Fully understanding the haphazard heteromorphism either in cultural ACCOMMODATION or in ACCULTURATION, we have enough reason to

Chapter 8 Language, Culture, and Society

introduce a newly developed theory for social learning in our classroom. It is called the theory of community of practice. By turning to this theory, we may regard the cultural enhancement in language learning as a social learning process characteristic of an everlasting practice of apprenticeship, starting from a peripheral member and ending up as a core member if we want to become active and competent language users. (Lave & Wenger, 1991) The good thing about this theory is that a natural way of learning is called for in the development of different skills, with language skills being included in our case.

8.4.2 Why Should We Teach Cultural Things in Our Classroom?

It is argued that effective language learning involves two types of knowledge: SYSTEMIC KNOWLEDGE for structural properties of a given language and SCHEMATIC KNOWLEDGE for social and cultural input of a certain culture. (Widdowson, 1990) Following this argument, we may say that while the former type of knowledge can be learned either in a natural situation of language acquisition or in a classroom of foreign language learning, the latter type of knowledge can only be gained in a social context where children learn how to complete the matching or "fit, or consistency, between the culture specific aspects of cognition and the native language." (Alptekin, 1993: 137) As our story above and more similar examples (Hu & Gao, 1997) indicate, due to the lack of an appropriate context to learn and cultivate this socially specific knowledge, the learning of this schematic knowledge always forms a detriment to language learners in a foreign language situation. This is definitely something that is worthy of further examination.

To better illustrate the relationships between culture and language learning, let us go back to the study of rhetorical organization again (Kaplan, 1966) and see what lessons we can learn from a culturally oriented paradigm in language teaching and research. As has been shown above, there has been a claim, though still full of debates and controversies at present, that our unique cultural background tends to produce a "filter" effect which will both perceptually influence our understanding of the world and linguistically determine our expression of ourselves. (Kaplan, 1966; Connor & Kaplan, 1987; Alptekin, 1988) Evidence from the domain of language learning, as has been summarized by Cem Alptekin (1993) below, shows that different rhetorical patterns were taken by student writers from separate cultural backgrounds.

> As a case in point, Clyne (1981) shows the fundamental contrast between English rhetorical patterns—which are generally characterized by linearity in the presentation of ideas—and German rhetorical patterns— which are marked not only by digressions, but also digressions from

> digressions. Similarly, Koch (1983) points out that, unlike Western modes of argumentation, which are based on a syllogistic model of proof, Arabic argumentative prose makes use of repetition as a device for textual cohesion and rhetorical effectiveness. In the same vein, Jenkins and Hinds (1987), speaking of audience awareness skills, indicate that while American business letters are reader oriented, the French ones are writer oriented, and the Japanese ones are oriented to the space between the writer and the reader. Finally, it is no secret that topical priorities change from one culture to another. (1993:138)

More recently, Colin Simpson (1995) claims that there exist several reasons for us to have in our language classroom sociolinguistics in general and cultural enhancement in particular.

> [F]irstly, students' motivation is often based on an enthusiasm for the cultures or societies which use a particular language as the main medium of expression; secondly, sociolinguistic studies offer a natural cultural backdrop to language studies, which is essential if language is to be seen as a living cultural asset; finally, the cultural area of language studies offers one of the best media through which cultural prejudices can be broken down and challenged, which is surely one of aims of every serious educator (1995: 51).

Depending on varying perspectives taken by individual researchers, one can provide far more reasons to the question concerned, of which we will dwell up the following five in some details to further highlight the importance of culture learning in any language classroom.

Facing a new world situation such as globalization and digitalization, a healthier philosophy of pedagogy should be developed in the field of language teaching so that due attention can be drawn to sociological and cultural studies. For educators, it has become an urgent and indispensable responsibility to make our students familiar with cultural differences. For instance, as early as in the 1980s, the European Cultural Foundation and the International Council for Educational Development stressed the view that "for effective international cooperation, knowledge of other countries and their cultures is as important as proficiency in their languages." (van Els, 1982 [quoted in Byram, 1986:324])

As Simpson (1995) rightly points out, learner's motivation could be greatly enhanced by virtue of the input of cultural things in a given language. Satisfactory mastery of a foreign language can never be achieved if we ignore the factors such as motivation and empathy in language learning. This is especially the case in China when the efficiency of college English has been challenged, which is basically test oriented and has less connection with one's carrier development in the future. Facing a situation like this, how to enhance

Chapter 8　Language, Culture, and Society

learners' motivation in their English learning becomes a critical thing to language instructors.

As a part of liberal education, the effort in this respect will provide our students with enough information to transcend their own culture and develop more objective consciousness of related issues to fight against CULTURAL STEREOTYPES of different kinds. For instance, the higher occurrence of some routine expressions like "Thank you" and "Thanks" in Anglo American culture does not necessarily mean that the speaker really thinks that he or she owes you something. These words and the expressions such as "please" and "Hello" or "Hi" are dubbed "the magic words" in the parental language use in an English speaking society and are internalized by means of SOCIOLIZATIONAL PROCESSES. In most cases, these expressions serve as a lip service or routine greetings to show politeness or cultivation. If members from another culture does not share this interpretation of language use, they may have a feeling that these British or American speakers are kind of falseness and insincerity, hearing these expressions exchanged so frequently between native speakers for some thing extremely trivial and worthy of no gratitude in their source culture. Or alternatively, they may even form a distorted negative image of their own culture, saying: "Look at these guys! Unlike our countrymen, they are so polite!"

As has been repeatedly testified, culture is always reflected in language and there is no separation between understanding language and understanding culture. A good interpretation of linguistic things has to do with a conscious understanding of the cultural background of the target language. Teaching culture in our language classroom will greatly facilitate the language learning process. A case in point is how to develop a higher degree of sensitivity to some culturally specific expressions in one's language learning. Below are some idiomatic expressions whose correct interpretation could never be ascertained without enough input from the target culture. (Yang, 1987: 9)

Table 8.1　A Comparison of Culturally Specific Expressions in English and Their Possible Chinese Interpretations

English Expression	English Explanation	Possible Semantic Interpretation Inferred by Chinese Students
harebrained	giddy; reckles	stimid; quiet
bird-brained	stupid	agile; clever
pigeon-toed	having the toes or feet turned inward	tiny; lovely
goose-step	balancing drill taught to army recruits	awkwardness; unsteadiness
athlete's foot	dermatophytosis	stoutness; powerfulness

Lastly, as theorists and practitioners, we should fully realize the difficulty and challenge that we may have in the teaching of culture in a language classroom. To know another culture is a rather difficult job. To act or behave appropriately in another culture is a more demanding task. A good understanding of the target culture, as Nida claims (Nida & JFL correspondent, 1998), will take more than a decade of time, thus forming a rather challenging task either to language learners or to language facilitators. Painstaking efforts should be made to issues such as teacher training, curriculum development, and proficiency evaluation if we hope for a fruitful reformation in this respect.

All this leads to a belief that a good understanding of structural things in some cases has much to do with a conscious understanding of the cultural background of the target language on the part of language learners. In other words, successful command of a given language has much to do with a deep appreciation of that culture. This is because, as we have shown so far, language and culture are correlated with each other at different levels of linguistic repertoire. Keeping these points in mind, we will take a more classroom-based perspective and examine the issue of what to be given in our classroom if cultural enhancement is really so important in the process of language learning. The interested reader can find more examples in relevant research. (Gao, 2000)

8.4.3 What Should We Teach about Culture in Our Classroom?

Before dealing with this instructional question, let us first see what has happened to the study of culture itself. Over the past decades, we have witnessed a lot of new academic specialties, of which cultural studies is definitely a fashionable one, though theoretically speaking, much remains to be done in this new subject. Some explanations should, however, be given to its apparent delay in the theoretic development if we want to have a whole picture of the situation.

Unlike the study of language teaching which may depend heavily on relevant sciences such as linguistics, psychology and cognitive sciences, cultural studies is commonly assumed to require "a broad base" (Byram, 1986: 325) and involves a variety of germane subjects such as geography, history, anthropology, ethnology, folklore, and even mass communication. The hetermorphical features of cultural studies make unpractical a unified theory or even a principled approach to the treatment of relevant issues in question. Nonetheless, Buttjes (1982 [cited in Byram, 1986: 323]) summarizes a set of three basic positions one may take in cultural studies, though how to adopt these positions in a language learning classroom remains something intangible:

The first perspective is a pragmatic communicative oriented position where learners are expected to use culture as a tool to solve communicative problems in language use.

The second perspective is an ideological understanding oriented position where learners are encouraged to know as much as possible about the target culture.

The last one is a political action oriented position where learners are hoped to resist a blind acceptance of a given culture by developing a more critical understanding of both the target culture and the source culture.

Practically, there are three types of culture available for a language classroom to adopt. (cf. Osburne, 1990) They are briefly summarized as follows while more explanation will be given soon.

1) Anthropological culture
2) History of civilization culture
3) Mini culture such as "pop culture, travel culture, scientific culture" (Alptekin, 1993: 142) or the culture embedded in the concept of WORLD ENGLISHES (cf. Kachru & Nelson, 1996)

While the first type of culture involves some fundamental features concerning the development of CULTURAL COMPETENCE in language learning (Wallace, 1988) and emphasizes the inclusion of a complex package of things such as belief, knowledge, attitudes, values, behavior, and thinking patterns in a given culture, the messages concerning geographical features, historical developments, and achievements of civilization and science of a certain culture are some necessary topics for the teaching of the second type of culture. The last type of culture indicates a rather loose definition to the scope of the subject and reflects a prolific source of materials that can be used to enhance learners' consciousness of the concept of "the international English" (Alptekin, 1993: 142) or the diversity of subculture in world Englishes.

Having specified the general scope of what to be taught in a language classroom, necessary caution should be taken in how to render the cultural stuff in practice. In any case, as language instructors, we should be fully aware of the possibility that when we teach something about a given culture, we should never form a new stereotype of another culture. Facing a dilemma like this and fighting against the negative influence from cultural colonization (cf. Alptekin & Alptekin, 1984), a sensible principle that should be followed in the teaching of culture can be summarized as this: Teach something about the target culture, but do not teach something of the target culture. Another pitfall we should equally eschew in our teaching practice is that a subject priority should be always given to the development of language and communication skills rather than to culture itself.

8.4.4 How Can We Use Public Signs to Enhance Learners' Awareness of Cultural Differences in Language Learning?

Over the past years, issues related to bilingual signs in China have attracted much attention both from the government and from the public. A key point spotted in this matter is that in the Chinese context, some English translations of public signs are unintelligible, if not funny, to speakers from English speaking society. A comprehensive survey of these problems will take much space than we can afford here. For this reason, what we present below are two case studies: One is related to the choice of "in case of" over "if" in warning signs; the other has to do with the choice of "mothers to be" over "pregnant women" in parking signs. Interested readers may go to our recent publications for more reference. (Yang & Liu, 2010; Yang & Zhao, 2010; Yang & Li, 2011; Yang & Lu, 2011)

How is "in case of" culturally different from "if" in warning signs?

As Figure 8.3 below shows, "In Case Of Fire, Do Not Use Elevators. Use Stairways."（如遇火情,勿乘电梯,请走逃生楼梯）is a sign one can see in many public places in the States. As bilingual signs show in cities of China, this fire sign was sometimes translated as "If there is fire, do not use elevators." Before we go deeper, let us see another English sign: "In Case Of Earthquake, Go To High Ground Or Inland."（如遇地震,朝高地或内陆方向疏散）By comparing these examples, it is clear that, though both "in case of" and "if" can be used to indicate a given condition, they are different in their usage. The former, more often than not, has an implication that involves something which should be avoided. For example, fire accidents and earthquake disasters are definitely something one would try hard to avoid or escape. Therefore, as warning signs "in case of" rather than "if" should be chosen. This interpretation of the usage depends much on the familiarity with the target culture and society, thus providing vivid feedback to cultural study in a language learning situation.

Figure 8.3 "In Case of Fire do not Use Elevators"
(Source: http://nmcsafety.com)

Chapter 8 Language, Culture, and Society

How is "mothers to be" culturally different from "pregnant women" in parking signs?

"Reserved Parking For Mothers To Be"（产妇孕妇专用车位）is another English sign that reveals more cultural information than just a notice one may have in a parking lot. In most bilingual signs in China, this sign was put as "Reserved Parking For Pregnant Women." Literally speaking, there is no difference between "mothers to be" and "pregnant women." But when used on public signs, they do make a difference: The former is more polite and hence more socially appropriate. "Stork Parking For New Mothers And Mothers To Be"（产妇孕妇专用车位）is another sign encoding the similar cultural information. In some English speaking countries, a stork has been traditionally regarded as a lucky bird that brings babies to a family. Figure 8.4 below vividly documents this tradition. Interestingly, 麒麟送子 is a cultural tradition we have held in China for a long time. Needless to say, knowledge like this will greatly enrich the teaching package of English instructors and make their work more appreciated by language learners, on the one hand, and more acknowledged by society, on the other.

Figure 8.4 "Stork Parking For New Mothers"
(http://www.smartsign.com)

8.4.5 What Contributions Has Sociolinguistics Made to the Field of Language Teaching?

In general, we may say that sociolinguistics has shed new and insightful light on some fundamental issues in language teaching and learning, which has made theorists and practitioners of the field know much more than before about what to teach and how to teach. More specifically, it is claimed that sociolinguistics has made at least six concrete contributions to the field of language teaching (Simpson, 1995; Berns, 1990; Lott, 1975):

1) Sociolinguistics has contributed to a change of emphasis in the

content of language teaching.

2) It has also brought about innovations in materials and activities for the classroom.

3) It has offered a fresh look at the nature of language development and use.

4) It has introduced a better framework in teacher training so that the cognitive faculties of the learner can be more efficiently fostered.

5) It has paved a more fruitful path to research in this field.

6) It has offered language learners a more global perspective in their learning.

Clearly, what is presented in the above list is far from comprehensive. The good thing about this classification is that it helps one see explicitly the important and colorful roles a sociolinguistic study of language can play in applied linguistics and language teaching. Based on the discussion in this section, a conclusion we can make here is that implications obtained from sociolinguistic studies can not only enrich our understanding of issues such as the relationships between sociolinguistics and language learning, the role of acculturation in language teaching, and a cultural perspective in curriculum development, but also highlight the question of how to develop a more optimal research paradigm in language teaching. (Firth & Wagner, 1997; Yang, 2000)

8.5 Summary

In our discussion above, we have introduced some important theories and practices in a sociocultural inquiry of language-related issues. The relationships between sociolinguistics and language teaching and learning have also been highlighted and discussed by examining some theoretical contributions and pedagogical implications the former has produced over the past decades to the latter. As we have indicated, the systematic pursuit of these issues did not start until the 1960s, with the occurrence of sociolinguistics as a new force in the study of language science. After almost 60 years' development, this innovative movement has gained much momentum and vitality by incorporating the insights from other relevant sciences and has gradually secured its position as a legitimate pursuit in linguistics. (cf. Chomsky, 1995; Hauser, Chomsky & Fitch, 2002)

On the other hand, as has been discussed in this chapter, the study of the interrelationships between language, culture, society, and language teaching and learning is a rather intriguing task. One of the difficulties observed in this attempt is the diversity in subject matters. The interdisciplinary nature of this pursuit requires good mastery of knowledge in relevant fields such as anthropology, social psychology, sociology, ethnology, cognitive sciences, and cross-cultural communication (cf. Rosch, 1975 & 1977) on the part of researchers and practitioners. Another problem we may face in this work is that complete ignorance of the cultural and social impact on language use will greatly jeopardize our understanding of language itself. Take an idiomatic expression in English for instance.

It has been claimed that sentences like "Would you like to have such a car?" and "I don't like such music." are typical mistakes committed by English learners. (Swan, 1980) The reason for this claim is that for the emphatic use of "such" phrases in modern English, one should use a "such + a(n) + adjective + noun" pattern rather than a bare "such + a(n) +noun" structure. A sociolinguistic survey of this issue, however, revealed that both of these uses are acceptable in contemporary English, and that the choice of one form over another is subculture, rather, gender specific: Women tend to use the bare structure more frequently than men. (Yang, 1990a & 1990b) More importantly, this study indicates that men and women do behave differently in a social context as far as the question of language use is concerned. To know the nature of language, we have also to know the diversity of language use as well, with so called SOCIAL DIALECTS being included.

Following this line of reasoning, we have to say that what is presented above is only a small part of the whole sociolinguistic edifice. Much of its beauty and fascination is still there waiting for conscious and courageous explorers to search and discover. That said, we suggest that the interested students go to the bibliographic part of this chapter for more information concerning their further study in this respect.

References

Alptekin, C. & M. Alptekin. 1984. "The question of culture: EFL teaching in non-English speaking countries," *ELT Journal* 38: 14—20.

Alptekin, C. 1993. "Target language culture in EFL materials," *ELT Journal* 47: 136—143.

Apte, M. L. 1994. "Language in sociocultural context," In *The Encyclopedia of Language and Linguistics*, 2000—2010. R. E. Asher (ed.). Oxford: Pergamon.

Austin, J. L. 1962. *How to Do Things with Words*. New York: Oxford University Press.

Backhaus, P. 2005. "Signs of multilingualism in Tokyo-A diachronic look at the linguistic landscape," *International Journal of the Sociology of Language*: 175—176, 103—121.

Backhaus, P. 2007. *Linguistic Landscapes: A Comparative Study of Urban Multilingualism in Tokyo*. Clevedon: Multilingual Matters.

Barnhart, C. L. & R. K. Barnhart (eds.). 1981. *The World Book Dictionary*. Chicago: World Book Children International, Inc.

Berns, M. 1990. "Why language teaching needs the sociolinguist," *The Canadian Modern Language Review* 46: 339—353.

Bloom, A. F. 1981. *Linguistic Shaping of Thought*. Hillsdale, N. J.: Lawrence Erlbaum.

Bolinger, D. 1980. *Language: The Loaded Weapon*. London: Longman.

Brumfit, C. J. & K. Johnson (eds.). 1979. *The Communicative Approach to Language Teaching*. Oxford: Oxford University Press.

Buttjes, D. 1982. "Landeskunde im fremdsprachenunterricht," *Newsprachliche Mitteilungen* 35: 2—16.

Byram, M. 1986. "Cultural studies in foreign language teaching," *Language Teaching* (The International Abstracting Journal of Language Teachers and Applied Linguists) 19: 322—336.

Carroll, J. B. (ed.) 1956. *Language, Thought, and Reality: Selected Writings of Benjamin Lee Whorf*. New York: MIT.

Chambers, J. K. 1995. *Sociolinguistic Theory: Linguistic Variation and Its Social Significance*. Oxford, U. K. & Cambridge, Massachusetts: Blackwell.

Chomsky, N. 1965. *Aspects of the Theory of Syntax*. Mass: MIT Press.

Chomsky, N. 1977. *Language and Responsibility*. Brighton: Harvester.

Chomsky, N. 1995. "Language and nature," *Mind* 104: 1—16.

Clyne, M. 1981. "Culture and discourse structure," *Journal of Pragmatics* 5: 61—66.

Crystal, D. 1985. *A Dictionary of Linguistics and Phonetics*. Oxford: Basil Blackwell.

Darnell, R. 1994. "Edward Sapir," In *The Encyclopedia of Language and Linguistics*, 3655—3656. R. E. Asher (ed.). Oxford: Pergamon.

Downes, W. 1998. *Language and Society*. (2nd ed.). London: Cambridge University Press.

Fasold, R. 1984. *The Sociolinguistics of Society*. Oxford: Black well.

Firth, A. & J. Wagner. 1997. "On discoursing, communication, and (some) fundamental concepts in SLA research," *The Modern Language Journal* 81: 285—300.

Fishman, J. A. 1972. "The sociology of language," In *Language and Social Context: Selected Readings*. P. P. Giglioli (ed.). Harmondsworth, England: Penguin.

Gao, Y. H. 2000.《语言文化差异的认识与超越》,北京:外语教学与研究出版社。

Geertz, C. 1960. "Linguistic etiquette," In *Sociolinguistics*. J. B. Pride et al., (ed.). New York: Penguin Books.

Greenberg, J. H. , C. A. Ferguson & E. A. Moravcsik (eds.). 1978. *Universals in Human Language*, Vol. I: *Method and Theory*. Stanford, CA: Stanford University Press.

Gregersen, E. 1979. "Sexual linguistics," In *Language, Sex and Gender: Does La Différence Make a Difference?* Judith Rorasanu et al (eds.). New York: New York Academy of Sciences. pp. 3—22.

Hall, E. T. 1959. *The Silent Language*. New York: Doubleday.

Halliday, M. A. K. 1973. *Explorations in the Functions of Language*. London: Edward Arnold.

Halliday, M. A. K. 1977. "Language structure and language function," In *New Horizons in Linguistics*. John Lyons (ed.). New York: Penguin Books. pp. 140—165.

Halliday, M. A. K. 1978. *Language as Social Semiotic*. London: Edward Arnold.

Harris, R. & T. J. Taylor. 1997. *Landmarks in Linguistic Thought I*. (2nd ed.). London: Routledge.

Hu, W. Z & Gao, Y. H. 1997.《外语教学与文化》(*Foreign Languages Teaching and Culture*),湖南:湖南教育出版社。

Hu, Z. L. 1990. 韩礼德语言学的六个核心思想,《外语教学与研究》1990(1): 2—8.

Hymes, D. 1972[1966]. "On communicative competence," Paper presented at the Research Planning Conference on Language Development among Disadvantaged Children, 1966. New York: Yeshiva University. Reprinted in J. B. Pride & J. Holmes (eds.). 1972. *Sociolinguistics: Selected Readings*. Harmondsworth, England: Penguin Books.

Hymes, D. 1973. "The scope of sociolinguistics," In *23rd Annual of Round Table—Sociolinguistics: Current Trends and Prospects*. Roger W. Shuy (ed.). Georgetown: Georgetown University Press. pp. 313—334.

Hymes, D. 2000. "The emergence of sociolinguistics: a response to Samarin," *Journal of Sociolinguistics* 4: 312—315.

Jenkins, S. & J. Hinds. 1987. "Business letter writing: English, French and Japanese," *TESOL Quarterly* 21: 327—349.

Kachru, B. B. & C. L. Nelson. 1996. "World Englishes," In *Sociolinguistics and Language Teaching*. Sandra Lee McKay & Nancy H. Hornberger (eds.). Cambridge: Cambridge University Press. pp. 71—102.

Kaplan, R. B. 1966. "Cultural thought patterns in inter-cultural education," *Language Learning* 16: 1—20.

Koch, B. J. 1983. "Presentation as proof: the language of Arabic rhetoric," *Anthropological Linguistics* 25: 47—60.

Kuhn, T. S. 1962. *The Structure of Scientific Revolutions*. Chicago: The University of Chicago Press.

Kuhn, T. S. 1970. *The Structure of Scientific Revolutions*. (2nd ed.). Chicago: The University of Chicago Press.

Lakoff, R. 1973. "Language and woman's place," *Language in Society* 2: 45—79.

Lakoff, R. 1991. "You are what you say," In *The Gender Reader*. Evelyn Ashton Jones & Gary A. Olson (eds.). Boston: Allyn & Bacon. pp. 292—298.

Landry, R. & R. Y. Bourhis. 1997. "Linguistic landscape and ethnolinguistic vitality: an empirical study," *Journal of Language and Social Psychology* 16: 23—49.

Lave, J. & E. Wenger 1991. *Situated Learning: Legitimate Peripheral Participation*. Cambridge: Cambridge University Press.

Lott, B. 1975. "Sociolinguistics and the teaching of English," *ELT Journal* 29: 272—277.

Malinowski, B. K. 1923. "The problem of meaning in primitive languages," Supplement to C. K. Ogden & I. A. Richards, *The Meaning of Meaning*. London: Routledge & Kegan Pual.

Mandelbaum, D. G. (ed.). 1963. *Selected Writings of Edward Sapir in Language, Culture, and Personality*. Berkeley, CA: University of California Press.

Mesthrie, R. 1994. "Linguistic variation," In R. E. *The Encyclopedia of Language and Linguistics*. Asher (ed.). Oxford: Pergamon. pp. 4900—4909.

Milroy, J. 1994. "Urban dialectology," In *The Encyclopedia of Language and Linguistics*. R. E. Asher (ed.). Oxford: Pergamon. pp. 4858—4863.

Newmark, L. & D. Reibel 1968. "Necessity and sufficiency in language learning," *International Review of Applied Linguistics* 6: 145—164.

Nida, E. A. 1964. "Linguistics and ethnology in translation problems," In *Language in Culture and Society: A Reader in Linguistics and Anthropology*. Dell Hymes (ed.). New York: Harper & Row.

Nida, E. A. 1998a. *Understanding English*（胡壮麟、黄倩译）．北京：外语教学与研究出版社。

Nida, E. A. & JFL Correspondent. 1998b. "An interview with Dr. Eugene Nida,"《外国语》2：1—5.

O'Barr, W. M. & B. K. Atkins. 1980. "'Women's language' or '"powerless language'," In *Women and Language in Literature and Society*. Sally McConnell Ginet et al., (eds.). New York: Praeger.

Osburne, A. 1990. *A Teaching Syllabus for TESOL*. Central Connecticut State University.

Palmar, F. R. 1981. *Semantics*. (2nd ed.). London: Cambridge University Press.

Rosch, E. 1975. "Cognitive representations of semantic categories," *Journal of Experimental Psychology: General* 104：192—233.

Samarin, W. J. 2000. "Sociolinguistics as I see it," *Journal of Sociolinguistics* 4：303—319.

Shohamy, E. & D. Gorter (eds.). 2009. *Linguistic Landscape—Expanding the Scenery*. New York: Routledge.

Simpson, C. 1995. "Lessons from sociolinguistics," *Language Learning Journal* 12：51—53.

Stam, J. H. 1994. "Benjamin Lee Whorf," In *The Encyclopedia of Language and Linguistics*. R. E. Asher (ed.). Oxford: Pergamon. p. 4983.

Trudgill, P. 1984. *Applied Sociolinguistics*. London: Academic.

von Els, T. 1982. De Bellagio Declaration. *Levende Talen* 374：597—599.

Wallace, C. 1988. *Learning to Read in a Multicultural Society*. New York: Prentice Hall.

Werner, O. 1994. "Sapir-Whorf hypothesis," In *The Encyclopedia of Language and Linguistics*. R. E. Asher (ed.). Oxford: Pergamon. pp. 3656—3662.

Whorf, B. L. 1939. "The relation of habitual thought and behavior to language," In *Language, Culture, and Personality*. L. Spier (ed.). Menasha, WI: Sapir Memorial Publication Fund.

Widdowson, H. G. 1990. *Aspects of Language Teaching*. Oxford: Oxford University Press.

Yang, Y. L. 1987. 文化比较研究与翻译（A Comparative Study of Cultures and Translation),《中国翻译》3：8—10.

Yang, Y. L. 1988. "The English pronoun of address: a matter of self-compensation," *Sociolinguistics* 17：157—180.

Yang, Y. L. 1990a. "Gender specific usage of 'SUCH + A + N' phrases: a sociolinguistic approach to pedagogic grammar research," *Connecticut Review* 12：21—36.

Yang, Y. L. 1990b. "Such a expressions in English: their grammatical status and gender basis," *Sociolinguistics* 19：160—184.

Yang, Y. L. 1991. "How to talk to the supernatural in Shakespeare," *Language in Society* 20：247—262.

Yang, Y. L. 1993. "Cultural differentiation and language misinterpretation: a case study of Chinese English learner's comprehension of some English expressions,"《山东外语教学》4：67—68。

Yang, Y. L. 1996. "Sex and level related difference in Chinese color lexicon," *Word* 47：207—220.

Yang, Y. L. 1997. 文化在英语新词构成中的表现——试析-*gate*及其合成词语,《西北师大学报》(哲社) 1：51—56。

Yang, Y. L. 2000. "Sex and skill differences in translation of English color words by Chinese students," *Perceptual and Motor Skills* 91: 1181—1192.

Yang, Y. L. 2008. 千门万门,同出一门——从美国的"水门事件"看文化"模因"现象,《外语教学与研究》5: 385—389。

Yang, Y. L. & Li, J. 2011. 双语标识译写研究——街名标识,《语言文字学》,5: 123—132.

Yang, Y. L. & Liu, Y. Q. 2010. 双语标识译写研究——理论方法篇,《外语电化教学》,2: 11—20.

Yang, Y. L. & Lu, B. Z. 2011. 中英双语标识译写研究——交通标识篇,《中国科技翻译》,1: 53—58.

Yang, Y. L. & Zhao, S. 2010. 公示语翻译的规范化——以北京地铁双语标识为例,《东方翻译》,5: 73—83.

Chapter 9

Cognitive Linguistics

9.1 Introduction

This chapter briefly introduces the enterprise of cognitive linguistics which is probably the most rapidly developing approach to the relationship between language, mind and sociophysical experience. Regarded as a modern movement or enterprise of linguistic thought and practice, cognitive linguistics originally emerged in the 1970s due to the dissatisfaction with Chomsky's formal approaches to language which was dominant then in linguistics and philosophy. Chomsky establishes the view that language is a cognitive phenomenon and holds that a "grammar" is a hypothesis about cognitive representation of a language. He argues linguistic knowledge is distinct from conceptual knowledge, social cognition, interpersonal skills, reasoning, etc., and their interaction; he insists in that linguistic knowledge itself consists of independent modules. To Chomsky, syntax, morphology and phonology are separate "components." Obviously, the Chomskyan approach has several by-products, say, an over-reliance on intuition and invented linguistic data, the postulation of invisible or inaudible elements and processes. Whereas, as a reaction to the excesses of the Chomskyan and the related approaches, cognitive approach to language largely lays the emphasis on human sociophysical experience in language and is increasingly influential in the interdisciplinary cognitive science. During its development and evolution, there were some important events happened in cognitive linguistics. In 1987, Langacker's *Foundations of Cognitive Grammar* (Volume 1) and Lakoff's *Women, Fire, and Dangerous Things: What Categories Reveal about the Mind* were published. And, other important cognitive linguists include L. Talmy, G. Fauconnier, J. Taylor, etc. contributed to the cognitive linguistic enterprise. By the early 1990s, there was a growing proliferation of research in this area, and of researchers who identified themselves as "cognitive linguists." In the spring of 1989, a symposium organized by Rene Dirven was held in Duisburg of Germany, which marked the birth of cognitive linguistics. And, the next year, International Cognitive Linguistics Association (ICLA) was established, together with the publication of journal *Cognitive Linguistics*. The Duisburg symposium was retroactively called the First International Cognitive Linguistics Conference (ICLC). Since then, the ICLC has been held biennially. The latest, the 11th International Cognitive Linguistics Conference was held in Xian of China in July of 2011. The eminent cognitive linguist Ronald Langacker (2002: xv) points out that the Duisburg symposium "marked the birth of cognitive linguistics as a broadly grounded, self conscious intellectual movement." Basically, cognitive linguists hold some guiding principles: language is symbolic; language is shaped by the way it is used and the general cognitive abilities. Cognitive linguistics has been strongly influenced by theories and findings from the other cognitive sciences that were prominent during the 1960s and 1970s, particularly cognitive psychology and Gestalt psychology. For example, John Taylor borrowed the idea of prototype from cognitive psychologist Eleanor Rosch, Leonard Talmy and Ronald Langacker applied the conceptions of figure and ground in Gestalt psychology to the analysis of structure of language, Charles Fillmore adopted the idea of human categorization from cognitive psychology and George Lakoff utilized the ideas of metaphor comprehension from experimental psychology. Also, the neural foundations of language and cognition have a longstanding influence on cognitive linguistic theories, for instance, Kay and Kempton worked on the visual biology constraints of colour-term systems.

Therefore, cognitive linguistics should be described as an "enterprise" because of its constitution on a number of commitments leading to a diverse range of complementary, overlapping and even competing theories. Cognitive linguists do not assume that "subsystems" of language are organized in significantly distinct ways. This is called as the Generalization Commitment which represents a commitment to investigating how the various aspects of linguistic knowledge emerge from a common set of human cognitive abilities upon which they draw rather than to assuming that they are produced in encapsulated modules of the mind. Consequently, cognitive studies of language focus on what is common among aspects of language by seeking to reuse successful methods and explanations across these aspects. For instance, just as word meaning displays prototype effects, there are better and worse examples of referents of given words related in particular ways, so, various cognitive studies apply the same principles to study the organization of morphology, syntax, and phonology. And, cognitive linguists assert that models of language and linguistic organization should reflect what is known about the human mind rather than purely the aesthetic dictates such as the use of particular kinds of formalisms or economy of representation. This is called as the Cognitive Commitment which represents a commitment to providing a characterization of the general principles for language that accord with what is known about human cognition from the other cognitive sciences and brain science. The concrete ramifications of this commitment are that linguistic theories cannot include structures or processes that violate known properties of the human cognitive system. For instance, if sequential derivation of syntactic structures violates time constraints provided by actual human language processing, then it must be jettisoned. Linguistic models that use known properties of human cognition to explain language phenomena are more parsimonious than those that are built from a priori simplicity metrics. For example, a theory that reduces word meaning to the same mechanisms responsible for categorization in other cognitive domains is simpler than one that hypothesizes a separate system for representing lexical semantics. Therefore, cognitive linguistic researcher attempt to find convergent evidence for the cognitive reality of components of any model or explanation of language.

Cognitive linguistics is approximately divided into two main areas of research: cognitive semantics and cognitive grammar, but we will discuss the general cognitive abilities and processes prior to discussing the concrete areas of cognitive semantics and cognitive grammar.

9.2 Cognitive Abilities and Cognitive Processes

The basic cognitive abilities and processes of human being include construal, attention, comparison, categorization, prototype, schema, metaphor, metonymy, conceptualization and conceptual blending and integration.

9.2.1 Construal

Construal is the ability to conceive and portray the same situation in alternate ways through specificity, different mental scanning, directionality, vantage point, figure-ground segregation etc. (Langacker, 2000: 25) Construal operations are conceptualizing processes used in language process by human beings; that is to say, construal operations are the underlying psychological processes and resources employed in the interpretation of linguistic expressions.

Cognitive linguists hold that language reflects our unique human construal of the world: our "world view," as it appears to us through the lens of our embodiment. For example, the sentences *Lily devoured the cake* and *The cake was devoured by Lily* stand in a sentence meaning relation of paraphrase. Traditionally, the truth-conditional model of meaning characterizes this meaning relation by describing the two sentences or the propositions they express as both hold true of the same state of affairs in the world. This truth-conditional model allows for precise statements that can be modelled by logic and it can only account for propositions, roughly, descriptions of states of affairs. However, many utterances such as questions, commands, greetings and so on do not express propositions, so, the truth-conditional model can only account for the meaning of a subset of sentence or utterance types. Cognitive semantics adopts the experientialist view which describes meaning in terms of human construal of reality. In cognitive linguistics, the same situation can be viewed, and therefore linguistically encoded, in multiple ways. For example, someone who is not easily parted from his money could be described either as *stingy* or as *thrifty*. Each of these words is understood with respect to a different background frame which provides a distinct set of evaluations. While *stingy* represents a negative assessment against an evaluative frame of GIVING AND SHARING, *thrifty* relates to a frame of HUSBANDRY (management of resources) against which it represents a positive assessment. In this way, lexical choice provides a different way of framing a situation, giving rise to a different construal. In other words, language is rarely "neutral," but usually represents a particular perspective, even when we are not consciously aware of this as language users.

Cognitive approaches view grammatical structure as independently meaningful. In cognitive linguistics, *construal* means the idea that different grammatical forms, like different words, give rise to distinct "ways of seeing." Consider the following examples.

(1) John kicked the ball.

(2) The ball was kicked by John.

From the perspective of truth-conditional semantics, these sentences both encode the same proposition and therefore express the same "meaning." From the perspective of cognitive semantics, a linguist tries to (i) say what the difference in meaning is, and, (ii) explain how it is encoded linguistically. Comment on what these examples reveal in terms of differing assumptions between cognitive semantics and formal semantics. Talmy and Langacker argue that grammar encodes schematic aspects of embodied experience and that attention, as a perceptual phenomenon, is one aspect of this. Linguistic expressions relate to conceived situations or "scenes." Attention is differentially focused on a particular aspect of a given scene. In Langacker's terms, this is achieved in language by a range of focal adjustments which "adjust the focus" on a particular aspect of any given scene by using different linguistic expressions or different grammatical constructions to describe that scene. The visual metaphor that the expression "focal adjustment" rests upon the emphasis of the fact that visual perception is central to how we focus attention on aspects of experience. By choosing a particular focal adjustment and thus linguistically "organizing" a scene in a specific way, the speaker imposes a unique construal upon that scene.

Construal can be thought of as the way a speaker chooses to "package" and "present" a conceptual representation, which in turn has consequences for the conceptual representation that the utterance evokes in the mind of the hearer. For example, the active construction focuses attention on the AGENT of an action (e. g. *George hid Lily's slippers*), while the passive construction focuses attention upon the PATIENT (e. g. *Lily's slippers were hidden by George*). Each of these constructions conventionally encodes a distinct construal.

One aspect of construal is the selection of a particular domain. This is illustrated by the examples in (3). In each example, the expression *close* selects a different domain and therefore contributes to a very different construal in each sentence.

(3) a. George's flat is quite close to Chapman Common. [SPACE]
   b. It's close to Lily's birthday. [TIME]
   c. Those roses are close to the colour she wants for her wedding dress. [COLOUR]
   d. Lily and her cat are very close. [EMOTION]

Even within a single domain, an expression like *close* can give rise to distinct construals. For example, an expression can select for differences of scale. Langacker (1987: 118) illustrates this idea with the examples in (4), which relate to the domain of SPACE.

(4) a. The two galaxies are very close to one another.
   b. San Jose is close to Berkeley.
   c. The sulphur and oxygen atoms are quite close to one another in this type of molecule.

The expression *close* selects for different scales in each of these examples: the distance between the two elements in each example ranges from the distance between galaxies to the distance between the subparts of a single molecule.

Therefore, construal is central to the choices that speakers make about how a scene is linguistically "packaged," and this in turn explains the availability of related yet distinct constructions. Construal is a central aspect of language and of its relation to thought, but it is constrained by convention as well as the experience itself.

9.2.2 Attention

A very general cognitive ability that human beings have is attention, together with the ability to shift attention from one aspect of a scene to another. For instance, when watching a tennis match we can variously attend to the umpire, the flight of the ball back and forth, one or both of the players or parts of the crowd, zooming "in and out," so to speak. Similarly, language provides ways of directing attention to certain aspects of the scene being linguistically encoded.

Attention, as a general ability manifested in language, is called profiling by Langacker (1987). One important way in which language exhibits profiling is in the range of grammatical constructions it has, each construction serves to profile different aspects of a given scene. For instance, given a scene in which a boy kicks over a vase causing it to smash, different aspects of the scene can be linguistically profiled:

(5) a. The boy kicks over the vase.
　　b. The vase is kicked over.
　　c. The vase smashes into bits.
　　d. The vase is in bits.

Sentence (5) a is an active sentence in which a relationship holds between the initiator of the action (the boy) and the object that undergoes the action (the vase). In other words, the boy is the AGENT and the vase is the PATIENT. From the AGENT to the PATIENT, there is a transfer of energy, reflecting the fact that the AGENT is acting upon the PATIENT. This represents the fact that the entire action chain is being profiled, which is the purpose of the active construction. Compare sentence (5)b a passive sentence. Here, both the energy transfer and the PATIENT are being profiled. However, the AGENT is not mentioned in the sentence and hence is not in profile, it must be understood as part of the background. After all, an action chain requires an AGENT to instigate the transfer of energy, the AGENT can be contextually understood but not in profile. The third sentence, example (5)c, profiles the change in the state of the vase: the fact that it smashes into bits. This is achieved via a subject-verb complement construction. A complement is an obligatory element that is required by another element in a sentence to complete its meaning. In (5)c, the complement is the expression *into bits*, which completes the meaning of the expression *smashes*. Finally, consider sentence (5)d, the grammatical form of this sentence is the subject-copula-complement construction; the copula is the verb *be* which is specialized for encoding a particular state. In sum, each of the constructions ACTIVE, PASSIVE, SUBJECT-VERB COMPLEMENT and SUBJECT-COPULA-COMPLEMENT is specialized for profiling a particular aspect of an action chain. In this way, linguistic structure reflects our ability to attend to distinct aspects of a scene. These examples demonstrate how linguistic organization reflects a more general cognitive ability: attention.

The constructions that have just been discussed are not restricted to encoding a canonical action chain involving the transfer of energy. For example, the active construction can often be applied in cases where an action is not involved. Consider stative verbs which can encode a relatively stable state that persists over time. This type of verb can appear in active or passive constructions, even though it describes a state rather than an action (e. g. ⟨6⟩ a-b):

  (6) a. John not Steve owns the shop on Trafalgar Street. [active]
   b. The shop on Trafalgar Street is owned by John not Steve. [passive]

  To sum up, we can direct our attention towards parts of the perceived scenery. In cognition, it has to do with the activation of conceptual structures. That is to say, we activate the most relevant concepts more than concepts that are irrelevant to what we're "thinking about." In this sense, we direct the attention towards the relevant concepts. Attention relates to language, because we use certain linguistic expressions to provoke certain patterns of activation.

9.2.3 Comparison

  German philosopher Kant considers comparison a fundamental cognitive faculty and judgment as a particular kind of it: "judgment in general is the faculty of thinking the particular as contained under the universal." (Kant 1952: 18) Cognitive linguist Langacker considers comparison to be a fundamental cognitive operation. (Langacker, 1987: 103 — 105) Thus, it is necessary to link the fundamental philosophical concept of judgment to the cognitive-psychological process of comparison. In the cognitive analysis of language, the choice of a linguistic category is based on comparing it to a prior situation frame and then construes the current situation in different ways, as in *fetus* vs. *unborn baby* or *thrifty* vs. *stingy*. In addition to the flexibility of framing a situation by comparing it to one or another prior situation, speakers also have the flexibility of comparing the current situation to a prior one and in effect redefining the frame. For example, upon entering a holding pattern over an airport, a pilot saying *We'll be on the path they call a racetrack; that's essentially a circle with two straight sides* expresses a significant reconceptualization of the category CIRCLE.

  An example of comparison is figure-ground alignment. Figure-ground alignment is strongly influenced by objective properties of the scene, although the objective properties can be overridden in various ways. The figure-ground distinction, derived from Gestalt psychology, is introduced into cognitive linguistics by Talmy (1972; 1983; 2000) to account for the expression of spatial relations in natural language. All spatial relations in language—both location (7)a or motion (7)b—are expressed by specifying the position of one object, the figure, relative to another object, the ground (sometimes more than one ground object, as in [⟨7⟩c-d]):

  (7) a. The book [figure] is on the floor [ground].
   b. Sheila [figure] went into the house [ground].

c. The Isaac CDs [figure] are between Compère [ground] and Josquin [ground].

d. Greg [figure] drove from San Rafael [ground] to Trinidad [ground] in five hours.

The figure and ground are asymmetrical. Although *near* is a spatially symmetrical preposition, (8)b sounds odd compared to (8)a:

(8) a. The bike is near the house.

b. ?? The house is near the bike.

Likewise, there is no preposition that functions as the inverse of *in* in (9)a, because the figure-ground orientation is quite unnatural:

(9) a. There's a crocodile in the water.

b. ?? There's water "being-a-suspending-medium-for" the crocodile.

Figure-ground relations can be manipulated. The same object can function as figure in one context and ground in another, as in (10) a—b; and the favoring contexts can also be overridden for the opposite figure-ground construal with appropriate contextualization, as in (11):

(10) a. The cat [figure] is on the table [ground].

b. I found a flea [figure] on the cat [ground].

(11) [The speaker is composing a scene for a photograph:]

I want the house [figure] to be behind Susan [ground]!

Figure-ground relations can be found in other domains, including relations between events. The main (figure)-subordinate (ground) event relation is construed asymmetrically in (12)a, compared to the symmetrical coordinate event relation in (12)b:

(12) a. I read while she sewed.

b. I read and she sewed.

The event in the ground/subordinate clause is conceptualized as the basis or ground—i.e., a cause or precondition—for the event in the figure/main clause. Figure-ground asymmetry may lead to outright anomaly, as in example (13):

(13) a. He dreamed while he slept.

b. * He slept while he dreamed.

The two events could be coextensive, but since dreaming is contingent on sleeping, sleeping must function as the ground and therefore (13) a is acceptable while (13)b is not.

For most figure-ground subordinators, there is no natural inverse for the figure-ground relation specified by the subordinator:

(14) a. She slept until he arrived.

b. ?? He arrived "immediately-and-causally-before-the-end-of" her sleeping.

(15) a. We stayed home because he had arrived.

b. ?? He arrived "to-the-occasioning-of-(the-decision-of)" our staying home.

In a few cases, it is syntactically simple to construct both a semantic relation and its inverse, for example *before* and *after*. However, there is a difference in construal depending on the choice of event as figure, see examples in (16)a—b:

(16) a. After Tom resigned, all hell broke loose.
b. Tom resigned before all hell broke loose.

In (16)a, Tom's resignation is presumed to let loose the forces of chaos; whereas, in (16)b, Tom succeeded in cutting out when he saw what was happening, or perhaps before the consequences of his actions became apparent to everyone.

Similarly, simultaneous subordinators such as *when* are temporally symmetrical, but inappropriate choice of figure and ground events leads to conceptual peculiarity, compare (17)b to (17)a:

(17) a. When Jerry was chair of the department, everything was all right.
b. ?? When everything was all right, Jerry was chair of the department.

In (17)a, the healthy state of affairs is presumed to be due to Jerry's chairmanship, on the other hand, example (17)b is odd, making Jerry look like an opportunist who has the extraordinary ability to take advantage of a healthy state of affairs to assume the chairmanship of the department.

Remember that figure-ground alignment is an example of comparison in that the two elements of the scene are compared to each other; the judgement based on comparison is one of contrast rather than similarity. By linking figure-ground to comparison, it is possible to argue that the typical figure-ground alignment falls out of the model of comparison as cognitive events of scanning a scene. The figure-ground alignment seems to apply to space with the ground as the prepositional object and the preposition expressing the spatial relational configuration. It also applies to the perception of moving objects since the moving object is typically the most prominent one; it is moving, it is typically the figure, while the remaining stimuli constitute the ground.

The process of comparison has to do with judging something by comparing it to something else. This is a very fundamental cognitive capacity, and, the cognitive operation of comparison is very fundamental to human experience.

9.2.4 Categorization

Categorization is one of the most basic human cognitive activities. Categorization is the process of classifying our experiences into different categories based on commonalities and differences. Categorization is a major ingredient in the creation of human knowledge and allows us to relate present experiences to past ones. Categorization involves the apprehension of some individual entity or some particular experience as an instance of something conceived abstractly that encompasses other actual and potential instantiations. For instance, a specific animal can be construed as an instantiation of the species DOG, a specific patch of color as a manifestation of the property RED, and so on. This abstract mental construct is called as a conceptual category which can be regarded as cognitive tools and can be usually credited with a number of general functions:

(a) *Learning*. The ability to learn from past experience and relate the present to similar aspects of past experience by putting them into the same conceptual categories. The learning ability would be severely impaired if we could not do so.

(b) *Planning*. The ability to formulate goals and to plans to achieve them that requires knowledge to be disassociated from individuals and packaged into concepts characterizing categories of entities.

(c) *Communication*. Language works in terms of generalities, say, in terms of categories. Any linguistic expression, in the end, represents only a category of referents.

(d) *Economy*. A significant amount of knowledge can be stored in relation to groups of individuals. New knowledge gained on the basis of interaction with one or more individuals can be easily generalized to other members of category. Conversely, on the basis of a limited number of criteria, knowing that an individual belongs to a particular category can give access to a much wider range of information about that individual. For instance, there is an important distinction to be made between generic concepts like CAT and TERRORIST and individual concepts like GEORGE BUSH and QUEEN ELISABETH.

The process of categorization presupposes a more basic one called "graded centrality"; that is to say, some members of a category are judged "better" or "more representative" of the category than others. The traditional model can offer no account of why category boundaries seem to be vague and variable (they are frequently described as "fuzzy"). Cognitive model of category structure provides a basis for an account of how we use categories in remembering, planning, reasoning and so on. Categories occur at different levels of inclusiveness, with more specific ones nested within more inclusive ones:

(18) a. vehicle-*car*-hatchback
b. fruit-*apple*-Granny Smith
c. living thing-creature-animal-*dog*-spaniel
d. object-implement-cutlery-*knife*-bread knife

  e. object-item of furniture- *table*-card table

  Normally, one level of specificity in each set, called the basic or generic level of specificity, has a special status, and importance (The basic level items in 〈18〉 are printed in bold italic.) Apart from the basic level, two further levels of specificity with different characteristics are usually identified: superordinate level and subordinate level. These are not defined simply by their position in the chain—there are substantive characteristics that distinguish one level from another.

  Basic level. The categories at the basic level are those that are most culturally salient and are required to fulfill our cognitive needs the best. This is the level where we perceive the most differences between "objects" in the world. All categories of dogs are different, but they still share enough to be distinguished from cats, birds, snakes, primates, etc. So it is at this level that we can find the idealized configuration of feature of a category. Consequently, basic level categories are also the most economical ones in that it is at this level that we can find the most relevant information. The information on our interactions with objects in the real world are stored at this level, which means that it is at this level that we conjure up the general gestalt of the category.

  Superordinate Level. Superordinate categories are the most general ones. The members of a superordinate category do not have enough features in common to conjure up a common gestalt at this level. But if someone asks us to think of a VEHICLE we might think of a CAR or a BUS or if someone asks us to think of a PLANT we might think of a TREE or a FLOWER. This is parasitical categorization. Actually, we borrow some features from a basic level category and apply them to the superordinate category. Of course, we pick a basic level category that is important to us somehow. The features that we have borrowed might seem representative of the entire superordinate category, but in fact they are very small proportion of its members.

  Subordinate Level. Subordinate categories have clearly identifiable gestalts and lots of individual specific features. At this level we perceive the differences between the members of the basic level categories. Often the names for subordinate categories are morphologically complex. They are typically composite forms. One such example is that of compound nouns. A composite form typically combines two or more words that signify basic level categories, like "rain coat" "apple juice" and "wheel chair." But the meaning of the composite form cannot be said to just be a combination of units it is composed of, since the subordinate level category behind the composite form typically has many more features than can be ascribed to the combined units. If we want to account for all the features of the meaning of the composite form, we'll have to look at its semantic frames.

9.2.5 Prototype

A prototype is a cognitive process of the abstract representation of a category. When judge category membership, we compare the items in terms of their representativeness of membership. So, prototype is the internal structure of the category defined by individuals' judgments of the degree to which members fit their "idea" or "image" of the category. The term prototype was first defined in Eleanor Rosch's study "Natural Categories" (1973) and as a stimulus which takes a salient position in the formation of a category as it is the first stimulus to be associated with that category. Later, Rosch redefined it as the most central member of a category.

Prototypes are those members of a category that most reflect the redundancy structure of the category. In other words, the more frequent a particular attribute is among members of a particular category, the more representative it is. The prototype structure of the category reflects this "redundancy" in terms of repeated attributes across distinct members or exemplars. This entails that another way of assessing prototype structure is by establishing the set of attributes that a particular entity has. The more category-relevant attributes a particular entity has, the more representative it is. Prototypes or proto instances combine the most representative attributes of a category. Prototypes are typical instances of a category that serve as benchmarks against which are the surrounding and less representative.

To prototype operation, prototype theory is postulated as a model of graded categorization in cognitive science where some members of a category are more central than others. For example, when asked to give an example of the concept *furniture*, *chair* is more frequently cited than *stool*. Formulated in the 1970s by Eleanor Rosch and others, prototype theory is a radical departure from traditional necessary and sufficient conditions as in Aristotelian logic which led to set-theoretic approaches of extensional or intensional semantics. Thus, in a definition based model, a *bird* may be defined as elements with the *features* [+feathers], [+beak] and [+ability to fly], instead, prototype theory considers a category like bird as consisting of different elements which have unequal status, for example, a *robin* is more prototypical of a *bird* than a *penguin*. This leads to a graded notion of categories which is a central notion in many models of cognitive science and cognitive semantics, e.g. in the work of George Lakoff (1987) and Ronald Langacker. (1987, 1991)

Rosch (1975) asked 200 American college students to rate on a scale of 1 to 7 whether they regarded the following items as a good example of the category *furniture*. The resulting ranks are as follows:
 1) chair
 2) sofa

3) couch

4) table

5) easy chair

6) dresser

7) rocking chair

8) coffee table

9) rocker

10) love seat

11) chest of drawers

12) desk

13) bed

...

22) bookcase

27) cabinet

29) bench

31) lamp

32) stool

35) piano

41) mirror

42) TV

44) shelf

45) rug

46) pillow

47) wastebasket

49) sewing machine

50) stove

54) refrigerator

60) telephone

While one may differ from this list in terms of cultural specifics, the point is that such a graded categorization is likely to be present in all cultures. Further evidence that some members of a category are more privileged than others came from experiments involving:

1) Response Times: in which queries involving a prototypical members (e. g. *is a robin a bird*?) elicited faster response times than for non-prototypical members.

2) Priming: When primed with the higher-level (superordinate) category, subjects were faster in identifying if two words are the same. Thus, after flashing *furniture*, the equivalence of *chair-chair* is detected more rapidly than *stove-stove*.

3) Exemplars: When asked to name a few exemplars, the more prototypical items came up more frequently.

Subsequent to Rosch's work, prototype effects have been investigated widely in areas such as colour cognition (Brent Berlin & Paul Kay, 1969), and for more abstract notions. Subjects may be asked, e. g. "to what degree is this narrative an instance of telling a lie?" [Coleman/Kay: 1981]. Similarly work was done on actions (verbs like *look*, *kill*, *speak*, *walk*), adjectives like "tall," etc.

9.2.6 Schema

Schemas form in the mental grammar when patterns of similarity are abstracted from utterances, giving rise to a more schematic representation or symbolic unit. A schema is a symbolic unit that emerges from a process of abstraction over more specific symbolic units called instances. The relationship between a schema and the instances from which it emerges is the schema-instance relation. This relationship is hierarchical in nature. Consider common nouns like *cats*, *dogs*, *books*, *flowers* and so on. Each of these expressions is a highly entrenched symbolic unit. For example, the symbolic unit *cats* might be represented by the formula in (19):

(19) [[[CAT]/[kæt]]-[[PL]/[s]]]

In the formula in (19), the representations in small capitals indicate the semantic poles and those in the International Phonetic Alphabet (IPA) font represent the phonological poles; the slash indicates the symbolic link between semantic and phonological poles and the hyphen indicates the linking of symbolic units to form a complex structure. Given that there are many cases of regular plural nouns in the linguistic inventory, this regular pattern is captured by a schematic symbolic unit which contains only schematic information about the construction. The schema for plural nouns is represented in (20).

(20) [[[THING]/[...]]-[[PL]/[s]]]

In this schematic representation, the semantic pole THING indicates a noun but its corresponding phonological unit is left blank to indicate that this construction represents nouns in general. Each fully specified unit corresponding to this schema (for example, the expressions *cats*, *dogs*, *books*, *flowers*) represents an instance of the schema. The hierarchical relationship between a schema and its instances is shown in Figure 9.1.

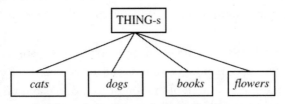

Figure 9.1 Schema-instance Relations

The schema-instance relation is not restricted to symbolic units. The schema is any superordinate (more general) element in a taxonomy and the instance is any subordinate (more specific) element. In other words, the schema-instance relation represents a type of categorization relation. For example, in phonological units, the phoneme is the schema and its allophones are instances, and, in semantic units, the concept *flower* is schematic in relation to the instances *rose*, *lily* and *gerbera*. An instance is said to elaborate its schema, which means that it provides more specific meaning. For example, *mammal* is more specific than *animal*, and in turn *monkey* is more specific than *mammal*.

Image Schema. An image schema is a recurring dynamic pattern of our perceptual interactions and motor programs that gives coherence and structure to our experience. (Johnson, 1987: xiv) Image schematic structures have two characteristics: they are preconceptual schematic structures emerging from our bodily experience and they are constantly operating in our perceptual interaction, bodily movement through space and physical manipulation of objects. Image schemas exist at a level of abstraction, operate at a level of mental organization between propositional structures and concrete images, and "serve repeatedly as identifying patterns in an indefinitely large number of experiences, perceptions, and image formation for objects or events that are similarly structured in the relevant ways." (Johnson, 1987: 28)

Center-periphery Schema. It involves a physical or metaphorical core and edge and degrees of distance from the core. For example, an individual's social sphere with family and friends at the core and others at the outside.

Containment Schema. It is an image schema that involves a physical or metaphorical boundary, enclosed area or volume, or excluded area or volume. A containment schema has additional optional properties such as transitivity of enclosure, objects inside or outside the boundary, protection of an enclosed object, the restriction of forces inside the enclosure, and, the relatively fixed position of an enclosed object.

Cycle Schema. It involves repetitious events and event series. Its structure includes the following: a starting point, a progression through successive events without backtracking, a return to the initial state. The schema often has superimposed lines or points on it's structure that builds toward a climax and then goes through a decline. Examples of cycle schemas are days, weeks, years, sleeping and waking, breathing, circulation, emotional buildup and release.

Force Schema. It involves physical or metaphorical causal interactions. It includes the following elements: a source and target of the force, a direction and intensity of the force, a path of motion of the source and target, a sequence of causation. Some kinds of force schemas are: an attraction schema, a balance schema, a blockage schema, a compulsion schema, a counterforce schema, a diversion schema, an enablement schema and a restraint removal schema.

A Link Schema. Such a schema consists of two or more entities connected physically or metaphorically, and the bond between them exists. Here are some examples of link schemas: a child holding her mother's hand, someone plugging a lamp into the wall, a causal "connection," kinship "ties."

Part-whole Schema. It involves physical or metaphorical wholes along with their parts and a configuration of the parts. For examples, the body and its parts, the family and the caste structure of India.

Path Schema. It involves physical or metaphorical movement from place to place, and, consists of a starting point, a goal, and a series of intermediate points.

Scale Schema. It involves an increase or decrease of physical or metaphorical amount and consists of any of the following: a closed-ended or open-ended progression of amount, a position in the progression of amount, one or more norms of amount, a calibration of amount. Here are some examples of scale schemas: physical amounts, properties in the number system.

Verticality Schema. It involves "up" and "down" relations. Here are some examples of verticality schemas: standing upright, climbing stairs, viewing a flagpole, watching water rise in a tub. Some image schemas also represent spatial orientations and relations: *up-down*, *front-back*, *part-whole*, *center-periphery*, and so on.

9.2.7 Metaphor and Metonymy

9.2.7.1 Metaphor

"Metaphor is for most people a device of the poetic imagination and the rhetorical flourish—a matter of extraordinary rather than ordinary language. Moreover, metaphor is typically viewed as characteristic of language alone, a matter of words rather than thought or action. For this reason, most people think they can get along perfectly well without metaphor. We have found, on the contrary, that metaphor is pervasive in everyday life, not just in language but in thought and action. Our ordinary conceptual system, in terms of which we both think and act, is fundamentally metaphorical in nature." (Lakoff & Johnson, 2003: 4)

Metaphor involves the comparison of two concepts in that one is construed in terms of the other. It's often described in terms of a target domain and a source domain. The target domain is the experience being described by the metaphor and the source domain is the means that we use in order to describe the experience. For example:

(21) We're wasting our time here.

This sentence is based on a metaphor "TIME IS MONEY" in which the target domain TIME is conceptualized in terms of the source domain of MONEY. Very often, abstract experiences are described in terms of more concrete ones. In cognitive linguistics, metaphors are represented by a simple formula: "X IS Y," in which X is the target domain and Y is the source domain. Conceptual metaphors are classified into 3 categories: ontological metaphors, structural metaphors and orientational metaphors.

Ontological metaphors. Ontological metaphors mean that human experiences with physical objects provide the basis for ways of viewing events, activities, emotions, ideas, etc., as entities and substances. Ontological metaphors can serve various purposes. By ontological metaphors we give bounded surfaces to less clearly discrete entities (mountains, hedges, street corners) and categorize events, actions and states as substances. In ontological metaphors, it is our experiences of interacting with physical bounded bodies, which provide the basis for categorizing events, activities, ideas, etc., as entities and substances. Take the experience of rising prices as an example, which can be metaphorically viewed as an entity via the noun *inflation*. This gives us a way to refer to experiences:

INFLATION IS AN ENTITY
(22) a. Inflation is lowering our standard of living.
 b. If there's much more inflation, we'll never survive.
 c. We need to combat inflation.
(23) a. Inflation is backing us into a corner.
 b. Inflation is taking its toll at the checkout counter and the gas pump.
 c. Buying land is the best way of dealing with inflation.
 d. Inflation makes me sick.

In these cases, regarding inflation as an entity allows human beings to refer to it, quantify it, identify it, treat it as a case, act with respect to it, and even believe that we understand it. Ontological metaphors are necessary for dealing with human experiences.

Structural metaphors. Structural metaphors play the most important role because they allow us to go beyond orientation and referring and give us the possibility to structure one concept according to another. This means that structural metaphors are grounded in our experience. Structural metaphors imply how one concept is metaphorically structured in terms of another. For example, ARGUMENT IS WAR leads to an English expression like "He attacked every weak point in my argument."

ARGUMENT IS WAR
(24) a. Your claims are indefensible.
 b. He attacked every weak point in my argument.
 c. His criticisms were right on target.

d. I demolished his argument.
   e. I've never won an argument with him.
   f. You disagree? Okay, shoot!
   g. If you use the strategy, he'll wipe you out.
   h. He shot down all of my arguments.

It is obvious that we don't just talk about argument in terms of war. We can actually win or lose arguments. We see the person we are arguing with as an opponent. We attack his positions and we defend our own. We gain and lose ground. We plan and use strategies. If we find a position indefensible, we can abandon it and take a new line of attack. Many of the things we do in arguing are partially structured by the concept of war.

Orientional Metaphors. Orientational metaphors give a concept a spatial orientation. They are characterized not so much by structuring one concept in terms of another, but by a co-occurrence in our experience. The orientational metaphors are grounded in an experiential basis, which links together the two parts of the metaphor. The link verb "is," part of the metaphor, should be seen as the link of two different co-occurring experiences. For example, MORE IS UP. This metaphor is grounded in the co-occurrence of two different kinds of experiences: adding more of a substance and perceiving the level of the substance rise.

Orientational metaphors are based on human physical and cultural experience. For example, in some cultures the future is in front of us, whereas in others it is in back of us. Let us read some orientational metaphors and give a brief hint about how each metaphorical concept might have arisen from human physical and cultural experience:

HAPPY IS UP; SAD IS DOWN

(25) a. I'm feeling up.
   b. That boosted my spirits.
   c. My spirits rose.
   d. You're in high spirits.
   e. Thinking about her always gives me a lift.
   f. I'm feeling down.
   g. I'm depressed.
   h. He's really low these days.
   i. I fell into a depression.

From these sentences, it is obvious that drooping posture typically goes along with sadness and depression, erect posture with a positive state.

9.2.7.2 Metonymy

Metonymy is another conceptual mechanism that is also central to human thought and language. Like metaphor, metonymy has traditionally been analyzed as a purely linguistic trope device. In recent years, some scholars have begun to suggest that metonymy may be more fundamental to conceptual organization than metaphor, and some have claimed that metaphor itself has a metonymic basis. Lakoff and Johnson (1980) argued that, like metaphor, metonymy is a conceptual phenomenon, but one that has quite a distinct basis. Consider example (26):

(26) The ham sandwich has wandering hands.

Imagine that the sentence in (26) is uttered by one waitress to another in a café. The use of the expression *ham sandwich* represents an instance of metonymy: two entities are associated so that one entity (the item the customer ordered) stands for the other (the customer). As this example demonstrates, linguistic metonymy is referential in nature: it relates to the use of expressions to "pinpoint" entities in order to talk about them. This shows that metonymy functions differently from metaphor. For example (26) to be metaphorical we would need to understand ham sandwich not as an expression referring to the customer who ordered it, but in terms of a food item with human qualities. Imagine a cartoon, for example, in which a ham sandwich sits at a café table. On this interpretation, human qualities would be attributed to a ham sandwich, motivated by the metaphor AN INANIMATE ENTITY IS AN AGENT. So, while metonymy is the conceptual relation "X stands for Y," metaphor is the conceptual relation "X understood in terms of Y."

Metonymy is motivated by physical or causal associations. It is expressed in terms of contiguity, a close or direct relationship between two entities. This is why the waitress can use the expression *the ham sandwich* to refer to the customer: there is a direct experiential relationship between the ham sandwich and the customer who ordered it.

Metonymy is represented by the formula "B for A," where "B" is the vehicle and "A" is the target, e. g. PLACE FOR INSTITUTION. This contrasts with the "A is B" formula that represents metaphor. For instance, in example (27) *Buckingham Palace* is the vehicle (PLACE) which stands for the BRITISH MONARCHY, the target (INSTITUTION):

(27) Buckingham Palace denied the rumours.

Metonymy is often contingent on a specific context. Within a specific discourse context, a salient vehicle activates and highlights a particular target. Hence, while metaphor is pre-conceptual in origin and is therefore motivated by the nature of our bodies and our environment, metonymy is motivated by communicative and referential requirements. Metonymy allows one entity to stand for another because both concepts coexist within the same domain. This explains why a metonymic relationship is based on contiguity or conceptual "proximity." The reason ham sandwich in (26) represents an instance of metonymy is because both the target (the customer) and the vehicle (the ham sandwich) belong to the same CAFÖ domain. Therefore, Metonymy is a cognitive process in which one conceptual entity, the vehicle, provides mental access to another conceptual entity, the target, within the same domain, or idealized cognitive model (ICM).

9.2.8 Conceptual Blending and Integration

"Blending" or "integration" is a cognitive operation whereby elements of two or more "mental spaces" are integrated via projection into a new, blended space with unique structure. Fauconnier (1997) illustrates the examples of blending, analyzes the blending process, provides a taxonomy of blends, and argues for the ubiquity and importance of blending as a cognitive resource.

Blending operates on two input mental spaces to produce a third space, the blend. The blend inherits partial structure from the input spaces and has emergent structure of its own. There are some conditions needed when two input spaces I_1 and I_2 are blended:

1) Cross-Space Mapping: there is a partial mapping of counterparts between the input spaces I_1 and I_2, as shown in Figure 9.2.

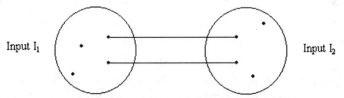

Figure 9.2　Cross-Space Mapping

2) Generic Space: It maps onto each of the inputs. It reflects some common, usually more abstract structure and organization shared by the inputs. It defines the core cross-space mapping between them, as in Figure 9.3.

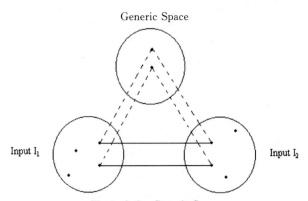

Figure 9.3　Generic Space

3) Blend: the inputs I_1 and I_2 are partially projected onto a fourth space, the blend, as in figure 9.4:

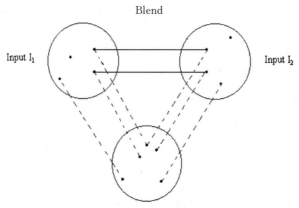

Figure 9.4 Blend

4) Emergent Structure: the blend has emergent structure not provided by the inputs. This happens in three interrelated ways (as shown in Figure 9.5):
  (a) Composition: Take together, the projections from the inputs make new relations available that did not exist in the separate inputs.
  (b) Completion: Knowledge of background frames, cognitive and cultural models, allows the composite structure projected into the blend from the inputs to be viewed as part of a larger self-contained structure in the blend. The pattern in the blend triggered by the inherited structures is "completed" into the larger, emergent structure.
  (c) Elaboration: The structure in the blend can then be elaborated. This is "running the blend." It consists in cognitive work performed within the blend, according to its own emergent logic.

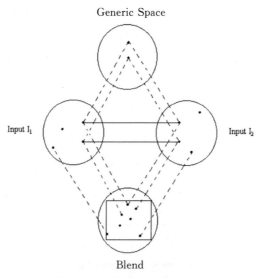

Figure 9.5 Emergent Structure

A full four-space blend looks in Figure 9.5. In the diagram, the square stands for the emergent structure in the blend. The diagram is meant to indicate that when counterparts are projected into the blend, they may be fused into a single element or projected separately. An additional possibility is that one of the counterparts is projected but not the other.

The blending theory suggests a new way of thinking about what constitutes a novel inference. Because the mapping operation involves integrated frames rather than isolated predicates, the choice of one particular framing over another necessarily results in a different set of attendant inferences. Besides the acquisition of unknown facts, a novel inference might involve a new construal of a well-understood phenomenon, a change in prominence of a particular element, or simply the availability of connected frames.

9.3 Cognitive Semantics

As a part of the cognitive linguistics movement, cognitive semantics mainly investigates the relationship between experience, the conceptual system, and the semantic structure encoded by language. Scholars in cognitive semantics investigate knowledge representation or conceptual structure and meaning construction and employ language as the lens through which the cognitive phenomena can be investigated. The main tenets of cognitive semantics are: 1) meaning construction is conceptualisation; 2) semantic structure is conceptual structure and conceptual structure is embodied and motivated by usage; 3) meaning representation is encyclopaedic; 4) the ability to use language draws upon general cognitive resources and not a special language module. Leonard Talmy, one of the original pioneers of cognitive linguistics, describes cognitive semantics in his influential masterpiece of cognitive semantics *Toward a Cognitive Semantics* (Volume 1) as follows: "Research on cognitive semantics is research on conceptual content and its organization in language." (Talmy, 2000: 4)

The cognitive semantics approach rejects the traditional separation of linguistics into phonology, syntax, pragmatics, etc. Instead, it divides semantics (meaning) into meaning construction and knowledge representation. Therefore, cognitive semantics studies much of the area traditionally devoted to pragmatics as well as semantics. The techniques native to cognitive semantics are typically used in lexical studies such as those put forth by Leonard Talmy, George Lakoff, Dirk Geeraerts and Bruce Wayne Hawkins. Some cognitive semantic frameworks, such as that developed by Talmy, take into account for syntactic structures as well.

Traditionally, semantics is interested in three big questions: what does it mean for units of language, called lexemes, to have "meaning"? What does it mean for sentences to have meaning? And, how is it that meaningful units fit together to compose complete sentences? These are the main points of inquiry behind studies into lexical semantics, structural semantics, and theories of compositionality, respectively. Classic theories in semantics tended to explain the meaning of parts in terms of necessary and sufficient conditions, sentences in terms of truth-conditions, and composition in terms of propositional functions. Each of these positions is tightly related to the others. According to these traditional theories, the meaning of a particular sentence may be understood as the conditions under which the proposition conveyed by the sentence holding true. For instance, the expression "snow is white" is true if and only if snow is, in fact, white. Lexical units can be understood as holding meaning either by virtue of set of things they may apply to (called the "extension" of the word), or in terms of the common properties that hold between these things (called its "intension"). The intension provides an interlocutor with the necessary and sufficient conditions that let a thing qualify as a member of some lexical unit's extension. Roughly, propositional functions are those abstract instructions which guide the interpreter in taking the free variables in an open sentence and filling them in, resulting in a correct understanding of the sentence as a whole.

Otherwise, cognitive semantic theories are typically built on the argument that lexical meaning is conceptual. For cognitive semanticists, meaning is not necessarily the reference to the entity or relation in some real or possible world. Instead, it corresponds with a concept held in the mind based on personal understanding. As a result, semantic facts like "All bachelors are unmarried males" are not treated as special facts about language practices; rather, these facts are not distinct from encyclopaedic knowledge. In treating linguistic knowledge as being apiece with everyday knowledge, cognitive semantics explains paradigmatically semantic phenomena like category structure by drawing upon theories from the related fields of cognitive psychology and cognitive anthropology. One proposal in cognitive semantics is to explain category structure in terms of nodes in a knowledge network. For example, cognitive semanticists employ the theory of prototypes from cognitive science to explain the cause of polysemy.

Cognitive semanticists argue that truth-conditional semantics is unduly limited in its account of full sentence meaning. While they are not on the whole hostile to truth-conditional semantics, they point out that it has limited explanatory power. That is to say, it is limited to indicative sentences, and does not seem to offer any straightforward or intuitive way of treating commands or expressions. By contrast, cognitive semantics seeks to capture the full range of grammatical moods by also making use of the notions of framing and mental spaces.

Cognitive semantics recognize meaning as a matter of construal and conventionalization. It argues that the processes of linguistic construal are the same psychological processes involved in the processing of encyclopaedic knowledge and in perception. The dynamic construal theory in cognitive semantics claims that words themselves do not have meaning but "default construals" which are the really just ways of using words. Therefore, compositionality can only be intelligible if pragmatic elements like context and intention are taken into consideration.

This section is to present a brief overview of some phenomena investigated within cognitive semantics so as to show and explain the nature and objective of the cognitive semantics.

9.3.1 The Bodily Basis of Meaning

Cognitive semantics concerns the bodily basis of meaning in that it assumes that conceptual structure is meaningful by virtue of being tied directly to meaningful bodily experience, much research within the cognitive semantics tradition investigates conceptual metaphors. And, conceptual metaphors give rise to systems of conventional conceptual mappings held in long-term memory, which may be motivated by image-schematic structure. If image schemas arise from bodily experience, then we may be able to explain conceptual metaphor on the basis that it maps rich and detailed structure from concrete domains of experience onto more abstract concepts and conceptual domains. Consider example (28):

(28) The number of shares has gone up.

The examples of this type are motivated by the highly productive conceptual metaphor based on our daily bodily experience of height.

(29) a. Mortgage rates have fallen.
  b. Inflation is on the way up.

Similarly, the metaphors in (29) relate the domains of QUANTITY and VERTICAL ELEVATION. In other words, we understand greater quantity in terms of increased height, and decreased quantity in terms of lesser height. This conventional pattern of conceptual mapping is directly grounded in ubiquitous everyday experience. This experiential correlation between height and quantity experienced from our early age motivates the conceptual metaphor *more is up* or known as *quantity is vertical elevation*.

9.3.2 Conceptual Structure

Cognitive semantics focuses on the conceptual structuring mechanisms apparent in linguistic structure, say, how language encodes and reflects conceptual structure. To uncover the conceptual structure in language, cognitive semanticists try to investigate the distinct functions associated with open-class and closed-class semantic systems. Talmy (2000) argues that the two systems encode our cognitive representation (CR) in language. The open-class semantic system is the system of meaning associated with content words and morphemes and provides the substantive content relating to a particular scene; the closed-class semantic system is the system of meaning associated with grammatical constructions, bound morphemes and grammatical words like *and* and *the*, which provides scene structuring representation. As illustrated in example (30), the distinction between the open-class and closed-class subsystems can be looked as the follow:

(30) The hunter tracked the tigers.

The declarative word order and the elements marked in bold form part of the system of closed-class semantics. They provide the "concept structuring" elements of the meaning described for this scene, the information about time of the event, the number of the participants involved, the familiarity of the participants to the speaker and hearer in the discourse, the assertion of speaker to information and so on. These closed-class elements can therefore provide a kind of frame or scaffolding, which forms the foundations of the meaning in this sentence. Words like *hunter*, *track* and *tiger* associate to an open-class semantic system and impose rich contentful meaning upon this frame: who the participants are and what the nature of event is.

9.3.3 Frame Semantics

Frame semantics, developed by Charles J. Fillmore (1975; 1985), attempts to explain meaning in terms of its relation to general understanding, not just in the terms laid out by truth-conditional semantics. Frame is meant by any concept that can only be understood if a larger system of concepts could also be understood. Frames are detailed knowledge structures or schemas emerging from everyday experiences. According to this point of view, knowledge of word meaning is, in part, knowledge of the individual frames with which a word is associated. Theory of frame semantics dedicates to reveal the rich network of meaning making up our knowledge of words.

Fillmore's Framing. Word meaning is an extension of our bodily and cultural experiences. For example, the notion of restaurant is associated with a series of concepts, like *food*, *service*, *waiters*, *tables* and *eating*. These contingent associations are intimately related to our understanding of "restaurant" and cannot be captured by an analysis in terms of necessary and sufficient conditions.

Traditionally, in semantic feature analysis, there is nothing more to the meanings of "boy" and "girl" than in example (31):

(31) BOY [+MALE], [+YOUNG]
     GIRL [+FEMALE], [+YOUNG]

However, language users regularly apply the terms "boy" and "girl" in ways that go beyond semantic features. For instance, people tend to be more likely to consider a young female a "girl" (as opposed to "woman") than to consider a borderline young male a "boy" (as opposed to "man"). This suggests that there is a latent frame made up of cultural attitudes, expectations and background assumptions, which is part of word meaning. These background assumptions go beyond the necessary and sufficient conditions corresponding to a semantic feature account. So, frame semantics seeks to account for the puzzling features of lexical items in certain systematic way.

Cognitive semanticists apply frame semantic paradigm as analytical tools to explain a wider range of semantic phenomena. Some words have the same definitions or intensions and the same extensions but subtly different domains. For example, the lexemes *land* and *ground* are synonyms, yet they naturally contrast with different things—*air* and *sea*, respectively.

The notion of framing is regarded as being of the same cast as the pragmatic notion of background assumptions. Consider example (32):

(32) The cat is on the mat.

In such a sentence, in order for the sentence to make any sense, the interpreter makes a series of assumptions: there is gravity, the cat is parallel to the mat, and the two touch. In order for the sentence to be regarded as intelligible, the speaker supposes that the interpreter has an idealized or default frame in mind.

Langacker's Profile and Base. An alternate strain of Fillmore's analysis can be found in the work of Ronald Langacker who makes a distinction between the notions of profile and base. The profile is the concept symbolized by the word itself, while the base is the encyclopedic knowledge the concept presupposes. For example, let the definition of "radius" be "a line segment that joins the center of a circle with any point on its circumference." If all we know of the concept *radius* is its profile, then we simply know that it is a line segment that is attached to something called the "circumference" in some greater whole called the "circle"; that is to say, our understanding is fragmentary until the base concept of circle is firmly grasped.

When a single base supports a number of different profiles, then it can be called a "domain." For instance, the concept profiles of *arc*, *center*, and *circumference* are all in the domain of *circle*, because each uses the concept of circle as a base. We are then in a position to characterize the notion of a frame as being either the base of the concept profile, or more generally, in a domain the profile is a part of it.

Therefore, knowledge representation can be described in terms of profile-base organization and every expression profiles some entity against background knowledge structures. For example, the concept *uncle* represents the notion of kinship relations, which in turn are based on notions of *family*, *gender*, *procreation*, etc. Also, the social role of an *uncle* is based on notions of *duties*, *responsibilities* and *affinities* within kinship networks. A full understanding of even this simple concept reaches into many areas of our conceptual knowledge.

9.3.4 Mappings

The forth theme in cognitive semantics is the idea of conceptual mappings. Three kinds of mapping operations have been identified (Fauconnier, 1997): 1) projection mappings; 2) pragmatic function mappings; and 3) schema mappings.

Projection Mappings project structure from one domain (source) onto another (target). Consider the examples in (33):

(33) a. Summer has just zoomed by.
 b. The end of term is approaching.
 c. The time for a decision has come.

In these sentences, temporally framed concepts corresponding to the expressions *summer*, *the end of term* and *the time for a decision* are structured in terms of motion. Temporal concepts cannot undergo literal motion because they are not physical entities. However, these conventional mappings allow us to understand abstract concepts TIME in terms of MOTION.

Pragmatic function mappings establish a connection between two entities by a shared frame of experience. For example, metonymy is an instance of a pragmatic function mapping because it depends on an association between two entities so that one entity can stand for the other. Once gain, consider example (34) which we analyzed in (26) in the context of metonymy (9.2.7.2):

(34) The ham sandwich has wandering hands.

Imagine the sentence in (34) uttered by one waitress to another in a restaurant. In this context, the salient association between a particular customer and the food he orders establishes a pragmatic function mapping.

Schema Mappings relate to the projection of a schema (another term for frame) onto particular utterances. As has been mentioned, a frame is a relatively detailed knowledge structure derived from everyday patterns of interaction. Suppose an abstract frame for purchasing goods, which represents an abstraction over specific instances of buying goods, such as buying a stamp in a post office, buying groceries in a supermarket, ordering a book through an on-line retailer, and so on. Each instance of PURCHASING GOODS involves a purchaser, a vendor, merchandise, money or credit card and so on. Consider example (35):

(35) The Ministry of Defence purchased twenty new helicopters from Westland.

The sense of this sentence could be made by mapping its various components onto the roles in the frame of PURCHASING GOODS. This frame enables us to understand the role assumed by each of the participants in this example: the Ministry of Defence is the PURCHASER, the contractor Westland is the VENDOR and the helicopters are the MERCHANDISE. The idea of schema mappings is addressed by two theories—Mental Spaces Theory and Conceptual Blending Theory (c.f. 9.2.8)

9.3.5 Idealized Cognitive Models

In the field of meaning studies, there is a question that has challenged philosophers and linguists for a long time: can word meaning be defined? George Lakoff (1987) argues words are categories that can be modeled and investigated using the theory of idealized cognitive models (ICM), which are highly abstract frames. In particular, Lakoff argues that lexical items represent the type of complex categories called as radial categories. A radial category is structured with respect to a composite prototype, and the various category members are related to the prototype by convention rather than being "generated" by predictable rules. As such, word meanings are stored in the mental lexicon as highly complex structured categories of meanings or senses.

Lakoff (1987) explored some of the consequences of the observations made by Eleanor Rosch (1975) and her colleagues for a theory of conceptual structure as manifested in language. These can account for certain kinds of typicality effects in categorization. For example, let's consider once more the concept BACHELOR. This is understood with respect to a relatively schematic ICM MARRIAGE. The ICM MARRIAGE includes the knowledge that bachelors are unmarried adult males. The category BACHELOR exhibits typicality effects. In other words, some members of the category BACHELOR (like eligible young men) are "better" or more typical examples than others (like the Pope). The knowledge associated with the MARRIAGE ICM stipulates that bachelors can marry. However, our knowledge relating to CATHOLICISM stipulates that the Pope cannot marry. It is because of this mismatch between the MARRIAGE ICM (with respect to which BACHELOR is understood) and the CATHOLICISM ICM (with respect to which the Pope is understood) that this particular typicality effect arises.

9.3.6 Polysemy

Another influential area in cognitive semantics is lexical semantics. Words or lexical items typically have more than one meaning associated with them. When the meanings are related, this is called polysemy. Polysemy appears to be the norm rather than the exception in language. In cognitive semantics, words are treated as conceptual categories, organized with respect to an idealized cognitive model or prototype. According to this viewpoint, polysemy arises because words are linked to a network of lexical concepts rather than to a single concept. However, there is usually a central or "typical" meaning that relates the others. In this respect, word meanings are a bit like the category BIRD (c. f. 9. 2. 5).

Briefly, cognitive semantics is primarily concerned with investigating conceptual structure and processes of conceptualization. Cognitive semanticists are not primarily concerned with studying linguistic meaning for its own sake, but rather for what it can reveal about the nature of the human conceptual system. Their focus on language is motivated by the assumption that linguistic organization will reflect, at least partially, the nature and organization of the conceptual system; this does not mean that language directly mirrors the conceptual system. In one word, for cognitive semanticists, language is a tool for investigating conceptual organization.

9.4 Cognitive Grammar

The title of this section should be "Cognitive approaches to grammar" rather than just "Cognitive grammar" because Cognitive Grammar is the name of a specific cognitive theory of grammar developed by Ronald Langacker. Cognitive approaches to grammar represent a collection of approaches united by theoretical assumptions rather than a single unified theory. Cognitive approaches to grammar focus directly upon the linguistic system in terms of the similar guiding principles, this is the reason for putting the various cognitive approaches to grammar in a unified title of "cognitive grammar." Two guiding principles of a cognitive approach to grammar are: the symbolic thesis and the usage-based thesis. A speaker's knowledge of language is represented as a structured inventory of conventional symbolic units that subsumes both open-class and closed-class symbolic units. These represent qualitatively distinct endpoints on a lexicon-grammar continuum between specific (content) meaning and schematic (grammatical) meaning. This inventory is structured in part by schema-instance relations which group specific instances together under a schematic representation of their shared properties. In cognitive approaches, the term "grammar" refers not only to the structure of words and sentences but also to the "mental grammar" or system of knowledge of language in the mind of the speaker.

In Langacker's Cognitive Grammar, the linguistic expressions are divided into two major categories: nominal predications (THINGS) and relational predications (PROCESSES and STATES). Nominal predications accounts for nouns which are schematically characterized as THING. Relational predications are divided into two subcategories: temporal relations and atemporal relations. Temporal relations accounts for verbs which are schematically characterized as PROCESS and atemporal relations account for a number of word classes including adjectives, adverbs, appositions and non-finite verb forms which can be schematically characterized as STATES. Two of the most important theoretical constructs in Langacker's theory are profile-base organisation and trajector (TR)-landmark (LM) organization. Langacker defines a construction as any expression with complex symbolic structure, and approaches constituency and head-dependent relations from the perspective of valence, based on conceptual autonomy and conceptual dependence. This model of constituency accounts not only for phrase structure, but also for word structure. Cognitive Grammar model also explore the clause structure, complements, modifiers, transitivity and case. Cognitive grammar analyses the tense, aspect, mood and voice of verbs. The verb string is analysed in terms of a grounding predication—either a tense morpheme or a modal verb—and a clausal head. For instance, in Cognitive Grammar, auxiliaries *have* and *be* are semantically related to non-auxiliary functions of the same verbs, and the past participle is also related to adjectival categories that share the same morphology. Tense and mood receive a unified semantic characterization in terms of the epistemic model, and the polysemy of modals is accounted for in force-dynamic terms.

Another model of cognitive grammar is Adele E. Goldberg's (1995) Construction Grammar in which she defines a construction as any form-meaning pairing whose properties cannot be predicted by its subparts. Goldberg adopts the usage-based thesis and assumes that knowledge of language consists of a structured inventory. She argues that certain clausal constructions have schematic meaning independent of the lexical items that instantiate them.

Two recently developed cognitive approaches to grammar are William Croft's (2001) Radical Construction Grammar and Embodied Construction Grammar developed by Benjamin Bergen and Nancy Chang (2005). In Radical Construction Grammar, every linguistic unit is a construction, regardless of complexity or arbitrariness. Everything in Radical Construction Grammar is arbitrary, since everything is construction-specific. In Embodied Construction Grammar, the emphasis is on language processing and the nature of the embodied knowledge with which the language system interacts rather than on the nature of the language system itself.

9.4.1 Cognitive Grammar

Cognitive grammar is the model of language developed by Ronald Langacker (1987). Langacker's model is called "Cognitive Grammar" because it represents an attempt to understand language not as an outcome of a specialized language module but as the result of general cognitive mechanisms and processes. According to this view, language observes the same general principles as other aspects of the human cognitive system. In his theory of cognitive grammar, Langacker attempts to delineate the principles of structure grammar and to relate these principles to aspects of general cognition. In his terminology, "grammar" is not used in a narrow sense to refer to a specific subpart of language in terms of syntactic or morphological knowledge; instead, it is used in the broad sense, where it refers to the language system as a whole, incorporating sound, meaning and morphosyntax.

Cognitive grammar takes a symbolic or constructional view of language and holds that there is no distinction between syntax and lexicon. The grammar consists of an inventory of units that are form-meaning pairings: morphemes, words and grammatical constructions. These units, called as symbolic assemblies, unite properties of sound, meaning and grammar within a single representation. An assembly can exhibit any degree of symbolic complexity and specificity (or conversely, schematicity) at the semantic pole and phonological pole. The assemblies usually recognized as lexical items which can be characterized as fixed expressions. In which, "fixed" refers to the status as conventional units, and, "expressions" to a substantial degree of semantic and phonological specificity. Grammatical markers are phonologically specific but schemas at the semantic pole. The schemas for constructions are symbolically complex, being merely the recurring commonalities abstracted from symbolically complex expressions. These construction schemas function as templates exploited in the formation of novel expressions.

Word Classes. Langacker argues that word classes have a conceptual basis. In other words, the linguistic categories noun, verb, adjective and so on are not "purely grammatical" categories with "purely formal" properties such as the affixes they take or their patterns of distribution within phrases and sentences. Rather, these categories have a conceptual basis and can therefore be semantically characterized. Langacker divides linguistic expressions into two broad categories: nominal predications and relational predications. This distinction relates to the nature of the schematic meaning encoded by nouns and noun phrases (nominals) on the one hand, and by other lexical classes like verbs, adjectives, prepositions and so on (relations) on the other. The term "predication" relates to meaning and refers to the semantic pole of a symbolic unit. Nominal predications are conceptually autonomous, that is, they relate to conceptually independent entities, for instance, the expressions *bed* or *slipper* invoke concepts that are independently meaningful. In contrast, relational predications are conceptually dependent, they rely on other units to complete their meaning, which are relational in nature. For example, in (36):

(36) George hid the slipper under the bed.

Where, the verb *hid* relates the conceptually autonomous entities GEORGE, SLIPPER and BED, establishing a relationship involving "hiding" between them. Similarly, *under* establishes a spatial relation between SLIPPER and BED.

Nominal predications: nominal predications describe entities. Noun category, as a nominal predication, has central and prototypical members. Schematic characterization of the noun class is as follow: a noun encodes a region in some domain, and a count noun encodes a bounded region in some domain. A region is a "set of interconnected entities." (Langacker, 2002: 67) The entities that comprise the region can be either homogeneous at least as far as the boundary (for example, *bleep*, *pond*) or being individuated (for example, *bicycle*, *cat*, *piano*, *constellation*). A region is bounded if there is some inherent limit to the set of entities that constitute it. For example, a CONSTELLATION is bounded because it is a bounded region in a "bigger picture" of SKY. A mass noun encodes an unbounded region in some domain. The concepts encoded by mass nouns can also differ in terms of how homogeneous or individuated the entities that compose them are (for example, compare *water* and *furniture*). Count nouns are replicable because they are bounded, this is why they can be counted, and this property does not hold for mass nouns.

Relational predications: relational predications describe relations between entities. The category of relational predications is divided into two subcategories: temporal and atemporal relations. Temporal relations are processes and are encoded by verbs. The category of atemporal relations is a more disparate category and contains prepositions, adjectives, adverbs and non-finite verb forms (infinitives and participles). The domain of TIME underlies the distinction between temporal and atemporal relations. In describing the role of time in this distinction, time is distinguished conceived time from processing time. Conceived time refers to the cognitive representation of TIME, where time is an object of conceptualization. Processing time can be thought as "real time," any cognitive process requires processing time in the sense. In this sense, processing time is a medium of conceptualization. Within conceived time, Langacker distinguishes the processes of summary scanning and sequential scanning, where "scanning" relates to how the aspects of a scene are perceived, visually or otherwise, and give rise to a conceptual representation. In summary scanning, aspects of a scene are scanned cumulatively and are simultaneously present in the conceptual representation. This gives rise to a Gestalt representation of time as a unified whole and characterizes static scenes. In sequential scanning, the aspects of a scene are scanned in a sequential fashion so that the aspects of the scene are not simultaneously present at any stage of the scanning. This gives rise to a conceptualization of time as a dynamic process and characterizes events. To understand distinction between summary scanning and sequential scanning, we can imagine the difference between looking at a photograph (summary scanning) and watching a film (sequential scanning). All aspects of a scene are simultaneously present in a photograph which presents a static scene, but a film involves a sequence of scenes, each different from the next.

Attention and Focal Adjustment. From a viewpoint of cognitive grammar of Langacker, grammar encodes schematic aspects of embodied experience, and attention, a perceptual phenomenon, is one aspect of this. Attention is differentially focused on a particular aspect of a given scene. This is achieved by a range of focal adjustments which "adjust the focus" on a particular aspect of any given scene by using different linguistic expressions or different grammatical constructions to describe that scene. By choosing a particular focal adjustment and thus linguistically "organizing" a scene in a specific way, the speaker imposes a unique construal upon that scene. Construal is the way in which a speaker chooses to "package" and "present" a conceptual representation, which in turn has consequences for the conceptual representation that the utterance evokes in the mind of the hearer. For example, in (37), the active construction focuses attention upon the AGENT of an action (37)a, while the passive construction focuses attention upon the PATIENT (37)b.

(37) a. George hid Lily's slippers.

b. Lily's slippers were hidden by George.

Focal adjustments can vary along three parameters: 1) selection; 2) perspective; and 3) abstraction. These parameters provide different ways of focusing attention on and construing a scene. **A. Selection**: profiling. Selection determines which aspects of a scene are attended to and relates to the notion of a conceptual domain. A conceptual domain, as the first aspect of selection, is a body of related knowledge within the conceptual system. Langacker (1987) proposes a number of basic domains tied directly to preconceptual embodied experience (Table 9.1). The second aspect of selection is related to profiling. Profiling involves selecting some aspect of a base, which is a conceptual entity necessary for understanding what a word means. So, words have profile-base organization. For example, the expression *elbow* profiles a substructure within the larger structure ARM, which is its base. As the predication necessarily includes both the profile and the base, the semantic pole of a symbolic unit is called its "predication" and the base represents the full scope of predication associated with an expression.

Table 9.1 Basic Domains Proposed by Langacker (1987)

Basic domain	Pre-conceptual basis
SPACE	Visual system; motion and position (proprioceptive) sensors in skin, muscles and joints; vestibular system (located in the auditory canal; detects motion and balance)
COLOUR	Visual system
PITCH	Auditory system
TEMPERATURE	Tactile (touch) system
PRESSURE	Pressure sensors in the skin, muscles and joints
PAIN	Detection of tissue damage by nerves under the skin
ODOUR	Olfactory (smell) system
TIME	Temporal awareness
EMOTION	Affective (emotion) system

Selection, related to profiling, is part of the process of coding. When a speaker wants to express a conceptual representation in language, he or she has choices over which linguistic expressions and constructions are used to "package" the conceptual representation. Coding is the process of "activating" the linguistic units. The process of coding is closely interwoven with construal, because decisions about how a situation is construed have consequences for the linguistic expressions selected to code the conceptualization.

B. Perspective: trajector-landmark organization and deixis. Perspective is the second parameter of focal adjustment. The perspective from which a scene is viewed has consequences for the relative prominence of its participants. The grammatical functions *subject* and *object* are reflections of perspective and thus have a conceptual basis. The distinction between *subject* and *object* relates to the prototype of an action chain, a cognitive model involving an active "energy source" (AGENT) that transfers energy to an "energy sink" (PATIENT). The semantic pole of the expression fulfilling the subject function is called the trajector (TR) which reflects the observation that the prototypical subject is dynamic. The semantic pole of the expression that fulfils the object function is called the landmark (LM) which reflects the observation that the prototypical object is inert. Tr-lM (or subject-object) organization in linguistic expressions is an instance of the more general perceptual and attentional phenomenon of figure-ground organization. Tr-lM organization is defined in terms of a conceptual asymmetry between participants in a profiled relationship: TR signifies the focal or most prominent participant, LM represents the secondary participant. In a sentence, TR (subject) comes first and LM (object) second. Consider example (38):

(38) a. George ate all the caviar. [active]
b. All the caviar was eaten by George. [passive]

In (38)a, the focal participant (TR) is *George* who is the AGENT of the action, and the secondary participant (LM) is *the caviar* which is the PATIENT. In (38)b, the situation is reversed and the PATIENT is now the focal participant (TR). In a passive sentence, the AGENT is the secondary participant (LM), but it is not the object because passivized verbs do not take objects. Instead, the *by*-phrase containing the object behaves more like a modifier and can be deleted without making the sentence ungrammatical. The distinction between these two sentences relates to a shift in perspective, which is effected by changing the relative prominence attached to the participants in the profiled relationship. Perspective also underpins the personal pronoun. The grammatical feature *person* distinguishes speaker, hearer and third party. However, person is a deictic category because SPEAKER, HEARER and THIRD PARTY are not fixed properties of any given individual but shift continually during conversation. Consider the following short conversation in (39).

(39) George: I love caviar!
     Lily: I hate it!

In the conversation, although an individual referred to as *I* both loves and hates caviar, there is no contradiction in *I* both loving and hating caviar because the participants in the conversation know that the first person singular pronoun *I* refers to a different individual in each utterance. In the case that George says *I*, it means GEORGE, and Lily says *I*, it means LILY. Speakers have no difficulty in "keeping track" of who *I* or *you* refer to at any given point in a conversation. It is our ability to adopt various viewpoints during a conversational exchange that underlies the ease with which we manipulate the person deixis: when George says *I*, Lily knows it means GEORGE is the speaker, because she momentarily adopts George's perspective as speaker. For deixis in perspective reflected in the grammatical system, Langacker uses the term *ground* to describe speech events, includes the participants, the time of speaking and the immediate physical context. Deictic expressions make specific reference to ground, and they are divided into two broad categories: those that place the ground "offstage" or in the background and those that place it "onstage" and focus attention upon the ground. For instance, temporal deictics *tomorrow* and *next week* place the ground offstage because they profile a point in time relative to the time of speaking, but the time of speaking which makes up part of the ground ("now") is backgrounded or implicit. In contrast, deictic expressions like *now* (temporal), *here* (spatial) and *you* (person deixis) place the ground onstage because they focus explicit attention upon aspects of the ground: time, place and participant. The difference between explicit mention of the ground and implicit dependence upon the ground is a difference of perspective.

C. Abstraction: profiling. This third focal adjustment operation relates to how specific or detailed the description of a scene is. It also has consequences for the type of construction selected. For example, read and think of sentences in (40):

(40) a. George threw a shoe at the TV and smashed it.
  b. George smashed the TV.

The scene in (40)b is more abstract (less detailed) than that in (40)a. Both of these examples share the same scope of predication, which involves an AGENT, a PATIENT and an INSTRUMENT. However, the more abstract description only profiles the AGENT and the PATIENT and leaves the INSTRUMENT as an unprofiled part of the base. In this way, abstraction, which relates to the level of attention paid to a scene, is paralleled by the kinds of linguistic constructions available to us in terms of level of detail.

Force-dynamics. "Force-dynamics" relates to our experience of motion energy. This experience gives rise to the knowledge that some entities have an inherent capacity for energy, whereas other entities only receive energy from external entities. The transfer of energy from AGENT to PATIENT results in a change of state of the PATIENT. This is called the action chain model manifested linguistically in profiling and the Tr-lM asymmetry. The unmarked status of the active transitive sentence with third-person participants arises from the fact that it represents the prototypical action from a canonical viewpoint perspective. Langacker argues that the grammatical notions of subject and object have their basis in this prototypical action chain model. The prototypical subject (TR) is the volitional "energy source" and the prototypical object (LM) is the passive "energy sink." The Tr-lM reversal effected by the passive construction could be modeled in terms of a shift of attention from AGENT to PATIENT within the action chain model. Grammatical features like voice and person, together with the grammatical functions subject and object, receive an experientially based semantic account within Langacker's Cognitive Grammar.

The Network Model in Grammar. Langacker develops a network model representing the structure of categories. According to this model, members of a category are viewed as nodes in a complex network and the links between nodes arise from a number of different kinds of categorizing relationships between the symbolic units stored in the grammatical inventory. One categorizing relationship is extension from a prototype, represented as [A] → [B], where A is the prototype and B shares some but not all attributes of A and is thus categorized as an instance of that category. Another categorizing relationship is the relationship between schema and instance, represented as [A] → [B]. The entrenched units that share a structural pattern give rise to a schematic representation of that structure. The schema structures then relate units as a category within the network, and novel expressions can be compared against such categories. The network can grow "upwards" via schematization, "outwards" via extension and "downwards" as more detailed instances are added.

The network model can be used to characterise polysemous open-class elements and underlies other linguistic categories such as sound, meaning and grammar. Word classes and grammatical constructions are also envisaged as nodes in a network. Some nodes such as morphemes are structurally simplex, and some nodes like the phonological units or phrase-level or sentence-level grammatical constructions have complex internal structure.

The open-class categories display polysemy in network and organize them in terms of prototype in nature, similarly, grammatical categories like closed-class words or bound grammatical morphemes are represented as discrete nodes in a complex network. For example, the modal auxiliaries represent a closed-class that shows a fixed and predictable participation in the grammatical behaviour of the verb string. The modal auxiliaries present a striking case of polysemy, according to their semantic contribution to the clause. For example, the examples in (41) illustrate the polysemous nature of the modal verb *can*:

(41) a. Mary can cook.
　　　b. You can leave now.

The modal in (41)a has a capacity meaning which conveys the speaker's judgment about Mary's capabilities, so, it presents a kind of epistemic modality because it relates to the speaker's knowledge. The other example reflects denotic modality related to obligation, say, (41)a encodes permission and (41)b encodes obligation.

9.4.2　Construction Grammar

Construction approach developed by Adele Goldberg (1995) is usage-based model. Influenced by the work of Kay and Fillmore and by the early work of George Lakoff on constructions, Goldberg developed a construction grammar to extend the constructional approach from "irregular" idiomatic constructions to "regular" constructions. Goldberg's approach focuses on the argument structure of sentence-level constructions such as the English ditransitive construction (e.g. ⟨42⟩a) and the English resultative construction (e.g. ⟨42⟩b).

(42) a. Lily knitted George a jumper.
　　　b. Lily drank herself stupid.

Most instances of these constructions are not idiomatic for their disconformities to the "regular" patterns of language, Goldberg argues that these constructions contain meaning that cannot be attributed to the lexical items in them, and the constructional approach is extended to account for regular instances as well as idiomatic instances.

The central thesis of construction grammar of Goldberg theory is that sentence-level constructions themselves are independently of the words in them and carry meaning. Constructions are theoretical primitives rather than "taxonomic epiphenomena" proposed by Chomsky (1991: 417). Although Goldberg does not deny that word level units contribute a great deal to the meaning and structure of sentences, she argues that a purely "bottom-up" or lexically driven model of grammar fails to provide the whole picture.

Unlike Langacker who defines a construction as any unit with a complex symbolic structure, Goldberg defines a construction as:

> C is a CONSTRUCTION if C is a form-meaning pair $<F_i, S_i>$ such that some aspect of F_i or some aspect of S_i is not strictly predictable from C's component parts or from other previously established constructions.
>
> (Goldberg, 1995: 4)

In this definition, F stands for "form" and S stands for "semantics," the subscripts represent the symbolic link between form and meaning, so, $<F, S>$ represents a symbolic unit. If any aspect of either the form or the meaning of a unit cannot be shown to be predictable from the properties of its component parts, then it has the status of a construction in Goldberg's model. Bound morphemes (like plural-*s*) and free morphemes (simplex words like *cat*) are constructions in Goldberg's construction theory. For Goldberg, neither the form nor the meaning of a morpheme is predictable from its component parts, since it lacks compositional structure. A complex word, phrase or sentence, will only count as a construction in Goldberg's model if some aspect of its form or meaning cannot be predicted from its subparts. Construction grammar blurs the boundaries between lexicon and syntax. Like other cognitive linguists, Goldberg also assumes the lexicon-grammar continuum. She refers to the lexicon-grammar continuum as the construction (the repository of constructions) because she makes no distinction between simplex and complex symbolic units (since either kind may count as a construction). Goldberg (1995: 5) also holds that knowledge of language is represented as a "highly structured lattice of interrelated information," and "knowledge of language is knowledge." In other words, she rejects the idea that knowledge of language is separate and distinct in nature from other kinds of knowledge and experience. Instead, Goldberg argues that the properties of language directly reflect human experience, conceptual organization and construal.

To understand Goldberg's approach, let us take argument structure alternations which received a considerable amount of attention in linguistics as an example. Consider the examples in (43) and (44):

(43) a. George brought Lily some breakfast.
     b. George brought some breakfast to Lily.
(44) a. *George brought the table some breakfast.

b. George brought some breakfast to the table.

As illustrated in these examples, the ditransitive verb *bring* can occur in two different construction types. Examples like (43)a and (44)a are called double object constructions (or dative shift constructions) because the verb is followed by two nominal objects, examples like (43)b and (44)b are called the prepositional construction, the indirect object (*Lily* or *the table*) is represented by a preposition phrase (PP). The point of interest here relates to the fact that while the prepositional construction allows the recipient to be either animate (43)b or inanimate (44)b, the double object construction requires that it be animate [compare (43)a with (44)a]. The issue arisen from this observation is how these differences are best captured in the model of the grammar. Goldberg argues that the most explanatory account associates these semantic restrictions directly with the grammatical construction itself rather than states the information in the lexical entries of individual verbs. Goldberg lists a number of properties that are specific to the ditransitive construction, which cannot be predicted either from the lexical items that fill the construction or from other constructions in the language. This issue of predictability is important, because the presence of unique or unpredictable semantic or syntactic properties is what identifies a construction in Goldberg's theory. The properties of the ditransitive construction are summarized in Table 9.2.

Table 9.2 Properties of the English Ditransitive Construction (Goldberg, 1995)

The English ditransitive construction: X CAUSES Y TO RECEIVE Z
Contributes TRANSFER semantics that cannot be attributed to the lexical verb
The GOAL argument must be animate (RECIPIENT rather than PATIENT)
Two non-predicative NPs are licensed in post-verbal position
The construction links RECIPIENT role with OBJ function
The SUBJ role must be filled with a volitional AGENT who intends TRANSFER

To sum up, Goldberg's model of construction grammar has several feature: 1) motivates the existence of the constructions by demonstrating that each has certain semantic and/or syntactic properties that cannot be predicted on the basis of the lexical items that fill the construction; 2) posits the central sense of the construction; 3) posits the syntactic frame that identifies the construction; 4) establishes the mapping between the argument roles of the construction and the participant roles of the lexical verb that fills the construction; and 5) explores inheritance links within the construction, focusing mainly on polysemy and metaphor.

In construction grammar of Goldberg, certain aspects of the meaning of a sentence as well as certain restrictions upon its structure arise directly from the properties of the skeletal grammatical construction rather than from the properties of the lexical verb. In addition, the verb contributes its own rich and specific (frame semantic) meaning and bringing with participant roles. It is in the interaction between the properties of the verb and the properties of the construction that both semantic and syntactic properties of the classes of sentences receive an explanation. Furthermore, Goldberg adopts the construction notion of inheritance in accounting for generalizations across constructions and relationships between constructions. She develops this idea into a taxonomy of inheritance links that enable certain shared properties between constructions to be explained in terms of polysemy and conceptual metaphor as well as in terms of more straightforward and predictable similarities.

9.4.3 Radical Construction Grammar

Radical Construction Grammar (RCG) model is developed by William Croft (2001) for exploring the implications of linguistic typology for syntactic theory. As a subdiscipline of linguistics, linguistic typology attempts to examine the structural properties of language from a cross-linguistic perspective and to describe patterns of similarity and points of diversity as well. In principle, typological studies can be theory neutral, relying on large-scale comparisons and statistical findings. Croft seeks to exploit in developing a model of language that marries typological insights with a meaning-based model of language structure.

In many respects, RCG is compatible with Langacker's Cognitive Grammar. For example, Croft assumes the lexicon-grammar continuum between specific and schematic meaning and the representation of the mental grammar in terms of a structured inventory. He also adopts the usage-based approach and the idea of entrenchment. However, in Croft's model, everything from a morpheme to a sentence is a construction. Croft's definition of construction is therefore different both from Langacker's definition and from Goldberg's. Table 9.3 represents Croft's taxonomy of constructions.

Table 9.3 RCG Taxonomy of Constructions (adapted from Croft, 2001: 17)

Construction type	Traditional name	Example
Complex and (mostly) schematic	Syntax	[NP be-TENSE VERB-en by NP]
Complex and (mostly) specific	Idiom	[pull-TENSE NP's leg]
Complex but bound	Morphology	[NOUN-s], [VERB-TENSE]
Atomic and schematic	Word classes	[NOUN], [VERB]
Atomic and specific	Lexical items	[the], [jumper]

In Croft's construction model, grammatical diversity is taken as a starting point to build a model that adequately accounts for patterns of typological variation rather than grammatical universal. To Croft, a constructional approach should best be placed to provide this type of model, since a constructional approach enables the articulation of the arbitrary and the unique, in contrast to most formal approaches which place the emphasis on generalization.

Five key features of RCG can be summed up. 1) Primitive units. Croft assumes that the construction is the only primitive unit in the grammar and may therefore be either simplex or complex in terms of structure and either specific or schematic in terms of meaning. In Croft's model, grammatical categories (for example, word classes like noun and verb, or grammatical functions like subject and object) have no independent status but are defined in relation to the constructions within which they occur. This explains why the relevant line in Table 9.3 is shaded: in RCG, word classes do not exist as primitive categories. This means that words cannot be categorized into word classes that have any independent reality, they are just part of individual constructions. In the RCG model, constructions are the primitives, and word classes, as they emerge from constructions, are epiphenomenal. From this perspective, the types of word classes that we observe from one language to another might be significantly different, and, because no universal word classes are posited, this cross-linguistic variation is not only unproblematic but predicted. Croft therefore argues against universal primitives and against the independent existence of word classes within any given language. Instead, Croft argues in favour of language-specific constructions and construction-specific elements (grammatical subparts) and components (semantic subparts).

2) Syntactic relations and constituent structure. The only syntactic relations admitted in the RCG model are the part-whole relations between the construction as a whole and the syntactic elements that fill it. In other words, the RCG model does not recognize grammatical functions like subject and object as having any independent reality outside of individual constructions. In this model, constituency is conceived in terms of grouping, grammatical units are identified in terms of contiguity and prosodic unity, and heads receive a semantic characterization as primary information bearing units.

3) Symbolic relations. The form and the meaning of a construction are linked in RCG by symbolic relations. In other words, each construction as a whole is a form-meaning pairing in the same way that each lexical item is a form-meaning pairing in the conventional view of the lexicon.

4) Functional prototypes. Both typological generalization and variation are characterized in terms of categorization and how function is linguistically encoded. That is to say, cross-linguistic similarities and differences are described in terms of functional typological prototypes: referring expressions relate to OBJECTS, attributive expressions relate to PROPERTIES and predicative constructions relate to ACTIONS. Essentially, OBJECTS, PROPERTIES and ACTIONS are semantic or conceptual categories and these

prototypes underlie the parts of speech in languages in the world.

5) Explaining linguistic universals. RCG explains linguistic universals (linguistic generalizations, in Croft's terms) not by assuming a set of universal grammatical primitives, but by assuming a universal conceptual space. In this respect, the RCG approach reflects one of the core assumptions of cognitive approaches to grammar: cross-linguistic patterns of grammatical structure are motivated by meaning, which in turn emerges from conceptual structure. Typologists generally adopt some version of a semantic map model. A semantic map is a language-specific typological pattern which rests upon a universal conceptual space. "Conceptual space represents a universal structure of conceptual knowledge for communication in human beings." (Croft, 2001: 105). Croft holds that the categories in constructions in human languages may vary from one language to the other but are mapped onto a common conceptual space, which represents a common cognitive heritage, the geography of the human mind.

Why Radical Construction Grammar can be described as radical. This approach questions and challenges basic assumptions that have defined theoretical and descriptive linguistics throughout the history of the discipline, for example, the existence of word classes and grammatical functions. From the perspective of radical construction model, what many linguists think of as the building blocks of language, say, its grammatical units, are epiphenomenal. In the place of these cross-linguistic universals, the RCG model emphasizes the universality of the conceptual system and explains typological patterns on this basis.

9.4.4 Embodied Construction Grammar

Embodied Construction Grammar (ECG) is a recent theory of construction grammar developed by Benjamin Bergen and Nancy Chang (2005). This approach assumes that all linguistic units are constructions, including morphemes, words, phrases and sentences.

The primary emphasis in ECG model is on language processing, particularly, language comprehension or understanding. The approaches we have discussed thus far place the emphasis on modelling linguistic knowledge rather than on on-line processing, whereas the ECG model takes it for granted that constructions form the basis of linguistic knowledge and focuses on exploring how constructions are processed in on-line or dynamic language comprehension. Moreover, ECG is centrally concerned with describing how the constructions of a given language relate to embodied knowledge in the process of language understanding. Therefore, much of the research to date in ECG has been focused on developing a formal "language" to describe the constructions of a language; this formal language also needs to be able to describe the embodied concepts that these constructions give rise to in dynamic language comprehension.

ECG claims that when a hearer hears an utterance he or she has two distinct tasks to perform. The first is analysis (parsing) which involves the hearer mapping the stimulus (the utterance) onto the structured inventory of constructions in his or her grammar and recognizing which constructions are instantiated by the utterance. The second is simulation which involves the activation of conceptual representations that underlie the interpretation of the utterance and the "re-enactment" of these conceptual representations. It is this process of simulation, together with contextual factors, that gives rise to the hearer's response. According to ECG, the conceptual representations that are accessed and simulated during language understanding are embodied schemas like the SOURCE-PATH-GOAL schema. In other words, it is embodied experience that gives rise to these conceptual representations, and, during language processing constructions are specified to prompt for these conceptual representations arisen from embodied experience. This explains why the approach is called "Embodied Construction Grammar." To take a concrete example, consider how a hearer might process the following utterance:

(45) Lily passed me a dead frog.

At the analysis stage, each of the phonetic forms maps onto a construction (form-meaning pairing) in the hearer's inventory of constructions at morpheme, word, phrase and sentence level. The hearer recognizes the ditransitive construction which brings with it the semantics of TRANSFER. The mapping of participant roles onto argument roles in the construction contributes to the interpretation of the utterance, and the context of the utterance enables the referent of the expression *me* to be identified (as the speaker). At the simulation stage, the interpretation of a ditransitive utterance like this activates three embodied schemas: FORCE APPLICATION, CAUSE-EFFECT and RECEIVE. Each of these is associated with schematic events and schematic roles such as ENERGY SOURCE and ENERGY SINK (Langacker, 1987), and, it is the mapping of constructions onto these schematic events and roles that gives rise to the simulation process. For example, in the sentence of (45), the construction instantiated by *Lily* is ENERGY SOURCE, and the construction instantiated by *me* is ENERGY SINK. This simulation process gives rise to an ordered set of inferences, some of which are represented in (46), where SMALL CAPS indicate participants and event schemas (Bergen & Chang, 2005):

(46) a. SPEAKER does not have FROG
  b. LILY exerts force via PASS
  c. FROG in hand of LILY
  d. LILY moves FROG towards SPEAKER

e. FROG not in hand of LILY
   f. LILY causes SPEAKER to receive FROG
   g. SPEAKER has received FROG

Although these inferences seem rather obvious in terms of deconstructing the meaning of the utterance, it is nevertheless important for a model of language processing to explain how such inferences arise in utterance comprehension. According to the ECG model, it is the hearer's own embodied experience that results in conceptual representations of that experience in terms of embodied schemas, which gives rise to these inferences via a simulation process. In this way, the hearer mentally re-enacts the event designated by the utterance.

We do not go into further detail on the ECG approach, this brief overview provides a sense of how a constructional approach can be extended to account not only for knowledge of language but also for the dynamic processing of language, while taking seriously the role of embodied knowledge and the notion of mental simulations as the outcome of language comprehension.

References

Bergen, B. K. & Chang, N. 2005. "Embodied construction grammar in simulation-based language understanding," in *Construction Grammars: Cognitive Grounding and Theoretical Extensions*. J.-O. Östman & M. Fried (eds.). Amsterdam: John Benjamins. pp. 147—190.

Berlin, B. & Kay, P. 1969. *Basic Color Terms: Their Universality and Evolution*. Berkeley: University of California Press.

Chomsky, N. 1991. "Some notes on economy of derivation and representation," in *Principles and Parameters in Comparative Grammar*. Robert Freidin (ed.). Cambridge, MA: MIT Press. pp. 417—454.

Coleman, L. & Kay, P. 1981. "Prototype semantics," *Language* 57:26—44.

Croft, W. 2001. *Radical Construction Grammar: Syntactic Theory in Typological Perspective*. Oxford: Oxford University Press.

Dirven, R. & Verspoor, M. 2004. *Cognitive Exploration of Language and Linguistics*. (2nd ed.). Amsterdam: John Benjamins.

Fauconnier, G. 1997. *Mappings in Thought and Language*. Cambridge: Cambridge University Press.

Fillmore, C. 1975. "An alternative to checklist theories of meaning," *Proceedings of the First Annual Meeting of the Berkeley Linguistics Society*. Amsterdam: North Holland. pp. 123—131.

Fillmore, C. 1982. "Frame semantics," in *Linguistics in the Morning Calm*. Linguistic Society of Korea (ed.). Seoul: Hanshin Publishing. pp. 111—137.

Fillmore, C. 1985. "Frames and the semantics of understanding," *Quaderni di Semantica* 6: 222—254.

Goldberg, A. 1995. *Constructions: A Construction Grammar Approach to Argument Structure*. Chicago: Chicago University Press.

Kant, I. 1952 [1790]. *The Critique of Judgment*. J. C. Meredith (trans.). Oxford: Clarendon Press.

Kay, P. & Fillmore, C. 1999. "Grammatical constructions and linguistic generalizations: the *what's X doing Y* construction," *Language* 75: 1—34.

Kay, P. & Kempton, W. 1984. "What is the Sapir-Whorf Hypothesis?" *American Anthropologist* 86(1): 65—79.

Johnson, M. 1987. *The Body in the Mind: The Bodily Basis of Meaning, Imagination and Reason*. Chicago: Chicago University Press.

Lakoff, G. 1987. *Women, Fire and Dangerous Things: What Categories Reveal about the Mind*. Chicago: University of Chicago Press.

Lakoff, G. & Johnson, M. 2003 [1980]. *Metaphors We Live by*. Chicago: University of Chicago Press.

Langacker, R. 1987. *Foundations of Cognitive Grammar, Volume I*. Stanford, CA: Stanford University Press.

Langacker, R. 1991. *Foundations of Cognitive Grammar, Volume II*. Stanford, CA: Stanford University Press.

Langacker, R. 2000. "A dynamic usage-based model," in *Usage-Based Models of Language*. M. Barlow and S. Kemmer (eds.). Stanford, CA: CSLI Publications. pp. 1—64.

Langacker, R. 2002. *Concept, Image, Symbol: The Cognitive Basis of Grammar*. (2nd ed.). Berlin: Mouton de Gruyter.

Talmy, L. 1972. *Semantic Structures in English and Atsugewi*. Ph. D. dissertation, University of California, Berkeley.

Talmy, L. 1983. "How language structures space," in *Spatial Orientation: Theory, Research and Application*. Herbert L. Pick, Jr. & Linda P. Acredolo (eds.). New York: Plenum Press. pp. 225—282.

Talmy, L. 2000. *Toward a Cognitive Semantics vol. 1: Concept Structuring Systems*. Cambridge, MA: MIT Press.

Taylor, J. 2003. *Linguistic Categorization*. (3rd ed.). Oxford: Oxford University Press.

Rosch, E. 1973. "Natural categories," *Cognitive Psychology* 4:328—350.

Rosch, E. 1975. "Cognitive representations of semantic categories," *Journal of Experimental Psychology: General* 104: 192—233.

Chapter 10

Pragmatics

10.1 Introduction

In the chapter on semantics, we said that the word "meaning" may have many different meanings, and we discussed some of them there. But there is one important type of meaning, SPEAKER'S MEANING, UTTERANCE① MEANING, or CONTEXTUAL MEANING, we did not touch on at all. This new type of meaning differs from the kinds of meaning we studied in semantics in that its interpretation depends more on the context. The discipline which concentrates on this kind of meaning is called PRAGMATICS②, which may also be defined as the study of LANGUAGE IN USE.

10.2 Speech Act Theory

This is the first major theory in the study of language in use, which originated with the Oxford philosopher John Langshaw Austin.

At the turn of the 20th century, there was a linguistic turn in western philosophy. Philosophers felt that many philosophical problems were in fact problems of language, and could be solved if we did a proper analysis of language. But there were different opinions about the adequacy of natural languages and whether only sentences which can be true or false are worth studying. Austin was in favour of NATURAL LANGUAGES. He thought

---

① "Utterance" may be defined as a piece of actually used language. In this sense we can divide the study of meaning into two types. One is concerned with the meaning of words and sentences, as abstract units of the language system; and the other is concerned with the meaning of utterances, as units of language in use. But the two terms "sentence" and "utterance" are not always clearly distinguished in the literature.

② In a sense there are two different approaches in pragmatics: the Anglo-American and the European Continental. The former regards pragmatics as a sub-branch of linguistics, comparable to syntax, semantics, etc. while the latter denies its componential nature, arguing that pragmatics should be seen as a perspective and every aspect of language, such as sounds, words and sentences, could be studied in the pragmatic way. In this chapter we largely follow the Anglo-American approach and will only touch upon the European Continental approach a little bit in the end.

there is no need to replace them by artificial, logical languages. And his speech act theory grew out of a conscious effort to combat the bias toward the study of sentences capable of being true or false only.

10.2.1 Performatives and Constatives

Austin's first shot at the theory is the claim that there are two types of sentences: PERFORMATIVES and CONSTATIVES. In his *How to Do Things with Words*, Austin argues that sentences like the following do not describe things. They cannot be said to be true or false. The uttering of these sentences is, or is a part of, the performance of an action. So they are called performatives. And verbs like "name" are called PERFORMATIVE VERBS.

(1) I name this ship the *Queen Elizabeth*.
(2) I bequeath my watch to my brother.
(3) I bet you six pence it will rain tomorrow.

In contrast, sentence (4) said by a chemistry teacher in a demonstration of an experiment is not a performative. It is a description of what the speaker is doing at the time of speaking. The speaker cannot pour any liquid into a tube by simply uttering these words. He must accompany his words with the actual pouring. Otherwise one can accuse him of making a false statement. Sentences of this type are known as constatives.

(4) I pour some liquid into the tube.

Though performatives cannot be true or false, there are still conditions for them to meet to be appropriate or felicitous. A simplified version of the felicity conditions suggested by Austin is as follows:

A. (i) There must be a relevant conventional procedure, and
   (ii) the relevant participants and circumstances must be appropriate.
B. The procedure must be executed (i) correctly and (ii) completely.
C. Very often, (i) the relevant people must have the requisite thoughts, feelings and intentions, and (ii) must follow it up with actions as specified.

However, Austin soon realized that these conditions only apply to some cases. There are other cases in which one does not need a conventional procedure to produce a performative. To make a promise, for example, one can either say "I promise" or "I give my word for it." There is no strict procedure for doing it. On the other hand, the so-called constatives may also be infelicitous in these ways. "The present King of France is bald" is infelicitous in the same way as "I bequeath my watch to my brother" said by somebody without a watch. They both presuppose the existence of something, which does not actually exist. And people making statements must also have requisite thoughts, feelings and intentions. One cannot say, "The cat is on the mat, but

I don't believe it. "

Then Austin explored the possibility of separating performatives from constatives on grammatical and lexical criteria. He noticed that typical performatives use first person singular subject, simple present tense, indicative mood, active voice, and performative verbs. But there are also counter examples. Passive performatives like "Pedestrians are warned to keep off the grass" are common. In informal situations, other moods and tenses are also possible. Instead of "I order you to turn right," one can simply say "Turn right." In place of "I find you guilty" the jury may say "You did it." What is more, even the most typical constative verb "state," which is used to describe things, may be used to do things. In uttering "I state that I'm alone responsible," the speaker has made a statement and undertaken the responsibility. In other words, it seems that the distinction between performatives and constatives cannot be maintained. All sentences can be used to do things.

10.2.2　A Theory of the Illocutionary Act

In the latter part of *How to Do Things with Words*, Austin made a fresh start on the problem and considered it from the ground up again, i.e. in what sense to say something is to do something.

In his opinion, there are three senses in which saying something may be understood as doing something. The first sense is an ordinary one. That is, when we speak we move our vocal organs and produce a number of sounds, organized in a certain way and with a certain meaning. In this sense, when somebody says "Morning!" we can ask a question like "What did he do?" instead of "What did he say?" And the answer could be that he produced a sound, word or sentence—"Morning!" The act performed in this sense is called a locutionary act. Within this act, however, Austin suggests that there is another act. "[I]n performing a locutionary act we shall also be performing such an act as: asking or answering a question, giving some information or an assurance or a warning, announcing a verdict or an intention, pronouncing sentence, making an appointment or an appeal or a criticism, making an identification or giving a description, and the numerous like." (1962: 98 – 99) For example, to the question "What did he do?" when the person concerned said "Morning!" we could perfectly well say "He offered a greeting."

In other words, when we speak, we not only produce some units of language with certain meanings, but also make clear our purpose in producing them, the way we intend them to be understood, or they also have certain forces as Austin prefers to say. In the example of "Morning!" we can say it has the force of a greeting, or it ought to have been taken as a greeting. This is the second sense in which to say something is to do something, and the act performed is known as an ILLOCUTIONARY ACT.

The third sense in which to say something can mean to do something concerns the consequential effects of a locution upon the hearer. By telling somebody something the speaker may change the opinion of the hearer on something, or mislead him, or surprise him, or induce him to do something, etc. Whether or not these effects are intended by the speaker, they can be regarded as part of the act that the speaker has performed. This act, which is performed through, by means of, a locutionary act, is called a PERLOCUTIONARY ACT.

Defined in this way, the locutionary act is what linguists have been studying all along. That is, how sounds, words and sentences are made, and what inherent meanings they have. The perlocutionary act involves many psychological, social factors, of which we are still more or less in the dark. So the illocutionary act is what Austin was really driving at. In this sense, speech act theory is in fact a theory of the illocutionary act.

In this general theory then, which applies to all sentences, the original performatives are only a special type in which the illocutionary force is made explicit by the performative verb.

10.2.3 Classes of Illocutionary Acts

In order to study illocutionary acts in depth, Austin attempted a preliminary classification of them in the last chapter of *How to Do Things with Words*. Since the illocutionary force of an utterance may be made explicit by a performative verb, the typical performative of the first person singular present indicative active form is used as a basis for the classification. By testing verbs in this form, Austin arrived at the following five classes.

(i) Verdictives

VERDICTIVES are concerned with the delivery of a verdict, a finding, a judgement, or an assessment, upon evidence or reasons. For example, when the jury acquit somebody of some crime, they give a verdict, a judgement on the basis of the evidence they hear. Typical verbs used in this class are: *acquit*, *convict*, *find* (as a matter of fact), *hold* (as a matter of law), *interpret as*.

(ii) Exercitives

EXERCITIVES are concerned with the exercising of powers, rights or influence. "It is a decision that something is to be so, as distinct from a judgement that it is so; it is advocacy that it should be so, as opposed to an estimate that it is so; it is an award as opposed to an assessment; it is a sentence as opposed to a verdict." (1962: 155) Typical verbs are: *appoint*, *degrade*, *demote*, *dismiss*, *excommunicate*.

(iii) Commissives

"The whole point of a COMMISSIVES is to commit the speaker to a certain course of action." (ibid.: 157) When someone promises, he undertakes the obligation to perform the action specified. Typical verbs are: *promise*, *covenant*, *contract*, *undertake*, *give* (my word).

(iv) Behabitives

BEHABITIVES have to do with attitudes and social behaviour, e. g. reaction to other people's behaviour and fortunes. There are seven sub classes for, respectively, apologies, thanks, sympathy, attitudes,[①] greetings, wishes, and challenges.

(v) Expositives

"EXPOSITIVES are used in acts of exposition involving the expounding of views, the conducting of arguments, and the clarifying of usages and of references." (ibid.: 161) There are also seven sub-classes, exemplified respectively by *affirm*, *remark*, *inform*,[②] *testify*, *accept*, *postulate*, and *begin by*.

But there are problems with this classification. One of them is that the classes are not clear cut. There are overlapping cases, as Austin himself concedes. And the most serious problem is that there is no consistent principle behind it. Austin claims that these classes are based on their illocutionary force and he uses the explicit performative verb in the first person singular present indicative active form as a test frame. This is, however, not even true of the sample verbs listed. Among the commissives, there is the verb "shall," which he clearly labels as a primary, i. e. implicit, performative. What is more, he groups "intending" and "promising" together on the ground that both can be expressed by the locutions "shall probably," "shall do my best to," and "shall very likely." (ibid.: 158)

10.2.4 Searle's Revisions

The American philosopher of language John Searle has introduced some revisions to Austin's theory. In this sub-section, we shall concentrate on his revisions about felicity conditions and classes of illocutionary acts.

In his *Speech Acts*, Searle argues that FELICITY CONDITIONS should not only be seen negatively as ways in which an utterance may go wrong, but also positively as rules, the observance of which constitutes or creates the speech act. For example, apart from general conditions like "Normal input and output conditions obtain," there are the following conditions on promises

---

① Under this sub-class, Austin lists verbs like "resent" "don't mind" "pay tribute" and "criticize."

② The third and fifth sub-classes are further divided into two finer classes, and the seventh is further divided into four finer classes.

and requests.

Table 10.1　Conditions on Premises and Requests

	propositional content condition	preparatory condition	sincerity condition	essential condition
PROM[①]	(a) S expresses the proposition that p in the utterance of T.[②] (b) In expressing that p, S predicts a future act A of S.	(a) H would prefer S's doing A to his not doing A, and believes H would prefer his doing A to his not doing A. (b) It is not obvious to both S and H that S will do A in the normal course of events.	S intends to do A.	S intends that the utterance of T will place him under an obligation to do A.
REQ	Future act A of H.	(a) H is able to do A. S believes H is able to do A. (b) It is not obvious to both S and H that H will do A in the normal course of events of his own accord.	S wants H to do A.	Counts as an attempt to get H to do A.

At that time, Searle thought it impossible to reduce illocutionary acts to some basic classes. But in "A taxonomy of illocutionary acts" published in 1975, he changed his mind and proposed a new classification of illocutionary acts. In his view, illocutionary acts may differ from each other in 12 dimensions, which therefore he uses as criteria for the classification. And the four important ones, most of which correlate to his felicity conditions, are: the illocutionary point, the direction of fit between words and the world, the psychological state expressed and the propositional content.

By ILLOCUTIONARY POINT is meant the point or purpose of an illocution. For example, "[t]he point or purpose of an order can be specified by saying that it is an attempt to get the hearer to do something. The point or purpose of a description is that it is a representation (true or false, accurate or inaccurate) of how something is. The point or purpose of a promise is that it is an undertaking of an obligation by the speaker to do something." (1979 [1975]: 2) This dimension corresponds to the essential condition.

The DIRECTION OF FIT between words and the world means whether there is reality first and we use words to describe it or there are words first and we follow them with actions to bring about the reality. ASSERTIONS, which

---

① "PROM" stands for "promise," and "REQ" below for "request."
② S is the abbreviation of *speaker*, H *hearer*, A *act*, p *proposition*, and T stands for *sentence*.

have as part of their illocutionary point to get the words to match the world, are of the former type. And promises and requests, which are involved in getting the world to match words, are of the latter type.

In the performance of an illocutionary act with a PROPOSITIONAL CONTENT, the speaker usually also expresses some attitude, some PSYCHOLOGICAL STATE, to that propositional content. "A man who states, explains, asserts or claims that *p expresses the belief that p*; a man who promises, vows, threatens or pledges to do A *expresses an intention to do A*; a man who orders, commands, requests H to do A *expresses a desire (want, wish) that H do A*; a man who apologizes for doing A *expresses regret at having done A*; etc." (ibid.: 4) And this dimension corresponds to the SINCERITY CONDITION.

The propositional content is concerned with the REFERENCE and PREDICATION of a locution. That is, who does what at what time. "The differences, for example, between a report and a prediction involve the fact that a prediction must be about the future whereas a report can be about the past or present." (ibid.: 6) And this dimension corresponds to the propositional content condition.

By these criteria, Searle establishes the five classes of assertives, directives, commissives, expressives and declarations.

(i) Assertives

The point or purpose of this class is to commit the speaker to something being the case, to the truth of the expressed proposition. The direction of fit is words to the world. The psychological state expressed is Belief (that). So this class is symbolized as $\vdash \downarrow B(p)$[①]. The simplest test of an assertive is: can you literally characterize it as true of false? In this sense, this class equals what Austin originally called constatives.

(ii) Directives

The illocutionary point of a DIRECTIVE is to get the hearer to do something. The direction of fit is the world to words. The psychological state expressed, or the sincerity condition, is Want (or Wish, Desire). And the propositional content is that the hearer H does some future action A. In Searle's view, questions are a sub-class of directives, since they are attempts by S to get H to answer, i.e. to perform a speech act. To use the exclamation mark for the illocutionary point of this class, the symbol for the directive is: ! $\uparrow W$ (H does A).

---

① The sign $\vdash$ is used by some philosophers for assertion. $\downarrow$ means the direction of fit is words to the world, $\uparrow$ means the opposite, and $\updownarrow$ means both words to the world and the world to words. B is the abbreviation of *belief*, and *p proposition*. Similarly, W below is the abbreviation of *want*, *C commissive*, *I intention*, *E expressive*, *D declaration* and D_a *assertive declaration*.

(iii) Commissives

The illocutionary point in this class is to commit the speaker to some future course of action. The direction of fit is the world to words. The sincerity condition is Intention. And the propositional content is that the speaker S does some future action. So it can be symbolized as $C \uparrow I$ (S does A).

(iv) Expressives

The illocutionary point is simply to express the psychological state specified in the sincerity condition about a state of affairs specified in the propositional content. But there is no direction of fit between words and the world. In performing an EXPRESSIVE, the speaker is neither trying to get the world to match the words nor the other way round, rather the truth of the expressed proposition is presupposed. The psychological state expressed in this class is a variable, depending on the illocutionary point. The propositional content ascribes some property (not necessarily an action) to either S or H, e.g. S's stepping on H's toe, H's winning a race, or H's good looks. Therefore it is symbolized as $E \emptyset (P^{①})$ (S/H + property).

(v) Declarations

The illocutionary point is to bring about some alteration in the status or condition of the referred to object. The successful performance of a DECLARATION guarantees that the propositional content corresponds to the world. If somebody successfully performs the act of appointing you chairman, then you are chairman. So the direction of fit is both words to the world and the world to words: $\updownarrow$. The saying of something causes something to become reality. In this sense, this class corresponds to the typical performative. There is no sincerity condition, since no personal attitude is involved in declarations. The speaker is acting as a spokesman of an institution. He is not expressing any psychological state of his own. The propositional content is also a variable, depending on the illocutionary point. Its symbol is: $D \downarrow \updownarrow (p)$.

But some members of this class overlap with members of the assertive class. When the judge declares "You are guilty," he has not only brought about some change in the status of the person referred to, but also asserts that it is true that you have committed a crime, and he believes in this verdict. So there is a difference of the illocutionary point, the direction of fit, and the psychological state in this sub-class, which may be called "ASSERTIVE DECLARATIONS" and symbolized as $D_a \downarrow \updownarrow B (p)$.

Searle's classification is an improvement on that of Austin's in that there is a principled basis—the revised felicity conditions. But there are also

---

① This capital P, different from the small p in the fourth position, refers to a psychological state.

problems here. One of them concerns the criterion of the direction of fit between words and the world. This is not a reflection of any inherent nature of illocutionary acts. Yet Searle attaches great importance to it. He wishes that he could build the taxonomy entirely around this distinction, and even tries to group directives and commissives together on the ground that they have the same direction of fit. A more serious problem is that the number of classes, i. e. five, is too small. Searle claims that the successful classification of illocutionary acts shows that "there are a rather limited number of basic things we do with language: we tell people how things are, we try to get them to do things, we commit ourselves to doing things, we express our feelings and attitudes and we bring about changes through our utterances." (ibid.: 29) If that is the case, then we may not need spend so much effort on it. Traditional grammar has already told us that we can use language to make statements, ask questions and issue orders. What we are really interested in are the specific functions of language, or the specific illocutionary acts we perform. The fact that in both Austin's and Searle's classifications there are sub classes also points to the need for more specific classes.

10.3 The Classical Theory of Implicature

The second major theory in pragmatics is the theory of CONVERSATIONAL IMPLICATURE. We divide this topic into two parts. In the present section we introduce the original theory as is presented by Herbert Paul Grice. And the next section will be devoted to relevance theory and neo-Gricean principles.

There is evidence that Grice began to formulate his ideas of this theory in 1950s at Oxford, but it was through the William James lectures he delivered at Harvard in 1967 that his theory first became known to the public. Part of the lectures was published in 1975 under the title of "Logic and Conversation," and the lectures were published in its entirety in 1989 posthumously.

10.3.1 The Cooperative Principle

Grice noticed that in daily conversations people do not usually say things directly but tend to imply them. For example, when A and B are talking about their mutual friend C, who is now working in a bank, and A asks B how C is getting on, B might answer "Oh, quite well, I think; he likes his colleagues, and he hasn't been to prison yet." Here B certainly implied something, though he did not say it explicitly. Grice argues that we can make a distinction between what B said in this case and what he implied, suggested or meant. In order to avoid the logical use of "implication," which we touched on in the section on logical semantics, Grice coined the term "IMPLICATURE." And he explored the question how people manage to convey implicature, which is not explicitly expressed.

His answer is that there is some regularity in conversation. "Our talk exchanges do not normally consist of a succession of disconnected remarks, and would not be rational if they did. They are characteristically, to some degree at least, cooperative efforts; and each participant recognizes in them, to some extent, a common purpose or set of purposes, or at least a mutually accepted direction." (1989: 26) In other words, we seem to follow some principle like the following: "Make your conversational contribution such as is required, at the stage at which it occurs, by the accepted purpose or direction of the talk exchange in which you are engaged." (ibid.) And this principle is known as THE COOPERATIVE PRINCIPLE, or CP for short.

To specify the CP further, Grice introduced four categories of maxims as follows:

Quantity

1. Make your contribution as informative as is required (for the current purposes of the exchange).

2. Do not make your contribution more informative than is required.

Quality

Try to make your contribution one that is true.

1. Do not say what you believe to be false.

2. Do not say that for which you lack adequate evidence.

Relation

Be relevant.

Manner

Be perspicuous.

1. Avoid obscurity of expression.

2. Avoid ambiguity.

3. Be brief (avoid unnecessary prolixity).

4. Be orderly. (ibid.:26—27)

Grice notes that there may be some overlap between the second Quantity maxim and the maxim of Relation. The excessive information will be something irrelevant. So perhaps the second Quantity maxim is not necessary. The exact interpretation of the Relation maxim has led to heated arguments among linguists later, which we will come to in detail in the discussion about post-Gricean developments.

The fact that the cooperative principle and its component maxims are expressed in the imperative has misled many readers to regard them as prescriptive: telling speakers how they ought to behave; while the truth is that the CP is meant to describe what actually happens in conversation. That is, when we speak we generally have something like the CP and its maxims in our mind to guide us, though sub-consciously, or even unconsciously. We will try to say things which are true, relevant, as well as informative enough, and in a clear manner. Hearers will also try to interpret what is said to them in this way. In the example of somebody working in a bank, A will assume that all the information provided by B is relevant. There must be a point in B's telling him that C likes his colleagues, and he hasn't been to prison yet. In this way, A will try to work out B's implied meaning, or the implicature.

In this sense, the CP may be compared to unwritten laws, such as, "Women and children are saved first from sinking ships"; "One is not supposed to make personal comments at academic conferences"; "礼尚往来"; "两军对阵,不斩来使".

10.3.2 Violation of the Maxims

The use of terms "principle" and "maxim" does not mean that the CP and its maxims will be followed by everybody at any time. People do violate them and tell lies. So the second half of Grice's "Logic and conversation" is devoted to a discussion of violations.

Concerning the first maxim of QUANTITY, he uses as an example an imagined reference letter by A for his past student X, who is applying for a lectureship in philosophy, and it reads: "Dear Sir, Mr. X's command of English is excellent, and his attendance at tutorials has been regular. Yours, etc." Grice comments "A cannot be opting out, since if he wished to be uncooperative, why write at all? He cannot be unable, through ignorance, to say more, since the man is his pupil; moreover, he knows that more information than this is wanted. He must, therefore, be wishing to impart information that he is reluctant to write down. This supposition is tenable only on the assumption that he thinks Mr. X is no good at philosophy. This, then, is what he is implicating." (ibid.: 33).

And tautologies like "Boys are boys" and "War is war" are extreme examples in which the first Quantity maxim is violated. At the superficial level, the level of what is said, they are totally uninformative. At a deeper level, the level of what is implicated, however, they are informative. They may convey implicatures like "Boys are naughty and mischievous by nature," "It's no use lamenting the tragedies of war. Terrible things always happen in it. That's its nature."

An example in which the second maxim of Quantity is violated will be:

(5) A: Where is X?

B: He's gone to the library. He said so when he left.

In a sense, the first part of B's answer is enough for A's question. But by adding the second part, the speaker may implicate that he is not sure whether X has really gone to the library. The examples Grice provides for the violation of the first Quality maxim are all traditional figures of speech like (2) and (3).

(6) He is made of iron.

(7) Every nice girl loves a sailor.

That is, at the level of what is said, they are false statements. No natural human being is made of iron, unless he is a robot. So (6) will not be taken literally. Instead we will interpret it as a metaphor, meaning this man has a character like iron. In the case of (7), the implicature is many girls love sailors.

In cases when we do not have adequate evidence, we will usually qualify our utterances by "It may be the case that..." or "I'm not sure but..."

As for the maxim of Relation, Grice thinks "Examples in which an implicature is achieved by real, as distinct from apparent, violation of the maxim of Relation are perhaps rare, but the following seems to be a good candidate. At a genteel tea party, A says 'Mrs. X is an old bag.' There is a moment of appalled silence, and then B says 'The weather has been quite delightful this summer, hasn't it?' B has apparently refused to make what HE says relevant to A's preceding remark. He thereby implicates that A's remark should not be discussed and, perhaps more specifically, that A has committed a social gaffe." (ibid.: 35)

When illustrating the violation of the "Avoid ambiguity" maxim, Grice uses as an example William Blake's lines "Never seek to tell thy love, Love that never told can be." In this case, "love" may refer to an emotion or the person one loves. And "Love that never told can be" may mean either "Love that cannot be told" or "Love that if told cannot continue to exist."

And the following may be seen as a case in which B is being deliberately obscure.

(8) A: Let's get the kids something.

B: Okey, but I veto I-C-E C-R-E-A-M-S.

If a reviewer has chosen (9)b rather than (9)a, then the prolixity implicates that Miss X's performance is so poor that the word "sing" cannot be applied.

(9) a. Miss X sang "Home sweet home."

b. Miss X produced a series of sounds that corresponded closely with the score of "Home sweet home."

At the end of the discussion, we may summarize conversational implicature as a type of implied meaning, which is deduced on the basis of the conventional meaning of words together with the context, under the guidance of the CP and its maxims. In this sense, implicature is comparable to illocutionary force in speech act theory in that they are both concerned with the contextual side of meaning, or 言外之意 in Chinese. And these two theories differ only in the mechanisms they offer for explaining the generation of this contextual meaning.

10.4 Post-Gricean Theories

The theory of conversational implicature has opened a new way of explaining the use of language, and caught the attention of linguists immediately. However, there is some inconsistency and redundancy among the CP and its maxims. Linguists of the post-Gricean period, therefore, have sought to boil down the maxims to a set of principles, which are truly indispensable and do not overlap at the same time. In this section, we shall discuss three such suggestions.

10.4.1 Relevance Theory

RELEVANCE theory was formally proposed by Dan Sperber and Deirdre Wilson in their book *Relevance: Communication and Cognition* in 1986. But the principle of relevance had already been around for some years through their articles written separately or jointly before then.

The first reference to this theory was made by Wilson in her book co-authored with Neil Smith *Modern Linguistics: The Results of Chomsky's Revolution* of 1979. She emphasizes there the crucial role played by judgements of relevance in the interpretation of utterances. For example, B's reply in (10) suggests that A's chocolates were gone.

(10) A: Where's my chocolates?

B: Where are the snows of yesteryear?

"However, it will not convey this suggestion unless it is construed as a relevant response to A. If it is construed as irrelevant—for example as the start of a poetry reading, a genuine inquiry in its own right, or a rhetorical response to a quite different question—then no such suggestion will arise." (Smith & Wilson 1979: 175) Similarly, if B's response is (11), it will suggest that the children may have eaten his chocolates, or may know where they are, on the condition that it is construed as a relevant answer to A's question.

(11) B: The children were in your room this morning.

If it is not construed as relevant, but as an attempt to change the subject or to dismiss A's question for some other reason, no such suggestion will arise either. And the definition of relevance then is:

A remark P is relevant to another remark Q if P and Q, together with background knowledge, yield new information not derivable from either P or Q, together with background knowledge, alone. (ibid.)

In 1981, Wilson and Sperber published an article entitled "On Grice's theory of conversation." In it they propose for the first time that all Gricean maxims, including the CP itself, should be reduced to a single principle of relevance, which is defined as "The speaker has done his best to be maximally relevant." (Wilson & Sperber, 1998 [1981]: 361) They argue that the principle of relevance may subsume not only the second Quantity maxim, as anticipated by Grice, but also the first Quantity maxim by providing a criterion for judging whether a given contribution is informative enough.

Concerning the Quality maxims, they maintain that to determine the relevance of an utterance, a hearer must make valid inferences on the basis of true premises. And the speaker, in general, will also have to tell the truth and have adequate evidence to achieve maximal relevance. So they may be subsumed by the principle of relevance as well. But when a patient says "I'm ill" to a doctor, he may not have adequate evidence. In the Gricean theory then the patient is said to have violated a maxim of Quality. In the relevance framework, however, as long as the speaker is sincere, his utterance will be relevant. Whether he is competent to proclaim he is ill is not important.

About the maxim of Relation, they do not see any difference between it and their principle of relevance.

Lastly, they think the principle of relevance subsumes the maxim of "Avoid obscurity." In their view, to determine the relevance of an utterance, the hearer must be clear about what is expressed. So, to be obscure is against the principle of relevance.

Similarly, to be ambiguous also violates the principle of relevance. However, they argue that the maxim of "Avoid ambiguity" is in fact misplaced. Utterances are in general all ambiguous one way or another. In other words, nobody follows this maxim.

The maxim of "Be brief," they hold, is at least misstated. First, Grice did not set a criterion. We do not know how to determine what is brief, whether by the number of syllables, words, word groups or by the syntactic and semantic complexity. Second, in some situations, the more prolix expression may be more relevant, for example, the (b) utterances below.

(12) a. Peter is married to Madeleine.
　　b. It is Peter who is married to Madeleine.
(13) a. Mary ate a peanut.
　　b. Mary put a peanut into her mouth, chewed and swallowed it.

On the other hand, the speaker of (14) has violated the principle of relevance. Its prolixity is only incidental.

(14) The baby is putting arsenic into his mouth, chewing and swallowing it!

In their view, the maxim of "Be orderly" mainly serves to indicate that "and" may have implicatures like "and then" "and so." So the two utterances in (15) mean differently.

(15) a. Jenny sang, and Maria played the piano.

b. Maria played the piano, and Jenny sang.

But different word orders may lead to different initial assumptions used for determining the relevance of an utterance. In this sense, the principle of relevance is more explicit than the maxim of "Be orderly."

As for the CP itself, they think it is not incompatible with their principle. Nevertheless, it does not seem right to characterize conversation as a cooperative effort. Conversation is basically egotistic, some degree of cooperation is only a price interlocutors have to pay.

In their 1986 book, Sperber and Wilson define the principle of relevance as:

> Every act of ostensive communication communicates the presumption of its own optimal relevance. (Sperber & Wilson, 1986: 158)①

To understand this definition, we need to be clear about the key notions in it: "OSTENSIVE COMMUNICATION" and "PRESUMPTION OF OPTIMAL RELEVANCE." They agree with Grice that communication is not simply a matter of encoding and decoding, it also involves INFERENCE. But they maintain that inference has only to do with the hearer. From the speaker's side, communication should be seen as an act of making clear one's intention to express something. This act they call ostensive act, or simply ostension. In other words, a complete characterization of communication is that it is OSTENSIVE INFERENTIAL. And "ostensive communication," or "inferential communication," is a shorthand.

To explain "presumption of optimal relevance," we shall first have a look at the three definitions of relevance in this book. The first definition relates it to a context.

> An assumption is relevant in a context if and only if it has some contextual effect in that context. (ibid.: 122)

But relevance is also, and more importantly, a comparative concept. Some assumptions may be more relevant than others. What is more, "The assessment of relevance, like the assessment of productivity, is a matter of balancing output against input." (ibid.: 125) It does not only depend on the effect produced by it but also on the effort required to process it. So they have improved on the previous definition by adopting an extent condition format:

> *Extent condition*1: an assumption is relevant in a context to the extent that its contextual effects in this context are large.

---

① In the second edition of 1995, Sperber & Wilson note that there are in fact two relevance-based principles. And they renamed this principle Communicative Principle of Relevance, and added the other, known as Cognitive Principle of Relevance, "Human cognition tends to be geared to the maximization of relevance." (Sperber & Wilson, 1995: 260)

Extent condition 2: an assumption is relevant in a context to the extent that the effort required to process it in this context is small. (ibid.)

Then they consider at length the question of what exactly context means. They find that sometimes context will have to include all the background information, otherwise it will be difficult to process some assumptions. Sometimes, however, some information must be excluded, otherwise the effort will be enlarged without increasing the effect. In other words, the size of context is determined by the assumption to process. It is not given, but chosen. It is not that there is a context, on which the relevance of an assumption depends. What is given is relevance. People generally assume that the assumption they are processing is relevant (otherwise they would not bother to process it), then try to find a context in which its relevance will be maximized.

Their second definition of relevance relates it to an individual as follows:

An assumption is relevant to an individual at a given time if and only if it is relevant in one or more of the contexts available to that individual at that time. (ibid.: 144)

And the last definition they offer involves the characterization of relevance "not just as a property of assumptions in the mind, but also as a property of phenomena (stimuli, e.g. utterances) in the environment which lead to the construction of assumptions." (ibid.: 150—151) A communicator cannot directly present an audience with an assumption. All a speaker, or a writer, can do is present a stimulus in the form of a sound, or a written mark. The presentation of this stimulus changes the cognitive environment of the audience, making certain facts manifest, or more manifest. As a result, the audience can mentally represent these facts as strong or stronger assumptions, and even use them to derive further assumptions. The notion of relevance extended in this way becomes:

A phenomenon is relevant to an individual if and only if one or more of the assumptions it makes manifest is relevant to him. (ibid.: 152)

Thus, by presumption of optimal relevance is meant:
(a) The ostensive stimulus is relevant enough for it to be worth the addressee's effort to process it. (Sperber & Wilson, 1995: 267)
(b) The ostensive stimulus is the most relevant one compatible with the communicator's abilities and preferences. (ibid.: 270)

That is, every utterance comes with a presumption of the best balance of effort against effect. On the one hand, the effects achievable will never be less than is needed to make it worth processing. On the other hand, the effort required will never be more than is needed to achieve these effects. In comparison to the effects achieved, the effort needed is always the smallest.

This amounts to saying "of all the interpretations of the stimulus which confirm the presumption, it is the first interpretation to occur to the addressee that is the one the communicator intended to convey." (ibid.: 168—169)

10.4.2 The Q-and R-principles

This is a less reductionist, bipartite model. These two principles, developed by Laurence Horn, were first proposed in his "Toward a new taxonomy for pragmatic inference: Q-based and R-based implicature" of 1984, and further elaborated in his "Pragmatic theory" of 1988. The Q-PRINCIPLE is intended to invoke the first maxim of Grice's Quantity, and the R-PRINCIPLE the Relation maxim, but the new principles are more extensive than the Gricean maxims.

The Q principle (Hearer-based):

MAKE YOUR CONTRIBUTION SUFFICIENT (cf. quantity$_1$)
SAY AS MUCH AS YOU CAN (given R)

The R principle (Speaker-based):

MAKE YOUR CONTRIBUTION NECESSARY (cf. Relation, Quantity$_2$, Manner)
SAY NO MORE THAN YOU MUST (given Q)

(Horn, 1984: 13) ①

The hearer-based Q-principle is a sufficiency condition in the sense that information provided is the most the speaker is able to. For example, (16) below implicates (17).

(16) Some of my friends are linguists.
(17) Not all of my friends are linguists.

The R-principle, in contrast, encourages the hearer to infer that more is meant. Typical examples are speech acts like (18).

(18) Can you pass the salt?

In his 1988 article, Horn describes the Q-principle as "a hearer based economy for the maximization of informational content, akin to Grice's (first) maxim of quantity," and the R-principle as "a speaker based economy for the minimization of form, akin to Zipf's (1949) 'principle of least effort.'" (Horn, 1988: 132)

10.4.3 The Q-, I-and M-principles

This tripartite model was suggested by Stephen Levinson. He first began

---

① As can be seen from the above the maxims of Quality are an exception. They are still there in the new theory.

to formulate his ideas along this line in 1981, when writing collaboratively with Jay David Atlas "*It*-clefts, informativeness and logical form: radical pragmatics." But it was in the two articles published in 1987—"Minimization and conversational inference" and "Pragmatics and the grammar of anaphor: a partial pragmatic reduction of binding and control phenomena"—that he formally put forward these principles.

In essence, Levinson says, the Q-, I-and M-principles are Grice's two maxims of Quantity and a maxim of Manner reinterpreted neo-classically. And the maxims of Quality, as is the case in Horn's theory, are kept intact.

Levinson does not agree with the treatment in both Sperber & Wilson's and Horn's accounts to subsume the second maxim of Quantity under a principle of relevance, or relation. In his view, the maxims of Quantity have to do with the quantity of information, while "relevance is a measure of timely helpfulness with respect to interactional goals," (1987b: 401) and "is largely about the satisfaction of others' goals in interaction, and the satisfaction of topical and sequencing constraints in discourse, as in the expectation that an answer will follow a question." (1989: 467) It is not, at least not primarily, about information. So he renames the second maxim of Quantity the PRINCIPLE OF INFORMATIVENESS, I-principle for short; and the first maxim of Quantity the Principle of Quantity, or Q-principle. And the contents of these principles are:

Q-principle

Speaker's Maxim: Do not provide a statement that is informationally weaker than your knowledge of the world allows, unless providing a stronger statement would contravene the I-principle.

Recipient's Corollary: Take it that the speaker made the strongest statement consistent with what he knows, and therefore that:

(a) if the speaker asserted A(W),[1] and <S, W> form a Horn scale[2] (such that A(S) ⊢ A(W)), then one can infer K ~ (A(S)), i.e. that the speaker knows that the stronger statement would be false;[3]

(b) if the speaker asserted A(W) and A(W) fails to entail an embedded sentence Q, which a stronger statement A(S) would entail, and {S, W} form a contrast set,[4] then one can infer ~ K(Q), i.e. the

---

[1] The letter A is the abbreviation of assertion, W that of weak, S that of strong, K that of know, and the sign ⊢ means "entail."

[2] This notion was originally proposed by L. Horn, referring to a set of quantitative elements, arranged in the order of informativeness as <all, most, many, some, few>, and <always, often, sometimes>.

[3] For example, (a) implicates (b) since *all* and *some* form a Horn scale <all, some>.

[4] Levinson makes a distinction between a Horn scale and a contrast set in that the former is clearly defined or strong and the latter loosely defined or weak.

speaker does not know whether Q obtains or not. ①(1987b: 401)

I-principle

Speaker's Maxim: the Maxim of Minimization

"Say as little as necessary," i. e. produce the minimal linguistic information sufficient to achieve your communicational ends (bearing the Q-principle in mind).

Recipient's Corollary: the Enrichment Rule

Amplify the informational content of the speaker's utterance, by finding the most SPECIFIC interpretation, up to what you judge to be the speaker's m-intended② point.

Specifically:

(a) Assume that stereotypical relations obtain between referents or events, UNLESS (i) this is inconsistent with what is taken for granted, (ii) the speaker has broken the maxim of Minimization by choosing a prolix expression.

(b) Assume the existence or actuality of what a sentence is "about" if that is consistent with what is taken for granted.

(c) Avoid interpretation that multiply entities referred to (assume referential parsimony); specifically, prefer coreferential readings of reduced NPs (pronouns or zeros③). (ibid.: 402)

To avoid possible clashes between the Q-and I-principles, Levinson proposes to restrict the scope of the Q-principle so that it operates only on Horn scales. And he also sets the following constraints on Horn scales:

For⟨S, W⟩to form a Horn scale,

(i) A(S) must entail A(W) for some arbitrary sentence frame A;

(ii) S and W must be EQUALLY LEXICALIZED (hence no Horn scale ⟨iff, if⟩to block "conditional perfection");

(iii) S and W must be "ABOUT" THE SAME SEMANTIC RELATIONS, or from the same semantic field (hence no scale⟨since, and⟩to block "conjunction buttressing"). (ibid.: 407)

On the other hand, implicatures are by definition cancellable in the face of inconsistent assumptions. "If the door is locked I have a key in my pocket" will not undergo "conditional perfection" to "If and only if..." because this would

---

① For example, (a) implicates (b) as *know* and *believe* do not form a Horn scale, but only a contrast set {know, believe}.

② This term was introduced into the literature by Grice in his article "Utterer's Meaning, Sentence-Meaning, and Word-Meaning," where he used "U [utterer] m-intends to produce in A [audience] effect E" as an abbreviation of "U intends to produce in A effect E by means of A's recognition of that intention." "M" stands for "meaning." (Grice, 1989: 122-123)

③ The term zero, sometimes written as Ø, refers to a linguistic unit which is not phonologically realized, e. g. *John came in and Ø sat down in the front row immediately.* It is also known as "gap."

be inconsistent with our assumption that keys do not automatically move to pockets when doors are locked.

Now let us turn to the M-principle. In his 1987 articles, Levinson did not give a specific formulation of it. He mixed the presentation of his own ideas with the criticism of Horn's principles. He accuses Horn of failing to draw a distinction between two kinds of minimization: a SEMANTIC MINIMIZATION and an EXPRESSION MINIMIZATION. The semantic, or content, minimization is equivalent to semantic generality. That is, the more general terms are more minimal in meaning, having more restricted connotation (in contrast to its more extended denotation); and the less general, the more specific, are less minimal, more maximal. For example, *ship* is more general than *ferry*, *flower* than *rose*, *animal* than *tiger*. The choice of the former instead of the latter is a process toward minimization. On the other hand, the expression, or form, minimization is some measure of surface length and complexity. It is concerned with the phonetic and morphological make up of a term. Thus the normally stressed terms are more minimal than their abnormally stressed counterparts. The shorter terms, those consisting of fewer constituents, are more minimal than longer ones, those consisting of more constituents, provided they are commeasurable in meaning, i. e. synonymous, such as *frequent* and *not infrequent*, *to stop a car* and *to cause a car to stop*.

In Levinson's view, only the semantic minimization has to do with the I-principle. The expression minimization, in contrast, is the domain of the principle of manner, as it concerns the form of a linguistic unit, the way to express something rather than what is expressed, or how much is expressed. He also criticizes Horn's division of pragmatic labour in this regard. "[T]he contrast involved in the Hornian division of labour is a contrast between marked and unmarked expressions, and more exactly a contrast between usual vs. unusual, or brief vs. prolix expressions. This distinction has nothing to do with quantity of information, the paired expressions being assumed to be synonymous; rather it has to do with surface form, and these implicatures are thus properly attributed to the maxim of Manner." (ibid.: 409)

Levinson (2000: 136) formulates the PRINCIPLE OF MANNER, or M-principle, as follows:

M-principle

Speaker's Maxim: Indicate an abnormal, nonstereotypical situation by using marked expressions that contrast with those you would use to describe the corresponding normal, stereotypical situation.

Recipient's Corollary: What is said in an abnormal way indicates an abnormal situation, or marked messages indicate marked situations, specifically:

Where S has said "p" containing marked expression M, and there is an unmarked alternate expression U with the same denotation D which the speaker might have employed in the same sentence-frame instead, then where U would have I-implicated the stereotypical or more specific subset d of D, the marked expression M will implicate the complement of the denotation d, namely $\Box d$ of D.

For example, *the man* in (20) is a marked form in contrast to *he* in (19), or the zero in (21), therefore it indicates an abnormal, or marked, non-coreferential interpretation. And the stressed HE in (22) is also a marked expression.

(19) John$_1$ came in and he$_1$ sat down in the front row immediately.
(20) John$_1$ came in and the man$_2$ sat down in the front row immediately.
(21) John$_1$ came in and $\emptyset_1$ sat down in the front row immediately.
(22) John$_1$ came in and HE$_2$ sat down in the front row immediately.

10.5 Recent Developments in Pragmatics

In recent years, there have been many new developments in the field of pragmatics. Cognitive pragmatics, for example, due to the cognitive appeals in relevance theory and the growing influence of cognitive linguistics in general, is a major strand of latest pragmatic developments. In this section, however, we shall concentrate on an interdisciplinary subject between pragmatics and discourse analysis, namely DISCURSIVE PRAGMATICS.

10.5.1 Pragmatics and Discourse Analysis

There are strong inherent connections between the two fields of pragmatics and discourse analysis ever since their respective inceptions in 1950s, though early practitioners of pragmatics like Austin and Grice seemed to be interested in isolated sentences only. [1]

Pragmatics, as we defined in the first section, is the study of language in use. And people do not just use single sentences in daily conversations, the sentences are connected with each other to form TEXTS, or DISCOURSES. [2] It is for this reason that Levinson in his authoritative textbook *Pragmatics* of

---

[1] Jenny Thomas (1995: 209) argues that a reason for using single sentences as examples in textbooks is that it is difficult to find a suitable text for all the illustrations. We believe this applies to the cases of Austin and Grice as well.

[2] Different authors use different terms. There may be a historical reason, so that people in Europe tend to use the word "text" while those in the US tend to use "discourse." There may also be a little difference in the senses of the terms in that "text" may be more concrete and therefore refers to the product more usually, and "discourse" may be more abstract and refers to the process quite often. But in general "text" and "discourse" are interchangeable most of the time.

1983 concludes with a chapter on the structure of conversation.①

On the other hand, the European Continental approach to pragmatics, mentioned in a note at the beginning of this chapter, maintains that pragmatics is a perspective and every aspect of language could be studied in the PRAGMATIC PERSPECTIVE. Therefore, text and discourse naturally fall within the domain of pragmatics in this approach as well.

Discourse analysts share this view on the relation between pragmatics and discourse analysis with pragmaticists. Brown and Yule, for example, define discourse analysis as "the analysis of language in use," (1983: 1) and they argue "'Doing discourse analysis' certainly involves 'doing syntax and semantics,' but it primarily consists of 'doing pragmatics.'" (ibid.: 26) Schiffrin, Tannen and Hamilton (2001: 1) also say that the three main categories of "discourse" are 1) anything beyond the sentence, 2) language use, and 3) a broad range of social practice, though there are different definitions of the term. And they (ibid.: 2) think Levinson's (1983) discussion of definitions of pragmatics includes "some which could easily cover either discourse analysis or sociolingustics."

10.5.2 The Discursive Turn in Pragmatics

2004 saw the publication of *Handbook of Pragmatics* edited by Laurence Horn and Gregory Ward, which represents the first conscientious attempt to combine the study of pragmatics with that of discourse analysis on the part of pragmaticists. There are four parts in this book: The Domain of Pragmatics (with 6 articles on basic concepts like implicature in pragmatics), Pragmatics and Discourse Structure (with 11 articles on important notions in discourse analysis like topic, focus, and information structure), Pragmatics and its Interfaces (with 9 articles on the relation between pragmatics and grammar, pragmatics and semantics, and so on), and Pragmatics and Cognition (with 6 articles on relevance theory, cognitive linguistics, etc.).

As one can see the second part on discourse analysis is obviously the focal part of the book with the sheer quantity of over one third of the articles. That there is a shift of emphasis to discourse analysis in pragmatic studies is also shown from the academic interests of the editors. Horn, as we have introduced, is a well-known neo-Gricean pragmaticist,② but Ward is definitely at the same time a discourse analyst, obtaining his PhD with a dissertation

---

① But Levinson seemed to have some prejudice against the methodology and techniques employed by some discourse analysts then.

② Though Horn has also written papers on topics relating to discourse analysis, for example, "Presupposition, theme and variations" of 1986 and "Given as new: when redundant affirmation Isn't" of 1991.

entitled *The Semantics and Pragmatics of Preposing* under the guidance of Ellen Prince in 1985. Ward and Betty Birner, the co-authors of "Informational structure and noncanonical syntax" in this handbook, have collaborated on a number of writings on information structure over the years. In 1998, they published a book *Information Status and Noncanonical Word Order in English*, in 2001 they wrote a paper of "Discourse and information structure" for *The Handbook of Discourse Analysis* edited by Schiffrin, Tannen and Hamilton, and in 2002 they wrote a chapter of "Information packaging" for *The Cambridge Grammar of the English Language* edited by Rodney Huddleston and Geoffrey Pullum. Ward has also written a paper entitled "Constraints on ellipsis and event reference" together with Andrew Kehler, who has independently written "Discourse coherence," another paper in this handbook, too.

What is more, articles in the other three parts have also touched on the topic of discourse. For example, Georgia Green's "Some interactions of pragmatics and grammar" in the third part is very similar to the one by Ward and Birner in that she discusses the influence of discourse structure on syntactic processes like preposing and inversion. Adele Goldberg in her "Pragmatics and argument structure" calls the treatment of information structure by writers like Halliday, Lambrecht, and Ward and Birner "conventional pragmatics," opposite to "conversational pragmatics" represented by Grice and Horn, and discusses the effects of these two types of pragmatics on argument structure. Julia Hirschberg goes into the details of the role of intonation in interpreting discourse, especially in distinguishing between the known information and new information and the determination of a topical structure in her paper "Pragmatics and intonation."

The paper "Historical pragmatics" by Elizabeth Traugott is on the historical change of meaning, but the author adopts "a methodology for text-based historical pragmatics." (2004: 554) In the analysis of "after all," for example, Traugott does not simply rely on logical speculations but bases her arguments on a computerized corpus of top stories issued by United Press International in the years of 1990 to 1992. On the historical origin of the adverbial "after all," there are suggestions by other writers that it derives from expressions like "after all that has been said and done." However, Traugott's own data show that the adversative "after all" arises in strongly adversative, largely dialogic contexts. And the justificational "after all" does not emerge until "after all" had come to be associated with an adversative generalized invited inference. Therefore, she concludes that "historical pragmatics requires going beyond decontextualized examples of semantic change, and paying attention to the discourse contexts in which the changes occur." (2004: 560)

So much so that even Daniel Jurafsky in his "Pragmatics and computational linguistics" argues that in computational linguistics we should not only take lexical and syntactic cues into consideration, but also discourse cues. The utterance "No, it isn't" is an agreement after a negative statement like "It isn't raining" but a disagreement after a positive statement like "It is raining." (2004: 596)

Of course, as we have shown in the first sub-section, there have been close connections between pragmatics and discourse analysis all along. In this sense the so-called "DISCURSIVE TURN" in pragmatics is really a "discursive return": pragmatics has come back to its original basis of language in use—discourse.

10.5.3 Discursive Pragmatics

If the *Handbook of Pragmatics* by Horn and Ward in 2004 represents an Anglo-American attempt to integrate discourse analysis into pragmatics, then *Discursive Pragmatics* edited by Jan Zienkowski, Jan-Ola Östman and Jef Verschueren, published in 2011 as the eighth volume of the series of *Handbook of Pragmatics Highlights*, constitutes the European Continental pragmaticists' attempt to bring pragmatics and discourse analysis together.

Apart from an introduction at the beginning, there are 15 chapters in it, namely, Appraisal, Cohesion and Coherence, Critical Linguistics and Critical Discourse Analysis, *Énonciation*: French pragmatic approach (es), Figures of speech, Genre, Humor, Intertextuality, Manipulation, Narrative, Polyphony, Pragmatic markers, Public discourse, Text and discourse linguistics, and Text linguistics, covering a wide variety of topics discourse analysts are interested in.

Now the authors are not simply discussing these topics in the usual discourse analytic way, they are dealing with them in terms of a pragmatic perspective. For example, cohesion and coherence is a central notion in discourse analysis, and there are heated arguments as to what exactly makes a text coherent. Wolfram Bublitz, the author of the paper on the topic in this volume, however, after a survey of researches on the relationship between cohesion and coherence, arrives at a pragmatics-oriented perspective. He thinks coherence is an interactive achievement resulting from negotiations between speaker and hearer within a specific socio-cultural setting. In other words, coherence becomes a "context dependent, user oriented and comprehension based notion" (Bublitz 2011: 45), and "it is not texts that cohere but rather people who make texts cohere." (ibid.: 46)

"Discourse analysis" is usually the term used in the US, as we noted earlier, in Europe the study on the properties of units larger than the sentence is known as "text grammar" and "text linguistics." Robert de Beaugrande, a prominent text linguist who co-authored an introductory book on the topic with Wolfgang Dressler in 1981, in his contribution recalls the historical development of text linguistics. In his view, "text linguistics has become strongly engaged with pragmatics" and "pragmatics forms the outermost framework for approaching syntax and semantics in terms of communicative activities." (de Beaugrande, 2011: 292)

He also thinks that text linguistics has entered the third and most recent stage, "dominated by 'textualization,' the social and cognitive processes entailed in the actual production and reception of texts." (ibid.: 293) At this stage, the pragmatics of text linguistics "could be a 'critical' view of communication as an ongoing interaction whereby the significance of a situation (real or hypothetical) is being negotiated, speaking turns are assigned, and relations of power or solidarity are enacted." (ibid.: 294)

Jan-Ola Östman and Tuija Virtanen in their turn argue that "Present-day text linguistics is just as interested in processual aspects of language as discourse analysis," hence they "use the phrase 'text and discourse linguistics' (TDL) as an umbrella-term for all issues that have been dealt with in the linguistic study of text and discourse." (Östman & Virtanen, 2004: 266)

Concerning the terms "discourse" and "pragmatics," Östman and Virtanen acknowledge that there has been competition between discourse analysts and pragmaticists about which one is more general. Although they have indicated the possibility of seeing discourse as a very general term, on the same level of abstraction as, or even more general than pragmatics, they have in this paper retained Morris' (1938) view of pragmatics as the most general term. (ibid.: 281)

Nevertheless, they maintain that to a certain extent, "this is a question of the hierarchization of traditional labels of academic subjects. A slightly more interesting response to this debate is that we are faced with different perspectives. Discourse and pragmatics have the same fields of interest, but different aspects in focus. Thus, discourse will typically require larger stretches of text or conversation, whereas for pragmatics this is not necessarily the case. The function of, for example, sound symbolism, or the specification of potential functional set-ups for pragmatic particles can be approached linguistically without explicit reference to a particular discourse." (ibid.: 281—282)

In other words, Östman and Virtanen think that discourse analysts and pragmaticists are interested in the same topics, though there is debate about which field is more general. On the other hand, they think that the difference between discourse analysis and pragmatics lies more on the focus, whether it is necessary to have larger stretches of text or conversation as data.

Now in my view the coming into existence of the interdisciplinary subject-discursive pragmatics, suggests at least that there will be more and more use of extended passages in pragmatics studies in the future. And this is a significant change for pragmatics.

For example, there are heated arguments whether all conversational implicatures are cancellable. And Matthew Weiner (2006) and Michael Blome-Tillmann (2008) each supplied highly contrived examples to substantiate their own positions. However, if we turn to extended authentic discourse①, the issue could be settled more easily.

There was a TV interview entitled 顾长卫、蒋雯丽做客《艺术人生》, hosted by 朱军 and shown in March, 2008, on the Central TV. At that time, Jiang Wenli had just returned from Rome, where she had won the best actress award in the film festival for her role as the heroine 王彩玲 in the film《立春》. This film therefore was naturally chosen as the first topic of the interview. One of the questions posed by Zhu Jun to Gu Changwei was why he had not decided at first to have Jiang Wenli play the role of Wang Cailing in this film. And without waiting for Gu's answer, Zhu Jun said that if he were the director, he would definitely first think of his wife, as the Chinese saying goes "肥水不流外人田。" Gu Changwei immediately responded with "我觉得你肯定是个好丈夫，" followed by Zhu Jun's retort "你的意思你不是个好丈夫。" In other words, Zhu Jun thought the utterance of "You must be a good husband" has the conversational implicature of "I'm not a good husband" here.

Then Gu Changwei went on as follows：

> 顾长卫：我觉得我不够，反正，至少是我在当时没有这个，这个。哦，就是实际的工作情况总是你很难，如果说你不是为了某一个，哦，什么明星去写一个故事，就为她写的话，我觉得这个过程还是在，哦，你在筹备在选演员的过程当中你才会慢慢去找这个人是谁，至少对我来说，我不是那样一个天才的导演，我，我就一读剧本，或者我一想就知道是谁了。

Gu Changwei first confirmed that he was not a good husband, at least not good enough. If an analyst of this dialogue simply quoted this first sentence, then he could perhaps claim that Gu's reply proves Zhu Jun's interpretation was right, in the sense that the uttering of "You must be a good husband" did have the conversational implicature of "I'm not a good husband" here.

But if we look further, we discover that Gu Changwei gradually changed his tone. He went on to say that it was a difficult task to decide the cast of a film and it usually took a long time, if the story was not written for a particular film star in the first place. And he was not such a talented director, who after reading the story for the first time, would immediately know who was to play the main character. In other words, the reason why Gu Changwei did not decide on Jiang Wenli at the beginning has something to do with his habit in

---

① The two modifiers "extended" and "authentic" are naturally related in that authentic data are usually extended in the sense that people do not usually use a word, or sentence, in isolation. There is always a co-text, and one text will be related to another in various ways as the study on intertextuality suggests.

choosing actors and actresses. It is simply a matter of his working procedure and has nothing to do with his being a good husband or not. In this sense the potential conversational implicature of "You must be a good husband," namely "I'm not a good husband," is cancelled in the end. ①

There is a special issue on Empirical Data and Pragmatic Theory in *Journal of Pragmatics* in August, 2008. The editor of the issue points out that all pragmaticists agree that pragmatics is the study of language in use, but not all of them agree that they should take samples of real-life examples into account, if not systematically, at least regularly. Some people maintain that theoretical advances in pragmatics can *only* be brought out by theorizing and that this theory is *only* attainable by deduction. The editor argues that "Studying language-in-use without paying any attention to the use of language is a methodological mistake." (Bordería 2008: 1354)

As a matter of fact, many arguments are virtually irresolvable without resorting to authentic data. For example, theoretically speaking, the possible conversational implicatures of an utterance like "You must be a good husband" could be an endless list, depending on the context, both situational and linguistic. One can always think up a hypothetical context in which there will, or will not, be a conversational implicature to support an argument. In this sense, authentic data, which is usually extended as we noted earlier, is of vital, crucial importance to the development of pragmatics. And discursive pragmatics by highlighting the necessity of studying larger stretches of text or conversation points to a promising direction for future pragmatics.

References

Austin, J. L. 1975 [1962]. *How to Do Things with Words*. (2nd ed.). Oxford: Clarendon Press.
Blome-Tillmann, M. 2008. "Conversational implicature and the cancellability test," *Analysis* 68(298): 156—160.
Bordería, S. P. 2008. "Introduction to the special issue on empirical data and pragmatic theory," *Journal of Pragmatics* 40: 1353—1356.
Brown, G. & Yule, G. 1983. *Discourse Analysis*. Cambridge: Cambridge University Press.
Bublitz, W. 2011. "Cohesion and coherence," In Zienkowski, J. Ostman J. & Verschueren, J. (eds.). *Discursive Pragmatics*: 37—49.
de Beaugrande, R. 2011. "Text linguistics," In Zienkowski, J., Östman, J. & Verschuren, J. (eds.). *Discursive Pragmatics*: 286—296.
de Beaugrande, R. & Dressler, W. 1981. *Introduction to Text Linguistics*. London: Longman.
Goldberg, A. E. 2004. "Pragmatics and argument structure," In Horn, L. R. & Ward, G. (eds.). *The Handbook of Pragmatics*: 427—441.

---

① For a more detailed discussion on this point, the reader is referred to 姜望琪 (2010).

Green, G. M. 2004. "Some interactions of pragmatics and grammar," In Horn, L. R. & Ward, G. (eds.). *The Handbook of Pragmatics*: 407—426.

Grice, H. P. 1975. "Logic and conversation," In *Syntax and Semantics* 3: *Speech Acts*. Cole, P. & Morgan, J. L. (eds.). New York: Academic Press. pp. 141—158.

Grice. H. P. 1989. *Studies in the Way of Words*. Cambridge, MA. : Harvard University Press.

Hirschberg, J. 2004. "Pragmatics and intonation," In Horn, L. R. & Ward, G. (eds.). *The Handbook of Pragmatics*: 56—637.

Horn, L. R. 1984. "Towards a new taxonomy for pragmatic inference: Q-based and R-based implicature," In *Meaning, Form, and Use in Context: Linguistic Applications*. Schiffrin, D. (ed.). Washington, D. C. : Georgetown University Press. pp. 11—42.

Horn, L. R. 1986. "Presupposition, theme and variations," *CLS 22, Part 2: Papers from the Parasessions on Pragmatics and Grammatical Theory*: 168—192.

Horn, L. R. 1988. "Pragmatic theory," In *Linguistics: The Cambridge Survey*. Vols. 1. Newmeyer, F. (ed.). Cambridge: Cambridge University Press. pp. 113—145.

Horn, L. R. 1991. "Given as new: when redundant affirmation isn't," *Journal of Pragmatics* 15: 305—328.

Horn, L. R. & Ward, G. (eds.). 2004. *The Handbook of Pragmatics*. Malden, MA. : Blackwell.

Jurafsky, D. 2004. "Pragmatics and computational linguistics," In Horn, L. R. & Ward, G. (eds.) *The Handbook of Pragmatics*: 578—604.

Kehler, A. 2004. "Discourse coherence," In Horn, L. R. & Ward, G. (eds.). *The Handbook of Pragmatics*: 241—265

Kehler, A. & Ward, G. 2004. "Constraints on ellipsis and event reference," In Horn, L. R. & Ward, G. (eds.). *The Handbook of Pragmatics*: 383—403.

Levinson, S. C. 1983. *Pragmatics*. Cambridge: Cambridge University Press.

Levinson, S. C. 1987a. "Minimization and conversational inference," In *The Pragmatic Perspective*. Verschueren, J. & Bertuccelli-Papi, M. (eds.). Amsterdam: John Benjamins. pp. 61—129.

Levinson, S. C. 1987b. "Pragmatics and the grammar of anaphora: a partial pragmatic reduction of Binding and Control phenomena," *Journal of Linguistics* 23: 379—434.

Levinson, S. C. 1989. "Review of *Relevance*," *Journal of Linguistics* 25: 455—472.

Levinson, S. C. 2000. *Presumptive Meanings: The Theory of Generalized Conversational Implicature*. Cambridge, MA. : MIT Press.

Östman, J. & Virtanen, T. "Text and discourse linguistics," In Zienkowski, J. , Östman, J. & Verschueren, J. (eds.). *Discursive Pragmatics*: 266—285.

Schiffrin, D. , Tannen, D. & Hamilton, H. E. (eds.). 2001. *The Handbook of Discourse Analysis*. Oxford: Blackwell.

Searle, J. R. 1969. *Speech Acts: An Essay in the Philosophy of Language*. Cambridge: Cambridge University Press.

Searle, J. R. 1975. *A Taxonomy of Illocutionary Acts*. Reprinted in Searle. 1979. *Expression and Meaning*. Cambridge: Cambridge University Press. pp. 1—29.

Smith, N. V. & Wilson, D. 1979. *Modern Linguistics: The Results of Chomsky's Revolution*. Harmondsworth: Penguin.

Sperber, D. & Wilson, D. 1986. *Relevance: Communication and Cognition*. Oxford:

Blackwell.

Sperber, D. & Wilson, D. 1995. *Relevance: Communication and Cognition*. (2nd ed.) Oxford: Blackwell.

Thomas, J. 1995. *Meaning in Interaction: An Introduction to Pragmatics*. London: Longman.

Traugott. E. C. 2004. "Historical pragmatics," In Horn, L. R. & Ward, G. (eds.). *The Handbook of Pragmatics*: 538—561.

Ward, G. & Birner, B. 2004. "Informational structure and noncanonical syntax," in Horn, L. & Ward, G. (eds.). *The Handbook of Pragmatics*: 153—174.

Ward, G. & Birner, B. 1998. *Information Status and Noncanonical Word Order in English*. Amsterdam: John Benjamins.

Ward, G. & Birner, B. 2001. "Discourse and information structure," In Schiffrin, D., Tannen, D. & Hamilton, H. E. (eds.). *The Handbook of Discourse Analysis*: 119—137.

Ward, G. & Birner, B. 2002. "Information packaging," In *The Cambridge Grammar of the English Language*, Chapter 16. Huddleston, R & Pullum, G. (eds.). Cambridge: Cambridge University Press.

Weiner, M. 2006. "Are all conversational implicatures cancellable?" *Anaysis* 66 (2): 127—130.

Wilson, D. & Sperber, D. 1981. "On Grice's theory of conversation," Reprinted in Kasher, A. (ed.). 1998. *Pragmatics: Critical Concepts*. Vol. 4. London: Routledge. pp. 347—368.

Zienkowski, J., Östman, J-O & Verschueren, J. 2011. *Discursive Pragmatics*. Amsterdam: John Benjamins.

姜望琪,2000,《语用学——理论及应用》(英文),北京:北京大学出版社。

姜望琪,2003,《当代语用学》,北京:北京大学出版社。

姜望琪,2008,从《语用学手册》看语用学的最新发展,《解放军外国语学院学报》第2期,第1—7页。

姜望琪,2010,语篇分析整体论,《语言学研究》第8辑,第3—11页。

Chapter 11

Issues of Stylistics

11.1 Introduction

Stylistics is an interdisciplinary subject. Its object of study is the style of language. It explains the relationship between the text and its context.

For Chinese learners of English, there are at least three areas of studies under the general head of STYLISTICS: Chinese stylistics, Western stylistics and Chinese studies of Western stylistics. Figure 11.1 illustrates these areas.

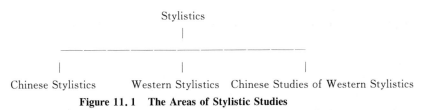

Figure 11.1   The Areas of Stylistic Studies

Chinese Stylistics

Systematic studies of Chinese stylistics may date back to a work of literary criticism, *The Carving of the Literary Mind* (《文心雕龙》) by Liu Xie (*circa* 465-*circa* 532 A.D.) in the South-North Dynasty. Later, there were generic classifications of the Tang Poetry(唐诗), the Song Prose Poems(宋词), the Yuan Verse Poems(元曲), and the Ming and Qing Novel(明清小说). Chen Wangdao's *Principles of Rhetoric* (1932) indicated the beginning of modern Chinese stylistics. The foundation of The Chinese Association of Rhetoric in 1980 marked the new era of Chinese stylistics, when more attention was paid to language and writing techniques. The publication of the *Stylistics Series*, edited by Tong Qingbing, in the mid 1990s showed that Chinese stylistics also borrows from the Western views of style and stylistics.

Western Stylistics

In the Western world, the Greeks' and the Romans' interest in style was combined with their study of rhetoric. They stressed the persuasive function of style. It was Longinus (213 — 273 A.D.), the alleged author of *On the*

Sublime, who paid more attention to the aesthetic function of style. Charles Bally's *Traité de stylistique française* (1909) was the beginning of Western modern stylistics. Its target of study was the style of oral language. In the 1960s and 1970s, stylistics was recognized as an independent discipline which focused its study on the form and function of style. In the 1980s discourse stylistics was in vogue with its emphasis on the mutual interaction between the two sides of the conversation participants. The 1990s witnessed the development of socio-historical/socio-cultural stylistics whose purpose was to reveal the implied relationship of ideology and power. Recently, the trend was that different schools of stylistics compete for development and new schools emerge every now and then. (Shen, 2000) For example, we have, for the time being, social stylistics, politicized stylistics, functional stylistics, forensic stylistics, feminist stylistics, pragmatic stylistics, contextualized stylistics, cognitive poetics, cognitive stylistics, interface studies, etc. (Bex, Burke & Stockwell, 2000; Chloupek & Nekvapil, 1993; Mills, 1995; Gaitet, 1992; Jucker, 1992; McMenamin, 1993; Stockwell, 2002; Semino, 2002)

Chinese Studies of Western Stylistics

Wang Zuoliang's article "Studies of English style" (1963) was the first Chinese study of Western stylistics. His article collection *Essays in English Style* (1980) marked the formal beginning of Chinese studies of Western stylistics. In 1985, the National Ministry of Education organized the designing of the *Teaching Syllabus* for the course "English Stylistics" and ever since then Stylistics has been a university course in the departments of foreign languages and literatures. The late 1990s witnessed new developments of stylistic studies: the first national conference on stylistics was held in Nanjing in 1999; the second in Jinan in 2000 and the third in Chongqing in 2002. The year of 2004 witnessed the foundation of "The China Society of Stylistics" and from 2006, the combined conferences of "The Chinese National Conference on Stylistics" and "The International Conference on Stylistics" became a well-established biyearly academic event.

Since the foundation of new China, 1128 articles and about 20 books on stylistics have been published. (Hu & Liu, 2000) Our statistic results revealed two very interesting points. Firstly, Chinese stylistic studies are carried out in the departments of Chinese and literature but Chinese studies of Western stylistics are carried out in the departments of foreign languages and literatures. However, there have been mutual influences between the two types of studies. Secondly, studies of stylistics are roughly divided into three

branches: literary stylistics, general stylistics and theoretical stylistics. ①
Figure 11.2 illustrates the branches of stylistics.

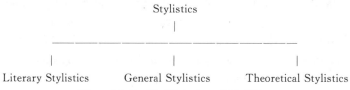

Figure 11.2　The Branches of Stylistics

Literary stylistics studies the styles of literary works. An example of literary stylistics is the chapter entitled "Language and literature" in Hu and Jiang's *Linguistics: A Course Book* (2001).② General stylistics studies the styles of all the varieties of language use other than that of literature. One acknowledged example of general stylistics is Crystal and Davy's *Investigating English Style* (1969).③ Theoretical stylistics is concerned with the concept of style and the theoretical models of stylistic analysis. The present book of advanced studies in linguistics is mainly concerned with this branch of stylistics.

11.2　Style and Stylistics

11.2.1　What Is Style?

STYLE is a rather elusive concept. It is not defined in a strictly logical way and specialists from different walks of life often have different views of style.

According to the artist, style refers to the constant form, elements, qualities and expression in the art of an individual or a group. It may also refer to the whole activity of an individual or society, as in speaking of a "life-style" or the "style of a civilization."

According to the archaeologist, style is exemplified in a motif or pattern, or in some directly grasped quality of the work of art, which helps to localize and date the work and to establish connections between groups of works or between cultures. It may be a symptomatic trait like the nonaesthetic features of an artifact and can be studied as a diagnostic means for its own sake as an important constituent of culture.

---

① See, Hu Zhuanglin, 2000. *Theoretical Stylistics*, Beijing: Foreign Languages Teaching and Research Press. p. 4.

② Liu Shisheng, "Language and literature", in Hu Zhuanglin and Jiang Wangqi, eds., 2001, *Linguistics: A Course Book* (2nd ed.) Bejing: Peking University Press.

③ D. Crystal and D. Davy, 1969. *Investigating English style*. London: Longman.

According to the historian of art, style is a means of tracing relationships between schools of art. It is a system of forms with a quality and a meaningful expression through which the personality of the artist and the broad outlook of a group are visible. It is a vehicle of expression within the group, communicating and fixing certain values of religious, social and moral life through the emotional suggestiveness of forms. It is a common ground against which innovation and the individuality of particular works may be measured.

According to the synthesizing historian of culture, style is a manifestation of the culture as a whole, the visible sign of its unity. The presence of the same style in a wide range of arts is often considered a sign of the integration of a culture. The style reflects or projects the "the inner form" of collective thinking and feeling.

According to the critic, style is a value term or a quality. For example, a painter has style. It is applied mainly to individual artists.

11.2.2 For Whom the Stylistician Works? Writer? Text? Reader? Context? Or Meaning?

According to Roman Jakobson (1960)[①], there are six constitutive factors in any speech event:

It seems that the analyses of style by different generations of stylisticians focus on certain factors of the speech event. These factors are, according to our understanding, writer, text, reader, context, and meaning. In the rest of this chapter, we shall discuss these issues of stylistics in a somewhat diachronic way.

11.3 Style as Rhetoric: The Initial Stage of Stylistics

Stylistics dates back to the study of rhetoric by the ancient Greeks and Romans.

According to Plato's account of Gorgias (485—380 B. C.), rhetoric is an art or a craft. It is the knowledge about speech. It makes men powerful at speaking and understanding the things they speak about. It is the power to

---

① Roman Jakobson, 1960. "Closing statement: linguistics and poetics," in Thomas A. Sebeok, ed. *Style in Language*. UN: The Belknap Press of Harvard University.

② Related to these factors, there are six functions.

persuade all the public bodies in which a large mass of citizens makes decisions. In other words, rhetoric is the manufacturer of conviction. What rhetoric induces is not knowledge (which is always true) but belief (which may be either true or false). Rhetoric is neutral between the good use and the bad use but the rhetor, the person who is skilful at using rhetoric, is more persuasive and powerful than other people who are not.

Plato (*circa* 428—*circa* 348 B. C.) thinks that, Gorgias' rhetoric is actually a practical skill in flattery, something less than an art, an ignoble technique. It is ignoble because it is bad for society and it is not an art because it cannot give any account of the nature of the things it offers... and so cannot explain the reason why it is offered. Plato tries to find the true form of rhetoric and the method he uses for the finding is that of the dialectic which consists in a joint use of collection and division.

The method of collection means that the art of rhetoric is taken as a whole and its function is to influence men's souls by means of words. The method of division means to set forth the conditions necessary to make speech-writing an art. That is, you must know the truth about the subject that you speak or write about. In other words, you must be able to isolate it in definition. You must know how to divide it into kinds until you reach the limit of the division. You must have a corresponding discernment of the nature of the soul, discover the type of speech appropriate to each nature, and order and arrange your discourse accordingly, addressing a variegated soul in a variegated style that ranges over the whole gamut of tones, and a simple soul in a simple style. We can see that Plato conceived a true art of rhetoric to be a consolidation of dialectic with psychological study-applicable to all discourse, public and private, persuasive and expository, which aims to influence men's souls.

To a certain extent, Plato focused on the content of rhetoric. His student Aristotle (384—322 B. C.), who was said to be the father of literary criticism and the analysis of style, in contrast, focused on the form. In his monograph, *Rhetoric*, Aristotle has a thorough analysis of rhetoric.

According to Aristotle, rhetoric is a counterpart of dialectic. Both deal with such subjects as fall within the scope of all men's knowledge and belong to no distinct science. Therefore all men have a share in both; for all men, up to a certain point, attempt to criticize and support an argument, and to conduct a defense and an accusation.

Aristotle defines rhetoric as the faculty of discovering all the available means of persuasion; he then divides means of persuasion or proof into the artistic, which is furnished by the speaker (bred by habit), and the nonartistic, which is furnished by the external evidence (without method).

Thus the method of rhetoric may be discovered. To discover method is the same as teaching an art. Both these methods, the artistic and the nonartistic, are possible. We can clearly reduce the processes to a system: for it is possible to investigate the causes of success in those who practice them with familiar knowledge, and those who practice them at random. Therefore we can find three kinds of persuasion: ethos, arising from the speaker's personal qualities; pathos, arising from the audience's emotions and logical proof, depending upon an argument.

The logical proof consists therefore chiefly in proofs, which are inferences. All inferences are syllogisms. And a logician, if he would observe the difference between a plain syllogism and an enthymeme, which is a rhetorical or elliptical syllogism, would make the best rhetorician. Armed with this knowledge of rhetoric, one will write good speeches. The speeches themselves may be forensic (judicial), deliberative (political) or epideictic (occasional), depending upon their ends, times, and subjects.

11.4 One Style or Several Styles?

The well-known Roman orator, politician and philosopher Cicero (106—43B. C.) thinks that in an oration, as in life, nothing is harder than to determine what is appropriate. That is, the orator must have an eye to propriety not only in thought but also in language.

The orator of eloquence will be one who is able to speak in court or in deliberative bodies so as to prove, to please, and to sway or persuade. To prove is the first necessity and one should use the plain style. To please is to charm people and one should use the middle style. To sway or persuade is to win victory and one should use the vigorous or grand style. The man who controls and combines these three varied styles needs rare judgment and great endowment; for he will decide what is needed at any point, and will be able to speak in any way which the case requires.

The plain style is restrained and plain. The orator follows the ordinary language. The audience is sure that they can speak in that fashion as well. The language will be pure Latin, plain and clear. The syntax should be loose but not rambling; so that it may seem to move freely but not to wander without restraint. For diction, the orator will not be bold in coining words and he will be modest in the use of metaphor, sparing in the use of archaisms, but somewhat subdued in using the other embellishments of language and of thought.

The middle style is fuller and somewhat more robust (marked by richness) than the plain style, but plainer than the grand style. There is a minimum of vigor, and a maximum of charm. All the ornaments are appropriate to this type of oration. Demetrius of Phalerum is a conspicuous example of this type in Greece. All figures of speech and many figures of thought belong to this style. E. g., "Dread Africa trembled with terrible tumult"; "I am bereft of citadels and towns."

The orator of the grand style is magnificent, opulent, stately, and ornate. He undoubtedly has the greatest power. This is the man whose brilliance and fluency have caused an admiring nation to let eloquence attain the highest power in the state. This eloquence has power to sway men's minds and move them in every possible way. It storms the feelings; it creeps in; it implants new ideas and uproots the old.

The eloquent orator is one who can discuss trivial matters in a plain style, matters of moderate significance in the tempered style, and weighty affairs in the grand manner. That is, he can discuss commonplace matters simply, lofty subjects impressively, and topics ranging between in a temperate style.

The previous scholars' interest in style was combined with their study of rhetoric. They stressed the persuasive function of style. But Longinus (213 — 273 A. D.), the alleged author of *On the Sublime*, pays more attention to the aesthetic function of style. Rather than declaring "poetic inspiration" a dangerous divine madness, as did Plato, Longinus inquires how it is best employed. His treatment of the sublime is an effort to balance and blend inspiration and rhetorical mastery. Thus, though he writes in the tradition of classical rhetoricians, devoting much space to a discussion of various rhetorical devices, he is not interested merely in persuasion and does not view tropes as merely supporting argument. Thus, the effect of elevated language upon an audience is not persuasion but transport or ecstasy. The reason is that our persuasions we can usually control, but the influences of the sublime bring power and irresistible might to bear, and reign sure over every hearer. Beethoven's Symphony Number 5, *The Fate*, is a very good example of this kind.

Then we must raise the question whether there is such a thing as an art of the sublime or lofty. Longinus' answer is yes. Sublimity is the echo of a great soul. A lofty tone is innate, and does not come by teaching; nature is the only art that can compass it. Yet the expression of the sublime is more exposed to danger when it goes its own way without the guidance of knowledge, when it is left at the mercy of mere momentum and ignorant audacity. So we can see that Longinus holds the view of style as sublimity. In other words there is only one style.

St. Augustine puts forward the view of Christian style. Since the Ciceronian rhetorical doctrine insists that three levels of style be employed, Augustine is careful to show that all three styles exist in the Scripture. He is unwilling to relegate rhetoric to the position of a mere preliminary study. Instead he wishes to use it in the active services of the ministry. His idea is that a Christian orator recognizes no absolute levels of subject matter; only the immediate context and purpose can tell him which level of style to employ. Therefore, a Christian orator's subject is always Christian revelation, and this can never be base (low or plain) or in-between (middle). Thus, there is no need for the classification of plain style or middle style or grand style. Actually, there is only one style: the Christian style.

11.5 Aspects of Style: The Writer-style as Writer's Individual/Personal Singularities

11.5.1 Buffon: Style Is the Man Himself

The Romantic movement, with its expressive poetics and cult of personality, encouraged and extended the idea of style, and the 19th century is notable for a flowering of many diverse and idiosyncratic styles. George Louis Leclerc de Buffon (1707—1788), a French naturalist, is one representative. His motto, *Le style, c'est l'homme même* (Style is the man himself), is a symbol of the time. His theory of style includes the following points: (Babb, 1972)

1) Absolute order. It is simply the order and movement one gives to one's thought. The writer must first form another more general and more absolute order, where only primary aspects and fundamental ideas shall enter. Style is a conscious activity because it involves careful planning. It is a single mold of a man's own. It cannot be subtracted from the work. But a good style is such only by virtue of the truths it presents. It involves personal experience and meditation.

2) The sublime. One must work on the soul, and touch the sensibilities by addressing the mind. The sublime style is to be found in lofty, noble topics. The sublime style can be attained only by one who surveys nature as an ordered whole from the highest vantage point, and who imitates it from this perspective.

3) Contrast. One aspect of an object is presented, while the remaining sides are put in shadow.

4) Substance (content) and form. Content refers to knowledge, facts, and discoveries. It is alterable and belongs to the realm of generality. These things are external to man. Style is the man himself. (This is

usually interpreted to mean that a writer's personality is somehow reflected in his style and that a careful examination of the style will uncover the man.)

5) External and internal factors. Whereas the subject-matter of a scientific treatise is external to the man, and would exist whether the man existed or not, the style, or the order in which the man arranges his thoughts on the subject-matter, springs from the man himself; the style is so much of the man as exist in the ordering of his thoughts. The facts are always there and belong to Nature, but the presentation, the style, are not natural but human or artificial.

So, to speak in one sentence, style is the man himself.

Buffon's concept of style has the following influences. The linguists apply the concept universally and ascribe to every individual speaking an "idiolect" or way of using language, which is unique. The literary critics take it as a useful and legitimate concept and regard the works by the same author as the literary articulation of the man. The idea that every writer displays his own unique "signature" in the way he uses language has been valuable in setting problems of authenticity.

But Buffon's concept of style also receives a lot of criticisms. One is that it is not very convincing because the conclusions reached are usually either circular or too general to mean anything. Another challenge is the degree of conscious control the writer has over his style. One view holds that the writer can exert no control over the style at all, all of it being determined by habits, associations, and conditioning. The other view is that the writer can consciously control and artistically shape every detail of his utterance. But in our opinion, some truth lies at both of these poles.

11.5.2 Spitzer: The Philological Circle and Its Methods

PHILOLOGY is the traditional term for the study of language history, as carried on by "comparative philologists" since the late 18th century. It also sometimes includes (though not in Britain) the study of literary texts, as in the study of texts as part of cultural or political research. The *raison d'être* of philology is as follows: 1) The soul of a nation can be found in its literature; 2) In the language of its outstanding works of literature can be found the spirit of the nation; and 3) One can distinguish the soul of a particular writer in his particular language, as Buffon and his followers did.

Spitzer used the methods of philology to do stylistic analysis and put forward the concept of "philological circle." This philological circle and its methods include the following points. 1) The individual stylistic deviation from the general norm must represent a historical step taken by the writer. 2) If there is a certain consistency of stylistic deviations, there must be "something the matter." 3) There must be a common denominator for all or most of these deviations. 4) These deviations indicate a common spiritual etymon, i. e. , the psychological root of several individual traits of style in a writer. 5) The writer has a pseudo-objective motivation in the use of deviations. 6) The writer is a kind of solar system into whose orbit all categories of things are attracted; language, motivation, plot, are all only satellites of this mythological entity. 7) The individual mind is a reflection of the mind of the nation of the 20th century. 8) Make the return trip to all the other groups of observations in order to find whether the "inward form" one has tentatively constructed gives an accent of the whole. 9) Work from the surface to the "inward life-center" of the work of art: first observe details, then group these details, seek to integrate them into a creative principle which may have been present in the soul of the artist, finally make the return trip to all the other groups of observation.

Spitzer's philological circle and methods received many criticisms. One strong criticism is against the circularity of arguments. That is, the explanation of a linguistic fact by an assumed psyche-logical process for which the only evidence is the fact to be explained. Spitzer argues that philological stylistics is not satisfied with psychologizing one trait but bases its assumptions on several traits carefully grouped and integrated. One should embrace all the linguistic traits observable with a given author.

Another criticism is about the "viciousness" of the philological circle. Harold Cherniss is against the "the biographical fashion in literary criticism." "The intuition" which discovers in the writings of an author the "natural law" and "inward form" of his personality, is proof against all objections, logical and philological; but, while one must admit that a certain native insight, call it direct intelligence of intuition as you please, is required for understanding any text, it is all the same, a vicious circle to intuit the nature of the author's personality from his writing and then to interpret these writings in accordance with the inner necessity of that intuited personality. Moreover, once the intuition of the individual critic is accepted as the ultimate basis of all interpretation, the comprehension of a literary work becomes a completely private affair, for the intuition of any one interpreter has no more objective validity than that of any other. Spitzer explains that the "circle" is vicious only when an uncontrolled intuition is allowed to exercise itself upon the literary works; the procedure from details to the inner core and back again is not in itself at all vicious. In fact, the intelligent reading is based precisely on that philological circle.

We can see that both the critics and Spitzer's views have their own reasons. When we do stylistic analysis, we usually take a short poem or a paragraph or page of prose, then read it over and over again and try our best to find something that matters. So the secret of the philological circle needs to be further studied.

11.6 Aspects of Style: The Text-style as Linguistic Sameness (Structural Equivalence)

Saussure's structural linguistics in the beginning decades of the 20th century initiated structural stylistics. Charles Bally was the first to apply structural linguistics to the analysis of style. Bally's *Traité de stylistique française* (1909) focuses on the description of oral language. Roman Jakobson and Richard Ohmann, however, are interested in the written, literary language. In this chapter we only have space to have brief discussions of Jakobson's projection theory and Ohmann's structural transformation theory.

11.6.1 Jakobson's Projection Theory: Style as Structural Equivalence

The 1920s and 1930s laid the foundations of American structuralism, which attained methodological perfection in these decades. Structuralism laid out a set of efficient techniques for discovering the structure of language. As Harold Whitehall (1951) claimed, "as no science can go beyond mathematics, no criticism can go beyond its linguistics." There are many structural stylisticians at that time but among all of them, Jakobson is the most representative. His theories of structural stylistics is explained in his "Closing statement: linguistics and poetics" [1] delivered at the first international conference on style and stylistics held in 1958 at Indiana University in the United States. The following are his theories.

11.6.1.1 Poetics and Linguistics

Poetics deals primarily with the question: What makes a verbal message a work of art? In other words, it deals with the problem of verbal structure. Since linguistics is the global science of verbal structure, poetics may be regarded as an integral part of linguistics. Linguistics is likely to explore all possible problems of relation between discourse and the "universe of discourse." Poetics, in contradistinction to linguistics, is concerned with evaluation.

Many poetic features belong not only to the science of language but also to the whole theory of signs, that is, to general semiotics. This statement is valid not only for verbal art but also for all varieties of language since language shares many properties with some other systems of signs or even with all of them. The question of relations between the word and the world concerns not

---

[1] In Thomas A. Sebeok, ed., 1960. *Style in Language*. Cambridge, Mass.: The M.I.T. Press.

only verbal art but also actually all kinds of discourse.

11.6.1.2 The Factors of Communication and the Functions of Language

Language must be investigated in all the varieties of its functions. An outline of these functions demands a concise survey of the constitutive factors in any speech event, in any act of verbal communication. Please see Section 11.2, "The analysis of style," and Footnote 2 Page 448, for these factors and the related functions. Notice that each of these six factors determines a different function of language but we could hardly find verbal messages that would fulfill only one function.

The REFERENTIAL function is denotative and cognitive; it is the leading task of numerous messages. The EMOTIVE function is a direct expression of the speaker's attitude toward what he is speaking about; it is represented by interjections. The CONATIVE function finds its purest grammatical expression in the vocative and imperative; it is not liable to a truth test; it is not convertible into interrogative sentences. The PHATIC function establishes, prolong, or discontinue communication; e. g. , it checks whether the channel works ("Hello" "Do you hear me?"). The METALINGUAL function is not only necessary in scientific research but also important in everyday usage, e. g. , when the addresser and/or the addressee need to check up whether they use the same code, speech is focused on the code ("What do you mean?" "What is 'sophomore'?"). The POETIC function is not the sole function of verbal art but only its dominant, determining function, whereas in all other verbal activities it acts as a subsidiary, accessory constituent.

11.6.1.3 The Empirical Linguistic Criterion of the Poetic Function

What is the empirical linguistic criterion of the poetic function? In particular, what is the indispensable feature inherent in any piece of poetry? The answer is that the SELECTION is produced on the basis of equivalence, similarity and dissimilarity, synonymy and anonymity (e. g. selection: child, kid, youngster, tot, etc.); the COMBINATION, the build up of the sequence, is based on contiguity.

The poetic function projects the principle of equivalence from the axis of selection into the axis of combination. Poetic language seeks in its CHAIN, or combinatory relationships—its syntactic elements—the same properties of close coherence that are to be found among the individual members of a CHOICE relationship, or paradigm.

Jakobson uses this theory to do stylistic analysis but the analytical work of Jakobson and his followers are said to be purely descriptive. They simply explore the nature of internal structures—that is, the relations between signs at different levels—phonic, syntactic, lexical, metrical, etc. Although the descriptions are indispensable as a first step, they have the disadvantage of providing no answer to important questions of interpretation. Jakobson does not analyze the function of the structure described and rejects the traditional criteria of code or author considered external to the message and stylistically irrelevant.

11.6.2 Ohmann's Structural Transformation Theory: Style as Transformation

According to Richard Ohmann, a style is a way of writing, a characteristic use of language—that is what the word means.

11.6.2.1 Deep Structure and Surface Structure

The basic precepts of TG grammatical theory, Ohmann shows, can characterize more exactly Buffon's famous statement, *le style, c'est l'homme meme*.

Language can be characterized at two levels of representation: deep structure and surface structure. The semantic interpretation proceeds from the deep structure but the phonetic interpretation proceeds from the surface structure. The two levels are related by an ordered set of transformations, which are meaning preserving. Given this theoretical framework, a writer's typical exploitation of particular kinds of transformation (particularly optional transformations) may be said to constitute his syntactic style.

A writer can vary the kinds of structures he employs in order to produce corresponding variations in style. Often a stylistic effect can be produced by just a slight shift in syntactic structure.

11.6.2.2 Four Kinds of Changes

A given sentence can be subjected to four kinds of changes.

1) Addition: a word, phrase or clause is added, e.g. *The poem is complex.* -> *The poem is, I think, complex.* This syntactic change covers such modifications as the insertion of adjectives before nouns, intensifiers before adjectives and adverbs, the doubling of items, parenthesis, polysyndeton, anaphora, parallelism, seriation, etc.

2) Omission: a word, phrase or clause is omitted, e.g. *The poem is, I think, complex.* -> *The poem is complex.* This syntactic change includes asyndeton (omission of the connective, e.g. *I came. I saw. I conquered.*) and ellipsis (leaving out duplicated parts of the structure, e.g. transitional words like *however, therefore, then* can be omitted).

3) Transposition: the elements are rearranged in different order. e.g. *On first reading, the poem is complex.* -> *The poem is complex on first reading.* With this syntactic change, the style variation opportunities are greater:

— Adjectives and some adverbs may occasionally be placed before or after the words they modify, e. g. enough money/money enough.

— Adverbial phrases and clauses may often be placed initially or finally, sometimes even medially.

— Sentence adverbs (however, therefore) may be placed almost anywhere in a sentence.

— Word order inversion.

— The periodic sentence and the loose sentence.

4) Substitution: an element is replaced by another, e. g. *The poem is complex.* -> *The poem is complicated.* A substitution provides the greatest range and number of options to the extent that these options should be further subdivided into lexical, morphological, syntactic, and figurative or rhetorical classes.

11. 6. 2. 3 Structures and Transformations

Ohmann applies these theories to his stylistic analysis. He selects brief passages from Faulkner, Hemingway, James, and Lawrence and reduces the passages to strings of kernel sentences. One of his main points is that writers who have a distinctive style often have a characteristic way of combining kernel sentences, that is, they have a favorite group of transformational rules. According to his analysis, Faulkner favors the relative clause transformation, the conjunction transformation and the comparative transformation, all of which are additive, that is, they add "information about a thing with a minimum of repetition." Hemingway relies on the transformations that produce indirect discourse. James' fondness for self-embedded constructions at the expense of the more normal right branching and left-branching ones. Lawrence favors the operation of deletion.

Ohmann also receives many criticisms. One is that the basic theory itself has avoided explicit discussion of style. Some transformationalists who dismiss instances of variation as stylistic seem to do so to imply that it is somebody else's job, not theirs, to discuss them in greater detail. Another criticism is that the description of English along transformational generative lines has not reached a stage whereby one can state exactly the degree of deviation in a particular instance (this is particularly true with regard to selection restriction rules) and indeed it is often only when one considers deviant sentences such as occur in literature that the extent of the problem becomes apparent.

11.7 Aspects of Style: The Text-style as Linguistic Difference (Deviation or Foregrounding)

Mukarovsky speaks of style as "foregrounding," i. e. bringing to attention, making new, "the violation of the norm of the standard." The systematic violation is what makes possible the poetic utilization of language; without this possibility there would be no poetry. The reason is that everyday usage, "autonomizes or conventionalizes language to the point that its users no longer perceive its expressive or aesthetic potential"; poetry must de-automatize or "foreground" language by violating the norms of everyday language. That is, there are, among other things, certain structural differences between poetic language and standard language. These violations or de-automatizations or foregroundings or differences are called "deviations." Geoffery Leech did a systematic study of these deviations.

11.7.1 Types of Deviation (Leech, 1969)

1) Lexical deviation
Neologism versus nonce-formations
NEOLOGISM refers to the invention of "new words." We call new words NONCE-FORMATIONS if they are made up "for the nonce," i.e. for a single occasion only, rather than as serious attempts to augment the English word-stock for some new need.

  ex. The widow-making unchilding unfathering deeps.
        ——Hopkins, *The Wretch of the Deutschland*

2) Grammatical deviation
An example of this type of deviation is illustrated in the repetition of generative construction.

  ex. Our hearts' clarity's hearth's fire, our thoughts' chivalry's throng's Lord.
        ——Hopkins, *The Wretch of the Deutschland*

3) Phonological deviation
This includes a number of cases: The omission of the unstressed syllable so that the line may conform to the metrical scheme:
  ex. What was th'impediment that broke this off?
The gradual and unintentional loss of the unstressed:
  ex. esquire-> squire
The loss of a final letter or syllable or more:
  ex. mine-> my
    curiosity-> curio
Special pronunciation for the convenience of rhyming:
  ex. The noun "wind" [wind] is pronounced like the verb "wind" [waind].
Certain 19th century poets placed word stresses in unusual places:
  ex. ba'luster (Tennyson)

bas'tard (Browning)

'July (D. G. Rossetti)

4) Graphological deviation

Two American poets who explore possibilities of purely visual patterning in Poetry are William Carlos Williams and E. E. Cummings. Capitalization, spacing, and punctuation become expressive devices, instead of symbols to be used according to typographic custom.

> ex. seeker of truth
> follow no path
> all paths lead where
> truth is here

5) Semantic deviation

It is reasonable to translate SEMANTIC DEVIATION mentally into "nonsense" or "absurdity," so long as we realize that "sense" is used in a strictly literal-minded way.

> ex. The child is the father of the man. (Wordsworth)

6) Dialectal deviation

DIALECTISM is the borrowing of features of socially or regionally defined dialects. It is quite often used by storytellers and humorists. For example, in *The Shepherd's Calendar*, Spencer uses homely provincial words like "heydeguyes" (a type of dance), "rontes" (young bullock), "weanell" (newly weaned kid or lamb), etc.

7) Deviation of register

Register borrowing in poetry is almost always accompanied by the further incongruity of register mixing, or the use in the same text of features characteristic of different registers.

> ex. To-day we have naming of parts. Yesterday,
> We had daily cleaning. And to-morrow morning,
> We shall have what to do after firing. But today,
> To-day we have naming of parts. *Japonica*
> *Glistens like coral in all of the neighboring gardens*, (our italics)
> And to-day we have naming of parts.
> ——Henry Reed, "Lessons of the War: 1. Naming of Parts"

Obviously, there are two registers in this stanza, that of rifle instruction and that of lyrical description. The effect of mingling these two registers is ironical in a bolder, more clear-cut, but nevertheless equally effective way.

8) Deviation of historical period

The poet is not restricted to the language of his own particular period. The medium of English poetry is the English language viewed as a historical whole, not just as a synchronous system shared by the writer and his contemporaries. James Joyce thought that a writer must be familiar with the history of his language—that he should be a philologist. T. S. Eliot insisted that "no poet ... has his complete meaning alone. His significance, his appreciation is the appreciation of the relation to dead poets and artists." What a poet sees as his linguistic heritage may even include dead languages such as Latin and Greek.

> ex. The association of man and woman
> In dausinge, signifying matrimonie—
> A dignified and commodious sacrament,
> Two and two, necessarye conjunction,
> Holding eche other by the hand or the arm
> Which betokeneth concorde.
> ——T. S. Eliot, "East Coker"

The alternation between ancient and modern, emphasized by spelling, is similar in inspiration and effect to the register mixing which Eliot employs extensively, both in this poem and elsewhere.

9) The use of foreign language

The use of foreign language may suggest the speaker's high education or an attempt to catch fashion. It is often found in literature. For example, Leo Tolstoy's famous Russian novel *Anna Karanina* has a lot of French in it. Qian Zhongshu's famous Chinese novel *The Citadel* has a lot of English in it. It can be also found in everyday language. China is in the WTO (the World Trade Organization) now and many Chinese people use some foreign language while speaking in Chinese.

> ex. 见了面说 hello,来是 come 去是 go.

11.7.2 The Significance of Deviation

Linguistic deviations (artistically) can be significant in the following situations.

1) When the deviation communicates something

> ex. My aunt suffers from terrible authorities.
> Like your plays?
> The Houwe of Commons.

They may convey quite a bit of information: malapropism (telling us something about the education, character, etc.), a foreigner's imperfect command of English, the printer's printing mistake, the author's careless proof-reading, etc.

2) When it communicates what was intended by its author

This definition of "significance" narrows the first one to exclude malapropism and other sorts of linguistic blunders.

3) When it is judged or felt by the reader to be significant

This is the most unsatisfactory of all: it merely says that the significance of a poem lies ultimately in the mind of the reader, just as beauty is said to lie in the eye of the beholder. We may say that what interpretation on it is to be given as a subjective matter.

11.8 Aspects of Style: The Reader-style as Reader's Response

With the style as structural equivalence theory, Roman Jakobson and Levi-Strauss and other structural stylisticians did a lot of descriptive stylistic analysis. But stylisticians like Michael Riffaterre, I. A. Richards, Stanley Fish, and others think that what counts most in the matter of style is neither the writer nor the text. Actually, style exists in the reader's understanding and appreciation process. In the present section we shall discuss Riffaterre's ideas in this respect.

Riffaterre attacks Jakobson and Levi-Strauss in the following points. 1) Some of the structures on which they build their reading are merely linguistic facts of the text. 2) They are not determinant stylistic facts. They cannot strike the reader as unpredictable and thus significant. 3) Jakobson and Levi-Strauss violate the rule which should govern comparative structural analysis—that comparison may not properly be made between the mere data appearing in different structures, but only between the structures themselves. Riffaterre's viewpoints are as follows.

11.8.1 Stylistic Facts versus Linguistic Facts

Stylistic facts	Linguistic facts
Style stresses	Language expresses
Writer's own attitude toward the message	Oriented toward communication of the message itself
Employing a number of unpredictable elements precisely to secure and control the attention of the reader	A high incidence of predictable verbal forms
Active, marked	Neutral, unmarked

11.8.2 Reader's Response

To isolate objectively the whole range of unpredictable elements, according to Riffaterre, the analyst should gather the responses of as many readers as he can—however various their literary training. The reason for this is that those responses will identify the "stylistic facts" which the analyst must take into account before proceeding to interpretation. That is, interpretation is a kind of reader-oriented process.

11.8.3 The Absence of the Reader

The literary text is a very special speech act: the speaker/poet is not present. Any attempt to bring him back only produces interference. The reason is that what we know of him we know from history. This knowledge is external to the message. Or we have found it out by rationalizing and distorting the message.

Therefore, the message and the addressee/reader are the only factors. The appropriate language of reference is selected from the message. The context is reconstituted from the message. Contact is assured by the control the message has over the reader's attention; it depends upon the degree of that control. All are designed to draw responses from the reader despite any wandering of his attention, despite the evolution of the code and despite the changes in esthetic fashion.

11.8.4 The Responses

The pertinent segmentation of the poem must therefore be based on these responses: they pinpoint in the verbal sequence the location of the devices that trigger them. The response itself testifies objectively to the actuality of a contact. The stylistician should guard against two possibilities. One is to empty the response of its content, i.e. a reader may rationalize his responses to fit into his sphere of interest and its technical terminology. The other is to multiply the response, i.e. a reader's response may be interfered with by his physical fatigue or the evolving of the language since the time the poem was coded.

11.8.5 The Superreader

Riffaterre invented the concept of SUPERREADER as his tool of stylistic analysis. This superreader follows exactly the normal reading process, perceives the poem as its linguistic shape dictates, starts at the beginning and screens pertinent structures (and only pertinent structures). Each point of the text that holds up the superreader is tentatively considered a component of the poetic structure. Such components or units of the text are always pointed out by a number of informants who usually give divergent rationalizations. These units are lexical elements of the sentence interrelated by their contrasting characteristics. The contrasts they create is what forces them upon the reader's attention. Those contrasts result from their unpredictability within the context.

11.8.6 Comments on Riffaterre's Theory

Riffaterre illustrates his theory with a detailed analysis of Baudelaire's poem "Les chat" (The Cats). He was criticized by others. Then he put forward the notion of Average Reader. But the "reactions of the reader" take us outside the message and show again the uselessness of a stylistics, which is purely formal and immanent to the text. Who is the reader anyway? Finally, even Riffaterre himself renounced his notion of Average Reader for some Ideal or Super Reader who seems to be very much the stylistician himself.

11.9 Aspects of Style: The Context: Style as Function

The linguists of the Prague School formulated the principles of the stylistic differentiation of the standard language in the context of the conception of language as an open dynamic system of signs functionally utilized.

11.9.1 Linguistics versus Stylistics

1) The integration of linguistic analysis

In linguistics, the lexical or grammatical analysis determines the different structural elements and processes. Stylistics regards speech as a unit and tries to establish general stylistic features of each utterance. The subject of stylistics is the structure of a concrete act of speech, and the mode of selection and utilization of its particular elements. It is the use of particular language devices in particular zones of the national language. This is the functional view of language.

2) The functional and the stylistic differentiation of the standard language

The functional aspect in the stylistics of the Prague School was elaborated mainly by B. Havranck. He distinguishes four types of language style:

— the communicative function in the area of everyday communication, the conversational form;

— the practical technical communication, the matter-of-fact or technically communicative form;

— the theoretical or scientific technical communication, the scientific form;

— the aesthetic function of the communication, the poetic form.

3) Functional styles

Language can be used to realize many functions, each of which has its own style. Some of these functional styles are as follows.

— matter-of-fact communication, information, e.g. classroom English;

— exhortation, appeal, e.g. the editorial language;

— general or popular explanation, e.g. textbooks;

— technical explanation, exposition, proof, e. g. scientific writing;

— codifying formulations, e. g. mathematic formulas.

4) Manner of response

There is a difference between the private functional style and the public functional style and they both have oral and written forms. Their combinations may be as follows.

— the private discourse: in dialogue or monologue;

— public speech-making: discussion or speech;

— the written private utterance: a personal letter;

— the written public utterance: a notice, poster, journalistic or book writing.

5) Functional style and functional language

The functional style is determined by the specific purpose or function of the given act of speech (parole). The functional language is determined by the over-all-purpose of the totality of means of expression, a function of the linguistic pattern (langue).

6) Individual and interindividual use

Within a standard national language we therefore distinguish

— the style of individual utterances;

— the style of utterances made by the same author;

— the objective, functional style (or style of language), e. g. the journalistic language, the scientific language, etc. ;

— the stylistic forms within particular objective styles, e. g. in the journalist style, there are leading articles, reports, etc.

In M. A. K. Halliday's terms, functional styles refer to the "field" (the ideational); the private functional styles and the public functional styles refer to the "tenor" (the interpersonal); the oral forms and the written forms refer to the "mode" (the textual).

11.9.2　Stylistic Factors and Differentiations

The different objective styles of standard language are determined by objective factors. The factors connected with meaning are:

1) The function of communication

— communicative: colloquial style;

— practically professional: style of the official, technical and professional language;

— theoretically professional: the scientific language;

— mass communications: journalistic style;

— aesthetically communicative: works of art.

2) The purpose of the act of speech

— objective statement: the interpretative style;

— appeal: the journalistic style.
3) The speaker's attitude to the theme
   — serious: official style;
   — humorous: the comical nature of the utterance;
   — depreciating: ironical or invective nature of the utterance.
4) The mode of the theme
   — dynamic: narration;
   — static: description.
5) The degree of spontaneity
   — the style of entirely spontaneous utterances;
   — that of prepared utterances.

The elements connected with the situation of the utterance:
1) Private or official setting: the style of the private or official utterances
2) Bilateral: the style of dialogues
   Unilateral speech: the style of monologue
3) The contact between the author and the addressee (in the colloquial utterance)
   — the addressee is present: style of situational utterances;
   — the addressee is absent: broadcasting style

The language substances used:
1) Phonic: the style of spoken utterances
2) Graphic: the style of written or printed utterances

The inner differentiation:

Apart from the differentiation of the principal functional styles of the standard language, it seems to be necessary to work out their inner differentiation. The great sphere of the technical functional style appears subdivided into a series of styles. Two examples may be given as follows:

The technical functional style may be divided into proper and popular styles. The proper style is subdivided into scientific and practical styles. The practical style may be further subdivided into styles of instruction, economics, law, administration, etc.

The technical functional style may be also divided into written and spoken styles. The spoken style is subdivided into styles of lecture (prepared), discussion (unprepared), monologue, and dialogue (debates).

Although this is only a rough picture, we can also see the complexity of different styles.

11.9.3 Main Features of the Basic Functional Styles of the Standard Language

The differentiation of the principle functional styles and their inner differentiation is connected with the determination of the principal features of the different styles of the standard language. According to B. Havranck, the basic functional styles of the standard language have three main features.

1) Intellectualization (or rationalization)

The intellectualization culminates in the scientific theoretical discourse, both in the lexical plan and in the grammatical structure. To approximate the expression as much as possible to the rigor of objective (scientific) thinking, in which the terms approximate concepts and the sentences approximate logical judgments.

LEXICAL

— the introduction of new words in technical terms;

— the change of the structure of the vocabulary;

— the number of unequivocal words, specialized words, and abstract summarizing terms, expressing existence, possibility, necessity, the relations of causality, finality, parallelism, etc.;

— a great number of nominal groups of adjectives with the noun;

— the use of the nominal prediction with formal verbs, etc.

GRAMMATICAL

— nominalizes two-member sentences;

— passive constructions;

— the hierarchy of clauses and sentences standing on different levels;

— specified conjunctions; etc.

2) Automation

Automation consists in a use of devices of the language, given in isolation or combination, which does not attract any attention.

3) Foregrounding

Foregrounding means the use of the devices of language in such a way that this use attracts attention and is perceived as uncommon, as non-automatic.

The degree and the mutual proportion of both these means of language characterize different functional styles. For examples, in conversation, both automation and foregrounding coexist; in scientific discourse, automation prevails; in poetic style/essay, foregrounding predominates.

11.9.4 Style as Foregrounding

The function of poetic language consists in the maximum of foregrounding of the utterance. Foregrounding is the opposite of automatization, that is, the deautomatization of an act; the more an act is automatized, the less it is consciously executed; the more it is foregrounded, the more completely conscious does it become. Objectively speaking, automatization schematizes an event; foregrounding means the violation of the scheme.

The standard language in its purest form avoids foregrounding. For example, a new expression, which foregrounds because of its newness, is immediately automatized in a scientific treatise by an exact definition of its meaning. Foregrounding is of course, common in the standard language, e. g. , in journalistic style, even in essays. But here it is always subordinate to communication: its purpose is to attract the reader's attention more closely to the subject matter expressed by the foregrounded means of expression.

In poetic language foregrounding achieves maximum intensity to the extent of pushing communication into the background as the objective of expression one of being used for its own sake; it is not used in the services of communication, but in order to place in the foreground the act of expression (the act of speech itself) for aesthetic purposes.

11.10 Aspects of Style: The Meaning: Style as Meaning Potential

M. A. K. Halliday regards a theory of language as the theory of meaning. His main studies of style are found in "The linguistic study of literary style" in Thomas A. Sebeok's *Style in Language* (ed. 1960) and "Descriptive Linguistics in literary studies" in G. Duthie's *English Studies Today* (ed. 1964).

11.10.1 Linguistic Stylistics

1) Application of linguistics

Linguistic stylistics must be an application, not an extension, of linguistics; this is the only way to ensure the theoretical validity of the statements made. The justification for using linguistic methods in literary analysis is that existing grammatical, lexical, phonological and phonetic theory is already valid and relevant for the purpose. If the linguistic analysis of literature is to be of any value or significance at all it must be done against the background of a general description of the language, using the same theories, methods and categories. A literary text has meaning against the background of the language as a whole, in all its uses.

2) Linguistic context or textual description

Linguistic context

Language does not operate except in the context of other event, any one point made about a piece of text which is under focus raises many further points extending way beyond it into the context. The only ultimately valid unit for textual analysis is the whole text.

Textual description

The linguistic study of literature is textual description, and it is no different from any other textual description; it is not a new branch or a new level or a new kind of linguistics but the application of existing theories and methods. What the linguist does when faced with a literary text is the same as what he does when faced with any text that he is going to describe.

3) Relative frequency and probability

If, for example, all clauses of a particular poem are shown to have the same structure, it is essential to know whether or not this is the only permitted clause structure in the language; if not, what its relative frequency is in a large sample representative of the language in general.

The originality of a person's use of his language consists in his selecting a feature not where it is impossible (has not been previously selected) but where another would be more probable—and even more in his balanced combination of the improbable with the probable, as in the lexis of "Leda and the Swan," which is an interesting blend of old and new collections.

Not only do we need to be able to state accurately the role or a particular pattern or item in the language, what it contrasts with what it may and may not combine with and so on; we way want to know its probability of occurrence under various definable conditions. A text is meaningful not only in virtue of what it is but also in virtue of what it might have been.

4) A comparative study

The most relevant exponent of the "might have been" of a work of literature is another work of literature. Linguistic stylistics is thus essentially a comparative study. All literary analysis, if one is at all interested in the special properties of the language of literary texts or of a particular genre, is essentially comparative. This makes it all the more essential to be consistent, accurate and explicit: to base the analysis firmly on a sound, existing description of the language. We also need to know the relative frequency of this clause structure in other works of the same period and the same genres.

5) Conclusion

We can therefore define linguistic stylistics as the description of literary texts, by methods derived from general linguistic theory using the categories of the description of the language as a whole; and the comparison of each text with others, by the same and by different authors in the same and in different genres. The same point applies to the comparison of texts: it is impossible to compare one text with another unless both have been described in the same way.

Linguistics is not and will never be the whole of literary analysis, and only the literary analyst—not the linguist—can determine the place of linguistics in literary studies. But if a text is to be described at all, then it should be described properly; and this means by the theories and methods developed in linguistics, the subject whose task is precisely to show how language works. The stylistician must have access to theories for the description of all levels of linguistic patterning—grammar, lexis, phonology and phonetics, and their graphic parallels. He must be able to see them in interaction as they must always interact in any language event.

11.10.2 Hallidayan Analysis

The best example of Halliday's stylistic analysis is found in his "Linguistic function and literary style: an inquiry into the language of William Golding's *The Inheritors* in Seymour Chatman's collection *Literary Style: A Symposium*" (ed. 1971).

1) Criteria of relevance

The problem of distinguishing between mere linguistic regularity which in itself is of no interest to literary studies, and regularity which is significant for the poem or prose work in which we find it.

2) A functional theory of language

A functional theory of language is a theory about meanings, not about words or constructions. It is used in the sense of "grammatical" function, e. g. "subject" and "object" are syntactic terms but "goal" and "actor" are semantic ones. It refers to the "functions" of language as a whole. For example, Karl Buhler has a three-way division of language function into the representational, the conative and the expressive functions.

Halliday's functional theory of language attempts to explain linguistic structure, and linguistic phenomena, by reference to the notion that language plays a certain part in our lives, that it is required to serve certain universal types of demand, i. e. the ideational, interpersonal, and textual functions. It is through these functions that language makes links with itself and with the situation; and discourse becomes possible, because the speaker or writer can produce a text and the listener or reader can recognize one.

3) Meaning potential

These three functions are differentiated semantically, as different areas of the "meaning potential." Language itself is a potential: it is the totality of what the speaker can do. Halliday's wording for this is "what might have been"; Chomsky's is the linguistic "competence" (or the structural knowledge).

All these functions are simultaneously embodied in the language user's planning procedures. All options are embedded in the language system: the system is a network of options, deriving from all the various functions of language.

4) Foregrounding

If we can relate the linguistic patterns to the underlying functions of language, we have a criterion for eliminating what is trivial and for distinguishing true foregrounding from mere prominence of a statistical or absolute kind.

Foregrounding is prominence that is motivated. A feature that is brought into prominence will be "foregrounded" only if it relates to the meaning of the text as a whole. Where that function is relevant to our interpretation of the work, the prominence will appear as motivated.

5) Prominence

Prominence versus norm/deviation

Is prominence to be regarded as a departure from or as the attainment of a norm? Prominence is a general name for the phenomenon of linguistic highlighting, whereby some feature of the language of a text stands out in some way. There are two types of prominences: deviation and deflection (over regularity). Deviation is a departure from a norm. Departure may in any case be merely statistical: we are concerned not only with deviations, ungrammatical forms, but also with deflections, departure from some expected pattern of frequency.

Statistical

To what extent is prominence a quantitative effect, to be uncovered or at least stated by means of statistics? Prominence may be of a probabilistic kind, defined by Bloch as "frequency distributions and transitional probabilities, which differ from those ... in the language as a whole." The notion that prominence may be defined statistically is not always accepted. Some say that since style is a manifestation of the individual, it cannot be reduced to counting.

Prominence due to subject matter

How real is the distinction between prominence that is due to subject matter and prominence that is due to something else? Ullmann's idea is that one must carefully avoid what have been called contextual words whose frequency is due to the subject-matter rather than to any deep-seated stylistic or psychological tendency. The concern here is with words that serve as indices of a particular author.

Each utterance has a thesis what is being talked about uniquely and instantially; and in addition to this, each utterance has a function in the internal organization of the text; in combination with other utterances of the text it realizes the theme, structure and other aspects. (Ruqaiya Hasan)

Every level is a potential source of motivation, a kind of semantic "situational norm," and since the role of syntax in language is to weave into a single fabric the different threads of meaning that derive from the variety of linguistic functions, one and the same syntactic feature is very likely to have at once both a deeper and a more immediate significance. Thus, we cannot really discount "prominence due to subject-matter," at least as far as syntactic prominence is concerned.

6) Semantic choice and syntactic choice

These refer to what the author chooses to say and how he chooses to say it. The one does not weaken or cut across the other but reinforces it. We have to do here with any interaction, not of meaning and form, but of two levels of meaning, both of which find expression in form, and through the same syntactic features. The immediate thesis and the underlying theme come together in the syntax; the choice of subject-matter is motivated by the deeper meaning, and the transitivity patterns realize both.

Language, because of the multiplicity of these functions, has a fugue-like quality in which a number of themes unfold simultaneously.

7) Analysis

Halliday chooses three passages from the novel *The Inheritors*. Passage A is the narrative of the people (the primitive tribe people); Passage B is the transition between Passage A and Passage C, which is concerned with the new people (the advanced people).

Through careful stylistic analysis, Halliday found that among the 56 clauses in Passage A, 21 are clauses of action, 14 are of location, 16 are of mental process, and 5 are attributive clauses. 46 clauses are of simple past tense. 19 of the 21 clauses of action describe simple movements, e. g. "turn" "rise" "hold" "reach" "throw forward," etc. (intransitive). These clauses of movement usually (16) specify location, e. g. "The man turned sideways in the bushes"; "A stock rose upright." The picture is one in which people act, but they do not act on things; they move, but they move only themselves, not other objects.

In Passage C, the majority of the clauses (48/67) have a human subject. More than half (25) are clauses of action, and most of these are transitive. Most of the perception is changed; the environment is enlarged. All indicate that the human subjects are acting on external objects.

11.11 Concluding Remarks: Linguistics, Literary Criticism, and Stylistics

11.11.1 Linguistics and Stylistics

Linguistics is the science of describing language and showing how it works. Stylistics is that part of linguistics, which concentrates on variation in the use of language, often, but not exclusively, with special attention to the most conscious, and complex uses of language in literature. Stylistics means the study of style, with a suggestion, from the form of the word. It is a scientific or at least a methodical study. All students of linguistic variation must face two tasks:

1) Describe the variant language, either as an independent system in its own right or as a subsystem derivable by explicit rules from some

known system;

2) They must make clear by whom, when, and where this particular variant is, or was, used.

There are different types of linguistic variation: regional, social, styles, registers, idiolects, etc. we should have at our disposal principles enabling us to decide which types and instances of variation are subordinate to others. The grammarian who describes his own orderly, reflective language describes only one kind of English. He writes not THE grammar of English but A grammar of English.

The grammarian is interested in each scheme separately and for its own sake. The stylistician is interested in comparing schemes, relating them to their contexts and observing the intricate patterns emerging from the interference of one with another.

11.11.2 Linguistic Critic

What specific contributions can linguistics make to literary studies? Three areas of advantages can be asserted.

1) The educational claim

Some knowledge of how language works is indispensable basic information for the student and critic of literature. Linguistics is a theory of how language works, how it is acquired, how it communicates meanings, what kinds of structures it employs, and so on. Literary criticism is an account of the use of language in some particular types of text. There is therefore a powerful argument for critics and students knowing about language—by knowing some general linguistics.

2) The technical claim

Certain areas of literary study demand close engagement with the mechanism of language (e.g. metrics); linguistics provides specific information and analytic technique. Such studies simply cannot be undertaken except by someone with an advanced descriptive competence in the relevant dimension(s) of linguistic structure. Any worthwhile statement in any of these fields must be based on a detailed, analytical awareness of the texture of language.

3) The theoretical claim

Linguistics is an advanced theoretical discipline, which provides certain insights into the nature of literature and criticism.

11.11.3 Literary Criticism

Instead of being guided towards techniques of individual interpretation, students are often provided with other people's interpretations so that his study of literature becomes identified with the study of literary criticism and commentary. As Widdowson comments, in most cases the individual can only respond to literature as a result of guidance.

Actually, literature as a subject has as its principal aim the development of the capacity for individual response to language use. What this amounts to is the study of literary works as kinds of discourse. If one defines the subject in this way, the reason for teaching literature to students of English becomes immediately apparent.

Stylistics provides a way of integrating the two subjects, English language and English literature. If literature is to be taught as a form of discourse then its textual features must be such as to relate to what the learner knows of English grammar and vocabulary. He must be introduced to other forms of discourse, of a conventional type, with which the literary discourse can be compared.

Literary studies provide something of educational value for the learners who will not be going on to more advanced study; they also provide a basis for those who will. The stylistic approach to literature can serve as a preparation both for those whose later studies will move towards the discipline of linguistics and for those who will move towards that of literary criticism.

11.11.4 Stylistics: An Area of Mediation

As Widdowson says, "By 'stylistics' I mean the study of literary discourse from a linguistics orientation and I shall take the view that what distinguishes stylistics from literary criticism on the one hand and linguistics on the other in that it is essentially a means of linking the two and has no autonomous domain of its own." One can conduct enquiries of a linguistic kind without any reference to literary criticism, and one can conduct enquiries in literary criticism without any reference to linguistics.

Some linguists have suggested that the latter is impossible since the literary critic must be involved in a discussion about language. But there are all kinds of ways of talking about language and the linguist's way is only one of them. The linguist would be the first to complain if everyone who talked about language claimed to be talking linguistics.

Stylistics, however, involves both literary criticism and linguistics, as its morphological make-up suggests: e.g. "style-" related to the former, and "-itics" related to the latter. Therefore, stylistics is an area of mediation between the two disciplines:

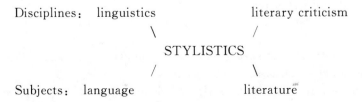

The literary critic is concerned with messages; the linguist, with the codes themselves. The literary critic is concerned with the meanings codes convey in particular instances of use; for the linguist, particular messages are of interest in so far as they exemplify the language system. For the literary critic, interpretation is the aim; for the linguist, interpretation is not an aim but an aid. The literary critic is interested in what aesthetic experience or perception of reality the poem is attempted to convey; the linguist is dependent on some prior interpretation of what the poem is about.

References

Beaugrande, Robert de. 2001. *Linguistic Theory: The Discourse of Fundamental Works*. Beijing: Foreign Language Teaching and Research Press/London: Longman Group.

Bennison, N. 1993. "Discourse analysis, pragmatics and the dramatic 'character': Tom Stoppard's *Professional Foul*," *Language and Literature* 2:2. 1. Bailey, Richard, & Dolores Burton. 1968. *English Stylistics*. Cambridge: MIT Press.

Birch, David & O'Toole, M. (eds.). 1988. *Functions of Style*. UK: George Allen & Unwin

Bradford, R. 1997. *Stylistics*. London: Routledge.

Brahim, Moussabbir. 1990. *Linguistic Models and the Literary Text: Stylistics and Poetics in America from the Fifties to the Eighties*. Unpublished Ph. D. dissertation of Indiana University.

Brown, G. & Yule, G. 1983/1987. *Discourse Analysis*. Cambridge: Cambridge University Press.

Brumfit, C. J. & R. A. Carter. 1986/1997/2000. *Literature and Language Teaching*. Oxford: Oxford University Press/Shanghai: Shanghai Foreign Languages Education Press.

Burke, B. 2005. "How cognition can augment stylistic analysis," in *European Journal of English Studies* 9(2): 185—195.

Burton, Dolores. 1990. "Reviewing the book *A Bibliography of Stylistics and Related Criticism*, 1967—1983," by James R. Bennett. *Style* 24(1): 153—159. Academic Search Elite, http:www.lib.tsinghua.edu.cn/NEW/EBSCO.htm

Carter, Ronald (ed.). 1982. *Language and Literature*. London: George Allen & Unwin.

Carter, R. and P. Simpson (eds.). 1989. *Language, Discourse and Literature: An Introductory Reader in Discourse Stylistics*. London: Unwin Hyman.

Chafe, W. 1994. *Discourse, Consciousness, and Time*. Chicago: University of Chicago Press,

Chatman, S. (ed.). 1971. *Literary Style: A Symposium*. Oxford: OUP.

Chatman, S. 2001. "Parody and style," in *Poetics Today* 22(1).

Chloupek, J. and J. Nekvapil(eds.). 1993. *Studies in Functional Stylistics*. Armsterdam: John Benjamins Publishing Company.

Cluysenaar, A. 1976. *An Introduction to Literary Stylistics*. London: B. T. Batsford Limited.

Cook, G. 1994/1995/1999. *Discourse and Literature*. Oxford: Oxford University Press / Shanghai: Shanghai Foreign Languages Education Press.

Cummings, M. & Simons, R. 1983. *The Language of Literature*. Oxford: Pergamen Press.

Currie, G. 1990. *The Nature of Fiction*. Cambridge: Cambridge University Press.

Eagleton, M. 1996. *Working with Feminist Criticism*. Oxford: Blackwell Publishers.

Fabb, Nigel. 1999. "A review of Paul Simpson's *language through literature: an Introduction*," Lingua 108: 217—221.

Feng, Z. & Shen, D. 2001. "The play off the stage: the writer-reader relationship in drama," *Language and Literature* 10 (1): 79—93.

Fowler, R. 1996. *Linguistic Criticism*. Oxford: Oxford University Press.

Fowler, R. 1998. "*Exploring the language of poems, plays and prose* (book review)," in *Style* 32(2). WilsonSelect, http://newfirstsearch.global.oclc.org/.

Fowler, R. (ed.). 1999. *A Dictionary of Critical Terms*. London: Routledge.

Freeman, Donald(ed.). 1981. *Essays in Modern Stylistics*. London: Methuen & Co Ltd.

Gaitet, P. 1992. *Political Stylistics*. London: Routledge.

Gee, J. P. 2000. *An Introduction to Discourse Analysis: Theory and Method*. Beijing: Foreign Languages Teaching and Research Press.

Genette, G. 1980. *Narrative Discourse: An Essay in Method*. New York: Cornell University Press.

Genette, G. 1988. *Narrative Discourse Revisited*. New York: Cornell University Press.

Halliday, M. A. K. and J. R. Martin. 1993. *Writing Science: Literacy and Discursive Power*. PA: University of Pittsburgh Press.

Haynes, J. 1989. *Introducing Stylistics*. London: Unwin Hyman.

Hatzfeld, Helmut. 1953. *A Critical Bibliography of the New Stylistics: Applied to the Romance Literature*, 1900—1952. Chapel Hill: University of North Carolina Press.

Holquist, M. 1990. *Dialogism: Bakhtin and His World*. London: Routledge.

Hough, G. 1969. *Style and Stylistics*. London: Routledge and Kegan Paul.

Jakobson, R. 1987/1996. *Language in Literature*. Cambridge, MA: The Belknap Press of Harvard University press.

Jucker, A. H. 1992. *Social Stylistics-Syntactic Variation in British Newspapers*. Berlin: Mouton de Gruyter.

Kachru, B. & Stahlke, F. W. (ed.). 1972. *Current Trends in Stylistics*. Edmonton: Linguistics Research, Inc.

Leech, G. 1969. *A Linguistic Guide to English Poetry*. London: Longman.

Leech, G. & M. Short. 1981. *Style in Fiction*. London: Longman.

McMenamin, G. R. 1993. *Forensic Stylistics*. UK: Elsevier Science Publishers B. V.

Milic, Lewis. 1967. *Style and Stylistics: An Analytical Bibliography*. London: The Free Press.

Miller, J. H. 1998. *Reading Narrative*. Oklahoma: University of Oklahoma Press.

Mills, S. 1995. *Feminist Stylistics*. London: Routledge.

Miner, E. 1990. *Comparative Poetics: An Intercultural Essay on Theories of Literature*. UN: Princeton University Press.

Mitchell, W. J. T. (ed.). 1981. *On Narrative*. Chicago: The University of Chicago Press.

Moore, C. N. & L. Lower. 1992. *Translation East and West: A Cross-Cultural Approach*. Hawaii: University of Hawaii.

Nickel, G. (ed.). 1978. *Rhetoric and Stylistics*. German: HochschulVerlag.

Oatley, K. 2003. "The future of cognitive poetics," in Joanna Gavins and Gerard Steen (ed.). *Cognitive Poetics in Practice*: 161—173.

Peer, W. Van. & Renkema, J. (eds.). 1986. *Pragmatics and Stylistics*. Acco (Academische Cooperatief s. v.), Leuven, Belgie.
Peer, W. Van. 1986. *Stylistics and Psychology-Investigations of Foregrounding*. London: Croom Helm.
Prince, G. 1987. *A Dictionary of Narratology*. UN: University of Nebraska Press.
Ricoeur, P. 1984. *Time and Narrative*. Vol. 1. K. MacLaughlin and D. Pellauer (trans.). Chicago: University of Chicago Press.
Ricks, C. 1998. *Essays in Appreciation*. Oxford: Oxford University Press.
Sebeok, Thomas (ed.). 1960. *Style in Language*. Cambridge: MIT Press.
Semino, E. 2002. "A cognitive stylistic approach to mind style in narrative fiction," in Elena Semino & Jonathan Culpeper (eds.). *Cognitive Stylistics*: 95—121.
Short, M. 1996. *Exploring the Language of Poems, Plays and Prose*. London: Longman.
Steen, G. & Joanna Gavins. 2003. "Contextualizing cognitive poetics," in Joanna Gavins & Gerard Steen (eds.). *Cognitive Poetics in Practice*: 1—12.
Stockwell, P. 2002. "Cognitive grammar," in *Cognitive Poetics*: 59—89.
Thomasson, A. L. 1999. *Fiction and Metaphysics*. Cambridge: Cambridge University Press.
Thornborrow, J. & S. Wareing. 2000. *Patterns in Language—An Introduction to Language and Literary Style*. London: Routledge/Beijing: Foreign Languages Teaching and Research Press. (刘世生导读)
Toolan, M. (ed.). 1992. *Language, Text and Context-Essays in stylistics*. London: Routledge.
Toolan, M. 1998. *Language in Literature—An Introduction to Stylistics*. London: Arnold.
Toolan, M. 2000. "'What makes you think you exist?': A speech move schematic and its application to Pinter's *The Birthday Party*," in *Journal of Pragmatics* 32: 177—201. www.elsevier..nl/locate/pragma.
Traugott E. C. & Pratt, M. L. 1980. *Linguistics for Students of Literature*. New York: Harcourt Brace Jovanovitch.
Tsur, Reuven. 1992. *Toward a Theory of Cognitive Poetics*. Amsterdam: North-Holland.
Wales, K. 1989. *A Dictionary of Stylistics*. London: Longman.
Weber, J. J. 1996. *Critical Analysis of Fiction-Essays in Discourse Stylistics*. Amsterdam: Rodopi B. V.
Weber, J. J. (ed.). 1996. *The Stylistics Reader-From Roman Jakobson to the Present*. London: Arnold.
Widdowson, H. G. 1979. *Stylistics and the Teaching of Literature*. London: Longman.
Widdowson, H. G. 1992/1999. *Practical Stylistics*. Oxford: Oxford University Press/Shanghai: Shanghai Foreign Languages Education Press.
Wright, L. and J. Hope. 1996/2000. *Stylistics: A Practical Coursebook*. London: Routledge/Beijing: Foreign Languages Teaching and Research Press.
胡壮麟,2000,《理论文体学》,北京:外语教学与研究出版社。
胡壮麟、刘世生,2000,文体学在中国的进展,《山东师大外国语学院学报》,2000年第1期。
刘世生,1998,《西方文体学论纲》,山东:山东教育出版社。
申 丹,1998,《叙述学与小说文体学研究》,北京:北京大学出版社。
申 丹,2000,西方现代文体学百年发展历程,《外语教学与研究》,2000年第1期,首届中国外语界面研究学术研讨会通知,第136页。

Chapter 12

Computational Linguistics

12.1 What Is Computational Linguistics?

COMPUTATIONAL LINGUISTICS is the scientific study of language from a computational perspective. It is a discipline between linguistics and computer science. While computer science is concerned with the computational aspects of the human language faculty, that is, theories and techniques for designing and implementing computer systems, linguistics contributes an understanding of the special properties of language data, and provides theories and descriptions of language structure and use. On the whole, computational linguists are interested in providing computational models of various kinds of linguistic phenomena. These models may be "knowledge based" ("hand crafted") or "data driven" ("statistical" or "empirical"). This assumption is in some cases motivated from a scientific perspective in that one is trying to provide a computational explanation for a particular linguistic or psycholinguistic phenomenon; and in other cases the motivation may be more purely technological in that one wants to provide a working component of a speech or natural language system. (Uszkoreit, 1996/2000; Ramsay, 2000)

Computational linguistics belongs to the cognitive sciences and overlaps with the field of ARTIFICIAL INTELLIGENCE(AI), a branch of computer science aiming at computational models of human cognition. Naturally, computational linguists are involved in all of these areas of research. Researchers and practitioners in other disciplines are also involved. For example, computer scientists, information scientists, engineers, professional programmers and even literary analysts are involved in designing and implementing shallow approaches to processing language data. However, natural language processing (NLP) is not just an engineering problem, because language data is different from other data, and it has special properties. What the computational linguist brings to the table is an understanding of these properties (Linguistics), an understanding of design, implementation, and computational techniques and issues(Computer Science), and an understanding of the intersection of these areas. Becoming a computational linguist is a harder job than simply becoming a linguist or a computer scientist.

All this suggests computational linguistics is an interdisciplinary enterprise which centers around the use of computers to process or produce human language or natural language. At this point, we cannot avoid mentioning the notion of "computing metaphor." The reason why the computing metaphor works so well is that language truly is a form of software. Just as the human brain was the model for computer hardware, human language was the model for computer software. It is no wonder that linguists were among the first scholars outside of the strictly technical fields to become generally computer literate. (Lawler & Dry, 1998)

According to Yu (2003), application of computer technology in language research and the research on algorithm regarding natural languages are the core research areas of computational linguistics. In a narrow sense, computational linguistics refers only to the above two aspects. But with the development of computational linguistics, its research areas have been constantly modified and broadened. Alexander Clark et al., (2010) states that "computational linguistics, together with its engineering domain of natural language processing, has exploded in recent years. It has developed rapidly from a relatively obscure adjunct of both AI and formal linguistics into a thriving scientific discipline. The focus of research in CL and NLP has shifted over the past three decades from the study of small prototypes and theoretical models to robust learning and processing systems applied to large corpora."

We are not able to cover every aspect of this discipline; in this introductory essay we will confine ourselves to the following areas: Machine translation (MT), corpus linguistics and information retrieval.

12.2 Machine Translation

MACHINE TRANSLATION (MT), different from computer-aided translation (CAT) and machine-aided human translation (MAHT), is the use of machine (usually computer software) to translate texts from one natural language into another. Rule-based MT and corpus-based MT are the two major approaches of machine translation. Corpus-based MT can be further classified into statistical and example-based MT. But a new approach, hybrid machine translation (HMT), which leverages the strengths of rule-based and statistical methodologies is becoming more popular. AppTek released a hybrid MT system in 2009. Several other MT companies (Asia Online, LinguaSys, Systran, PangeaMT, UPV) are also claiming to have a hybrid approach using both rules and statistics.

Machine translation has always been a chief concern in computational linguistics in spite of its ups and downs in the course of development, which has been well summarized by John Hutchins(1995; 1999; 2001) and Martin Kay (online).

12.2.1 History of Development

12.2.1.1 The Independent Work by MT Researchers

The first period began with the memorandum from Warren Weaver in 1949, which effectively launched MT research. In the early 1950s, research was necessarily modest in its aims, as it was constrained by the limitations of hardware, in particular, inadequate memories and slow access to storage, and the unavailability of high level programming languages. Apart from this, research was done inadequately without necessary assistance from the language experts in those fields of syntax and semantics. The first public machine translation exhibition was held in 1954, with very limited vocabulary of 250 English-Russian words, 6 basic grammatical rules and 49 selected sentences as sample translation. Early researchers also suggested the major involvement of human translators both for the pre-editing of input texts and for the post-editing of the output. They advocated the development of controlled languages and the restriction of systems to specific domains.

Rule-based machine translation, also called traditional machine translation, was the only method in the early period. Actually it had remained to be the only predominant method of MT before 1990s. Rule-based MT can be further divided into three types:

Direct Translation (also called "word-for-word" translation)

It is to render all the words or phrases in the source language into those in the target language, with no attention paid to the word order of the two languages.

But the interlingual structural divergencies preclude a word-for-Word translation, making this kind of MT close to gibberish in some cases. Direct translation can be found nowadays in translating web pages so as to facilitate reading for those who are foreign language illiterates.

Interlanguage Translation

Interlanguage can be any natural language, logic language or artificial language. For example, DLT in Holland takes Esperanto as its interlanguage. The procedure of this type is as the following:

(SL)—(Analysis)—(Interlanguage)—(Generating Rules)—(TL)

Transformational Method

The following procedure demonstrates how this method is working:

(SL)—(Analysis)—(Interstate of SL)—(Transformation)—(Interstate of TL)—(Generate)—(TL)

Interstate is the deep structure of language. By taking into consideration deep structure in MT, there seems to be a possibility to overcome the structural difference between two languages. But unfortunately the degree of explicitness of sentences leaves a lot to be desired. There are a lot of sentences which are entirely different on the deep-structure level, but can have a similar, or even identical, surface structure. Another drawback is the incompetence of this method in dealing with ambiguities, either syntactic or semantic.

12.2.1.2 Perfectionism

At the end of the 1950s, researchers in the United States, Russia, and Western Europe began to see things in an optimistic way. They were confident that high quality machine translation of scientific and technical documents would be possible within a very few years. This might also be a response to the emergence of greatly improved computer hardware, the first programming languages, and above all developments in syntactic analysis. Since it was not clear which methods would prove most successful in the long run, U.S. agencies had to support a large number of projects. As a result of enthusiasm for MT throughout the world, the emphasis of research was on the search for theories and methods for the achievement of "perfect" translations.

Of course, one could still hear voices which sounded different from the dominant "perfectionism." For instance, researchers at Georgetown University and IBM accepted the long term limitations of MT in the production of usable translations. In 1960, Bar Hillel, once an enthusiast of MT, was strongly critical of the theory-based projects, particularly those investigating interlingua approaches and the non-feasibility of FULLY AUTOMATIC HIGH QUALITY TRANSLATION(FAHQT).

12.2.1.3 The "Quiet" Period

In 1966, the Automatic Language Processing Advisory Committee of the United States issued a report which highlighted the "failure" of MT research to meet its promises. For some years after ALPAC report, researches continued but on a much reduced scale, and resources were redirected towards more fundamental questions of language processing that would have to be answered before any translation machine could be built. This period lasted until about 1975.

12.2.1.4 The Development of Translation Tools

Dismayed by the perfectionist approach, researchers began to look for sophisticated translation tools, that is, translation workstations, which can make their work more productive.

Some successes could be shown in three main strands: Computer-based tools for translators, operational MT systems involving human assistance in various ways, and "pure" theoretical research towards the improvement of

MT methods.

The development of translation tools was made possible due to the fact that real-time interactive computer environments were available since the 1960s, word processing appeared in the 1970s, and micro computers together with networking and large storage capacities were mass-produced in the 1980s. The most recent addition has been the "TRANSLATION MEMORY" (TM) facility which enables the storage of and access to existing translations for later (partial) reuse or revision or as sources of example translations. There are over 20 brands of TM systems nowadays in the market, with TRADOS as the most popular. It has also been recognized that all current commercial and operational systems output must be edited or revised if it is to be of publishable quality.

12.2.1.5 The Corpus-based Methods and the Example-based Translation

In the early 1990s, research on MT was envigorated by the coming of corpus-based methods, notably the introduction of statistical methods and of example-based translation. Statistical (stochastic) techniques have brought liberation from the increasingly evident limitations and inadequacies of previous exclusively rule-based (often syntax-oriented) approaches. Problems of disambiguation, anaphora resolution and more idiomatic generation have become more tractable with corpus-based techniques. On their own, statistical methods are no more the answer than rule-based methods have been, but there are now prospects of improved output quality which did not seem attainable a decade ago. Example-based MT is quite promising. For rule-base MT, if the two languages are vastly different in word order and structure, the problems of structural transformation is almost impossible to be solved. For example-based MT, if the corpus is large enough and similarity metric can be properly handled, satisfactory translations can be achieved theoretically. As many observers have indicated, the most promising approaches will probably integrate rule-based and corpus-based methods, which is called hybrid method. Even outside research environments integration is already evident: many commercial MT systems now incorporate translation memories, and many TM systems are being augmented by MT methods.

12.2.2 Research Methods

MT research methods can be represented from two perspectives, one being from the application of linguistic theories, another from what has been actually practiced by MT researchers.

12.2.2.1 The Linguistic Approach

MT research has been regarded as a field in which new linguistic formalisms or new computational techniques can be tried out. In other words,

MT has been seen as a test-bed for linguistic theories, because the quality of MT and translation can be judged by non-experts.

The relevant theories were information theory, categorical grammar, transformational generative grammar, dependency grammar, and stratificational grammar in the 1950s and 1960s; artificial intelligence, non-linguistic knowledge bases; formalisms such as lexical-functional grammar, generalized phrase structure grammar, head-driven phrase structure grammar, definite clause grammar, principles and parameters, Montague semantics in the 1970s and 1980s, neural networks, connectionism, parallel processing, and statistical methods and others in the 1990s.

It has been found out later that these new theories, which were successful in their initial trials on small samples, have turned out to be problematic in the end.

12.2.2.2 The Practical Approaches

These approaches can be further divided into 3 strands.

a. The transfer approach

According to the majority transfer view of machine translation, a certain amount of analysis of the source text is done in the context of the source language alone and a certain amount of work on the translated text is done in the context of the text language, but the bulk of the work relies on comparative information about the specific pair languages. This is argued for on the view that translation is, by its very nature, an exercise in comparative linguistics. The massive Eurota system, in which groups from all the countries of the European Union participated, was a TRANSFER system. The Japanese share the general perception that the transfer approach offers the best chance for early success.

b. The interlingual approach

The method is taken as a move towards robustness and overall economy in that translation between all pairs of a set of languages in principle requires only translation to and from the "INTERLINGUA" for each member of the set, if there are n languages, n components are therefore required to be translated into the interlingua and then into the target language.

c. Knowledge-based approach

A transfer system takes on much of the flavour of an interlingual system while not making the commitment in linguistic universality that may be seen as the hallmark of the interlingual approach. Such semantic transfer systems are attracting quite a lot of attention. This can also be seen to some extent as a compromise between the mainly linguistically based approaches and the so-called KNOWLEDGE-BASED systems. Translation relies heavily on information and abilities that are not specifically linguistic. It is only because we take their common sense and knowledge of the everyday world for granted.

The only major new lines of investigation that have emerged in recent years have involved the use of existing translations as a prime source of information for the production of new ones. EXAMPLE-BASED machine translation, a system of otherwise fairly conventional design, is able to refer to a collection of existing translations. A much more radical approach, championed by IBM, is the one in which virtually the entire body of knowledge that the system uses is acquired automatically from statistical properties of a very large body of existing translation.

12.2.3 Evaluation of MT and Translation Tools

It has to be admitted that there have been faults in all actual translations produced. One can find some errors that no human translators would ever commit, such as, wrong pronouns, wrong prepositions, garbled syntax, incorrect choice of terms, plurals instead of singulars, wrong tenses, etc. Sometimes this cannot be avoided because there are languages like French in which pronouns must show number and gender, Japanese where pronouns are often omitted altogether, Russian where there are no articles, Chinese where nouns do not differentiate singular and plural nor verbal present and past, and German where flexibility of the word order can leave uncertainties about what is the subject and what is the object.

This will not pose a problem if systems remain research prototypes and poor quality has little public impact. When it comes to commercial systems the whole MT industry will suffer from the poor quality translation. This is why evaluation methodology has been the subject of much discussion in recent years. (E. g. Arnold et al. , 1993; Falkedal, 1994; AMTA, 1992)

There are generally two paradigms of machine translation evaluation: 1) Glass Box evaluation, which measures the quality of a system based upon the internal mechanisms of the translation system, and 2) Black Box evaluation, which measures the quality of a system based solely upon its output. (Olive et al. , 2011) Evaluation of machine translation can be done automatically, semi-automatically (human-in-the-loop) or by human judgments.

As in other areas of natural language processing, three types of evaluation are recognized:

1) ADEQUACY EVALUATION: to determine the fitness of MT systems within a specified operational context. Adequacy evaluation is typically performed by potential users and/or purchasers of systems (individuals, companies, or agencies);

2) DIAGNOSTIC EVALUATION: to identify limitations, errors and deficiencies, which may be corrected or improved (by the research team or by the developers). Diagnostic evaluation is the concern mainly of researchers

and developers;

3) PERFORMANCE EVALUATION: to assess stages of system development or different technical implementations. Performance evaluation may be undertaken by either researchers/developers or by potential users.

12.2.4 MT and the Internet

In recent years, we have seen many systems designed specifically for the translation of Web pages and of electronic mail. There is clearly an urgent need for translating systems developed specifically to deal with the kind of colloquial (often ill formed and badly spelled) messages found on the Internet. Obviously, we cannot depend on those old linguistics rule-based approaches. Although corpus-based methods making use of the voluminous data available on the Internet itself are appropriate, there has been little research on such systems.

It is all agreed that the INTERNET is having further profound impacts that will surely change the future prospects of MT. One of the predictions is that the stand-alone PC will be replaced by NETWORK COMPUTERS which would download systems and programs from the Internet as and when required. In this case, the one-off purchase of individually packaged MT software, dictionaries, etc. would be replaced by remote stores of MT programs, dictionaries, grammars, translation archives, specialized glossaries, etc., which would presumably be paid for according to usage.

Another profound impact of the Internet will concern the nature of the software itself. What users of Internet services are seeking is in formation in whatever language it may have been written or stored. Users will need an integration of information retrieval, extraction and summarization systems with translation. So it is probable that in future years there will be fewer "pure" MT systems but many more computer-based tools and applications where automatic translation is just one component.

12.2.5 Speech Translation

The most widely anticipated development in the new century must be that of spoken language translation or SPEECH TRANSLATION. Pioneer work was done at British Telecom and at the ATR laboratories near Osaka, Japan. The latter has been a major well-funded project supported by government and industry. When research projects were begun in the late 1980s and early 1990s, it was known that practical applications were unlikely, but it was assumed that once basic principles and methods had been successfully demonstrated on small scale research systems it would be merely a question of finance and engineering to create large practical systems. When visiting the Panasonic Laboratory in Santa Barbara, California in 1992, the present writer was asked to read several

English sentences into the microphone, my reading was translated into written English and Japanese on the screen quickly. The researcher told me at that time that it was not a matter of software, but the power of the hardware. With the advent of more and more powerful computer, the computer could translate more and more sentences as well as texts. His prediction has partially come true as I noticed, during my recent trip to the U. S. in 2001, some new models of TV are equipped with an inbuilt device, which can translate spoken English into written captions almost synchronously on the screen.

Speech translation presents another issue, namely speech recognition, for automatic translation besides the ad hoc difficulties of MT. Although speech recognition has improved considerably over the past decades, it is still far from being a solved problem. A speech recognition process can be divided into three parts: feature computation, acoustic modeling, and language modeling. According to some scholars (Olive et al., 2011), all speech recognizers currently use the so-called Hidden Markov Models (HMMs) as the basic methodology for performing speech recognition. But because of differences across languages, it is not an easy job to build general model which is competent for all natural languages.

12.2.6　MT and Human Translation

Even since the idea of using computers to translate natural language, translators hold different attitudes toward this enterprise.

The first of these attitudes found expression as early as in 1951 in a report for UNESCO by J. E. Holmström. He believed that from a MT system, "the resulting literary style would be atrocious and full of 'howlers' and false values than the worst that any human translator produces." The reason was that "translation is an art; something which at every step involves personal choice between uncodifiable alternatives; not merely direct substitutions of equated sets of symbols but choices of values dependent for their soundness on the whole antecedent education and personality of the translator." (Holmström, 1951)

The second attitude has also persisted to the present day. Computer-based translation systems are not rivals to human translators, but aids to enable them to increase productivity in technical translation or provide means of translating material which no human translator has ever attempted. In this context we must distinguish 1) machine translation (MT), which aims to undertake the whole translation process, but whose output must invariably be revised; 2) computer aids for translators (translation tools), which support the professional translator; and 3) translation systems for the "occasional" non-translator user, which produce only rough versions to aid comprehension. These differences were not recognized until the late 1980s. (Hutchins, 2001)

When we look at the beginning of the new century, it is already apparent that MT and human translation can and will co-exist in relative harmony.

When translation has to be of "publishable" quality, both human translation and MT have their roles. Machine translation is demonstrably cost-effective for large scale and/or rapid translation of (boring) technical documentation, (highly repetitive) software localization manuals, and many other situations where the costs of MT plus essential human preparation and revision or the costs of using computerized translation tools are significantly less than those of traditional human translation with no computer aids. For instance, A human translator can translate about 2,000 to 3,000 words in a day, SYSTRAN's MT system translates 3,700 words per minute; human translation costs anywhere from US $20 cents to US $60 cents per word, whereas the cost of a high-end MT solution pays for itself within the first year of use. (Systran, 2001) By contrast, the human translator is and will remain unrivaled for non-repetitive linguistically sophisticated texts (e.g. in literature and law), and even for one-off texts in specific highly specialized technical subjects.

For the translation of texts where the quality of output is much less important, MT is often an ideal solution. For example, to produce "rough" translations of scientific and technical documents that may be read by only one person who wants to merely find out the great content and information and is unconcerned whether everything is intelligible or not, and who is certainly not deterred by stylistic awkwardness or grammatical errors, MT will increasingly be the only answer.

For the one-to-one interchange of information, there will probably always be a role for the human translator, e.g. for the translation of business correspondence (particularly if the content is sensitive or legally binding). But for the translation of personal letters, MT systems are likely to be increasingly used; and, for electronic mail and for the extraction of information from Web pages and Computer-based in formation services, MT is the only feasible solution.

As for spoken language translation, there must surely always be a market for the human translator. But MT systems are opening up new areas where human translation has never featured; the production of draft versions for authors writing in a foreign language, who need assistance in producing an original text; the real-time on-line translation of television subtitles; the translation of information from databases, and no doubt, more such new applications will appear in the future as the global communication networks expand and as the realistic usuality of MT becomes familiar to a wider public.

12.3 Corpus Linguistics

In the previous section, we were led to know that one of the MT approaches is working on an example-based system, that is, a system "able to refer to a collection of existing translations." This presupposes a very large corpus concerning existing translations. Although American structural linguists all used a corpus-based methodology(Kennedy, 1998), thanks to the development of computer technology, the marriage between "corpus" and "linguistics" has been made possible. In this section we will mainly deal with the computer corpora.

12.3.1 Definition

There are various definitions concerning "corpus" and "corpus linguistics." The following is one representing a linguist's view.

> Corpus, plural corpora. A collection of linguistic data, either compiled as written texts or as a transcription of recorded speech. The main purpose of a corpus is to verify a hypothesis about language—for example, to determine how the usage of a particular sound, word, or syntactic construction varies.
>
> Corpus linguistics deals with the principles and practice of using corpora in language study. A computer corpora is a large body of machine-readable texts. (D. Crystal, 1992: 85)
>
> A corpus in modern linguistics, in contrast to being simply a body of text, might more accurately be described as a finite-sized body of machine-readable text, sampled in order to be maximally representative of the language variety under consideration. (McEnery, Wilson, 2001:32)

The definition by McEnery and Wilson specifies what a modern corpus is. A difference should be made between an electronic archive and a modern sense of corpus, which is a large body of machine-readable texts and can be processed with computer tools. A corpus is stored in such a way that it can be studied non-linearly, and both quantitatively and qualitatively.

The importance of corpus to language study is aligned to the importance of EMPIRICAL DATA. Empirical data enable the linguist to make objective statements, rather than those which are subjective, or based upon the individual's own internalized cognitive perception of language. Starting from the point, we shall find corpora can play important roles in a number of different fields of study related to language, such as, speech research, lexical studies, grammar, semantics, pragmatics, discourse analysis, sociolinguistics, stylistics, historical linguistics, dialectology, variation studies, psycholinguistics, social psychology, cultural studies, etc. In view of the huge amount of corpus-based linguistic research, selective examples are cited in Hu and Jiang (2001).

12.3.2 Key Terms

12.3.2.1 Word, Type, Token, Hapax

The following paragraph is from a Chinese novel:

> The rickshaw pullers of Beiping fall into many different categories. There are strong, fleet-footed young men who rent smart rickshaws and work round the dock, starting work or knocking off whenever they please. They pull their rickshaws to a rickshaw-stand or the gate of some big house and wait for fares who want a fast runner. With luck, a single trip can net one or two silver dollars; but it may happen too that they spend the whole day idle, not even recouping their rickshaw rent. Still, they take this all in their stride.

If someone asks us "How many 'words' are there in this paragraph?" We usually say there are 94 words. That is, 94 sequences of letters separated by spaces or punctuations. This is the figure that the word-count function of a word-processing program gives. In other words, there are 94 tokens.

However, many of these words occur more than once:

the 12 times

there 13 time

they 4 times

rickshaw 5 times

Counting each repeated item once only, so that only different words are counted, gives a total of 65 items, which are called types using corpus terminology.

The words that occur only once are called hapax legomena or hapaxes.

12.3.2.2 Lemma, Word-Form

There is a further factor to be taken into account when dealing with "words" in a corpus. In the paragraph quoted above, it could be argued that *rickshaw* and *rickshaws* are in a sense the "same word," because one is simply the plural form of the other.

We might say, in technical terms, that *rickshaw* and *rickshaws* are two word-forms belonging to the same lemma: rickshaw.

In the same way, am, is, are, was, been, were and being are word-forms belonging to the same lemma: BE.

12.3.2.3 Tag, Parse, Annotate

All the three terms refer to the adding of more information to the corpus.

A corpus may exist in two forms: unannotated (in their existing raw states of plain text) or annotated (enhanced with various types of linguistic information).

Tag is normally used to refer to the addition of a code to each word in a corpus, indicating mostly the part of speech. For example, "Claire collects shoes." is tagged as "Claire_NP1 collects_VVZ shoes_NN2."

Corpus parsing is the analysis of text into constituents, such as clauses and groups.

12.3.3 Development, Categorization and Taxonomy

The use of collections of text in language study is not a new idea. In the Middle Ages work began on making lists of all the words in particular texts, together with their contexts. Other scholars counted word frequencies from single texts or from collections of texts and produced lists of the most frequent words.

Here, we will move on to look at some important stages in the contemporary development of corpus linguistics by focusing on some central corpora. (University of Essex, 1998)

12.3.3.1 The First Generation

The first modern, electronically readable corpus was the *Brown Corpus of Standard American English*. The corpus consists of one million words of American English texts printed in 1961. To make the corpus a good standard reference, the texts were sampled in different proportions from 15 different text categories: Press (reportage, editorial, reviews), Skills and Hobbies, Religious, Learned/Scientific, Fiction (various subcategories), etc.

The Brown Corpus lay-out has been imitated by other corpus compilers, such as the LOB (*Lancaster Oslo Bergen*) *Corpus for British English* and the *Kolhapur Corpus for Indian English*. They both consist of 1 million words of written language (500 texts of 2,000 words each), sampled in the same 15 categories as the *Brown Corpus*.

Another important "small" corpus is the *London Lund Corpus of Spoken British English* (LLC). The corpus was the first computer readable corpus of spoken language, and it consists of 100 spoken texts of approximately 5,000 words each. The texts are classified into different categories, such as spontaneous conversation, spontaneous commentary, spontaneous and prepared oration, etc. The texts are orthographically transcribed and have been provided with detailed prosodic marking.

12.3.3.2 The Big Corpus Generation

It soon turned out, however, that for certain tasks, larger collections of texts were needed. In 1980, COBUILD started to collect a corpus of texts on computer for dictionary making and language study. The compilers of the *Collins Cobuild English Language Dictionary* (1987) had daily access to a corpus of approximately 20 million words. New texts were added to the corpus, and in 1991 it was launched as the *Bank of English* (BOE). More and more data have been added to the BOE, and the latest release (1996) contains some 320 million words! New material is constantly added to the corpus to make it "reflect[s] the mainstream of current English today."

In 1995 another large corpus was released; the *British National Corpus* (BNC). This corpus consists of some 100 million words. Like the BOE it contains both written and spoken material, but unlike the BOE, it is finite—no more texts are added to it after its completion. The BNC texts were selected according to carefully pre-defined selection criteria with targets set for the amount of texts to be included from different text types. The texts have been encoded with "mark-up" providing information about the texts, authors, speakers.

12.3.3.3 Modern Diachronic Corpus

Diachronic corpus is also called monitor corpus. Linguists believe that language is a changing phenomenon, and language change can in principle be observed in corpus data. These two points are considered to be the motivation for the development of the modern diachronic corpus.

The concept of a diachronic, or "monitor," corpus had been raised as a theoretical possibility back in 1982 by Sinclair. (Johansson, 1982) But it was not until 1990 that the first "dynamic" corpus was finally established at Birmingham, with texts from the *Times* newspaper dating back to 1988. The second "dynamic" corpus of this kind was set up in the ACRONYM (The Automated Collocational Retrieval of Nyms) project at Liverpool in 1994, this time with *Independent* news texts.

There are three types of corpora which currently support diachronic study, each representing different approaches to diachronic study. The first generation corpora Brown and LOB have been enlarged to be Frown and FLOB. They are the first type of this kind of diachronic corpora, because they comprise the small, synchronic but parallel "standard" corpora, Brown, Frown, LOB and FLOB; the second type is the chronologically-ordered corpus of text samples of the English language reaching into the 20th century, known as the *Archer Corpus* (Universities of Arizona, Southern California, Uppsala and Freiburg). The third type is represented by the unbroken, chronological data flow of

Times, and more recently of *Independent* and *Guardian* journalistic text (now at the University of Central England, Birmingham).

12.3.3.4 Specialized Corpora

This can be sub-categorized into the following types.

a. Historical corpora

Historical linguists saw the potential usefulness of computerized HISTORICAL CORPORA. A diachronic corpus with English texts from different periods was compiled at the University of Helsinki. *The Helsinki Corpus of English Texts* contains texts from the Old, Middle and Early Modern English periods, 1.5 million words in total. Another historical corpus is the recently released *Lampeter Corpus of Early Modern English Tracts*. This collection consists of "[P]amphlets and tracts published in the century between 1640 and 1740" from six different domains.

b. Corpora for special purposes

The corpora described above are general collections of texts, collected to be used for research in various fields. Many of these are used for work on spoken language systems. Examples of such are the *Air Traffic Control Corpus*, created to be used "in the area of robust speech recognition in domains similar to air traffic control" and the *TRAINS Spoken Dialogue Corpus* collected as part of a project set up to create "a conversationally proficient planning assistant." (railroad freight system)

c. International/multilingual corpora

There are a growing number of corpora available in other languages as well. Some of them are monolingual corpora—collections of texts from one language. Here the *Oslo Corpus of Bosnian Texts* and the *Contemporary Portuguese Corpus* can be mentioned as two examples.

A number of multilingual corpora also exist. Many of these are "PARALLEL CORPORA," corpora with the same text in several languages. These corpora are often used in the field of Machine Translation. The *English Norwegian Parallel Corpus* is one example, the *English Turkish Aligned Parallel Corpora* another. The Linguistic Data Consortium (LDC) holds a collection of telephone conversations in various languages: CALLFRIEND and CALLHOME.

Parallel corpus, multilingual corpus and comparable corpus are considered to be the three types of translational corpus. TEC (*Translational English Corpus*) is reported to be the first translational corpus which was designed and developed at the Centre for Translation and Intercultural Studies (CTIS) in Manchester University. The total size of TEC is 50 million words. Four text categories are represented: Newspapers (1.34%), Biography (14.1%), Fiction (81.5%) and Magazines (3.09%).

Ball (1997) showed that the taxonomies of corpora fall into the following groups:

a. by medium: printed, electronic text, digitized speech, video (e. g. for ASL), mixed

b. by design method: balanced, pyramidal, opportunistic

c. by language variables:

—monolingual vs. multilingual;

—original vs. translations (unmatched; matched);

—native speaker vs. learner (e. g. corpora of learner compositions)

d. by language states: synchronic vs. diachronic (e. g. Brown corpus vs. Helsinki Diachronic corpus)

e. by plain vs. annotated

12.3.4 Constructing a Corpus

There is no consensus in the community as to the procedure to be followed in corpus design (balanced, opportunistic, statistically sophisticated and definitely naive approaches all struggle with each other for acceptance). Come what may, the following questions should draw our attention:

—Who are the intended users? (e. g. personal research vs. a general resource)

—What is the purpose of the corpus? (e. g. as a basis for a dictionary; to create a word frequency list; to study some linguistic phenomenon; to study the language of a particular author or time period; to train a NLP system; as a teaching resource for non native speakers; to study language acquisition...)

—How much data is needed/realistic? What variables should be anticipated?

—Sampling? or exhaustive? (e. g. the complete OE corpus is available on-line; a complete Early Middle English corpus is feasible; a complete 20th C. British or American English corpus is not feasible.)

—perfectly plain: (e. g. Project Gutenberg texts, produced by scanning; no information about text.)

—marked up for formatting attributes: (e. g. page breaks, paragraphs, font sizes, italics, etc.)

—annotated with identifying information, such as identified with edition date, author, genre, register, etc. and annotated for part of speech, syntactic structure, discourse information, etc.

If corpus is said to be unannotated—it appears in its existing raw state of plain text. Unsurprisingly, the utility of the corpus is increased when it has been annotated, making it no longer a body of text where linguistic information is implicitly present, but one which may be considered a repository of linguistic information. The implicit information has been made explicit through the process of concrete annotation. For example, the form gives contains the implicit part of speech information "third person singular present tense verb," but it is only retrieved in normal reading by recourse to our pre-existing knowledge of the grammar of English. However, in an annotated corpus the form *gives* might appear as "gives-VVZ," with the code VVZ indicating that it is a third person singular present tense(Z) form of a lexical verb(VV). Such annotation makes it quicker and easier to retrieve and analyze information about the language contained in the corpus.

Leech (1993) describes 7 maxims which should apply in the annotation of text corpora:

1) It should be possible to remove the annotation from an annotated corpus in order to revert to the raw corpus.

2) It should be possible to extract the annotation by itself from the text.

3) The annotation scheme should be based on guidelines which are available to the end user.

4) It should be made clear how and by whom the annotation was carried out.

5) The end user should be made aware that the corpus annotation is not infallible, but simply a potentially useful tool.

6) Annotation schemes should be based as far as possible on widely agreed and theory neutral principles.

7) No annotation scheme has the *a priori* right to be considered as a standard.

It has to be pointed out that some of Leech's maxims are not easy to observe. Take Maxim 1 for example, at times this can be a simple process—for example removing every character after an underscore e. g. "Claire-NP1 collects-VVZ shoes-NP2" would become *Claire collects shoes*. However, the prosodic annotation of the *London Lund Corpus* is interspersed within words— for example "g/oing" indicates a rising pitch on the first syllable of the word going, meaning that the original words cannot be so easily reconstructed.

12.3.5 Concordances and Corpora

CONCORDANCE, in its simplest form, is an alphabetical listing of the words in a text, given together with the contexts in which they appear. The most common form of concordance today is the Keyword-in-context (KWIC) index, in which each word is centered in a fixed length field (e. g. 80 characters). The example given below was produced by Conc 1.70 (Macintosh), from a plain ASCII text version of the first book of Dickens' *A Tale of Two Cities*. Note that the line numbers are as calculated by Conc. (Ball, 1997)

Table 12.1   Concordance of *Poor* in *Tale of Two Cities*, Book1

1320	taste it is that such	poor cattle always have in their mouths
948	of sparing the	poor child the inheritance of any part of
778	small property of my	poor father, whom I never saw-so long
1870	desolate, while your	poor heart pined away, weep for it
947	Miss, if the	poor lady had suffered so intensely
1884	the love of my	poor mother hid his torture from me
1615	stockings, and all his	poor tatters of clothes, had, in a long
1577	faded away into a	poor weak stain. So sunken and
1001	on your way to the	poor wronged gentleman, and, with a
1036	detachment from the	poor young lady, by laying a brawny hand

To create a rudimentary concordancer is a simple programming task: it is a matter of indexing words to lines, sorting the words alphabetically, and displaying each word in a fixed amount of context. However, most of the generally available concordancers have many additional features, including options for producing full or partial concordancers, sorting in a variety of orders, searching for collocations, and producing basic text statistics.

Concordances can usually be sorted alphabetically in an ascending or a descending manner, and with spans as another option, allowing linguistic patterns to be more easily observed by humans. When the computer has been trained to identify characters, word-forms, and sentences, it can produce different kinds of statistics. This can be very useful in comparing texts, or searching for texts with particular characteristics. (Sinclair, 1991)

Concordance can not only test hypothesis, but also reveal discrepancies between language in actual use and our intuitions. With the help of concordance, we get to know the notion of collocation is not as simple as it looks. Current work in lexicography shows that, for many common words, the most frequent meaning is not the one that first comes to mind and takes pride of place in most dictionaries. Some new evidence is challenging our current linguistic descriptions quite fundamentally. Such evidence has not been available before, and its assimilation should contribute to the maturation of linguistics as a discipline. (Sinclair, 1991)

12.4 Information Retrieval

12.4.1 Scope Defined

In this section, we will be concerned only with AUTOMATIC

INFORMATION RETRIEVAL, "automatic" as opposed to "manual" and "information" as to "data" or "fact." A straightforward definition was given by Lancaster(1968): "An information retrieval system does not inform (i. e. change the knowledge of) the user on the subject of his inquiry. It merely informs on the existence (or non existence) and whereabouts of documents relating to his request."

Information retrieval (IR) is different from data retrieval (DR), document retrieval, and text retrieval, though there is overlap in the usage of the terms. IR is interdisciplinary, based on computer science, mathematics, library science, information science, information architecture, cognitive psychology, linguistics, and statistics.

Automated information retrieval systems are used to reduce what has been called "information overload." Information retrieval is finding material (usually documents) of an unstructured nature (usually text) that satisfies an information need from within large collections (usually stored on computers). Now, it is not only a research area for professionals, but also an activity of hundreds of millions of people who use a web search engine or search their emails. Information retrieval is becoming the dominant form of information access, overtaking traditional database-style searching .

With high speed computers available for non-numerical work, many thought that a computer would be able to "read" an entire document collection to extract the relevant documents. But we could find many problems were left unsolved. First, automatic characterization in which the software attempts to duplicate the human process of "reading" is a very sticky problem. "Reading" involves attempting to extract information, both syntactic and semantic, from the text and using it to decide whether each document is relevant or not to a particular request. The difficulty is to know not only how to extract the information but also how to use it to decide reference. Next, the purpose of an automatic retrieval strategy is to retrieve all the relevant documents at the same time retrieving as few of the non-relevant as possible.

12.4.2 An Information Retrieval System

An information retrieval system can be distinguished by the scale at which they operate. There are usually three prominent scales: web search, personal information retrieval and enterprise, institutional, and domain-specific search. (Christopher D. et al. , 2009)

A typical IR system can be illustrated by the following diagram, which shows three components: input, processor and output.

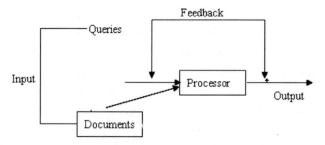

Starting with the INPUT, the main problem here is to obtain a representation of each document and query suitable for a computer to use. It is to be pointed out that most Computer-based retrieval systems store only a representation of the document (or QUERY), which means that the text of a document is lost once it has been processed for the purpose of generating its representation. A document representative could be a list of extracted words considered to be significant. Rather than have the computer process the natural language, an alternative approach is to have an artificial language within which all queries and documents can be formalized.

When the retrieval system is on-line, it is possible for the user to change his request during one search session in the light of a sample retrieval, thereby, improving the subsequent retrieval run.

Secondly, with respect to the PROCESSOR, that part of the retrieval system concerned with the retrieval process, the process may involve structuring the information in some appropriate way, such as classifying it. It will also involve performing the actual retrieval function, that is, executing the search strategy in response to a query. In the diagram, the documents have been placed in a separate box to emphasize the fact that they are not just input but can be used during the retrieval process in such a way that their structure is more correctly seen as part of the retrieval process.

Finally, we come to the OUTPUT, which is usually a set of citations or document numbers. In an operational system the story ends here.

12.4.3 Three Main Areas of Research

There are many ways to subdivide the topic of information retrieval, but three main areas of research make up a considerable portion of the subject. The three areas are content analyses, information structures, and evaluation.

12.4.3.1 Content Analysis

CONTENT ANALYSIS is concerned with describing the contents of documents in a form suitable for computer processing. The approach pioneered by Luhn (1957) is typical by the use of frequency counts of words in the document text to determine which words were sufficiently significant to represent or characterize the documents in the computer. Thus a list of what might be called KEYWORDs (or TERMs) was prepared for each document. In addition the frequency of occurrence of these words in the body of the text could also be used to indicate a degree of significance.

Information retrieval systems, both operational and experimental, have been keyword-based. Some have become quite sophisticated in their use of keywords. Some use distributional information to measure the strength of relationships between keywords or between the keyword descriptions of documents. The limit of our ingenuity with keywords seemed to have been reached when a few semantic relationships between words were defined and exploited.

12.4.3.2 Information Structure

INFORMATION STRUCTURE is concerned with exploiting relationships between documents to improve the efficiency and effectiveness of retrieval strategies. The development in information structures has been fairly recent. The main reason is that for a long time no one realized that computers would not give an accurate retrieval time with a large document set unless some logical structure was imposed on it.

12.4.3.3 Evaluation

To put the problem of EVALUATION in perspective we should answer three questions: 1) Why evaluate? 2) What to evaluate? 3) How to evaluate? The answers to these questions pretty well cover the whole field of evaluation.

The answer to the first question is mainly a social and economic one. The social part is to put a measure on the benefits (or disadvantages) to be got from information retrieval systems. The economic answer amounts to a statement of how much it is going to cost you to use one of these systems, and coupled with this is the question "is it worth it?"

The second question boils down to what we can measure that will reflect the ability of the system to satisfy the user. Cleverdon (1966) listed six main measurable quantities:

—The *coverage* of the collection, that is, the extent to which the system includes relevant matter;

—The *time lag*, that is, the average interval between the time the search request is made and the time an answer is given;

—The form of *presentation* of the output;

—The *effort* involved on the part of the user in obtaining answers to his search requests;

—The *recall* of the system, that is, the proportion of relevant material actually retrieved in answer to a search request;

—The *precision* of the system, that is, the proportion of retrieved material that is actually relevant.

It is claimed that the first four points are readily assessed. It is "RECALL" and "PRECISION" which attempt to measure what is now known as the *effectiveness* of the retrieval system. In other words it is a measure of the ability of the system to retrieve relevant documents while at the same time holding back non relevant ones. It is assumed that the more effective the system the more it will satisfy the user. (Salton, 1989: 248)

The final question has a large technical answer. It is interesting to note that the technique of measuring retrieval effectiveness has been largely influenced by the particular retrieval strategy adopted and the form of its output. For example, when the output is a ranking of documents an obvious parameter such as rank position is immediately available for control. Using the rank position as cut-off, a series of precision recall values could then be calculated, one part for each cut off value. The results could then be summarized in the form of a set of points joined by a smooth curve. The path along the curve would then have the immediate interpretation of varying effectiveness with the cut-off value. Unfortunately, the kind of question this form of evaluation does not answer is, for example, how many queries did better than average and how many did worse?

12.5 Looking into the Future

From the above discussion, we can notice several common goals underlying all these fields, which determine the development of computational linguistics in future research. (Uszkoreit, 2000)

1) User-friendly software can listen and talk

Natural language interfaces enable the user to communicate with the computer in English, French, German, Chinese, or any other human languages. Some applications of such interfaces are database queries, information retrieval from texts, so-called expert systems, and robot control. Further breakthroughs in the recognition of spoken language will improve the usability of many types of natural language systems. We are sure that communication with computers using spoken language will have enormous influence upon the work environment. Completely new areas of application for information technology will open up. However, spoken language needs to be combined with other modes of communication such as pointing with mouse or finger. If such multimodal communication is finally embedded in an effective general model of cooperation, we will have found an amicable partner in the machine.

2) Computers help people communicate with each other

We have been faced with communication problems between people with different mother tongues for thousands of years. No wonder, fully automatic translation between human languages will still be one of the aims of applied computational linguistics. Machine translation students have realized that there's still a long way to go with regard to these aims.

3) Language forms the fabric of the web

The rapid growth of the Internet/WWW and the emergence of the information society invite exciting new challenges to language technology. In spite of the fact that the new media combine text, graphics, sound and movies, the whole world of multimedia information can only be structured, indexed and navigated through language. For browsing, navigating, filtering and processing the information on the web, we need software that can get at the contents of documents. Language technology for content management is a necessary precondition for turning the wealth of digital information into collective knowledge. The increasing multilinguality of the web constitutes an additional challenge for our discipline. The global web can only be mastered with the help of multilingual tools for indexing and navigating. Systems for cross-lingual information and knowledge management will surmount language barriers for e-commerce, education and international cooperation.

4) The new emerging enterprise is to be marked by its diversity

People from different walks of life will all benefit from this new emerging enterprise, therefore we not only need efforts on the part of computer scientists and linguists, but also on the part of educationalists, translators, psychologists, sociologists, literary critics, librarians, etc.

References

Aijmer, K. & Alterberg, B. (eds.). 1991. *English Corpus Linguistics: Studies in Honour of Jan Svartvik*. London: Longman.

Aijmer, K., Alterberg, B. & Johansson, M. 1996. "Text based contrastive studies in English," Presentation of a Project. In 73—85. *Languages in Contrast Papers from a Symposium on Text-based Cross-linguistic Studies*. Aijmer, K., Altenberg, B. & Johansson, M. (eds.). Lund: Lund University Press.

Alexander Clark, Chris Fox & Shalom Lappin. 2010. *The Handbook of Computational Linguistics and Natural Language Processing*. West Sussex: Wiley-Blackwell Publishing Ltd.

Alexander Gelbukh (ed.). 2011. *Computational Linguistics and Intelligent Text Processing*. 12th International Conference, CICLing 2011 Tokyo, Japan, February 20—26, 2011 Proceedings. New York: Springer.

Altenberg, B. & Granger, S. (eds.). 2002. *Lexis in Contrast: Corpus-based Approaches*. Amsterdam: John Benjamin's Publishing House.

AMTA. 1992. *MT Evaluation: Basis for Future Directions*. Proceedings of a Workshop. 2—3 November 1992, San Diego, California. Washington, D. C.: Association for Machine

Translation in the Americas.

Arnold, D. et al. (eds.). 1993. "Special issue on evaluation of MT systems," *Machine Translation* 8(1—2): 1—126.

Arnold, D. et al. 1994. *Machine Translation: An Introductory Guide*. Manchester/Oxford: NCC/Blackwell.

Baker, M. (ed.). 1998. *Routledge Encyclopedia of Translation Studies*. London: Routledge.

Baker, Mona. 1993. "Corpus linguistics and translation studies: implications and applications," In Mona Baker, Gill Francis & Elena Tognini-Bonelli (eds.). *Text and Technology: in Honour of John Sinclair*. Amsterdam and Philadelphia: Amsterdam: John Benjamins Publishing Company. pp. 233—250

Ball, Catherine. 1997. *Concordances and Corpora*. Online.

Ball, Catherine. 1998. *Introduction to Computational Linguistics*. On line.

Banerjee, S. & Lavie, A. 2005. *METEOR: An Automatic Metric for MT Evaluation with Improved Correlation with Human Judgments* in Proceedings of Workshop on Intrinsic and Extrinsic Evaluation Measures for MT and/or Summarization at the 43rd Annual Meeting of the Association of Computational Linguistics (ACL—2005), Ann Arbor, Michigan, June 2005

Biber, D., Conrad, S. & Rappen, R. 2000. *Corpus Linguistics*. Beijing: Foreign Language Teaching and Research Press.

Christopher D. Manning, Prabhakar Raghavan & Hinrich Schütze. 2009. *An Introduction to Information Retrieval*. Cambridge: Cambridge University Press.

Cleverdon, C. W., Mills, J. & Keen, M. 1966. *Factors Determining the Performance of Indexing Systems*, Vol. 1, Design, Vol. II, *Test Results*, ASLIB Cranfield Project, Cranfield.

Crystal, David. (ed.). 1992. *An Encyclopedic Dictionary of Language and Languages*. Oxford: Oxford University Press.

Davies G., Walker R., Rendall H. & Hewer S. 2011. "Introduction to Computer Assisted Language Learning (CALL)," Module 1.4 in Davies G. (ed.). *Information and Communications Technology for Language Teachers* (ICT4LT), Slough, Thames Valley University [Online]: http://www.ict4lt.org/en/en-mod1—4.htm.

Engwall, Gunnel. 1994. "Not chance but choice: criteria in corpus creation," In B. T. S. Atkins, et al. (eds.). *Computational Approaches to the Lexicon*. Oxford: OUP. pp. 49—82.

Falkedal, K. (ed.). 1994. *Proceedings of the Evaluators' Forum*, April 21st—24th, 1991, Les Rasses, Vaud, Switzerland. Geneva: ISSCO.

Freedman, Alan. (ed.). 1998. *The Computer Glossary*. (8th ed.). UN: Amacom.

Garrett, N. 1991. "Technology in the service of language learning: trends and issues," *Modern Language Journal* 75(1): 74—101.

Gupta P. & Schulze M. 2011. "Human language technologies (HLT)," Module 3.5 in Davies G. (ed.) *Information and Communications Technology for Language Teachers* (ICT4LT). Slough, Thames Valley University [Online]: http://www.ict4lt.org/en/en-mod3—5.htm.

Halliday, M. A. K. 1991. "Corpus studies and probabilistic grammar," In *English Corpus Linguistics: Studies in Honour of Jan Svartvik*. Aijmer, K. & Alterberg, B. (eds.). London: Longman. pp. 30—43.

Halliday, M. A. K., Teubert, W., Yallop, C. & Cermakova, A. 2004. *Lexicography and Corpus Linguistics*. London: Continuum.

Holmstrom, J. E. 1951. *Report on Interlingual Scientific and Technical Dictionaries*. Paris: Unesco.

Hu, Zhuanglin & Jiang Wangqi (eds.). 2001. *Linguistics. A Course Book*. Beijing: Peking University Press.

Hu, Zhuanglin. 1997. "Exploiting the research function of Email," *Waiyu Jiaoshi Shangwang shouce (Handbook of Internet for FL Teachers). Contemporary Foreign Language. (Supplement)*

Hubbard P. (ed.). 2009. *Computer-Assisted Language Learning*. Volumes I – IV. Routledge: London and New York: http://www.stanford.edu/~efs/callcc/

Hutchins, John. 1986. *Machine Translation: Past, Present, Future*. Chichester(UK): Ellis Horwood.

Hutchins, John. 1999. "Retrospect and prospect in computer-based translation," Paper presented at the MT Summit, Singapore, 1999.

Hutchins, John. 1988. "Recent developments in machine translation," In: Maxwell, D. et al. (eds.). *New Directions in Machine Translation*. Conference proceedings, Budapest 18—19 August 1988. Dordrecht: Foris. pp. 7—63.

Hutchins, John. 1993. "Latest developments in machine translation technology," *MT Summit* 4: 11—34.

Hutchins, John. 1995. "Reflections on the history and present state of machine translation," Paper presented at the *MT Summit*, Luxenbourg.

Hutchins, John. 2001. "Machine translation and human translation: in competition or in complementation?" *International Journal of Translation* 13: 1—2 Jan-Dec20.

Johansson, S. (ed.). 1982. *Computer Corpora in English Language Research*. Bergen: NAVF.

Johansson, S. 1998. "On the role of corpora in cross-linguistic research," In *Corpora and Cross-linguistic Research: Theory, Method, and Case Studies*. Johansson, S. & Oksefjell, S. (eds.). Amsterdam: Rodopi.

Johnson, Keith & Helen Johnson. 1998/1999. *Encyclopedic Dictionary of Applied Linguistics—A Handbook of Language Teaching*. Oxford: Blackwell Publishers.

Kay, Martin. 2001. *Machine Translation*. Xerox Palo Alto Research Center. Palo Alto, California. Online.

Kennedy, Graeme. 1998. *An Introduction to Corpus Linguistics*. Addison Wesley: Longman.

Kenny, D. 2001. *Lexis and Creativity in Translation: A Corpus-Based Study*. Manchester: St. Jeorme Publishing.

Kyto, M., Ihalainen, O. & Rissanen, M. (eds.). 1988. *Corpus Linguistics, Hard and Soft*. Amsterdam: Rodopi.

Lancaster, F. W. 1968. *Information Retrieval Systems: Characteristics, Testing and Evaluation*. Wiley, New York: Badford Academic and Education Ltd.

Lawler, John & Helen Aristrar Dry. (eds.). 1998. *Using Computer in Linguistics*. London: Routledge.

Leech, G. 1993. "Corpus annotation schemes," *Literary and Linguistic Computing* 8(4): 275—281.

Luhn, H. P. 1957. "A statistical approach to mechanized encoding and searching of library information," *IBM Journal of Research and Development* 1: 309—317.

Manning, Christopher D. et al. 2008. *Introduction to Information Retrieval*. Cambridge: Cambridge University Press.

McEnery, T. & Hardie, A. 2012. *Corpus Linguistics Method, Theory and Practice*. Cambridge: CUP.

McEnery, T. & Wilson, A. 2001. *Corpus Linguistics*. Edinburgh: Edinburgh University Press.

Oliver, J. et al. (eds.). 2011. *Handbook of Natural Language Processing and Machine Translation*. New York: Springer

Ooi, V. B. Y. 1998. *Computer Corpus Lexicography*. Edinburgh: Edinburgh University Press.

Ramsay, Allan. 2000. *Introduction to Computational Linguistics*. Online.

Richards, Jack C., John Platt, Heidi Platt. 1998. *Longman Dictionary of Language Teaching and Applied Linguistics* (English Chinese edition). Beijing: Foreign Language Teaching and Research Press.

Salton, Gerard. 1989. *Automatic Text Processing: The Transformation, Analysis, and Retrieval of Information by Computer Reading*. MA: Addison Wesley.

Simpson, R. C. & Swales, J. M. (eds.). 2001. *Corpus Linguistics in North America*. Michigan: The University of Michigan Press.

Sinclair, J. 1991. *Corpus, Concordance, Collocation*. Oxford: OUP.

St. John, Elke. 2001. "A case for using a parallel corpus and concordancer for beginners of a foreign language," *Language Learning and Technology* 5(3): 185—203.

Summers, D. 2001. "Computer lexicography-the importance of representativness in relation to frequency," In *Using Corpora for Language Research*. Jenny Thomas & Mick Short (eds.). Beijing: Foreign Language Teaching and Research Press. pp. 260—266.

Svartvik, J. (ed.). 1992. *Directions in Corpus Linguistics*. Berlin: Mouton de Gruyter.

Systran, S. A. 2001. *Machine Translation*. Online.

Taylor, M. B., & Perez, L. M. 1989. *Something to do on Monday La Jolla*. CA: Athelstan.

Thomas, J. & Short, M. (eds.). 2001. *Using Corpora for Language Research*. Beijing: Foreign Language Teaching and Research Press.

Tognini-Bonelli, E. 2001. *Corpus Linguistics at Work*. Amsterdam: John Benjamins Publishing Company.

University of Essex. 1998. *Corpus Linguistics*. Online.

Uszkoreit, Hans. 1996/2000. "What is computational linguistics?" *The Association for Computational Linguistics*. On line.

Walker, D. E. 1994. "The ecology of language," Proceedings of the International Workshop On Electronic Dictionaries. Japan Electronic Dictionary Research Institute. 1991. Also in Antonio Zampolli, Nicoletta Calzolari, and Martha Palmer (eds.). *Current Issues in Computational Linguistics: In Honour of Don Walker*. Dordrecht: Kluwer. pp. 359—376.

Wang, Lixun. 2001. "Exploring parallel concordancing in English and Chinese," *Language Learning and Technology* 5(3): 174—184.

Warschauer, Mark. 1996. "Computer Assisted Language Learning: an introduction," In *Multimedia Language Teaching*. S. Fotos (ed.). Tokyo: Logos International.

pp. 3—20
Wolfgan, T. & Ramesh, K. (eds.). 2008. *Corpus Linguistics: Critical Concepts in Linguistics*. London and New York: Routledge.
Zhang, Delu. 1998. *Functional Stylistics*. Jinan: Shandong Educational Press.
俞士汶,2003,《计算语言学概论》,北京:商务印书馆。

Chapter 13

Second Language Acquisition

13.1 Introduction

The study of second language acquisition (SLA) aims to reveal the process of learning the second language (L2) and those factors relating to success and failure in this learning. It is generally held that SLA established itself as an independent discipline around 1970, ① particularly after the publication of Selinker's seminal paper "Interlanguage" in 1972. The term *interlanguage* (IL) is now used widely to refer to learners' developing L2 system that gradually approximates the target language or the language being learned. Nowadays L2 researchers often use "L2 learning" as a cover term to refer to the learning of any language other than the learner's native language. In this sense, L2 learning may refer to the learning of a second or third or fourth language. Some researchers make a distinction between L2 learning in a naturalistic environment (e. g. a Chinese speaker learning English in Britain) and that in a foreign language context (e. g. learning English in China). They reserve "L2 acquisition" for the former and "L2 learning" for the latter. In this chapter we use the two terms interchangeably, as environmental factors are not particularly emphasized.

Although researchers study L2 learning from varied perspectives, their current interests can be generally categorized into four main areas: the internal mechanisms, the first language, the psychological variables, and the social and environmental factors. (Mitchell & Myles, 1998: 40) These four research areas can serve as a guide for us to navigate through the mammoth literature for a good understanding of what is happening in the present-day SLA field. Due to the limit of space, this chapter focuses on some major theories and findings related to each of the four areas rather than attempting a comprehensive overview of the whole field. By so doing, selection of materials to be included in this chapter is inevitably subject to the author's discretion and

---

① There are L2 researchers who maintain that Corder's (1967) paper "The significance of learners' errors" marks the beginning of SLA as an independent discipline.

leaves some important points unattended. For example, we have devoted more space to the discussion of internal mechanisms due to the predominant interest in the cognitive process involved in L2 learning in present-day SLA research. Fortunately, a number of SLA books in the original such as Ellis' *Study of Second Language Acquisition* are available in bookstores these days. They provide us with detailed and systematic knowledge of SLA. For more up-to-date information in this field, four major journals are of great help. They are *Language Learning*, *Studies in Second Language Acquisition*, *Second Language Research*, and *Applied Linguistics*.

13.2 The Role of Internal Mechanisms

Over the past 20 years or so, exploring the underlying mechanisms responsible for IL changes has become one of the most intriguing issues in L2 learning research. This issue has been studied from different perspectives, among which the Universal Grammar (UG) approach is thus far the most influential. L2 researchers often use it as a yardstick against which other approaches are compared. For this reason, we begin with an introduction of this line of research and then turn to other approaches.

13.2.1 The UG Approach

Universal Grammar has been postulated to account for how the first language (L1) is acquired. It has been noted that children are universally able to acquire whatever language to which they are exposed[①] in spite of the fact that the language input children hear around them is full of degenerate data such as false starts, incomplete sentences. This is called the *poverty of the stimulus argument*. The mismatch between children's linguistic attainment and the impoverished input is known as *the logical problem of language acquisition* or *the learnability problem*. Since external or environmental factors fail to account for this logical problem, one can only turn to the internal structure of the human brain for an explanation. Based on this reasoning, the American linguist Norm Chomsky posits the existence of Universal Grammar, a biological device inside the human brain. UG is an endowment that all children are born with and the initial state from which children proceed to acquire their first language.

The goal of linguistics, according to Chomsky, is to specify UG in Chomsky's framework, UG represents the language knowledge of the adult human mind and takes the form of universal *principles* and variable settings for

---

① This phenomenon is known as "equipotentiality."

parameters. The universal principles, which are part of the human mind, require no learning. They specify the limited possibilities of variation in the form of parameters which need to be fixed in the course of language learning. The process of learning the parameter values is called triggering the setting for the parameters. The triggering is predominantly caused by *positive evidence*, i. e. the grammatical sentences actually present in the language input. UG plays down the role of *negative evidence* either in its direct or indirect form. Direct negative evidence refers to the explicit correction of children's errors. Indirect evidence refers to the non-occurrence of a linguistic feature in the language input. This conceptualization accords with the observation that children acquire a language through positive evidence. Negative evidence is generally not available and, if provided, helps little in child language acquisition. UG-based conceptualization of language acquisition points to a direction in which we can work towards solutions to the learnability problem.

In what follows, we will illustrate what UG principles and parameters are like. Let us begin with an oft-cited example: the *Structure-dependency* principle. This principle dictates that the elements (phrases) of a sentence in any language are hierarchically arranged. When elements of the sentence are moved to form, say, a question, this movement hinges on the structural relationship of the sentence rather than the linear order of words. Look at the following sentences:

(1) Is the man who is tall a basketball player?
(2) *Is the man who tall is a basketball player?

English allows (1) but not (2). The moving of "is" depends on its position in the hierarchical structure of the sentence rather than a word in an arbitrary position, say, the second word. Here it is the "is" in the main clause (the second "is"), not the one in the relative clause (the first "is") that is movable to form a question. This knowledge of language is part of human mind.

While UG is intended to maximize the generalization of universal principles, it also has to account for the differences across languages. This task is left to be fulfilled by parameters. We might as well use the *head parameter* to illustrate how this is done. Languages may differ in the order in which the elements of a phrase is arrayed. A phrase consists of a head and its complements. In English, for example, the head of a verb phrase is the verb. In the phrase *to break a cup*, *to break* is the head, which precedes *a cup*, the complement. In the prepositional phrase *with some flowers*, the head *with* comes before the complement *some flowers*. Other types of English phrases also have the head followed by the complement. But not all languages have this positional array. Japanese, for example, is a language with the complement preceding the head. Based on this crosslinguistic comparison, English is categorized as a *head-first* language and Japanese as a *head-last* language.

The crosslinguistic differences between English and Japanese enable us to see more clearly the relationship between principles and parameters. Here we have a universal principle which states that languages are structured into phrases containing a head and optional complements. The positional array of the head and the complement in a phrase may vary across languages. This variation is captured by the head parameter with two possible settings either in the first or the last position. Following this line of thinking, one can explain why children are capable of acquiring all the complexities of language within a few years in spite of their relatively inferior cognitive abilities as compared with adults. This is because they are endowed with knowledge of universal principles such as structure-dependency and the limited possibilities with respect to the settings of parameter values such as the binary head parameter. "Given such an assumption, the child could set the parameter correctly on the basis of minimal linguistic experience." (Radford, 1997:22)

In the 1990s, the above UG conceptualization of language acquisition was modified by Chomsky (1995). He advanced what he called the Minimalist Program. In this new framework, the universal principles remain the same as before, but parameters are contained within the lexicon rather than bearing on specific principles. As learning a language involves settings of parameters, this amounts to saying that all that requires learning is the lexicon of a language since languages differ from one another in their lexicons which contain a great deal of grammatical information. In short, to learn a language is to learn its lexicon.

13.2.2 UG and SLA

UG theory has arisen out of the need to account for the logical problem of L1 acquisition. It thus follows that applicability of this theory to L2 acquisition hinges on whether such a logical problem also exists in L2 acquisition. It is well known, and perhaps least controversial, that IL contains rules of learners' own creation, which stem from neither L1 nor L2 input. Gregg (1996:52—53) holds that, if the learner's IL grammar is underdetermined by the input data, the logical problem exists however "imperfect" the acquired grammar may be. Therefore, UG must also be operative in L2 learning. This reasoning has motivated L2 researchers to apply UG theory to the study of L2 acquisition. The point is that, given the mismatch between IL grammar and input data, whether the logical problem in L2 learning is of the same kind as in L1 remains a moot question. This is because L2 acquisition differs from L1 acquisition in important ways. Bley-Vroman (1989) points out some crucial differences between child L1 learning and adult L2 learning, which include the following: L2 learning generally lacks success, reaches a stage where progress ceases (a phenomenon known as *fossilization*), and involves L1 transfer, more matured cognitive abilities and different motivations for learning a L2. Because of these differences, Bley-Vroman advanced what he called the *Fundamental Difference Hypothesis* (FDH), claiming that unlike child L1 acquisition, L2 learners do not have access to UG. Rather, what they know of language universals is constructed through their L1. Furthermore, they rely on their general problem-solving abilities to learn the L2. But not all researchers agree on FDH. The debate over the differences between L1 and L2 learning has given rise to four hypotheses regarding accessibility of UG to L2 acquisition.

1) Full access hypothesis: Like children acquiring the L1, L2 learners rely on UG principles and can successfully reset parameters where the L2 differs from the L1.
2) No access hypothesis: UG is no longer available to L2 learners after they reach a certain critical age and learners have to resort to other learning mechanisms such as problem-solving abilities to help acquire the L2.
3) Indirect access hypothesis: UG is available to L2 learners via the L1. L1 acquisition results from the operation of UG principles and parameter-setting and impinges on subsequent L2 learning.
4) Partial access hypothesis: Some aspects of UG are available and others not. L2 learners are able to set some parameters but not others.

Hypotheses 1 and 2 are in direct opposition. They are relatively easy to test as they are a matter of all or none. But researchers who take either stance would find supporting evidence. These two hypotheses are the major source of debate during 1980s and 1990s. Hypothesis 3 and particularly Hypothesis 4 are more a compromise than an independent stance. In spite of the differences, all four hypotheses presuppose that UG is responsible for L1 learning.

Despite its avowed relevance to L1 acquisition, UG has appeal for SLA study as well. This is largely because UG theory has done much to uncover the abstract and specific properties of human language underlying our daily use of language and make cross-linguistic comparison possible. An accurate description of linguistic properties is a prerequisite to our understanding of the language learning process. As Wexler and Culicover (1980: 486) put it, "Without a precise characterization of what is to be learned, the question of whether it can be learned is virtually meaningless." The UG framework has provided us with a tool to delve into the L2 learning process and generated a lot of intriguing topics that are researchable, as evidenced in the copious UG-based research in 1980s through 1990s. It has influenced SLA research because it has been considered as a powerful linguistic theory. The upshot of such research is that L2 learning study is no longer a consumer of theories but has its own contributions to make to the linguistic theory and can be exploited to verify UG for its crosslinguistic nature.

In applying UG theory to the study of SLA, some L2 researchers such as Gregg (1996: 53), drawing on Chomsky's distinction between *competence* (the abstract and hidden mental system) and *performance* (the observable behavior in actual use of language), emphasize that the goal of the domain of SLA theory should be the underlying competence rather than the linguistic performance. This dual distinction has manifested itself in the present-day SLA research. To measure competence, grammaticality judgement tasks have been used, though not without controversy. As competence has to be inferred from performance anyway, one might query why to bother making such a distinction. In fact this is what some other theories examining learning mechanisms set out to do. In what follows we introduce two such theories: connectionism and the information-processing model.

13.2.3 Connectionism and SLA

At the turn of this century, UG-based SLA research is no longer in vogue, as evidenced by an apparent decrease in publications in major international SLA journals. Instead, usage-based linguistics, which represents a school of thoughts that emphasizes language knowledge as experience, is gaining momentum in its influence on SLA. And connectionism belongs to this school. Although connectionism is not intended specifically to account for language learning, it deserves special mention here partly because, as an approach radically different from not only UG but also from other cognitive approaches, it offers important insights into the L2 learning process and partly because its application to L2 learning research is quite a recent event, starting in the 1990s.

Connectionism models cognition on the assumption that human mind is predisposed to look for associations between elements and create links between them. The connectionist framework is composed of a system of neural networks interrelated by information nodes in a complex manner. The links between these nodes can be strengthened through repeated activation or weakened without activation. The processing is highly distributed throughout the entire system, hence the name *Parallel Distributed Processing* (PDP). "There are no task-specific modules, discrete symbols, or explicit rules that govern the operation." (Wilson & Keil, 1999: 186) In this conceptualization, learning a language is not to learn rules. Rather, it is to change the strength of associations between nodes through activation. Learners are sensitive to regularities in the language input such as adding *-s* or *-es* to form plural nouns, and able to extract probabilistic patterns on the basis of these regularities. Repeated exposure and activation of these patterns lead to learning. Consequently associative patterns are what learners need to establish in order to acquire the ability to use language.

The connectionism-based SLA research is relatively scanty. Two such studies are worth mentioning here. Sokolik and Smith (1992) investigated the process of learning to identify the gender of French nouns within the framework of connectionism. In French, a noun can be either masculine or feminine. There are some formal regularities associated with the gender of nouns, which are manifest in their endings. The researchers set out to make the connectionist network in the computer learn the gender features of a set of nouns. Through repeated activation, the computer established some associative patterns as the links between nodes in the network become strengthened. Based on this learning experience, the computer can assign correct gender to a new noun by relying on the ending of this noun. Learning in this case does not depend on extraction of rules. Rather, it comes about through building up the association between the gender and its formal features. The association yields probabilistic patterns, which, in turn, can be used to make judgements about new cases.

By adopting a connectionist approach, N. Ellis and Schmidt (1997) conducted a study of the adult acquisition of plural morphology using an artificial language. They found that associative mechanisms were all that were needed in order to explain the acquisition of plural morphology and it is not necessary to invoke underlying rule-governed processes.

The connectionist view that learning a language is to develop probabilistic patterns rather than knowledge of rules has psychological reality. Language learning does not depend solely on rules. Grammar leaks. For example, an English grammar rule states that the plurality of nouns is formed by adding -*s* or -*es*. There are nouns that violate this rule such as *women* and *sheep*. Due to exceptions, a rule can vary in its coverage of the linguistic data it accounts for. This means that some rules may be 90% correct, others 80% correct, still others 50% correct, and so on. It is doubtful that a "rule" with a generality lower than 50% is still counted as a rule that can be incorporated into a grammar book. Technically, such low-generality rules ought to exist and the difference between them and the high-generality ones is a matter of degree. As native speakers, we may intuitively feel the existence of rules of varying generality but cannot articulate them. This tacit knowledge is stored in our mind in the form of the so-called "language sense," which makes creative use of language possible. Such language sense constitutes none other than the probabilistic patterns in connectionist's terms. Given this "leaking" nature of grammar rules, if we follow rules to the letter in speaking, we will inevitably make errors and communication will be likely to break down. But this rarely happens in L1 use. Why? In the course of acquiring a linguistic structure in a naturalistic environment, we are simultaneously exposed to contextual information. The linguistic form is parasitic on such non-linguistic information and the two are intertwined in a complex way. In other words, when we are acquiring our native language, linguistic structures are contextually coded and constitute only a portion of what is acquired. Apparently, non-linguistic information has an important role to play in the acquisition process and in the accurate and fluent use of language. Use of rules is probabilistic. Without the aid of authentic context, language acquisition is incomplete, as is often the case with L2 learning in a foreign language setting.

13.2.4 The Information Processing Approach to SLA

The information processing model, which has its origin in cognitive psychology, proceeds from the notion that complex behavior builds on simple processes that can be studied separately. Human information-processing mechanisms bear on different processing systems including perceptual systems, output systems, memory systems, and systems for intrinsic reasoning. (See McLaughlin & Heredia, 1996: 213) Because the human mind is a limited-capacity processor and only so much attention is available at one time, it has to develop effective ways to deal with information. In learning a complex and difficult task, one can break it down into components. Once a component has become automatized, attention can be freed up to take care of the other components. Thus the originally difficult task can be tackled eventually. This learning process involves two basic modes of processing: *automatic processing* and *controlled processing*. (Shiffrin & Schneider, 1977) Automatic processing has to do with the activation of the nodes in memory in which the same input is mapped onto the same activation pattern through repeated trials, thus building up associative connections. Automatic processes occur rapidly and are difficult to suppress. Controlled processing involves a temporary activation of nodes which are under attentional control. As attention is required, controlled processes are capacity-limited and slow in activation. Thus, learning a skill is aimed at transition from controlled to automatic processing in conformity with the old saying "Practice makes perfect."

The notion of automaticity offers a fairly convincing explanation of the fossilization issue. (Mitchell & Myles, 1998) Fossilization, a phenomenon characteristic of L2 learning, refers to the fact that L2 learners seem unable to get rid of some non-native-like structures in their L2 no matter how much exposure they receive. Fossilization occurs because the structures involved have become automatized and difficult to change.

There are cases, however, that practice does not make perfect. Performance may degenerate in the course of learning a structure. For example, it is well documented that English-speaking children begin with correct use of the past tense forms of verbs such as *went, broke, came*. At a certain stage of learning, such irregular verbs become regularized and *goed*, *breaked*, *comed* appear in children's utterances. The correct forms come back again later. This learning pattern, sometimes called *the U-shaped pattern*, is believed to take place as a result of the change in the mental representations of the English verbs. When regularization appears, children apply a rule across-the-board. What is initially learned as memorized discrete items now becomes rule-governed. The seemingly degenerate use comes about due to *restructuring* of the representation of the linguistic subsystem. Restructuring is seen as a qualitative and discontinued change in mental representation. Another oft-quoted case illustrating restructuring is learners' use of the strategy to memorize formulaic structures. Learners begin by memorizing some unanalyzed *chunks* or sentences without knowing their internal structure and use them as a whole for communicative purposes. Gradually, they may arrive at a stage where the complex chunks become analyzed into simpler and shorter structures. "The shift from formulaic speech to rule analysis is an example of transition from exemplar-based representations to more rule-based representations." (McLaughlin & Heredia, 1996: 217) At this stage, restructuring is believed to have occurred.

13.2.5 Skehen's Information Processing Framework

A good example of applying the information processing theory to the study of SLA is Skehan's (1998) attempt to incorporate some important findings in the SLA field into a coherent framework in line with this theory. The framework, which gives us a comprehensive picture of the L2 learning process, composes three stages: input, central processing, and output, as shown in the following diagram.

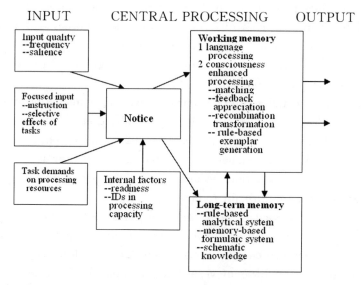

In the input stage, noticing occupies a central place. Unless it is noticed, input will not be processed and turn into intake. (Schmidt, 1990) So, noticing has a crucial role to play in the change of the IL system. The crux of the matter is what factors enhance noticing. Schmidt identifies six such factors.

1) Frequency. The more frequent a form, the more likely it is to be noticed and then becomes integrated in the IL system.
2) Salience. The more a form stands out in the input stream, the more likely it is that it will be noticed.
3) Instruction. Teaching makes aspects of input salient and brings into awareness what otherwise would have been missed.
4) Individual differences in processing ability. Some people process input more effectively and rapidly due to their greater working memory capacity.
5) Readiness to notice. The current state of the IL system predisposes learners to be ready to attend to certain input.
6) Task demands. Task requirements may overload or fit in with the limited capacity system, leading to the ease or difficulty in processing.

In addition to the above, Skehen proposes one more factor. That is the selective effects of tasks. Some task characteristics may make certain forms salient and more likely to be noticed. We might also add one factor, which is the effect of learners' native language on noticing since the L1 system is so deeply rooted and may direct our attention to certain input.

In Skehen's framework, the seven factors are arranged into four boxes under the headings of input qualities, focused input, task demands, and internal factors. Except the internal factors, other three sets of factors are external influences. As external factors are controllable, they have important implications for L2 teaching and learning research. By activating these factors, we can enhance the effects of instruction and observe these effects on IL development.

The central processing system is made up of working memory and long-term memory. Skehen attaches much importance to two assumptions with respect to the workings of the two closely related memory systems. One is Schmidt's (1990) consciousness assumption that awareness of working memory operations adds to their efficiency. The other is a dual mode of processing which is built on the rule-based system on the one hand and the memory-based formulaic (exemplar) system on the other. Conscious awareness in working memory helps in focusing on matching, feedback appreciation, recombination, and transformation. These processes facilitate restructuring in long-term memory from a rule-based perspective.

Long-term memory consists of a rule-based analytic system, a memory-based formulaic system, and general schematic knowledge. These representational systems interact through the mediating action of working memory. The rule-based system is analytic, generative and flexible, but demanding in real processing time, while exemplar memory system may be rigid, but its access is more rapid and effective. Given our limited information processing capacity, using exemplars from the previous rule generation or using unanalyzed formulaic structures (chunks) under communication pressure can ease our processing load and enables us to plan our speech ahead more smoothly.

The output stage within Skehen's framework draws heavily on Schmidt's (1992) views on the psychological mechanisms underlying fluency. Three approaches are involved, which are based on accelerating models, restructuring models, and instance models. Briefly, accelerating models emphasize developing automaticity in language use. Restructuring models involve reorganization of mental representation such as sorting out underlying rules, which leads to improvement of performance. Instance models, similar to the dual coding system, assume that fluency is achieved either through the use of exemplars or through the use of rule-based systems to generate future exemplars which then operate autonomously.

Relevant to the discussion of Skehen's framework are VanPatten's (1996) proposals of three principles for input processing, two of which are mentioned here: (a) learners process input for meaning before they process it for form; and (b) for learners to process form that is non-meaningful, e. g. third person -s, they must be able to process informational or communicative content at no or little cost to attentional resources. These two principles suggest that form-processing for learners is a luxury in real processing time. This is why use of exemplars helps. Presumably it is the exemplars or chunks that we more likely resort to under communication pressure. But from the learning perspective, developing the rule-based system through restructuring is more significant as this qualitative change makes creative use of language possible. Furthermore, the rule-based system is conducive to generating structures that can be used as chunks to facilitate communication. In other words, chunks help in performance while rule-development increases competence, if we make this dual distinction. But chunks may become analyzed and analysis is a matter of degree. Note that the role of formulaic language in L2 learning and performance has received little attention until recently. Skehen's specification of the dual-coding representation in long-term memory and the role of formulaic system in real processing time is a significant contribution to our understanding of the L2 learning process.

13.3 The Role of Native Language

One of the most striking features that distinguish adult L2 learning from child L1 learning is the fact that, prior to L2 learning, L2 learners have already had a fully developed native language system in their mind and do not start the L2 learning task completely new. To what extent L1 knowledge facilitates or impedes L2 learning has been a perennial issue in the SLA field. In the 1950s when behaviorism was in its heyday, the L1 was construed as the single most important factor influencing L2 learning. Motivated by pedagogical purposes, Contrastive Analysis (CA) was the predominant tool used to locate surface L1-L2 similarities and differences, according to which learning difficulties were predicted. The *Contrastive Analysis Hypothesis* (CAH) assumes that those elements that are similar are easy to learn and those elements that are different difficult to learn.

The pendulum swung to another extreme following Chomsky's severe attack on behaviorist's view of language learning around 1960. L1 influence was minimized in the 1970s as reflected in the *Creative Construction Hypothesis* that L2 learning is guided by universal innate principles and treated as identical to L1 learning. Supporting evidence comes from the well-known *morpheme order study*. Following Brown's (1973) original morpheme study in child L1 acquisition, a group of L2 researchers (Dulay & Burt, 1974) conducted a series of experiments investigating the order in which a set of grammatical morphemes such as progressive *-ing* and the third person singular *-s* were acquired by L2 learners. Based on the results of these studies, they claimed that, like child L1 acquisition, L2 learners followed a natural order of acquiring L2 structures regardless of L1 influence. This finding has been incorporated in Krashen's (1982) Monitor Model as the natural order hypothesis. The morpheme study has exerted a lasting influence on SLA research more for its avowed theoretical stance than for the worth of a few grammatical structures under investigation.

In spite of the downplay of L1 influence in the 1970s and the following years thereafter, there has been a renewed interest in L1 transfer in the past 20 years or so. This is because L1 transfer is a ubiquitous phenomenon throughout L2 learning, which researchers cannot afford to ignore in their endeavor to reveal the cognitive mechanisms underlying L2 learning. It has become clear that an explanatory account of L2 acquisition cannot be given on the basis of the target language alone. (Gass, 1996:321) In fact, L1 transfer results from a myriad of factors and constraints. What gets transferred, and under what conditions and when L1 transfer occurs still fascinate L2 researchers. There have been numerous studies investigating these issues. For example, drawing on evidence from German children learning English, Wode (1984, cited from Gass, 1996:322) claimed that the acquisition of prerequisite structures must occur before transfer can take place and a crucial prerequisite for L1 transfer is a certain amount of similarity between L1 and L2 structures.

An oft-quoted example in the literature concerning language transfer is a cross-linguistic study by Schachter (1974) to investigate the role of L1 in the production of English relative clauses by Chinese, Japanese, Persian, and Arabic students. She found that Chinese and Japanese students used far fewer relative clauses than the Persian and Arabic students. This was attributed to the positional difference in relative clauses between Chinese and Japanese on the one hand and English on the other. The former languages have relative clauses in prenominal position while English clauses are in postnominal position. This difference does not obtain in the Persian and Arabic languages. The linguistic difference slowed down progress for the Chinese and Japanese learners who tended to avoid using the English relative clauses. A study by Bialystok (1997) demonstrates that L1-L2 differences constitute a major factor affecting L2 learning. These studies give us reason to believe that the observation made by the proponents of the Contrastive Analysis is not far too wrong. That is, L1-L2 differences cause learning difficulty. The point is that surface differences are not the only source of difficulty and prediction of difficulty cannot be based on such differences alone.

One important constraint on L1 transfer has been identified by Kellerman (1979), whose name is associated with his coinage *psychotypology*. According to Kellerman, transferability depends on learners "perception of the distance between L1 and L2 on the one hand, and the structural organization of learners' L1 on the other." Perception is psychological while structural differences have to do with language typology. Hence the term psychotypology. The dual aspects of psychotypology suggest that both the learner factor and the linguistic factor work together to determine transferability. Rutherford (1983) moved a step further by proposing that L2 learners might perceive discourse-related information as more universal than syntax-related information and thereupon more available for transfer, and it was discourse rather than syntax that guided the overall L2 development.

Researchers working along the UG line put L1 transfer in a new perspective. According to the parameter-setting model of language learning, L2 learners start with L1 values for all parameters. Gass (1996:333) identified three possibilities in terms of the learnability of L2 parameter values: 1) appropriate L2 values are learnable through positive evidence of the L2, guided by knowledge of UG; 2) appropriate L2 values are not learnable unless they are available through surface facts of the L2; 3) L2 learners begin with UG and acquire the L2 much as a child does, and in this case, there should be no effect of the L1 parameter value. The first possibility presupposes that UG is available to L2 learners. Given this is true, positive evidence will help parameter resetting and L1 values will not be too much of a learning problem to overcome. The second possibility suggests that where L2 surface structures (positive evidence) are not available, learners will not be able to learn. In this case, L1 values will get transferred unless negative evidence is available to get rid of inappropriate use resulting from transfer of L1 values. In fact, Gass (1995) investigated this issue with the finding that L2 learners were not able to make use of the underlying and abstract things and it was through the surface similarities that the underlying and abstract structures are detected and learned. The third possibility is highly questionable. Few researchers identify L2 learning entirely with L1 learning. Even if UG principles are available to L2 learning, the L1 continues to exert major force. (Gass, 1996:332)

White (1992) holds that, within the UG framework, L1 transfer can be conceptualized differently from Contrastive Analysis. Sentences can have surface and underlying structures and L1 transfer can occur at either level of linguistic representation. For example, in the sentence *Flying planes can be dangerous*, *flying planes* can refer either to the human action of flying or to the planes that are flying. Contrastive Analysis uses surface differences alone to predict L1 transfer. Predictability of this kind is poor because surface differences may camouflage underlying complexity. It is likely that learning difficulty has more to do with underlying than with surface differences.

Connectionism, with its emphasis on the previous learning experience in tackling current learning tasks, is particularly germane to the concept of L1 transfer. The connectionist network responds to incoming information through analogy with previously stored information. Both L1 structures and the learned L2 structures constitute such previous knowledge. Due to analogy, the probabilistic patterns associated with the L1 system are activated. Since the L1 system is highly automatized through repeated activation, L1 transfer occurs inevitably, which is often manifest in the beginning stage of L2 learning when learners do not have a rich store of L2 patterns to rely on.

Wang (2012) summarizes his view on language transfer in light of the more recent development in L2 research along the usage-based line. According to him, this line of study emphasizes interaction among variables related to language learning and has done much to deepen our understanding of language transfer. The L2 learning process entails a multitude of variables, linguistic and non-linguistic, interacting with each other at different levels, "not only within the language system, but also within the social environment and the psychological make-up of an individual." (de Bot, 2007) As N. Ellis (1998) put it, "language representations emerge from interactions at all levels from brain to society... Ultimately, everything humans know is organized and related to other knowledge in some meaningful way or other, and everything they perceive is affected by their perceptual apparatus and perceptual history. Language reflects this embodiment and this experience." This interactive view on language learning concurs with the *dynamic systems theory* (*DST*), a theory that studies changes and views our world as constantly changing systems of various magnitude, which are each made up of interconnected variables. Interaction and interconnectedness of variables are two basic characteristics of DST (de Bot & Larsen-Freeman, 2011). Application of the theory to the study of second language development is a fairly recent event (see de Bot et al., 2007) and L2 learners are conceived of as a dynamic system that is constituted by a network of many interconnected L2 learning variables, psychological, cognitive and social.

Interaction and interconnectedness of L2 learning variables suggests that accurate and appropriate use of a linguistic form depends on what contextual variables are involved in the learning process. For this, Wang (2009) has advanced what he calls the learn-together-use-together principle. That is, what co-occurs with a linguistic form being learned will affect its use and retrieval. The principle maintains that the right kind of contextual variables concomitant with a linguistic form being learned enhances the likelihood of its correct use, whereas inappropriate contextual variables that co-occur with the form increase its deviant uses. Activating one variable within a dynamic system would inevitably trigger other interrelated variables. Viewed in this way, language transfer can be conceptualized as a process of activating one language in the use of another and as an outward manifestation of the internal workings of the dynamic system. Such an interactive view implies that language transfer is bidirectional rather than a one-way track from L1 to L2. In fact, there is evidence supporting this conception. In a study that examines the domain of manner of motion using intermediate L2 learners of English, Brown and Gullberg (2008) find parallel influences exist of L1 on L2 and vice versa, not necessarily an effect of advanced bilingualism, and such cross-linguistic interactions occur regardless of proficiency. This finding demonstrates that the L2 can influence L1 use in the beginning of L2 learning due to interactions that occur within the L2 learner as a dynamic system.

It is noteworthy that contextual interactions in light of DST blurs the distinction between language transfer and language use: both draw on linguistic forms previously encountered; both are related to contextual interactions during the language learning process; and both are influenced and primed by contextual variables. In other words, language transfer can be viewed as a form of language use. Just as language use is intimately tied up with learning, so language transfer as a form of language use is inseparable from language learning.

Also note that the learn-together-use-together principle gives an account of language transfer at the conceptual level, which is reminiscent of *conceptual transfer*. (see Odlin, 2008) The notion of conceptual transfer is based on a distinction between language-mediated and language-independent conceptual representations and concerned with "the influence of the language-mediated conceptual categories of one language on verbal performance in another language." (Jarvis & Pavlenko, 2008: 115) However, no such a distinction is made in the learn-together-use-together principle. Accordingly all contextual variables co-occurring with a linguistic form being learned are capable of facilitating or impeding recall and retrieval of the form. In the absence of L2-based context to support L2 learning, L1 contextual knowledge serves to fill the gap and thereupon activates associated L1 forms, resulting in L1 transfer.

13.4 Input, Interaction and Output

No learning will occur without input. Yet to what extent input contributes to language development as compared with our internal mechanisms remains largely inconclusive. In child L1 acquisition study, there is a long tradition of investigating the role of caretakers "speech in L1 development." As input data, the *child directed speech* (CDS), which refers to caretakers' interactions with children, has aroused considerable controversies. UG theorists such as Chomsky are skeptical about its usefulness in L1 acquisition. (See Snow, 1994) Nevertheless, there is no lack of researchers who believe that CDS with all its facilitative features has a role to play in child language development. For example, a common feature of CDS is the use of *recasts* in caretakers' utterances. Recasts refer to the expansion of children's utterances by providing grammatically correct versions (e. g. Following a child's utterance "Fix Lily," her mother responded with "Oh ... Lily will fix it."). Sokolov and Snow (1994) argue that recasts in CDS provide negative evidence that helps children test hypotheses about the workings of the target language.

In a similar vein, L2 researchers also examine the features of the input which L2 learners receive. Corresponding to CDS, there is the *foreigner talk discourse* (FTD) in L2 research. It refers to the speech that native speakers (NSs) simplify and adjust in talking to non-native speakers (NNSs). Since 1970, some L2 researchers (e. g. Ferguson, 1971) have studied the FTD to determine whether it facilitates L2 comprehension or acquisition.

With respect to the study of L2 input, Krashen's Input Hypothesis is highly influential. It is the most developed of the five hypotheses in Krashen's Monitor Model. ① This hypothesis claims that "humans acquire language in only one way—by understanding messages or by receiving 'comprehensible input.'" (Krashen, 1985:2) According to Krashen, input that is useful for L2

---

① The other four hypotheses are the Acquisition/Learning Hypothesis, the Monitor Hypothesis, the Natural Order Hypothesis, and the Affective Filter Hypothesis.

acquisition must be neither too difficult nor too easy to understand and ought to be tuned just right to learners' current level, represented as i. In the course of acquiring the L2, learners progress from one level to another. The next level is called $i+1$. For $i+1$ to occur, the input has to be slightly beyond the level at which learners are well proficient. The gap between i and $i+1$ is bridged by comprehensible input, which is the information drawn from the context and previous experience. Comprehensible input is considered both necessary and sufficient for L2 acquisition to occur and output plays little role. In other words, L2 learning takes place because the data to which learners are exposed contain comprehensible input.

The Input Hypothesis has prompted two other important hypotheses: the Interaction Hypothesis and the Output Hypothesis. Not long after the Input Hypothesis was made known, Long (1980) conducted a study which gave rise to what is known as the Interaction Hypothesis. In the study, NSs and NNSs were required to carry out some oral activities in pairs. NS-NNS pairs were found to use more such conversational tactics as repetitions, confirmation checks and clarification requests. Long argued that interaction of this kind, between more and less fluent speakers, should be facilitative of L2 learning. As the less proficient speakers were trying hard to understand their partners, they negotiated all their way through the difficult language points to achieve comprehension. This *negotiation for meaning* provides comprehensible input, namely $i+1$, and facilitates language acquisition according to the Input Hypothesis. In an updated version of the Interaction Hypothesis, Long (1996: 451—454) emphasizes the facilitative effect of negotiation for meaning in linking the features of input or linguistic environment with the internal learner capacities since the learner's current L2 knowledge and built-in acquisition processes influence learning. An important feature of negotiation for meaning is that it provides negative evidence for the structures in the target language.

The Input Hypothesis, however, is not without criticism. Swain (1985; 1995) argues that comprehension of L2 input is possible without the need for a full grammatical analysis. If our purpose is to achieve comprehension, we do not have to take the trouble to learn grammar. But when we are trying to say something in the L2, we are compelled to pay attention to the structural organization of sentences and rely on grammar to put words together. This process enables us to test the hypotheses about the target language and notice the gap between what we want to know and what we can say, leading to the recognition of the learning problem. Therefore, syntactic processing in the course of generating output is more conducive to L2 learning than merely comprehension of $i+1$. This view on the role of output in L2 learning is called the Comprehensible Output Hypothesis or the Output Hypothesis for short. Note that the Output Hypothesis is not so much a negation of the importance of input as a complement and reinforcement of the input-based approaches to L2 acquisition. (Izumi & Bigelow, 2000) It simply says that comprehensible input is not sufficient to drive L2 learning. Ever since its appearance, the Output Hypothesis has prompted copious research on the issue whether conscious use of L2 forms facilitates L2 acquisition.

The Input Hypothesis has also been criticized for being too general (e. g. the comprehensible input is difficult to pin down). As its outgrowth, the Interaction Hypothesis and the Output Hypothesis inherit the same weaknesses. Even so, interest in and research on these two hypotheses continue unabated.

13.5 Non-language Influences

Unlike child L1 acquisition which normally ends up in full linguistic competence, adult L2 learners differ widely in their ultimate attainment of the L2. To account for this difference, factors that affect learning outside the linguistic domain have been examined. This area of study is often called *individual differences* in L2 learning. Some of these factors are sometimes labeled affective factors such as motivation, attitude, confidence, locus of control, and self-concept. Others, which also fall into the affective domain, are called personality factors such as extroversion, introversion, field independence, anxiety, and risk-taking. Still other factors that demonstrate variations in L2 learning are age, aptitude, learner strategies. Owing to the space limit, we cannot go to the details of the role of each factor in L2 learning. For more knowledge about these factors, two good references are Peter Skehen's (1989) book *Individual Differences in Foreign Language Learning* and Dörnyei's (2005) *The Psychology of the Language Learner: Individual Differences in Second Language Acquisition*. In this section we concentrate only on the age factor, because it has aroused much interest among L2 researchers throughout the past 40 years or so and almost all sub-areas of the SLA study are connected with the age issue.

In 1967, Lenneberg published his influential book entitled *Biological Foundations of Language* in which the famous *Critical Period Hypothesis* (CPH) was formulated. According to CPH, there is a critical period, roughly between age 2 and puberty, for language acquisition. Once this period is closed, full linguistic competence will become difficult to attain due to a loss of neural plasticity. This hypothesis claims that successful acquisition of language is subject to maturational constraints. Although CPH was not originally intended to specifically address L2 learning issues, it nevertheless has sparked a great deal of research in this field.

The central issue concerning the age effect on L2 learning is whether a critical period exists for L2 learning. If adult learners could learn a new language just as easily as children learn the L1, then there would have been no CPH. As one grows older, the decline of the language learning ability seems to be obvious. However, decline does not presuppose a critical period because the term "critical" suggests a cut-off point beyond which language learning is difficult, if not impossible. Furthermore, researchers always find cases that native-like competence is attainable after the critical period. Thus, individual differences are a powerful weapon used to reject CPH. Confronted with such criticisms, proponents have delimited CPH to some extent. Some researchers (e.g. Scovel, 1969) single out pronunciation as supporting evidence and maintain that native-like pronunciation is impossible to achieve beyond puberty. Others (e.g. Seliger, 1978) posit multiple critical periods, suggesting that learning different aspects of language follows different timetables and is subject to different maturational constraints. Still others replace "critical period" with "sensitive period" to relax the term "critical." Following a comprehensive review of relevant literature, Krashen, Long, and Scarcella (1979) concluded that older learners acquire L2s faster, but in the long run younger learners become more proficient. This "younger = better" position is called "the consensus view" by Singleton (1995). There is nothing unexpected about this view as it applies to any number of skills. Language learning would be really exceptional if older individuals are better learners.

A well-known study in support of CPH is Johnson and Newport's (1989) investigation into the relationship between learners' proficiency and ages of arrival (AOA) in the United States. The subjects' range of AOA was from 3 to 39. Results showed that there existed a linear relationship between L2 syntactic knowledge and AOA up to puberty. After that, learners' performance on the linguistic tasks deteriorated and correlated poorly with AOA. But this finding has been challenged by other studies. For example, Bialystok (1997) reanalyzed Johnson and Newport's data and, on the basis of two empirical studies, found that the maturational variable is not a determining factor affecting success of L2 learning and the significant factors were the L1-L2 differences.

There have been attempts to explain why the critical period exists if CPH holds. Birdsong (1999: 3—18) summarizes the following possible mechanisms underlying the age-related declines in language learning ability after the closure of the critical period:

    1) Neural plasticity in the brain is lost. Due to the change in cerebral functions, the neural substrate that is required for language learning is not fully available.

    2) Language learning faculty is lost. UG is no longer available.

    3) Less is more. As one grows older, cognitive maturity becomes a

disadvantage for language learning. Children's limited processing capacity allows them to process only a few morphemes from the linguistic input and success is more likely.
4) Use it then lose it. Early learning of language is biologically favoured over later learning because we may reap the benefits of linguistic communication over a longer stretch of our lifetime. To retain the learning faculty would be uneconomical.
5) Use it or lose it. The language learning faculty atrophies with lack of use over time.
6) Learning inhibits learning. In line with the connectionist networks, after the L1 probabilistic patterns of weights have been developed and strengthened, they are difficult to undo.

All the above proposed mechanisms cannot possibly occur abruptly. Take 6 for example. Once the L1 system has been fixed, learning a new language would become difficult, suggesting that only L1-L2 differences pose learning difficulty. Where the L1 and the L2 are the same, no learning is required. However, differences are always there regardless of learners' age. If L1-L2 differences are the cause of learning difficulty, then this difficulty should be the same for both children and adults alike and learning a L2 during and after the critical period should make no difference. There ought to be no maturational constraint on L2 learning. (see Bialystok, 1997) Learning a L2 is virtually to learn what it differs from one's L1. Since L1-L2 differences can vary from language to language, it follows that a L2 can be more or less difficult to learn.

Although evidence against CPH abounds, there is "a general consensus that older individuals cannot reasonably hope to ever achieve a native accent in a second language. There is no such consensus about other areas of language." (Gass & Selinker, 2001:337) This suggests that pronunciation is the only aspect of language which is subject to maturational constraint. Other language skills do not relate to the critical period. We would argue that the relationship between pronunciation and CPH has important consequences to L2 learning and it is due to this relationship that the critical period appears to make sense. Affect is the common denominator underlying the learning of pronunciation and other language skills.

Compared with other affective factors, *self-concept* seems to be more closely related to the learning of L2 pronunciation. According to Burns (cited in Child, 1986:244), self-concept "is the individual's percepts, concepts and evaluations about himself, including the image he feels others have of him and of the person he would like to be, nourished by a diet of personally evaluated environmental experience." Psychologically, an individual is always trying to protect his or her self-concept against external threats. Human language faculty can be conceptualized as a mental organ with pronunciation as its external expression. Like our eyes or nose, the "looks" of our mental organ, namely our pronunciation, has an effect on our self-concept. Those learners whose pronunciation is poorly learned may feel embarrassed or psychologically threatened. They may choose to keep silent at best and give up learning altogether at worst. Difficulty in learning pronunciation after puberty can have a detrimental effect on adult L2 learners' self-concept, which in turn affects the learning of other aspects of language. Based on this reasoning, we presume that pronunciation bears on CPH and has an extended effect on the learning of other language skills because of affect. This explanation of CPH seems to fit in with our intuition. Affective factors may not necessarily be the cause for learning, but they serve as a starting machine capable of activating learning mechanisms. Unless this machine is in operation, no learning is likely to occur.

Although it has been extensively studied for several decades, CPH remains as controversial today as ever before. Even so, interest in research along this line shows no sign of dwindling partly because CPH has become a unified concept that brings almost all research areas of SLA together and does much to deepen our understanding of the L2 learning process.

13.6 Summary

In this chapter, we have reviewed some major issues in SLA study. These issues include internal mechanisms of L2 learning, the role of the native language, the role of input and output, and non-language influences. Discussion of internal mechanisms centers around three approaches based on three theoretical models: Universal Grammar, connectionism, and information processing. Each model offers unique insights into the L2 learning process. The role of native language receives much attention in present-day SLA study because it is a distinguishing feature of L2 learning and a crucial factor responsible for its variable success. Input is important for the simple reason that, without it, no learning will occur. But how input interacts with internal mechanisms to facilitate interlanguage development still remains an open issue. The Input Hypothesis is intended to address this issue and has sparked off two more influential hypotheses: the Interaction Hypothesis and the Output Hypothesis. Non-language influences cover many factors, but only the age factor has been singled out for a focused discussion due to its relevance to almost all sub-areas of SLA research.

References

Bialystok, E. 1997. "The structure of age: in search of barriers to second language acquisition," *Second Language Research* 13: 116—137.

Birdsong, D. 1999. "Introduction: whys and why nots of the critical period hypothesis for second language acquisition," *Second Language Acquisition and the Critical Period*. In Birdsong, D. (ed.). New Jersey: Lawrence Erlbaum. pp. 1−22.

Bley-Vroman, R. W. 1989. "What is the logical problem of foreign language learning?" In *Linguistic Perspectives on Second Language Acquisition*. Gass, S. & Schachter, J. (eds.). Cambridge: Cambridge University Press. pp. 41−68.

Brown, G. 1973. *A First Language: The Early Stages*. Cambridge, MA: Harvard University Press.

Brown, A. & Gullberg, M. 2008. "Bidirectional crosslinguistic influence in L1−L2 encoding of manner in speech and gesture," *Studies in Second Language Acquisition* 30: 225−251.

Child, D. 1986. *Psychology and the Teacher*. (4th ed.). London: CASSELL.

Chomsky, N. 1995. *The Minimalist Program*. Cambridge, MA: MIT press.

Corder, P. 1967. "The significance of learners' errors," *International Review of Applied Linguistics* 5: 161−169.

de Bot, K. 2007. "A dynamic systems theory approach to second language acquisition," *Bilingualism: Language and Cognition* 10: 7−21.

Dörnyei, Z. 2005. *The Psychology of the Language Learner: Individual Differences in Second Language Acquisition*. Mahwah, NJ: Lawrence Erlbaum Associates.

Dulay, H. & But, M. 1974. "Natural sequences in child second language acquisition," *Language Learning* 24: 37−53.

Ellis, N. C. & R. Schmidt. 1997. "Morphology and longer distance dependencies," *Studies in Second Language Acquisition* 19: 145−171.

Ellis, N. 1998. "Emergentism, connectionism and language learning," *Language Learning* 48: 631−664.

Ferguson, C. 1971. "Absence of copula and the notion of simplicity: a study of normal speech, baby talk, foreigner talk and pidgins," In *Pidginization and Creolization of Languages*. Hymes, D. (ed.). Cambridge: Cambridge University Press. pp. 141−150.

Gass, S. 1995. "Universals, SLA and language pedagogy: 1984 revisited," In *The Current State of Interlanguage*. Eubank, L., Selinker, L. & Sharwood Smith, M. (eds.). Amsterdam: John Benjamins. pp. 31−42.

Gass, S. 1996. "Second language acquisition and linguistic theory: the role of language transfer," In *Handbook of Second Language Acquisition*. Ritchie, W. C. & Bhatia, T. (eds.). San Diego: Academic Press. pp. 316−345.

Gass, S. & Selinker, L. 2001. *Second Language Acquisition: An Introductory Course*. (2nd ed.). New Jersey: Lawrence Erlbaum.

Gregg, K. R. 1996. "The logical and developmental problems of second Language acquisition," In *Handbook of Second Language Acquisition*. Ritchie, W. C. & Bhatia, T. (eds.). San Diego: Academic Press. pp. 50−84.

Izumi, S. & Bigelow, M. 2000. "Does output promote noticing and second language acquisition?" *TESOL Quarterly* 34: 239−278.

Jarvis, S. & Pavlenko, A. 2008. *Crosslinguistic Influence in Language and Cognition*. New York: Routledge.

Johnson, J. & Newport, E. 1989. "Critical period effects in second language learning: the influence of maturational state on the acquisition of ESL," *Cognitive Psychology* 21: 60—99.

Kellerman, E. 1979. "Transfer and non-transfer: where we are now," *Studies in Second Language Acquisition* 2: 37—57.

Krashen, S. 1982. *Principles and Practice in Second Language Acquisition*. Oxford: Pergamon.

Krashen, S. 1995. *The Input Hypothesis: Issues and Implications*. London: Longman.

Krashen, S. D., Long, M., & Scarcella, R. 1979. "Age, rate, and eventual attainment in second language acquisition," *TESOL Quarterly* 13: 573—582.

Long, M. H. 1980. *Input, Interaction and Second Language Acquisition*. Doctoral dissertation, University of California, Los Angeles.

Long, M. 1996. "The role of the linguistic environment in second language acquisition," In *Handbook of Second Language Acquisition*. Ritchie, W. C. & Bhatia, T. (eds.). San Diego: Academic Press. pp. 413—468.

McLaughlin, B. & Heredia, R. 1996. "Information-processing and approaches to research on second language acquisition and use," In *Handbook of Second Language Acquisition*. Ritchie, W. C. & Bhatia, T. (eds.). San Diego: Academic Press. pp. 213—228.

Mitchell, R. & Myles, F. 1998. *Learning Theories*. London: Arnold.

Odlin, T. 2008. "Conceptual transfer and meaning extensions," In *Handbook of Cognitive Linguistics and Second Language Acquisition*. Robinson, P. & Ellis, N. (eds.). New York: Routledge.

Rutherford, W. 1983. "Language typology and language transfer," In *Language Transfer in Language Learning*. Gass, S. & Selinker, L. (eds.). Rowley, MA: Newbury House.

Radford, A. 1997. *Syntax: A Minimalist Introduction*. Cambridge: Cambridge University Press.

Schachter, J. 1974. "An error in error analysis," *Language Learning* 24: 205—214.

Schmit, R. 1990. "The role of consciousness in second language learning," *Applied Linguistics* 11: 17—46.

Schmit, R. 1992. "Psychological mechanisms underlying second language fluency," *Studies in Second Language Acquisition* 14: 357—385.

Scovel, T. 1969. "Foreign accents, language acquisition, and cerebral dominance," *Language Learning* 19: 245—253.

Seliger, H. 1978. "Implications of a multiple critical period hypothesis for second language learning," In *Second Language Acquisition Research*. Ritchie, W. (ed.). New York: Academic Press. pp. 11—19.

Selinker, L. 1972. "Interlanguage," *International Review of Applied Linguistics* 10: 209—231.

Shiffrin, R. M. & Schneider, W. 1977. "Controlled and automatic human information processing: II. perceptual learning, automatic attending, and a general theory," *Psychological Review* 84: 127—190.

Singleton, D. 1995. "Introduction: a critical look at the critical period hypothesis in second language acquisition research," In *The Age Factor in Second Language Acquisition*. Singleton, D. & Lengyel, Z. (eds.). London: Multilingual Matters Ltd., Clevedon. pp. 1—29.

Skehen, P. 1998. *A Cognitive Approach to Language Learning*. Oxford: Oxford University

Press.

Snow, C. 1994. "Beginning from baby talk: twenty years of research on input and interaction," In *Input and Interaction in Language Acquisition*. Gallaway, C. & Richards, B. R. (eds.). Cambridge: Cambridge University Press. pp. 3—12.

Sokolik, M. E. & M. E. Smith. 1992. "Assignment of gender to French nouns in primary and secondary language: a connectionist model," *Second Language Research* 8: 39—58.

Sokolov, J. L. and Snow, C. E. 1994. "The changing role of negative evidence in theories of language development," In *Input and Interaction in Language Acquisition*. Gallaway, C. & Richards, B. R. (eds.). Cambridge: Cambridge University Press. pp. 38—55.

Swain, M. 1985. "Communicative competence: some roles of comprehensible input and comprehensible output in its development," In *Input in Second Language Acquisition*. Gass, S. M. & Madden, C. G. (eds.). Rowley, MA: Newbury House. pp. 235—253.

Swain, M. 1995. "Three functions of output in second language learning," In *Principles and Practice in Applied Linguistics: Studies in Honour of H. G. Widdowson*. Cook, G. & Seidlhofer, B. (eds.). Oxford: Oxford University Press. pp. 125—144.

VanPatten, B. 1996. *Input Processing and Grammar Instruction*. New York: Ablex.

Verspoor, M. H., de Bot, K. & Lowie, W. (eds.). 2011. *A Dynamic Approach to Second Language Development*. Amsterdam: John Benjamins.

Wang, C. 2012. Context and language transfer. ms.

Wexler, K. & Culicover, P. 1980. *Formal Principles of Language Acquisition*. Cambridge, MA: MIT Press.

White, L. 1992. "Universal Grammar: Is it a new name for old problems?" In *Language Transfer in Language Learning*. Gass, S. & Selinker, L. (eds.). Amsterdam: John Benjamins. pp. 219—234

Wilson, R. A. & Keil, F. C. 1999. "The MIT encyclopedia of the cognitive sciences," Cambridge: The MIT Press. (上海:上海外语教育出版社,2000 年出版)

王初明,2009,学相伴 用相随——外语学习的学伴用随原则,《中国外语》5: 53—59。

Chapter 14

Modern Theories and Schools of Linguistics

Theories without facts may be barren, but facts without theories are meaningless.

Kenneth E. Boulding (*Economic Analysis*: *Microeconomics*. New York: Harper & Row, 1966.)

14.1 The Beginning of Modern Linguistics

Modern linguistics began from the Swiss linguist Ferdinand de Saussure (1857—1913), who is described as "father of modern linguistics" (Culler, 1976: 7) among many other sources thereafter. Indeed, Saussure has been so important a figure that he is not only frequently referred to in the field of modern linguistics, but also by many more in the fields such as semiotics, literary theory, and philosophy.

Although Saussure is well known for his posthumous publication *Cours de linguistique générale* /*Course in General Linguistics*, he did not write the book, which was a collection and expansion of his teaching notes taken by his students. During the years from 1907 to 1911, Saussure lectured on general linguistics in the University of Geneva. After his death in 1913, his colleagues and students thought that his ideas were original and insightful and should be preserved. Two of his students, Charles Bally and Albert Sechehaye, collected lecture notes from fellow students and put them together to produce the *Cours* in 1916.[①] It has been one of the seminal works of the 20th century, since Saussure's innovative ideas, principles and methods formed the central tenets of structural linguistics.

After Rudolf Engler had a two-volume critical edition of the *Cours* published between 1967 and 1974, with all the students' notes from which the *Cours* was originally constructed, it became possible to go beyond the constructed text for Saussure's ideas. As Culler (1976: 17) points out among

---

[①] Two English editions are the 1959 translated by W. Baskin and the 1983 translated by R. Harris. Since 1916, more than 400 editions have been published in about 30 languages and held by over 2,000 libraries worldwide.

other things, Bally and Sechehaye's edition might not be Saussure's order of presentation and his potential logical sequence of argument. Saussure had told friends that he was writing up the lectures himself but no evidence was found until 1996, when a manuscript in Saussure's hand was discovered in the orangerie of his family house in Geneva. This proved to be the missing original of the great work and was published in English for the first time as *Writings in General Linguistics* (2006). Although Saussure's knowledge was passed on in a somewhat extraordinary manner, a fact remains that the *Cours/Course* is still the major source of Saussure's ideas, influence and reputation.

14.1.1 Sources of Saussure's Ideas

Saussure's idea son linguistics were developed along five lines: linguistics, sociology, psychology, economics, and philosophy.

1) *Linguistics*. Saussure was influenced by the Neogrammarians and particularly from the American linguist William Dwight Whitney (1827—1894), who was working within essentially the Neogrammarian tradition but raised the question of the SIGN. Whitney argued that language is in fact an institution, founded on social conventions. In stressing the institutional and conventional nature of language, Whitney distinguished human communication from the merely instinctive animal communication. Saussure said that by insisting on the concept of arbitrariness of the sign to emphasize that language is an institution, Whitney brought linguistics onto the right track. For Saussure, meaning exits only because there are differences of meaning, and it is these differences of meaning that enable one to establish the articulation of linguistic forms. Forms can be recognized not because of their historical continuity, but because of their different functions, their ability to distinguish and to produce distinct meanings.

2) *Sociology*. Since language was seen as different from biological species, what is the notion of linguistics as an academic discipline? If languages are not living species, in what sense can things be studied at all? Following the French sociologist Emile Durkheim (1858—1917), Saussure answered these questions in terms of the new science of sociology: language is an example of the kind of entity which certain sociologists call "social facts." Social facts, according to Durkheim, are ideas in the "collective mind" of a society. The collective mind of a society is something that exists over and above the individual members of the society, and its ideas are only indirectly and imperfectly reflected in the minds of the people who make up that society. In this view social facts are radically distinct from individual psychological acts, since they are of a general nature and exercise constraint over the individual.

Language is a social fact, since it is general throughout a community and exercises a constraint on the speakers. It consists in our lack of any alternative and it is imposed on us by education, but when we master it, we are no longer aware of any constraint. Against this backdrop, Saussure found the answer to the ontological problem. A language, whether English or French or Chinese, is not a thing in the same sense as a chair or a table. But there is a category of "things" which includes legal systems and structures of convention, then language surely fits into the category too. What is actually observed of a language (sequences of vocal sounds, printed texts and so on) are physical phenomena, but there is a distinction between observable physical facts and the underlying general system. In Saussure's terms, they are *langue* and *parole*. What individual speakers say (*parole*) exemplifies the system (*langue*) that only exists within a collectivity.

3) *Psychology*. Saussure was also influenced by the Austrian psychologist Sigmund Freud (1855—1939), who discussed the prohibition of incest and other social taboos and the Oedipus Complex. Freud postulated a historical crime in primitive times: a jealous and tyrannical king, who wished to keep all women round and drove his sons away as they reached maturity, was killed and devoured by the sons who had banded together. In devouring him they sought to take on his power and his role. This "memorable and criminal deed" was the beginning of social organization, of moral restrictions, and of religion, because guilt and remorse created taboos. Freud recognized that in making the deed the historical cause of social norms and psychic complexes which still existed, he was postulating the continuity of a collective psychic, which he called the unconscious. How could otherwise a single act continue to exercise such profound effects on humanity? Part of the explanation is that in our psychical system, feelings of guilt may arise from wishes as well as from actual deeds, and this creative sense of guilt helps to keep the consequences of the deed alive. Indeed, he admits that it is possible that the original deed never actually took place, remorse may have been provoked by the sons' fantasy of killing the father. Even so, "no damage would thus be done to the causal chain stretching from the beginning to the present day."

4) *Economics*. Saussure was also influenced by Western economic theories of the time. His linguistic theories on the nature of the linguistic sign, *langue* vs. *parole*, syntagmatic vs. paradigmatic, and synchronic vs. diachronic, can find their traces in the economic theories of "the Old Historical School" and "the New Historical School" founded by German economists W. G. F. Roscher and G. von Schmoller respectively, "the Marginal Utility School" initiated by the Swiss economists Antoine Auguste Walras (1801—1866) and Marie E'spril Leon Walras (1834—1910), the Austrian economist Carl Menger (1840—1921), and the British economist William Stantley Jevons (1835—1882). Since value and value theory have been a central issue in almost all Western schools of economics, Saussure held that both linguistics and economics were sciences

Chapter 14 Modern Theories and Schools of Linguistics 457

of studying values. While historicism aimed to study the causes of values, synchronicity aimed at understanding the effects of values without being concerned about where they came from. Saussure's serial dichotomies and his preferences on one over the other in developing theories of language brought linguistics onto a scientific road.

5) *Philosophy*. In order to be explicit about the nature of signification and to develop a science of signs, Saussure based his theories on the classical relationship in most western philosophies between "presence" and "absence," which is a distinction between virtual worlds and actual worlds. For Saussure, *langue* is "absence" in the virtual world and *parole* is "presence" in the actual world. Absence/virtual systems are considered stable and invariable, while presence/actual systems are considered unstable and variable. The advantage of this formulation is that, in the discussion of the virtual system of *langue*, one would theoretically be working with a stable, unchanging system rather than with the unpredictable activities of an actual system of *parole*. This theory in fact underpins most systems of thought and science in the west. By designing and building models of virtual systems or *langue*, one is not principally concerned with actual systems of *parole*, or what people actually say or what appears on the page, but the structures of a system that gives the potential for the words on the page or the utterances of speech to exist. This principle is in fact the key to understanding part of the fundamental philosophy of structuralism and its consequence for the academic inquiries in the 20th century.

Ideas from these different academic sources form useful ways of explaining how certain systems can be simultaneously unknown yet effectively present. If a description of any system counts as the analysis of what is being observed, it is because the system is something not immediately given to the presence yet seemed to be always present and always at work in any human behaviour.

14.1.2 Saussure's Theorizing

Together with other social scientists, Saussure discovered that although human behaviour is objective, it is different from the objects of study for natural scientists. Unlike natural scientists, social scientists have to take into account human subjective impressions on behaviour, and they are part of the behaviour that has social meaning. Social sciences do not deal with the social reality itself, but a combination of social facts and their social meanings.

Saussure was the first to notice the complexities of language. He saw human language as an extremely complex and heterogeneous phenomenon. Even a single speech act involves an extraordinary range of factors and can be considered from many different, even conflicting points of view: sounds, sound waves and hearing mechanism, the signifying intention of the speaker, reference, the communicative context, the conventions between speakers and listeners, grammatical and semantic rules, the history of language, etc. Confronted with all these aspects of language, the linguist must ask himself what he is trying to describe. Saussure believed that language is *a system of signs*. Noises count as language only when they serve to express or communicate ideas; otherwise they are nothing but noise. To communicate ideas, they must be part of a system of conventions, part of a system of signs.

Saussure's theories are extremely important, since they serve to direct attention to essentials of language and make clear the object of study for linguistics as a science. He writes, "Linguistics never attempted to determine the nature of the object it was studying, and without this elementary operation a science cannot develop an appropriate method." Some of his ideas can be summarized as follows:

1) *The essential nature of the linguistic sign*. Saussure holds that the linguistic sign unites, not a thing and a name, but a concept and a sound-image. It is the combination of the two that makes up the whole of the linguistic sign. Saussure calls the concept signified and the sound-image signifier, thus separating the two from each other and from the whole of which they are parts. The word *tree*, for example, is a linguistic sign; its sound-image /tri:/ is the signifier and the plant it refers to is the signified. The particular combination of the signifier and the signified is an arbitrary entity.

Related to the arbitrary nature of the linguistic sign is the linear nature of the signifier. The signifier is auditory and therefore is unfolded solely in time. As a result of this, the signifier represents a time span and the span is measurable in one single dimension, the dimension of time. The linear nature of the signifier is as important as the arbitrary nature of the sign. Because of this, the elements of the signifier are represented in succession—they form a chain, which makes the processing of them possible. This feature becomes more obvious when elements of the signifier are represented in writing, in which case the spatial line of graphic marks is substituted for succession in time.

2) *The relational nature of linguistic units*. Since the relation between the signifier and the signified is arbitrary, there is no necessary reason for one concept rather than another to be attached to a given signifier. Consequently, there is no defining property which the concept must retain in order to count as the signifier of that signified. The signifiers are nothing but members of a system and they are defined by their relations to the other members of that system. Saussure writes, in all cases, we find not "pre-existing ideas" but "values emanating from the system." (1959: 117) When we say that these values correspond to concepts, it is understood that these concepts are purely

Chapter 14　Modern Theories and Schools of Linguistics

differential, not positively defined by their content but negatively defined by their relations with other terms of the system. Their most precise characteristic is that they are what the others are not.

3) *The distinction of* langue *and* parole. This distinction is an opposition between the linguistic system and its actual manifestation. Saussure writes, in separating *langue* from *parole*, we are at the same time separating "what is social from what is individual" and "what is essential from what is accessory and more or less accidental." (1959: 14) He argues that the task of the linguist is to study *langue*. The linguist, in analyzing language, is not to describe speech acts, but to determine the units and rules of combination which make up the linguistic system.

The distinction between what belongs to particular linguistic facts and what belongs to the linguistic system itself is important at many levels. It led to the distinction of phonetics and phonology, and between studies of utterance and of sentence. It is, in fact, essentially a distinction between institution and event, between the underlying system which makes possible various types of behaviour and actual instances of such behaviour. By this distinction, Saussure gave linguistics a suitable object of study and gave the linguist a much clearer sense of what he was doing.

4) *The distinction of synchrony and diachrony*. The difference between synchrony and diachrony of linguistics is that between static linguistics and evolutionary linguistics. Saussure explained his point with a comparison between the functioning of language and a game of chess. First, the state of language is very much like that of the set of chessmen. The respective value of the pieces depends on their position on the chessboard just as each linguistic term derives its value from its opposition to all other items. Second, the system is always momentary, varying from one position to the next. Although the values depend on an unchangeable convention, the set of rules that exists before a game begins persists after each move. Rules that are agreed upon once and for all exist in language too. Third, to pass from one state of stability (or synchrony) to the next, only the chess pieces have to be moved. Some changes bring about great effects; other changes bring about minor effects. In spite of that, the move does affect the whole system. A certain move can revolutionize the whole game and even affect the pieces that are not immediately involved.

However, this distinction faces some challenges, because it is not easy to draw a sharp line between these two aspects of language studies. There are several reasons for this. First, languages are in a constant state of changing. There is never a moment when a language remains static for our description. We can never be too certain whether a new word or phrase was introduced and accepted today or yesterday, this year or last year. The process of change is usually long and gradual. Second, the language of any speech community is never uniform. Different groups of people speak a somewhat different variety of the language. Which variety is to be described is quite a matter of decision, for there is always the possibility for someone to challenge the description by "*But I never say that.*" Third, when a language changes, it is not the case that one set of features is suddenly replaced by another set of features.

In a diachronic study, the different states of a language compared should be relatively removed from one another in time; otherwise the changes will not be obvious or typical. By the statement that synchronic descriptions are prior to diachronic descriptions, it is meant that one has to describe the states first before he can compare them. It is never meant that in describing one state of the language, some knowledge of its previous state is unnecessary. In fact we often need to know what the language was like previously in order to describe with insight what it is like today. In short, there is a close relation between the study of diachronic changes on the one hand and synchronic variations on the other.

14.1.3 Saussure's Legacy

Although originally interested in historical linguistics, Saussure developed a more general theory of semiotics for a number of disciplines, and his thoughts were adapted by French intellectuals (Roland Barthes, Jacques Lacan & Claude Lévi-Strauss) to literary studies, philosophy, psychoanalysis, and anthropology.

Saussure is the first scholar to point out that the semiological perspective was central to any serious study of language. Where there are signs there are systems, and if one is to determine their essential nature, one must treat them not in isolation but as examples of semiological systems. In this way, aspects that are often hidden or neglected will become apparent, especially when language is seen as one of the many types of semiotic systems or non-linguistic signifying practices are considered as "language."

Linguistics may serve as a model for semiology because in the case of language the arbitrary and conventional nature of the sign is especially clear. Non-linguistic signs may often seem natural to those who use them, and it may require some effort to see that the politeness or impoliteness of an action is not a necessary and intrinsic property of that action but a conventional meaning. Saussure (1959: 68) says,

> In fact, every means of expression used in a society is based, in principle, on collective behaviour or—what amounts to the same thing— on convention. Polite formulas, for instance, though often imbued with a certain natural expressiveness (as in the case of a Chinese who greets his

Chapter 14   Modern Theories and Schools of Linguistics

emperor by bowing down to the ground nine times), are nonetheless fixed by rule; it is this rule and not the intrinsic value of the gestures that obliges one to use them. Signs that are wholly arbitrary realize better than the others the ideal of the semiological process; that is why language, the most complex and universal of all systems of expression, is also the most characteristic; in this sense linguistics can become the master-pattern for all branches of semiology although language is only one particular semiological system.

Saussure's theory of semiology not only opened up a new discipline, but also founded a methodology applicable to many social sciences. A young science as semiology is, it has proved that the relations between the signifier and the signified exist in numerous phenomena, and that the underlying system that gives special values to social semiotics is worth studying. It is now realized that many daily happenings that have been taken for granted are governed by underlying customs, institutions, and social values. The development of semiology owes much to the great thinker and modern linguist Saussure.

Saussure actually exerted two kinds of influence on modern linguistics. First, he provided a general orientation, a sense of the task of linguistics which has seldom been questioned. He is the first in emphasizing this sense of the task of linguistic investigation and it is in this sense that he has been called the father of modern linguistics. Second, he influenced modern linguistics in the specific concepts, the distinction between *langue* and *parole*, the separation of the synchronic and the diachronic perspectives, and the view of language as system of syntagmatic and paradigmatic relations operating at various hierarchical levels. Although these concepts are not strictly original to him, Saussure's contributions lie in his efforts to promote them. Many of the developments of modern linguistics can be described as the investigations of the precise nature and import of these concepts. Saussure's fundamental perception is of revolutionary significance. It is he that pushed linguistics into a brand new stage and all linguistics in the 20th century are Saussurean linguistics.

14.2   The Prague School and the Copenhagen School

14.2.1   The Prague School

The first meeting of the Linguistic Circle of Prague was held under the leadership of Vilem Mathesius (1882—1946) in 1926. Activists in this school included Roman Jakobson (1896—1982) and Nikolai Trubetzkoy (1890—

1938). This school practised a special style of synchronic linguistics, and its most important contribution to linguistics is that it sees language in terms of function. It has been an extremely important source of influence in linguistics, even unparalleled in some cases, as has been stated that "No other European group has wielded quite as much influence as this one," and it "has influenced every important development in the United States." (Bolinger, 1968)

The first common task for the Prague School linguists was the formulation of collective theses to be presented to the First International Congress of Slavists in Prague in the summer of 1929. These theses were later published in Volume I of the *Travaux du Cercle Linguistique de Prague*. It was through the eight volumes of these collections of papers, which were published until 1939, that the Prague Circle became known abroad. In 1930, on the initiative of the Circle, the first international phonological conference was convened in Prague in preparation for the International Linguistic Congress in Geneva in 1931. From then onwards the members of the Prague Circle prepared joint theses for several other international linguistic gatherings. Their work was somewhat interrupted by World War II. The last collective preparation of papers was in 1948 when the Sixth International Congress was held in Paris. The Circle formally ceased to exist in 1950. At present, it has two successors. The Linguistic Association comprises mainly specialists in general linguistics, in phonetics and in Slavic languages, and in Czech and Slovak linguistics, while the Group for Functional Linguistics at the Circle of Modern Philologists represents linguists in the field of English, Germanic and Romance Languages. These organizations are not only active in Prague, but have several branches in many parts of the country. In the 1960s Czechoslovak linguists again felt the need to publish collective volumes of those papers in order to prove the continuity of the Linguistic Circle of Prague.

Of the many ideas developed in Prague School, three points are of special importance. First, it was stressed that the synchronic study of language is fully justified as it can draw on complete and controllable material for investigation but no rigid theoretical barrier is erected to separate diachronic study. Second, there was an emphasis on the systemic character of language. It was argued that no element of any language can be satisfactorily analysed or evaluated if viewed in isolation: assessment can only be made if its relationship is established with the coexisting elements in the same language system. In other words, elements are held to be in functional contrast or opposition. Third, language was looked on as functional in another sense, that is, as a tool performing a number of essential functions or tasks for the community using it.

Following Saussure's distinction between *langue* and *parole*, they argued that phonetics belongs to *parole* whereas phonology belongs to *langue*. On this basis, they developed the notion of the "phoneme" as an abstract unit of the sound system as distinct from the sounds actually produced. To determine these phonemes, they employed, for example, commutation tests, by which significant features of sounds bringing about changes in meaning, e. g. bat / bet / bit, could be established. In recent years Prague School ideas have been developed with reference to syntax, semantics and stylistics of English and Salvic languages. In what follows, we shall mainly discuss the School's contribution to phonology and its functional analysis of language.

14. 2. 1. 1 Phonology and Phonological Oppositions

The Prague School is best known and remembered for its contribution to phonology and the distinction between phonetics and phonology. The name of the most influential scholar in this connection is Trubetzkoy, whose most complete and authoritative statements of principle are formulated in his *Principles of Phonology* published in 1939. This is the result of his 16-year research, dictated on his bed and published posthumously. When the book was near its completion short of only 20 pages, he died at the age of 48, on June 25, 1938. After his death, the manuscript was published in German, French, and Russian.

Trubetzkoy followed Saussure's theory in the discussion of the phoneme. He said, phonetics belongs to *parole*, and phonology belongs to *langue*. He found that for each abstract sound, there is a range than a point in which speakers are allowed to make the actual realisation of it different from every other realisation by themselves and also distinct from every other realisation by other people. Try to pronounce the /t/ in *tea*, *two* and *tar*. Within this range, every realisation can do the job it is expected to do. But if the realisation is beside the range, we will be understood as producing another sound or saying something else. If we ignore the meaning of the sounds, we can find features peculiar to each realisation. Some features have no significance; they make no differences to the meaning of the word. Some make differences; they are significant sounds or distinctive sounds, because they have the function of distinguishing words or meaning. The criterion for determining which sounds are significantly contrastive is meaning; phonetic differences that do not signal semantic differences are not distinctive but are phonemic. Indeed, it is not the sound itself that serves to differentiate the phonological unit, the phoneme, which is actually a sound's contrastive function. A phoneme, therefore, may be defined as the sum of these differential functions. It is not a thing, but an *abstraction*. Sounds in themselves are not phonemes; they are phonemes in so insofar as they serve to distinguish meaning. As a founder and a leading scholar of the Prague School, he called his particular approach to the study of language "phonology," which he defined as the study of the function of speech-sounds, and because of this emphasis he and other Prague linguists are called "functionalists."

Trubetzkoy tried to classify these distinctive features. Not only did he wish to know the difference between /p/ and /b/, but also wished to know the nature of the difference in the phonological system. In classifying phonological oppositions, he proposed three criteria: 1) their relation to the whole contrastive system; 2) relations between the opposing elements; and 3) their power of discrimination. These can be summarized as follows:

1. Bilateral opposition: If the features two phonemes share belong only to them, they are bilateral opposition; In other words, the features they have in common do not occur simultaneously in any other phoneme. /p/ and /b/ share the feature of "bilabial."

2. Multilateral opposition: a more loosely established relationship: /a/ and /ɪ/ for instance are alike only to the extent that both are vowels, a quality shared by any other pairs of vowels.

3. Proportional opposition: Two phonemes are proportional if the same contrastive features also serve as the differentiating criterion for other pairs of phonemes. For example, sonority (voiced/voiceless) is the contrastive feature between not only /p/ and /b/, but also /t/ and /d/.

4. Isolated opposition: If the contrastive feature is unique to the pair, that is, it is not a contrastive feature of any other pairs of phonemes in the language, it is isolated opposition. In English, /v/ and /l/, the former is labial-dental fricative, the latter is lateral voiced. The German /t/ and /x/—a dental stop and a velar fricative. These oppositions are not shared by any other pair of phonemes in the same language.

5. Privative opposition: One member of a contrastive pair may be characterized by the presence of a certain feature, the other by its absence: aspiration vs. lack of aspiration (/p/ and /b/), nasalization versus lack of nasalization (/m/ and /b/), and so on.

6. Gradual opposition: If the pairs share different degrees of a feature, their relation is gradual opposition; in a language with seven-vowel system:

    ɪ   ʊ
    e   o
    ɛ   ɒ
        ɑ

the relation between /ʊ/ and /o/ is gradual, for sharing the same feature of tongue height (of the vowel) is a third vowel /ɒ/.

7. Equipollent opposition: If the pair is not in gradual opposition, nor in privative opposition, they are logically equipollent. For example, /t/

Chapter 14 Modern Theories and Schools of Linguistics

and /p/, /t/ and /k/ in English.
8. Neutralisable opposition: the opposition occurs when two sounds contrast in some positions but not in others. English /p/ and /b/ do not contrast after /s/. In German, the voiced consonants at the end-position become voiceless: *Rat* ("persuade") and *Rad* ("wheel") are pronounced the same way; but their plurals are different.
9. Constant opposition: The pair of sounds occurs in all possible positions without neutralising effect. For example, in Nupe (a language spoken in Nigeria) the normal phonological structure is a consonant followed by a vowel, except in very few cases. The opposition between /t/ and /d/ is constant in all positions for consonants.

Trubetzkoy's contributions to phonological theory concern four aspects. First, he showed distinctive functions of speech sounds and gave an accurate definition for the phoneme. Second, by distinguishing phonetics and phonology, stylistic phonology and phonology, he defined the sphere of phonological studies. Third, by studying the syntagmatic and paradigmatic relations between phonemes, he revealed the interdependent relations between phonemes. Finally, he put forward a set of methodologies for phonological studies, such as the method of extracting phonemes and the method of studying phonological combinations.

14.2.1.2 Functional Sentence Perspective (FSP)

Functional Sentence Perspective (FSP) is a theory of linguistic analysis which refers to an analysis of utterances (or texts) in terms of the information they contain. The principle is that the role of each utterance part is evaluated for its semantic contribution to the whole. The notion of "communicative dynamism" (CD) has been developed as an attempt to rate these different levels of contribution within a structure, particularly with reference to the concepts of *Theme* and *Rheme*.

Some Czechoslovak linguists devoted considerable attention to problems of analysing sentences from a functional point of view. They believe that a sentence contains a point of departure and a goal of discourse. The point of departure is equally present to the speaker and to the hearer—it is their rallying point, the ground on which they meet. This is called the theme. The goal of discourse presents the very information that is to be imparted to the hearer. This is called the rheme. It is believed that the movement from the initial notion (Theme) to the goal of discourse (Rheme) reveals the movement of the mind itself. Language may use different syntactic constructions, but the order of ideas remains basically the same. Based on these observations, they created the notion of Functional Sentence Perspective (FSP) to describe how information is distributed in sentences. FSP deals particularly with the effect of the distribution of known (or given) information and new information in discourse. The Known information refers to information that is not new to the reader or hearer. The New information is what is to be transmitted to the reader or hearer. As we can see, the subject-predicate distinction is not always the same as the *Theme-Rheme* contrast. For example, *Jane* is the grammatical subject in both of the following sentences, but the Theme in (1)a and the Rheme in (1)b.

(1) a. Jane stood on it   b. On it stood Jane
      Subject   Predicate   Predicate   Subject
      Theme   Rheme   Theme   Rheme

We can approach a sentence at three levels and distinguish between the grammatical sentence pattern (GSP), the semantic sentence pattern (SSP), and the communicative sentence pattern (CSP). It would be possible to imagine a context in which the semantic and grammatical structure (*John has written a poem*) would function as utterance event following the Agent-Action-Goal SSP, the Subject-Verb-Object GSP, and the Theme-Transition-Rheme CSP. This shows that there is a distinction between sentence and utterance.

In research into the relation between structure and function, Jan Firbas developed the notion of "communicative dynamism." This notion is based on the fact that linguistic communication is not a static phenomenon, but a dynamic one. CD is meant to measure the amount of information an element carries in a sentence. The degree of CD is the effect contributed by a linguistic element, for it "pushes the communication forward." Thus if examined in its non-marked use, the sentence *He was cross* could be interpreted in regard to the degree of CD as follows: The lowest degree of CD is carried by *He*, and the highest is carried by *cross*, the degree carried by *was* ranking between them.

Any element—sentence, phrase, word, morpheme—may be singled out in order to establish a sharp opposition, as in "*John WAS reading the newspaper.*" The stressed *WAS* indicates it is the information that is to be imparted, in opposition to the present tense, and that all other elements are Given information. Under this circumstance, the only element conveying New information is contextually independent, whereas all the other elements conveying Known information are contextually dependent. Consequently contextually dependent elements carry the lowest degree of CD owing to the operation of the context. Strictly speaking, contextual dependence or independence is determined by the very purpose of the communication. Thus in the sentence "*John has gone up to the window,*" *the window* may not be known from the preceding context, but since the purpose of the communication is the expression of the direction of the movement, *the window* necessarily appears contextually independent. A contextually independent object in "*I have read a nice book*" will carry a higher degree of CD than the finite verb.

This is because the object expresses an essential amplification of the verb and is therefore more important. Similarly, a contextually independent adverbial element of place will have a higher degree of CD than a verb expressing motion, as in "*He was hurrying to the railway station.*" This is because the adverbial element indicates the direction of the motion and is therefore more important than the motion itself.

Normally the subject carries a lower degree of CD than the verb and/or the object and/or adverbial provided either the verb or object and/or adverbial are contextually independent. This is because a known or unknown agent expressed by the subject appears to be communicatively less important than an unknown action expressed by the finite verb and/or an unknown goal (expressed by the object or the adverbial element of place) at or towards which the action is directed. For example, in "*A man broke into the house and stole all the money,*" the ultimate purpose of the communication is to state the action (*the breaking into* and *stealing*) and/or its goal (*the house* and *the money*), not the agent (*a man*). However, if the subject is accompanied by a verb expressing "existence or appearance on the scene" (possibly also by an adverbial element of place or time) and is contextually independent, then it will carry the highest degree of CD. This is because an unknown person or thing appearing on the scene is communicatively more important than the act of appearing and the scene itself, i. e. the local and temporal settings. For example, "*An old man appeared in the waiting room at five o'clock.*" If the subject is contextually dependent, a contextually independent adverbial of time or place becomes an important local and temporal specification, carrying greater degree of CD than both the subject and the finite verb, as in "*The old man was sitting in the waiting room.*"

In all the structures exemplified above, the semantic contents and relations contribute to the degree of CD and they are not directly related to the positions the elements occupy within the linear arrangement. However, not all semantic contents and relations are capable of signalling degrees of CD in the same way. The following are illustrations of how the linear arrangement itself operates on the level of FSP when unhampered either by context or semantic structure. For example, a contextually independent infinitive of purpose carries lower degree of CD when occurring finally, as in "*He went to Prague to see his friend*" in contrast to "*In order to see his friend, he went to Prague.*" Similarly, with the direct and indirect object, if they are contextually independent, the one coming later within the linear arrangement carries a higher degree of CD, as is shown in the difference in "*He gave a boy an apple*" and "*He gave an apple to the boy.*"

Firbas defined FSP as "the distribution of various degrees of CD." This can be explained as: the initial elements of a sequence carry the lowest degree of CD, and with each step forward, the degree of CD becomes incremental till the element that carries the highest. However, there are often exceptions to this rule: the Theme at the beginning, the Transition in the middle, and the Rheme at the end of the sentence. And sometimes the distributional field may be entirely contextually independent (e. g. "*A girl broke a vase*"), so the Theme may not always be contextually dependent. Contextually dependent elements, however, are always thematic. On the other hand, non-thematic elements are always contextually independent, but not every contextually independent element is non-thematic.

14.2.2 The Copenhagen School

Inspired by the Linguistic Circle of Prague, Louis Hjelmslev (1899—1965) and a group of Danish colleagues founded the Linguistic Circle of Copenhagen in September 1931. Hjelmslev aimed at establishing a framework for understanding communication as a formal system, and developed precise terminology for describing different parts of linguistic systems and their interrelatedness. The basic theoretical framework, called "glossematics" was laid out in his two main works, *Prolegomena to a Theory of Language* and *Résumé of a Theory of Language*. However, since Hjelmslev's death in 1965 left his theories mostly on the programmatic level, the group that had formed around him dispersed. While the Circle continued to exist, it was not really a "school" united by a common theoretical perspective.

Rooted in European structuralism, glossematics is a theory of language characterized by a high degree of formalism and an emphasis on the nature and status of linguistic theory and its relationship to description. It also developed a distinction between system and process, where for every process there is a corresponding system through which the process can be described. One of the principal features of glossematics is the emphasis of the study of relationships and not of things. Things can be seen rather as the points of conjunction of dependencies or functional. Combined with Hjelmslev's views on the dichotomies between form and substance, expression and content, and expressed in a terminology unique to glossematics, this points to the abstract focus and nature of much of his work. Nonetheless, its influence can be observed up to the present particularly in stratificational linguistics.

Hjelmslev had a persistent interest in the structure and status of linguistic theory. His *Principes de grammaire générale* (1928) is an invaluable source. He believed that word order was of general significance and that the study of expression preceded the study of meaning. During the 1930s Hjelmslev wrote *La catégorie des cas*, in which he analysed the general category of case in detail, with abundant empirical evidence supporting his hypotheses. He believed that the study of meaning would precede the study of expression, as case could not be defined in sense groups but would have to be defined and categorized on semantic grounds. Finally, by introducing the terms "glosseme" "ceneme" "prosodeme" and "plereme" (analogous to "phoneme" "morpheme", etc.) as linguistic units, he took to a highly abstract approach and argued that the system of language consisted of relationships and that those relationships rather than elements manifesting them should be the focus of linguistic study.

Hjelmslev's representative work is *Omkring sprogteoriens grundlæggelse* (1943)[①], probably the best summary of his theoretical position on various aspects of linguistics. Seeing the prevailing methodologies in linguistics up till his time as descriptive and unsystematic, he proposed a theory to form the basis of a more rational linguistics. Following Saussure to take language as a system of signs, he argued that a theory of semiotics should be consistent within itself.

In his *Prolegomena*, Hjelmslev discussed a range of issues. He put forward a number of criteria for linguistic theory and its resulting descriptions to meet. He argued that linguistic theory should be immanent, i.e., it should analyse language as a self-sufficient structure and it should also be arbitrary and appropriate. It should aim to provide a procedure for description and this description should be consistent, adequate and simple. He also elaborated dual dichotomies between form and substance and expression and content which interlock in his theory of the linguistic sign. It is not easy to see how much of this abstract theorising could be put into practice and it could be argued that, had Hjelmslev used fewer and less individualistic terms, his theory might have been better and more widely understood.

Hjelmslev's development of Saussure's views and his new observations on the nature of linguistic signs had enormous influence on modern linguistics. He emphasized that the true focus of linguistics should be language and the human culture that continually reinvents it, and all society's memory of its accumulated knowledge preserved through language. His theory of "glossematics" is also known as "Neo-Saussurean Linguistics," much appreciated by M. A. K. Halliday, who developed Systemic-Functional Grammar.

14.3 The London School

The London School generally refers to the kind of linguistic scholarship in England, a country that has both an unusually long history in linguistics and peculiar features in modern linguistics. The man who turned linguistics proper into a recognized distinct academic subject in Britain was John Rupert Firth

---

① English edition, *Prolegomena to a Theory of Language* (1953/1961).

(1890—1960), the first Professor of General Linguistics in Great Britain (1944). The majority of university teachers of linguistics in Britain were trained under Firth and their work reflected Firth's ideas. Hence, although linguistics eventually began to flourish in a number of other locations, the name "london school" is quite appropriate for the distinctively British approach to the subject.

Firth was influenced by the Polish-born British anthropologist Bronislaw Kasper Malinowski (1884—1942) at the University of London. In turn, he influenced his student, the well-known linguist Michael Alexander Kirkwood Halliday (1925—). The three men all stressed the importance of context of situation and the system aspect of language. Thus, London School is also known as systemic linguistics and functional linguistics.

14.3.1 Malinowski

Malinowski was Professor of Anthropology at the London School of Economics from 1927 onwards. He has been held as one of anthropology's most skilled ethnographers, especially because of the highly methodical and well theorized approach to the study of social systems. He emphasized the importance of detailed participant observation and argued that anthropologists must have daily contact with their informants if they are to adequately record the "imponderabilia of everyday life" that are so important to understanding a different culture. In his *Argonauts of the Western Pacific* (1922), Malinowski stated that the goal of the anthropologist, or ethnographer, is "to grasp the native's point of view, his relation to life, to realize his vision of his world."

The most important aspect of Malinowski's theorising, as distinct from his purely ethnographic work, concerned the functioning of language. For Malinowski, to think of language as a "means of transfusing ideas from the head of the speaker to that of the listener" was a misleading myth. He said that "language is to be regarded as a mode of action, rather than as a counterpart of thought." According to him, the meaning of an utterance does not come from the ideas of the words comprising it but from its relation to the situational context in which the utterance occurs.

Malinowski's assertion is based on two kinds of observations. First, in primitive communities there is no writing, and language has only one type of use. Second, in all societies, children learn their languages in this way. He imagined that, for children, a name for a person or object that bears it has certain magic powers. Children act with the aid of sounds, and people around them respond or react to the sounds. Therefore, the meaning of the sounds is the external reaction for them, and these reactions are human activities.

Malinowski believed that utterances and situation are bound up inextricably with each other and the context of situation is indispensable for the

Chapter 14 Modern Theories and Schools of Linguistics

understanding of the words. There is no way to characterise the meaning of utterances on the basis of internal considerations about the language alone. The meaning of spoken utterances could always be determined by the context of situation. He distinguished three types of context of situation:
1. situations in which speech interrelates with bodily activity;
2. narrative situations;
3. situations in which speech is used to fill a speech vacuum—"phatic communion."

By the first type of situation Malinowski meant that the meaning of a word is not given by the physical properties of its referent, but by its functions. When a savage learns the meaning of a word, the process is not accompanied by explanation but by learning to handle it. Likewise, a verb, a word for an action, receives its meaning through an active participation in this action. For the second type, Malinowski further distinguished "the situation of the moment of narration" and "the situation referred to by the narrative." The first case is "made up of the respective social, intellectual and emotional attitudes of those present," and the second case derives its meaning from the context referred to (as in a fairy tale). Malinowski believed that although there is no relationship between the meaning of narration and the situation in which language is used, narration can change the hearer's social attitudes and emotions. The third refers to cases of "language used in free, aimless, social intercourse." Such use of language is not the least related to human activities, and its meaning cannot possibly come from situations in which language is used, but from the "atmosphere of sociability and ... the fact of the personal communion of these people." For example, the function of a polite utterance has nothing to do with the meaning of the words in it. Malinowski called such utterances "phatic communion."

In his *Coral Gardens and Their Magic* (1935), Malinowski developed his theories on meaning and put forward two points. First, he prescribed the data for linguistic studies. He held that isolated words are only imagined linguistic facts, and they are the products of advanced analytical procedures of linguistics. Since an utterance may sometimes be an autonomous unit, even the sentence cannot be regarded as reliable data for linguistic studies. According to him, the real linguistic data are the complete utterances in actual uses of language. The second point is that when a certain sound is used in two different situations, it cannot be called one word, but two words having the same sound, or homonyms. He said that in order to assign meaning to a sound, one has to study the situations in which it is used. Meaning is not something that exits in sounds, but something that exists in the relations of sounds and their environment.

Malinowski's concepts of "linguistic environment" and "meaning as functions in the context of situation" provided useful background for further development of linguistics carried out by his student Firth.

14.3.2 Firth

J. R. Firth was Professor of English at the University of the Punjab from 1919 to 1928, and worked in the Phonetics Department of University College London before he became Professor of General Linguistics at the School of Oriental and African Studies until his retirement in 1956. While inheriting the tradition by taking up some of Saussure's and Malinowski's views, Firth developed their theories and put forward his own original ideas.

On the nature of language. Influenced by Malinowski, Firth regarded language as a social process, as a means of social life, rather than simply as a set of agreed-upon semiotics and signals. He held that in order to live, human beings have to learn, and learning language is a means of participation in social activities. Language is a means of doing things and of making others do things. It is a means of acting and living.

Following Saussure, Firth held that language consists of two elements: system and structure. While "structure" is the syntagmatic ordering of elements, "system" is a set of paradigmatic units, each of which can be substituted by others in certain places. Thus, structure is horizontal and system is longitudinal.

```
              S
              Y
              S
     STRUCTURE
              E
              M
```

On the grammatical level, some sentences are the same, for example:

(2)   *John helped Mary.*
       John met Mary.
       John greeted Mary.
       John liked Mary.

All these four sentences have the "Subject + Verb + Object" structure, where *helped*, *met*, *greeted*, and *liked* are elements of a system of verbs. On the phonological level, for example, the ordering of *pit*, *bed*, *file*, and *vase* are C_1VC_2, which is "structure," and there are three different systems at the same time: 1) /p/, /b/, /f/, /v/; 2) /ɪ/, /e/, /aɪ/, /ɑː/; and 3) /t/, /d/, /l/, /s/. Thus Firth pointed out that the system prescribes the positions where linguistic elements can occur, i. e. the rules for collocation. The structure is not simply a matter of ordering, for there are relations of mutual

Chapter 14   Modern Theories and Schools of Linguistics

expectancy between elements.

Firth did not fully agree with Saussure on the distinction of *langue* and *parole*, nor did he agree that the object of linguistic study is *langue*. He believed that language exists neither in the collective mind nor in the individual, but that individuals in the society are like a group of characters on the stage, each having a role to play. Like individuals that are born in nature and brought up by nurture, language has three implications:

1. Language has a natural tendency. Behind our use of sounds, gestures, semiotics and symbols, there is a strong wish and motive.
2. Language is systemic. As a result of our being nurtured, we learn traditional systems and customs of speech, which are fossilized by social activities.
3. Language is used to refer to the speech of many individuals and numerous speech events in social life.

Firth did not see language as something wholly inborn or utterly acquired. He seemed to adopt a riding-on-the-wall attitude, seeing language as something both inborn and acquired. Thus he insisted that the object of linguistic study is language in actual use. And the goal of linguistic inquiry is to analyse meaningful elements of language in order to establish corresponding relations between linguistic and non-linguistic elements. The method of linguistic study is to decide on the composite elements of language, explain their relations on various levels, and ultimately explicate the internal relations between these elements and human activities in the environment of language use. That is to say, Firth attempted to integrate linguistic studies with sociological studies: because human beings are inseparable from cultural values, and language is an important part of cultural values, linguistics can help reveal the social nature of human beings.

Prosodic analysis. Firth's initial goal for phonological analysis was to list the general phonetic contexts, or syllable types, of each language, and to list the entities that substitute for one another in given positions in these syllable types and in words, which are made up of sequences of syllables. In his 1937 description of the Chinese monosyllable, he added a third goal, which was to list those phonetic features that must be considered as properties of entire syllables rather than of designated positions within them. In his 1948 paper presented at London Philological Society, Firth announced a new and distinctive phonological theory that took as its objective the meeting of the three goals listed. For the entities that substitute for each other in the various positions of the various syllable types he proposed the term "phonematic unit"; for the list of the syllable types, and the entities characteristic of syllables (and words) as a whole, he suggested the term "prosodic unit."

Firth'sown method of prosodic analysis is called prosodic phonology. The term "prosody" has a special meaning. Since any human utterance is a continuous speech flow made up of at least one syllable, it cannot be cut into independent units. In order to analyse the functions on various levels, mere phonetic and phonological descriptions are insufficient. Phonological description only deals with paradigmatic relations, leaving syntagmatic relations out of consideration. Firth pointed out that in actual speech, it is not phonemes that make up the paradigmatic relations, but "phonematic units." There are fewer features in phonematic units than in phonemes, because some features are common to phonemes of a syllable or a phrase (even a sentence). When these features are considered in syntagmatic relations, they are all called prosodic units, which Firth did not define but obviously included such features as stress, length, nasalization, palatalization, and aspiration, not to be found in one phonematic unit alone.

Another principal feature of Firth's prosodic phonology is that it is "polysystemic," in opposition to the concept of "monosystemic." Take the English word *ski* for example, the monosystemic method would do no more than pointing out an ordering of two consonants and a vowel. But the polysystemic method would reveal many more features of the same word by representing it $C_1 C_6 V_6$. This means that before the consonant /k/ there is only one phoneme /s/ in order to form a consonant cluster, there are six phonemes (/p/, /t/, /k/, /l/, /w/, /y/) that can follow the phoneme /s/ to form a consonant cluster. The vowel /iː/ belongs to another system of six vowels (/iː/, /e/, /aː/, /ɔː/, /o:/, /uː/).

An emphasis on polysystemic analysis does not mean a neglect of structural analysis. Firth actually attached great importance to syntagmatic relations. He held that the basic unit in analysing speech is not word, but text, text in particular contexts of situation. Dissecting text into levels is only for the sake of analysis. It does not matter much which level should be analysed first, since levels are abstracted from text. However, whichever level we analyse, we should analyse the prosodic units of the text.

Prosodic analysis and phonemic analysis both consider basically the same phonological facts. However, prosodic analysis is advantageous in categorizing data and revealing the relations between linguistic data. It can discover more units on various levels and attempts to explicate the interrelationships between units on these levels.

In the years of teaching, Firth influenced a generation of linguists by encouraging his students to carry out research on African and Oriental languages (e.g. T. F. Mitchell on Arabic and Berber, Frank Palmer on Ethiopean languages, and M. A. K. Halliday on Chinese), along with students of languages other than English (e.g. Arab linguists Ibrahim Anis and Tammam Hassan). By drawing insights from work done by his students in Semitic and Oriental languages, Firth made a great departure from the linear analysis of phonology and morphology to syntagmatic and paradigmatic analyses which lay emphasis on the distinction between the two levels of phonematic units and prosodies.

The study of meaning. Throughout this later period Firth maintained intact his understanding of "meaning" as expressed earlier in "Technique of semantics" (1935). He devoted his paper "Modes of meaning" (1951) to going over approximately the same ground. However, one of the five dimensions of meaning, the lexical dimension (or mode), received much greater attention, and the meaning that was supposedly contributed by this mode was also given a new name, "meaning by collocation." (1957: 144)

Firth held that meaning is use, for "each word, when used in a new context, is a new word." (Firth, 1957: 190) Since the statement of meaning "cannot be achieved by one analysis, at one level," meaning is the relationship between an element at any level and its context on that level.

Firth took a sociological approach and his term of meaning does not simply cover lexical and grammatical meanings, but is a larger concept covering the meaning in the context of language use. He discussed meaning at various levels. On the phonological level, he believed that sounds have function by virtue of the place in which they occur and the contrast they show with other sounds that could occur in the same place. On the lexical level, he recognized that the meaning of words is not only determined by the usual referential sense, but also by collocation or the "company a word keeps." On the situational level, he recognized the difficulty in determining all the factors that make up a situation, but he wrote in his paper "Personality and language in society" that context of situation can be "best used as a suitable schematic construct to language events" and it is "a group of related categories at a different level from grammatical categories but rather of the same abstract nature." So in linguistic work it brings into relation the following categories:

1. The relevant features of participants: persons, personalities.
   (i) The verbal action of the participants.
   (ii) The non-verbal action of the participants.
2. The relevant objects. [①]
3. The effect of the verbal action.

According to Firth, contexts of situation and types of language function can be "grouped and classified." And context of situation is "a convenient abstraction at the social level of analysis and forms the basis of the hierarchy of techniques for the statement of meanings." (Firth, 1957: 182—183).

Firth held that the meaning of any sentence consists of five parts, i. e.

[①] In a later essay, "A synopsis of linguistic theory, 1930—1955," Firth revised it as "The relevant objects and non-verbal and non-personal events." (Palmer, 1968: 177)

1) the relationship of each phoneme to its phonological context; 2) the relationship of each lexical item to the others in the sentence; 3) the morphological relations of each word; 4) the sentence type of which the given sentence is an example; and 5) the relationship of the sentence to its context of situation.

Accordingly, there are actually four levels of analysis: 1) phonological; 2) lexical and semantic; 3) grammatical (morphological and syntactic); and 4) that of context of situation. By analysing the positions of sounds in relation to other sounds on the first level, one can find out the phonological functions. Analyses on the lexical and semantic levels aim not only to explain the referential meaning but also the collocative meaning. On the grammatical level, (a) morphological: inflections are studied; (b) syntactic: the syntagmatic relationship of grammatical categories, or "colligation," is studied. On the last level, the context of situation, non-linguistic elements such as objects, behaviour, and events, together with the effects of linguistic behaviour are studied. Firth said that this kind of study makes no distinction between words and ideas. And by doing this, we can explain why certain utterances are used in certain contexts of situation, and we can therefore equate "use" and "meaning." By "context of situation," Firth meant a series of contexts of situation, each smaller one being embedded into a larger, to the extent that all the contexts of situation play essential parts in the whole of the context of culture.

Typical contexts of situation. Firth's own study only focused on the context of situation as Malinowski did. Along the line of thoughts of Philipp Wagener, Allen Gardiner, and Malinowski, Firth made more specific and more detailed contextual analyses. For example, he defined the context of situation as including the entire cultural setting of speech and the personal history of the participants rather than as simply the context of human activity going on at the moment. Recognizing that sentences are infinitely various, he used the notion of "typical context of situation" so that some generalizations can be made about it.

By a typical context of situation, Firth meant that social situations determine the social roles participants are obliged to play; since the total number of typical contexts of situation they will encounter is finite, the total number of social roles they will assume is also finite. He also put forward the idea that in analysing a typical context of situation, one has to take into consideration both the situational context and the linguistic context of a text, which are as follows:

1. The internal relations of the text
    (a) the syntagmatic relations between the elements in the structure;
    (b) the paradigmatic relations between units in the system and find their values.

2. The internal relations of the context of situation
   (a) the relations between text and non-linguistic elements, and the general effects;
   (b) the analytical relations between words, parts of words, phrases and the special elements of the context of situation.

In connection with his concept of "context of situation," practically nothing of what Firth has to say in his later discussions goes beyond his 1935 paper, due to his observation (1957: 9) that "no linguist has yet set up exhaustive systems of contexts of situation such that they could be considered mutually determined in function or meaning," as if this goal were readily achievable, when in fact no one as yet has shown how even a single utterance can be semantically characterized by its context of situation.

Views on syntax. During the later period, Firth, together with his colleagues made no substantive theoretical contribution to the study of syntax or morphology. Practically no further work was done to refine the notion "context of situation." The only means by which we can evaluate Firth's view of syntax is by studying the terminological suggestions he made, since he published no syntactic descriptions during his lifetime.

Firth and his colleagues have explicitly rejected the validity of universal grammar, and indeed of universal phonology; and he strongly criticized Malinowski's assumptions concerning universal grammar in 1951. In phonology, Firth stated that the phonematic and prosodic units should be "systematically stated *ad hoc* for each language."

14.4 Halliday and Systemic-Functional Grammar

M. A. K. Halliday has developed the ideas stemming from Firth's theories in the London School. His systemic-functional grammar (SFG) is a sociologically oriented functional linguistic approach and one of the most influential linguistic theories in the 20th century, having great effect on various disciplines related to language, such as language teaching, sociolinguistics, discourse analysis, stylistics, and machine translation.

Halliday took a BA honours degree in modern Chinese Language and Literature at London University in 1947. From 1947 to 1949 he studied under the supervision of Luo Changpei at Peking University. From 1949 to 1950 he studied at Lingnan University, South China, tutored by Wang Li. Then he worked for his Ph. D. degree under the supervision of Firth. By 1955, he finished his doctoral dissertation "The language of the Chinese *Secret History of the Mongols*," on his studies of the work written in a northern Chinese dialect in the 14th century. From 1955 to 1963, he taught linguistics at Cambridge University and Edinburgh University. From 1963 to 1970, he worked at the

University College London and the University of London. From 1970 to 1972, he was visiting professor at Yale University, Brown University, and Nairobi University. From 1972 to 1973, he worked as research fellow in the Center for Advanced Study in the Behavioural Sciences at Stanford, California. From 1973 to 1974 he was Professor of Linguistics at the University of Illinois. From 1974 to 1975, he was Professor at Essex University. In 1975, he moved to Australia and founded the Department of Linguistics at the University of Sydney, working there till his retirement in 1988.

Halliday is well known for his grammatical theory and descriptions, outlined in his *An Introduction to Functional Grammar* (1985), second edition (1994), and third edition (2004, in collaboration with Christian Matthiessen). Systemic-Functional Grammar has two components: systemic grammar and functional grammar. They are two inseparable parts for an integral framework of linguistic theory. Systemic grammar aims to explain the internal relations in language as a system network, or meaning potential. And this network consists of subsystems from which language users make choices. Functional grammar aims to reveal that language is a means of social interaction, based on the position that language system and the forms that make it up are inescapably determined by the uses or functions which they serve.

Systemic-Functional Grammar is based on two facts: 1) language users are actually making choices in a system of systems and trying to realise different semantic functions in social interaction; and 2) language is inseparable from social activities of man. Thus, it takes actual uses of language as the object of study, in opposition to Chomsky's TG Grammar that takes the ideal speaker's linguistic competence as the object of study.

14.4.1 Systemic Grammar

Like Firthian phonology, Systemic Grammar is primarily concerned with the nature and import of the various choices which one makes (consciously or unconsciously) in deciding to utter one particular sentence out of the infinitely numerous sentences that one's language makes available. The notion of system is a central explanatory principle, the whole of language being conceived as a "system of systems." Systemic Grammar is concerned with establishing a network of systems of relationships, which accounts for all the semantically relevant choices in the language as a whole.

On a very general level, there is the horizontal chain system and the vertical choice system, based on the axis of choice and the axis of chain, which represent the syntagmatic and paradigmatic relations. Associated with the axis of choice is the concept of contrast, without which language would work. While the axis of chain deals with the surface aspects of grammar, the axis of choice deals with the meaning aspects of grammar.

Chapter 14　Modern Theories and Schools of Linguistics

The central component of a systemic grammar is a chart of the full set of choices available in constructing a sentence, with a specification of the relationships between choices. A system is a list of things between which it is possible to choose. So they are meanings, which the grammar can distinguish. The items in a system are called options. To enter a particular system, the options must meet the entry conditions. That is, the items must have something in common or belong to the same area of meaning, as "singular" and "plural" enter the system of "number" whereas "singular" and "negative" do not, although they are different, their difference is not so sharply defined as that between "negative" and "positive," or between "singular" and "plural."

Take the system of "transitivity," for example,

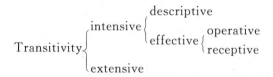

All systems have three essential characteristics. First, the terms in a system are mutually exclusive. The selection of one precludes the selection of any of the others. Second, a system is finite. It is possible to fix a limit for a system and to say that it consists of a certain countable number of terms, no more and no less. Third, the meaning of each term in a system depends on the meaning of the other terms in the system. If the meaning of one term is changed, the meaning of other terms will also change.

In the Transitivity system, for example, there are six types of processes (i. e. Material, Behavioural, Mental, Relational, Verbal, and Existential Processes); and in the Material processes there are two types of choices, Action (*John kicked the ball*) and Event (*The train left five minutes ago*). Then the Action process can be further distinguished into Intention and Supervention. Likewise, the Mental process can be distinguished into the Internalised (*I like it*) and the externalized (*It puzzled everybody*), which can be further distinguished into Perception, Reaction, and Cognition processes.

There is another kind of relationship possible between systems, that of simultaneity. A system is simultaneous with another system if it is independent of the other system but has the same entry conditions as the other system. When two systems are simultaneous, their terms can combine freely; and a term from one system can combine with any term from the other system. There can be many more other systems in English, and the notion of a systemic grammar is that we take a general area of meaning and gradually break it into smaller and smaller sub-areas. The dimension that recognizes increasing depth of detail is called delicacy. In each stage, we gradually make finer and finer distinctions in meaning and arrange systems on a scale according to the fineness of the distinction, called "scale of delicacy."

When we express meanings, we are intentionally making choices in the system network. On this basis, choice is meaning. Halliday believes that there are realization relationships between various levels. The choice of meaning (on the level of semantics) is realised by the choice of the "form" (on the level of lexicogrammar), which is in turn realised by the choice of "substance" (on the level of phonology). In other words, "what can be done" is realised by "what is meant to be done," which is realised by "what can be said." In this view, we can regard language as a multi-level code system, in which one sub-system is embedded in another. For example,

```
MEANING                 SEMANTICS
    is coded by             ↘
WORDING                 LEXICOGRAMMAR (SYNTAX)
    which is coded by       ↘
SOUND (or WRITING)      PHONOLOGY
```

The relations of realisation are represented by an arrow "↘".

The system network in Systemic Grammar chiefly describes three components of function, or three metafunctions. Each of the metafunctions is a complex system consisting of other systems, and choices are simultaneously made from the three metafunctions. This is the close relationship between Systemic Grammar, which is functional, and Functional Grammar, which is systemic.

14.4.2 Functional Grammar

Halliday's emphasis has been on the functional part of grammar, i.e. "the interpretation of the grammatical patterns in terms of configurations of functions." Since he sees these functions as particularly relevant to the analysis of text (by which he means "everything that is said or written"), Halliday defines a functional grammar as "essentially a 'natural' grammar, in the sense that everything in it can be explained," on the belief that language is what it is because it has to serve certain functions.

Halliday views language development in children as "the mastery of linguistic functions," and believes "learning a language is learning how to mean." So he proposes seven functions in children's model of language: 1) the instrumental function; 2) the regulatory function; 3) the interactional function; 4) the personal function; 5) the heuristic function; 6) the imaginative function; and 7) the informative function.

According to Halliday, the adult's language becomes much more complex and it has to serve many more functions, and the original functional range of the child's language is gradually reduced to a set of highly coded and abstract functions, which are metafunctions: the ideational, the interpersonal, and the textual functions. These metafunctions appear at a new level in the linguistic system, taking the form of "grammar." The grammatical system has, as it were, a functional input and a structural output; it provides the mechanism for different functions to be combined in one utterance in the way the adult requires.

14.4.2.1 The Ideational Function

The Ideational Function (consisting of "experiential" and "logical") is to convey new information, to communicate a content that is unknown to the hearer. Present in all language uses, the ideational function is a meaning potential, because whatever specific use one is making of language he has to refer to categories of his experience of the world.

The whole of the transitivity system is part of the ideational component. In this respect, this function not only specifies the available options in meaning but also determines the nature of their structural realizations. For example, *John built a new house* can be analysed as a configuration of the functions:

> Actor: *John*
> Process: Material: creation: *built*
> Goal: affected: *a new house*

Here the Actor, Process, Goal, and their subcategories reflect our understanding of phenomena that come within our experience. Hence this function of language is that of encoding our experience in the form of an ideational content. The notions of Actor, Process and the like make sense only if we assume an ideational function in order to satisfy some theory of linguistic functions; an analysis in something like these terms is necessary if we are to explain the structure of clauses. The clause is a structural unit, and it is the one by which we express a particular range of ideational meanings, our experience of process, the process of the external world, both concrete and abstract, and the processes of our own consciousness, seeing, liking, thinking, talking and so on.

14.4.2.2 The Interpersonal Function

The Interpersonal Function embodies all uses of language to express social and personal relations. This includes the various ways the speaker enters a speech situation and performs a speech act. Because the clause is not confined to the expression of transitivity, there are non-ideational elements in the adult language system. These elements are grouped together as this metafunction in the grammar, covering a whole range of particular uses of language.

The Interpersonal Function is realised by mood and modality. Mood shows what role the speaker selects in the speech situation and what role he assigns to the addressee. If the speaker selects the imperative mood, he assumes the role of one giving commands and puts the addressee in the role of one expected to obey orders. Modality specifies if the speaker is expressing his judgement or making a prediction. For example, *Give me that teapot*!

According to Halliday, of the various speech roles, two are the most basic: giving and demanding. In interpersonal communications, the commodities exchanged can also fall into two kinds: goods-&-services and information. thus, speech roles and commodities exchanged make up four principal speech roles: offer, command, statement, and question.

Table 14.1　Giving and Demanding

Role in exchange \ Commodity exchanged	(a) goods-&-services	(b) information
(i) giving	"offer" Would you like this teapot?	"statement" He's giving her the teapot.
(ii) demanding	"command" Give me that teapot!	"question" What is he giving her?

(Halliday, 1994: 69)

When the two variables are taken together, they define the four primary speech functions of offer, command, statement and question. These, in turn, are matched by a set of desired responses: accepting an offer, carrying out a command, acknowledging a statement and answering a question, as are in the following table of "Speech Functions and Responses":

Table 14.2　Offer, Command, Statement and Question

		Initiation	expected response	discretionary alternative
give	goods-&-services	offer	acceptance	rejection
demand	goods-&-services	command	undertaking	refusal
give	information	statement	acknowledgement	contradiction
demand	information	question	answer	disclaimer

(ibid.)

14.4.2.3　The Textual Function

The Textual Function refers to the fact that language has mechanisms to make any stretch of spoken or written discourse into a coherent and unified text and make a living passage different from a random list of sentences. Although two sentences may have exactly the same ideational and interpersonal functions, they may be different in terms of textual coherence.

Chapter 14 Modern Theories and Schools of Linguistics

The textual function fulfils the requirement that language should be operationally relevant, having texture in a real context of situation that distinguishes a living passage from a mere entry in a grammar or a dictionary. It provides the remaining strands of meaning potential to be woven into the fabric of linguistic structure. For example, if we compare the two sets of sentences:

(3) a. *Mary had a very bad cold last week. Mary went to the doctor. The doctor examined Mary. The doctor said there was nothing serious with Mary. The doctor gave Mary some medicine. The doctor told Mary to take a rest for a few days. Mary took some medicine. Mary took the doctor's advice. Mary got better on the third day. Mary started to work on the third day.*

b. *Mary had a very bad cold last week and went to the doctor, who examined her and said there was nothing serious. He gave her some medicine, and told her to take a rest for a few days. She took the medicine and the advice, got better on the third day, and started to work right away.*

We can see that the two are exactly alike in their ideational and interpersonal components but differ only in their textual component. While the first is a group of 10 sentences that hardly make a coherent and unified text, the second is more cohesive and compact by avoiding lexical repetitions and adding various binding devices, which are known collectively as the cohesion of a text.

The Textual Function can also highlight certain parts of the text. For example, in

(4) *Authority* I respect, but *authoritarianism* I deplore.

both "authority" and "authoritarianism" are highlighted. Each is acting as a complement, and has been placed in front of its subject and predicator, laying emphasis and drawing attention.

According to Halliday, a clause is the simultaneous realisation of ideational, interpersonal, and textual meanings. For example,

Table 14.3 Ideational, Interpersonal and Textual Meanings of a Clause

Ideational *Material Process* *Action/passive*	This house	was built		by John Smith
	Goal/Affected	Process: Material, Action		Actor: Agent Animate
Interpersonal *Declarative*	Mood		Residue	
	Subject	Fin	Pred	Adjunct
Textual Unmarked Theme	Theme	Rheme		
	Given			New

The concept of the social function of language is central to the interpretation of language as a system. The internal organisation of language is not accidental: it embodies the function that language has evolved to serve in the life of social man. Because language serves as a generalized "ideational" function, we are able to use it for all the specific purposes and types of context which involve the communication of experience. Because it serves a generalized "interpersonal" function, we are able to use it for the specific forms of personal expression and social interaction. In order for the ideational and interpersonal functions to be effective, language must be a text, related to itself and to its contexts of use. Without this "textual" component of meaning, we are unable to make meaning at all.

If we want to pursue this line of interpretation further, we shall have to go outside language to some theory of social meanings. From the point of view of a linguist the most important work in this field is that of Bernstein, whose theories of cultural transmission and social change are unique in the respect, that language is built into them as an essential element in social processes.

14.4.3 Further Developments

During the years, Halliday has been further developing and refining his functional theory of language, ranging from linguistic theory and description, studies of grammar, grammatics, to text and discourse analysis, etc. Meanwhile, he has influenced a large number of linguists who have been developing the Systemic-Functional paradigm by incorporating register theory, genre theory, etc. While Halliday and Hasan (1985) see register and genre as concepts on the same semantic level, Martin (1992) takes register as another name for context of situation, thus taking register as a concept on the cultural level.

Based on Halliday's Interpersonal Function in which Mood, Modality, Polarity, and Modal expressions make up a complex appraisal system, Martin further developed the system in the 1990s and early 2000s, defining appraisal as related to value judgments. In Halliday's Modality System, what is at work is grammar, whereas in Martin's Appraisal System, what is at work is lexicon. Martin and White's (2005) comprehensive account of the Appraisal Framework focuses on analyzing the linguistic realization of attitudes, judgments and emotions and the ways in which these evaluations are negotiated interpersonally. They explain and justify the underlying linguistic theory and apply this flexible tool to a wide variety issues in text and discourse analysis, with sample text analyses from a range of registers, genres and fields.

Inspired by Halliday and Hasan's (1985: 4) observation that a culture can be defined as "a set of semiotic systems, a sets of systems of meaning, all of which interrelate," Kay L. O'Halloran (2004, 2011) developed "multimodal discourse analysis," which is both systemic and functional in nature and concerned with the theory and practice of analyzing meaning arising from the use of multiple semiotic resources in discourses which range from written, printed and electronic texts to material lived-in reality. In such a grammatical description as part of a social semiotic approach to language, the multidimensional architecture of language reflects what Halliday (2003: 29) calls "the multidimensional nature of human experience and interpersonal relations."

Informed by Halliday's (2007) notion of appliable linguistics on the belief that "the value of a theory lies in the use that can be made of it," a lot of research has been done on everyday real-life language-related problems, both theoretical and practical, in diverse social, professional and academic contexts. A notable work is Ahmar Mahboob and Naomi K. Knight's *Appliable Linguistics* (2010), a collection of papers that offers an initial step in pursuit of "an appliable linguistics." In short, such a linguistics illuminates the many ways language is used, since language has evolved in the human species as a fundamental resource with which we build and negotiate relationships, shape experience and deal with the many issues and challenges of life. As can be seen from the 16 papers on a range of issues including translation, education, language teaching/learning, multimodality, media, social policy and action, and positive discourse analysis, SFL theory can best meet the needs for being an "appliable" linguistics such as appliable discourse analysis among many others.

14.4.4 Functional Grammars

In its broad sense, the term "functional grammar" refers to a range of functionally-based approaches to linguistics, including functional discourse grammar developed in Amsterdam by Simon C. Dik (1978); danish functional linguistics founded in Copenhagen; lexical functional grammar developed by Joan Bresnan and Ronald Kaplan in the 1970s; functional unificational grammar developed by Martin Kay; and role and reference grammar developed by William Foley and Robert Van Valin, Jr. in the 1980s, etc.

Dik's description of "a functional view of natural language" differs from Halliday's only in terminology. While Halliday begins from the premise that language has certain functions for its users as a social group, so that it is primarily sociolinguistic in nature, Dik concentrates on speakers' competence. While Halliday makes no distinction between grammatical and pragmatic competence and sees his grammar as a meaning potential shared by a language and its speakers, Dik sees his grammar as a theory of the grammatical component of "Communicative Competence" which consists of grammatical competence and pragmatic competence. Dik shares, in some measure, Chomsky's view of grammar as a part of cognitive psychology.

Danish Functional Linguistics is a framework that drew on the work and ideas of Hjelmslev and the functional frameworks of cognitive semantics and Dik's functional grammar, represented by Harder's *Functional Semantics* (1996). Lexical Functional Grammar is theoretically a type of phrase structure grammar, as opposed to a dependency grammar. Initiated in reaction to the direction research in TG Grammar, it focuses on syntax, including its relation with morphology and semantics, viewing language as made up of multiple dimensions of structure, each of which is represented as a distinct structure with its own rules, concepts, and form. Functional Unification Grammar seeks to accomplish the functionalist linguists' aim of describing language at all levels in terms of the functions if fulfils for its users by means of "a clean, simple formalism." It is a competence grammar, written formally to expresses linguistic universals. It has proved particularly successful in machine parsing of natural language and has been applied in machine translation.

Role and Reference Grammar incorporates many of the points of view of current functional grammar theories. In such a grammar, the description of a sentence in a particular language is formulated in terms of its logical (semantic) structure and communicative functions, and the grammatical procedures that are available in the language for the expression of these meanings.

Of course the most influential and appliable of functional grammars is the Systemic-Functional Grammar (SFG), or FG, which sets out to explain how spoken and written texts construe meanings and how the resources of language are organized in open systems and functionally bound to meanings. It does not describe language as a finite rule system, but describes language in use, creating systematic relations between choices and forms within the strata of grammar, phonology, context of situation, and context of culture rather than exploring them as autonomous systems. It treats the definition of language as a resource rather than as grammaticality by focusing on the relative frequencies of choices made in uses of language which reflect the probability that choices are made from available resources. While Chomsky takes linguistics as a sub-branch of psychology, Halliday investigates linguistics more as a sub-branch of sociology, paying much more attention to pragmatics and discourse semantics, among many others.

It is an important and admirable part of the London School tradition to believe that different types of linguistic description may be appropriate for different purposes. Although the advocates of SFG do not normally suggest that it is more successful than any other grammatical theory at carrying out the task for their purposes, it is obvious that their theory is much more relevant and appliable.

14.5 American Structuralism

American descriptive linguistics, generally called American structuralism, is a branch of synchronic linguistics which emerged independently in the United States at the beginning of the 20th century. It developed in a very different style from that of Europe, under the leadership of the anthropologist Franz Boas (1858—1942), whose tradition has actually influenced the whole of the 20th-century American linguistics.

While linguistics in Europe started more than two thousand years ago, linguistics in America started at the end of the 19th century. While traditional grammar plays a dominating role in Europe, it has little influence in America. While many European languages have their own historical traditions and cultures, English is the dominating language in America, where there is no such a tradition as in Europe. In addition, the pioneer scholars who took an interest in linguistics in America were anthropologists, who found that the indigenous languages of the American Indians were dying out rapidly and they felt the urgent need to record these languages before they died out. Because there were no written record of these languages, when the last speaker of a language dies, the language can be said to have perished. However, these languages were characterized by features of vast diversity and differences which are rarely found in other parts of the world. There are probably well over one thousand American Indian languages grouped into 150 families. It is said that in California alone there are more languages than in the whole of Europe. To record and describe these exotic languages, it is probably better not to have any presuppositions about the nature of language in general. This explains why there was not much development in linguistic theory during this period but a lot of discussion on descriptive procedures.

14.5.1 Early Period: Boas and Sapir

Specialized in the anthropology of North America, Franz Boas worked as organizer of a survey of the many indigenous languages of America north of Mexico. The result of the survey was the book *Handbook of American Indian Languages* (1911). Boas wrote several chapters for the book and an important introduction, which is still a good summary of the descriptive approach to language. Boas trained the men who investigated other languages. For decades, all the great names of American linguists learned their subject from Boas at first or second hand.

Boas was a self-taught linguist, having never received any formal training in linguistics. This lack of professional qualification (in the modern eye) was in fact an advantage rather than a hindrance to his work. Unlike the Europeans who stressed the universals of language, Boas held that there was no ideal type or form of languages, since human languages were endlessly diverse. Although the structure of a language in some primitive tribe might sound very arbitrary and irrational, there was no basis of truth in such a judgement, because European languages would appear just as irrational to a member of that tribe. Boas was strongly opposed to the view that language is the soul of a race, and he proved that the structure and form of a language has nothing to do with the evolution of a race and the development of a culture. Because of historical reasons, people in the same race may have started using different languages, the same language can be used by different races, and speakers of languages of the same family can belong to quite different cultures. Thus, there were only differences in language structure, while there is no difference between languages in terms of being more or less reasonable or advanced.

In the Introduction to his *Handbook*, Boas discussed the framework of descriptive linguistics. He held that such descriptions consist of three parts: the sound of languages, the semantic categories of linguistic expression, and the process of grammatical combination in semantic expression. Boas noticed that every language has its own system of sounds and its own grammatical system. He held that the important task for linguists is to discover, for each language under study, its own particular grammatical structure and to develop descriptive categories appropriate to it. His methodology in processing linguistic data of American Indian languages is analytical, without comparing them with such languages as English or Latin. Starting from an anthropological view, Boas regarded linguistics as part of anthropology and failed to establish linguistics as an independent branch of science. But his basic theory, his observation, and his descriptive methods paved the way for American descriptive linguistics and influenced generations of linguists.

Like Boas, Edward Sapir (1884—1939) was an eminent anthropological linguist. Before meeting Boas in New York, Sapir was pursuing his Master's degree in Germanic studies and felt confident that he understood the nature of language quite well. After meeting Boas, Sapir said he felt as though he had everything to learn. As a result, Sapir undertook the description of American Indian languages after Boas's method, using a native informant in his own cultural surroundings. This is a novel experience for Sapir and radical departure from the traditional practice of trying to impose the grammatical categories of Indo-European languages upon all other languages. His idea on language and thought was later developed by his student, B. L. Whorf (1897—1941), and is known as the Sapir-Whorf hypothesis.

Sapir's work is best summed up in his *Language* (1921). He started from an anthropological viewpoint to describe the nature of language and its development, with his main focus on typology. The aim of the book is to "give a certain perspective on the subject of language rather than to assemble facts about it. It has little to say of the ultimate psychological basis of speech and gives only enough of the actual descriptive or historical facts of particular languages to illustrate principles. Its main purpose is to show what I conceive language to be, what is its variability in place and time, and what are its relations to other fundamental human interest—the problem of thought, the nature of the historical process, race, culture, art." He defines language as "a purely human and non-instinctive method of communicating ideas, emotions and desires by means of a system of voluntarily produced symbols." He also compares speech with walking, saying that walking is "an inherent, biological function of men," and it is "a general human activity that varies only in circumscribed limits as we pass from individual to individual," and its variability is "involuntary and purposeless." His *Language* deals with a wide range of problems, such as the elements of speech, the sounds of language, form in language, grammatical process, grammatical concepts, types of linguistic structure, and historical changes.

In discussing the relations between speech and meaning, Sapir holds that the association of speech and meaning is a relation that may be, but need not be, present. In discussing the relation between language and thought, Sapir holds that although they are intimately related, they are not to be considered the same. Language is the means, and thought is the end product: without language, thought is impossible.

Sapir also noticed the universal features of language. He says that all human races and tribes, no matter how barbaric or underdeveloped, have their own languages. In spite of the formal differences, their basic frameworks (distinct phonetic systems, concrete combinations of sound and meaning, and various means of representing all kinds of relations, etc.) are highly developed. Language is the oldest human legacy, and no other aspects of any culture can be earlier than its language. Without language, there is no culture.

Sapir's objective attitude toward and his respect for linguistic facts has remained a significant heritage for American linguists after his making American linguistics fully descriptive. After Boas, Sapir emphasized the necessity of describing specific languages, but failed to formulate complete analytical methods and procedures.

14.5.2 Bloomfield

It is Boas that created the tradition which was carried forward and which influenced many other American linguists, but the principal representative of American descriptive linguistics is Leonard Bloomfield (1887—1949). Bloomfield is such a landmark figure in the history of American linguistics that the period between 1933 and 1950 is known as Bloomfieldian Age, in which

American descriptive linguistics formally came into being and reached its prime development.

Bloomfield's *Language* was once held as the model of scientific methodology and the greatest work in linguistics on both sides of the Atlantic in the 20th century. For Bloomfield, linguistics is a branch of psychology, and specifically of the positivistic brand of psychology known as "behaviourism." Behaviourism is a principle of scientific method, based on the belief that human beings cannot know anything they have not experienced. Behaviourism in linguistics holds that children learn language through a chain of "stimulus-response reinforcement," and the adult's use of language is also a process of "stimulus-response." When the behaviourist methodology entered linguistics via Bloomfield's writings, the popular practice in linguistic studies was to accept what a native speaker *says* in his language and to discard what he *says about* it. This is because of the belief that a linguistic description was reliable when based on observation of unstudied utterances by speakers; it was unreliable if the analyst had resorted to asking speakers questions such as "*Can you say ... in your language?*"

In his *Language* (1933), Bloomfield used an example to explicate his process of stimulus-response theory. Suppose a boy and his girlfriend are taking a walk. The girl is hungry and sees some apples on the tree. She makes some sounds and the boy jumps over the fence, climbs up the tree, picks an apple, gives it to the girl, and the girl eats it. This series of acts can be divided into the act of speech and the practical event. And the story can be divided into three parts: 1) the practical event prior to the act of speech; 2) speech; and 3) the practical event after the act of speech. In 1), the girl's hunger, the sight of apples on the tree, and her relationship with the boy constitute the speaker's stimulus. In 3), the boy's practical acts are called the hearer's reaction. The result of the girl's act of speech is that she has got an apple without her having to get it from the tree. Thus, Bloomfield's first principle is: *when one individual is stimulated, his speech can make another individual react accordingly.* Individuals in a society vary in their abilities, but as long as someone is able to climb trees or to catch fish, other people in the community will have apples and fish. Thus, Bloomfield's second principle is: *the division of labour and all human activities based on the division of labour are dependent on language.* Finally, the girl's articulation is speech reaction to external stimulus (hunger). When the sound waves reach the boy's ears, the ears stimulate his nerves and he hears the girl's speech. This is the stimulus to the boy. This shows that humans react to two kinds of stimuli, practical stimulus and speech stimulus. Thus, Bloomfield's third principle is: *the distance between the speaker and hearer, two separate nervous systems, is bridged up by sound waves.* From this, Bloomfield put forward the well known formula:

$$S \to r \cdots\cdots s \to R$$

Here S stands for practical stimulus, r stands for the substitute reaction of speech, s stands for the substitute stimulus, and R stands for external practical reaction.

In grammatical description, Bloomfield distinguished "free form" and "bound form." A dependent form is called a bound form (-y in *Billy* or -ing in *dancing*), and an independent form is called a free form (*Bill*, *dance*). He also introduced the concept of "morpheme," a form that has no phonological and semantic commonness with other forms.

In the last chapter, Bloomfield touched upon the application of linguistics to language teaching and criticized traditional grammar. He pointed out that the 18th- and 19th-century grammarians were mostly laying down rules about what English should be like. In fact, all variations are genuine English. He asserted that traditional grammarians, who were mostly prescriptive, intended to prescribe linguistic categories by borrowing concepts from philosophy, and therefore dogmatic. Thus, in language teaching, instead of paying too much attention to graphetic forms, we should give priority to the teaching of pronunciation. Concerning the popular practice of foreign language teaching in America, he said that learning a language involves constant practice and repetition in real situations rather than merely teaching language learners grammatical theories; traditional practice, being sometimes confusing and far from being economical, cannot help the learners much.

As a textbook, Bloomfield's *Language* started American structuralism as a school of thought. Over half a century ago, Bloch (1949: 92) wrote,

> It is not too much to say that every significant refinement of analytic method produced ... has come as a direct result of the impetus given to linguistic research by Bloomfield's book. If today our methods in descriptive analysis are in some ways better than his, if we see more clearly than he did himself certain aspects of the structure that he first revealed to us, it is because we stand upon his shoulders.

14.5.3 Post-Bloomfieldian Linguists

Influenced by Bloomfield's *Language*, American linguists such as Z. Harris, C. Hockett, G. Trager, H. L. Smith, A. Hill, and R. Hall further developed structuralism, characterized by a strict empiricism. With the advent of the electronic computer in the 1950s, some linguists came to feel that an appropriate goal for general linguistics was to devise explicit "discovery procedures" to enable the computer to process raw data about any language and form a complete grammar without intervention by the human linguist.

Therefore, post-Bloomfieldian linguistics focused on direct observation: a grammar is discovered through the performing of certain operations on a corpus of data, i. e. through discovery procedures. The corpus of data consists of speech, so the operation has to start from a phonological analysis of the stream of sounds as phonemes. Since phonemes form a variety of types of structures, they can be grouped into minimal recurrent sequences, or morphs, which are the members of the same morphemes. Based on the discovery of morphemes of the language, the task of the linguist is to discover how the morphemes may be combined in order to write a grammar. The post-Bloomfieldian linguists also took an interest in the discourse level in order to develop discovery procedures for structure above the sentence level.

Harris's *Methods in Structural Linguistics* (1951) is generally taken as marking the maturity of American descriptive linguistics. In this book, Harris gave the fullest and most interesting expression of the "discovery procedure" approach to linguistics, characterized by accurate analytical procedures and high degree of formalization. The Italian linguist Giulio C. Lepschy regarded this book as the symbol and turning point of "Post-Bloomfieldian Linguistics." (Lepschy, 1970: 160)

Harris formulated a set of strict descriptive procedures which took the logic of distributional relations as the basis of structural analysis. This method has greatly influenced American descriptive linguistics and Harris is therefore regarded as one of the most distinguished linguists in the post-Bloomfieldian era. However, Harris has also been criticized. Some have pointed out that Harris's theory is circular: units are derived from distribution, which depends on environments, which are made up of units. Others have criticized Harris's extreme attitude toward meaning, saying that while Harris tried to do without meaning, actually he depended heavily on meaning. Whatever criticisms there may be, Harris's method as one of the many possible ones of description is of great significance.

Hockett was both a linguist and anthropologist, remaining firmly within the structuralist paradigm. In addition to his contributions to phonemic, morphemic and grammatical analysis and to general linguistics and its relationship with other disciplines, he offered a stimulating and spirited defence of his structuralist views while questioning many of the basic and often seemingly unchallenged assumptions underlying transformational grammar.

Hockett's *A Course in Modern Linguistics* (1958) is a well-known textbook in the American descriptive tradition. It contains and develops many of the insights gained from the work carried out within the structuralist paradigm from the 1930s onwards. In its Preface, Hockett says that the book is intended to be a textbook for college readers in linguistics. While he did not run after any "school" of linguistics, evidence of his being influenced by

Chapter 14 Modern Theories and Schools of Linguistics

American linguistics, especially by Bloomfield, can be found on every page.

The most significant figure in continuing the structuralist tradition may be Kenneth Pike, who and his followers have a special name for their technique of linguistic analysis—"tagmemics."

For Pike, a language has its own hierarchical systems independent of meaning. Not only are there hierarchies in language, but that everything in the world is hierarchical, consisting of different layers in the system from small to big, from bottom to top, from simple to complex, from part to whole. Thus, all languages have three interrelated hierarchies: phonological, grammatical, and referential. On each level of the three hierarchies, there are four linguistic units having the four following features: slot, class, role, and cohesion. These basic units are called grammatical units, or tagmemes. Generally speaking, the Slot specifies whether a certain tagmeme is in the position of the Nucleus or of the Margin in the structure. The Slot can be a subject slot, predicate slot, object slot, and additive slot. The Class tells what the linguistic entity is in the position of Slot, such as suffix, noun, noun phrase, verb root, etc. The Role shows the functions of the tagmeme concerned in the structure, such as Actor, Undergoer, Benefitee, Associated Agent, Scope, Time, etc. The Cohesion shows whether a certain tagmeme is dominating others or dominated by others. (Since this is not easily observable, Cohesion is not quite explicit.) The formula is

$$\text{Tagmeme} = \begin{array}{c|c} \text{Slot} & \text{Class(es)} \\ \hline \text{Role} & \text{Cohesion} \end{array}$$

Each of the four components in the diagram is called a cell. Some tagmemes are obligatory and are marked by "+", while optional tagmemes are marked by "−". With this formula or four-cell notation, a verb can be represented as:

$$V = + \quad \begin{array}{c|c} \text{Nuc(lear)} & \text{VRt (verb root)} \\ \hline \text{Pred(icate)} & - \end{array}$$

$$V = \pm \quad \begin{array}{c|c} \text{Mar(gin)} & \text{TsSuf (Time Suffix)} \\ \hline \text{Tm (time)} & \text{Tm} > \end{array}$$

The ultimate aim of tagmemics is to provide a theory which integrates lexical, grammatical, and phonological information. This theory is based on the assumption that there are various relations in language, and these relations can be analysed into different units. However, to believe that language is part of human behaviour, one needs to recognise that language cannot be strictly formalized. Since no representational system can account for all the relevant facts of language, tagmemics accepts various different modes of representation for different purposes, and does not insist that there is only one correct grammar or linguistic theory.

14.5.4 Structural Grammar: Summary

Levin (1960) saw the "structural way" in those decades as a significant change in the attitudes of people interested in the study of language and a different way of looking at language. He held that structuralists, unlike traditionalists, are interested in making only what have been called "vulnerable" statements about grammar, and it is primarily because of this that structural linguistics has a right to being called a science.

Structural grammar is based on the assumption that grammatical categories should be defined not in terms of meaning but in terms of distribution, and that the structure of each language should be described without reference to the alleged universality of such categories as tense, mood and parts of speech. Structural analysis is said to be formal, in the sense that the units of the analysis are defined internally in relation to each other, rather than externally in relation to psychological or logical categories that are not part of the language system. Yet, in no way is it free of problems. Firstly, structural grammar is descriptive, describing everything that is found in a language instead of laying down rules. However, the aim of structural grammar is confined to the description of languages, without explaining why language operates the way it does. Secondly, structural grammar is empirical, aiming at objectivity in the sense that all definitions and statements should be verifiable or refutable. It has, however, produced almost no complete grammars comparable to any comprehensive traditional grammars. Thirdly, structural grammar examines all languages, recognizing and doing justice to the uniqueness of each language. But it does not give an adequate treatment of meaning. Lastly, structural grammar describes even the smallest contrasts that underlie any construction or use of a language, not only those discoverable in some particular use.

14.6 Chomsky and Transformational-Generative Grammar

In the late 1950s, Avram Noam Chomsky (1928—) put forward a new theory that violently punched the prevailing structuralist descriptive linguistics. As a student of Hebrew with the structuralist methodology, Chomsky tried to open up a new route when he found that the classification of structural elements of language according to distribution and arrangement had its limitations. From this practice Chomsky gradually established the well-known Transformational-Generative (TG) grammar. The publication of his *Syntactic Structures* (1957) marked the beginning of the Chomskyan Revolution.

Important as Chomsky's TG Grammar is in modern linguistics, the theory has been very much controversial: some people follow it closely; some recognise its importance but disagree on many details; others totally reject the theory. In a review "Chomsky's revolution in linguistics," John Searle (1972) wrote, Chomsky's work is one of the most remarkable intellectual achievements of the present era, comparable in scope and coherence to the work of Keynes or Freud. It has created a new discipline of generative grammar and is having a revolutionary effect on two other subjects, philosophy and psychology. Not the least of its merits is that it provides an extremely powerful tool even for those who disagree with many features of Chomsky's approach to language.

In the introduction to his *Chomsky*, John Lyons (1991: 9) assumed a more objective tone and wrote, Chomsky's position is not only unique within linguistics at the present time, but is probably unprecedented in the whole history of the subject... There are at least as many recognizably different "schools" of linguistics throughout the world as there were before "Chomskyan revolution." But the "transformationalist," or "Chomskyan," school is not just one among many. Right or wrong, Chomsky's theory of grammar is undoubtedly the most dynamic and influential; and no linguist who wishes to keep abreast of current developments in his subject can afford to ignore Chomsky's theoretical pronouncements. Every other "school" of linguistics at the present time tends to define its position in relation to Chomsky's views on particular issues.

From its birth to the present day, TG Grammar has seen five major stages of development. The first is the Classical Theory (1955—1965), which aims to make linguistics a science. The second is the Standard Theory (1965—1970), which deals with how semantics should be studied in a linguistics theory. The third is the Extended Standard Theory (1970—1980), which focuses the discussion on language universals and universal grammar. The fourth is the Revised Extended Standard Theory (1980—1992), which focuses the discussion on government and binding, and is also called the GB Theory. The fifth is the Minimalist Program (starting from 1992), which is a further revision of his previous theory. The new century has witnessed his efforts in interdisciplinary inquiries, including biolinguistic approaches, on the faculty of language in the broad and narrow senses. Since there are too many aspects of Chomsky's theory to be discussed and not all of them can be taken up within the space of a few pages, we shall have to be content with a brief discussion of some important points.

14.6.1　The Innateness Hypothesis

　　Chomsky believes that language is somewhat innate, and that children are born with what he calls a language acquisition device (LAD), which is a unique kind of knowledge that fits them for language learning. He argues the child comes into the world with specific innate endowment, not only with general tendencies or potentialities, but also with knowledge of the nature of the world, and specifically with knowledge of the nature of language. According to this view, children are born with knowledge of the basic grammatical relations and categories, and this knowledge is universal. The categories and relations exist in all human languages and all human infants are born with knowledge of them. Thus, the study of language or the structure of language can throw some light on the nature of the human mind. This approach is a reaction against behaviourism in psychology and empiricism in philosophy, making linguistics a branch of psychology.

　　Chomsky's innateness hypothesis is based on his observations that some important facts can never be otherwise explained adequately. Children learn their native language very fast and with little effort. While the input is degenerate data, the output is a perfect language system; while they learn in very different environments, they reach uniform levels of competence; while they may be good at different things, they show amazingly small differences in their first language acquisition; while they learn during a limited period of time, they can produce and understand not only sentences they have heard, but also those they have never heard before. All these suggest that although babies are not born knowing a language (as they are born being able to see), they are born with a predisposition to develop a language in much the same way as they are born with a predisposition to learn to walk. Like the ability to walk, the ability to speak and understand spoken language seems to be a natural human activity. Though children would certainly not learn a language if they did not hear speech, it is not more necessary to teach babies to talk than it is to teach them to walk.

　　The Innate Hypothesis states that there are aspects of linguistic organisation that are basic to the human brain and that make it possible for children to acquire linguistic competence in all its complexity with little instruction from family or friends. But this is not the whole picture yet. Chomsky argues that LAD probably consists of three elements: a hypothesis-maker, linguistic universal, and an evaluation procedure.

　　This observation suggests that children are born with an innate faculty for language in general, a blueprint for languages, not just for any particular language. From this, we would then suppose that if children are predisposed for learning any language, human languages in the world must have the same underlying principles in common. This is what Chomsky called language universals or linguistic universals.

14.6.2 What Is a Generative Grammar?

By a "generative grammar," Chomsky simply means "a system of rules that in some explicit and well-defined way assigns structural descriptions to sentences." He believes that every speaker of a language has mastered and internalized a generative grammar that expresses his knowledge of his language. "Thus a generative grammar attempts to specify what the speaker actually knows, not what he may report about his knowledge." (Chomsky, 1965: 8)

A generative grammar is not limited to particular languages, but to reveal the unity of particular grammars and universal grammars. It does not describe one language as an end, but as a means to explore the universal rules in the hope of revealing human cognitive systems and the essential nature of human beings.

In order to reach this ultimate goal, Chomsky puts forward three different levels to evaluate grammars on. They are the "observational adequacy" level, the "descriptive adequacy" level, and the "explanatory adequacy" level. On the first level, grammars are able to produce correct explanations for raw linguistic data. On the second level, grammars should not only produce correct explanations for raw linguistic data, but also produce correct explanations for the linguistic competence of the speaker and hearer. On the third, and the highest, level, grammars that are sufficiently described should reveal linguistic competence and then relate it with universal grammars in order to be related to the initial state of the human mind for the purpose of revealing human cognitive systems. It is after successful descriptions of many languages and subsequent generalizations of universal features of human language that it is possible to explore the initial state of the human mind that contains universal grammars. In a sense, the way a linguist does his work is just contrary to the way a child learns his native language. While a child develops his particular grammar from a universal grammar, a linguist tries to discover a universal grammar from particular grammars.

Contrary to Bloomfield's data-oriented discovery procedure, Chomsky insists on the "hypothesis-deduction" method and his research is called evaluation process. Chomsky holds that while structuralist grammarians' IC analysis can reveal some of the structural features, it is seriously defective. For example, IC analysis cannot appropriately explain the difference between *John is easy to please* and *John is eager to please*, between the two interpretations of *Visiting relatives can be tiresome*, and between *John saw Mary* and *Mary was seen by John*. The process of transforming *John saw Mary* into *Mary was seen by John* can be represented algebraically as:

$$NP_1 + Aux + V + NP_2 \rightarrow NP_2 + Aux + be + en + V + NP_1$$

Thus, TG method cannot only describe the surface structure of a sentence, but also interpret the internal grammatical relationships within a sentence, getting closer to the truth of language than IC analysis.

14.6.3 The Classical Theory

In the classical theory, Chomsky's aim is to make linguistics a science. This theory is characterized by three features: 1) emphasis on generative ability of language; 2) introduction of transformational rules; and 3) grammatical description regardless of meaning. The main ideas can be found in Chomsky's *Syntactic Structures* (1957).

Chomsky puts forward three kinds of grammar: finite state grammar, phrase structure grammar, and transformational grammar. He considers first that a finite state grammar is inadequate. A grammar should be finite, that is, it cannot be simply a list of all morpheme sequences, since there are infinitely many of these. Suppose we have a machine that can be in any one of a finite number of different internal stages, and suppose that this machine switches from one state to another by producing a certain symbol (a word). One of these states is an initial state, runs through a sequence of states, and ends in the initial state. Then we call the sequence of words that has been produced a "sentence." Each such machine thus defines a certain language. Any language that can be produced by a machine of this sort we call a finite state language. And we call the machine a finite state grammar.

A finite state grammar is the simplest type of grammar which, with a finite amount of apparatus, can generate an infinite number of sentences. But they are all very simple in their structure. We can prove its inadequacy by considering tested dependency:

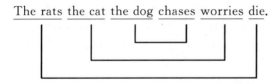

And there are even more complex sentences than this. English is not a finite-state language. It is impossible to construct an observationally adequate English grammar which is a finite-state grammar. The point of Chomsky's devising such a grammar is to show the impracticality of organizing language from a left-to-right order, and such a process is not feasible in studying natural languages. While this theory is appropriate to describe the "Stimulus-Response" process of learning, it is inappropriate to explain the complexities of the human cognitive system. So Chomsky believes that it is necessary to work out a grammar that, with a finite set of rules, can generate all the grammatical sentences in a language without generating a single non-grammatical sentence. Then a grammar is seen as a system of finite rules generating an infinite number of sentences, and the rules must meet the following requirements:

1. Generative: the rules must automatically generate sentences;
2. Simple: the rules must be represented by symbols and formula;
3. Explicit: everything must be stated precisely, leaving nothing to chance;
4. Exhaustive: the rules should cover all linguistic facts, leaving nothing uncovered;
5. Recursive: the rules can be repeatedly applied so as to generate an infinite number of sentences.

This is what is called the phrase structure grammar, the second model put forward by Chomsky, which consists solely of phrase-structure (PS) rules that formalize some of the traditional insights of constituent structure analysis. This grammar has greater generative powers than a finite state grammar because it can process sentences that cannot be processed by the latter. The phrase-structure rules are as follows:

1. S→ NP + VP
2. VP→ Verb + NP
3. NP→ NP (single)
   NP (plural)
4. NP(s)→ D + N
5. NP (p)→ D + N + s
6. D→ the
7. N→ {man, ball, door, dog, book, ...}
8. Verb→ Aux + V
9. V→ { hit, take, bite, eat, walk, open, ... }
10. Aux→ Tense (+M) (+ have + en) (+be + ing)
11. Tense→ Present
    Past
12. M→ {will, can, may, shall, must, ...}

The arrow means "can be rewritten as." phrase structure rules are called rewriting rules. The generative process of a sentence is the process of rewriting one symbol into another. For example, to generate a sentence *"The man hit the ball,"* we have to use the rules and represent them by bracketing as:

(NP(Det(the)N(man)) VP(V((hit) NP(Det(the) N(ball))))

or in a tree diagram as:

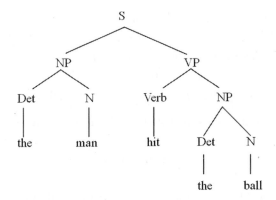

Bracketing applies mathematical principles, where "x(y + z)" is different from "xy + z". When the sequence of computation is different, the results are certainly different: "(old men) and women" is different from "old (men and women)." This shows explicitly 1) the word classes (sometimes number, tense, and the structure); 2) the categories and formation of phrases; and 3) relations between phrases. Tree diagramming has the same functions. It is a hierarchical system, explicitly showing the relations between elements: *man* (belonging to NP) is related to *hit* (belonging to VP) only through a node.

In his *Syntactic Structures*, Chomsky lists sixteen transformational rules for English. For example, English mostly depends on "not" for negation, and its occurrences have certain regular rules, as in

(5) a. *She might not visit us today*.
　　b. *John has not finished his work*.
　　c. *Jane is not reading*.
　　d. *He didn't kiss his mother*.
　　　　1　　2　　　3

The first part of each sentence is an NP. The second parts can be analysed into a concord element[①], represented by C, and a modal verb, *have*, *be*, and *do* respectively, that is, "C + M" "C + have" "C + be" and "C + do." The third parts, elements after the negative form are of no importance and can be represented with an ellipsis. (...)

　　　　Structural analysis: NP-C + M...
　　　　　　　　　　　　　　NP-C + have-...
　　　　　　　　　　　　　　NP-C + be-...
　　　　　　　　　　　　　　NP-C + do...[②]

With the three parts of each sentence substituted with X_1, X_2, and X_3, the transformational rule for negation can be written as:

---

① The concord element is responsible for the realization of the inflected forms like "has" "is" etc.
② Chomsky's original form is "NP-C-V..."

Chapter 14 Modern Theories and Schools of Linguistics

Structural changes: $X_1\text{-}X_2\text{-}X_3 \rightarrow X_1\text{-}X_2 + \text{n't-}X_3$

And another rule, "*do*-insertion," must be added to it: $\# \text{Af} \rightarrow \# \text{do} + \text{Af}.$ ①

This is a commonly used rule, as in the transformation of general questions:

Structural analysis: NP-C-V...
NP-C + M...
NP-C + have-...
NP-C + be-...

Structural changes: $X_1\text{-}X_2\text{-}X_3 \rightarrow X_2\text{-}X_1\text{-}X_3$

(6) *Did he kiss his mother?*
Might she visit us today?
Has John finished his work?
Is Jane reading?

Chomsky has distinguished transformational rules into two kinds: obligatory and optional. The transformation of auxiliaries and particles are obligatory, and the transformation of negation, the passive voice, etc. are optional. The reason for different types of sentences is that they have experienced different transformational processes. According to Chomsky, the following eight sentences have undergone different transformations:

(7) a. *The man opened the door.*
b. *The man didn't open the door.*
c. *Did the man open the door?*
d. *Didn't the man open the door?*
e. *The door was opened by the man.*
f. *The door was not opened by the man.*
g. *Was the door opened by the man?*
h. *Wasn't the door opened by the man?*

The first sentence has only undergone obligatory transformations, and such a simple, active, and positive declarative sentence is called a "kernel sentence." The sentences that follow have undergone the transformation of negation (7)b, the transformation of interrogation (7)c, the transformation of negative interrogation (7)d, passive transformation (7)e, the transformation of passive negation (7)f, the transformation of passive interrogation (7)g, and the transformation of passive negative interrogation (7)h. These eight types of sentences are derived from the same deep structure.

Chomsky's Classical Theory is the beginning of formalizing linguistic

---

① Affix.

description. In spite of his efforts in borrowing mathematical symbols and reducing his operations, there are serious defects in his theory. Later, Chomsky revised the model and put forward the Standard Theory.

14.6.4 The Standard Theory

The Standard theory is marked by *Aspects of the Theory of Syntax* (1965). After the publication of his *Syntactic Structures*, Chomsky found serious problems that called for solution in order to reach his theoretical goals. The first problem is that the transformational rules are too powerful. An ordinary sentence can be transformed at will, negated, passivized, with certain elements added or deleted, without restrictions. The second problem is that his rules may generate ill-formed sentences as well as well-formed ones. For example, with the rules S → NP + VP, and VP → V + NP, there might be generated the following two:

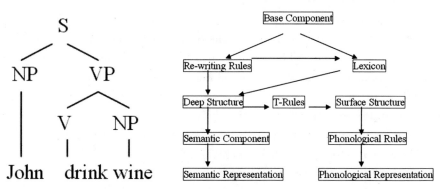

This indicates that there are certain selectional rules between the verb and the noun. The third problem is that the transformational rules for the passive voice cannot be used at will, for some of the English verbs do not have passive structures. We can say *John married Mary*, but *Mary was married by John* means something different (that is, John is the priest who presided over Mary's wedding). We can say *John resembles his father*, but cannot transform this sentence into *His father was resembled by John*. These facts show that the transformational rules are not universally applicable. In this period, Chomsky noted that application of the transformational rules should not change the meaning of the original sentence, and that the noun must be restricted by the verb.

In his *Aspects* (1965), Chomsky made a remarkable change by including a semantic component in his grammatical model. He says that a generative grammar should consist of three components: syntactic, phonological and semantic. The syntactic component can be called the base component, which consists of re-writing rules and the lexicon. It is the re-writing rules that generate the deep structure of the sentence, and the transformational rules, in turn, transform the deep structure into surface structure. The semantic component makes semantic interpretations on the deep structure, and the phonological component makes phonological interpretations on the surface structure. The relationships of the three components can be illustrated by the following diagram:

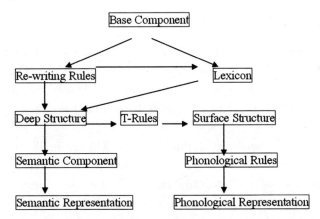

The Standard Theory improved a lot on the Classical Theory. Firstly, transformations can only change the forms of sentences and are not allowed to alter the meaning. Secondly, to rule out the generation of sentences like *Wine drinks John*, there is now a selectional restriction to ensure that the animate noun (*John*) appears before the verb (*drink*) and the inanimate noun (*wine*) appears after the verb (*drink*). Thirdly, restrictions are put on transformations in order not to generate ill-formed sentences. Fourthly, in rewriting rules, the symbol S is introduced on the right of the arrow, so that there are rules like: VP → V + S and NP → NP + S. This means that sentences can be embedded. By means of this rule, this theory not only covers simple sentences but also complex ones:

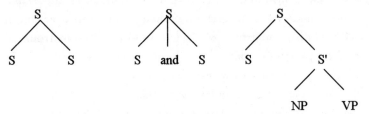

Fifthly, the rules are properly ordered and there is a set order in which the rules apply. It makes a great difference which rule comes first and which comes next. For example, the Reflexive Rule says that in simple sentences, if a noun appears twice, the second noun should be in reflexive form (*John kills John = John kills himself*), and the Imperative Rule says, "delete the noun before the verb in an imperative." (*You come here! = Come here!*) Clearly, in a simple statement, the Reflexive Rule applies first, e.g. *John kills John → John kills*

himself, and the Imperative Rule does not apply, since *John kills John* is not an imperative and it can not be transformed into * *Kills John* or * *Kills himself*. Likewise, in an imperative, the Imperative Rule applies first and the Reflexive Rule does not apply, since in *You come here* the noun (*you*) does not appear twice.

14.6.5 The Extended Standard Theory

In the Extended standard theory, Chomsky revised his Standard Theory twice. The first revision is called the "Extended Standard Theory" (EST). The second revision is called the "Revised Extended Standard Theory" (REST). The two revisions are generally called the "Extended Standard Theory" (EST).

In spite of the revisions of the Classical Theory made in the Standard Theory, there are still a lot of problems to be solved. Firstly, the transformational rules are still too powerful, for they can move or delete linguistic segments, change the categories, keep the original meaning intact, and vary according to specific circumstances. Secondly, the Standard Theory holds that derived nouns such as *criticism* and *explanation* have the same semantic properties with their corresponding verbs, thus the following sentences are bizarre:

(8) a. * *The square root of 5 's criticism of the book.*
b. * *The square root of 5 criticized the book.*

Later it was found that the relations between derived nouns and their corresponding verbs are irregular not only in terms of syntactic features, but also in phonological and semantic relations, which are too difficult to generalize. Thirdly, the Standard Theory holds that semantic interpretations are determined by the deep structure, and transformational processes will not change the sentence meaning. Later this was found to be impossible, for any kind of transformations will certainly change the sentence meaning. For example, (8)c is different from (8)c', and (8)d is different from (8)d':

c. *Everyone loves someone.*
c'. *Someone is loved by everyone.*
d. *Tom doesn't go to town very often.*
d'. *Very often Tom doesn't go to town.*

Chomsky also admitted that sentences would change their presuppositions after transformations. For example,

e. *Beavers build dams.*
e'. *Dams are built by beavers.*

While (8)e focuses on the nature of beavers, (8)e' focuses on the nature of dams, the two strings meaning quite different things. Fourthly, the Standard Theory cannot explain gapped structures as:

f. *John ate some spaghetti, and Mary some macaroni.*

Here the item *ate* can be omitted in the second clause according to the deletion rule, which can only be applied after semantic interpretation. This is, therefore, contrary to the model of the Standard Theory. Fifthly, investigations of more types of structures showed that many transformational rules must have complex constraints in order that they do not produce ungrammatical sentences. On the one hand, there should be one transformational rule for some universal phenomena. On the other hand, there are exceptions that have to be constrained. For example, a lot of verbs may occur in the following two structures:

g. *John gave a book to Mary.* (_____ NP PP)
h. *John gave Mary a book.* (_____ NP NP)

At the same time, a lot of verbs can only appear in the first structure:

i. *John donated a book to Mary.* (_____ NP PP)
j. ** John donated Mary a book.* (_____ NP NP)

As a result, the part that is transformed becomes a set of rules and the conditions for a set of restrictive rules. When efforts are made later to find universal features in the restrictive rules, new rules arise.

In his first revision of the Standard Theory, Chomsky moved part of semantic interpretation to the surface structure. Take the categories of the logical component for example, in the following two sentences,

k. *Not many arrows hit the target.*

l. *Many arrows didn't hit the target.*

their deep structure is "NOT. [many arrows hit the target]" Through transformations, the two sentences differ semantically due to the logical component NOT. This shows that semantic interpretation does play certain roles in the surface structure, but Chomsky still believed that semantics is determined by the deep structure.

Chomsky's second revision involves the whole theoretical framework, which can be illustrated by the following diagram.

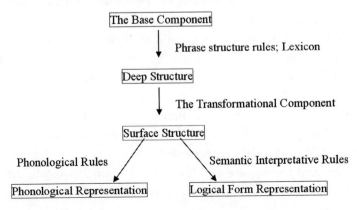

The most remarkable change is that Chomsky now completely puts semantic interpretation in the surface structure. And, accordingly, from semantic interpretative rules is derived logical form representation. Hence, semantics was left out of the domain of syntax.

14.6.6 GB and Minimalism

In the 1980s, Chomsky's TG Grammar entered the fourth period of development with the theory of government and binding (GB). It consists of X-bar Theory, θ-Theory, Bounding Theory, Government Theory, Case Theory, Control Theory, and Binding Theory. Although all others, with the exception of the θ-Theory, had been mentioned in EST, GB further developed and complemented the discussions in EST.

In his Pisa Lectures in 1979, published as *Lectures on Government and Binding* (1981), Chomsky made strong claims regarding universal grammar: that the grammatical principles underlying languages are innate and fixed, and the differences among the world's languages can be characterized in terms of parameter settings in the brain (such as the pro-drop parameter, which indicates whether an explicit subject is always required, as in English, or can be optionally dropped, as in Spanish), which are often likened to switches. This is often referred to as the principles and parameters approach. In this view, a child learning a language need only acquire the necessary lexical items, and determine the appropriate parameter settings, which can be done based on a few key examples.

GB directs our attention to a new orientation, i.e. the empty category (EC). Chomsky believes that through the empty category, we can further get to know about the mechanism of language. Chomsky's further efforts have thrown new light on exploring the nature of human language, although it is still not certain whether the various principles concerning empty categories are applicable to all languages and whether these categories are universal.

In 1992, Chomsky wrote an essay "A minimalist program for linguistic theory," collected in his *The Minimalist Program* (1995), marking a new stage of his generative theory. The minimalist program is motivated by two related questions: 1) What are the general conditions that the human language faculty should be expected to satisfy? 2) To what extent is the language faculty determined by these conditions, without a special structure that lies beyond them?

Compared with its immediate predecessor, GB, this new version is characterized by several remarkable changes. First, some of the discrete analytical models in the GB are discarded and the two levels of analysis, the deep structure and the surface structure, are left out. Second, the important concept of "government" in the previous theory is rejected and the facts

Chapter 14 Modern Theories and Schools of Linguistics

interpreted by the theory of government are replaced by several revised concepts, thus the theory of government has turned from a subsystem of universal grammar into the interpretative constraint of the output condition.

Based on the last chapter of *The Minimalist Program*, Chomsky has further developed the minimalist theory in his *Minimalist Inquiries: The Framework* (1998). In this work, Chomsky reconsiders the motivation for the Minimalist Program in order to give it a clearer explanation. He makes the emphasis that the minimalist inquiries are the results of work from collective minds. However, this work is loaded with terms that are new to other linguists, and his discussions go on in terms of abstract symbols with few examples.

Chomsky holds that the initial states of human languages are the same whereas the states of acquiring different languages are not. A universal grammar is a theory for studying the initial states, and particular grammars are theories for studying the states of acquisition. While the faculty of language consists of a cognitive system that stores information such as sound, meaning, and structure, the performance system retrieves and uses the information. He raises a profound question: How well is the language faculty designed?

Chomsky imagines a case in which a certain primate is comparable to human beings except for its lack of the faculty of speech. Suppose some event has reorganized its mind by giving it such faculty. In order for the new mechanism to be operable, it must meet the "legibility conditions," and the other systems of the mind/brain must be able to understand the expressions generated by the new mechanism. On the other hand, the directions given by the new mechanism must be recognized and accepted by the other systems of the mind/brain. Thus, Chomsky puts forward the strongest minimalist thesis: Linguistic mechanism is the ideal solution to the problem of legibility conditions.

Given that a human language is a way of relating sound and meaning, the Minimalist Program seeks to establish that there are no levels except the "interface" levels PF (phonetic form) and LF (logical form). Later, Chomsky suggests that even PF and LF as specific levels of representation in the technical sense are non-existent. Rather, throughout the derivation, the syntactic structure thus far created is encapsulated and sent off to the interface components for phonetic and semantic interpretation. The Minimalist Program further maintains that derivations and representations conform to an "economy" criterion demanding that they be minimal in a sense determined by the language faculty: no extra steps in derivations and no extra symbols in representations.

14.6.7 Interdisciplinary Inquiries

After the turn of the new century, Chomsky shifted his attention to interdisciplinary perspectives and the biological aspects of the faculty of language. In their joint article "The faculty of language" (Hauser *et al*, 2002), Chomsky, together with two Harvard psychologists, argue that an understanding of the faculty of language requires substantial interdisciplinary cooperation, on the belief that linguistics can be profitably wedded to work in evolutionary biology, anthropology, psychology, and neuroscience. They make a distinction between the faculty of language in the broad sense (FLB) and in the narrow sense (FLN). The former includes a sensory-motor system, a conceptual-intentional system, and the computational mechanisms for recursion, while the latter only includes recursion and is the only uniquely human component of the faculty of language. They believe that since FLN may have evolved for reasons other than language, comparative studies might look for evidence of such computations outside of the domain of communication.

In an article "Biolinguistic explorations," Chomsky (2005) traces the development of biolinguistics from its early philosophical origins through its reformulation during the cognitive revolution of the 1950s and outlines his views on where the biolinguistic enterprise stands now. He suggests that the growth of language in the individual depends on three factors: genetic factors, experience, and principles that are not specific to the faculty of language. The best current explanation of how language is recursively generated is through merge, an operation that takes objects already constructed, and reconstructs a new object from them, generating a "language of thought," perhaps in a manner close to optimal, with externalization (hence communication) a secondary process. Finally, he offers several objectives for future research in the field, such as accounting for: 1) the atoms for computation (lexical items, concepts), with their apparently unique human characteristics; 2) the rewiring of the brain that made unbounded Merge available for generating structured expressions from these atoms; 3) the operations of externalization that map expressions to the sensory-motor interface; 4) whatever else remains in UG after "why" questions have been answered by resort to third-factor principles; and 5) interface operations.

Chomsky justifies this list by saying that little is known about the evolution of human thought and about the brain to proceed from the very first thing in a useful way. By formulating the goals with reasonable clarity and moving step by step towards principled explanation, we gain a clearer grasp of the universals of language, although much work is needed before we can understand the problems concerning the "organical structure of the brain" and the "creative and coherent ordinary use of language."

Chapter 14 Modern Theories and Schools of Linguistics

The development of Chomskyan thought can be regarded as a process of constantly minimalizing theories with one logical step after another. Although his grammar has involved putting forward, revising, and cancelling of many specific rules, hypotheses, mechanisms, and theoretical models, its aims and purposes have been consistent, i.e. to explore the nature, origin and the uses of human knowledge on language.

14.6.8 Chomsky's Fundamental Contributions

Chomsky fundamental contributions are many. First, he has offered a different view on the nature of language by defining language as a set of rules or principles. Second, he set a new goal for linguistics by producing a generative grammar which captures the tacit knowledge of the native speaker of his language, touching upon the question of learning theory and the question of linguistic universals. Third, he has used a different type of data in analysis that can reveal the native speaker's tacit knowledge on their own intuition. Fourth, he has proposed a new methodology, hypothesis-deduction, which works on grammars for particular languages and general linguistic theory. Finally, he views language learning in a different way by following rationalism in philosophy and mentalism in psychology.

Chomsky is responsible for the "cognitive revolution," a great shift in American psychology from being primarily behavioral to being primarily cognitive, with his critique of Skinner's *Verbal Behavior* in 1959. In his *Cartesian Linguistics* (1966) and subsequent works, Chomsky lays out explanations of human language faculties that have become the model for certain areas of psychological investigation. With his unusual knowledge of philosophy, logic, and mathematics, he developed and revised one model after another for half a century. It is fair to say that Chomsky is the first persuasive scholar that has seriously addressed the questions concerning, and heavily influenced our present conception of, how the mind works.

His ideas have had a strong influence on studies of language acquisition in children, though many researchers (such as Elizabeth Bates and Michael Tomasello) have argued very strongly against him and advocated connectionist theories to explain language with a number of general processing mechanisms in the brain that interact with the extensive and complex social environment in which language is used and learned.

His work in phonology, in collaboration with Morris Halle (1968), has had a great impact on the development in the field, and has been considered the precursor of some of the most influential phonological theories today.

NeilSmith (1999: 212) writes that practical applications of Chomsky's work are not obvious. Although one might expect that Chomsky's ideas on language acquisition would have implications for second language teaching and that his ideas on the nature of language would reverberate in therapy for aphasic stroke victims, there is no such thing as Chomskyan school of language teaching or speech therapy. To avoid misunderstanding the nature of Chomsky's achievement, we have to bear in mind that his work is about understanding and explanation rather than applications and implementation.

14.7 Revisionist/Rebellious Theories

In the latter half of the 20th century, many more schools of linguistics flourished, mostly in America. In spite of certain differences, these schools have one thing in common: making attempts to explain language phenomena in greater depth. Notable ones include Stratificational Grammar, Case Grammar, Generative Semantics, Relational Grammar, Montague Grammar, Chafe Grammar, Interface Grammar, and Cognitive Linguistics. Although not as influential as TG Grammar or SF Grammar, each of them contributed to the explanation of language in its own way. Here is a brief account of some of these schools.

14.7.1 Stratificational Grammar

Stratificational grammar started from the American linguist Sydney M. Lamb. In 1957, Lamb proposed taking language as a model consisting of three levels: phoneme, morpheme, and morphophoneme. This laid the foundation for his theory of Stratificational Grammar, which saw rapid development in the 1960s.

Lamb (1966:3) says that linguistic analysis can perhaps best be understood as a process of simplifying. It is a process that involves both simplification and generalisation. For example, as in algebra,

$$abc + abd + abe + abf + abg$$

can be reduced to

$$ab(c + d + e + f + g).$$

The latter expression is simpler than the former and it contains a generalisation not present in the former. It is simpler precisely by virtue of the fact that it expresses the generalisation. So the linguist can do similar things as a student of algebra does. For example,

blueberry, cranberry

can be reduced to

$$\begin{bmatrix} \text{blue} \\ \text{berry} \end{bmatrix} \text{cran}$$

Lamb claims that language, by its nature, relates sound to meaning, and vice versa, and while the relationship is complex it can be seen as series of connected stratal systems or strata. Each stratal system has its own rules of combination within the stratum and the different strata are interconnected on the basis of realisation. Lamb not only developed this view in an original manner but he devised an effective representational system to match it.

Like Chomsky, Lamb believes that language relates sound to meaning. This view is not without its critics. But much as Chomsky seeks to connect "semantic representations" to "phonetic representations," Lamb seeks to show the relationships that obtain between the hypersememic stratum and the hypophonemic stratum. His view has the advantage of being neutral with respect to speaker or hearer. Unlike Chomsky, however, Lamb's grammar does not involve transformations. It represents the complex linguistic combinations and arrangements on and between the postulated strata. It does not seek to derive one structure from another but rather seeks to show how things are related.

Like every other theory, Stratificational Grammar is hailed by some and criticized by others. It is criticized because Lamb himself might not be sure how many strata there are in language. It is hailed because stratificational analysis gives a better account of the relations between sound and meaning.

While other theories tend to take grammar as abstraction from the analysis of linguistic phenomena, paying virtually no attention to human mind, Lamb's theory aims to know about the language system in the human mind. Thus, Lamb named his theory as "cognitive stratificational theory." As more and more people began to use the term "cognition" while their theories do not deal with the relationship between language structure and the human mind, Lamb distinguished his theory by the term "neurocognitive linguistics." The main ideas can be found in his paper, "Neuro-cognitive structure in the interplay of language and thought" (1998) and his monograph, *Pathways of the Brain: The Neurocognitive Basis of Language* (1999). Lamb feels that the most urgent task at present is to develop computer programs to check theories of language, not only theories of learning hypotheses but also the details of network structure and its related aspects.

14.7.2 Case Grammar

Case grammar is an approach that stresses the relationships in a sentence. It is a type of generative grammar developed by Charles J. Fillmore in the late 1960s. In this grammar, the verb is regarded as the most important part of the sentence, and has a number of relationships with various noun phrases. These relationships are called "CASES." For example, in the sentences

(9) *Smith killed the policeman with a revolver.*

This revolver killed the policeman.

with a revolver and *This revolver* have different syntactic functions, but their semantic relationships with the verb *kill* are the same in both sentences. The revolver is the instrument with which the action of the verb *kill* was performed, *with a revolver* indicates the manner in which the killing action took place.

Fillmore sees his Case Grammar as a "substantive modification to the theory of transformational grammar" (Fillmore, 1968: 21) as represented by Chomsky. Chomsky's model was unable to account for the functions of the items in the clause as well as for their categories. It only showed, for instance, that the expressions like *in the room*, *towards the moon*, *on the next day*, *in a careless way*, *with a sharp knife*, and *by my brother* are of the category PP, without showing that they simultaneously indicate the functions, location, direction, time, manner, instrument, and agent respectively. Fillmore suggests that this problem would be solved in the following way. The underlying syntactic structure of prepositional phrases can be analysed as a sequence of a noun phrase and an associated prepositional case marker. This noun phrase and the prepositional case marker are both dominated by a case symbol that indicates the thematic role of that prepositional phrase. He also suggested that in fact every element of a clause which has a thematic role to play should be analysed in terms of case markers and case symbols.

Fillmore's argument is based on the assumptions that syntax should be central in the determination of case and that covert categories are important. "Case" is used to identify "the underlying syntactic-semantic relationship," which is universal. The term "case form" identifies "the expression of a case relationship in a particular language." The notions of subject and predicate and of the division between them should be seen as surface phenomena only. In its basic structure, the sentence consists of a verb and one or more noun phrases, each associated with the verb in a particular case relationship. The various ways in which cases occur in simple sentences define sentence types and verb types of a language.

The obvious attractions of Case Grammar include the clear semantic relevance of notions such as agency, causation, location, advantage to someone, etc. These are easily identifiable across languages, and are held by many psychologists to play an important part in child language acquisition. According to Lyons, however, Case Grammar is no longer seen by the majority of linguists working within the general framework of TG Grammar as a viable alternative to the Standard Theory. The reason is that when it comes to classifying the totality of the verbs in a language in terms of the deep-structure cases that they govern, the semantic criteria which define these cases are all too often unclear or in conflict.

In spite of the defects of the theory and methods of analysis, Case Grammar has been an important undertaking in drawing the attention of an initially sceptical tradition of linguistic study to the importance of relating semantic cases or thematic roles to syntactic descriptions.

14.7.3 Generative Semantics

Generative semantics was developed in the late 1960s and early 1970s, as a reaction to Chomsky's syntactic-based TG Grammar. The leading figures of this approach are John R. Ross, George Lakoff, James D. McCawley, and Paul Postal. Generative Semantics considers that all sentences are generated from a semantic structure. This semantic structure is often expressed in the form of a proposition that is similar to logical propositions in philosophy. Linguists working within this theory have, for example, suggested that there is a semantic relationship between such sentences as:

(10) *This dog strikes me as being his new master.*

and

This dog reminds me of his new master.

because they both have the semantic structure of

X perceives that Y is similar to Z.

Generative Semantics holds that there is no principled distinction between syntactic processes and semantic processes. This notion was accompanied by a number of subsidiary hypotheses. First, the purely syntactic level of deep structure posited by Chomsky's *Aspects of the Theory of Syntax* (1965) cannot exist. Second, the initial representations of derivations are logical representations identical from language to language. Third, all aspects of meaning are representable in phrase-marker form. In other words, the derivation of a sentence is a direct transformational mapping from semantics to surface structure. The initial generative semantic model can be represented by the following model:

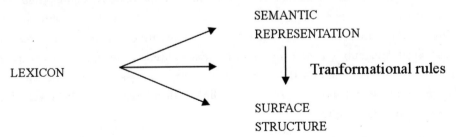

As the figure indicates, the question of how and where lexical items entered the derivation was a controversial topic in Generative Semantics. McCawley (1968) dealt with this problem by treating lexical entries themselves as structured composites of semantic material (the theory of lexical decomposition), and thus offered the entry for *kill* as:

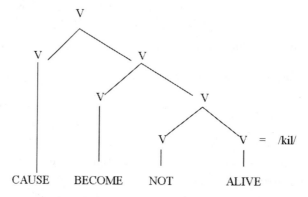

Generative semanticists realised that their rejection of the level of deep structure would be little more than word-playing. For, the transformational mapping from semantic representation to surface structure turned out to be characterized by a major break before the application of the familiar cyclic rules-particularly if the natural location for the insertion of the lexical items was precisely at this break. They therefore constructed a number of arguments to show that no such work existed. The most compelling were moulded after Morris Halle's classic argument against the structural phoneme. Generative semanticists attempted to show that the existence of a level of deep structure distinct from semantic representation would demand that the same generalisation be stated twice, once in the syntax and once in the semantics. (Postal, 1970)

Generative Semantics had collapsed well before the end of the 1970s. While Generative Semantics is no longer regarded as a viable model of grammar, there are innumerable ways in which it has left its mark on its successors. First, it was generative semanticists that started an intensive investigation of syntactic phenomena which defied formalisation by means of transformational rules. Second, many proposals originally disputed by generative semanticists have since appeared in the interpretivist literature. Finally, the important initial studies which Generative Semantics inspired on the logical and sub-logical properties of lexical items, on speech acts, both direct and indirect, and on the more general pragmatic aspects of language are becoming more and more appreciated as linguistic theory is finally developing means to incorporate them.

14.7.4 Relational Grammar

After the advent of the TG theory, many attempts were made in order to discover universals of human language. In so doing, there were a lot of controversies and some scholars called TG theory into question, on the grounds that the deep structure in the TG theory is not justified, others argued that there is no such thing as transformation. David Perlmutter and Paul Postal (1977) put forward the view that the relations between the active and the passive voices in natural languages cannot be accounted for by either word order or case, but can only be accounted for by the relations between the subject and the object. Against such a background, relational grammar became a discipline when increasing attention was being paid to the relationship between grammatical units.

Perlmutter and Postal take grammatical relation as a primitive concept and word order as a derived concept. Their theory broke away from traditional studies of syntactic structure and semantic structure in the hope of discussing common problems relating to all languages by resorting to pure grammatical relations. And it soon gained wide acceptance and became popular in the mid-1970s as Relational Grammar, next to Chomsky's TG theory.

One reason for the popularity of Relational Grammar is that it takes grammatical relations of subject and object as the primitives and makes direct syntactical descriptions by the use of relational networks. The linear order of words and phrases are derived from these primitives. Thus, the grammatical model is powerful enough to account for phenomena unaccountable by other models based on the linear order. It also reveals some universal principles unaccountable by models other than the relational grammatical model. Another reason for its popularity is its inclusion of descriptions which Chomsky's model had failed to include. In this sense, relational grammarians can more justifiably claim their origin of theory as traditional grammar rather than TG grammar.

The description of language by Relational Grammar lays emphasis on universal aspects. Hence it deals with particular aspects of different languages (such as word order, case, and the problem of expressing certain grammatical relations by way of words) according to specific features of the language in question. For this purpose, Relational Grammar attempts to represent these particulars and account for them by the component of "side effects." It holds that when this universal grammar is applied to particular languages, there would be such side effects. However, the theory itself is applicable to all languages. The model of Relational Grammar can be expressed as follows.

Semantics→Grammatical→Transformational→Relational→Side
            Relations   Rules   Network Effects
                              ↑
                         Relational
                           rules

Grammatical relations and multi-level analysis of syntax are two essential conditions for syntactical description. The description includes grammatical relations, grammatical rules, and relational rules. In analysing natural language structure, Relational Grammar starts from the transformation of grammatical relations. This is where peculiar features of the relational theory lie.

Popular as it was in the mid-1970s, Relational Grammar is somewhat short-lived. In the late 1970s, it lost its popularity due to various reasons. For one, the theorists failed to present a complete and timely account of their work to the linguistic circle in the world. For another, some linguists strongly dissatisfied with certain arguments of Generative Semantics found that the same problems existed in Relational Grammar, accompanied by obscure terminology. What is more important is that this theoretical model failed to consider in depth the relationship between syntax and semantics. Paradoxically, such a theoretical model not involving too much of the relationship between syntax and semantics is just what it is special for. It is the peculiar theory and analytical methods that make Relational Grammar innovative in the 1970s.

14.7.5 Cognitive Linguistics

Unlike many less influential schools of linguistics of the late 20th century, cognitive linguistics (CL) has unique paths of development and has presented a different picture. Closely associated with semantics but distinct from psycholinguistics, CL arose in the 1970s and has been prospering till the present day. It grew out of the work of a number of researchers interested in the relation of language and mind and against Chomskyan grammar which treats meaning as interpretive and peripheral to the study of language; and against the prevailing tendency to explain linguistic patterns by means of appeals to structural properties internal to and specific to language. Instead of attempting to segregate syntax from the rest of language in a "syntactic component" governed by a set of principles and elements specific to that component, their research was to examine the relation of language structure to things outside language, including principles of human categorization, pragmatic and interactional principles, and functional principles in general, such as iconicity and economy.

Influential linguists on cognitive principles and organization include Wallace Chafe, Charles Fillmore, George Lakoff, Ronald Langacker, and Leonard Talmy, each having his own approach to language description and linguistic theory, centered on a particular set of phenomena and concerns. One of their common assumptions is that meaning is so central to language that it must be a primary focus of study. Structures express meanings and hence the mappings between meaning and form are a prime subject of linguistic analysis. In this view, linguistic forms are closely linked to the semantic structures they are designed to express, and semantic structures of all meaningful linguistic units can and should be investigated.

In a broader sense, linguists working in a cognitive direction in the 1970s also included Joan Bybee, Bernard Comrie, John Haiman, Paul Hopper, Sandra Thompson, and Tom Givon, in functional linguistics; Sydney Lamb who developed Stratificational Grammar and later Neurocognitive Linguistics; Dick Hudson who developed word grammar; and Elizabeth Traugott and Bernd Heine whose work on historical linguistics along functional principles led to principles of grammaticalization. Much work of the time in child language acquisition was influenced by Piaget and by the cognitive revolution in psychology, so that the field of language acquisition had a strong functional/cognitive strand through this period.

Linguistic theories in the late 1980s were fundamentally important. Fillmore's ideas had developed into frame semantics and, in collaboration with others, construction grammar. With the publication of Lakoff (1987) and Langacker (1987), researchers made explicit references to them in linguistic inquiries into problems from a cognitive standpoint. Langacker is known for his space grammar and cognitive grammar; Talmy is known for his influential papers on linguistic imaging systems; Giles Fauconnier developed a theory of mental spaces and, in collaboration with Mark Turner, developed it into a theory of conceptual blending, meshing with both Langacker and Lakoff's theories.

During the 1990s the work of Lakoff, Langacker, and Talmy formed the leading strands of the CL theory. By the mid-1990s, CL was characterized by a defining set of intellectual pursuits and summarized in "Cognitive Linguistics" (Geeraerts, 1995: 111—112), with a recognition of close connections between CL and functional linguistics, linguistic description, psycholinguistics, pragmatics, and discourse studies.

Cognitive Linguistics is characterized by adherence to three central positions: 1) it denies the existence of an autonomous linguistic faculty in the mind; 2) it understands grammar in terms of conceptualization; and 3) it claims that knowledge of language arises out of language use. Although cognitive linguists do not necessarily deny that part of the human linguistic ability is innate, they deny that it is separate from the rest of cognition. They argue that knowledge of linguistic phenomena is essentially conceptual in nature, and that the storage and retrieval of linguistic data is not significantly different from the storage and retrieval of other knowledge. Departing from the tradition of truth-conditional semantics, cognitive linguists view meaning in terms of conceptualization. Instead of viewing meaning in terms of models of the world, they view it in terms of mental spaces. Finally, cognitive linguists argue that language is both embodied and situated in a specific environment.

This can be considered a moderate offshoot of the Sapir-Whorf Hypothesis, in that language and cognition mutually influence each other, and are both embedded in the experiences and environments of its users.

14.8 Concluding Remarks

The development of linguistics has undergone three stages, from *prescription* to *description* and to *explanation*. Traditional grammar in the two-millennium long period before the 19th century was prescriptive. Historical and comparative linguistics in the 19th century and structural linguistics in the first half of the 20th century were descriptive. Many schools of linguistics starting from TG Grammar in the second half of the 20th century have been explanatory.

In fact, various schools of linguistics in the past two centuries have been shifting between approaches of description and explanation. In the new period starting from Saussure till the mid-20th century, the main trends of linguistic inquiry focused on describing the linguistic systems of various languages. When linguists found that mere description of languages is insufficient for their purposes of accounting for language faculty in human beings, new theories of linguistics evolved for explanatory purposes. Chomsky's formalist approach starting from the 1950s and Halliday's functionalist approach starting from the 1970s are both explanatory, with the only difference that the former is psychologically oriented and the latter is sociologically oriented.

With the development of modern sciences, man is being armed with tools whose powers may go far beyond our imagination in inquiring into the human mind. Faced with various existing theories that keep developing and new ones that keep arising, the serious learner should take an unbiased attitude: Never follow or reject any theory blindly. Popularity is only a relative term, and every theory is subject to further verification. Some theories may be (even some classical theories may still be) far ahead of our time, and their value may not be fully appreciated at the present state of our knowledge. On the one hand, every "new" theory may have its theoretical origins in the past. On the other hand, no "old" theory is easily obsolete, however likely it may seem.

> ...*by far the greatest danger in scholarship (and perhaps especially in linguistics) is not that the individual may fail to master the thought of a school but that a school may succeed in mastering the thought of the individual.* (Sampson, 1980: 10)

References

Bloch, B. 1949. "Leonard Bloomfield," *Language* 25(1): 87—89.

Bloch, B. & Trager, J. L. 1942. *Outlines of Linguistic Analysis*. Baltimore: Waverly Press.

Bloomfield, L. 1933/1955. *Language*. London: George Allen & Unwin Ltd.

Boas, F. 1911. *A Handbook of American Indian Languages*. Washington, DC: Smithonian Institution.

Bolinger, D. 1968/1975. *Aspects of Language*. New York: Harcourt Brace Jovanovich.

Bresnan, J. 2001. *Lexical Functional Syntax*. Oxford: Blackwell.

Chafe, W. 1971. *Meaning and the Structure of Language*. Chicago: University of Chicago Press.

Chomsky, N. 1957. *Syntactic Structures*. The Hague: Mouton & Co.

Chomsky, N. 1965. *Aspects of the Theory of Syntax*. Cambridge, MA: MIT Press.

Chomsky, N. 1972. *Studies on Semantics in Generative Grammar*. The Hague: Mouton.

Chomsky, N. 1981. *Lectures on Government and Binding: The Pisa Lectures*. Berlin and New York: Mouton de Gruyter.

Chomsky, N. 1986. *Knowledge of Language: Its Nature, Origin, and Use*. New York: Praeger.

Chomsky, N. 1994. *Language and Thought*. London: Moyer Bell.

Chomsky, N. 1995. *The Minimalist Program*. Cambridge, MA: MIT Press.

Chomsky, N. 1998. *Minimalist Inquiries: The Framework*. Cambridge, MA: MIT Press.

Chomsky, N. 2005. "Biolinguistic explorations: design, development, evolution," *International Journal of Philosophical Studies* 15(1): 1−21.

Culler, J. 1976. *Saussure*. London: Fontana/Collins.

Dik, S. 1978. *Functional Grammar*. Amsterdam: North-Holland.

Dowty, D. Wall, R. & Peters, S. 1981. *Introduction to Montague Semantics*. Dordrecht: Reidel.

Fauconnier, G. & M. Turner. 2003. *The Way We Think*. New York: Basic Books.

Fillmore, C. 1966. "Toward a modern theory of case," in *Modern Studies in English*. D. Reibel & S. Schane (eds.). Englewood Cliffs: Princeton Hall.

Fillmore, C. 1968. "The case for case," in *Universals in Linguistic Theory*. E. Bach & R. T. Harms (eds.). New York: Holt, Rinehart and Winston.

Fillmore, C. 1971. "Some problems for case grammar," in *Report of the 22nd Annual Round Table Meeting on Linguistics and Language Studies*. R. J. O'Brien (ed.). Washington, DC: Georgetown University Press. pp. 35−56.

Fillmore, C. 1977. "Thecase for case reopened," in *Syntax and Semantics*, Vol. 8: *Grammatical Relations*. P. Cole and J. M. Sadock (eds.). New York: Academic Press. pp. 59−81.

Firth, J. R. 1957. *Papers in Linguistics 1934−1951*. London: Oxford University Press.

Firth, J. R. 1968. *Selected Papers of J. R. Firth 1952−1959*. F. R. Palmer (ed.). London: Longman.

Foley, W. A. & R. D. Van Valin, Jr. 1984. *Functional Syntax and Universal Grammar*. Cambridge: Cambridge University Press.

Geeraerts, D. 1995. "Cognitive linguistics," *Handbook of Pragmatics* (Blackwell Handbooks in Linguistics). Oxford: Blackwell. pp. 111−112.

Halliday, M. A. K. 1978. *Language as Social Semiotic*. London: Edward Arnold.

Halliday, M. A. K. 1985/1994. *An Introduction to Functional Grammar*. London: Edward

Arnold.

Halliday, M. A. K. 2002. *Linguistic Studies of Text and Discourse*. J. Webster (ed.). London: Continuum.

Halliday, M. A. K. 2003. *On Language and Linguistics*. J. Webster (ed.). London: Continuum.

Halliday, M. A. K. 2005. *On Grammar*. J. Webster (ed.). London: Continuum.

Halliday, M. A. K. 2006. *The Language of Science*. J. Webster (ed.). London: Continuum.

Halliday, M. A. K. 2007. "Applied linguistics as an evolving theme," *Language and Education*. J. Webster (ed.). London: Continuum. pp. 1—19.

Halliday, M. A. K. 2010. "Pinpointing the choice: meaning and the search for equivalents in a translated text," in Mahboob & Knight (eds.). *Appliable Linguistics*: 13—24.

Halliday, M. A. K. & Hasan, R. 1985. *Language, Context, and Text: Aspects of Language in a Socio-semiotic Perspective*. Victoria: Deakin University Press.

Halliday, M. A. K. and Matthiessen, C. 2004. *An Introduction to Functional Grammar*. (3rd ed.). London: Hodder Arnold.

Harder, Peter. 1996. *Functional Semantics: A Theory of Meaning, Structure and Tense in English*. Berlin and New York: Mouton de Gruyter.

Harris, Z. S. 1951. *Methods in Structural Linguistics*. Chicago: University of Chicago Press.

Hauser, Marc D., Noam Chomsky, & W. Tecumseh Fitch. 2002. "The faculty of language: what is it, who has it, and how did it evolve?" *Science* 298(5598): 1569—1579.

Hjelmslev, L. 1928. *Principes de Grammaire Générale*. København: A. F. Høst & Søn.

Hjelmslev, L. 1953. *Prolegomena to a Theory of Language*. Francis J. Whitfield (Trans.). Baltimore: Waverly Press.

Hjelmslev, L. 1961. *Prolegomena to a Theory of Language*. Francis J. Whitfield (Trans.). Madison: University of Wisconsin Press.

Hjelmslev, L. 1975. *Résumé of a Theory of Language*. (Edited and translated with an introduction by Francis J. Whitfield). Madison: University of Wisconsin Press.

Kay, M. 1985. "Parsing infunctional unification grammar," in D. Dowty *et al* (eds.). *Natural Language Parsing: Psychological, Computational, and Theoretical Perspectives*. Cambridge: Cambridge University Press. pp. 125—138.

Kress, G. & Van Leeuwen, T. 2001. *Multimodal Discourse: The Modes and Media of Contemporary Communication Discourse*. London: Edward Arnold.

Lakoff, G. 1987. *Women, Fire, and Dangerous Things. What Categories Reveal about the Mind*. Chicago: University of Chicago Press.

Lamb, S. 1966. *Outline of Stratificational Grammar*. Washington, DC: Georgetown University Press.

Lamb, S. 1999. *Pathways of the Brain: The Neurocognitive Basis of Language*. Amsterdam: John Benjamins.

Langacker, R. W. 1987. *Foundations of Cognitive Grammar* Vol. 1: *Theoretical Prerequisites*. Stanford: Stanford University Press.

Langacker, R. W. 1990. *Concept, Image, and Symbol. The Cognitive Basis of Grammar*. Berlin: Mouton de Gruyter.

Langacker, R. W. 1991. *Foundations of Cognitive Grammar* Vol. 2: *Descriptive*

Application. Stanford: Stanford University Press.

Lepschy, G. C. 1970. *A Survey of Structural Linguistics*. London: Faber and Faber.

Levin, S. 1960. "Comparingtraditional and structural grammar," *College English* 21(5): 260—265.

Lyons, J. 1968. *Introduction to Theoretical Linguistics*. London: Cambridge University Press.

Lyons, J. 1991. *Chomsky*. (3rd ed.). London: Fontana.

Malinowski, B. 1922. *Argonauts of the Western Pacific*. London: Routledge and Kegan Paul.

Malinowski, B. 1923. "The problem of meaning in primitive languages," supplement to C. K. Ogden & I. A. Richards. *The Meaning of Meaning*. London: Routledge and Kegan Paul. pp. 451—510.

Malinowski, B. 1935. *Coral Gardens and Their Magic*. London: Routledge and Kegan Paul.

Mahboob, A. & N. K. Knight. 2010. *Appliable Linguistics*. London: Continuum.

Martin, J. R. 1992. *English Text: System and Structure*. Philadelphia/Amsterdam: John Benjamins.

Martin, J. R. & White, P. R. R. 2005. *The Language of Evaluation: Appraisal in English*. New York: Palgrave Macmillan.

Newmeyer, F. 1986[1980]. *Linguistic Theory in America*. (2nd ed.). New York: Academic Press.

Newmeyer, F. 1986. "Hasthere been a 'Chomskyan revolution' in linguistics?" *Language* 62 (1): 1—18.

O'Halloran, K. L. (ed.). 2004. *Multimodal Discourse Analysis*. London: Continuum.

O'Halloran, K. L. 2005. *Mathematical Discourse: Language, Symbolism and Visual Images*. London and New York: Continuum.

O'Halloran, K. L. 2008. "Inter-semiotic expansion of experiential meaning: hierarchical scales and metaphor in mathematics discourse," in *New Developments in the Study of Ideational Meaning: From Language to Multimodality*. C. Jones & E. Ventola (eds.). London: Equinox.

O'Halloran, K. L. 2011. "Multimodal discourse analysis," in *Companion to Discourse*. K. Hyland & B. Paltridge (eds.). London and New York: Continuum.

O'Toole, M. 1994. *The Language of Displayed Art*. London: Leicester University Press.

Perlmutter, D. 1980. "Relational grammar," in *Syntax and Semantics*, Vol. 13: *Current Approaches to Syntax*. Moravcsik and Wirth (eds.). New York: Academic Press.

Perlmutter, D. (ed.). 1983. *Studies in Relational Grammar* 1. Chicago: University of Chicago Press.

Perlmutter, D. & Rosen, C. (eds.). 1984. *Studies in Relational Grammar* 2. Chicago: University of Chicago Press.

Pike, K. 1982. *Linguistic Concepts: An Introduction to Tagmemics*. Lincoln, NE and London: University of Nebraska Press.

Postal, P. 1970. "On the surface verb 'remind'," *Linguistic Inquiry* 1(1): 37—120.

Postal, P. 1982. "Some arc pair grammar description," in *The Nature of Syntactic Representation*. Jacobson and Pullum (eds.). Dordrecht: Reidel.

Sampson, G. 1980. *Schools of Linguistics: Competition and Evolution*. London: Hutchinson.

Sapir, E. 1921. *Language: An Introduction to the Study of Speech*. New York: Harcourt Brace Jovanovich, Inc.
Saussure, F. de. 1916. *Cours de linguistique générale*. Paris: Payot.
Saussure, F. de. 1959. *Course in General Linguistics*. W. Baskin (trans.). New York: Philosophical Library.
Saussure, F. de. 1967—1974. *Cours de linguistique générale*. Critical edition by Rudolf Engler, Two volumes, four fascicules. Miesbaden: O. Harrassowitz.
Saussure, F. de. 1983. *Course in General Linguistics*. R. Harris (trans.). London: Duckworth.
Saussure, F. de. 2006. *Writings in General Linguistics*. S. Bouquet, R. Engler, C. Sanders, & M. Pires (ed.). London & New York: Oxford University Press.
Searle, J. 1972. "Chomsky's revolution in linguistics," *New York Reviews of Books*. New York: New York Review, Inc.
Smith, Neil. 1999. *Chomsky: Ideas and Ideals*. Cambridge: Cambridge University Press.
Talmy, Leonard. 2000. *Toward a Cognitive Semantics* (2 volumes). Cambridge, MA: MIT Press.
Trubetzkoy, N. S. 1969. *Principles of Phonology*. (1st edition 1939, translated from German by C. A. M. Baltaxe). Berkeley and Los Angeles: University of California Press.
Vachek, J. 1964: *A Prague School Reader in Linguistics*. Bloomington: Indiana University Press.
Waterman, J. T. 1970. *Perspectives in Linguistics*. Chicago: University of Chicago Press.
封宗信,2000,论生成文体学的功能主义思想,《外语与外语教学》1:15—18。
封宗信,2003,诚信原则在人际交流中的制约功能,《清华大学学报》(哲学社会科学版)5:76—80。
封宗信,2005,语言学的元语言及其研究现状,《外语教学与研究》6:403—410。
封宗信,2006,《现代语言学流派概论》,北京:北京大学出版社。
封宗信,2008,格莱斯原则四十年,《外语教学》5:1—8。
封宗信,2011,系统功能语言学中的情态系统:逻辑、语义、语用,《外语教学》6:1—5。
封宗信,2012,系统功能语言学理论中的逻辑学性质,《语言研究与外语教学》,北京:高等教育出版社。
胡壮麟,2000,《功能主义纵横谈》,北京:外语教学与研究出版社。
胡壮麟、朱永生、张德禄,1989,《系统功能语法概论》,长沙:湖南教育出版社。
胡壮麟等,2005,《系统功能语言学概论》,北京:北京大学出版社。
黄国文、常晨光、戴凡,2006,《功能语言学与适用语言学》,广州:中山大学出版社。
刘润清,1995,《西方语言学流派》,北京:外语教学与研究出版社。
刘润清、封宗信,2003,《语言学理论与流派》(英文版),南京:南京师范大学出版社。
向明友,2000,《索绪尔语言理论的经济学背景》,《外国语》第2期。
赵世开,1989,《美国语言学简史》,上海:上海外语教育出版社。